New Testament Foundations

Centre for
Faith and Spirituality
Loughborough University

D1386658

New Testament Foundations:
A Guide for Christian Students

Revised Edition

VOLUME 2

The Acts

The Letters

The Apocalypse

by

RALPH P. MARTIN

WM. B. EERDMANS PUBLISHING COMPANY
GRAND RAPIDS, MICHIGAN

THE PATERNOSTER PRESS
EXETER

*This book is dedicated
to the memory of
T. W. Manson
(1893-1958)
from whom the author learned
so much of what is contained
in this volume.*

Copyright © 1978 by William B. Eerdmans Publishing Company
All rights reserved
Printed in the United States of America

Revised edition published jointly 1986 by Wm. B. Eerdmans Publishing Co.,
255 Jefferson Ave. SE, Grand Rapids, Mich. 49503 and
The Paternoster Press Ltd, 3 Mount Radford Crescent,
Exeter EX2 4JW, England

Library of Congress Cataloging-in-Publication Data

Martin, Ralph P.
New Testament foundations.

Bibliography: p. 439
Includes indexes.
Contents: v. 2.   The Acts, the Letters, the Apocalypse.
1. Bible.   N.T. — Introductions.   I. Title.
BS2330.2.M28   1986   225.6'1   86-16235

ISBN 0-8028-0076-9   (v. 2)

Paternoster ISBN 0-85364-441-1

Contents

Acknowledgments

In several of the following chapters I have drawn on some material which first appeared in various books and journals. In particular these are sections and essays published in *Vox Evangelica,* Vol. 1 (1962), and Vol. 2 (1963); in the Scripture Union Bible Study book on *Acts* (1968); in the New Century Bible commentaries on *Philippians* (1976) and *Colossians and Philemon* (1974); in *Worship in the Early Church*[2] (1975); and in an essay on "Authority" in the *Evangelical Quarterly,* 40 (1968). On Ephesians I have also used a few paragraphs from my section in the *Broadman Bible Commentary,* Vol. 11 (1971), and from a contribution to the *Expository Times,* 79 (1968), 296–302. For the acknowledged use of this material editorial and publishers' permission has been sought and generously granted.

Preface

The present volume fulfils the promise made at the opening of *New Testament Foundations,* Vol. 1 (1975), to provide a companion guide to the Acts of the Apostles, New Testament letters, and the Apocalypse. The aim of both books is to offer a simply written and constructive handbook to assist students and other readers in their understanding of the New Testament.

As before I pay tribute to those whose questions, comments, and criticisms in a classroom context have clarified my own thinking. Several student assistants have contributed significantly: in particular, Eric Behrens, Lynn A. Losie, James L. Resseguie, Allan R. Selander, and John S. Piper. The last-named, now professor in Bethel College, St. Paul, Minnesota, has been responsible for compiling Part Seven, and I am grateful for his work.

Ann Lausch, secretary in the Graduate Office, has taken care of the preparation of the manuscript, and I am in her debt for this service so willingly rendered.

This preface is being written during sabbatical leave at Spurgeon's College, London; and it is again appropriate to acknowledge the congenial surroundings in which the book is taking its final form, and the generous sabbatical arrangement of Fuller Seminary that makes this concentrated work possible.

RALPH P. MARTIN

Fuller Theological Seminary
Pasadena, California

For this reprint I have taken the opportunity to review the following pages, to correct a small number of misprints, to emend an occasional sentence or paragraph that was obscure or misleading, and to supplement the footnotes with additional bibliography. The temptation to add references indiscriminately has, I trust, been resisted.

I am indebted to Richard E. Menninger for help in preparing these bibliographies.

R. P. M.

Introduction

This book is a companion to the first volume, which aimed at providing a student's guide to the four Gospels. Both volumes contain material that has been used in lectures over a decade and a half both in a British university and in several seminaries in the USA. The goals that the author has set himself and his students ought here to be acknowledged; and it will be apparent that the pattern of the following volume follows that already used for the treatment of the Gospels. Each book is designed to provide the groundwork for instruction covering thirty hours of classroom teaching, either in a university academic year or a seminary semester. This explains why, especially in the present volume, much has had to be omitted and certain important topics are only briefly glanced at. The bibliographies have been curtailed accordingly; and there is a certain amount of cross-referencing and some repetition for the sake of emphasis.

The opening sections of Parts One and Two aim at awakening interest and providing some general orientation to a study of the epistles. The chapters on the world of the early church offer a bird's-eye view of the historical, political, cultural, and religious setting of the first century; and their purpose is to plot the existence of the early Christian communities within the coordinates of world events and contemporary thought.

We are indebted to the author of the two biblical volumes addressed "to Theophilus" for our understanding of the primitive church, its mission, and expansion—though Luke's purpose in writing the Acts of the Apostles is still debated. Students will need to know, however, what are the main lines of the development of the Christian mission. The several chapters which cover the story in Acts are devoted to this purpose.

The apostle Paul towers over the world of the New Testament. Successive chapters aim at placing his letters in their historical and pastoral context, with special attention given to the theological and ethical problems that confronted the Pauline churches. Again, no claim to an exhaustive coverage is made, and alert readers will detect many gaps. Since supplementary readings are assigned in W. G. Kümmel, *Introduction to the New Testament,* now available in a revised edition (Abingdon/SCM Press, 1975), and D. Guthrie, *New Testament Introduction* (Inter-Varsity, 3rd ed., 1970), a lot of material has been safely omitted on the understanding that students can quickly make good the deficiency. Wherever possible, however, later bibliographical data have been supplied, on the assumption that the most recent treatments usually build on the work of predecessors.

Because this is not a book of New Testament criticism (in the technical sense) I have included in Part Five a miscellany of themes related to Paul's writings, ranging from a discussion of Paul's letters in the framework of ancient styles of correspondence to a brief consideration of what may be said about Paul's authority on the modern church scene. At this point I have an interest to declare in terms of my confessional position. A reviewer of the earlier volume objected that it stood in an academic no-man's-land between the competing claims of scholarly objectivity and Christian commitment. That no such neutral stance was intended should have been clear, which other reviewers noted in their labeling the book "confessional"; but any lingering doubt may be dispelled by what appears in Chapter 21.

The remaining New Testament literature is covered in Part Six. With Part Seven the reader is given an opportunity to interact with the text itself, as three selected passages of 1 Corinthians are introduced and annotated as an aid to exegesis. What has been learned in the preceding pages is now called into service to elucidate representative Pauline pericopes.

In some quarters exception has been taken to the subtitle "A Guide for Christian Students." Obviously no denominational or ecclesiastical bias is implied in this; nor should the impression be given that the author has in view only a particular type of student. Rather, as one kind reviewer observed, what is meant is really students who are "open-minded and teachable," though my conviction remains that New Testament study is of special relevance to those who stand within the household of Christian faith. But this conviction is not to be interpreted in any narrow sectarian or exclusive fashion.

With a desire that the book, like its partner, may serve the purpose of laying a foundation on which readers may build by fuller exposure to the New Testament texts and deeper appreciation of its contents, I send out this volume.

Abbreviations

AJT	*American Journal of Theology*
ANQ	*Andover Newton Quarterly*
ATR	*Anglican Theological Review*
BA	*Biblical Archaeologist*
BGU	Aegyptische Urkunden, Berlin Museum
BJRL	*Bulletin of the John Rylands University Library of Manchester*
BT	*Biblical Theology*
BTB	*Biblical Theology Bulletin*
BZ	*Biblische Zeitschrift*
CBC	Cambridge Bible Commentary
CBQ	*Catholic Biblical Quarterly*
EQ	*Evangelical Quarterly*
ET	English Translation
ETL	*Ephemerides Theologicae Lovanienses*
EvTh	*Evangelische Theologie*
Expos	*Expositor*
ExpT	*Expository Times*
Harper-Black	*New Testament Commentaries* published by Harper and Row/A. and C. Black
HE	*Ecclesiastical History* of Eusebius
HJ	*Heythrop Journal*
HTR	*Harvard Theological Review*
HzNT	Handbuch zum Neuen Testament
ICC	International Critical Commentary
IDB	*Interpreter's Dictionary of the Bible* (ed. G. A. Buttrick)
IDB, Supp. Vol.	*Interpreter's Dictionary of the Bible, Supplementary Volume* (ed. K. Crim)
Int	*Interpretation*
ISBE	*International Standard Bible Encyclopedia* (revised)
JAAR	*Journal of the American Academy of Religion*
JAC	*Jahrbuch für Antike und Christentum*
JBL	*Journal of Biblical Literature*
JEH	*Journal of Ecclesiastical History*
JETS	*Journal of the Evangelical Theological Society*
JHS	*Journal of Historical Studies*
JNES	*Journal of Near Eastern Studies*
JSNT	*Journal for the Study of the New Testament*
JSS	*Journal of Semitic Studies*

JTS	*Journal of Theological Studies*
LXX	Septuagint
MNTC	Moffatt New Testament Commentary
MT	Masoretic Text
NBD	*New Bible Dictionary* (ed. J. D. Douglas)
NCB	New Century Bible
NEB	New English Bible
n.f.	neue folge
NICNT	New International Commentary on the New Testament
NLCNT	New London Commentary on the New Testament
NIDNTT	*New International Dictionary of New Testament Theology* (ed. C. Brown)
NIGTC	New International Greek Testament Commentary
NovT	*Novum Testamentum*
n.s.	new series
NTF	*New Testament Foundations* (R. P. Martin)
NTS	*New Testament Studies*
o.s.	old series
POxy	Oxyrhynchus Papyri
RB	*Revue biblique*
RE	*Review and Expositor*
RTR	*Reformed Theological Review*
SBT	*Studia Biblica et Theologica*
SE	*Studia Evangelica*
SEÅ	*Svensk Exegetisk Årsbok*
SJT	*Scottish Journal of Theology*
SNTS	Society for New Testament Studies
ST	*Studia Theologica*
TB	*Tyndale Bulletin*
TDNT	*Theological Dictionary of the New Testament* (edd. G. Kittel, G. Friedrich; tr. G. W. Bromiley)
TEV	Today's English Version = The Good News Bible
TLZ	*Theologische Literaturzeitung*
TNTC	Tyndale New Testament Commentary
TS	*Theological Studies*
TU	Texte und Untersuchungen
TZ (ThZ)	*Theologische Zeitschrift*
VC	*Vigiliae Christianae*
VE	*Vox Evangelica*
WBC	Word Biblical Commentary
WTJ	*Westminster Theological Journal*
ZKT	*Zeitschrift für katholische Theologie*
ZNTW	*Zeitschrift für die neutestamentliche Wissenschaft*
ZThK	*Zeitschrift für Theologie und Kirche*

PART ONE

Introducing the Letters and Apocalypse

Apart from the Gospel records, the remaining parts of the New Testament literature represent different types of writing. These may be classified as Acts, Letters, and Apocalyptic writing. In another place I have summarized the understanding of these genres in recent scholarly discussion.[1] Here it will be enough to comment that these documents, various in literary form and style and emanating from different authors or schools of early Christianity, are yet united in a particular way. They represent the literary deposits of a set of Christian communities, pulsating with life in Christ and conscious of an identity which marked them off from other religious groups in the first century.

As in Gospel study, where the completed wholes of the evangelical records represent the end product of a line of development from public proclamation through the oral period to the gradual collection of pericopes into units of tradition, so it is with the investigation of the Epistles and the Apocalypse. The apostolic writers and their disciples seem consciously to be drawing on earlier traditions of creed and catechism, sermon and scriptural teaching, song and liturgical praise. The plentiful evidence for this will occupy these pages.

Above all, the New Testament represents the literary creations, under God, of these apostolic assemblies, who both wanted to conserve the best of the past thus ensuring continuity as the generations lengthened, and to be responsive to the Spirit's direction in new situations and challenges. Tradition and freedom combine to shape the background out of which the New Testament Letters and Apocalypse came.

---

[1] See my essay in *New Testament Interpretation*, ed. I. H. Marshall (1977), pp. 220-51.

CHAPTER ONE

What to Look for in the Epistles

If we follow the traditional order in which the New Testament books appear in the English Bible, we naturally assume that the Gospels came before the Epistles. This assumption is valid in the sense that the historical record of what is contained in the Gospels—the life and ministry of Jesus of Nazareth—is foundational for the writers of the early church. No epistle would have been written if there had been no "Jesus of history." But it is just as surely the case that no Gospel would have been composed unless the influence and power of the risen Lord had first been known in the lives of men and women who made up the apostolic church; and the epistles are the literary deposits of that community of faith. The leading epistles (that is, the Pauline writings and, quite likely, 1 Peter) pre-date the Gospels in order of appearance; yet their writers presuppose, at least in basic outline, the historical happening of the coming of Jesus as a figure on the stage of Palestinian history. Indeed, to explain both types of literature, we need to postulate both the historical "having-happenedness" of Jesus' life and ministry and his new existence in the church as the Lord of Easter and the dispenser of life-in-the-Spirit. The victory of the crucified Jesus and the consequent coming of the Holy Spirit made possible the birth of the church, which in due course became a letter-writing and letter-receiving community as well as a company of people who wanted to express their faith in the form of written Gospels.[1]

As we approach the study of the New Testament Letters, we should keep several factors constantly in view. The import of these observations may be more telling at the close of our study, but we place them here as a sort of prolegomenon and as an incentive to alertness as we proceed.

---

[1] For a recent discussion of the interrelation of Gospels and Epistles in the New Testament see Neil Alexander, "The Epistle for Today," in *Biblical Studies: Essays in Honour of William Barclay,* edd. J. R. McKay and J. F. Miller (1976), pp. 99–118.

THE HISTORICAL BACKGROUND

While it is undeniable that the voice of God is heard in every age through his word in Scripture in ways not dependent on or determined by scientific study, the only safe way to read Scripture is with regard to its historical and contextual setting.[2] For only thus are we safeguarded both from the subjectivism that finds in Scripture what it wants to discover and from the illegitimate use of the church's holy book which reduces the reading of it to an exercise in severely personal piety based on impressions. We need the perspective supplied by the historical-critical method. By this we mean that Scripture is properly understood in its right context only when it is seen as emerging from a distinct and distinctive historical, cultural, and religious setting. When we have sought to ascertain its meaning in that milieu we shall be in a position to discover what God is saying, whether directly or obliquely, to his people in our time.

Specifically, that background falls into well-defined areas. The first is the history of the times in which the early church appeared, grew, suffered, thrived, and developed. There is more to this than the outer frame or shell of world history: it is clear that historical events (e.g., Claudius's edict, Nero's pogrom, the fall of Jerusalem) played a formative part in shaping the response of Christians to the events around them and in providentially conditioning the shape and substance of the message now recorded in the apostolic literature.

Then, the cultural matrix in which the faith was born and nursed must equally be respected. The formative influences were the Jewish ancestral religion, in which most if not all of the New Testament writers were nurtured; Greek ways of thought and expression, particularly in the widespread use of *koinē* Greek and the prevailing atmosphere of Hellenism that emerged directly from the time of Alexander the Great; and Roman society, with its characteristic emphasis on law and order within a framework of world peace and easy communication (see Chapters 2 and 3 below). It does not tax the imagination much to see how the combination of these factors was significant in leading the church to the conclusion that Christianity had been born "in the fulness of time."

Here, too, the nature of the documents that make up the New Testament is to be considered. All are based on *theological convictions*. All are theological works, written out of a living faith to express that faith in God, whose revelation and redemption in Christ they presuppose and proclaim. Even the obvious specimens such as James and Acts, which seem to belong respectively to the genres of moral tract and history-writing, are not really exceptions to this general description.

---

[2] See my essay "Approaches to New Testament Exegesis," in *New Testament Interpretation*, for further discussion of this.

Moreover, the theology which underlies and informs the New Testament writers' task is experiential in character. Though there are snatches of credal and doctrinal formulation, often seen just beneath the surface as in 1 John and 1 Peter, the letters are in the main transcripts of vital experience, at once personal and corporate, of the common life in the body of Christ in the world.[3] The New Testament is a handbook of experiential religion, a conviction that is visible as much in Paul as in James and 2 Peter.

Finally, while we do well to appreciate the contributions of the individual authors who wrote or were indirectly responsible for these New Testament writings, we must never overlook the fact that they are the literary deposits of an ongoing and shared life within the Christian communities in the Mediterranean world of the first century. "Paul's theology" may rightly be deduced or read off from his letters, but it is equally important that these letters contain in written, tangible form the liturgical, confessional, and proclamatory materials cherished and practiced by Christian groups both before and during Paul's ministry.

THE DOMINANCE OF PAUL

Coming to the New Testament without a previous knowledge of it, the reader would quickly gain the impression that Paul was dominant among the men and women who cross the stage of the early church. We will see later (pp. 92, 143f.) how, both in the Acts of the Apostles and in the epistolary literature represented within the twenty-seven books of the New Testament canon, the personality and influence of this man play a major part.

But some fresh perspective needs to be entertained if we are not to draw a false conclusion from the extant evidence. We need to exercise some deliberate restraint in attributing this role to Paul, for it is clear that in the New Testament period Paul was only one among several men and women who claimed, rightly or wrongly, to be church leaders and apostolic figures (cf. 2 Cor. 10–13, esp. 11:13; 1 John 4:1; 2 Pet. 2:1; Rev. 2:2, 20). Of course, it is virtually impossible to put the clock back and recapture such a perspective, undoing the hagiographical influences of later centuries which turned Paul of Tarsus into St. Paul, apostle and martyr. Nor would we want to demote Paul from a pinnacle of eminence, if we accept his own self-witness to his being an "eschatological apostle"[4] and acknowledge the importance that is his due to his later influence on the development of Christian theology as represented in Augustine, Luther, Calvin, Wesley, and Barth.

---

[3] J. S. Stewart's study of Paul's theology, *A Man in Christ* (1935), demonstrated this. See also P. G. S. Hopwood, *The Religious Experience of the Primitive Church* (1936), and, more recently, J. D. G. Dunn, *Jesus and the Spirit* (1975).

[4] See A. Fridrichsen, *The Apostle and his Message* (1947).

Nonetheless, we must always remind ourselves that Paul never stood alone in solitary splendor. All we will learn about the traditional materials on which he drew and to which he was indebted (although he may have edited and adapted them) is confirmed by his own admission that there were others before him who were already Christians when he came on to the scene (Rom. 16:3–16).[5]

Besides, as we become familiar with first- and early second-century literature, we will learn of representatives of several diverse traditions and understandings of the Christian faith, its expression, and its experience. Among these are the so-called Asia Minor tradition, seen in the Johannine literature; the strand seen in Hebrews, which may well represent Christianity as understood in Rome against a Judaeo-Christian backdrop; also there are diverse traditions in the literature outside the New Testament emanating from Egypt, in a distinctive Syrian brand of Christianity seen in the *Didache* or "Teaching of the Twelve Apostles" and in the Pseudo-Clementine literature for Christianity at Edessa, which give evidence of Jewish Christianity.

This notion of the geographical distribution of New Testament and early church Christianity is an important reminder that the apostolic faith took on many forms of expression in the first decades of its life.[6] It expressed itself in response to cultural, social, political, and religious pressures. Sometimes we can easily identify these, such as the need to respond to the new situation after the fall of Jerusalem in AD 70 and the end of Jewish cultus centered in the Temple.[7] On a different level, the delay in the arrival of the Lord's *parousia* created problems (seen in 2 Pet. 3:3ff.) and Christians had to address themselves to such questions.[8] The inevitable dying out of the apostolic figures who had been eyewitnesses of the Lord meant also that some adjustment to a new set of circumstances was needed to ensure continuity with the past.

These factors meant that the type of Christianity as expressed by Paul in his generation would inevitably alter to meet emergent needs. Yet certain constants remain.[9] If we take seriously the claim that the living Lord is the head of the church, his abiding presence would be known as often as believers met to share the fellowship meal. The Lord's Supper ritual may have varied (witness the divergent traditions in

---

[5] This is the thesis of A. M. Hunter's seminal *Paul and his Predecessors* (1940; 2nd ed., 1961).

[6] See W. Bauer, *Orthodoxy and Heresy in Earliest Christianity* (ET 1971).

[7] S. G. F. Brandon, *The Fall of Jerusalem and the Christian Church* (1951; 2nd ed., 1957), has rightly called attention to this important event as it affected both Jews and Christians, though some of his conclusions are to be challenged. See R. P. Martin, *Mark: Evangelist and Theologian* (1972), pp. 75–78; also J. A. T. Robinson, *Redating the New Testament* (1976), pp. 13–30.

[8] A. L. Moore, *The Parousia in the New Testament* (1966), surveys the leading issues.

[9] On the unity underlying the chief New Testament writers, see A. Fridrichsen, "Jesus, St John and St Paul," in *The Root of the Vine,* ed. Fridrichsen (1953), pp. 37–62; A. M. Hunter, *The Unity of the New Testament* (1943); G. E. Ladd, *The Pattern of New Testament Truth* (1968). See later, pp. 419f.

Matthew-Mark, in Luke-Paul, in John-the *Didache,* and in Justin Martyr);[10] but the important element—the presence of the risen Christ in the company of the faithful—persisted. Apart from this vital and abiding element, it is difficult to account for the continuance and centrality of the meal-rite in an emerging institutional Christianity.

Cultural influences also modified the practice of the Christian liturgy, as we can see from comparing worship practices derived from Syria with the later Egyptian or Roman rite.[11] Paul's influence lived on, if sometimes in the shadows. It was never completely submerged and lost; and we can point to its partial recovery in Marcion in the mid second-century, which prepared for fuller apprehension of the Pauline gospel in Irenaeus, Tertullian, and the later fathers. But the Johannine strain of "mystical" Christianity is well represented also in Ignatius, while moralistic emphases discoverable in Matthew, James, and 2 Peter find later formulation in the literature of Jewish Christianity.[12]

THE OVERLAP OF THE APOSTOLIC, POST-APOSTOLIC, AND SUB-APOSTOLIC AGES

For assessing the development and evolution of Christian teaching a customary time division has been used, distinguishing the "apostolic age" from the "post-" and "sub-apostolic" periods, though the latter terms are not always treated as the same. Conventionally, three eras may be designated:

> *Apostolic age:* from Pentecost to the martyr deaths of Paul and Peter (AD 65).
>
> *Post-apostolic age:* after AD 65 to the close of the New Testament canon, traditionally held to be around AD 100 with the demise of John the apostle at Ephesus.
>
> *Sub-apostolic age:* from the turn of the century to the age of the Apologists, *c.* 117–161, and including non-canonical literature from the first and second centuries which is represented by 1 and 2 Clement, the *Didache,* Diognetus, Barnabas, Ignatius, Polycarp, and Hermas—the so-called "Apostolic Fathers."

Whatever value these neat classifications have as pedagogical aids, it is now evident that the categories are misleading. There is a trend toward defining the distinction between canonical and non-canonical literature less sharply than orthodox Christianity, with its belief in a fixed and

---

10 Cf. E. Schweizer, *The Lord's Supper According to the New Testament* (ET 1967).
11 H. Lietzmann, *Mass and Lord's Supper* (ET 1953ff.); cf. A. J. B. Higgins, in *ExpT,* 65 (1954), 333–36.
12 For a survey of the literature of Jewish Christianity, see J. Daniélou, *The Development of Christian Doctrine before the Council of Nicaea,* Vol. 1: *The Theology of Jewish Christianity* (ET 1964).

closed canon, allows. For those scholars such a compartmental division gives a false importance to the canonical literature.

But even if the line between the documents that are canonical and those that are not is preserved, it is still historically prejudicial to set the New Testament books apart from a historical continuum. The fact is that some sub-apostolic books are simultaneous with or even earlier in date than the latest New Testament books, as far as we can tell. For instance, the *Didache* is credibly to be dated in the same period as Hebrews, the Apocalypse, and 2 Peter, while 1 Clement may be earlier than 1–3 John.[13] And in content and background there is a shared background between many of the books of the period, regardless of their precise dating. Moreover, there are no invisible time lines that separate off the three segments. It must be admitted that these divisions have outlived their usefulness and should be discarded or at least relegated to an area of only symbolic value.

THE IMPETUS TO WRITING

A later section (pp. 241–47) is devoted to the literary genre "letters." There we shall note how the New Testament letters fit into ancient letter-writing categories, and how they served the important functions of communication and establishing contact between separated parties. Here our purpose is to inquire whether we can detect motivations that led the New Testament authors to express their mind in epistolary form. It is not difficult to tabulate some of the more obvious reasons before we consider motives beneath the surface of the documents.

Undoubtedly the chief impulse that governed Paul's letter-writing practice was *pastoral*. All he says about his apostolic ministry in terms of his authoritative attitude to his churches (esp. in Gal. and 2 Cor. 10–13) needs to be counterbalanced by those other descriptions of his relationship where he calls himself a father (1 Thess. 2:11; 1 Cor. 4:15), a mother in labor (Gal. 4:19), a nurse (1 Thess. 2:7), and a beloved friend to his congregations (Phil. 4:1).

It is not surprising, then, that his letters reflect tones of anxious solicitude for the well-being of the people to whom he writes. He will address them as a pastor, a designation that recalls both his own demeanor and the ideal he sets before the church leaders of Ephesus (cf. Acts 20:18–35).

In 1 Corinthians (perhaps earlier, too, in the Thessalonian correspondence) Paul appears to be responding to inquiries from church

---

[13] First Clement is usually dated *c.* AD 96, though there have been recent attempts to place it considerably earlier. See A. E. Wilhelm-Hooijbergh, "A Different View of Clemens Romanus," *HJ*, 16 (1975), 266–88; J. A. T. Robinson, *op. cit.*, pp. 327–35.

members. They had sent him a letter, and he had picked up snatches of information from the visits of Stephanas, Fortunatus, and Achaicus (1 Cor. 16:17) as well as from "gossipy" items relayed to him from the entourage of Chloe's family (1 Cor. 1:11). He evidently makes allusion to these sources of information in his reply (1 Cor. 5:1; 7:1). This would lead the modern reader to suspect that Paul might well cite parts of the Corinthian documents in his replies. It has been plausibly argued that such quotations *do* appear in 1 Corinthians 6 and 7, and it certainly contributes to a better understanding of the apostle's mind if we regard some statements, especially in 6:12, in 7:1, and in 8:1,4, as containing quoted remarks from the Corinthian church, which Paul reproduces before giving his own evaluation of the position they represent (see later, p. 295). At Colossae Paul is dependent on what he has learned from Epaphras (1:7; 4:12), and his letter reflects the information supplied by this man, who was his representative in the Lycus valley.

Second, Paul's letter-writing habits include the use of *catechetical material*, which he draws on and uses by way of reminder to the churches. The often reiterated appeals, "Don't you know . . . ?" and "Are you ignorant . . . ?" (see examples in Rom. 6:3,16; 7:1; 11:2; 1 Cor. 3:16; 5:6; 6:2,3,9,15,16,19; 9:13,24; 10:1; 2 Cor. 1:8; 1 Thess. 4:13; cf. Rom. 6:17) suggest a conscious allusion to traditional teaching that is the common property of the church members. In a later chapter (pp. 248ff.) we shall have occasion to investigate more closely the indebtedness of Paul to the fund of traditional teaching-forms already current in the church. What is easily demonstrable in the case of the apostle to the Gentiles is just as evident as we inspect 1 Peter, Hebrews, James, and the Johannine letters and Apocalypse, all of which make use of catechetical forms of instruction, credal expressions, and possibly snatches of hymnic and baptismal liturgy.[14]

We should not lose sight of the powerful psychological factor involved in this practice. New Testament writers often give the appearance of being on the defensive in their writings, seeking to win over elements in the congregations who were either hostile or indifferent to their theological positions.[15] It is likely that one sure way to enlist support and promote concurrence would be to use traditional materials that were the shared, common possession of both writers and their readership. This would dispel the notion that the writers were introducing new-fangled ideas and would give solidity and confidence to the appeals they were making.

14 For a discussion see G. W. H. Lampe, "The Evidence in the New Testament for Early Creeds, Catechisms and Liturgy," *ExpT*, 71 (1959–60), 359–63; and below, pp. 251ff.
15 See E. E. Ellis, "Paul and his Opponents: Trends in Research," in *Christianity, Judaism and Other Greco-Roman Cults: Studies for Morton Smith at Sixty*, Part 1, ed. J. Neusner (1975), pp. 264–98 = *Prophecy and Hermeneutic in Early Christianity* (1978), pp. 80–115.

The same desire to communicate with their readers by *sharing an understanding of the Old Testament,* on which agreement with the teaching may be expected, is a third prominent feature of the New Testament authors' method.[16] Several issues are involved in this statement, and reference to the practice of embodying types of exegesis as a teaching model will be made in the course of this book. It is a truism to say that the Old Testament was appealed to mainly as a witness to the church's Lord and to buttress the claim that the new age of prophetic fulfilment had indeed dawned in his coming and in the life of the church. More questionable is whether the specimens of exegetical method found in the New Testament were used as weapons of polemic to oppose "erroneous" interpretations of the Old Testament text. Conceivable examples are found in Romans 10:6–10,[17] 1 Corinthians 1:18—4:5 (the nature and propriety of "true" wisdom), 15:44–46 (the proper order of the resurrection body),[18] and Ephesians 5:32. The Ephesians passage has been cited as an instance of the writer's opposing a current interpretation of the Old Testament. His remark, "I for my part refer it to Christ and to the church" (NEB), seems clearly slanted against those (gnosticizing) teachers who understood "the two shall become one" (Gen. 2:24) as a union of the cosmic powers, the aeons which filled the *pleroma* of interstellar space. The Pauline theologian opposes this treatment of an Old Testament text and offers his own christological and ecclesiological interpretation to refute and replace it.[19]

This observation brings us to the importance of seeing, in the fourth place, at least some of the emphases in the letters as *polemically oriented to false teaching.* We may recognize immediately part of the purpose of Galatians, Colossians, 1 John, and 2 Peter as unmasking and repelling false ideas about the person of Christ and the way of salvation in him. The root errors are quickly identifiable as (1) trust in nomistic righteousness, implying that circumcision was valued as the badge of the Christian profession (Gal.; cf. Rom. 3 and 4; Phil. 3); (2) false understanding of the Christian life as an invitation to antinomian license

---

[16] On this see D. M. Smith, "The Use of the Old Testament in the New," in *The Use of the Old Testament in the New and Other Essays: Studies in Honor of William Franklin Stinespring,* ed. J. M. Efird (1972), pp. 3–65.

[17] Jewish literature derived from Deut. 30:11–14 the teaching that "God in his goodness has brought this hidden Wisdom 'near' in the Torah." Paul opposes this interpretation by equating Wisdom with Christ. Cf. M. J. Suggs, "'The Word Is Near You,'" in *Christian History and Interpretation: Studies Presented to John Knox,* edd. W. R. Farmer, C. F. D. Moule and R. R. Niebuhr (1967), pp. 289ff., esp. 299–312.

[18] See H. Conzelmann, *First Corinthians* (ET 1975), *ad loc.*; E. E. Ellis, "'Wisdom' and 'Knowledge' in 1 Corinthians," *TB,* 25 (1974), 82–98 = *Prophecy and Hermeneutic in Early Christianity* (1978), pp. 45–62.

[19] Cf. H. Schlier, *Christus und die Kirche im Epheserbrief* (1930), pp. 60–75. This interpretation is opposed by E. Percy, *Die Probleme der Kolosser- und Epheserbriefe* (1946), p. 327. Most commentators attach no significance to the introductory words of vs. 32.

(Rom. 3:8; 6:1ff.; parts of Gal. 5, 6; cf. the same ethical laxity, set on a gnostic background in 2 Pet. 2); (3) a Christology which demoted Jesus Christ to the level of one angelic power in a hierarchical system (Col.) or which made him a spiritual power who had no real contact with humanity and touched human life only tangentially as a heavenly figure wearing the guise of a mortal man (1 John; Col.; the same docetic error is also to be seen in the Corinthians' attitude to Jesus, according to one plausible interpretation of 1 Cor. 12:3).[20]

These aberrations, both doctrinal and practical, evoked the letter-writing practices of the apostles and those of their followers who claimed their authority in exposing and rebutting heretical tendencies. But there were also incipient false ideas that needed attention. The threat of a gnosticizing depreciation of a historical incarnation and a gnosticizing denial of God's purpose in history leading up to a final appearing of Christ, along with an attempt to sever the roots of the new faith from its soil in the Old Testament Scriptures—these are real dangers posed to the Pauline writer of Ephesians[21] and the Petrine disciple whose work we read as 2 Peter.

Nor were libertine practices absent. There is abundant evidence of how quickly the narrow line between "salvation by grace without works" and an irresponsible attitude of "live as you please" was rubbed out, as (Gentile) Christians failed to perceive the ethical demands of the gospel as well as its offer of free grace and acceptance apart from merit. In his lifetime Paul had to refute these travesties of his teaching; doubtless after his death overzealous followers carried part of his teaching to an unwarranted extreme. The reaction to this swing of the pendulum is visible in James, 2 Peter, Revelation, and Matthew, while Mark was written to rescue Paul's Christology of the heavenly Christ from losing contact with the earthly figure of the lowly Jesus of Galilee.[22]

Above all else, the New Testament writers were concerned to *explicate the nature of the Christian life.* Two discussions of the data helpfully focus on the guidelines set up by these writers to assist Christians in appreciating the genius and heartbeat of the life in Christ.[23] The following outline displays the evidence.

1. "Once this was hidden, now it is revealed" (Rom. 16:25f.; 1 Cor. 2:7f.; Col. 1:26f.; Eph. 3:4f., 9f.). The subject is the plan of God for including humanity in the era of salvation. Previously this *Heilsplan*

---

[20] See W. Schmithals, *Gnosticism in Corinth* (ET 1971), pp. 124ff.
[21] For a recent statement of these purposes underlying Ephesians, see C. L. Mitton, *Ephesians* (1976), pp. 29–32.
[22] R. P. Martin, *Mark: Evangelist and Theologian*, Ch. 6.
[23] R. Bultmann, *Theology of the New Testament*, Vol. I (ET 1952), 105f.; N. Dahl, "Formgeschichtliche Beobachtungen zur Christusverkündigung in der Gemeindepredigt," in *Neutestamentliche Studien für Rudolf Bultmann*, ed. W. Eltester (1957), pp. 3–9 = ET in *Jesus in the Memory of the Early Church* (1976), pp. 30–36.

(saving plan) lay covered in obscurity; now in the new age it is made known, and believers are invited to live in its light (see Eph. 5:8–17) by appreciating both the offer and the demand of the new period of history into which they have been ushered at the coming of Christ.

In the non-Pauline corpus the same emphasis is found: what was promised or given at the foundation of the world is now revealed (1 Pet. 1:18–21; 1 John 1:1–3; cf. 2 Tim. 1:9–11; Titus 1:2f.; Ignatius, *Magn.* 6:1; Hermas, *Sim.* 9:12).

2. A soteriological setting to this scheme of revelation is provided in another group of verses, where a contrast is set up: "once [ποτέ/τότε] you were this, but now [νυνὶ δὲ] you are that." The lines of contrast are clear in Ephesians 2:11–22; 5:8; Galatians 4:8f. (cf. 3:23ff.); Romans 6:17–22; 7:5f.; 11:30; 1 Corinthians 6:9ff.; and 1 Peter 2:10,25.

A variation of this theme makes the second member of the statement a report of what God or Christ has done. Thus, "once you were this, but now God/Christ has done that [for you]" (see Col. 1:21ff.; Eph. 2:1–10; Titus 3:3–7; cf. Gal. 4:3–9; Col. 2:13f.; 1 Pet. 1:14ff.; 2 Clem. 1:6ff.).

3. The ethical pattern of conformity to Christ is often appealed to as a motive for Christian living, again with several variations.

Paul favors the recall of Christ's love for his people and his action on the church's behalf as a foundation on which he builds his ethical appeal (see Rom. 15:3f., 7f.; 2 Cor. 8:9; Eph. 5:2,25,29; cf. 4:32; and Col. 3:13). There is, however, no appeal to the historical details of Jesus' earthly life, so it is not quite accurate to speak of "imitation of Christ." Rather Paul makes the total impression of Christ's self-effacement and self-giving in love the basis for his admonition to act likewise.

Philippians 2:5–11 presents its own problems. Interpretations vary according to the meaning attached to verse 5: "Have this mind among yourselves, which you have in Christ Jesus" (RSV). Is it the "mind of Christ" that is inculcated as an example for the Philippians to accept and adopt in their situation? Or is Paul appealing to them to adopt the disposition that should be theirs as those who are "in Christ Jesus," that is, members of his church? The recital of verses 6–11 shows the character of the once incarnate and now exalted Lord, and it is this character that is to be practiced, according to the first view. But there are weighty objections to this.[24] We should therefore conclude that Paul is citing the "hymn of salvation" in verses 6–11 to enforce the appeal of verse 5 and to show that the new life "in Christ Jesus" is possible only on

---

[24] See R. P. Martin, *Philippians* (NCB, 1976), pp. 92f.; and the author's *Carmen Christi: Philippians 2:5–11* (²1983), pp. xii–xix, seeking to respond to recent critics, notably L. W. Hurtado, "Jesus as Lordly Example in Philippians 2:5–11," in *From Jesus to Paul. Studies in Honour of Francis Wright Beare,* edd. P. Richardson and J. C. Hurd (1984), pp. 113–26.

the basis of the lordship of Christ. He came to his glory along a road of obedience and suffering. The Philippians are called to live under that lordship (vs. 12) and to conform their congregational life, not according to Christ's earthly characteristics, but rather according to a life that confesses his kingly authority over their lives.

Imitatio Christi, it would seem, is not a Pauline category of ethical endeavor, even if it can be seen in 1 Peter 2:21-24; Hebrews 12:1-3; and possibly Revelation 14:4,5 (the example of the martyrs).[25]

4. What has been termed a *teleological motif* is seen in statements which open with a declaration of what Christ has done for his people and glide into an implicit call for them to accept the benefit he has secured for them. His action was purposeful, and they are bidden to accept and live by the purpose for which he called them. We may instance the following varieties of application:

a. Christ for us ... therefore/in order that we ... (1 Thess. 5:9f.; 2 Cor. 5:14f.,21; Gal. 3:13f.; 4:4f.; 1 Pet. 2:21-24);

b. Christ for us ... in order that God (Christ) may ... (Gal. 1:4; Eph. 5:25f.; Titus 2:13f.; 1 Pet. 3:18f.);

c. Christ for us ... (no explicit reason given) (Rom. 14:9; Eph. 2:15f.; 4:10; Heb. 2:14f.).

5. There is finally the use of the verbs "beseech," "entreat," "exhort."[26] Such appeals, couched in the first person of the verb, often gain authority from the accompanying phrase "in the Lord" or "in the name of the Lord" (see 1 Thess. 4:1ff.; 5:1ff.; 2 Thess. 3:12; Rom. 15:30; 1 Cor. 1:10; 2 Cor. 10:1; Phm. 9,10; 2 Tim. 4:1; cf. 1 Tim. 5:21; 6:13).

In these various ways and by means of differing motifs the constant appeal to accept the full implications of the Christian life is enforced. To drive home this insistence, as both a gracious offer and a total demand, may be said to be the chief aim of apostolic preaching, with its stress on the celebration of God's gracious act in Jesus Christ for human salvation, and the practical-hortatory application that appeals to Christians "not to accept the grace of God in vain" (2 Cor. 6:1) but to receive and live by all that the gospel offers. This is clearly a prominent factor, if not the *leitmotif,* of the apostolic preaching to the community. It is certainly a powerful impetus that produced the New Testament literature.

---

[25] See E. J. Tinsley, *The Imitation of God in Christ* (1960); R. Schnackenburg, *Christian Existence in the New Testament,* Vol. I (ET 1968), pp. 114-27.

[26] Dibelius' discussion of these verbs of "exhortation," *From Tradition to Gospel* (ET 1936), pp. 238-40, has been considerably extended by C. J. Bjerkelund, *Parakaló: Form, Funktion und Sinn der parakaló-Sätze in den paulinischen Briefen* (1967). He comments on the use of the allied verbs παρακαλῶ and ἐρωτῶ as one in which the writer expresses concern for both practical and "spiritual" (*geistliche*) interests (p. 87) and goes on to define the scope of παρακαλῶ as expressing a summons in a dignified, well-bred way, free from a tone of either injunction or submissiveness (p. 110). See H. Boers, "The Form Critical Study of Paul's Letters," *NTS,* 22 (1975-76), 140-158, esp. 154ff.

PART TWO

The Ancient World:

The Setting of the New Testament in Graeco-Roman Civilization

The two chapters of this section complement the corresponding chapters in Volume 1 and offer the same general approach. The purpose of this sketch is to provide some background to the world of the New Testament church in the political, cultural, social, and religious currents that ran through the civilization of Greece and Rome from the age of Augustus to the first decades of the second century.

The church of the apostles lived in the framework provided by the Roman Empire with its network of cities and political institutions. The social ethos of the age is equally important for understanding the setting of the Christian message, as some recent studies on the sociological dimension of the early church have illustrated.[1] But the really formative background is that of the philosophical and religious presuppositions of the age. It is worthwhile to look closely at some of the trends in popular religion, and we shall be reading several texts of that period, including some more well-defined formulations of Epicureanism and Stoicism.

---

[1] R. Scroggs, "The Earliest Christian Communities as Sectarian Movement," *Christianity, Judaism and Other Greco-Roman Cults,* ed. J. Neusner, Part 2 (1975), pp. 1–23; see L. E. Keck, "On the Ethos of Early Christians," *JAAR,* 42 (1974), 435–52; J. Gager, *Kingdom and Community: The Social World of Early Christianity* (1975); A. J. Malherbe, *Social Aspects of Early Christianity* (1977); R. F. Hock, *The Social Context of Paul's Ministry* (1980); H. C. Kee, *Christian Origins in Sociological Perspective* (1980); D. Tidball, *The Social Context of the New Testament* (1984); C. Osiek, *What Are They Saying about the Social Setting of the New Testament?* (1984).

Special mention should be made of W. A. Meeks, *The First Urban Christians. The Social World of the Apostle Paul* (1983); and E. A. Judge, "Cultural Conformity and Innovation in Paul: Some Clues from Contemporary Documents," *TB,* 35 (1984), 3–24.

CHAPTER TWO

The World of the Early Church: The Roman Empire

This chapter offers a brief overview of the political and social factors prominent in the Roman world of the first century.[1] It was in this world of Roman political conditions and administration that the early church was born and grew. The religious and philosophical setting of that world will be taken up in the subsequent chapter.

THE ORGANIZATION OF THE EMPIRE

Let us put two quotations side by side. The first is attributed to the Emperor Augustus, who in an edict dated 27 BC expressed the fond hope that when he "had secured the frontiers of the Empire, pacified the turbulent provinces, got the administration running smoothly, and brought about political harmony at home,"[2] he would hand over the reins of power to the Roman senate and people. The second, also referring to an edict, is more familiar to the Christian reader.

> May it be granted to me to establish the commonwealth on its foundations so safely and soundly, and to receive the reward for that action that I seek, that I may be called the author of the best state of things and when I die may carry with me the hope that the foundations of the commonwealth that I have laid will remain unshaken (Suetonius, *Life of Augustus* 28.2).

> In those days a decree was issued by the Emperor Augustus for a general registration throughout the Roman world (Luke 2:1, NEB).

Both quotations introduce the concept of the Roman world (οἰκουμένη) and name its ruler Augustus (27 BC—AD 14).

---

[1] In organization and content this chapter owes a great deal to H. Carey Oakley, on whose essay in *Vox Evangelica*, 1 (1962), I have gladly drawn with his permission. More recent books consulted include G. W. Bowersock, *Augustus and the Greek World* (1965); A. H. M. Jones, *Augustus* (1970); R. Syme, *The Roman Revolution* (repr. 1967); P. A. Brunt, *Social Conflicts in the Roman Republic* (1971); A. N. Sherwin-White, *Roman Society and Roman Law in the New Testament* (1963); B. H. Warmington, *Nero, Reality and Legend* (1969); R. M. Grant, *Augustus to Constantine* (1970); and E. Lohse, *The New Testament Environment* (ET 1976), Part II; H. Koester, *Introduction to the New Testament*. Volume One: *History, Culture, and Religion of the Hellenistic Age* (ET 1982).

[2] Jones, *op. cit.*, p. 78.

In the preceding century, from about 133 BC, the social life of the empire was disfigured by several blemishes. A corrupt municipal oligarchy and an unruly city mob at Rome, rival warlords in the provinces (of which Appian gives a graphic account in his *Civil Wars*),[3] and threats of invasions from the north and east had brought the Roman Republic to the verge of ruin.

A succession of military dictatorships under Sulla, Marius, and Cinna gave way at length to the wars of Lucullus, Pompey, and Crassus, which were followed by the conflict between Crassus, Pompey, and Caesar. There were also popular uprisings led by Lepidus (78–77 BC) and Spartacus (73 BC), the latter a slave revolt with wide social repercussions.[4]

The eventual result was the establishment of the sole rule of Julius Caesar, which in turn was abruptly halted by his murder in March of 44 BC. The reins of power were quickly seized by his grandnephew Gaius Octavius, who at that time was a student in Greece. He claimed the title Octavian as successor to Julius Caesar, put in a bid for the allegiance of the legions, and entered into a triumvirate with the generals Mark Antony and Lepidus. Unhealthy rivalry finally led to a showdown and, after the Battle of Actium (31 BC), Octavian was left as the undisputed master of the Roman world.

Octavian set about the task of refurbishing the constitution, with results that led to his being presented by the senate with the title of honor "Augustus."[5] An example of his reforming work was his desire to equalize the burden of taxation throughout the Empire and to introduce new and more equitable forms of tax liability. The registration of which Luke speaks was a part of this scheme.[6] Yet the return of peace and order associated with Augustus' principate was not secured without cost. As the quotation above implies, the emperor kept a firm grip on national leadership and control. He chose to call himself the *princeps* (leading citizen of the Republic), yet he carefully retained within his own authority certain key powers that had formerly been at the discretion of the Senate.[7] In particular, he virtually controlled the army single-handedly, and freedom of speech, long cherished by orators in the Forum, was somewhat curtailed. But the citizens were ready to surrender some of their liberties for the gift of peace, and it was the benevolent dictator Augustus who gave peace to the Roman world. *Otium*—peace

---

[3] Cf. Brunt, *op. cit.*, p. 153; Syme, *op. cit.*, p. 17.

[4] Brunt, *op. cit.*, pp. 112ff.

[5] Jones, *op. cit.*, pp. 46f.

[6] *Ibid.*, p. 119.

[7] *Ibid.*, p. 85; cf. Brunt, *op. cit.*, p. 147. Augustus cloaked his claim in high-sounding altruistic language as later benevolent dictators have sought to do. See his *Res Gestae*, as quoted in C. K. Barrett, *The New Testament Background: Selected Documents* (1956), pp. 2–4.

and order—became a happy reality, as Tacitus reported and Horace and Vergil celebrated.[8]

The Mediterranean Sea was a Roman lake: countries bordering on it were directly or indirectly subject to Rome. The centrality of the Mediterranean gave the Empire cohesion, and Augustus finally came to see, when his legions were defeated by Arminius in Germany, that there were limits to Rome's colonial and territorial ambitions.[9] "He left," says Tacitus, "an empire bounded by the Ocean and distant rivers" (*Annals* 1.9). To the west was the Atlantic; to the north the Rhine and the Danube; to the east the Euphrates formed a natural boundary; and to the south lines of civilization were drawn by the North African desert. These geographical points of the compass mark the "inhabited world" of which Luke writes. To the far east were the mysterious Parthian tribes and to the north the unruly barbarian peoples whose forces Augustus could only partly contain.

Within these frontiers peace was secured by the Roman army and justice administered, on the whole impartially, by provincial prefects, the most powerful of whom were directly responsible to the Emperor and client kings.[10] There were exceptions, of course. Judaea suffered from a number of unfortunate prefects, including Pontius Pilate (see Vol. 1, pp. 66–68). One of the most notorious was the Greek freedman Felix, brother of Claudius' favorite Pallas, who (in the words of Tacitus) "with every kind of cruelty and lust exercised the power of a tyrant in the spirit of a slave" (*Histories* 5.9). Yet, on the whole, Rome deserved its reputation for even-handed justice. The words of the late Roman poet Rutilius, himself a Gaul, are true: "Under your rule the lawless have only gained by their defeat" (*De reditu suo* 64).

THE UNIFICATION OF THE EMPIRE

Augustus and his successors were concerned to draw the peoples of the Empire together. Under the Republic, there had been a great gulf between the rulers and the ruled; under the Empire this distinction gradually disappeared. This was partly effected by the spread of Roman citizenship to the provinces.[11] At first, the imperial citizenship was confined to Italians and a few favored communities and individuals outside Italy, but gradually it was extended more widely, in spite of Augustus' fears that the body of citizens might be contaminated by the influx of

---

[8] Brunt, *op. cit.*, p. 148. Horace's *Odes* (e.g., III.14; IV.15; see M. Hengel, *Christ and Power* [ET 1977], p. 9) and *Carmen Saeculare* and Vergil's fourth *Eclogue* display the euphoria of the Augustan Age. See Barrett, *op. cit.*, pp. 6–10; also J. B. Mayor, W. W. Fowler, and R. S. Conway, *Virgil's Messianic Eclogue* (1907).

[9] Suetonius, *Augustus* 23 (cited by Jones, *op. cit.*, pp. 76f.).

[10] Jones, *op. cit.*, pp. 107–16.

[11] Sherwin-White, *op. cit.*, Ch. 7 and pp. 178f.

manumitted slaves and foreign freedmen.[12] The emperor Claudius (41–54) followed a particularly liberal policy, and double citizenship became possible: Paul was proud to be a citizen of Tarsus—"no undistinguished city" (Acts 21:39)—but he also rejoiced in and took advantage of the privileges of being a citizen of Rome.

With Roman citizenship went Roman customs, Roman dress, and the Latin language. In the time of Agricola (77–84), Tacitus reports, the sons of British chieftains received a liberal education and were encouraged to rival the Gauls as orators in Latin (*Agricola* 21). There was apparently no racial or color prejudice, and a man of industry and ability might rise from a humble origin to a high position in the imperial service. As early as AD 70 a Roman general, addressing Gauls, could say: "All is common between us; you often command our legions, you govern these and other provinces. There is no privilege, no exclusion" (Tacitus, *Histories* 4.74). To quote another late Roman poet: "She [Rome] alone has received the vanquished into her bosom."[13]

IMPERIAL PROPAGANDA

There were also more subtle means by which the emperors sought to win the loyalty of their subjects. Augustus was a master of propaganda and he set the pattern for his successors. In the absence of a popular press, radio, and television, the two most effective means of propaganda were buildings and coinage. Suetonius reports a boast of Augustus that he found Rome a city of brick (*latericia*) but left it a city of marble (*marmorea*) (*Augustus* 28.3). In architecture and design he indulged his taste for the magnificent. Emblems and inscriptions on the coins were carefully chosen and frequently changed. As they passed from hand to hand they were closely scrutinized and carried their message far and wide. "'Whose likeness and inscription is this?' They said, 'Caesar's'" (Matt. 22:20f.). Vespasian (69–79) issued gold coins showing "Judaea captured" to mark the Roman destruction of Jerusalem in 70. The blessings of imperial rule were brought home by figures representing peace, valor, good fortune, abundance, providence, and many others. Scholars have only recently come to appreciate the far-reaching influence of the imperial coinage.[14]

[12] Jones, *op. cit.*, pp. 133ff.
[13] Claudian, *On Stilicho's Consulship* 3.150. Typical of this sentiment is the full quatrain from Claudian (3.150–4) in a modern verse:

Rome! Rome alone has found the spell to charm
The tribes that fell beneath her conquering arm,
Has given one name to the whole human race,
And clasped and sheltered them in fond embrace.

Cf. R. P. Martin, *Philippians* (1959, rev. 1986) on Phil. 1:27.
[14] See H. Mattingly, *Roman Imperial Civilisation* (1957), pp. 46–55 with plates; and E. Stauffer's use of numismatic data in *Christ and the Caesars* (ET 1955); cf. H. St. J. Hart, "Judaea and Rome: The Official Commentary," *JTS* 3 n.s. (1952), 172–98.

Emperors also influenced public opinion by creating a personal relationship between themselves and their subjects. All soldiers swore an oath of allegiance to their *imperator* and acclaimed him after every victory won by his subordinates. Claudius, though the least soldierly of men, recognized the importance of this personal link with the army, and came to Britain especially to witness the crossing of the Thames at London by his victorious troops and to receive their acclamations. With the civilian population, too, the emperor strove to establish a personal bond of allegiance. He was *pater patriae,* the father of his country, as Augustus claimed for himself in AD 2.[15] All the inhabitants of the Empire were under his protection and his relation to them was that of patron to client. Oaths of allegiance to the emperor made it easy for the enemies of the early Christians to bring them before the local magistrates on the charge that they were disloyal to the emperor "saying that there is another king, Jesus" (Acts 17:7).

EMPEROR-WORSHIP

Emperor-worship was another means Augustus adopted to link together the peoples of the Empire in loyalty to the ruling power.[16] Since the days of Alexander the Great, who claimed divine honors in his lifetime, it had been common in the east to accord such honors to monarchs and benefactors. Such deification was not unnatural in a polytheistic society, with its legends of heroes like Hercules, who had been deified after death as benefactors of mankind. Euhemerus, in the third century BC, had theorized that all the gods of Greek mythology were originally kings and conquerors, to whom humanity had showed gratitude by worshiping as gods. The distinction between divine and human, especially made by Lucretius, who regarded the gods as removed from mankind yet still addicted to pleasure, was thus blurred for all except the Jews.

Augustus played down worship of himself in Rome by refusing the honors which the Senate, the equestrian order, and the Roman people endeavored to offer him; but he did allow the worship of his "genius" or guardian spirit. At his death his stepson Tiberius extolled him as a god.[17] In 29 BC Augustus permitted the city of Pergamum to erect a temple to Rome and Augustus. Possibly it is this temple to which reference is made in Revelation: "I know where you dwell, where Satan's throne is" (2:13) (but see below, p. 375). Seeing in such a cult an expression of loyalty to the Empire and himself, Augustus not only encouraged it in the east, where it was spontaneous, but introduced it in the west, where there was no precedent for it. Further, starting with Julius Caesar, emperors were deified after death, unless their memory had

---

[15] Jones, *op. cit.,* p. 60. The titles *pater patriae* along with *pontifex maximus* are, however, regarded only as honorific and added nothing to Augustus' powers.
[16] See Grant, *op. cit.,* p. 5; Jones, *op. cit.,* pp. 150–52; Bowersock, *op. cit.,* pp. 112–21.
[17] Cf. Dio Chrysostom 56.36.4–5; 39.5; 41.9.

been condemned, and temples and priests were assigned to them. Such temples were symbols of Roman rule. The rebel Britons, in AD 61, regarded the temple of Claudius at Camulodunum (Colchester) as "a citadel of perpetual tyranny" (*arx aeternae dominationis*) (Tacitus, *Annals* 14.31).

Emperor worship brought together the various communities in a province and enabled them to present their petitions to the emperor; it also symbolized the wider unity of different races within the Empire. But it remained a formal and official cult and was conducted in a perfunctory manner. Jews were exempt from it. Christians could not conform to it: refusing to offer a few grains of incense before the emperor's image was a test of a person's sole allegiance to Jesus Christ as Lord.[18] What to the pagan was a mere formality, for the Christian meant the denial of his faith.

COMMUNICATIONS BY LAND AND SEA[18a]

Strong Roman rule made travel in the Mediterranean area during the first century of our era safer and easier than any time until the late 19th century. "Caesar," says Epictetus, "seems to provide us with profound peace; there are no wars nor battles any more, no great bands of robbers or pirates; we are able to travel by land at any hour and to sail from sunrise to sunset" (*Discourses* 3.13.9). Rome was the center of a vast system of roads covering the whole Empire, most of them military in origin, for swift and easy movement of troops was vital to the safety of the Empire. Road-building was one of the regular tasks of the Roman soldier when he was not fighting. Under the Empire the central government seems to have been responsible for maintaining the chief roads, though local communities were sometimes called upon to share the cost. Skilfully planned, these roads were built so solidly that stretches of them remain today. In Macedonia one can still see part of the Egnatian Way, the great arterial road from the Adriatic to Constantinople, along which Paul traveled from Neapolis to Philippi and then to Thessalonica.

Augustus instituted an imperial courier service (*cursus publicus*) on the model of that organized by Darius of Persia, to keep in close touch with the provinces. Rest-houses were provided at intervals of twenty-five miles and changes of horses at shorter distances. An imperial courier could cover fifty miles a day and reach the Bosporus from Rome in twenty-five days. These facilities were strictly limited to official use; ordinary travelers proceeded much more slowly.[19]

---

[18] See the illustration of this test in *Martyrdom of Polycarp* 9; cf. O. Cullmann, *The Earliest Christian Confessions* (ET 1949), pp. 25–32.

[18a] See for this topic L. Casson, *Travel in the Ancient World* (1974).

[19] See R. P. Martin, *Philippians* (NCB, 1976), pp. 41f.; P. N. Harrison, *Polycarp's Two Epistles to the Philippians* (1936), pp. 113–16; Harrison in *NTS* 2 (1955–56), 260.

Among the perils Paul mentions on his missionary journeys was "danger from robbers" (2 Cor. 11:26). Brigandage had not been entirely stamped out, though it was much less prevalent than under the late Republic. The imperial government took seriously its duty to ensure the safety of travelers. In some places troops kept order along the roads, and provincial governors hunted out highwaymen, kidnapers, and thieves. The usual punishment for these offenses was crucifixion or death in the arena.

Four years before Augustus was born Pompey had cleared the Mediterranean of pirates, and during the first centuries of the Christian era travelers could sail the seas without fear of molestation. In the summer the Etesian winds from the northwest made for swift voyages between Rome and Alexandria, but the return took much longer. Storms made sailing dangerous from mid-September to mid-November, and after that all navigation ceased on the open sea for the rest of the winter. It was because the captain refused to winter at Fair Havens that the ship on which Paul traveled ran into bad weather and was wrecked.[20] The ship on which Paul sailed was doubtless one of the grain fleet, organized and protected by the Roman government, which supplied Rome with corn from Alexandria (cf. Acts 27:6,38). Outside the Mediterranean there were regular sailings from the Red Sea to India and Ceylon, the modern Sri Lanka.

EXCHANGE OF GOODS AND IDEAS

By these land and sea routes goods circulated freely. No barriers to trade existed except for moderate customs dues, which were not protectionist. Much of the trade was in the hands of Greek and Syrian merchants. We find Lydia, from Thyatira in Asia Minor, selling the purple dye for which her city was famous three hundred miles away in Philippi (Acts 16:14).

No less free was the circulation of ideas. The traveler on a Roman road might meet the priests of a Syrian goddess, preying on the superstition of simple country folk; or Cynic philosophers, "the mendicant friars of antiquity," with their staff, scrip, and rough cloak, preaching the simple life and the vanity of riches and learning; or more cultivated philosophical missionaries like Dio Chrysostom, many of whose speeches have come down to us. Exiled from Italy under Domitian, he spent years traveling through the Balkans and Asia Minor, sometimes, like Paul, working with his hands, attacking the moral evils of the day, convinced of his divine mission as a doctor of the soul. Slaves from the east and soldiers returning from service there brought oriental customs and cults to Rome, so that Juvenal, writing at the end of the first cen-

[20] See F. F. Bruce, *The Acts of the Apostles* (1951), *ad* Acts 27:9.

tury, complains that "long ago Syrian Orontes has flowed into the Tiber" (*iam pridem Syrus, in Tiberim defluxit Orontes*).[21]

Among Christian travelers, besides Paul and his companions, we might find Phoebe, a deaconess of the church at Cenchreae, journeying from Corinth to Rome and taking with her Paul's letter to the Romans; or Epaphroditus traveling from Philippi to take the love-gift of the Philippian church to the apostle in prison. In John's third epistle we learn of traveling Christian teachers of a generation later, who "have set out for his sake and have accepted nothing from the heathen" (3 John 7). The *Didache* spells out careful instructions for receiving such itinerant teachers.

> Let every apostle who comes to you be received as the Lord, but let him not stay more than one day, or if need be a second as well; but if he stay three days, he is a false prophet. And when an apostle goes forth, let him receive nothing but bread until he reaches his night's lodging; but if he ask for money, he is a false prophet (11.4–6).

When the risen Lord issued his instructions to the apostles, "Go into all the world," the routes by land and sea lay open and ready for their obedience.

THE CITIES OF THE EMPIRE

The nodal points in the system of Roman roads were the great cities of the Empire.[22] A city-state in origin, with a population in New Testament times estimated at over 700,000,[22a] Rome fostered city life wherever it was found and created it where it did not exist. The city became the unit of administration within the province, and to each city was attached the country around it as its "territory." In the east, particularly in Asia Minor and Syria, Rome took over many cities founded by Alexander or his successors in the policy of hellenization. The amount of local independence allowed to the cities varied. Most favored were the Roman colonies, like Philippi and Corinth, which were communities of Roman citizens including military veterans settled at key points in the Empire. The constitution of the cities conformed to a general pattern. Each had annually elected magistrates, a senate drawn from the landed aristocracy, and a popular assembly. Rome considered the upper classes more sympathetic to its rule, and common people thus had little power. Occasionally, however, they were aroused to noisy demonstrations, as in the uproar in the theater at Ephesus. From the vivid account in Acts we see that the civic authorities were much concerned at such riots, fearing Roman intervention (Acts 19:29ff.; cf. 16:21; 17:7f.).

The first century of our era was the golden age of city life in the

---

[21] Juvenal, *Satires* 3.62; cf. G. La Piana, *HTR* 20 (1927), 183–403 (esp. 193–95, 227–32, on the presence of Jews in Rome).

[22] See Grant, *op. cit.*, p. 10.

[22a] An estimate of 800,000–1 million is offered by K. Hopkins, *Conquerors and Slaves* (1979), pp. 96–98.

Roman Empire. City vied with city in the magnificence of public buildings, town halls, temples, theaters, baths, aqueducts. Rich men, some of
whom had risen to high positions in the emperor's service, delighted to
honor their native towns with munificent gifts. Their reward was to
have statues of them set up, carefully recording all the offices they had
held. Existing ruins at Ephesus are an eloquent witness to the magnificence of civic architecture in the Graeco-Roman world.[23]

Acts gives a vivid contemporary picture of life in the cities of the
eastern Mediterranean. Paul, a native of a Greek city, based his missionary strategy on these cities. His starting point was Antioch, the
third city in the empire (after Rome and Alexandria),[24] the capital of the
province of Syria, and the metropolis of Gentile Christianity. On his
first missionary journey he visited the cities of south Galatia, finding in
city after city a synagogue of Jews settled centuries before by the successors of Alexander. To synagogue worship many "God-fearing" Gentiles
had been attracted, and through these the pagan population became
interested in Paul's message. Moreover, Greek was spoken in all the
cities of the eastern Mediterranean (though in out-of-the-way Lystra the
inhabitants used "the speech of Lycaonia" among themselves—as Acts
14:11 reports) and so the missionaries' preaching was understood
everywhere. Later, Paul visited Thessalonica, the capital of Macedonia;
spent eighteen months in Corinth, the great commercial city on the
isthmus, with the trade of the world flowing through its ports on two
seas; and was in Ephesus, another great commercial city on the main
route from Rome to the east for almost three years.[25] From these
centers, through which sailors, merchants, and other travelers were
constantly passing, the Christian message sounded forth (cf. 1 Thess.
1:8).

SOCIAL LIFE AND ITS PROBLEMS FOR CHRISTIANS

Society in these cities presented difficult problems to the early Christians. "Even the streets and the market-places," said Tertullian later,
"the baths and the taverns and our very dwelling-places, are not altogether free from idols. Satan and his angels have filled the whole
world."[26] The immorality of some of the cities was notorious. In the park
of Daphne, five miles from Antioch in Syria, the worship of Artemis and

---

[23] D. Magie, *Roman Rule in Asia Minor* (1950), pp. 583–85; for the most recent study
of the Ephesian monuments see E. Akurgal, *Ancient Civilisations and Ruins of
Turkey*[3] (1973), pp. 142–71.

[24] Strabo writes that Antioch was only a little less important than Alexandria as the
"metropolis of Syria . . . and the royal residence for rulers of the country. It does
not fall much short . . . of Alexandria" (*Geography* 16.2.5; 17.1.13).

[25] On the importance of Ephesus in the first-century world see G. E. Bean, *Aegean
Turkey: An Archaeological Guide* (1966), Ch. 7.

[26] *De Spectaculis* 8, cited in W. R. Halliday, *The Pagan Background of Early Christianity* (1925), p. 25.

Apollo was tainted with the immoral practices connected with the Syrian goddess Astarte and her consort. Corinth had its temple of Aphrodite with its priestess-courtesans whose sacred prostitution was part of the worship of the goddess.[27] Many Christians, such as the Galatian believers before their conversion (Gal. 4:8–10), had followed such practices as part of their religion. Hence the frequent and urgent warnings in the epistles against immorality.

Another difficulty was concerned with the "guilds" (*collegia*) which flourished in these cities.[28] These were not trade unions, but voluntary associations of people with common interests. Guilds of artisans and traders of every kind are mentioned in the many surviving Roman inscriptions. No doubt it was the guild of silversmiths at Ephesus to whom Demetrius appealed for action in the face of the danger Paul's preaching occasioned (Acts 19:24–28). Most common were burial clubs, which ensured decent burial for the poor freedman or slave. Many such guilds had religious connections and held their banquets in heathen temples.

Could a Christian conscientiously eat a meal in an idol's temple? This was a burning question in the church at Corinth (cf. 1 Cor. 8–10).[28a] Some, who claimed superior knowledge, argued that for a Christian all things were lawful; they were prepared to treat the matter with indifference. The view persisted that compromise was admissible, and we meet it again in the letters to the seven churches of Revelation. The Nicolaitans, mentioned there in the letters to Ephesus and Pergamum, seem to have been a sect prepared to accommodate to pagan standards in matters of sexual morality and idolatrous worship (Rev. 2:6,15). Some conscientious Christians, on the other hand, could not feast with their guild when it met in an idol's temple, nor could they take part in emperor worship. This led people generally to regard Christians as antisocial killjoys. Once hostile public opinion had been aroused, more positive charges emerged—such as the accusations that Christians practiced incest and cannibalism at their meetings.

Hence Tacitus describes the Christians as "a class hated for their abominations . . . criminals who deserved extreme and exemplary punishment" (*Annals* 15.44).[29] He tells us that Christians "were convicted on account of hatred of the human race" (*odio humani generis convicti sunt*), a charge similar to that which he brings against the Jews, who, he says, were animated by "enmity and hatred towards all other people" (*Histories* 5.5). "The Jews," he adds bitterly, "regard as profane

---

[27] On Corinth see Pausanias' (2nd cent. AD) description of his visit to the city; cf. G. Roux, *Pausanias en Corinthe* (1958); and below, pp. 170f.

[28] On the importance of such *collegia* see E. A. Judge, *The Social Pattern of Christian Groups in the First Century* (1960).

[28a] See A. Ehrhardt, *The Framework of the New Testament Stories* (1964), ch. 12.

[29] See P. Winter, "Tacitus and Pliny: The Early Christians," *Journal of Historical Studies,* Vol. 1, Autumn 1967, 31–40.

all that we hold sacred, and permit all that we abhor." All these charges were rooted in the refusal of both Jews and Christians to join in social activities connected with pagan deities. The Jews, though unpopular, were recognized as a people demanding special treatment, and their religion was protected by law (an exemption referred to as the practice of *religio licita*). So long as the Roman government did not distinguish between Jews and Christians, a similar toleration was extended to Christianity. But some time after the fire of Rome in 64, for which Nero made the Christians scapegoats, to confess the name of Christ became an offense punishable by arrest and death.[30] Public opinion sided with the government, believing the Christians to be guilty of anti-social and subversive activities.

SLAVERY

The world in which Christianity grew up recognized slavery as an institution, and many of the early Christians were slaves.[31] Moreover, there was a strain of cruelty in the Roman character that had made the lot of the slave in Rome less happy than it had been in Athens.

Under the influence of Stoicism, a more humane attitude to slaves was gaining ground. The classical expression of this is found in a letter (*Ep.* 47.10) of Seneca. "Remember," he says, "that he whom you call your slave sprang from the same stock, is smiled upon by the same skies, and on equal terms with yourself breathes, lives and dies. It is just as possible for you to see in him a free-born man as for him to see in you a slave." Furthermore, slaves in Rome, especially Greek slaves, were often better educated than their masters and were entrusted with important business including the supervision of children.[32] The Christians "of Caesar's household," whose greeting Paul sent to the Philippians (4:22), were slaves and freedmen in the imperial service. Funeral inscriptions testify to the love of slaves for their masters and of masters for their "humble friends." Slaves were allowed to associate with free men on an equal footing in the guilds. Manumission was common from Augustus' time onwards,[33] and a slave could usually buy his freedom by the savings (*peculium*) his master allowed him to accumulate. So when

---

[30] The pogrom under Nero was local and the charge of incendiarism personal. "The basis of the persecutions, properly so called, was somewhat different after the death of Nero" (Warmington, *op. cit.*, p. 127). There was "no specific statute or legislative act which made the profession of Christianity a criminal offence" until the time of Decius in the mid-third century (D. L. Stockton, *"Christianos ad Leonem,"* in *The Ancient Historian and his Materials: C. E. Stevens Festschrift*, ed. M. B. Levick (1975), p. 207.

[31] See M. I. Findley, *Slavery in Classical Antiquity* (1960); S. Scott Bartchy, *MALLON CHRĒSAI: First-Century Slavery and 1 Corinthians 7:21* (1973).

[32] Cf. the role of παιδαγωγός in Gal. 3:24.

[33] Jones, *op. cit.*, pp. 133ff.; W. Westermann, *The Slave System of Greek and Roman Antiquity* (1960), pp. 102f.

Christianity, while accepting the institution of slavery as part of the contemporary order of things, struck at its roots by proclaiming that in Christ there is neither "slave nor free" (Gal. 3:28; Col. 3:11), its teaching was not wholly alien to the spirit of the times. Nevertheless, Paul's attitude to Onesimus and his counsel to Philemon strike notes lacking in the best of Stoic thought.[34] See later, pp. 312–14.

---

[34] R. P. Martin, *Colossians and Philemon* (NCB, 1974), pp. 149f. See K. Hopkins (with P. J. Roscoe), *Conquerors and Slaves,* ch. 3: "Between Slavery and Freedom: On Freeing Slaves at Delphi."

CHAPTER THREE

The World of the Early Church: The Religious and Philosophical Framework

When we turn from the external world of the Roman Empire to the world of ideas, we are struck by the strength of Greek and Oriental influences in the thought of the first century. The Greeks, less successful than the Romans in the art of government, were intellectually far superior. In Horace's words: "captured Greece took her savage conqueror captive, and brought the arts into rural Latium."[1] The Greeks with whom we are dealing here were not the pure Greeks of the age of Pericles, but the product of the fusion of Greek and Oriental civilizations begun with the conquests of Alexander the Great and carried further by his successors in the process called Hellenization (Vol. 1, pp. 53–55).[2] To this mix Greece contributed abstract thought and technical skill, while the East brought her mysticism often mingled with superstition. Moreover, the first-century Greek was not the citizen of a small and independent city-state that controlled a small, manageable area; rather, he was involved in the life of a great empire, mingling with other people and often exposed to a wide variety of cultural influences.

A MATERIALISTIC AND FATALISTIC AGE

The age in which the New Testament was written was a materialistic one. The inhabitants of the cities were interested, first and foremost, in making money and enjoying the comforts and luxuries it provided. It was an age in which fortunes could be made quickly by judicious commercial ventures, like that of Trimalchio in Petronius's novel, who started as a favorite slave, inherited his master's money, and invested it in commercial enterprises, especially the wholesale wine trade. He

---

[1] Horace, *Epp.* 2.1.156: "*Graecia capta ferum victorem cepit, et artes intulit agresti Latio.*"

[2] See M. Hengel, *Judaism and Hellenism* (ET 1974) for the pervasive influence of Greek culture on Judaism. But cf. the critical review by A. Momigliano, *JTS*, n.s. 21 (1970), 149–53; and his *Alien Wisdom: The Limits of Hellenization* (1975).

finished up as the owner of a beautiful villa in Campania, living on the income from his large estates and the interest on his investments. In such a society a man's value was what he was worth, and very little more.[3]

Part of the reason for this materialism was the failure of the old Graeco-Roman religion. The temples of the great gods were still thronged at festival time, and the games of Greece were still celebrated in honor of the Olympian gods. Cities still had their tutelary deities. Artemis of the Ephesians is familiar to readers of the New Testament; and at Lystra Barnabas and Paul were thought to be Zeus and Hermes when the priest of Zeus, whose temple was before the city, brought oxen and garlands to the gates to make sacrifice to them (Acts 14:11-13). The Athenians were described by Paul as "uncommonly scrupulous in everything that concerns religion."[4] But the effect of all this outward ceremonial on people's conduct and values was small. At best, the old religion had been a matter for the state or the family rather than for the individual. A man shared the worship as a member of a group and there was little idea of personal communion with the deity. The basis of this religious orthodoxy was contractual:

> If the gods will at least listen to prayers, and will at times accept sacrifices, the state will do all that organized effort can accomplish to maintain friendly relations with the gods by such means. So temples and cult images, processions and sacrifices, hymns and dances, are the answer of the state to this demand.[5]

Now in the wider world, often separated from his native city and his family, a Greek of this period was without spiritual roots. It was easy for him to conclude that life held nothing beyond this world and its goods. "I was not, I was, I am not, I don't care" runs a common form of Roman epitaph, and many an epigram in the Greek anthology says the same thing in less laconic language.

Ancient paganism ultimately failed for two reasons: moral laxity and intellectual muddle.[6] Although the gods punished murder and perjury, their own character, as depicted in the myths from Homer to Ovid, was essentially immoral. They could not be taken as models either for the individual or for society. In the East particularly their worship was carried on with grossly immoral rites, as revolting to the best thought of paganism as it is to us. In the world in which Christianity

---

[3] *Credite mihi: assem habeas, assem valeas: habes, habeberis*—"Believe me, if you have a penny, that's your worth. What a man has, is his value"; Petronius, *Satyricon* 77.6, cf. line 43 for remarks on the character of the money-grubber.

[4] Acts 17:22 (cf. NEB). The Greek δεισιδαιμονεστέρους here should be compared with Theophrastus' character, "The Superstitious Man" (ὁ δεισιδαίμων). See below, p. 36.

[5] William Chase Greene, *Moira: Fate, Good and Evil in Greek Thought* (1944), p. 48.

[6] H. Mattingly, *Roman Imperial Civilisation*, p. 218.

grew up, there was a growing feeling that the gods should be worshiped not merely with ceremonial ablutions, but with a pure heart.

On the intellectual side, it was difficult to make sense of the "many 'gods' and many 'lords'" (1 Cor. 8:5) of polytheism. In the later Empire, an attempt was made to do this by syncretism, merging the various deities into one and assimilating their rites. Thus worshipers of Isis claimed that she was worshiped under many names in many lands, but "the Egyptians call her by her right name, the Queen Isis."[7] Similarly, various Baals worshiped in the east were identified with Jupiter or with *Sol Invictus,* "the unconquerable sun." But neither syncretism nor the monotheistic tendency (which, as we shall see, was fostered by Stoicism) could in the end make polytheism acceptable to thoughtful people.

The basic cause of the onset of despair in the Hellenistic age is the view of the cosmos provided by Greek science. The new geocentric astronomy adumbrated by Heraclides (c. 360 BC) and earlier by Eudoxus (c. 408–355 BC), was formulated by Hipparchus (c. 190–126 BC) and immediately and enthusiastically brought into relation with everyday life through astrologers, who were interested in locating the realms of the gods or the forces governing human life in the sphere of the fixed stars. On this view, the planets did much to alter the scheme of human life, and the region below the moon was a source of constant daemonic interference. The geocentric cosmology taught that the earth floated freely in space, surrounded by seven or eight concentric spheres which rotated about it, always in perfect harmony and obedient to eternal laws. The effect of this newer scientific theory on religion was to require a drastic re-thinking of the Homeric theology. No place could be found for the pantheon on Mount Olympus, and the realm of the gods could not be located in any mundane sphere. There was no place for them except the outer regions of starry space, unless they were to be identified with the stars.

This identification came about, chiefly through the advent of Oriental astrology, which "with its accompanying astral religion and dominant fatalism, lay like a nightmare upon the soul"—or, to change the metaphor, "fell upon the Hellenistic mind as a new disease falls upon some remote island people."[8] The new scientific world-view, which placed emphasis on transcendence, universal law, and cosmic order, pushed religion into a phase of pessimism and despair. Scientists had given an important place to the stars and planets in their systems. Astrologers made capital of this by teaching that everything in this

---

[7] Apuleius, *Metamorphoses* 11.5.
[8] The first assessment is P. Wendland's "Hellenistic Ideas of Salvation in the Light of Ancient Anthropology," *AJT,* 17 (1913), 345–51; the second Gilbert Murray's *Five Stages of Greek Religion*[2] (1935), p. 144.

world—including the lot of humanity—was determined by astral powers indifferent to the individual. The doctrine of Destiny, earlier applied only to public affairs, was now transferred to private life. All things were ruled by an evil Necessity (ἀνάγκη) and Destiny (εἱμαρμένη) which from birth—and the particular constellation or conjunction of the stars or planets under which a person was born was of decisive importance— determined "the entire course of our lives, and . . . nothing can enable us to escape."[9]

But escape was promised along certain paths: mysticism, occultism, and ascetic practices met the yearning of Hellenistic man for "salvation" and a sense of harmony with the remote eternal world of the divine. He might seek fellowship with a mighty god, who was able to raise his protégés above the hopeless round of Necessity and above the regions controlled by the powerful astral deities;[10] or he might take refuge in the cults of Serapis, Isis, and Asclepius, hailed by contemporary writers as mightier than εἱμαρμένη, who offered victory over Destiny (τύχη) to their devotees;[11] or he might take the route of renunciation, asceticism, and magic. Men confessed that life was one of uncertainty and fear and sought to escape from the mesh of inevitability. The universe seemed cold and unfriendly; indeed, the stars—earlier deified by religious thought—were now seen as positively malevolent and hostile. Life lacked any sense of purpose or significant meaning. The heart's cry of this man was that expressed in A. E. Housman's words:

> I, a stranger and afraid
> In a world I never made.

Or, as Belloc's lines put it:

> Strong God, which made the topmost stars
> To circulate and keep their course;
> Remember me, whom all the bars
> Of sense and dreadful fate enforce.[12]

SOME ANSWERS TO THE PHILOSOPHICAL AND RELIGIOUS PROBLEMS

How, in fact, did men and women seek to overcome the spiritual crisis occasioned by the breakdown of the old religious ideas of the Homeric theology? Escape, deliverance, and religious satisfaction were attempted along these diverse routes.

1. *Demonology.* If the Olympian gods seemed too remote to have much practical bearing on men's lives, demons were very near and very

---

[9] A.-J. Festugière, *Personal Religion among the Greeks* (1960), p. 41.
[10] Wendland, *loc. cit.*, 347.
[11] As quoted in Festugière, Isis is greater than εἱμαρμένη and has power to deliver man, *HTR*, 42 (1949), 209f., 223, 233f.
[12] Quoted by F. C. Grant, *Roman Hellenism and the New Testament* (1962), p. 48.

real. Belief in *daemones* as intermediaries between the gods and men had been developed by Xenocrates on the basis of some utterances of his master Plato. God was seen as absolute and transcendent, able to be brought into relation with an imperfect and changing world only through subordinate and intermediate spiritual agents. These *daemones* were responsible for the creation of the world around us. They lived in the air beneath the moon, but also wandered about the earth, particularly around tombs. They had human defects and passions; some were good, others bad. Plutarch, who considered the doctrine of *daemones* one of the greatest advances made by philosophy, ascribed to them oracles that turned out to be lies along with all the revolting features in pagan ritual. "I will never think," he says, "that those [things were] done on any of the gods' account, but rather to avert, mollify, and appease the wrath and fury of some bad demons."[13]

In the first century of our era belief in evil demons was widespread. The superstitious lived in dread of their evil activities. The New Testament refers to them as evil powers existing in the spiritual world and often having their abode in human beings (1 Cor. 12:2). Paul identifies them with the recipients of heathen sacrifices (1 Cor. 10:20). Yet he distinguishes between a meal in an idol temple, which he forbids to the Corinthians (vs. 14) and a social occasion when a pagan neighbor might invite a Christian to dine in his home (vs. 27). In the latter case, food may be eaten without scruple. But if it is specifically identified as food formerly "offered in sacrifice," it is to be refused on the grounds of conscience and not wishing to give offense to the informant.

An invitation to such a meal in a shrine of the god Serapis has survived from the second century and illustrates the type of situation in view in this chapter:[14]

Ἐρωτᾷ σε Χαιρήμων δειπνῆσαι εἰς κλείνην τοῦ κυρίου Σαράπιδος ἐν τῷ Σαραπείῳ αὔριον, ἐστὶν ιε, ἀπὸ)ὥρας θ.

"Chaeremon invites you to dine at the table of the lord Serapis in the Serapeum tomorrow, that is, the 15th, from the 9th hour."

Notes
POxy 110

This is an invitation to an unnamed friend to join the host at dinner in honor of the god Serapis at a retreat house called the Serapeum, an accommodation where persons in sickness or trouble

---

[13] Quoted by Halliday, *The Pagan Background of Early Christianity*, p. 180, from *De def. orac.* 14.417c. The basis of this is Plutarch's dualism, epitomized in his statement: "If nothing happens without a cause, and a good being can produce nothing evil, there must be in nature a special principle of evil as there is of good" (*De Iside et Osiride* 369a-d). See Greene, *op. cit.*, p. 310.

[14] For the latest discussion see Chan-Hie Kim, "The Papyrus Invitation," *JBL*, 94 (1975), 391-402.

sought the help of the god and were regarded for the time being as "possessed" by the god or at least under his special protection and influence. This practice is further illustrated by a British Museum papyrus (No. 42; 168 BC), which explains how the writer's husband Hephaestion had been "shut up" with other devotees of the god in the Serapeum at Memphis in Egypt, but after a period was "released" from his retreat (κατοχή). The vows, therefore, were not permanent but limited to the time the "inmates" (κάτοχοι) sought asylum in the Serapeum.

Cultic meals were held in the temples of the gods. Josephus (Ant. 18:65ff.) speaks of members of the Isis-community being invited to a meal in the temple of the goddess. It is more likely that the present text is an invitation to a ceremonial banquet than to a private meal, although invitations to meals in private homes at a time of celebration have been found. The passage in 1 Corinthians may refer to a meal either in a temple (as suggested by 8:10 and 10:44ff.) or, more likely, in a private home, as in POxy 523 (see notes below). Parties in homes were held to celebrate birthdays or weddings (POxy 524).

ἐρωτᾷ σε is a standard verb of invitation (cf. Luke 7:36; 11:37). The host puts himself in the third person. His name is given (Χαιρήμων), but the addressee is not named, suggesting that the invitation was not a letter as such but the script from which the messenger read out the invitation in front of the guest. Supporting evidence for this procedure is found in the Gospel of Thomas, 64. A single invitation could thus be used for several guests in turn.[15] In BGU 596 (from the Fayûm, AD 84) an invitation to a festival does call the addressee by name.

Notes

δειπνῆσαι: the invitation is for a meal, "dinner," or even a "banquet."

Εἰς κλείνην: κλ(ε)ίνη means "table," thus also what is represented by the table, a meal. 1 Cor. 10:21 uses τράπεζα, which is roughly equivalent.

ἐν τῷ Σαραπείῳ: "at the Serapeum." POxy 523 gives the location of a meal in honor of Serapis as ἐν τοῖς Κλαυδ(ίου) Σαραπίω(νος) "in the house of Claudius Serapion." For ἐν τοῖς . . . meaning "in the home of" cf. Luke 2:49.

αὔριον, ἥτις ἐστὶν ιε: letter-numerals after the adverb are common. Αὔριον implies that the invitation was sent out the day preceding the meal, even for wedding celebrations. The name of the month is not ordinarily supplied.

ἀπὸ ὥρας θ: the eighth or ninth hour (2 or 3 pm) was a fairly standard time for the meal to begin.

2. *Astrology.* Originating in Babylonia, the teaching that the stars determine human fortunes had entered the Hellenistic world from

[15] *Ibid.*, 397.

the east and became a powerful force in this age. Alexandria, the meeting place of east and west, was the center of the study of astronomy, and the accurate knowledge of the stars gained by the Alexandrian astronomers helped astrology to pose as a pseudo-science. Working out the position of the stars at a person's birth in order to determine his life and destiny was a complicated astronomical and mathematical problem.[16] Tacitus derogated the *mathematici* (as the Romans called astrologers) as "a class of men who deceive the ambitious, although those in power distrust them—a class that in our state will always be forbidden and always retained among us" (*Histories* 1.22.2).[17] He tells us how the emperor Tiberius had his own private astrologer Thrasyllus, whom he trusted implicitly and kept among his intimate friends (*Annals* 6.21.4).[18] Vespasian, when in command against the Jews, had been encouraged by astrologers to make a bid for the throne, and later kept an astrologer, Seleucus, to help him by his advice and prophecy (*Histories* 2.78). Astrology led logically to atheism, as Tiberius saw, but most simple folk thought of the planets as gods to be appeased by prayer or sacrifice or mastered by magic.

3. *Magic.* Alone and adrift in a frightening world, surrounded by daemonic activity, oppressed by the weight of inevitable necessity, controlled by the movement of the planets, what was the ordinary man or woman to do?

On the lowest level, the answer was magic. Unlike the religious person, who approaches a higher power with humble petition, the magician claims to use certain formulas or rites to compel the higher power to do his will. Sometimes the magician identifies himself with the particular god or spirit concerned. Magic was commonly used to compel the affection of a loved one or procure the destruction of an enemy. In the second idyll of Theocritus, the girl Simaetha, madly in love with Delphis, who has forsaken her, goes out into the moonlit night with her magic wheel and endeavors to subdue him by spells and by invoking the moon-goddess. Magic might also be used to exorcise a demon. We meet magicians in the Acts of the Apostles: Simon Magus in Samaria, of whom the people said "this man is that power of God which is called Great" (8:10), and Elymas, the magician of Sergius Paulus, who withstood Paul and Barnabas when they were invited to speak before the governor (13:8). Ephesus, famous in antiquity for books of magic, which are sometimes called "Ephesian writings," was the location of an open confession by new believers that they had been using magic spells. Many of them collected their books and burned them publicly—at a considerable financial loss (19:18ff.). In Egypt magical papyri dating

---

[16] For a fragment of a "technical" astrological work from an Egyptian papyrus, see Barrett, *The New Testament Background*, p. 35.

[17] For attitudes toward astrology, see Greene, *op. cit.*, Appendix 63.

[18] *Ibid.*, Appendix 61.

from the early centuries of the Christian era have been discovered, containing "magical recipes, conjurations, descriptions of sorceries, and methods for procuring appearances of gods and *daemones* and predictions of the future."[19] Amid much unintelligible mumbo-jumbo, they contain invocations of Egyptian gods, of Jao (the Egyptian form of Yahweh), and of Jesus.[20]

Probably the most illuminating illustration of the pervasive influence of magical ideas in ordinary life is Theophrastus' character "The Superstitious Man," ὁ Δεισιδαίμων. Theophrastus was born around 370 BC. He came to Athens, where he studied under Plato and later Aristotle. When Aristotle died in 322, Theophrastus succeeded him and established the School (the Lyceum) as an institution in its own right. He continued to direct its work until he died in 287 BC. The *Characters* was composed in 319 BC. As a satire on popular religion the character called "The Superstitious Man" stands out. There is obviously some exaggeration here but it is just as clear that his portrait "would lose all point if it had no basis in everyday experience."[21]

'Αμέλει ἡ δεισιδαιμονία δόξειεν ἂν εἶναι δειλία πρὸς τὸ δαιμόνιον, ὁ δὲ δεισιδαίμων τοιοῦτός τις, οἷος ... ἀπονιψάμενος τὰς χεῖρας καὶ περιρρανάμενος ... οὕτω τὴν ἡμέραν περιπατεῖν. καὶ τὴν ὁδὸν ἐὰν ὑπερδράμῃ γαλῆ μὴ πρότερον πορευθῆναι, ἕως διεξέλθῃ τις.... καὶ τῶν λιπαρῶν λίθων τῶν ἐν ταῖς τριόδοις παριὼν ἐκ τῆς ληκύθου ἔλαιον καταχεῖν καὶ ἐπὶ γόνατα πεσὼν καὶ προσκυνήσας ἀπαλλάττεσθαι.... καὶ πυκνὰ δὲ τὴν οἰκίαν καθᾶραι δεινός.... καὶ οὔτε ἐπιβῆναι μνήματι οὔτ' ἐπὶ νεκρὸν οὔτ' ἐπὶ λεχὼ ἐλθεῖν ἐθελῆσαι, ἀλλὰ τὸ μὴ μιαίνεσθαι συμφέρον αὑτῷ φῆσαι εἶναι. καὶ ταῖς τετράσι δὲ καὶ ταῖς ἑβδομάσι ἐξελθὼν ἀγοράσαι μυρρίνας, λιβανωτόν, [πίνακα] [πόπανα].... καὶ ὅταν ἐνύπνιον ἴδῃ, πορεύεσθαι πρὸς τοὺς ὀνειροκρίτας, πρὸς τοὺς μάντεις, πρὸς τοὺς ὀρνιθοσκόπους, ἐρωτήσων τίνι θεῷ ἢ θεᾷ εὔχεσθαι δεῖ.... μαινόμενον δὲ ἰδὼν ἢ ἐπίληπτον φρίξας εἰς κόλπον πτύσαι.

Superstitiousness,[a] I need hardly say, would seem to be a sort of cowardice with respect to the divine.... The superstitious man ... will not go out for the day till he has washed his hands and sprinkled himself....[b] And if a cat[c] crosses his path he will not proceed on his way till someone else has gone by.... When he passes one of the smooth stones set up at the crossroads[d] he anoints it with oil from his flask, and will not go his way until he has knelt down[e] and worshiped it.... He is forever purifying his house[f].... He will not set foot on a grave,[g] nor come near a dead body[h] nor a woman in confinement; he must keep himself unpol-

---

[19] M. P. Nilsson, *Greek Piety* (1948), p. 174.
[20] Barrett, *op. cit.*, p. 31, gives a translation of part of the Paris Magical Papyrus.
[21] A. A. Long, *Hellenistic Philosophy: Stoics, Epicureans, Sceptics* (1974), p. 42.

luted. . . . On the 4th and 7th days of the month[i] he . . . goes out to buy myrtle-boughs, frankincense, and a holy picture[j]. . . . He never has a dream but that he runs to the diviner or the soothsayer or an interpreter of visions[k] to ask what god or goddess he should pray to. . . . If he catches sight of a lunatic or an epileptic, he shudders and spits in his bosom.[l]

Notes

[a]δεισιδαίμων can be used in two ways, favorably as "showing respect before the divine" (Aristotle) or "religious" (the accepted NT use; Acts 17:22, 25:19), but Theophrastus' use has a pejorative sense, found in the contemporary comedy of Menander. Epicurus is praised for having freed men from δεισιδαιμονία in this sense.

[b]"Washing and sprinkling hands" are his daily exercise, unlike ordinary persons who would sprinkle themselves only after special defilement.

[c]A common warning-sign was meeting an unclean animal. The γαλέη (a cat or weasel, a herald of death in popular folklore, associated by Aristophanes with earthquake) would set up a magical barrier whose spell would need to be broken by another person to whom the omen was transferred.

[d]Cairns, piled up at points where three roads met, were regarded as crude altars dedicated to the triform goddess, Hecate, Trioditis, and Trivia. Worship conducted at "smooth stones" is mentioned by Clement of Alexandria in his *Stromateis*. Of this primitive practice traces are found in the Old Testament (Gen. 28:18) and in the Phrygian Mother-goddess cult (see Acts 19:35).

[e]"Knelt down": ordinarily a non-Greek posture for worship. See the discussion in my *Carmen Christi* (1967), pp. 264f.

[f]The "purifying of the house" recalls the purging of the house of Atreus from the stain of murder in Euripides' tragedy.

[g]Inscriptions from the ancient world contain warnings to and curses on those who violate graves or even burial sites; e.g., "Never set foot on ground where a corpse has been burned" (*locum in quo bustum est*).

[h]"He will not . . . come near a dead body": normally ablutions were performed outside a room with a dead person in it in order to cleanse the visitor as he left and to prevent those who passed the door from incurring defilement. See Euripides, *Alcestis*, ll. 98ff., where the Chorus, debating the question Is she alive or dead?, remarks, "I do not see before the doors the spring-water for ablution (χέρνιψ), as is the custom at the doors of the dead."

The superstitious man is not content with this antidote against defilement. He steers clear of any contact with the dead, and declines the duty of kinship and friendship (called εὐσέβεια, piety).

ʲThe fourth day of the month was sacred to Hermes, the seventh to Apollo. Hermes' consort's birthday (Aphrodite) fell on the seventh day. He respects them as household divinities.

ʲIf πίναχα is the correct reading, a painted picture-board is intended; the variant πόπανα would mean flat cakes used as a votive offering.

ᵏDreams in the ancient world were held to be significant. The point here is that any trivial vision in his dream is a source of great distress to the superstitious man. "Soothsaying" (μαντική) was an art of forecasting the future, either by observing the appearance of the victim (ἱερομαντία) or the contours of the flame (πυρομαντεία) in the sacrifice.

ˡThe practice of spitting to avert an evil spell is based on the idea that one can avoid evil by acts or words that show repugnance to it. Paul faced the issue of the spell cast by an evil eye, familiar to the Galatians; but he has his own antidote found in the cross of Jesus (Gal. 3:1). It is an open question whether Theophrastus in this passage has an eye at all on Jewish ceremonials as well as on Greek superstitiousness. It would seem likely that much of post-exilic Judaism would have been unintelligible and quite abhorrent to Theophrastus.

4. *Mystery religions.* To pass from magic to the mystery religions is to move from rank superstition to something akin to worship. Many in this age were sincerely seeking "a way of salvation"— deliverance from the grip of Destiny or Fate, personal communion with the deity in this life, and assurance of immortality beyond death— through initiation into the mysteries. The initiate prepared by ceremonial purification and fasting for the actual rites, which were kept strictly secret. Some of the myths on which the mysteries were based told of the death and resurrection of a god, and it would seem that during initiation a person passed through a great and terrible darkness and emerged into a dazzling light. This experience typified death and resurrection, and the one who passed through it felt himself united with the deity he worshiped. Sometimes he partook of a sacred meal, through which it was supposed that he received a share of the divine power.

The fullest account we have of such rites is the story of the initiation of Lucius, the hero of Apuleius' romance *The Golden Ass,* into the mysteries of Isis. The account is deeply moving, probably autobiographical in part. After a long wait, Isis appears to Lucius in a vision and tells him that the day he had wished for so long is at hand; she has appointed her principal priest to prepare him. The priest instructs him from sacred books, washes and purifies his body, and bids him fast for ten days eating no flesh and drinking no wine. Then, clothing him in a new linen robe, he takes him to the most secret part of the temple. What he sees there he is not allowed to tell, but he summarizes his experience thus:

I drew near to the borders of death; when I had set my foot upon the threshold of Proserpine, I returned, carried through all the elements; in the middle of the night I beheld the clear radiance of the sun; I approached the gods both infernal and celestial and worshiped them face to face.

The next morning, ceremonially dressed and carrying a lighted torch, he is shown to a crowd of worshipers, and with them he celebrates a feast and addresses a prayer to Isis which ends thus: "I will always keep thy divine appearance in remembrance and close the imagination of thy most holy godhead within my breast" (Apuleius, *Metamorphoses* 11.22-26).[22]

The cults from which the mystery religions were derived differed so much among themselves that no "mystery theology" can be constructed from our knowledge of them. In any case, their appeal was to the emotions, not the intelligence. Aristotle said that those initiated into the mysteries of his time learned nothing but were put into a certain receptive disposition.[23] We do not know how the sights and the sounds were produced, but they were carefully designed to give the initiate an impression of contact with the supernatural. Of the sincerity and devotion of many of the worshipers there can be no doubt.

Some writers have held that Paul's thought was deeply influenced by the mystery religions and that Christianity borrowed much from them. Certainly Paul used terms familiar to adherents of mystery-religions among his readers,[24] but he gave this language a content of his own. At decisive points the Christian gospel stands diametrically opposed to the claims and procedures of the Hellenistic mysteries.

5. *Gnosis*. Another route of escape from the grip of Fate was by gnosis, secret knowledge communicated by revelation. Those who followed this way believed that the material world was evil. The human soul, sometimes typified in a myth of a primal Man, had fallen from the transcendent world of light where God dwells, through the seven spheres controlled by the world-rulers (κοσμοκράτορες), and was imprisoned in the material sphere. Yet it contained a divine element, and by "knowledge" might free itself and win its way back to the sphere from which it came. This "salvation" was attained by intellectual illumination, assisted by abstinence and asceticism. In these beliefs there were elements derived from the teaching of Zoroaster, from Babylonian astrology, and from the account of the fall of man in the Old Testament. These ideas were widespread in the Hellenistic world of the century before and after the birth of Christ. Possibly they are represented in the knowledge (*gnōsis*) on which Paul's opponents at Corinth prided themselves and in the heresy he had to combat at Colossae and maybe also

---

[22] Tr. in Barrett, *op. cit.*, pp. 97–100; cf. Halliday, *op. cit.*, pp. 252ff.; A. D. Nock, *Conversion* (1933), Ch. 9; Lohse, *op. cit.*, pp. 237ff.

[23] Fragment 45, quoted by Nilsson, *op. cit.*

[24] See H. A. A. Kennedy, *St. Paul and the Mystery Religions* (1913); G. Wagner, *Pauline Baptism and the Pagan Mysteries* (ET 1967).

Galatia and Philippi.[25] Amalgamated with Christianity they produced the gnostic sects of the second century.[26] In a pagan context they formed the background of the Hermetic documents later current in Egypt.[27]

6. *Philosophy*. The philosophy to which many thoughtful men turned for guidance in the first century of our era was not the disinterested attempts of Plato and Aristotle to solve by pure reason the problems of mind and matter. The emphasis had shifted from metaphysics to ethics, from the nature of reality to the conduct of the individual. Moreover, philosophy had been popularized; it was no longer taught in the lecture room only, but at the street-corners and along the roads that linked the cities of the Empire.[28]

On his visit to Athens, Paul encountered philosophers of the Epicureans and of the Stoics (Acts 17:18). The founders of both these schools of philosophy had taught at Athens in the closing years of the fourth century BC. Zeno, the founder of the Stoics, came to Athens from Citium in Cyprus in 300 and was probably of Semitic origin. The aim of both Epicureanism and Stoicism was to formulate a way of life based on a rational and consistent explanation of the universe.[29]

a. *Epicureanism*. Epicurus (born in 341 BC) taught that happiness consists in "freedom from disturbance" (ἀταραξία); all that disturbs body or mind is to be shunned. This was part of his overall interest in philosophy—"a strange mixture of hard-headed empiricism, speculative metaphysics, and rules for the attainment of a tranquil life."[30] Physical pain must be endured, as Epicurus himself endured it; when acute, it does not last long; when protracted, it is less severe. And "all living creatures from the moment of birth take delight in pleasure and resist pain from natural causes independent of reason" (Diogenes Laertius). The violent passions—love, hatred, ambition—are to be avoided. The philosopher will take no part in public life, but will withdraw from the world and "live unobtrusively."

One of Epicurus' main aims was to free man from fear of the gods and of punishment after death. He explained that the soul like everything else consists of atoms. These fly apart at death, so that the soul ceases to exist. Lucretius, who set forth the Epicurean doctrine in exalted poetry, offered twenty-eight proofs of the soul's mortality, and

---

[25] For the maximum correspondence to be drawn between the "Corinthian theology" and later gnosticism, see W. Schmithals, *Gnosticism in Corinth* (ET 1971). But see later Ch. 24. See too Lohse, *op. cit.*, Ch. 3. For a recent report on gnostic studies see K. Rudolph, *Gnosis. The Nature and History of Gnosticism* (ET 1983).

[26] See R. M. Grant, *Gnosticism and Early Christianity* (1959) and *Gnosticism: An Anthology* (1961).

[27] Cf. Barrett, *op. cit.*, pp. 80–90, on the Hermetic documents.

[28] *Ibid.*, pp. 75f.

[29] On Epicureanism and Stoicism in the Graeco-Roman period, see Long, *op. cit.*; on Epicureanism see also B. Farrington, *The Faith of Epicurus* (1967); J. M. Rist, *Epicurus, An Introduction* (1969).

[30] Long, *op. cit.*, p. 19.

concluded that death is not to be feared. His argument runs thus: events prior to our birth did not disturb us, because we did not *feel* them. So there is no logical need to fear death, since we simply pass into unconsciousness at the end of life. He sums up: "We may be assured that there is nothing to be feared in death and (that) he who no longer exists cannot be troubled" (*scire licet nobis nil esse in morte timendum nec miserum fieri qui non est posse*) (*De rerum natura* 3.865f.).

Epicurus did not deny the existence of the gods, but taught that they were entirely unconcerned with human affairs and lived a life of perfect detachment in the "spaces between the worlds" (*intermundia*).[31] It was foolish to fear them or to address petitions to them, though one might contemplate them as embodying the perfect ideal of happiness after which he was himself imperfectly striving.

> The divine nature everywhere enjoys life everlasting in perfect peace, sundered and separated far away from our world. For free from all grief, free from danger, mighty in its own resources, never lacking anything we could give, it is not won by our well-doing nor angered when we do ill (Lucretius, *De rerum natura* 2.646-51).[32]

Religion for Epicurus is adoration, by which one may be helped "to live a life worthy of the gods" (*De rerum natura* 3.322).

Epicureanism was never widely held in the Roman world. Its rejection of the popular religion was too radical—Epicureans were classified with Christians as "atheists"—and its moral ideal, based on the gods who—like true Epicureans—dwell in *sedes quietae* ("tranquil resting-places"),[33] was too quietistic for the active Roman temperament.

b. *Stoicism*. More successfully than Epicureanism Stoicism adapted itself to the ideas of the age. Resting on a religious basis, it made a strong appeal to the Roman character. For the Stoic, the universe itself was God. The ultimate substance of the universe was a "fiery breath" or "spirit" (πνεῦμα πυρῶδες), which was distributed throughout in varying degrees of tension.[34] This "spirit" was alive and rational. In its manifestation as reason (λόγος) it introduced order into the world. The matter of which the world was composed was itself mind. The "fiery spirit" was also god;[35] it was divine, the Stoics argued, because nothing could be more excellent. Moreover, human reason—"a particle of the divine breath" in man himself—meant that man is capable of adoring and entering into communion with the supreme reason.

The Stoics identified their god with the supreme deity of the

---

[31] Cicero, *De natura deorum* 1.18; see A.-J. Festugière, *Epicurus and His Gods* (ET 1955).
[32] Cf. Farrington, *op. cit.*, p. 117.
[33] A. A. Long, *op. cit.*, p. 45, referring to *De rerum natura* 3.18-24.
[34] For the background in the pre-Socratics, *ibid.*, p. 150.
[35] *Ibid.*, pp. 155f. The distinction between "active" (*logos* or *pneuma*) and "passive" (matter) principles in cosmology goes back to Heraclitus.

Greeks and Romans, Zeus or Jupiter. Cleanthes, Zeno's successor as head of the Stoic school in Athens, had dominant theological interests; he wrote a "Hymn to Zeus," which began

> Most glorious of immortals, Zeus all-powerful,
> Author of nature, named of many names, all hail!
> Thy law rules all, and the voice of the world may cry to thee,
> For from thee we are born, and alone of living things
> That move on earth are we created in God's image.[36]

In the same poet, Zeus is coupled with "Fate":

> Lead me, O Zeus, and thou, my Destiny,
> To that one place which you will have me fill.
> I follow gladly. Should I strive with thee,
> A recreant, I needs must follow still.[37]

Unlike the Epicurean the Stoic did not see fate as a blind mechanistic process, but as the providence of the god who is the universal reason. In later Stoicism, especially in Epictetus (AD 50—120) we find a communion between this supreme deity and the philosopher, which leads to prayer.

Epictetus offers, in his *Discourses* and his *Handbook* (*Encheiridion*), one of the most compact and coherent statements of Stoic religious belief and practice. Arrian's valuable record of the *Discourses* reports the actual words of his teacher in what appears to be a kind of classroom

---

[36] Barrett, *op. cit.*, p. 63, has useful notes on this text. "For from thee we are born" recalls the statement of Aratus of Cilicia that men are "the offspring" of God, alluded to by Paul in Athens (Acts 17:28). "In him we live and move and have our being" in the same verse is from Epimenides of Crete (cf. Titus 1:12) who addressed the deity in these words. The setting of Paul's speech is given as the Hill of Ares (*Areios pagus*), but it is likely that the court met close to the northwest corner of the *agora* (marketplace), near the *Stoa poikilē*, the Painted Colonnade, from which Zeno and his friends derived their name, the Stoics. On this location, see C. J. Hemer, "Paul at Athens; A Topographical Note," *NTS*, 20 (1973-74), 341-50. Paul's remarks in vs. 25 seem designed to appeal to both Epicureans and Stoics (vs. 18). That God does not lack anything and has no need of human service is exactly what the Epicureans held; while the Stoics would applaud the teaching that the divine is the source of all life. See F. F. Bruce, *The Speeches in the Acts of the Apostles* (1944), p. 18. Neither group would tolerate the thought of resurrection, and would have recalled Apollo's words in Aeschylus' *Eumenides:* "But when the earth has drunk up a man's blood, / Once he is dead, there is no resurrection." The attitude in vs. 32 is typical.

[37] The problem here is that of evil or, as Greene puts it (*Moira*, pp. 331-54), how to reconcile fatalism and freedom (p. 351). Cleanthes argues that though everything that comes through providence is also fated, not all that is fated is providential. Further, the moral responsibility for evil is laid on man, since Cleanthes evidently also believes that God can make evil contribute to good: "Thou knowest to make the crooked straight. / Chaos to thee is order." The notion of God's "providential care" (πϱόνοια) is one of the most attractive features of Stoicism, as is clear from Epictetus' discussion.

context, and we may overhear, with simple directness, the voice of the master in the student's transcription.

Epictetus was the son of a slave woman and a slave himself for many years. This experience (which may or may not account for his lameness) left an indelible mark on him, and no theme pervades his writings more than that of freedom and human dignity. His beliefs were those of conventional Stoicism, stressing virtue as the only good; and the good is that which leads to happiness (εὐδαιμονία) based on an even flow of life (εὔροια βίου). All else—health, prosperity, pleasure—are matters of indifference (ἀδιάφορα).

To know the good is not enough. There must be practical application (ἄσκησις); and it is with the practical outworking of Stoic philosophy that he was concerned. The touchstone of practice is a man's duty (τὸ καθῆκον), which Epictetus applied to social relationships. On the strictly theological plane, God's overruling providence embraces both good and evil and works only for what is good. Man's duty is to rise to the level of this understanding and to see the range of life steadily and wholly from this perspective. His happiness is assured as he fills the niche God's providence appoints for him, by "cooperating with the inevitable" (ἑκόντα δέχεσθαι τὰ ἀναγκαῖα) and thereby becoming a co-worker with God. The noble sentiment of this aim in life parallels much New Testament teaching, yet for all his earnest desire to be free and happy independent of circumstances (*Discourses* 2.6.17), to "be as God wants man to be," his philosophy is one of self-sufficiency. "That which is within our power" (τὸ ἐφ' ἡμῖν) is a common phrase in Epictetus, and his doctrine of the brotherhood and unity of mankind is based on a common share in the Logos, which is God. A highwater mark of Epictetus' teaching is seen in *Discourses* 1.16: "On Providence."

(1) God's providence is seen in his gifts.

καίτοι νὴ τὸν Δία καὶ τοὺς θεοὺς ἓν τῶν γεγονότων ἀπήρκει πρὸς τὸ αἰσθέσθαι τῆς προνοίας τῷ γε αἰδήμονι καὶ εὐχαρίστῳ. καὶ μή μοι νῦν τὰ μεγάλα· αὐτὸ τοῦτο τὸ ἐκ πόας γάλα γεννᾶσθαι καὶ ἐκ γάλακτος τυρὸν καὶ ἐκ δέρματος ἔρια τίς ἐστιν ὁ πεποιηκὼς ταῦτα ἢ ἐπινενοηκώς; "οὐδὲ εἷς" φησίν. ὢ μεγάλης ἀναισθησίας καὶ ἀναισχυντίας.

By Zeus and the gods, one gift of nature would be enough to make a man who is reverent and grateful perceive the [divine] providence. Don't talk to me now of great matters. Take the fact that milk is produced from grass, and cheese from milk, and that wool grows from skin. Who has created or contrived these things? "No one," someone says. O what great stupidity and shamelessness!

(2) Providence and the sexes.

Ἄγε ἀφῶμεν τὰ ἔργα τῆς φύσεως, τὰ πάρεργα αὐτῆς θεασώμεθα. μή τι ἀχρηστότερον τριχῶν τῶν ἐπὶ γενείου; τί οὖν; οὐ συνεχρήσατο καὶ ταύταις ὡς μάλιστα πρεπόντως ἐδύνατο; οὐ διέκρινεν δι᾽ αὐτῶν τὸ ἄρρεν καὶ τὸ θῆλυ; οὐκ εὐθὺς μακρόθεν κέκραγεν ἡμῶν ἑκάστου ἡ φύσις "ἀνήρ εἰμι· οὕτω μοι προσέρχου, οὕτω μοι λάλει, ἄλλο μηδὲν ζήτει· ἰδοὺ τὰ σύμβολα"; πάλιν ἐπὶ τῶν γυναικῶν ὥσπερ ἐν φωνῇ τι ἐγκατέμιξεν ἁπαλώτερον, οὕτως καὶ τὰς τρίχας ἀφεῖλεν.... διὰ τοῦτο ἔδει σῴζειν τὰ σύμβολα τοῦ θεοῦ, ἔδει αὐτὰ μὴ καταπροίεσθαι, μὴ συγχεῖν ὅσον ἐφ᾽ ἑαυτοῖς τὰ γένη τὰ διῃρημένα.

Let us leave the [main] works of nature, and see what are her lesser works. Is there anything less useful than the hairs on the chin?[a] What then? Has not nature used even these in the most fitting way possible? Has she not by these means distinguished the male and the female? Has not the nature of each one of us immediately cried out from a distance, "I am a man; on this basis approach me, speak to me, seek nothing else; here are the signs?" Again, in the case of women, just as [nature] has mingled something gentler in their voice, so likewise she has taken away the hair [of the chin][a].... For that reason, we ought to maintain the signs which God has given; we ought not to throw them away; we should not confound, so far as we can, the sexes which have been kept distinct in this way.

(3) Providence and man's duty.

Ταῦτα μόνα ἐστὶν ἔργα ἐφ᾽ ἡμῶν τῆς προνοίας; καὶ τίς ἐξαρκεῖ λόγος ὁμοίως αὐτὰ ἐπαινέσαι ἢ παραστῆσαι; εἰ γὰρ νοῦν εἴχομεν, ἄλλο τι ἔδει ἡμᾶς ποιεῖν καὶ κοινῇ καὶ ἰδίᾳ ἢ ὑμνεῖν τὸ θεῖον καὶ εὐφημεῖν καὶ ἐπεξέρχεσθαι τὰς χάριτας; οὐκ ἔδει καὶ σκάπτοντας καὶ ἀροῦντας καὶ ἐσθίοντας ᾄδειν τὸν ὕμνον τὸν εἰς τὸν θεόν; "μέγας ὁ θεός, ὅτι ἡμῖν παρέσχεν ὄργανα ταῦτα δι᾽ ὧν τὴν γῆν ἐργασόμεθα· μέγας ὁ θεός, ὅτι χεῖρας δέδωκεν, ὅτι κατάποσιν, ὅτι κοιλίαν, ὅτι αὔξεσθαι λεληθότως, ὅτι καθεύδοντας ἀναπνεῖν." ταῦτα ἐφ᾽ ἑκάστου ἐφυμνεῖν ἔδει καὶ τὸν μέγιστον καὶ θειότατον ὕμνον ἐφυμνεῖν, ὅτι τὴν δύναμιν ἔδωκεν τὴν παρακολουθητικὴν τούτοις καὶ ὁδῷ χρηστικήν. Τί οὖν; ἐπεὶ οἱ πολλοὶ ἀποτετύφλωσθε, οὐκ ἔδει τινὰ εἶναι τὸν ταύτην ἐκπληροῦντα τὴν χώραν καὶ ὑπὲρ πάντων ᾄδοντα τὸν ὕμνον τὸν εἰς τὸν θεόν; τί γὰρ ἄλλο δύναμαι γέρων χωλὸς εἰ μὴ ὑμνεῖν τὸν θεόν; εἰ γοῦν ἀηδὼν ἤμην, ἐποίουν τὰ τῆς ἀηδόνος, εἰ κύκνος, τὰ τοῦ κύκνου. νῦν δὲ λογικός εἰμι· ὑμνεῖν με δεῖ τὸν θεόν. τοῦτό μου τὸ ἔργον ἐστίν, ποιῶ αὐτὸ οὐδ᾽ ἐγκαταλείψω τὴν τάξιν ταύτην, ἐφ᾽ ὅσον ἂν διδῶται, καὶ ὑμᾶς ἐπὶ τὴν αὐτὴν ταύτην ᾠδὴν παρακαλῶ.

Are these the only works of providence in our case? What language is adequate to praise them all, or to make us aware of them? For, if we had sense, would we be doing anything else in public or private than offering hymns, praising the deity,[b] and extolling his benefits? Should we not, as we dig and plow and eat,[c] sing the hymn of praise to God (in these words):

Great is God, who has provided these tools for us to till the earth. Great is God, who has given us hands, and power to swallow, and a stomach,[d] and power to grow when we are not aware of it, and to breathe while we sleep.

This is what we ought to sing about on every occasion, and above all to sing the greatest and most divine hymn, that God has given us the ability to investigate[e] these things and to follow the path of service.

What then? Since most (of you) have become blind, should not there be someone to make good this deficiency, and on behalf of all to sing the hymn of praise to God? Why, what else can I, a lame old man,[f] do but sing hymns to God? If, indeed, I were a nightingale, I should sing as a nightingale. If I were a swan, as a swan. But, since I am a rational person,[g] I must be singing hymns of praise to God. This is my task. I do it and I will not give up this post, as long as it is given[h] me to fill it; and I encourage you to join me in the same song.

Notes

[a]Paul's discussion of human hair (1 Cor. 11:14f.) should be compared with Epictetus' remarks; although the apostle has in mind hair that grows on the head, his conclusion is akin: "let us not confound the sexes."

[b]See 1 Cor. 14:26 for the exercise of a hymn (ὕμνος) in the Corinthian assembly.

[c]"As we dig and plow and eat" is reminiscent of 1 Cor. 10:31: "Whether you eat or drink, or whatever you do, do all to the glory of God."

[d]κοιλία: "stomach." What is meant is either the capacity to ingest food or the sexual capacity to reproduce (cf. 1 Cor. 6:12–20).

[e]τὴν παρακολουθητικὴν: παρακολουθέω means either to investigate or to understand. The verb occurs in Luke 1:3 with a similar ambiguity. If the former meaning is preferred, man is unique in the exercise of his reason (νοῦς, λόγος); if the second sense is better, man is a "thinking reed" (Pascal) and has the power of self-reflection (cf. 'A both

3:15 quoted in *New Testament Foundations*, I, 78). Epictetus had a powerful effect on Pascal.

ᶠ"lame old man" is autobiographical. An anonymous epigram ran: Δοῦλος Ἐπίκτητος γενόμην καὶ σωμ' ἀνάπηρος καὶ πενίην Ἴρος καὶ φίλος ἀθανάτοις: "I, Epictetus, was both poor as Irus and lame, yet became a friend of the immortal (gods)."

ᵍλογικός εἰμι: "I am a being possessing λόγος, reason." Cf. Rom. 12:1, where presenting one's person as a "living sacrifice" is a part of λογικὴ λατρεία (spiritual worship); cf. also *Odes of Solomon* 16:1: "As it is the farmer's business to plow, so it is my business to praise God."

ʰδιδῶται: the passive suggests "given by God," as his calling to me.

Stoicism set before its followers a high standard of conduct, which was "to live according to nature," that is, according to man's own nature and the nature of the universe, in harmony with the divine reason. This might seem an impossibly high ideal, attainable by only the "wise man" to whom all mundane matters are indifferent. But the later Stoic teachers, beginning with Panaetius, who lived at Rome in the second half of the second century before Christ, tried to adapt Stoic ethics to the needs of the Roman nobility.[38] They emphasized the active virtues of benevolence and magnanimity and taught that one must do his duty to his family and to the state. The Stoic was encouraged to play his part (in the words of Marcus Aurelius' *Meditations* 2.5) "as a Roman and as a man" in the affairs of his day and to regard the world of action as the arena in which God's athlete shows how he has been trained for the conflict (Epictetus, *Discourses* 4.4). So Stoicism produced men like Brutus and Cato in the last days of the Republic, Seneca in the reign of Nero, and in the second century of our era, the emperor Marcus Aurelius.

In its stricter form Stoicism offered no hope of personal immortality.[39] At death the soul was liberated to be united with the divine fiery essence of which it was a part. Nevertheless, some Stoics held that while bad souls, in whom the divine spark had been quenched, perished quickly after death, the souls of the good might survive till the general conflagration which would destroy the whole of the sensible world and resume its fiery elements into the great central fire (ἐκπύρωσις). Among some Stoic thinkers a doctrine of purgatory, derived from Plato, taught that the souls of the good are gradually purified and made fit to rejoin the divine fire.[40] This doctrine, however, finds no place in Epictetus or Marcus Aurelius, who hesitate to be dogmatic about the survival of the individual soul.

[38] F. H. Sandbach, *The Stoics* (1975), Ch. 8; J. M. Rist, *Stoic Philosophy* (1969), Ch. 10, "The Innovations of Panaetius," pp. 173–200. But cf. Long, *op. cit.*, p. 211.
[39] Cf. Long, *op. cit.*, p. 213.
[40] Greene, *op. cit.*, pp. 339f.

It is worth drawing attention to the marked contrast which the Christian attitude to death shows over against contemporary Stoic thought. One of the most vividly contrasting documents outside the New Testament (where Mark 5:35-43; 1 Cor. 15:42-57; 1 Thess. 4:13-18 come readily to mind as expressing the Christian's confidence and hope in the face of death) is Oxyrhynchus Papyrus 115, dated in the second century of our era. This papyrus presents a letter from a lady Irene to her friend Taonnophris and her husband Philon. The letter is meant to console the recipients on the loss of their son; the writer herself is recently bereaved also. Her note expresses the bitterness of bereavement and a pious resignation—strongly in the Stoic tradition—that little can be done. Even Christian inscriptions, with their laconic θαρρεῖ, οὐδεὶς ἀθάνατος: "Cheer up, no one lives for ever," betray a similar sentiment, though Christian conviction of the certainty of death's conquest is also amply found.

Εἰρήνη Ταοννώφρει καὶ Φίλωνι εὐψυχεῖν. Οὕτως ἐλυπήθην καὶ ἔκλαυσα ἐπὶ τῶι εὐμοίρωι ὡς ἐπὶ Διδυμᾶτος ἔκλαυσα, καὶ πάντα ὅσα ἦν καθήκοντα ἐποίησα καὶ πάντες οἱ ἐμοί, Ἐπαφρόδειτος καὶ Θερμούθιον καὶ Φίλιον καὶ Ἀπολλώνιος καὶ Πλαντᾶς. Ἀλλ' ὅμως οὐδὲν δύναταί τις πρὸς τὰ τοιαῦτα. Παρηγορεῖτε οὖν ἑαυτούς. Εὖ πράττετε. Ἀθὺρ α.

Irene to Taonnophris and Philon, good cheer![a] I similarly grieved and wept over your blessed one,[b] as I wept for Didymas, and everything that was fitting I did[c] and all who were with me, Epaphroditus[d] and Thermouthron and Philion and Apollonius and Plantas. But truly there is nothing anyone can do in the face of such things. Do therefore comfort one another.[e]
Goodbye. October 28.

Notes
[a]The ordinary greeting is χαίρειν (Acts 15:23; James 1:1); here the more tender εὐψυχεῖν (see Phil. 2:19) is used, in view of the contents and character of the letter.

[b]εὔμοιρος is not a proper name (meaning "well off, fortunate") but a description of the deceased son's state; it is found also in Christian inscriptions in Egypt.

[c]This would include the rites and prayers appropriate to his burial. Her son or close relative is mentioned by name. "Everything . . . fitting" (πάντα . . . καθήκοντα) recalls the Stoic motto to do what is one's duty to the living and the dead.

[d]Epaphroditus ("charming") was a common name (see Phil. 2:25; 4:18).

[e]The call is to comfort one another (ἑαυτούς = ἀλλήλους, as in

Col. 3:16). The sentiment looks superficially like that in 1 Thess. 4:18 where Paul writes: "Comfort one another (παρακαλεῖτε ἀλλήλους) with these words," but the setting is quite different.

Paul had just written: you "do not grieve (λυπῆσθε, the same word as in the letter) as those do who do not have hope" (v. 13). Irene grieves as a person bitterly conscious that nothing can be done to express hope: the most that lies in one's power is the pious duty (εὐσέβεια) of burial and an acceptance of the inevitable (cf. Epictetus, *Discourses* 1.2,21: "when did I ever tell you that I was immortal?").

Stoicism showed a remarkable ability to assimilate or come to terms with popular religious beliefs. Essentially monotheistic, it nevertheless made room for the gods of polytheism by explaining them as allegorical representations of various aspects of the activity of the supreme deity, "the gifts of God called by the names of gods" (Cicero, *De natura deorum* 2.23,60). Later the Stoics borrowed from Neo-Platonism in explaining the gods of mythology as good and evil *daemones* subordinate to the supreme God. Their interest in the stars, in whose regular movements they saw a confirmation of their belief in the reason inherent in the universe, led them to countenance the popular belief in astrology. But Panaetius rejected astrology; in this he seems to be alone, according to Cicero (frag. 74). Posidonius even sought to justify divination from the entrails of animals, as practiced at Rome, by the "sympathy" which exists between all parts of the universe, because of the presence in them of the "fiery breath" which is god (Cicero, *De divinatione* 1.3,6,55,125; 57,130). The ability of Stoicism to adapt itself to the beliefs of the age proved in the end a weakness, for it gave popular superstitions a spurious respectability.

CONCLUSION

We have tried in these last two chapters to sketch the world into which Christianity was born. It was a world made ready for the coming of the Christian message. In the *Pax Romana,* in the Roman roads and the common language of the Hellenistic East, we have seen the way made ready for the spread of the gospel. In the failure of the old religion, in the prevailing fear of demons, in the attempts to escape from Fate by magic and astrology, in the craving for communion with God and personal immortality to which the mystery religions bore testimony, in the attempts of philosophy to solve the problems of the universe and of man, we can see the deep need of the Graeco-Roman world for the Christian message as εὐαγγέλιον, good news.

We may notice, in closing, some ways in which Christianity differed from the religions and philosophies we have been considering.

First, Christianity was rooted in history, not in myth like the mystery religions, or in some theory of the constitution of the universe like the contemporary philosophies. It spoke of one whose birth, life, death, and resurrection were appealed to as facts of history, to which its first preachers bore witness with a certainty that carried conviction to their hearers.

Second, Christianity like Judaism refused to compromise with polytheism. No doubt there was a tendency to monotheism both in the popular religion and in the philosophy of the age; but the pagan who was at heart a monotheist was prepared to give lip service to other gods or to explain them away as the Stoics did. The Christians' refusal to sacrifice to the gods, including the emperor, exposed them to charges of "stubbornness and unbending obstinacy" (*pertinacia et inflexibilis obstinatio*) or "sheer cussedness" (ψιλὴ παράταξις) which in the eyes, respectively, of good men like Pliny the Younger (*Epp.* 10.96,3) and Marcus Aurelius (*Meditations* 11.3), was a crime worthy of death. But the Christians could not compromise on this issue and therein lay their strength.

Third, Christianity demanded repentance for past sins and gave the assurance of forgiveness through the atoning death of Jesus and the offer of a power through the Spirit to overcome sin in the future. This was a new message. The pagan myths told of gods who died and rose again. But they were dramatizations of fertility rites, in which vegetation deities were pictured as dying and rising. These acts were not thought to redeem their worshipers from sin. The initiate in the mysteries felt himself for a moment united with the deity, but that union held no promise of a permanent indwelling of the deity resulting in a changed life. The promise of "reborn eternally" was not taken at face value, since the ceremony of renewal was repeated.[41]

Finally, Christianity was unique in its emphasis on the motive power of love. In Stoicism the appeal was ultimately to self-respect and self-help;[42] the good man must act worthily of the divine spark within him. Hence there was a distrust of the emotions. "Sympathy is allowable, but only if it does not disturb the soul's serenity. You may sigh with your friend, but your inner being must remain unmoved. Similarly, pity is viewed with suspicion and affection must be kept within strict limits."[43] In strong contrast, the love of God in Christ awoke in the

---

[41] Barrett, *op. cit.*, p. 97, gives the reference to *taurobolium* (baptism in bull's blood). See too Wagner, *op. cit.*, pp. 244 54. This Mithraic rite was efficacious twenty years (Halliday, *op. cit.*, p. 307). This means that the phrase *renatus in aeternum*, even when applied to the renewal of the rite, was more a pious hope than a cherished conviction (*ibid.*, p. 308).

[42] See Sandbach, *op. cit.*, p. 177.

[43] Cf. P. E. Matheson, Introduction to *Epictetus: The Discourses and Manual* (1916), Vol. 1, p. 20.

Christian an answering love for God and for his neighbor, which was the mainspring of his conduct.[44]

[44] The list of differences could be extended. J. B. Skemp mentions, e.g., that "The real difference between Greek doctrines of immortality and Jewish and Christian doctrines may be said to lie in the corporate nature of the resurrection doctrine and the individual character of the Greek doctrine"; *The Greeks and the Gospel* (1964), p. 85. This important distinction lay at the root of much misunderstanding in the Pauline churches, which were composed of Hellenistic congregations.

    We have stressed dissimilarities between Christianity and its contemporary religions. There were also points of contact—of providence, the existence of moral evil in the human passions, moral values—taken over by the later Greek church fathers. J. G. Gager, *Kingdom and Community*, 132–42, discusses early Christianity and its three main rivals: Mithras, philosophical schools, and Judaism, and indicates both the external factors and the internal processes by which Christianity became in the first centuries of its era the dominant world religion.

PART THREE

Cameos of the Early Church

Eusebius, who died around 339, is traditionally regarded as the father of church history; and this description is justifiably endorsed by his ten books of Church History, which appeared in 325. But there were earlier attempts at writing the history of the Christian church, and one could maintain that the author of the Acts of the Apostles in the New Testament canon set in motion the desire to record the outlines of the Christian church's story for posterity to read.

Why Luke wrote the Acts is hotly debated, as we shall observe in a chapter on how recent criticism has viewed the book. Thereafter we look at the leading issues of the "three crucial decades" (to use Floyd V. Filson's phrase) from Pentecost, which marked the church's beginning, to Paul's arrival in Rome and subsequent martyrdom there, about AD 64/65. These thirty years are intrinsically important and Luke's record of events and their meaning is indispensable. Throughout, there are outstanding highlights that illumine the landscape of the rise, progress, problems and influence of the Christian movement; and to them we devote the successive chapters of this section.

CHAPTER FOUR

The Acts of the Apostles as a Historical and Theological Document

Early church fathers and writers such as Marcion in the mid-second century summed up the New Testament books as "the Gospel and the Apostle." By these terms they meant roughly our Gospels and Epistles. These are natural groupings, but there is an obvious lack, namely, a description of the rise and development of the church. The Acts of the Apostles provides such a bridge.[1] Its name πράξεις [τῶν] ἀποστόλων needs to be seen in this light. It is not a history of all the apostles nor a set of biographical studies, but the "true testimony of the acts and teaching of the apostles" (Irenaeus, *Adv. Haer.* 3.15.1), who laid the foundation of the church (Eph. 2:20; Rev. 21:14). The precise words may reflect the ancient idea that a title should convey what is prominent in the first pages of a book, and in Acts 1 and 2 there are extensive sections devoted to the presence and work of the apostles in Jerusalem.[2]

THE PURPOSE OF ACTS

The plan and purpose of the book are closely related, and modern scholars are divided over Luke's intention in this composition.

1. By some Luke is seen as a *church historian,* exercising literary and artistic skill as a chronicler of past events, either for his own

---

[1] A. Harnack, *The Origin of the New Testament* (ET 1925), pp. 42ff., 63ff.; cf. F. F. Bruce, *Commentary on the Book of Acts* (NICNT, 1952), p. 15, who comments on how Acts "played an indispensable part in relating the two collections to each other." See C. K. Barrett, *Luke the Historian in Recent Study* (1961), p. 53.

[2] The first extant reference to the title of the book is in the anti-Marcionite Prologue to Luke, where the plural "apostles," with the addition of "all", may have been intended to counter Marcion's overemphasis on Paul. M. Dibelius, however, believes its title may be earlier than this (*Studies in the Acts of the Apostles* [ET 1956], pp. 89, 147f.). Clearly the plural could be misleading: only at 1:13 are most of the apostles mentioned, and many prominent names in the story were not apostles. Yet the concept of an apostolic "college" is frequently alluded to (2:14; 5:18; 6:2; 8:14; 9:27; 11:1; 15:2–22). This body of evidence gives support to the idea (see later, pp. 62f.) that the author meant in part to demonstrate that the nascent church rested on solid apostolic foundation (as in Luke 1:1–4) and that Paul had an honored place in that group.

sake or in order to influence Theophilus. Many classicists (E. Meyer, E. M. Blaiklock, F. F. Bruce) take this view, and this is the popular understanding.[3] But W. G. Kümmel objects that a number of key characteristics of history-writing are missing in Acts: complete coverage of the material, precision in historical detail, full chronology, and a biographical interest.[4] These standards are more relevant to the designation of a modern rather than a first-century historian. More striking is another line that critics like Kümmel pursue, arguing that Luke cannot be considered as a historian recording objectively "what actually happened" in a non-committal way. His preoccupation is rather with "kerygmatic" history (see Vol. 1, pp. 42–47). A test issue in which Luke is said to have abandoned the role of the first church historian is his treatment of the resurrection narratives. In contrast to Mark and Matthew, who place the resurrection appearances in Galilee, Luke focuses on Jerusalem. This is taken to reflect his theological interest in Jerusalem as the center of God's saving purposes.[5]

2. At the other end of the scale are those who view Luke as a *theologian,* using historical records as a vehicle for preaching, clearly exercising a creative role to edify the church *in his own day.*[6] Hence, Haenchen's description of Luke's two-volume work as "a book of edification."[7]

---

[3] For Meyer see *Ursprung und Anfänge des Christentums* (1921–23), esp. Vol. III, pp. 7, 15n2; also A. T. Olmstead, "History, Ancient World, and the Bible," in *JNES,* 2 (1943), 26. For Blaiklock, *The Acts of the Apostles* (TNTC, 1959), p. 9; and "The Acts as a Document of 1st-Century History," in *Apostolic History and the Gospel,* edd. W. W. Gasque and R. P. Martin (1970), pp. 41–54. For Bruce, see his two commentaries on Acts (1951 and 1952). On others (e.g., Ramsay, Zahn, Harnack) who considered Luke as a historian, see Gasque, *A History of the Criticism of the Acts of the Apostles* (1975), Ch. 7.

[4] W. G. Kümmel, *Introduction to the New Testament*[2] (ET 1975), pp. 161f.; see also W. C. van Unnik, "The 'Book of Acts'—the Confirmation of the Gospel," *NovT,* 4 (1960), 44.

[5] H. Conzelmann, *The Theology of St. Luke* (ET 1960), discussed in *NTF,* Vol. 1, pp. 138, 246f.

[6] See E. Lohse, "Lukas als Theologe der Heilsgeschichte," *EvTh,* 14 (1954), 256–75. This viewpoint is shared by Conzelmann in his commentary (1963) and "Luke's Place in the Development of Early Christianity," in *Studies in Luke-Acts,* P. Schubert *Festschrift,* edd. L. E. Keck and J. L. Martyn (1968), pp. 298–316. The names that follow are mostly Continental scholars, but for an ambitious American attempt to place Luke among the theologians see C. H. Talbert, *Luke and the Gnostics* (1966); and "The Redactional Critical Quest for Luke the Theologian," in *Jesus and Man's Hope* (1970), pp. 171–222.

[7] *The Acts of the Apostles* (ET 1971), p. 103: "Of course Luke firmly believed that the history of Christian beginnings was edifying in itself, but to present it as such he had to employ a special technique"—later described as one of dramatic interest (p. 418) by which Luke qualifies for the role of "dramatist" (p. 106). "The question of the historical reliability of the book of Acts does not touch the central concern of the book. By telling the history of apostolic times through many individual stories, the book primarily intends to edify the churches, and thereby contribute its part in spreading the Word of God farther and farther, even to the ends of the earth" ("The Book of Acts as Source Material," in Keck-Martyn, *op. cit.,* p. 278). There is both

In this view the church belongs to the sub-apostolic age, and as an institution it betrays features of ecclesiastical life which mark it as belonging to the time of "early catholicism."[8] "Luke" (the name is thought to be the pseudonym of an unknown author rather than the Luke mentioned in Paul's letters)[9] confronts a present situation by drawing lessons from a past age of the church.

Four such lessons, listed in recent studies of the purpose of Acts, are that the church's ministry is a safeguard against heresy of a gnostic type;[10] that the apostolic ministry is the only true custodian and interpreter of Scripture;[11] that Paul's gospel had to—and unquestionably did—overcome rivals (though "Luke" has a distorted view of the historical Paul);[12] and that a futuristic eschatology, which anticipates the Lord's return at any moment, needs to be corrected to account for the non-appearance of the *parousia* (so Vielhauer and E. Lohse, and, classically, the commentaries of E. Haenchen and H. Conzelmann), and because of the postponement of the imminent *parousia,* Luke has taken the fateful step of transforming early Christian eschatology into salvation-history.[13]

---

truth and misconception in this summary statement. True, Acts may very well have served to build up the church in the writer's day, but this intention does not prejudge the issue of the writer's concern for historical reliability (cf. Gasque, *op. cit.,* p. 246).

[8] E. Käsemann, *New Testament Questions of Today* (ET 1969), p. 21: "early catholicism" is defined as "the Church's defence mechanism in the face of the threat of a gnostic takeover."

[9] Kümmel (*op. cit.,* pp. 180f.) cites three instances which show that "the author of Acts is so misinformed that he can scarcely have been a companion of Paul on his missionary journeys." But this conclusion is by no means so certain, and valiant attempts have been made to overcome the difficulties.

[10] A thesis elaborated by C. H. Talbert, *Luke and the Gnostics* (1966); and in "An Anti-Gnostic Tendency in Lucan Christology," *NTS,* 14 (1967-68), 259ff. See also C. K. Barrett, *Luke the Historian in Recent Study* (1961), pp. 62f. Talbert appeals to Acts 20:29f. in support of his thesis that Paul's words are a warning against threatening false teaching of the gnostic variety. See, however, Kümmel, *op. cit.,* p. 162, and W. C. van Unnik, "Die Apostelgeschichte und die Häresien," *ZNTW,* 58 (1967), 240ff.

[11] Talbert, *op. cit.,* Ch. 2, is devoted to this theme, concluding that "when faced with a Gnostic misinterpretation of Scripture, Luke appealed to apostolic authority as a guarantee for the church's exegesis of the Old Testament" (p. 48).

[12] Vielhauer's allegation that there is not a single "specifically Pauline idea" in Acts ("On the 'Paulinism' of Acts," in *Studies in Luke-Acts,* p. 48) is exaggerated and needs some qualification. We may concede that his Christology is "pre-Pauline"; cf. C. F. D. Moule, "The Christology of Acts," *ibid.,* pp. 159-85; S. S. Smalley, "The Christology of Acts," *ExpT,* 73 (1961-62), 358-62; and "The Christology of Acts Again," in *Christ and Spirit in the New Testament: Festschrift* for C. F. D. Moule, edd. B. Lindars and S. S. Smalley (1973), pp. 79-93. But that concession does not require the conclusion that Acts was written years later than Paul when his message was forgotten. Besides, the use of the title παῖς θεοῦ ("servant of God") in the speeches of 3:13,26 and 4:27 as well as the erratic Christology in 3:20f., is an unexplained problem if the outlook of Acts is held to reflect early catholic Christianity.

[13] E. Käsemann, *loc. cit.,* p. 21.

3. Since unresolved problems face both these ways of looking at Acts, a more satisfactory view should steer a middle course, doing justice to some well-attested facts. In the first place, no biblical writer composed history for its own sake as a dispassionate academic exercise. Each had a theological purpose in view (compare the purpose underlying such different history books as 1-2 Kings, 1-2 Chronicles, Judith, 2 Maccabees; and the intention of the gospel writers).[14] Second, there is evidence to show that while Luke was a second-generation Christian he was in touch with and faithfully portrayed the early period of the church's life, ethos, and theology. Acts "reflects the outlook of a man writing in the seventies or eighties of the (first) century who has known Christianity in the fifties and sixties."[15]

We do well to think of the author of Acts as Luke *the pastor* (a descriptive term supported by S. G. Wilson),[16] whose chief interests are to be seen in his concern for the church of his day, but who has access to his own experience as Paul's companion (the so-called "we"-sections in Acts) and to sources which go back to early Palestinian Christianity by way of his sojourn with the apostle in Caesarea about AD 60.[17] He writes as a Christian teacher who claims to have done his homework conscientiously and with integrity (Luke 1:1-4). The pastoral problems he faced may be seen from the book itself.

Let us examine one test case in which his purpose seems clear. The key passage is Acts 1:1-11, where Luke is addressing two situations

---

[14] See A. A. T. Ehrhardt, "The Construction and Purpose of the Acts of the Apostles," *ST,* 12 (1958), 45-79: "The whole purpose of the Book of Acts ... is no less than to be the Gospel of the Holy Spirit" (p. 55). See R. F. O'Toole, *The Unity of Luke's Theology. An Analysis of Luke–Acts* (1984); J. Jervell, "The Acts of the Apostles, and the History of Early Christianity," *ST,* 37 (1983), 17-32.

[15] R. P. C. Hanson, *The Acts* (New Clarendon Bible, 1967), p. 48.

[16] S. G. Wilson, *The Gentiles and the Gentile Mission in Luke-Acts* (1973), p. 266; cf. *NTF,* Vol. 1, pp. 249f.

[17] In the "we"-sections (11:28 [D-text]; 16:10-17; 20:5—21:18; 27:1—28:6) the narrative moves into the first person plural and gives a *prima facie* impression that the narrator is thereby indicating his own personal presence in the scenes described. H. J. Cadbury, "'We' and 'I' Passages in Luke-Acts," *NTS,* 3 (1956-57), 128ff., and J. Dupont, *The Sources of Acts* (ET 1964), pp. 99ff., 131, believe the prologue to Luke's Gospel (1:1-4; cf. *NTF,* Vol. 1, pp. 120f.) prepares for the "we" in Acts on the ground that παρακολουθέω means "I have participated in all events." There is little confirming support for this translation. Cf. E. Haenchen, "'We' in Acts and the Itinerary," ET in *Journal for Theology and the Church* (1965), pp. 95-99. Yet A. J. B. Higgins, "The Preface to Luke and the Kerygma in Acts," in *Apostolic History and the Gospel,* edd. Gasque and Martin, pp. 78-91, rightly wants to see παρακολουθηκότι at least partly implying the writer's active participation in the events narrated (p. 82).

The issue of Luke's use of sources, including the summary narratives (2:42ff.; 4:32ff.; 5:12ff.) and the speeches, which occupy roughly one fifth of the entire book, is exceedingly complex. In addition to Dupont's survey above, see F. F. Bruce, "The Speeches of Acts—Thirty Years After," in *Reconciliation and Hope,* L. Morris *Festschrift,* ed. R. Banks (1974), pp. 53-68; W. W. Gasque, "The Speeches of Acts: Dibelius Reconsidered," in *New Dimensions of New Testament Study,* edd. R. N. Longenecker and M. C. Tenney (1974), pp. 232-50.

which had conceivably arisen in the church and led to two extremes.[18]

On the one hand was an apocalyptic presumption which produced a self-willed and fanatical anticipation of the end of the age. This is countered by the Lord's rebuke (vv. 6-8) to those who inquire feverishly when the fulfilment of God's purpose in history will be. Luke's answer to this impatience is that the question of when the end will come is a foolish one; and preoccupation with apocalyptic speculation on one side and false quietism on the other need correction by the call to the worldwide missionary task, given in the Lord's words in verse 8. In the power of Christ's "other person," the Holy Spirit who *has* come upon the church (ch. 2: Pentecost guarantees the Spirit's presence and power), the believing community must address itself to specific missionary tasks, following the example of the apostolic church.

On the other hand, despair had set in that the *parousia* would ever occur. Doubt had arisen that the finale, a grand climax to history and the victory of God's purposes, would ever take place. Luke meets this extreme situation by recording the angelic assurance of vs. 11 that "this Jesus... will come in the same way as you saw him go into heaven." The Lord *will* come. It will not be soon; nonetheless, the hope is secure and the end is certain.[19]

In conclusion, Luke's interests are not speculative or even theological; rather, they are pastorally motivated. The Ascension of the risen Lord links the ministry of Jesus with his later work in the church through the Holy Spirit. The Spirit is the linking factor uniting Jesus and the church in every age. Indeed, only as the risen, ascended Lord pours out the Spirit (2:33) does the church's life and mission get under way. So the Ascension of Jesus is the concrete event leading to the Holy Spirit's presence and the expansion of the church. These are ruling themes in Acts and they control the author's purpose. To understand Luke's purpose as pastoral means appreciating him as both historian and theologian—though these terms need careful definition. W. C. van Unnik's emphasis at this point provides the needed caution:

> Luke [appears] no longer as a somewhat shadowy figure who assembled stray pieces of more or less reliable information, but as a theologian of no mean stature who very consciously and deliberately planned and executed his work.... Luke was not primarily a historian who wanted to give a record of

---

[18] On Acts 1:1-11 see S. G. Wilson, "The Ascension," *ZNTW*, 59 (1968), 269-81; and "Lukan Eschatology," *NTS*, 16 (1969-70), 330-47.

[19] This motif regarding the arrival of the *parousia*—the Lord will come certainly but not in the near future—is characteristic of the Third Gospel. See *NTF*, Vol. 1, p. 261. The idea of a postponement of the *parousia* is usually thought to have occasioned Luke's attenuated eschatological hope, yet it is clear from Luke-Acts that a delay is not the same as a denial of the final coming of the Lord. From the volume referred to in Vol. 1, p. 157n.74 comes another intriguing typographical error, turning the phrase "the delay of the *parousia*" into "the decay of the parousia." No such abandoning of hope is envisaged in Luke-Acts!

the past for its own sake, but a theologian who, by way of historical writing, wanted to serve the church of his own day amid the questions and perils that beset her.[20]

LEADING THEMES OF ACTS

We can test the validity of our suggestions about Luke's aim by setting down the main features of his work.

1. The first chief theme was to show that the universal spread of the church was begun and maintained by the power of the Holy Spirit, whose coming to the church was a consequence of the exaltation of the risen Lord. This is clear from the data of 2:33; 3:13–16; 5:31f.; 7:55,56,59; 10:40–45; 13:2–4.

This theme has many facets. First, emphasis is placed on the Holy Spirit at every critical phase of the church's development.[21] Second, emphasis is placed on central figures, who carry forward the expansion of the church (Stephen, the Gentile missionaries, Philip, Cornelius, the team of Paul-Barnabas, and then Paul as "a chosen instrument" (σκεῦος ἐκλογῆς).[22] Third, there is indirect emphasis on Paul's journey to Rome, which is never lost sight of or frustrated, though many attempts are made to thwart the divine plan (see 19:21; 23:11; chs. 27, 28).

These sections of the Acts narrative from Paul's arrest in Jerusalem (21:33), his detention in protective custody, the threat on his life, his removal to Antipatris (23:31), his final appeal to Caesar (25:10–12), and his journey to Rome by ship are full of interest. Why does Luke pack so much biographical and dramatic detail into this part of the story (e.g., 23:16–22, where Paul's nephew acts as liaison between Paul and the tribune Claudius Lysias)? This travel-narrative reaches its climax with Paul's arrival in Rome, and it plays an important role because of the following points of interest.

[20] W. C. van Unnik, "Luke-Acts: A Storm Center in Contemporary Scholarship," in *Studies in Luke–Acts*, pp. 23f. An invaluable study is R. Maddox, *The Purpose of Luke–Acts* (1982). Also see V. E. Vine, "The Purpose and Date of Acts," *ExpT*, 96 (1984), 45–48.

[21] A. A. T. Ehrhardt (*loc. cit.*, p. 55) rightly calls attention to the prominence of the Holy Spirit in Luke's record. To suggest that the book ought exclusively to be titled "The Acts of the Holy Spirit" would, however, be a mistake. The writer is much more concerned to emphasize the present activity of the risen Lord through the Spirit and in the church, as the Christian cause advances from Jerusalem to Rome (1:8). See B. Reicke, "The Risen Lord and His Church: The Theology of Acts," *Interpretation*, 13 (1959), 157–69; F. F. Bruce, "The Holy Spirit in the Acts of the Apostles," *Interpretation*, 27 (1973), 166–83. Notice too E. Haenchen's classification of a selection of the 62 occurrences of πνεῦμα in Acts (*Acts of the Apostles*, p. 187); see also J. H. E. Hull, *The Holy Spirit in the Acts of the Apostles* (1967).

[22] G. Klein has contended in *Die zwölf Apostel* (1961) that the presentation of Paul in Acts seeks to devalue his position in early Christianity, e.g., by denying to him the title of "apostle" (except in 14:4, 14). C. Burchard, *Der dreizehnte Zeuge* (1970), p. 174, rightly rejects this, concluding that "Luke insists on placing Paul's witness, though non-apostolic, on the same footing as that of the twelve apostles."

    a. It conforms to Luke's programmatic outline of his book in 1:8, by which the witness is sustained from the center of Judaism to the Imperial City (the phrase ἕως ἐσχάτου τῆς γῆς—"to the ends of the earth"—is a veiled allusion to Rome).[23]

    b. It tells how Paul's wish (19:21) was fulfilled as part of the divine plan for a Christian presence to be established in the Imperial City (23:11), although Paul came to Rome in a way he would not have chosen for himself, namely, in chains (28:20) as a prisoner of Rome.

    c. It demonstrates the overruling purpose of God, which was to preserve the apostle alive in spite of the many dangers, from persons and from the elements, which beset him. In the latter category are "wonder-stories" about the storm (27:14-44) and the venomous snake (28:1-6). On Acts 27, H. Chadwick has perceptively written:

> The story occupies a quite disproportionate amount of space, and one asks why St. Luke thought it so important. The commentaries either tell us that the story is there because it is an eyewitness account—it happened—or that it was invented by a fertile imagination, constructed out of the literary conventions of contemporary adventure stories. The answer is surely that the story is there to underline the extreme improbability that the apostle would ever reach Rome.... For the author of Acts the preaching of the apostle of the Gentiles in the capital of the Gentile world is a supernatural fact.[24]

In view of this statement Luke's purpose can be seen clearly. He is intent on supplying Theophilus with these hair-raising details, interlaced with tokens of divine providence and control, in order to show that Paul's presence in Rome was God's will and that the Gentile mission of the church had the approving stamp of God upon it. This certificate would be a cogent appeal to Theophilus to believe that his embryonic faith was firmly grounded in an enterprise attested by historical events.[25]

    d. The same travel narrative brings Paul to his destined place (cf. 1 Clem. 5:7) and so provides the satisfying climax on which Luke's

---

[23] There is evidence in Psalms of Solomon 8:15 that this phrase was a cipher for the Imperial City. On the other hand, in an essay on the phrase W. C. van Unnik draws attention to several Old Testament references, e.g., Isaiah 49:6 (= Acts 13:47), to argue that Luke's intent is simply to show that Christian witness spread "to the entire world." See *Studia Biblica et Semitica: Festschrift* for Th. C. Vriezen, edd. van Unnik and A. S. van der Woude (1966), pp. 3-49 (reprinted in *Sparsa Collecta*). Haenchen, "The Book of Acts as Source Material for the History of Early Christianity," in *Studies in Luke-Acts*, p. 278, sees a twofold purpose: to indicate the triumphal procession of the Word of God from Jerusalem to Rome; and to point to the need for peaceful coexistence between the pagan state and the Christian church.

[24] *The Circle and the Ellipse* (1959), p. 16.

[25] The tie-in between Jesus' resurrection and ascension and his commission to the apostles by which the Gentile mission, itself unheard of and unexpected in contemporary Judaism, is launched provides D. P. Fuller, *Easter Faith and History* (1965), pp. 192ff., with his understanding of the *leitmotif* of Acts.

book can end. With Paul at Rome Luke's tale of two cities may be rounded off suitably, for he has told his story of how the gospel was brought from Jerusalem to Rome, from the center of Judaism to the capital of the Empire. And his last word "unhindered" (ἀκωλύτως) is both a triumphant assertion of God's overarching providence and a timely reminder that Rome's attitude can do nothing to stand in the way of the ongoing march of the gospel as it reaches out to conquer all lands.[26] As Paul was divinely chosen, inspired, and successful—and his Roman contemporaries would be compelled to acknowledge this—it is the mark of a wise man in Theophilus' day to accept this too and throw in his lot with a movement now manifestly shown to be "of God" (Acts 5:39).

2. In the second place, Luke composed his two-volume work to offer an apologetic that would convince Theophilus—or confirm him in the belief—that the Christian church was not politically dangerous and that the apostles no less than their Lord (Luke 23:2f.) were innocent of the charges leveled against them.[27]

a. The crucifixion of Jesus was construed as a miscarriage of justice for which Jews were responsible (Acts 3:13,14,17; 7:52–53; 10:39; 13:28). These reconfirm the thrust of those texts in Luke's Gospel which place the Roman authorities in a consistently good light and by contrast—especially in the Passion narrative (Luke 22, 23)—put the onus on the Jewish leaders.[28]

---

[26] The adverb is purposely chosen and placed so as to epitomize the motif of the two-volume work, according to F. Stagg, *The Book of Acts* (1955), p. 1.

[27] One of the few "assured results" in recent *Actaforschung*. Kümmel (*op. cit.*, pp. 162f.) writes: "the aim of defending the Christians against the charge of enmity toward the state is unmistakable." For this consensus, see J. Dupont, "Le salut des Gentils, etc.," in *NTS*, 6 (1959–60), 133; W. C. van Unnik, *NovT*, 4 (1960), 40f.; J. C. O'Neill, *The Theology of Acts* (1961), pp. 171f.; Haenchen's commentary, pp. 403f., 642ff., 657f. Clearly the same data can lead to diverse conclusions from this single premise; e.g., M. Schneckenburger (1804–48) argues that Luke's historical, eyewitness record is calculated to place Paul in an attractive light in order to win over Jewish Christians in the late 60s. E. Zeller, F. C. Baur's son-in-law and protégé, wanted to see Acts as directed toward Jewish Christians at Rome, and so dated its publication in the early second century, when the Roman government was taking up a hostile attitude to the church; *Die Apostelgeschichte nach ihrem Inhalt und Ursprung kritisch untersucht* (1854); cf. Gasque, *op. cit.*, pp. 44–50; Horton Harris, *The Tübingen School* (1975), pp. 55–77. That Luke intended to confirm Theophilus in his recent acknowledgment of the faith is argued by J. H. Crehan, "The Purpose of Luke in Acts," *SE*, 2 (1964), 354–68, though there has been much discussion as to the identity of Theophilus (see *NTF*, Vol. 1, pp. 245f.).

[28] See R. P. Martin, "Salvation and Discipleship in the Gospel of Luke," *Interpretation*, 30 (1976), 366–80. A partial analogy to this situation may help. Dorothy L. Sayers' dislike of newspaper reporters and the press in general comes out in her detective novels, in which there is a similar placing of the press in an unfavorable light. See Janet Hitchman, *Such a Strange Lady: A Biography of Dorothy L. Sayers* (1975), p. 131.

b. A variety of officials show good will to Paul and have no cause for political complaint (Acts 13:7,12; 16:37ff.; 18:12ff.; 19:31,35ff.; 23:29; 25:12,14–21,25; 26:31,32).

c. Roman military men are consistently impressed with Jesus and Paul. Paul's arrest leads to free detention (*libera custodia*) in Acts 28:30f.

d. Jews were unable to make any charge against the apostles and Paul stick (Acts 18:14; 19:38,39; 23:29; 25:25; 26:32; 28:18,19).[29]

3. Then, in a more oblique fashion, Luke sets out to demonstrate that the church came out of Judaism to form "one new man" (cf. Eph. 2:11–22). Yet the multiracial church—in Luke's day predominantly Gentile in ethnic balance—has links with salvation-history which cannot be severed,[30] and Luke's purpose is to show that the Apostle to the Gentiles was no iconoclast or moral freewheeler.[31]

The theological themes of Acts can be illustrated by comparing it with another New Testament document, whose motif is to demon-

---

[29] An older view saw Acts as a written legal brief defending Paul at his trial, in an extreme form holding that Theophilus was the magistrate who heard Paul's case. This explains the abrupt ending, since 28:30f. brings things right up to the trial. See D. Plooij, in *Expositor*, 8th series, 8 (1914), 511–23; *ibid.*, 13 (1917), 108–24; Harnack, *The Date of Acts* (ET 1911), pp. 90–125. A. J. Mattill believes Acts was written against Jewish-Christian attacks on Paul during his imprisonment; "The Purpose of Acts," in *Apostolic History and the Gospel*, pp. 108–22. Trocmé argues for an even earlier date and sees Acts as a defense against Judaizing claims that Pauline Christianity subverts the state and breaks with Jerusalem Christianity; *Le "livre des Actes" et l'histoire* (1957), pp. 52ff. Kümmel indicates that all such "defense" theories are based on only fragmentary evidence in Acts and presuppose too early a setting for the book; *op. cit.*, p. 162. C. K. Barrett, *Luke the Historian*, p. 63, minces no words: "No Roman official would ever have filtered out so much of what to him would be theological and ecclesiastical rubbish in order to reach so tiny a grain of relevant apology."

[30] For the exegetical grounding of the recent consensus that Luke's scheme of "salvation history" involves a nexus of Old Testament promise and gospel fulfilment, see N. A. Dahl, "The Story of Abraham in Luke-Acts," in *Studies in Luke-Acts*, pp. 139–58. In the modern debate the technical expression "salvation history" is understood in quite different ways. Some see Luke as the one who connects the Gospel events and their continuance in the church with the fulfilment of Old Testament anticipations. But in Continental scholarship "salvation history" has the pejorative connotation that Luke's theology abandons Paul's eschatological understanding of the Christ-event by which the church lives in the (short) interval between the cross and the imminent *parousia*. So Käsemann in *New Testament Questions of Today*, p. 21. Haenchen expresses the contrast thus: "For Paul salvation history is hidden in history (and only perceived by faith: *theologia crucis*); for Luke salvation history is already visible in history"; "Tradition und Komposition in der Apostelgeschichte," *ZThK*, 52 (1955), 225n.; cf. Gasque, *op. cit.*, p. 238.

[31] Hence Paul's "Jewish behavior" in Acts 21. The author thereby demonstrates Paul's essential faithfulness to his ancestral convictions as *au fond* a Jew, a lifestyle that can be confirmed from his epistles (e.g., 1 Cor. 9; Rom. 14). For the problems with this, recognized by Harnack (who thought that none was insuperable) see Gasque, *op. cit.*, pp. 150–55.

strate God's purpose in bringing to birth a universal church in which Paul's role is paramount—the Epistle to the Ephesians.

At least part of Luke's theological purpose in writing and publishing the Acts of the Apostles was to portray the Palestinian origin of the church and the essentially Jewish matrix of its birth. Using Old Testament "prooftexts" as witnesses to the new age of salvation in Christ is a frequent device, many of these being set in the frame of prayers, praises, and speeches to Jewish audiences. This has a counterpart in the use of messianic canticles in the Gospel, chapters 1 and 2. Paul is introduced as a faithful Jew, who stays loyal to his ancestral heritage throughout, though part of Luke's task is to show how he was commissioned by the risen Lord as "apostle to the Gentiles" *par excellence* (Acts 9:15; 22:21; 26:20,23). Even when rejected by his brethren, he remains a prisoner for "the hope of Israel" (Acts 28:20).

The data for a comparison of Luke-Acts and Ephesians may be assembled, though we can do no more than offer a ground-plan of the full discussion.[32]

a. Certain linguistic parallels have been noted by J. Moffatt, who drew attention to several interesting correspondences. First is the common teaching on the Ascension, in the light of G. B. Caird's observation that it is only in these two documents that a distinction is drawn between the Ascension and the gift of the Spirit on the one hand and the events of Easter on the other. Also, a peculiar vocabulary is shared by the Lukan writings and Ephesians (see later, pp. 230ff.). An interesting feature of this is the use of verbs in Acts with the prefix προ- (Acts 2:23; 3:18,20; 4:28; 7:52; 13:24; 22:14; 26:16) and a heavy concentration on the divine election motif (using nouns and verbs with the same prefix) in Ephesians 1. Abbott's statistical study shows, further, that of the thirty words in Ephesians found elsewhere in the New Testament but not represented in the Pauline corpus, twenty-five *are* found in Luke-Acts. Fourth, the special interest of Acts 20:17–38 has close links with Ephesians 1. Some metaphors (e.g., building imagery) are not exclusive to these two documents, but a case could be made out for certain other terms that have a distinctive usage in Luke-Acts and Ephesians (e.g., βουλή = divine counsel, which outside Luke-Acts and Ephesians carries this sense only in Hebrews; 1 Cor. 4:5, moreover, uses the term in the plural in a totally different sense).

b. Many of the leading ideas of Ephesians are also found in Luke-Acts.[33] The ecclesiology in both documents runs parallel, for instance the concept of "one church" as God's purchased possession, called to be a holy people. In a later section (pp. 232f.) we shall note the role of

---

[32] What follows draws upon my article, "An Epistle in Search of a Life-Setting," *ExpT*, 79 (1968), 296–302, which includes bibliographical details. Further support comes from J. L. Houlden, *Paul's Letters from Prison* (1970); C. L. Mitton, *Ephesians* (NCB, 1976), pp. 15–17.

[33] See E. Käsemann, "Acts and Ephesians," in *Studies in Luke-Acts*, pp. 288–97.

the apostolate as a bulwark against the inroads of heresy. This is envisaged in both documents with clearly stated descriptions of very similar kinds, especially in Paul's address to church leaders in Acts 20. The church's life in this world where resistance to evil forces is a Christian duty is a feature in both Acts and Ephesians. In both the church must expect to be "a church persecuted and struggling."

Of the two most notable elements these two parts of the New Testament have in common one is the description of the church as a structured society with an ordered and "sacramental" life, on the way to becoming institutionalized. This development is inevitable once the church comes to take its place on earth as a settled institution. Both documents have much to say about "church orders" and ministerial oversight, with the apostolate occupying a preeminent place in both ecclesiologies.

The second notable shared idea is that the "naturalization" of the church in this world stems partly from a recession of the hope of an imminent *parousia*. Luke's Acts does contain some futuristic references to the Lord's return (1:11; 3:19,20) but the place of this teaching in the Acts-kerygma is not at all secure, as T. F. Glasson has pointed out (see p. 77n below). It would certainly be against the evidence to suppose that Luke envisages the church waiting on tiptoe for the cleaving heavens and the returning Lord. And this awareness that the church has a future on earth indefinitely is precisely the purport of Ephesians in such passages as 3:21 and 4:15. About the latter verse Ch. Masson has commented:

> The eschatological event is the creation and growth of the body of Christ in which humanity finds its unity and shares the divine fullness. This eschatology is different from that of St. Paul. . . . Already united to Christ as the body to the head, the church grows towards Christ; *she no longer waits for him to come to her.*[34]

Ephesians 5:27 places Christ's preparation for his bride at a more distant future, intimating that the church has a life in this world before the consummation of its destiny.

From the above discussion, we may tentatively conclude that Acts shares in this singular concern to show how the mission of the apostle led to the establishment of a worldwide Christian community, whose life on earth is relatively fixed and settled and whose future is bound up with a task to embrace the nations within its fold.[34a]

THE DATING OF ACTS

Discussions of the purpose of Acts depend partly on the date of its writing, and that issue in turn involves matters like authorship and histori-

---

[34] *L'épître aux Ephésiens* (1953), p. 199; italics added to my translation.
[34a] See R. J. Karris, *What Are They Saying about Luke and Acts? A Theology of the Faithful God* (1979), for a useful treatment of the themes of Acts.

cal worth. Three possibilities gain support from various interpretations of these data.

1. The chief modern proponent of a second-century dating of Acts is J. C. O'Neill, whose argument builds on the author's attitude to Jews and Jewish Christianity, the theological content, and the formal structure of the book.[35] He concludes that Acts has theological and literary kinship with second-century apologists (especially Justin, AD 150) and is to be dated by this affinity. An older view tried to show that "Luke" had read (and misread) Josephus (AD 90–95) at 5:36f. and 21:38, and so must have written later than the first century.[36] But if he was a second-century Christian, Luke's ignorance of Paul's letters is hard to explain, since there is every probability that the corpus of Paul's letters was in existence no later than the first decade of the second century. Furthermore, Marcion accepts Acts as canonical, and he was roughly a contemporary of Justin. It is difficult to believe that he would have done so if the publication of Acts were dated in his lifetime or nearly so.

2. If we take Lukan authorship as a premise, we may accept a dating in the 60s, following F. F. Bruce, T. W. Manson, and C. S. C. Williams.[37] This argument builds on the importance of persecution at Rome (65) and the Jewish War (66–70). The first event led to Rome's hostility to the church; the second was the outcome of Jewish fanaticism. So Acts becomes a statement that Christians, unlike Jews, are not disloyal to the Roman Empire.

We can enumerate difficulties with this reconstruction as well. A teasing question is whether Acts presupposes the Fall of Jerusalem. If Acts is later than Luke's Gospel (as 1:1 naturally suggests), does not Luke 21:20–24 (plus 19:42–44) picture the catastrophe of AD 70 as *vaticinium ex eventu*, i.e., "a prophecy after the event" and already fulfilled? This point can be deflected by postulating that the words "former treatise" refer to a proto-Luke, that is, the first edition of Luke's Gospel, written before Luke settled with Paul at Caesarea in AD 60.[38] But this

---

[35] *The Theology of Acts in its Historical Setting* (1961); in the 2nd rev. ed. (1970) the author's understanding of the purpose of Acts has not changed, but he is more open to the possibility that "Luke" has used sources.

[36] Luke's alleged dependence on Josephus goes back to the last part of the nineteenth century and was a factor in H. H. Wendt's commentary (1899); cf. Gasque, *op. cit.,* pp. 103f.

[37] F. F. Bruce, *The Acts of the Apostles* (1951), pp. 11–13, lists seven reasons for a date near the end of Paul's two-year detention in Rome (c. AD 61). T. W. Manson, *Studies in the Gospels and Epistles* (1962), pp. 62–67, and C. S. C. Williams, *A Commentary on the Acts of the Apostles* (1957), pp. 13–15, prefer a slightly later dating, though before AD 70. See also J. A. T. Robinson, *Redating the New Testament* (1976), pp. 86–117.

[38] C. S. C. Williams, "The Date of Luke-Acts," *ExpT,* 64 (1952–53), 283f. Against the objection that Luke 21 reflects a situation *after* AD 70, he appeals to C. H. Dodd whose essay "The Fall of Jerusalem and the 'Abomination of Desolation,'" repr. in his *More New Testament Studies* (1968), pp. 75–79, maintains that the writing of

is a forced concession to our ignorance. Secondly, Paul's death is unrecorded in Acts. If Luke knew of it in AD 66–68, why did he not mention it? Some suggest that he did allude to it in a roundabout way in Acts 20:25,29, but it remains strange that writing so soon after the apostle's martyrdom he should pass it by, and leave Paul in relative freedom in Rome (28:30,31). Ignorance of Paul's letters is again a problem if Acts appeared in the 60s, unless some good reasons can be suggested for Luke's choosing not to use them.

3. A publication date in the 80s, either with or without Lukan authorship, has been proposed to answer the problems with both suggestions. At one extreme, the setting of the book in the ninth decade, coupled with a denial of Lukan authorship, chimes in with the view of Conzelmann and Haenchen that "Luke" is a theologian whose outlook reflects the church situation in 80–90, when Paul's memory was under a cloud. We may ask about the evidences for the disparity that sets Paul against "Luke." Recent Continental scholars argue that there is a set of contrasts between the historical Paul and the author of Acts:[39] "Luke" is pre-Pauline in Christology but post-Pauline in natural theology, understanding of the law, eschatology, and ecclesiology;[40] also there are disagreements over history, e.g., visits of Paul to Jerusalem, the setting of the Apostolic Council (Acts 15), and even a complete fabrication of so-called historical detail on Luke's part;[41] above all, the church as "body of

---

Luke 21 borrows from the Old Testament imagery of siege warfare, not the historical circumstance of the first Jewish war. See too B. Reicke, "Synoptic Prophecies on the Destruction of Jerusalem," in *Studies in the New Testament and Early Christian Literature, Festschrift* for A. P. Wikgren, ed. D. E. Aune (1972), pp. 121–34; and J. A. T. Robinson, *op. cit.,* Ch. 2.

[39] This dichotomy is usually attributed to Vielhauer, "On the 'Paulinism' of Acts" (ET of a 1950 essay, in *Studies in Luke-Acts,* pp. 33–50). E. Haenchen, *Acts,* p. 48, regards this essay as marking "the new development" in the more recent phase of *Actaforschung.*

[40] These four points of distinction between the "Lukan Paul" and the "historical Paul" (represented in the main epistles of Rom., Gal., and 1–2 Cor.) have evoked some critical review. See Gasque, *op. cit.,* pp. 284–91, for a summary of the issues. Even more telling are the criticisms from within the group of European scholars that looks back to Dibelius as mentor, e.g., U. Wilckens, "Interpreting Luke-Acts in a Period of Existentialist Theology," in *Studies in Luke-Acts,* pp. 60–83. He comments significantly, "It is Paul, interpreted existentially, who is so sharply set against Luke as the great but dangerous corrupter of the Pauline gospel. But the existentially interpreted Paul is not the historical Paul" (p. 77).

[41] E.g., a critical axiom is to deny the historicity of the so-called first missionary journey (Acts 13–14) as an apologetic invention to show the effectiveness of the Pauline mission in converting a Roman official (13:12), his heroic character as powerful speaker and leader (13:13, 16; 14:12) and the victory of the gospel over magic (13:6–11). Or else, the narrative has been written up from the tradition in 2 Tim. 3:11. The skepticism of Haenchen (*Acts,* pp. 400–404) and Conzelmann, *Die Apostelgeschichte,* pp. 72–81, who makes the entire travel-report into a fiction, had earlier been anticipated by Zeller and Loisy. Such efforts are highly subjective and should not be treated as axiomatic, as R. H. Fuller, *A Critical Introduction to the New Testament* (1966), p. 9, is inclined to do.

Christ" in Paul becomes for later "early Catholicism" an institution dispensing salvation (*Heilsanstalt*).[42]

On the other hand, even when Acts is dated in the ninth decade, it is possible to appeal to a series of counterbalancing evidences for Luke's access to early and reliable sources.[43] We may instance the presence of Aramaisms, or at least Semitisms, in the early chapters; the use, in the main, of correct terminology for Roman officials; the fact that Luke is in touch with Asia Minor geographical detail and the administrative practices which prevailed in that part of the world; and the affirmation that an author's interest in theology does not necessarily mean a disdain of history.[44]

We may reach a tentative conclusion. Luke wrote in the 80s, but he told his story using sources which are trustworthy for the 40s and the 50s of the first century. His task was pastoral[45] and proclamatory,[46]

[42] For Käsemann's dictum that "Luke is . . . the first representative of evolving early catholicism" see n. 8 above. Haenchen (*Acts*, p. 49) finds fault with this statement, and questions (p. 132) whether Käsemann may not after all have put too big a hiatus between the apostolic times and the later church age. See also C. K. Barrett, *Luke the Historian*, p. 74, on the incorrectness of calling Luke's concept of the church that of an "institution." Barrett's questioning of the propriety of the term "early catholicism" in Acts is reinforced in his *Church, Ministry and Sacraments in the New Testament* (1985), pp. 78–80, 89, 99.

[43] This is an important question, for if it can be shown (inferentially, to be sure) that he did so draw on such materials, his connection with the apostolic age he purportedly describes can be more firmly established. Such sources naturally include the "we"-sections, on which Barrett comments (*op. cit.*, p. 22): "This means, not necessarily, that the author was an eye-witness but that he had some sort of access to eye-witness material for this part of the narrative." Other possibilities are an itinerary-document, a catalog of the places Paul visited (so Dibelius, *Studies in the Acts of the Apostles*, p. 199); or even a "diary" as an *aide-mémoire* written by a companion of Paul (so Trocmé, *op. cit.*, pp. 134–40; cf. Haenchen, *op. cit.*, pp. 84ff., for a favorable regard accorded to this hypothesis; Gasque, *op. cit.*, p. 270). Haenchen is instructive on Luke's use of written sources (pp. 87–89), esp. the argument based on Acts 18:18–22.

[44] On Semitisms see M. Wilcox, *The Semitisms of Acts* (1965); D. F. Payne, "Semitisms in the Book of Acts," in *Apostolic History and the Gospel*, pp. 134–50. Luke's correct nomenclature for Roman officials was first appealed to by Lightfoot (opposing Baur); cf. Gasque, *op. cit.*, p. 120. Most of this argument stands, with qualifications supplied by Sherwin-White, *Roman Society and Roman Law in the New Testament*, who maintains Acts' "basic historicity" (p. 189) with residual uncertainty regarding correct naming of officials (e.g., 16:22). On geography see W. M. Ramsay, *The Bearing of Recent Discovery on the Trustworthiness of the New Testament* (1915); B. Van Elderen, "Some Archaeological Observations on Paul's First Missionary Journey," in *Apostolic History and the Gospel*, pp. 151–56. On contemporary administrative practices, 23:34f. is a case in point, involving the custom of *forum domicilii*, by which an accused person was referred back to the jurisdiction of his native province. To the question why Felix did not send Paul back to Cilicia under this provision, the answer is that Cilicia was dependent on the Syrian province in 52, and was not made a separate province until the Flavian period (69–96). Luke thus follows a reliable tradition here; see Sherwin-White, *op. cit.*, pp. 55f. On history and theology see W. C. van Unnik, "Luke-Acts: A Storm Center," *loc. cit.*

[45] S. G. Wilson, "Lukan Eschatology," *NTS*, 16 (1969–70), 347.

[46] Cf. Dibelius, "The Speeches of Acts," *Studies in the Acts of the Apostles*, pp. 182ff.: "Luke narrates but while he does this, he also preaches." This is not to endorse Dibelius' negative connotation ("*not* a historian, *but* a preacher")—which suggests

namely, to recall his contemporaries to the church's ministry in the apostolic age. He was a second-generation pastor harking back to a first-generation model. By using the past history of the church as material, he meant to recall the church of his own day to apostolic norms and ministry, and in particular, to apostolic zeal in outreach based on a fresh experience of the dynamism of the Holy Spirit.

AUTHORSHIP

The earliest attestation of traditional Lukan authorship comes in the Muratorian canon (c. 170–200), though the translation of the text is debated. The implication is that Luke is silent about Peter's martyrdom at Rome and Paul's journey to Spain because he was not a personal witness of these events, whereas he was of the preceding history. This is obviously a misstatement, as is clear from much of what Acts contains. The Anti-Marcionite prologue to Luke (c. 160–180) puts a clear identity-label on both the Gospel and the Acts, ascribing both to Luke, "an Antiochean of Syria, a doctor by profession, a disciple of the apostles, and one who later accompanied Paul until his martyrdom." Irenaeus explicitly (*Adv. Haer.* 3.1) mentions Luke as *sectator Pauli,* "a companion of Paul," and thereafter the evidence builds up (in Clement of Alexandria, Tertullian, and Eusebius). Jerome, however, is the first church father to say expressly that Acts was written immediately after the two-year imprisonment (Acts 28), and Jerome is dependent on Eusebius.

The internal evidence from the Gospel and Acts is inferential, since both books have no author's name. It seems indisputable that both come from the same hand, since the same style, language, and interest are shared. A. C. Clark's singular attempt to discredit common authorship has been judged to have failed, and it was effectively demolished by W. L. Knox.[47]

The presence of the narrator as a companion of Paul is seen traditionally by the so-called "we"-sections (11:28, Codex Bezae; 16:10–17; 20:5—21:18; 27:1—28:6). Why were these "diary" extracts incorporated if not as the personal memoirs of one of the apostle's companions? The simplest response, that Luke is here calling on his personal memoirs, is by no means universally endorsed.[48] Most scholars, how-

a false antithesis; cf. I. H. Marshall, *Luke: Historian and Theologian* (1970), Chs. 2, 3. Marshall now prefers to regard Luke as an "evangelist" ("Early Catholicism in the New Testament," in *New Dimensions in New Testament Study,* edd. Longenecker and Tenney, p. 220, though in his earlier title he refrained from this description.

[47] A. C. Clark, *The Acts of the Apostles* (1933), pp. 393–408; W. L. Knox, *The Acts of the Apostles* (1948), pp. 2–15, 100–109.

[48] J. Dupont, *The Sources of Acts* (ET 1964); D. Guthrie, *New Testament Introduction*³ (1970), pp. 363–77; and see E. Haenchen, *Acts,* Ch. 6, "The Source Question," for the parameters of the debate.

ever, agree that Luke is dependent on a carefully articulated tradition that has certain claims to reliability (see note 17 above).

Luke's name does not appear in the "we"-sections. Yet the suggestion that he is author is, if a guess, an educated one, partly because of the imprisonment epistles (Col. 4:10ff.) and partly in view of the medical language attributed to the "beloved physician" (Col. 4:14).[49] The latter evidence, however, has been much questioned since H. J. Cadbury's demonstration that there is nothing exclusively and uniquely "medical" in Luke's vocabulary.[50] More centrally decisive for or against Lukan authorship are the witness of Luke 1:1-4 and the question whether it may be taken at face-value, especially the claim that the author personally participated in the events he describes (see note 17 above); and the theological tendency of Luke-Acts and its manifestly non-Pauline theology.

The test issues raised by Vielhauer are as follows:[51]

1. The account of Paul's apostleship in 1 Corinthians is said to be at odds with the record of Acts, which does not know of any claim to the title "apostle" that Paul emphasized. But Acts does not deny the title (cf. Acts 13:4; 14:4,14), and recent study has focused on Luke's interest in the apostolic ministry.[52]

2. The Pauline kerygma in Romans 1-8 is held to differ from the statements in Acts 17 on the question of natural theology. But there are basic agreements between Romans 1:18ff. and Acts 14:15-17, and the extent of discord between Paul's teaching in his Epistles and his speeches in Acts has been overrated; the emphases can be understood in the light of different purposes that are in view in the two sets of writing.

3. Paul's heavy concentration on the redeeming virtue of Christ's death hardly appears in Acts (except at 20:28). This raises the problem of a disparity between the Paul of the Epistles and the Paul ostensibly known to the author of Acts. But we should recognize that the Epistles give the content of Paul's church teaching, whereas Acts is concerned chiefly with a missionary situation.

Our conclusion would be that the evidence of tradition rests on good ground and that Acts was written by an author who had known Paul firsthand. The alleged misunderstanding of Paul is to be explained more by Luke's later perspective of what he knew concerning the apostle's history than by either ignorance or misrepresentation of the mis-

---

[49] W. K. Hobart, The Medical Language of St. Luke (1882; repr. 1954).

[50] The Style and Literary Method of Luke, Part 1: The Diction of Luke and Acts (1919), pp. 39-72. "The style of Luke bears no more evidence of medical training and interest than does the language of other writers who were not physicians" (p. 50). For a critique of Cadbury see J. Moffatt, in Expositor, 8th series, 24 (1922), 1-18.

[51] P. Vielhauer, "On the Paulinism of Acts," in Studies in Luke-Acts, pp. 33-50.

[52] C. Burchard, Der dreizehnte Zeuge; E. Käsemann, "Acts and Ephesians," in Studies in Luke-Acts, pp. 295ff.

sionary significance of the great apostle to the Gentiles (see later for Luke's adaptation of Paul's teaching to new situations, pp. 224ff.).[53, 54]

---

[53] W. C. van Unnik, *loc. cit.*, p. 26. See now W. G. Kümmel, "Current Theological Accusations against Luke," *ANQ*, 16 (1975), 131–45, summarized by C. H. Talbert in *Interpretation*, 30 (1976), 390ff., now in *Interpreting the Gospels* (1981), ed. J. L. Mays, pp. 208–13.

[54] Literary analysis of Acts is a chief feature of G. Krodel's commentary (Proclamation Commentaries, 1981), a highly suggestive treatment to be complemented by C. H. Talbert's semi-popular edition in Knox Preaching Guides series (1984). Both writers seek to find rather elaborate parallels and correspondences in the literary structures of Acts. More traditional in its approach is I. H. Marshall, *The Acts of the Apostles* (TNTC, 1980), and even more so C. Rowland's clearly and cogently written section, "From Messianic Sect to Christian Religion," in his *Christian Origins* (1985), pp. 236–308. See too M. Hengel, *Acts and the History of Earliest Christianity* (ET 1979).

CHAPTER FIVE

Pentecost and the Church at Jerusalem

Acts 1–5 is by no means the earliest or only source of information about the historical origins of the church, but its witness is indispensable to our understanding of how the Christian movement began. Neither an objective historical report nor a biased and invented reconstruction of history, it is a combination—or better, a confluence—of event and interpretation in which "history" is present, but it is history seen and understood through the eyes of faith.

Thus, we may say about the story of Pentecost that, on the one hand, it records a historical happening which (the "objective" historian might conclude) can be explained as an outburst of enthusiastic behavior within a Jewish messianic sect, as the Christian movement was evidently regarded (Acts 24:5, 14; 28:22).[1] On the other hand, for the men and women of faith to whom Luke is addressing this report, and for Theophilus, a sympathetic inquirer anxious to know more, the validity of this chapter in history lies precisely in its significance as an episode in redemptive history by which the prophetic Scriptures of the Old Testament were fulfilled and a fresh beginning in God's dealings with mankind opened up. For this reason, we should concede that Acts 1–5 describes the first days of the church's life with a purpose in mind—a purpose at once theological (God is at work among his people of the new covenant, who stand at the turning point of the ages, marking the transition from the old order to the new) and apologetic (in this new creation of the church the last word of God to man is spoken).

[1] On the story of Pentecost, see C. A. A. Scott, "What Happened at Pentecost," in *The Spirit,* ed. B. H. Streeter (1919), pp. 117–58; K. Lake, *The Beginnings of Christianity,* edd. F. J. Foakes Jackson and K. Lake, Vol. 5, note X: "The Gift of the Spirit and the Day of Pentecost," pp. 111–21. On this latter essay see R. N. Flew, *Jesus and His Church*[2] (1943), pp. 99ff. Cf. J. D. G. Dunn, *Baptism in the Spirit* (1970), Ch. 4; *Jesus and the Spirit* (1975), Ch. 6, esp. section 26: "What Happened at Pentecost?" (pp. 146–52); and "Pentecost, Feast of," *NIDNTT,* 2 (1976), 783–88. Cf. I. H. Marshall, "The Significance of Pentecost," *SJT,* 30 (1977), 347–69; A. T. Lincoln, "Luke's Pentecost: Theology and History," *ExpT,* 96 (1985), 204–9. Well worth tracking down and considering is B. Noack, "The Day of Pentecost in Jubilees, Qumran, and Acts," *Annual of the Swedish Theological Institute,*I (1962), 73–95.

This picture has to be filled out by other sources of information at our disposal. We shall investigate these shortly, when we consider Paul's letters, which incorporate pre-Pauline materials, such as early credal forms, hymnic specimens, and possible "words of Jesus" (see below, pp. 251ff.). Another fruitful field of inquiry is the catechetical tradition: how did early Christians begin to teach new converts and disciples in preparation for baptism and with a view to including them in the family and household of the church (see below, p. 254)? Nor should we overlook various pieces of information from the Synoptic Gospels. These data bear hallmarks of an origin long before their eventual inclusion in the completed Gospels. For instance, it is commonly agreed that the material peculiar to the Gospel of Matthew (e.g., Matt. 10:23; 15:21-28) goes back to an early Palestinian community that preserved sayings and teachings of Jesus. This material gives evidence, both on stylistic grounds (by Semitic constructions) and in content (portraying a limitation of the Christian mission to Israel) of the mind of the Lord in reference to the Jewish Christian community in Palestine.[2] We may use this material to reconstruct, however tentatively, the life of the church in Jerusalem and beyond in the early days of its existence.

PENTECOST

The first part of Acts 2 contains the tantalizing account of the descent of the Holy Spirit on the disciples and the coming into being of the community of the new Israel. Several answers have been proposed to the enigmatic question, When did the Christian church originate? These fall into two main categories, as T. W. Manson remarks.[3] On the one side are those who see the church as already existing before Jesus' crucifixion; who hold, for example, that it was born—or at least was conceived and was existing in embryo—at the calling of the Twelve,[4] or at the time of Peter's confession at Caesarea Philippi,[5] or at the supper table when Jesus gathered his disciples as a nucleus of what later became recognized as the church.[6] On the other hand are those who insist that there

---

2 For a history of the interpretation of Matt. 10:23 see M. Künzi, *Das Naherwartungslogion Mt 10,23: Geschichte seiner Auslegung* (1970); cf. D. R. A. Hare, *The Theme of Jewish Persecution of Christians in the Gospel according to St. Matthew* (1967), pp. 96-114. On Matt. 15:21-28, see J. Jeremias, *Jesus' Promise to the Nations* (ET 1958), pp. 26ff. For the particularities of Matthean Christianity see R. E. Brown and J. P. Meier, *Antioch and Rome. New Testament Cradles of Catholic Christianity* (1983), pp. 45-72; cf. M. Hengel, *Acts and the History of Earliest Christianity* (ET 1979), p. 98.

3 T. W. Manson, "The New Testament Basis of the Doctrine of the Church," *JEH*, 1 (1950), 1-11.

4 *Ibid.*, p. 1; R. N. Flew, *op. cit.*, pp. 87f.; A. M. Hunter, *The Unity of the New Testament* (1943), p. 55.

5 G. Gloege, *Reich Gottes und Kirche im Neuen Testament* (1929), pp. 227, 275. The argument is that there is no church without messiahship.

6 K. L. Schmidt, *TDNT*, 3 (ET 1965), 521: "In this light the so-called institution of the Lord's Supper is shown to be an act in establishment of the Church," with reference to Kattenbusch's study in the Harnack *Festgabe* (1921), p. 169.

was no church in the true sense of the word until after the work of the Lord was achieved in his cross, his triumph, his ascension, and his gift of the Holy Spirit. Just as the coming of the kingdom, even if present proleptically in Jesus' ministry, awaited the outworking of God's purpose in his passion and triumph (cf. Mark 9:1), so the church may be said to exist as a potential during Jesus' earthly life, but its historical establishment did not take place until the completion of Messiah's task in Jerusalem. Kingdom and church belong together on the post-Easter side of Jesus' death and victory, which in turn made possible the coming of the Spirit.[7] The evidence of the Epistles as well as Acts would seem to support the second position. Augustine described the day of Pentecost correctly, therefore, as the birthday of the church, its *dies natalis*.

1. The antecedents of Pentecost are seen in the use made of Old Testament Scripture (specifically Joel 2:28–32) to account for the phenomenon the hearers and spectators found so puzzling. This prophecy also explained the promise of Jesus (Acts 1:5) about the baptism of the Holy Spirit in the Synoptic tradition.[8] Perhaps most important from the theological standpoint, Pentecost follows on the ascension of the Lord, which in both Lukan (Acts 2:33) and later church theology (e.g., Eph. 4:7–10; John 16:7) makes possible the coming of the Spirit and the life of the church.[9]

2. The historical narration, on its face value, is written to convey an obvious meaning, though we should note that Luke's descriptions are partly veiled ("*as* of fire" in Acts 2:3 matches "*like* the rush of a mighty wind" in vs. 2;[10] both phenomena are only partially comprehensible and remain *au fond* mysterious) and partly symbolic. Fire and wind are familiar Old Testament signs of the presence and activity of Yahweh, Israel's covenant God. The obvious sense of the narrative, taken at face value, is to declare that the Spirit, which is God's gift promised at the end-time, has come to believers in Jesus, Israel's messianic Savior, and that by this coming the new era of messianic salvation and blessedness is inaugurated.

Several things show that the gift of the Holy Spirit comes in circumstances which unmistakably demonstrate to the Jewish onlookers that this is not a repetition of past times in Israel's history but it is startlingly new and novel. For one thing, the entire company of 120 believers in Jesus is blessed, and the Spirit's presence is not restricted to select individuals such as prophets and leaders of the nation (2:4; cf. Num. 11:29). Furthermore, the Spirit's presence, first given at Pente-

---

[7] G. Gloege cites H. E. Weber's dictum: "The church is, since the kingdom of God is" (*op. cit.,* p. 202n1). This position is elaborated by J. D. G. Dunn, *Baptism in the Holy Spirit*, Ch. 4, "The Miracle of Pentecost," esp. pp. 44f.

[8] Cf. J. D. G. Dunn, "Spirit-and-Fire Baptism," *NovT*, 14 (1972), 81–92.

[9] J. G. Davies, *He Ascended into Heaven* (1958), pp. 60–68.

[10] E. Schweizer, *TDNT*, 6 (ET 1968), 406n478.

cost, is the abiding possession of the community. Thus, while the Spirit fills the company again in Acts 4:31, there is no hint that he had been withdrawn in the interval. John 14:16—"He will give you another Counselor (*Paraclete*), to be with you *for ever*"—endorses this Christian conviction that the Spirit's presence in the church is not fitful and intermittent, requiring the Psalmist's petition "Take not thy holy Spirit from me" (51:11), but rather that the presence is permanent and enduring. Moreover, a facet of the Spirit's new activity in the early church is that its signs are in the realm of moral and spiritual renewal, strength and grace. Little is said of the Spirit's endowment of physical prowess (such as occurred when the *rûaḥ 'Adonai* came upon Saul or Samson), nor does he lead the believers to eccentric types of behavior comparable to the stripping naked of the pre-canonical prophets and Saul (1 Sam. 10:9-13; 19:23f.) or the strange antics of Ezekiel (Ezek. 3, 4).[11]

3. The symbolic motifs of what happened at Pentecost would escape the attention neither of the Jews who witnessed the event nor of Luke's readers, who were evidently intended to read between the lines of the full details which are given.

a. In the background is a conviction, attested in Jewish apocalyptic expectation, that in the end-time there would be only one language. This is seen in Isaiah 66; verse 18, following the Septuagint, has Yahweh saying: "I am coming to gather all nations and tongues"—ἔρχομαι συναγαγεῖν πάντα τὰ ἔθνη καὶ τὰς γλώσσας (cf. Test. Judah 25:3).[12] In this way, what transpired at Pentecost, when the disciples spoke a common language which all their hearers could understand, even though they came from the many lands of the Dispersion (2:8-11), was a reversal of Babel (Gen. 11:1-9). This is shown by the verbal correspondences between the Old Testament story and the Acts account, and also by the setting of the latter in the context of its message concerning a new beginning in salvation-history.[13]

b. Another indirect witness to the renewal of God's covenant purposes may be seen in 2:3, with its motifs of a revelation of the divine will for the new age. "Tongues of fire" on the believers' heads then become tongues to proclaim the mighty works of God in verse 11. There is a new beginning in salvation history as those same fiery tongues sit on the heads of the new Israel, replacing the Shekinah ("glory of God") thought in rabbinic Judaism to rest and remain on students of the Torah

---

[11] For the Old Testament meanings of *rûaḥ* see N. H. Snaith, *Distinctive Ideas of the Old Testament* (1944), pp. 143-58; E. Jacob, *Theology of the Old Testament* (ET 1958), pp. 121-27; cf. A. A. Anderson, "The Use of 'Ruah' in 1QS, 1QH, and 1QM," *JSS*, 7 (1962), 293-303. See also D. Hill, *Greek Words and Hebrew Meanings* (1967), pp. 202ff., esp. pp. 257ff.

[12] See K. Lake, *loc. cit.*, p. 115; E. Schweizer, *TDNT*, 6, 410f.

[13] J. G. Davies, "Pentecost and Glossolalia," *JTS*, 3, n.s. (1952), 228-31.

(cf. Mishnah, '*Abôth* 3:2: "if two [students] sit together and words of the Law [are spoken] between them, the Divine Presence rests between them").

c. Another token of Luke's conscious purpose is the way he accentuates the date and setting of Pentecost.[14] It fell at the Feast of Weeks (Deut. 16:9f.; Lev. 23:15ff.). The offering of the loaves at Weeks completed the Passover sheaf-offering; and while the point of connection between Easter and Pentecost in the Christian calendar is not here made explicitly, the discerning reader of Luke's story could not fail to observe the link, as Paul does (1 Cor. 5:7,8; 15:20; Rom. 8:23; 16:5). Festal joy, so obvious in the Jewish harvest (Deut. 16:10f.), is represented in the descriptions which follow of the Holy Spirit's work in Christian hearts (Acts 2:46; 5:41; cf. 13:52) leading to joy as a hallmark of their life together.

The extra dimension some interpreters associate with the Feast of Weeks, the renewal of the Sinai covenant, is disputed.[15] But some points of contact seem too clear to be fortuitous. At this festival the anniversary of the law-giving was celebrated, and a covenant renewal was observed, stretching back to the covenant with Noah (Gen. 9:8f.; cf. Jubilees 6:1–21; 1QS 2). It looks as though Luke wished to contrast the first law-giving at Sinai, in which Israel alone was the beneficiary, with the new covenant of the messianic era, which embraces all the families of the earth (so anticipating the Gentile mission of Acts 1:8; 13:1ff.).[16]

d. Still in the realm of symbolism we should include the phenomenon of the "tongues" (*glossolalia*). In the context here the term (vs. 4) probably means no more than "ability to communicate in an intelligible speech," which for this audience, drawn from the Jewish world of the Diaspora, would be *koinē* Greek and/or Aramaic.[17] The language is thus not the same as the type of speech Paul depicts in 1 Corinthians 14, where "ecstatic speech" is possibly, but not certainly, meant. If this distinction is made, it becomes possible to interpret the Pentecostal *glossolalia* more in terms of what was said than of the unusual manner of speaking.[18] Such a focus on what arrested the hearers' interest and

---

[14] E. Lohse, *TDNT*, 6, 44–53, with bibliography. For the Feast of Weeks, cf. R. de Vaux, *Ancient Israel* (ET 1961), pp. 490f.

[15] See J. H. E. Hull, *The Holy Spirit in the Acts of the Apostles* (1967), p. 53. But see Dunn, *NIDNTT*, 2, 785.

[16] On the correlation between Sinai and Pentecost, see L. Cerfaux, "Le symbolisme attaché au miracle des langues," *ETL*, 13 (1936), 258f.; J. Dupont, "Ascension du Christ et don de l'Espirit d'après Actes 2:33," in *Christ and Spirit in the New Testament: Festschrift* for C. F. D. Moule (1973), pp. 219–28, sees Pentecost as a new Sinai bestowing the Spirit in place of the Torah.

[17] Esp. since the Old Testament in 2:14–20 is quoted in LXX. See A. W. Argyle, "The Theory of an Aramaic Source in Acts 2,14–40," *JTS*, 3, n.s. (1952), 213f.

[18] On this see J. G. Davies, "Pentecost and Glossolalia," *loc. cit.*; R. H. Gundry, "'Ecstatic Utterance' NEB," *JTS*, 17, n.s. (1966), 299–307; Dunn, *Jesus and the Spirit*, p. 152, for the claim that *glossolalia* was ecstatic speech. Perhaps this type

curiosity, the declaring of the "mighty works" of God (Acts 2:11) in fulfilment of Scripture and as a sign of the new age, has much in its favor.

The external trappings of the Pentecostal sign of tongues must not obscure our appreciation of Luke's twofold main purpose. First, he records the coming of the Spirit as a universal, divine gift linked in a cause-and-effect relationship with the exaltation of the risen Lord (2:33). This in turn is explained in the light of the scriptural evidence for the conclusion that "the mighty works of God" (2:11) are seen in the new age begun by the Spirit's presence and power. Second, he calls attention to the common language at Pentecost in order to focus interest on Peter's message. There the signs of the messianic age are appealed to as confirmation that God is acting in a new way and in decisive power.

PETER'S SERMON

The central theme of this sermon is the triumphant declaration that Christians are living in a new era of God's dealings with men and women.[19] That era opened with the resurrection of the Messiah. The Jewish expectation of what was to take place beyond history at the end of the age is boldly asserted to have taken shape within history and on the third day after Messiah's rejection. The life of the first believers is thereby cast in "the last days" of eschatological purpose (2:16, 17). The end will come soon (cf. 3:20,21). In the interim Peter calls for repentance for the Jewish rejection of Jesus the Messiah; and the pledge is given that the door to an entry into messianic fellowship is open to all Jews willing to go through it (2:38-40).

1. The structure of the sermon follows an orderly pattern. There are three sections, each set in a three-part framework. First, an address is directed to the hearers (2:14; 2:22; 2:29). Next comes a statement of Christian truth (2:15f.; 2:22-24; 2:29-33). Third, Peter appeals to an Old Testament text for a testimony to and proof of the assertion made (2:17-21; 2:25-28; 2:34-35).

An illustration is the final section. Having alluded to the Psalm-

---

of utterance had to do with how biblical prophecies were applied to the current situation and their immediate fulfilment claimed by the apostles. See G. J. Sirks, "The Cinderella of Theology: The Doctrine of the Holy Spirit," *HTR*, 50 (1957), 77–89. He observes that γλῶσσα may mean "tongue" or "language" or "a word or a part of Scripture which requires exposition, an altered or new exposition given by commentators." Then it begins to mean the explanation itself (84). Sirks interprets the Pentecostal γλῶσσαι as "chosen passages of Scripture" (85). Peter's preaching becomes not ecstatic talk but decisive expository preaching (86). For "tongues" at Corinth see R. P. Martin, *The Spirit and the Congregation: Studies in 1 Corinthians 12–15* (1984), esp. pp. 60–74.

19 On the setting and meaning of Peter's sermon in Luke's theological perspective, see R. F. Zehnle, *Peter's Pentecost Discourse: Tradition and Lukan Reinterpretation in Peter's Speeches of Acts 2 and 3* (1971). Cf. A. R. George, *ExpT*, 58 (1947), 312ff.

ist's hope in Psalm 16, Peter goes on to explain what that hope meant.[20] Though written by David, the Psalm cannot refer only to him because he died (vs. 29). It does, however, express the confidence that death and decay will not befall God's anointed king, whom David prefigured. The only possible conclusion, then, is that David was speaking prophetically of the Messiah (vv. 30, 31). He, too, died and was buried, but when men had done their worst he was vindicated by God in the resurrection.

Three proofs of the resurrection, the central emphasis of the sermon, are supplied: first, only a bodily resurrection of Messiah can make sense of prophetic Scripture; second, the apostles themselves are living witnesses to his personal victory over death (vs. 32; cf. 10:41 for an even clearer reference by Peter to the reality of Jesus' bodily resurrection); and third, only the exaltation of the living Christ can satisfactorily explain the phenomena which his hearers have seen and heard (vs. 33).

Justification for mentioning the Lord's exaltation comes from Psalm 110:1.[21] The dialogue is between God, in his Old Testament name Yahweh, and his anointed king. David prefigured the Messiah (so all Jews and Christians believe: 2 Sam. 7:12-14; 4Q Flor in the Dead Sea Scrolls), but he never ascended to heaven. He must, therefore, again have been speaking of the Messiah, "great David's greater Son" (vv. 34f.).

For Peter the conclusion is irresistible (vs. 36). As Jesus of Nazareth alone fulfils the aspiration expressed in both Psalms, he is the true Messiah now installed in the place of honor. His messiahship, once concealed, is now displayed; and his title to worship as Lord (*kyrios*) is proved. Romans 1:3,4 represents this fact in a two-part confessional fragment, representing a pre-Pauline credal formulary describing Jesus' earthly life as David's Son and his heavenly status as Lord.

2. Several clearly defined emphases emerge in the Pentecostal preaching: the Jews put Jesus to death, but God raised him and exalted him as Lord (Acts 2:22-24); all this was foretold in the Old Testament (2:25-31); witnesses confirm the truth announced (2:32-36); and there is a call to repentance and allegiance to the exalted Lord (2:38-41).

Interestingly, this pattern is reproduced in other sermons in Acts (e.g., 3:13-19; 4:10-12; 5:30-32); and the same outline lies beneath 1 Corinthians 15:3-11 (another pre-Pauline *credo* cited by him), where the notes of Jesus' death and resurrection, the attestation of these events as occurring "in accordance with the scriptures," and the appeal to witnesses are sounded.

---

[20] On Ps. 16 in Peter's sermon see J. W. Doeve, *Jewish Hermeneutics in the Synoptic Gospels and Acts* (1954), pp. 168ff.

[21] See D. M. Hay, *Glory at the Right Hand* (1973), on "one of the fundamental texts of the kerygma" (C. H. Dodd, *According to the Scriptures* [1952], p. 35).

C. H. Dodd's pioneering work on the *kerygma* in Acts endeavored to show that this pattern was more or less stereotyped. Criticism has challenged this argument, and has led to a general admission that there is more flexibility and variety than Dodd was willing to grant.[22] However, his chief contention is sound: the Acts-report of early Christian preaching is set in a pattern of standardized forms with recognized features present in each instance where sermons are reported.

THE EARLY CHURCH'S SENSE OF MISSION

The tragic death of Jesus—so it must have seemed to most of his followers until the Easter message broke upon them (Luke 24:18-24 gives a typical reaction to the suggestion that death was not the end of his story)—left the disciples in great perplexity. But shortly thereafter there arose a fellowship of his followers in Jerusalem and possibly in Galilee (Luke 24; cf. Mark 14:28; 16:7) who gathered in the common conviction that they had a future and a hope. The essence of that confidence was that God had raised up the crucified one and enthroned him in the place of honor. Because of him God had sent his Spirit into their midst. The crucified was the promised one, and as such he would appear in glory very soon. This, we gather, is what Luke intended his readers to understand about the theological undergirding of the Palestinian community.[23]

The church immediately after Pentecost remained within the community of Israel and showed that adherence by its practices and ethos.[24] Circumcision was practiced as a badge of fidelity to the ancestral covenant (Gen. 17; "those of the circumcision group" is an identifying designation in Acts; e.g., 11:2; cf. 15:1-5; Col. 4:11). Jewish observance of the dietary laws of clean and unclean foods was retained (Acts

---

[22] C. H. Dodd, *The Apostolic Preaching and its Developments* (1936), Ch. 1. Among those agreeing with Dodd were A. M. Hunter, C. T. Craig, F. V. Filson, and F. F. Bruce; cf. R. C. Worley, *Preaching and Teaching in the Earliest Church* (1967), pp. 27ff. For contrary views, P. E. Davies, "Unity and Variety in the New Testament," *Interpretation*, 5 (1951), 182; G. B. Caird, *The Apostolic Age* (1955), p. 38. Others have charged that Dodd's summary needs supplementing; T. F. Glasson, "The Kerygma: Is our Version Correct?", *HJ*, 51 (1953), 129-32; R. H. Mounce, *The Essential Nature of New Testament Preaching* (1960), pp. 60ff. An assault on Dodd's confidence in the authenticity of the speeches was made by C. F. Evans, "The Kerygma," *JTS*, 7, n.s. (1956), 25-41, who holds that speaking of "one kerygma" is mistaken in view of the pluralism in Acts' descriptions of Christian proclamation and also in recognition of Luke's purpose for using the speeches in his story of the early church. For an attempt to vindicate the general reliability of the speeches, see A. A. T. Ehrhardt, "The Construction and Purpose of the Acts of the Apostles," in *The Framework of the New Testament Stories*, esp. pp. 86-88. For an overall assessment Worley's book, esp. pp. 83-86, is most valuable.

[23] See L. Goppelt, *Jesus, Paul, Judaism* (ET 1964), pp. 100ff.

[24] For one understanding of Luke's purpose in the descriptive scenes in Acts, see E. Haenchen, *The Acts of the Apostles*, pp. 188f.

10). The Temple services (Acts 3) and the Jewish calendar (Acts 20:16) were still respected. And James' summary in Acts 21:20 talks of "thousands" of believing Jews who were all jealous for the Jewish law as Jewish Christians. If we include in our evidence the M stratum in Matthew's Gospel, especially in chapters 5–7 and 23, we can amplify this remark and point to a Jewish Christian church, practicing tithing, fasting, almsgiving, and liturgical praying at this period of its existence.

In the eyes of the parent Jewish authority these "Nazoraeans," as they are called both in Acts and in the *Shemoneh Esreh* or synagogue public prayers of Eighteen Benedictions, would constitute a "fellowship" (*hăbûrāh*) within the larger structure and family of Israel. The term αἵρεσις is used of them (24:5,14; 28:22), as Jewish writers use it of other groups such as the Pharisees. They would, of course, be distinguished from the latter by certain features; for example, their firm messianic hope and the assertion that Messiah had come and that his name was Jesus of Nazareth; their prayers in his name (4:24–31) and their daring invocation of Jesus in prayer as *mārān,* "our Lord," inviting his presence at their fellowship meals and even bidding him to come back (*mārānâ ta* in 1 Cor. 16:22 is almost certainly an invocation, not a statement: "our Lord, come!" is preferable to "the Lord is coming," as we see from Rev. 22:20; *Didache* 10:6).[25] They may even have addressed him as Lord of the resurrection.[26] Also, the common meal was held in his name, and the "breaking of bread" (a Jewish term) was the occasion when they expected and experienced his unseen yet real presence (Luke 24:35) in a continuation of the fellowship the disciples had known in Galilee and Jerusalem (Acts 10:41; cf. 1:4 RSV mg.). Of special significance was the knowledge of the risen Lord in the midst of his own. His promises of such a personal presence (Matt. 18:20) and the stories of the Easter experience (e.g., John 20:19–29) would be recalled and reenacted as they waited in an expectant faith for him to reveal himself.

This special sense of belonging to "Messiah's people," the congregation of the end-time, gave them a self-conscious identity as members of "my church" (Matt. 16:18). They met together in this group consciousness (seen in Acts 4:23 as permeating a company of "friends"), and when attacked they drew strength from their close-knit common life (κοινωνία). Yet the followers of Jesus were separated from contemporary

---

[25] On *mārānâ thâ,* see R. P. Martin, "Approaches to New Testament Exegesis," in *New Testament Interpretation,* pp. 243f.

[26] B. Gustafsson, "The Oldest Graffiti in the History of the Church?", *NTS,* 3 (1956–57), 65–69, wishes to accept the equivalence of ἀλώθ on the Talpioth ossuary with the Hebrew verb '*ālāh* (infin. '*ālôt*) and to interpret the graffito as "Jesus, (let him who rests here) arise," thus providing a remarkable testimony to the oldest church's faith in Jesus as the risen Lord. But see J. P. Kane's later discussion, "By No Means 'The Earliest Records of Christianity,'" *Palestine Exploration Quarterly* (1971), pp. 103–108.

sects within Judaism by possessing and exhibiting a missionary faith which gave them a concern for their fellow-Jews. Unlike the recognized groups—the Pharisees (cf. Matt. 23:15) and Sadducees—and unlike the sectarian protest movements on the fringe of first-century Judaism—such as the Essenes at Qumran, they actively sought adherents to join with them.[26a] Peter's sermon closes on the notes of appeal (Acts 2:38), warning (2:40), and invitation to the hearers to join the newly formed Christian movement (2:39; the same emphases are present in 3:17,19,26).

Clearly the basis of Peter's appeal was that if his compatriots repented of their sin in rejecting Jesus as God's final messenger, they would be welcomed by God and given a place in the new Israel. "Times of refreshing" (3:19) are promised to all who obey the call; and the final hope of Israel is seen in the pledge that Jesus will come as Messiah to the Jewish people (vs. 20).[27]

No clearly defined theology of this hope is worked out, but it is a plausible suggestion of several scholars that the lines of argument run as follows.[28] Faced with the paradox of a sense of continuing identity with old Israel and yet an eager desire to act on Jesus' example of a wider ministry (e.g., Mark 7:24–37), the early Jerusalem church found the answer in a determination to concentrate their mission on national ethnic Israel, hoping that by means of a converted Israel the salvation of the Gentiles would come about. The Old Testament basis for this expectation is found in such passages as Isaiah 2:2ff. and 49:6, which speak of Jerusalem as the center of redemptive history and the focal point to which the nations come in the end-time to seek Israel's God (cf. Zech. 8:20–23).[29] The word of the Lord proceeds from the Holy City to call the Gentiles to the future God has prepared (Isa. 25:6). Israel, when it is true to its vocation and destiny as Yahweh's servant, and when it is restored to its pristine integrity with Jerusalem as the holy city of God (Isa. 1:21–31; 4:2–6), will be the messenger to the nations.

The business of the followers of Jesus as Israel's Messiah (whether Messiah in fact or only an appointee to that title as *Messias designatus* or *Messias futurus*) was to stay in Jerusalem, concentrating

---

[26a] The extent of Judaism's proselytizing endeavor is disputed; see J. N. Sevenster, *The Roots of Pagan Anti-Semitism in the Ancient World* (1975), pp. 201–18.

[27] See J. A. T. Robinson, "The Most Primitive Christology of All?", *JTS*, 7, n.s. (1956), 177–89; repr. in *Twelve New Testament Studies* (1962), pp. 139–53.

[28] L. Goppelt, *op. cit.*, pp. 100ff.; *Apostolic and Post-Apostolic Times* (ET 1970), Ch. 2; F. V. Filson, *Three Crucial Decades*, pp. 101ff. See too P. T. O'Brien, "The Great Commission of Matthew 28:18–20," *RTR*, 35 (1976), 66–78.

[29] B. Gerhardsson, *Memory and Manuscript* (1961), pp. 214ff., 275f., refers to the evidence as understood in rabbinic Judaism; see also J. Munck, *Paul and the Salvation of Mankind*, pp. 303f. J. Jeremias' essay, "The Gentile World in the Thought of Jesus," *SNTS Bulletin*, 1–3 (1950–52), 18–28, is of fundamental importance.

their efforts on winning over fellow-Jews to an acknowledgment of their past failures with a promise of repentance and national forgiveness, and to await the stream of Gentiles which would flow into Zion to hear the word of the Lord at the end-time. This seems to be the underlying tenor of such descriptions as Acts 2:39; 3:19-26; 4:10-12.

The divine purpose did not work out like this, as the cross had intimated in advance, and as the exaltation of Jesus as Lord of the world clearly proved to men such as Stephen, the men of Cyprus and Cyrene (Acts 11:19-24), and Paul. That is the cause of the tension running through Acts. Part of the tragedy of this mistaken hope of Jewish Christianity was that, even when old Israel was given a second opportunity to respond to Jesus, it turned away. The representatives of the Jewish nation still proved obdurate, and the mission to Israel on Judaistic terms collapsed largely under the weight of a monumental failure. The future lay rather with those who perceived that the Christian gospel had a universal appeal independent of Israel's response or lack of it (Rom. 9-11) and that the church was not a sect of Judaism but a new creation, a re-created humanity, a third race of men and women (Gal. 6:15,16; Eph. 2:11-22; 1 Cor. 10:32).

LIFE IN THE JERUSALEM CHURCH

Several aspects of the corporate life of the Palestinian church claim our attention.[30]

1. There was a communal responsibility evidenced by a pooling of material resources to meet the social needs of the community. The common life of the body of Christ expressed itself in their concern to share their goods (2:45) as well as to participate in common meals (vs. 46; cf. 4:32ff.). There are parallels to this common life in the Pythagoreans of the Greek world and among the monks of Qumran in the Jewish world.[31] But what stands out in the Christian experiment in communal living was its voluntary nature. The fatal mistake of Ananias and Sapphira (5:1-11) was not their refusal to give everything they possessed, but their deceitful ways in pretending to give all, namely, the full price of their property, while they kept back a portion for their own use (so 5:2, 8).[32]

---

[30] For various viewpoints see B. Reicke, *Glaube und Leben der Urgemeinde* (1957); R. Bultmann, *Theology of the New Testament*, I, 33-62; F. F. Bruce, *New Testament History* (1969), pp. 195-205; H. Conzelmann, *History of Primitive Christianity* (ET 1973), Ch. 4.

[31] The evidence is given in H. Conzelmann's *Apostelgeschichte* (1963), p. 31, and discussed by S. E. Johnson in *The Scrolls and the New Testament*, ed. K. Stendahl (1958), pp. 129ff. Cf. *TDNT*, 3 (ET 1965), 789ff. (F. Hauck).

[32] Ph.-H. Menoud, "La mort d'Ananias et de Saphira," in *Aux sources de la tradition chrétienne: Mélanges offerts à Maurice Goguel* (1950), pp. 146-54.

Pooling goods involved selling lands and properties, and liquidating capital assets followed (4:34, 37). Early commentators saw here a cause for the later poverty of the Jerusalem church (Acts 11:29; 2 Cor. 8, 9). Luke makes no such value judgment, but simply reports the facts as a proof of Christian concern for the well-being of all—at least for the immediate future—and as a lesson in generosity. No indication is given that the Christians got rid of their goods because they expected an imminent end of the world. Perhaps Luke recorded an experiment in communal living with a common purse to point the church of his own day back to a simpler way of life lost by the established church. Luke is honest enough to tell the whole story—of failure (Acts 5:1-11; 6:1) as well as success.

2. Another aspect of the social life of the early believers was their self-consciousness as the people of God. Especially interesting is the descriptive picture in Acts 2:42: "And they devoted themselves to the apostles' teaching and fellowship, to the breaking of bread and the prayers." Recent study has examined the four parts of this description, identifying not only four component parts of early Christian social life (including a regular worship at the Temple, as the verb "devoted themselves," προσκαρτερεῖν, suggests—1:4; 2:46; 6:4—and a fellowship meal) but also a sequence of early Christian worship. J. Jeremias suggests that these several parts are: *teaching,* especially the apostles' setting up of a catechumenate for the instruction of new converts; *koinōnia,* table-fellowship expressed either in almsgiving (see Acts 6:1; Rom. 12:13; 15:26) or in the common meal, called the *agapē* feast or shared meal; "*the breaking of bread,*" which he takes to be an allusion to the eucharist as a meal in continuation of the last supper of Jesus and the disciples; and "*the prayers,*" where the definite article indicates the continued adherence to the set prayers in the Temple daily service.[33]

3. We should not overlook the facets of early church life which show that the people did not regard themselves as an amorphous, transient group soon to be dissipated and dispersed throughout Judaism. They were the nucleus of a new society, committed to one another as well as to the Lord and his apostles and determined to stay together. Those who came to join them united in their company (Acts 2:41, 47) and their numbers grew as their popularity increased. Threats and punishments served only to give the group greater cohesion (Acts 4:23ff.; 5:41f.), inspired by Peter's courageous leadership and refusal to be daunted (4:19, 20; 5:29-32). The desire was to stay together, to thrive under pressure of persecution, and to continue to proclaim the message of God, assured of the presence with them of the living Lord (4:33), to whom they were witnesses.

---

[33] J. Jeremias, *The Sermon on the Mount* (ET 1961), p. 21; *The Eucharistic Words of Jesus* (ET² 1966), pp. 118-21, contains some modification of his earlier views.

Their rudimentary church life and its ethos can hardly be better summarized than by George Johnston in this paragraph:

The existence of the Church was a result of divine activity and of human obedience to the word of God. Its members became partners in a great fellowship, baptized into a single society where, by union to the Lord, they could enjoy a certainty of final salvation, were able to worship God in reality, in praise and prayer and the Eucharist. Through Jesus Christ incarnate, crucified and risen, Jew and Gentile alike shared an experience of forgiving grace. Invisible bonds of the Spirit joined the widely separated congregations to one another. This spiritual Israel was a new community, one in faith and loyalty to the expected Messiah and Lord, a divine family, itself a word of God to the nations as it witnessed to Jesus Christ.[34]

---

[34] *The Doctrine of the Church in the New Testament* (1943), p. 132.

CHAPTER SIX

Stephen, the Hellenists and the Early Gentile Mission

Having surveyed the Acts-account of Jewish Christianity and noted its sense of mission, we should now look at how the Christian mission moved outward and forward.

We can discern Luke's purpose in his selection and use of the story which centers in Stephen.[1] Two lengthy chapters in his record are occupied with the case of the church's first martyr. Luke's desire to place great emphasis here led him to a detailed account of the circumstances of the dispute between Stephen and his opponents, concluding with a long (7:2-53) report of Stephen's defense. Why did Luke attach such value to this man and his public utterance?

In the first place, Stephen represented a vital link in the outward-reaching mission of the church. His martyrdom demonstrated that the Jewish hierarchy in Jerusalem could not be moved even by so eloquent a plea and so heroic an example. So, "Stephen's arrest and trial and lynching mark the final failure of the mission to the capital."[2] Furthermore, Stephen's thought, as represented by his defense, catches the chief points in a theology of Christian mission. In particular, he was convinced that the Christian message could not be confined within the narrow bounds of Jewish particularism.[3] And a third reason for focusing

[1] Among recent studies of Stephen in early Christianity are W. Manson, *The Epistle to the Hebrews* (1951); H. P. Owen, "Stephen's Vision in Acts vii.55-6," *NTS*, 1 (1954-55), 224-26; A. F. J. Klijn, "Stephen's Speech–Acts vii.2-53," *NTS*, 4 (1957-58), 25-31; M. Simon, *St. Stephen and the Hellenists in the Primitive Church* (ET 1958); M. H. Scharlemann, *Stephen: A Singular Saint* (1968); J. Bihler, *Die Stephanusgeschichte* (1963). O. Cullmann, *The Christology of the New Testament* (ET 1959), p. 183, speaks for many: "Apart from Paul, Stephen was perhaps the most significant man in the early Church. According to the little we know of his theological views, he grasped what was new in Jesus' thought better than almost anyone else." The possible exception is Apollos, we suggest; at least after the incident in Acts 18:26. M. Hengel's *Between Jesus and Paul* (ET 1983) contains some excellent chapters on the early church's mission in the light of the role given to Stephen. See too F. F. Bruce, *Peter, Stephen, James and John* (British title, *Men and Movements in the Primitive Church* (1979), ch. 2; P. Trudinger, "Stephen and the Life of the Primitive Church," *BTB*, 14 (1984), 18-22.

[2] J. C. O'Neill, *The Theology of Acts*[2] (1970), p. 85.

[3] Manson's thesis, contained in his view that the outcome of Stephen's influence is seen in the Epistle to the Hebrews (*op. cit.*, pp. 27ff.); see also his essay in his *Jesus and the Christian* (1967), pp. 199-207, esp. p. 202.

on Stephen is that with him the reader is prepared to be introduced to his successor, Paul. Paul is, as it were, waiting in the wings while Stephen is the chief actor on the stage. Acts 6:9 may well contain a veiled allusion to Saul of Tarsus as a member of the party of "those from Cilicia" and elsewhere who disputed with Stephen;[4] and there is the explicit witness to the influence of Stephen on Saul in 7:58, 8:1, and 22:20.

In summary, Stephen plays an important and distinctive role in Luke's unfolding drama of missionary expansion because he showed a powerful grasp of the universal character of the gospel, which went beyond all national and religious and racial boundaries. He typified that species of Hellenistic Christianity which sprang out of Judaism but went far beyond it. He sparked off a decisive missionary movement, carried forward by those infected with his spirit (11:19–26), which produced the missionary genius of the apostle to the Gentiles (11:25f.; 13:1–3). Nor may we overlook the personal impact of Stephen's character and example as the first Christian martyr, whose suffering and death are modeled on those of his Master as recorded in Luke 22 and 23.[5]

THE RISE OF THE HELLENISTS

1. *The background.* The appointment of the seven Hellenists came about as a result of a social disagreement in the church. The allotment of funds to needy widows was attended to by the apostles, who gave the Hellenists a share in the administration, for all seven names listed in 6:5 apparently belonged to that wing of the fellowship. One of them, Nicolaus, was not a born Jew but a proselyte, that is, a pagan convert to Judaism.

The people appointed these men (often called deacons in view of the description in 1 Tim. 3:8–13), and the apostles confirmed the choice by a solemn rite of ordination, modeled on the Jewish pattern of "setting apart" persons for specific tasks. The seven are described as "serving tables," which is usually taken to mean some financial work in connection with the common fund. But it may be that they were to have responsibility for the *agape*-meal (Acts 2:46) or love-feast. Associated with that meal was the custom of sharing out to the poor, a custom probably derived from the *tamḥui* or "tray" of charitable provision for the needy in the Jewish community.[6]

---

[4] W. Neil, *The Acts of the Apostles* (1973), p. 106. This is especially likely if Acts 22:28 implies that Paul's father or forebear received his citizenship by manumission, thereby rendering Paul a freedman (*libertinus*).

[5] There are contrasts, too, noted by G. N. Stanton, *Jesus of Nazareth in New Testament Preaching* (1974), pp. 35f., against C. H. Talbert, *Luke and the Gnostics* (1966), pp. 71–76, and others. But the close parallel, at least in ideas, between Luke 23:34 and Acts 7:60 cannot be fortuitous. See too C. H. Talbert, *Literary Patterns, Theological Themes and the Genre of Luke-Acts* (SBL Monograph, vol. 20 [1974]), p. 97.

[6] On this service to the poor see Lake, *Beginnings of Christianity*, Vol. 5, Note XII, pp. 148f. On the ordination of the seven, see E. Ferguson, "The Laying On of Hands: Its Significance in Ordination," *JTS*, 26, n.s. (1975), 1–12.

Of the seven men mentioned, Stephen and Philip are more renowned for their preaching ministry, though all of them were required
to have a spiritual quality of life.

2. *Who were the Hellenists?* Acts 6:1 introduces us to a new
situation in the church and a new term to describe some of the people
involved. The new scene is "the first suggestion of some diversity in the
Palestinian church."[7] The situation described here arose because of the
pooling of resources practiced in the Jerusalem church (2:44f.; 4:34f.)
and the continuing influx of new converts (5:14; 6:7). But the significance of the story is its evidence of a division of the church on a cultural
and linguistic basis. "Hebrews" (vs. 1) obviously refers to original converts to the faith from Judaism, typified by the Twelve. But who are the
Ἑλληνισταί?

a. One view sees them as Jewish proselytes, born Gentiles who
had experienced a double conversion—first to Judaism, then to Christianity.[8]

b. Others take them to have been pagan Greeks. But this would
require us (improbably) to believe that there were Gentiles among the
Jewish community at this very early date.[9]

c. The same critique can be brought against G. P. Wetter's view
(shared by H. Windisch) that the word means Christians who did not
live according to the Jewish law.[10]

d. M. Simon argues for identifying them with a radical reforming party of Gentile origin within Judaism, while Cullmann tries to
equate them in a rough way with Qumran sectaries, of syncretistic
origin.[11]

e. There is a growing modern consensus, however, that the term
is linguistic above all else. The term Ἑλληνισταί means Jews who were
bilingual.[12]

The seven were Hellenists. They have Greek names; their leader
was Stephen; and they stand for a more liberal, relaxed view of the new
faith. The data for all this come in Stephen's speech.

---

[7] J. A. Fitzmyer, "Jewish Christianity in Acts in the Light of the Qumran Scrolls,"
in *Studies in Luke-Acts*, p. 237.

[8] E. C. Blackman, "The Hellenists of Acts 6:1," *ExpT*, 48 (1936–37), 524f.

[9] H. J. Cadbury, *Beginnings of Christianity*, Vol. 5, Note VII: "The Hellenists," pp.
59–74.

[10] G. P. Wetter (ref. in Cadbury, *loc. cit.*, p. 70); H. Windisch, *TDNT*, 2 (ET 1964),
512.

[11] Simon, *St. Stephen*, Ch. 1: "Who were the Hellenists?" Cullmann, "The Significance of the Qumran texts for Research into the Beginnings of Christianity," in
The Scrolls and the New Testament, ed. K. Stendahl, pp. 18–32. But Cullmann's
later views are strikingly different; see *The Johannine Circle* (ET 1976), pp. 41,
53ff., 89ff.

[12] C. F. D. Moule, "Once More, Who were the Hellenists?", *ExpT*, 70 (1959), 100–102.
Recent discussion has emphasized how much the "Hebrews" and the "Hellenists"
had in common, and there is a danger in setting off one against the other on a
cultural basis. See I. H. Marshall, *The Origins of New Testament Christology*
(1976), pp. 36–42.

3. *Stephen*. The most prominent member of the seven was Stephen. A man of some personal charisma as well as an effective representative of the Hellenists, he is introduced in a way that establishes Luke's point that he was a true member of the apostolic college (compare 6:8 with 5:12). But he met opposition head-on. His opponents, from a synagogue called a meeting-place for Freedmen, who represented Hellenistic Jews from the world of the Dispersion (vs. 9), challenged him to debate. He overwhelmed them (vs. 10). This led to an indictment, maliciously framed (Luke's account of Jesus' passion did not mention that element, though Mark 14:56 and Matthew 26:60 suggest that Jesus faced the same strategy),[13] that Stephen had spoken out against the sacrificial system, the venerable place of the Temple, and the final authority of the Torah. Evidently (vs. 11) this assault was seen as directed at "Moses": the personal name of the Jewish father had come to stand for all that was holiest and most valued in rabbinic religion and to deny him was to strike at the divine authority and validity of the entire Jewish system.

This was a radical attack on Judaism, which the earlier Jewish Christian leaders had not made. Stephen had grasped the full implicates of what the gospel tradition, both early (Mark 2:21f.) and late (John 2:19–21), was to report, namely, that the Christian movement was not a revamped Judaism but a new creation from God, and that the Jerusalem Temple as a center of worship now gives place to the new temple of the body of the risen Lord. Stephen stands in direct antithesis to the old religion of law represented in Moses, but he catches Moses' radiance (Ex. 34:29f.) as God's approving light shines on him (vs. 15; cf. 2 Cor. 3:17–18).

STEPHEN'S SPEECH

What Stephen said to the Jewish council is sometimes called his defense (i.e., an answer to legal charges),[14] but it is clearly more of an *apology*—that is, a statement of the teaching which had led to his arrest and prosecution. And as his interpretation of the Christian message touched the vital questions of the validity of Judaism and Stephen's own "blasphemy" against God, his address turns out to be an *apologia* for his own life.

There are three chief ideas that his lengthy retelling of the Old Testament story is designed to emphasize: first, the Jewish people

---

13 Cf. Haenchen, *Acts of the Apostles*, p. 227. The reason why Luke transfers the false witness to Stephen's trial is discussed by A. A. Trites, *The New Testament Concept of Witness* (1977), p. 187.

14 See the denial of this in Lake and Cadbury, *Beginnings of Christianity*, Vol. 4, p. 69. Their allegation that the speech "is not a rebuttal of the charges brought against him" is answered by J. C. O'Neill, *The Theology of Acts²*, pp. 78f.

throughout their long history have been inveterate rebels against God and his accredited messengers; second, God does not live in nor want a material and fixed shrine, for his presence is not confined to sacred sites but accompanies his people, who are to be always a "pilgrim church" on earth; and third, as a subsidiary theme, the Jewish people have not only rebelled against God and their leaders, but they have consistently rejected the saviors whom God sent to them—the outstanding proof of this being their recent rejection of their Messiah.[15]

Stephen draws a couple of examples from Israel's history. First, God spoke to Abraham while he lived on "foreign" soil in Mesopotamia; thence he called him to the Promised Land. With a change of geographical locale in Egypt, Joseph was God's answer to the threat of patriarchal extinction, but he suffered much indignity at the hands of his brothers (Acts 7:9).[16] Moses, too, in a later period appeared as a heaven-sent deliverer, but he met opposition and misunderstanding (vv. 23ff.). In so emphasizing these points, Stephen is patiently laying the foundations of his argument. Later, he will draw some conclusions unwelcome to his hearers.

Stephen's recital of Israel's history continues in 7:30–53. The purpose of this long paragraph on Moses' call by God and his unique place as both deliverer (vv. 30–36) and lawgiver (vv. 37f.) is simply to show that of all Israel's national figures he surely enjoyed divine appointment and authority.[17] But, in spite of these clear signs of attestation from God, he met with opposition and disbelief. Notice the asides which Stephen cleverly inserts in verses 25, 35, and 39.

A further indication of the failure of the Jewish nation, even though blessed with so outstanding a man of God as Moses, is the positive acts of idolatry and apostasy which they committed (vv. 40,41,53). It was bad enough that they rebelled against Moses; it was far worse that they lapsed into flagrant idol worship and astrology (vs. 42).[18]

At the same time as they practiced a heathen worship, they imagined that God could be localized in a man-made shrine (built by Solomon, vs. 47); and further they contrived to placate God by a multitude of sacrifices. Both these errors indicate bad religion, as the eighth-century prophets in Israel had been quick to expose. But this prophetic protest went unheeded.[19]

---

[15] Cf. Lake and Cadbury, loc. cit., on the unity connecting the several parts of Stephen's speech.

[16] On Stephen's speech and the accounts in Genesis, see Cadbury, The Book of Acts in History (1955), pp. 102f.

[17] The Moses/Messiah typology is discussed by J. Jeremias, in TDNT, 4 (ET 1967), 863.

[18] See W. D. Davies, "A Note on Josephus, Antiquities 15:136," HTR, 47 (1954), 135ff., referring the phrase δι' ἀγγέλων to the prophets as ambassadors of God.

[19] For Stephen's critique of the Temple and its cult, see J. C. O'Neill, op. cit., pp. 79f.

Stephen found the same hard core of resistance in his hearers; and his impassioned peroration (vv. 51-53) drove home the personal application in the light of the ample evidence. The closing section of Stephen's speech is its climax. Neutrality was impossible in the face of his forthright declarations. The violent language of verse 54 makes it clear that he had touched his hearers on a tender spot; and they reacted by cutting short his sermon in an outburst of rage. One final "blasphemy"—from their point of view (vv. 55f.)—called forth the murderous spite of verses 57 and 58.

Stephen died, like his Master, with a prayer of committal and forgiveness on his lips (Luke 23:34,46).[20] His death was more a lynching than a judicial execution for blasphemy. No trial took place, and there was no respect for Jewish law, which had an elaborate arrangement to safeguard the person accused of blasphemy—and therefore condemned to death by stoning (Mishnah, *Sanhedrin* 6)—so that if he should recant or if a witness for the defense should suddenly appear the stoning would be stopped. It seems clear that no such precautions were made for Stephen, and he fell victim to the mob violence of an uncontrolled crowd.[20a]

The most impressionable person in this sordid scene seems to have been Saul, who looked after the witnesses' clothes. These witnesses for the prosecution were required to carry out the sentence (Lev. 24:14; Deut. 17:7; cf. John 8:7). By his complicity, Saul agreed with the rough "justice" meted out. He never forgot this awful sight (Acts 22:20) or his personal involvement in the violence (cf. 1 Tim. 1:13).[21] Yet Augustine believed that this martyrdom may have been the turning point in his life: "If Stephen had not prayed, the Church would not have had Saul." Nonetheless, Paul never explicitly refers to its influence.

Stephen's vision is full of meaning, and gives the key to his whole thought. He sees the exalted Jesus as victorious Son of man, destined like the celestial figure of Daniel 7:13ff. to possess world-dominion, and worthy of worship. Here is the clear statement of Stephen's Christology: he "saw that the Messiah was on the throne of the Universe,"[22] and so by implication the head of a worldwide church. His characteristic name for Jesus is "Lord," which has the same implication, and he calls upon him in prayer (thereby confessing his place within the Godhead).[23] The links with Luke's Passion story are impor-

---

[20] On his dying prayer, see J. Jeremias, *The Central Message of the New Testament* (1965), pp. 48f.

[20a] See now D. R. Catchpole, *IDB, Supp. Vol.* (1976), p. 917.

[21] Lake and Cadbury (*loc. cit.,* p. 85) speak of "a genuine Pauline reminiscence" in 7:58.

[22] W. Manson, *The Epistle to the Hebrews,* p. 32; but cf. M. Simon, *op. cit.,* pp. 67-74.

[23] Bruce terms Stephen's calling on Jesus as Lord "an early, if tacit, testimony to the Christian belief in our Lord's essential deity"; *Acts* (NICNT), p. 171.

tant. Stephen captured the spirit of the dying Jesus, who rises to greet the first Christian martyr.

We may conclude by tabulating some of the leading features in Luke's presentation of Stephen.

1. He was the best known example of Hellenistic Christianity.

2. This group of Hellenistic Christian leaders had a social conscience and showed the church's care for the needy.[24]

3. Their chief importance was theological. They opposed the Temple cult; they denied the permanent validity of the Law; and their understanding of Christology (cf. 7:54-60) opened a new dimension, which represents either an esoteric (Cullmann) or cosmic (W. Manson) or martyr (Tödt) Christology.[25] The main implication of the Son of man's standing posture here is probably that he is about to vindicate his servant by his *parousia,* which is seen as a personal experience and an event shortly to be realized, so that Luke is pointing to the non-imminence of the general *parousia* and conceding that Christians may die in the interim before the Lord returns.[26] The range of Stephen's thought should be observed, especially if it links up with other parts of the New Testament (Hebrews, as Manson suggests, and Phil. 2:6-11).

4. The opposition of Paul is depicted; and he appears as joining in Stephen's murder. This consent will throw into greater relief the vast change from enemy to friend that followed his conversion and will demonstrate its miraculous quality. There was no predisposition on Saul's part to accept the Christian message.

5. Stephen's prayer and invocation of Jesus as *mārē'* (Lord) played a significant role in Luke's program in preparing for the preaching to the Greeks (11:20f.) and bringing the Pauline apostolic mission into view, since it was Saul's allegiance to Jesus as Lord that laid the theological basis for the Gentile mission.

6. The resultant persecution in Acts 8 and the opening of the Samaritan mission followed. More importantly, a direct linear connection is established with the mission undertaken by Gentile Christians to pagan Greeks (11:19-21).

[24] C. E. B. Cranfield, "Diakonia in the NT," in *Service in Christ: Essays Presented to Karl Barth on his 80th Birthday,* edd. J. I. McCord and T. H. L. Parker (1966), p. 46.

[25] O. Cullmann, *The Christology of the New Testament,* pp. 157ff., argues that Stephen's titles for Jesus give evidence of a Christology that drew its ideas from the Danielic-Enoch strain in Jewish "Son of man" literature. For Manson, *op. cit.,* pp. 30-36; for Tödt, *The Son of Man in the Synoptic Tradition* (ET 1965), pp. 303-305.

[26] This follows C. K. Barrett's conclusion, "Stephen and Son of Man," in *Apophoreta: Festschrift* for E. Haenchen, ed. W. Eltester (1964), pp. 32-38. This essay covers most of the essential issues raised by the verses and has a good bibliography. See too C. Colpe, *TDNT,* 8 (ET 1972), 461-63; P. Doble, "The Son of Man Saying in Stephen's Witnessing: Acts 6:8-8:2," *NTS,* 31 (1985), 68-84.

THE EARLY GENTILE MISSION

It is possible to chart the steps by which, according to the Lukan record, a mission to the Gentile world was seen to be God's will for the church and fully (if not quite freely) embraced, in spite of antagonisms and opposition.

As we suggested (p. 79), the Jewish-Christian community in Jerusalem (Acts 1–5) apparently saw their immediate task as witnessing to fellow Jews in the hope that a converted nation would be God's instrument for the evangelization of the Gentile races.[27] But they had not thought through the implications of this restriction and were later to be disillusioned by the obduracy of the nation of Israel. In Romans 9–11 Paul wrestles with the problems occasioned by Israel's unbelief and refusal to heed the Christian message.

The first impulse to Gentile witness came from the Hellenistic wing of the church represented by Stephen and Philip. Stephen was the thinker behind the new venture, as we may deduce from his cultural ties to the Dispersion and his speech with its philosophy of history and Christology. His critique of Judaism as a religion bound to one land, one city, a central Temple and a system of animal sacrifices carries the implication that Jesus' coming has given a new center to religion and antiquated certain existing types of worship on a national basis. Stephen saw God's purpose as wider than the nation of Israel and its geographical setting in the holy land. His Christology envisaged a heavenly Son of man, destined to be world ruler, not limited to one land or religious system. Stephen catches the vision of the exalted Lord as Son of man (Dan. 7:13), who receives the kingdom of the saints of the Most High God (Dan. 7:14,18). As we have seen, his title Son of man is a token of his office as head of a worldwide community. Stephen's characteristic name for Jesus is "Lord," which has the same implications. Perhaps the well-known "cosmic Christology" of Philippians 2:6–11 came out of Stephen's school; in any event, this is clearly a missionary theology.[28]

---

[27] The persecution of the Jerusalem community after Stephen's death left the apostles untouched (Acts 8:1). Haenchen notes that "by remaining [in the city], these [apostles] preserve the continuity of the community" (*op. cit.*, p. 293), whereas the followers of Stephen were dispersed. The Western text reads "except the apostles *who remained in Jerusalem*"—an addition regarded as "doubtless a correct interpretation" (*Beginnings of Christianity*, Vol. 4, p. 87). Either the apostles were not persecuted because they were still regarded as good Jews, while the attack was directed against the Hellenists, or the note is intended to demonstrate that the leaders of the *Urgemeinde* were still obedient to the charge "not to leave Jerusalem" (1:4), where they anticipated the mass response of the Jews.

[28] R. P. Martin, *Carmen Christi: Phil. 2:5–11* (²1983), pp. 297ff., 312f.; D. Georgi, "Der vorpaulinische Hymnus: Phil. 2, 6–11," in *Zeit und Geschichte*, Bultmann *Festschrift*, ed. E. Dinkler (1964), pp. 263–93. Links between Phil. 2 and Hebrews have been discussed by O. Hofius, *Der Christushymnus, Phil. 2, 6–11* (1976), pp. 75–102.

Preparatory missionary work to the Gentiles was done by Philip—in Samaria among a racially mixed people, and in his contact with the Ethiopian eunuch who was both racially and physically outside of Judaism.

1. *The Samaritan Mission* (Acts 8). O. Cullmann attached great importance to this episode as marking "the actual beginnings of the Christian mission" to a non-Jewish community.[29] He believed that the ground for this movement was prepared by Jesus himself in John 4, with its sequel that the woman returned to the city as a faithful witness. The sowing (in John 4) is to be followed by a time of reaping (vs. 38). But he asked, Who are the "others" who are praised for having "labored" (κοπιᾶν)? This verb is used of missionary service in the early church. The suggestion commends itself then that it is the Hellenistic missionaries like Philip who are the middle link in the chain: Jesus-Hellenists-apostles (Peter, John). That the Johannine Christ is supportive of the Hellenistic attitude to the Temple is clear from allusions in the Gospel itself (2:13ff.; 4:21-24; 8:48). Not all, however, are persuaded by this suggestion.[30]

2. *The Mission to Gentiles.* Chronologically, from the death of Stephen we should pass on to Acts 11:19ff., where the men of Stephen's school carry his teaching and influence to their logical outcome in active outreach to pagans. The intervening incidents (Acts 10-11) play a significant role in describing the convincing of Peter; but clearly the Hellenists needed no further encouragement. At Antioch the Gentile mission was consolidated in response to a preaching of Jesus as Lord, and a church was formed (Acts 13).

---

[29] O. Cullmann, "Samaria and the Origins of the Christian Mission," in *The Early Church* (ET 1956), pp. 185-94; and *The Johannine Circle*, p. 16. Cf. L. Goppelt, *Jesus, Paul and Judaism*, pp. 176ff.; R. F. O'Toole, "Philip and the Ethiopian Eunuch (Acts VIII.25-40)," *JSNT*, 17 (1983), 25-34.

[30] E.g., J. A. T. Robinson, "The Others of John 4:38," in *Twelve New Testament Studies* (1962), pp. 61-66; J. D. G. Dunn, *Baptism in the Holy Spirit*, Ch. 5; E. Haenchen, *The Acts of the Apostles*, pp. 301ff. See also C. H. H. Scobie, "The Origins and Development of Samaritan Christianity," *NTS*, 20 (1972-73), 390ff.

CHAPTER SEVEN

Paul's Conversion: History and Faith Meet

Acts 8:1 and 9:1–30 introduce us to a man who may be said to dominate on the human side the New Testament literature. About one-fifth of the New Testament consists of his letters; and nearly a half of Acts is devoted to him. Statistically speaking, more than a fourth of the New Testament is given over to Paul. But two caveats are needed lest we draw some false conclusions.

First, he himself would have drawn back from this assessment. He saw his life as essentially Christ-centered, and any claim to a place in history he cherished would have been as "an apostle of Jesus Christ" and his "slave" (δοῦλος), a term that emphasizes his sense of privilege and mission, such as Israel's prophets enjoyed.[1]

Also, we make our value-judgments from the standpoint of later history, with the advantage of hindsight. We say Paul dominates the New Testament because of the twenty-seven books in our canon. But we do not know what other letters were being written at the same time by other apostles and circulated among the early churches. Paul is for us a magisterial figure, but it is obvious that not everyone was so enthusiastic or positively drawn to him (2 Cor. 5:13; 10:10; 11:5f.; 12:6).

Yet the fact remains that Paul entered the fellowship of Christ's people to become a person of significance in his day and of monumental importance in the later history of the church. How can we make sense of Augustine, Luther, Wesley, or Barth without this apostolic character, who turned decisively from persecuting Christians, and who subsequently offered yeoman service to Christ and his church?

Four aspects are to be noticed in our study of the early days of the historical Paul.

---

[1] G. Sass, "Zur Bedeutung von δοῦλος bei Paulus," *ZNTW*, 40 (1941), 24–32. The word signifies that God is acting through the human agent: "In this sense, δοῦλος remains limited to a few men who are entrusted by God with special tasks in and for the church." See also F. W. Beare, *Philippians* (1959), p. 51, *ad* Phil. 1:1.

PAUL'S BACKGROUND IN JUDAISM AND HELLENISM

Saul was born into an environment rich and varied, combining the religion of the Hebrews, the civilization of the Greeks, and the political and administrative genius of the Romans.[2] He was proud of his relation to all three, though the most powerful of them was undoubtedly the religious atmosphere in which he was nurtured.

1. *Paul's Israelite background.* Several texts (Phil. 3:5; 2 Cor. 11:22; Gal. 1:14) reflect Paul's love for his ancestral race (Rom. 9:3). He inherited some basic beliefs from the Judaism in which he was cradled: that there is one, righteous and holy God who entered into covenantal relationship with the patriarchs and Moses; that he elected Israel to be his people; that the Torah was the unique revelation of God; and the hope of Messiah, which the Pharisees especially cherished (see Vol. 1, pp. 84ff., 103ff.).

2. *Paul's Greek inheritance* (Acts 21:39; 22:3). The apostle's birthplace Tarsus was a large and prosperous city in Cilicia, situated on the Cydnus river near where it emptied into the Mediterranean, and at the foot of a famous pass through the Taurus mountains, down which commerce flowed. Intellectually and aesthetically Tarsus was a Greek city. It was a center of Greek civilization and a university town. It showed a Greek ethos in its literature and in its sports and games.

There are some indications that Paul recalled his Greek past. He quotes Greek poets (Menander in 1 Cor. 15:33; cf. Epimenides in Titus 1:12; and Aratus, a fellow-citizen of Tarsus, is appealed to in his Areopagus speech of Acts 17:28). He borrows illustrations from the games: running, boxing, wrestling, the arena. He used Greek and Roman ideas as illustration of the processes of law (especially the Roman custom of adoption). He employs words from moral philosophy, such as "virtue" and "conscience," and he uses the Stoic doctrine of the law engraved on the conscience of man (Rom. 2:14f.).[3] Terms from the

---

[2] The question of Paul's debt to his heritage, culture, environment, and early training has been much canvassed, with little agreement. In particular, the type of Judaism he knew in Israel and the Diaspora is still actively debated; see the ground-breaking works of E. P. Sanders, *Paul and Palestinian Judaism* (1977) and *Paul, the Law and the Jewish People* (1983). The relevance of this discussion to Paul's message is evident in C. Rowland, *Christian Origins* (1985), pp. 215–35; and for one individualistic treatment see J. C. Beker, *Paul the Apostle* (1980). In a preface to his second edition (1984) Beker responds to his reviewers and clarifies some less than clear points in his argument. Both Beker and Rowland fruitfully employ the correlation of contingency (Paul's involvement with his world and its conditioning factors) and coherence (the constants in Paul's thought as a Christian apostle). Rowland's preferred terms are situation and system, but they are less desirable (see later, p. 143).

[3] On the alleged indebtedness of Paul to Stoicism (above, pp. 27f., 48f.), see J. N. Sevenster, *Paul and Seneca* (1961), who has important contributions on Paul's use of Stoic terms in Phil. 4 (pp. 152–56). "Conscience," as employed by Paul, owes its place to its use by the Corinthians, not to Paul's Stoicism, according to C. A. Pierce, *Conscience in the New Testament* (1955).

mystery religions, such as "initiate" and "perfect," are also found in his writings.[4]

But the idea that he was a zealous student of Greek letters or was deeply influenced by Stoic philosophy is not to be taken seriously. Rather, in the eyes of sophisticated Corinthians, he was a "plain man" (2 Cor. 10:10; 11:6). The mental ability and intellectual grasp he displays were probably due not to any education at Tarsus, but to the long training which he enjoyed at the "school of Gamaliel," compounded with a sensitivity to his environment in the Graeco-Roman world.[5]

3. *Paul's Roman milieu.* The Mediterranean was a Roman lake in Paul's lifetime. One sailing from Palestine to Gibraltar would have the Empire on both sides practically all the way. To the south, Roman dominion did not penetrate very far, but to the north it included the whole of Asia Minor and all Europe south of the Danube and west of the Rhine. It reached even to Britain. Westward it was bounded by the Atlantic, eastward by the Euphrates.

Roman law and customs prevailed throughout this vast territory. Paul's acceptance of Roman citizenship—either by inheritance (so Paul's own witness in Acts: his father must have been a man of position, probably of some wealth) or purchase—is an attested fact (Acts 22:28).[6]

Paul valued this privilege. Because of it he wrote as he did in Romans 13, and possibly 2 Thessalonians 2:6,7, if "restrainer" there is to be equated with the Empire and the structures of society. We may ponder whether he would have written differently had he survived Nero's outburst. The Jews claimed special treatment as adherents of a *religio licita*, that is, a religion permitted to exist in the pluralistic society of the Empire, retaining some of its exclusive features, with certain safeguards. Paul was additionally glad to accept whatever privileges he could, both as a Jew and as a Roman, to gain freedom for the gospel.

PAUL'S CONVERSION

In addition to the threefold account of Paul's conversion in Acts 9, 22, and 26,[7] there is scattered information that helps us piece together a

---

[4] H. A. A. Kennedy, *St. Paul and the Mystery Religions* (1913), is still valuable, to be supplemented and updated by G. Wagner, *Pauline Baptism and the Pagan Mysteries* (ET 1967).

[5] W. C. van Unnik, *Tarsus or Jerusalem. The City of Paul's Youth* (ET 1962), contends, on the basis of Acts 22:3; 26:4, that Paul was exclusively brought up and educated in Jerusalem; for a challenge to this case see N. Turner, "Where Was Saul Brought Up?", in his *Grammatical Insights into the New Testament* (1965), pp. 83–85.

[6] On this verse, see A. N. Sherwin-White, *Roman Society and Roman Law in the New Testament*, pp. 151–55.

[7] The *Tendenz* of each of these accounts is discussed later, p. 99. In each the call to preach to the Gentiles is connected with the event. See W. D. Davies, *Paul and Rabbinic Judaism*[2] (1955), p. 67; J. G. Gager, "Some Notes on Paul's Conversion," *NTS*, 27 (1981), 697–704; E. Best, "The Damascus Road Experience?" *Irish Biblical Studies*, 7 (1985), 2–7.

picture of Paul's conversion experience and its personal meaning to him in 1 Corinthians 9:1; 15:8; 2 Corinthians 4:6; Galatians 1:15f.; and Philippians 3:4–10.

Several interpretations of this pivotal event in early Christianity have been proposed. Popular among many preachers is an approach based on the study of the psychology of religion. Prior to the encounter on the Damascus road, it is said, Saul was caught in the throes of an emotional struggle, caused by his sense of failure to keep the law perfectly (so apparently Acts 26:14). Other preparatory factors may be mentioned—in particular, the witness of the Christians and the death of Stephen:

> The steadfastness and religious submission with which Stephen went to his death cannot have failed to make some impression upon him. The question would have arisen in his mind: can the Master, whose disciples die like this for Him, really be a will-o'-the-wisp? But he suppresses this doubt within himself, and kills it as he surrenders himself fully at last to his persecuting zeal. The psychological law which becomes apparent here is well known. How many a man seeks to hides his inner uncertainty behind some particularly zealous deed![8]

His conversion came—in Weiss's much-quoted phrase—as "the final outcome of an inner crisis."[9]

A side issue here is the type of Judaism with which Saul had been acquainted. C. G. Montefiore's view is that Saul as a Diaspora Jew was burdened by the law, and as such he was glad to be released from its dark oppressiveness, which inspired in him a sense of abject failure.[10]

A second type of explanation is the rationalistic approach. The phenomena of Paul's conversion may be accounted for as the result of an attack of epilepsy or as part of a legendary tale.[11] Some have called on

---

[8] W. von Loewenich, *Paul His Life and Work* (ET 1960), p. 36; for criticism see W. Manson, *Jesus and the Christian*, pp. 149–59. A vigorous denial of this viewpoint is found in K. Stendahl, *Paul among Jews and Gentiles* (1977), pp. 1–77. But some of his exegetical positions are to be questioned; see R. P. Martin, *Reconciliation: A Study of Paul's Theology* (1981), pp. 24–31, for a reassertion of the "new" elements in Paul's conversion call, a counterargument to be reinforced by S. Kim, *The Origin of Paul's Gospel* (1982), esp. ch. 3.

[9] J. Weiss, *Das Urchristentum* (1917), p. 138 (ET *Earliest Christianity*, 1 [1959], 190).

[10] The Judaism of the Dispersion Montefiore calls "colder, less intimate, less happy because it was poorer and more pessimistic" than the best elements in the rabbinic Judaism of Palestine; *Judaism and St. Paul* (1914), p. 93. This thesis is critically examined by W. D. Davies, *Paul and Rabbinic Judaism*,[2] Ch. 1. Rom. 7 is often appealed to as showing Paul's sense of frustration and failure in his pre-Christian days. But there are serious objections to this interpretation; see J. D. G. Dunn, "Romans 7:14–25 in the Theology of Paul," *ThZ*, 31 (1975), 257–73. Other useful discussions of the place of Rom. 7 in this debate are C. L. Mitton, *ExpT*, 65 (1953–54), 78–81, 99–103, 132–35; and W. G. Kümmel, *Man in the New Testament* (ET 1963).

[11] For epilepsy, J. Klausner, *From Jesus to Paul* (ET 1944), p. 326. For the legendary approach, W. Prentice, "St. Paul's Journey to Damascus," *ZNTW*, 46 (1955), 250–55, who regards Gal. 1:15–17 as the only reliable source of information. The rest, he avers, is popular legend and his conversion is an affair of pure psychology.

mystical experience to interpret Paul's conversion as ecstasy (so W. Prokulski, who draws attention to Paul as a mystic according to 2 Cor. 12:2-4 and 1 Cor. 14:6ff.).[12] "Mysticism" may, indeed, describe the form of the experience, but not its nature, which appears as unique and (as far as Paul describes the experience in later life) objective.[13] We do best to interpret the event as christological and set it in a theological framework. But even this designation can be taken in a number of ways, and we must ask, What does faith do with the history? Let us look at a number of points.

First, the format of the story is colored by Old Testament and Jewish material used or implied in the background, especially Isaiah 49:1-6 (Gal. 1:15); Jeremiah 1:4ff. (Acts 26:17); and Ezekiel's vision as modified in Enoch 14:8—16:4, with the common features of a bright light and a sight of the glory of Yahweh, with the effects of this seen in a man falling to the ground, and the call to prophesy.[14]

Strictly speaking, there is no real previous history or preparation, since Saul's conversion is a sovereign act of God, as his autobiographical remarks confirm (1 Cor. 9:1; 15:8; 2 Cor. 4:6; Gal. 1:15-17; Phil. 3:4-10). On these last verses Manson comments perceptively, summing up what conversion meant for Paul:

> ... a radical change from a self-centred to a Christ-centred life, a complete submission to Jesus Christ in which he becomes a disciple of the Master and a servant of the Lord, and ... his entrance into the Kingdom of God on earth into that apostolic service which is the task of the Christian community.[15]

Even the summons to surrender to the heavenly *kyrios* overtook him against his will, if we accept at face value the witness of 1 Corinthians 9:15-18 and Philippians 3:12.

At one level, there was an intellectual revolution, involving an exchange of beliefs. The crucified one was the Messiah of prophecy.[16] But there was more than this. A spiritual experience is involved. Saul's encounter with the living Lord was nothing less than an ethical and

---

[12] W. Prokulski, "The Conversion of St. Paul," *CBQ*, 19 (1957), 453-73; cf. J. Munck, *Paul and the Salvation of Mankind*, pp. 11-35. But see also B. Rigaux, *The Letters of St. Paul* (ET 1968), pp. 40-55 (esp. 51ff.).

[13] There are problems associated with this term. See J. E. Alsup, *The Post-Resurrection Appearance Stories in the Gospel Tradition* (1975); and F. F. Bruce, "Was Paul a Mystic?", *RTR*, 34 (1975), 66-75.

[14] Cf. Munck, *op. cit.*, pp. 24ff. See too G. Lohfink, *The Conversion of St. Paul* (ET 1976) on the "apparition dialogue" (pp. 61-69).

[15] T. W. Manson, *On Paul and John* (1963), pp. 13f. ἔκτρωμα (abortion) (1 Cor. 15:8) suggests a forceful removal from his previous way of life by the "powerful intervention" of Christ; J. Schneider, *TDNT*, 2 (ET 1964), 465ff.; cf. J. Munck, "Paulus tanquam abortivus," in *New Testament Essays: Studies in Memory of T. W. Manson*, ed. A. J. B. Higgins (1959), pp. 180-93.

[16] See Ph.-H. Menoud, "Revelation and Tradition: The Influence of Paul's Conversion on his Theology," *Interpretation*, 7 (1953), 131-41. Cf. A. D. Nock, *St. Paul* (1946), p. 74: "Paul's conversion meant for him the recognition that the condemned criminal was in fact the Anointed One of God, living now...."

spiritual union with Christ (Gal. 2:20). J. Dupont shows that much of Saul's passion as a persecutor may be expressed in terms of his zeal for the law. At his conversion this zeal was redirected into an ardent love for Christ and his people. The key to the conversion is soteriology. The pursuit of righteousness by the law was later seen as a failure (even though he attained perfection in that occupation), and he needed to be converted to God's way of saving sinners at the cross.

Above all, Paul was converted to Christ, not Christianity or to any religious or ethical system. And his subsequent Epistles tell the story of what this personal transformation meant in terms of an intimate union with the risen, directing Lord.[17] In summary, conversion meant for Paul a personal encounter with the living Christ, seen to be vindicated by God as Messiah and Lord; an awareness of the close connection between Christ and his people (Acts 9:4), which Paul theologized as the doctrine of the church as the body of Christ (1 Cor. 8:12; 12:12–13); and a vision of a waiting world and a summons to be a missionary apostle to it (Acts 9:15).

PAUL'S EARLY YEARS AS A CHRISTIAN

Our information about Paul's early days as a Christian is not altogether clear, and it cannot be easily harmonized with the data of the Epistles. But a fairly likely order of events can be deduced.

If we date Paul's conversion in 35 (two years after the crucifixion of Jesus), we have a tentative starting point.[18] Three years of silence follow (Acts 9:23 = Gal. 1:18), though the experience described in 2 Corinthians 11:32f., a hurried exit from Damascus, may be equated with the events of Acts 9:24f.

In Acts 9:26–30 we read of his visit to Jerusalem as a Christian believer, a visit parallel with that in Galatians 1:18–24. But there are problems with this identification.[19] If we accept it, we may place it in 37 or 38. This meeting was a private visit lasting two weeks.

Paul, his life under attack, went off to Tarsus, and the story of his life breaks off (Acts 9:30), not to be resumed until Barnabas finds him in Tarsus and brings him to Antioch (11:25). This period must have

---

[17] J. Dupont, "The Conversion of Paul, and Its Influence on His Understanding of Salvation by Faith," in *Apostolic History and the Gospel*, edd. Gasque and Martin, pp. 176–94; H. G. Wood, "The Conversion of St. Paul: Its Nature, Antecedents and Consequences," *NTS*, 1 (1954–55), 276–82.

[18] See J. A. T. Robinson, *Redating the New Testament*, p. 36, for a dating two years earlier. On the chronology here and elsewhere see the contrasting interpretations of such data as there are by R. Jewett, *A Chronology of Paul's Life* (1979); A. J. M. Wedderburn, "Keeping Up with Recent Studies. VIII. Some Recent Pauline Chronologies," *ExpT*, 92 (1980–81), 103–8; and G. Luedemann, *Paul, Apostle to the Gentiles. Studies in Chronology* (ET 1984). See J. Murphy-O'Connor, "Pauline Missions before the Jerusalem Conference," *RB*, 89 (1982), 71–91.

[19] See G. Ogg, *The Chronology of the Life of Paul* (US title, *The Odyssey of Paul*, 1968), Ch. 6.

covered seven or eight years. The famine-relief visit is dated in the winter of 45–46, so pushing back the year at Antioch to 45.

During these several years Paul spent part of that time in Syria and Cilicia (Gal. 1:21), and there is evidence (Acts 15:41) that his initial evangelism in those districts stood the test of time. W. C. van Unnik suggests that these were years of study, centering on Greek culture and especially the Greek Old Testament.[20]

Why does Luke pass over this long period with virtual silence? Perhaps he had no information; perhaps telling all he knew lay outside his immediate purpose. If the latter is the case, the question arises whether Luke presents his material about Paul in such a way as to depict him as an ideal apostle (see below). In any case, it was not until his apostolic mission to the Gentiles began that Paul's life took on significance as the career of a "chosen instrument" (9:15). So Luke can afford to neglect the early period in order to highlight the tremendous significance of what began at 13:1ff.

LUKE'S PARADIGMATIC APOSTLE[20a]

The characterization of Paul in Acts justifies designating him as something of an ideal figure. This is seen most obviously in the prominence given to his apostolic life and labors. From Acts 13:9 (where Saul's birth-name is changed to his Roman *cognomen* Paulus) and 13:13 (where the interesting phrase is "Paul and his followers," οἱ περὶ Παῦλον, a classical expression to denote Paul as a leader of men: cf. 14:20), it is Paul who dominates the story, and he is given a prominence which none apparently disputed, at least in Luke's presentation.

The various ways Paul's unique place in Acts—and therefore, according to this record, in the early church—is displayed may be summed up in the statement of Ephesians 2:20, that the church is built on "the foundation of [or, laid by] the apostles and prophets" or more specifically, in the same epistle (3:1–13), in the descriptions given of the special stewardship of grace for the Gentiles entrusted to Paul. Paul's sufferings on behalf of Gentile Christians were significant (Eph. 3:13; Col. 1:24); and it cannot be accidental that those same sufferings, endured while establishing Gentile congregations in Asia and Europe, occupy much of the descriptive writing of Luke in Acts.

In particular, we may note the following ways Luke deliberately accentuates Paul's apostolic ministry.

1. *The threefold account of Paul's conversion.* This is a remarkable feature of Acts, since the three sections tell the story in virtually the same way. Luke evidently intended monumental importance to be attached to this part of his narrative.[21]

---

[20] *Op. cit.,* pp. 56ff.

[20a] This is also M. Hengel's designation: see *Acts and the History of Early Christianity,* p. 59.

[21] D. M. Stanley, "Paul's Conversion in Acts: Why the Three Accounts?" *CBQ,* 15 (1953), 315–38. There is no need to postulate that the triple tradition arose in

The three accounts differ in detail. They agree *verbatim* only in the dialogue by which the risen Christ identifies himself with the church.[22] The variation of detail seems to be deliberate, with each account highlighting a different motive in the author's mind. In Acts 9:3–9 the emphasis falls on Paul's really having seen Christ. So he is rightfully categorized with those who meet the apostolic qualification of Acts 1:22 (see 1 Cor. 9:1; 15:8f., where seeing the Lord is linked with apostleship). Acts 22:6–16, on the other hand, picks up the unique character of the meeting. Paul of all the apostles has seen the Christ exalted in glory (22:11,14). This, if anything, would give Paul's claim to be apostle to the Gentiles an added endorsement—that the glorified Lord addressed his servant in a way that only he could understand (22:9).[23] Finally, in Acts 26:12–23 the setting is that of an inaugural vision, such as the prophets and seers received (motifs drawn from Isaiah, Jeremiah, Ezekiel, and Enoch are included). There may be intentional links with Acts 1 and 2 in terms of the prophetic witness now realized (2:17 = Joel 2:28–32), which put Paul's experience on a par with that of the original eye-witnesses of Pentecost. Moreover, Paul's vocation is spelled out in terms of Isaiah's suffering servant (26:18 = Isa. 42:7, 16)—a destiny which belonged uniquely to the apostle Paul and his entourage, as in Acts 13:47ff., in which the mission to the Gentiles is prophetically authorized.

2. *Special emphasis on the call and commission at Antioch* (13:1–3). The key terms here are heavy with significance to stress that the innovation of a mission to the Gentiles was no humanly devised enterprise or expedient. It was undertaken in obedience to the voice of the Spirit and subsequently discharged in the power of the same Spirit (vv. 2, 4). Clearly Luke intended to focus on the divine initiative and approval, and to clear Paul of any suspicion that he acted pragmatically or according to his own devices in launching the mission to the non-Jewish world, itself an unheard-of departure within Judaism.[24]

3. *The tragic refusal of the synagogue to respond favorably.* This led to the wider expansion of the mission, as indicated in 13:46–49. But implicit in this new sphere of missionary operations was the responsibility the apostles still felt for Israel. The program is identical to that

---

three centers (Acts 9 from Paul himself; Acts 22 from Jerusalem; Acts 26 from Antioch), as K. Lake, *Beginnings of Christianity,* Vol. 5, note XV, pp. 188–95, does. G. Lohfink, *op. cit.,* pp. 87ff., gives a useful discussion.

[22] We may compare a similar phenomenon in the pronouncement stories of the Synoptic Gospels, which have variant accounts and differing circumstantial details but agree in the punch-line of a logion of Jesus. See Matt. 8:5–13 = Luke 7:1–10, and the present writer's study in the *Festschrift* for George E. Ladd, ed. Robert A. Guelich (1978). Another example is B. Reicke, "The Synoptic Reports of the Healing of the Paralytic. Matt. 9, 1–8, with Parallels," in *Studies in the New Testament Language and Text: Essays in Honour of George D. Kilpatrick,* ed. J. K. Elliott (1976), pp. 319–29, esp. p. 322.

[23] On the relation of Acts 9:7 and 22:9 see N. Turner, *op. cit.,* pp. 87–90.

[24] See D. P. Fuller, *Easter Faith and History* (1965), pp. 192ff.

referred to in Romans 1:16*b* and 11:1–32, and amplified and theologized in Ephesians 2:11–22.

4. *The context of Luke's designation of Paul as apostle.* It is in the account of this so-called first missionary journey that this designation is most often found. Indeed, the evidence is clearer. Only in chapter 14 (vv. 4 and 14) is Paul explicitly called an apostle in the book of Acts; and it is in this setting of his apostolic work of founding churches in areas where Christ's name was unknown (Rom. 15:20) that his consolidating work of arranging a rudimentary ministerial order (14:23) is mentioned also (cf. Phil. 1:1).

5. *The task of the apostle is bearing witness* (Acts 9:15; 22:15; 26:16). Hence it was Luke's design in writing to bring the chief witness to Rome. En route he stands before representatives of imperial Rome, Herod Agrippa II (25:23ff.) and then Nero Caesar (27:24). With Paul at Rome, Luke's narrative can close. Though he may well have known the outcome of Paul's imprisonment and trial, his purpose as narrator is served when he has shown how, in divine providence, Paul reached the place of his appointed destiny and bore testimony as apostle *par excellence.* As 1 Clement 5:7 puts it: "After reaching the furthest limits of the west, and bearing his testimony before kings and rulers, he passed out of this world and was received into the holy places. In him we have one of the greatest of all examples of endurance" (see below, p. 299).

Luke the pastor is thus using Paul's faithful example in order to call his church to follow the apostle in mission and devotion, as it acknowledges his supreme, God-given role in establishing the "one body of Christ" in the world.

CHAPTER EIGHT

Cornelius' Conversion and the First Missionary Journey

The narrative sections of Acts 10–14 cover three significant events in Luke's account of the origin and rise of the Christian faith.

CORNELIUS

Martin Dibelius in an important essay treats the account in Acts 10:1—11:18 form-critically and attempts to disentangle an original "harmless" story of Cornelius' baptism by Peter from alleged Lukan embellishments, which add details of the vision and turn the composite narrative into a discussion of theological principles which center on whether Christians may or may not eat unclean foods. This exercise is open to question.[1]

Luke attaches much importance to this story, using it to show the progress of the church in an ever-widening evangelistic endeavor. Yet the ultimate scope of the Gentile mission still awaits the activity of the men from Cyprus and Cyrene (Acts 11:20) and the logical outcome in the Pauline mission (13:1ff.). The discussion of Cornelius confirms this. Peter needs a vision from God to enter a Gentile house, to accept the abolition of *kosher* food rules, and to baptize Gentiles without raising the issue of their need to observe Jewish rituals. But the entire story accents the special character of all this, and the Jewish Christians' concurrence is given on the tacit understanding that Cornelius is a unique case, not the first in a new army of converts to the faith.

Cornelius was a Gentile "God-fearer," not a proselyte who had

---

[1] M Dibelius, "The Conversion of Cornelius," in *Studies in the Acts of the Apostles*, pp. 109–22. J. Munck, *Paul and the Salvation of Mankind*, pp. 228–31, criticizes Dibelius, arguing that the story "cannot lose its epoch-making character by having parts here and there removed from it. It is presumably correct that the allusion to unclean foods in 11:3 is due to Luke, who knew about the narrative that follows about the Council at Jerusalem and the food laws for the Gentile Christians; but it is incorrect to make that a reason for relating the vision (10:10–16) to foods and not to people" (p. 229).

accepted baptism and admission to the Jewish fold. On the fringe of the synagogue, he was still technically a pagan in Jewish eyes. Hence Peter's fears of defilement were real (10:28).

The vision (10:9–16) was of a great sheet holding a menagerie of the animal kingdom. The point to notice is that clean and unclean animals (Lev. 11) jostle together indiscriminately, and the divine command (vs. 13) makes no distinction: "Get up, Peter. Kill ritually (θύειν) and eat the *kosher* food." The cancellation of the Jewish food laws is the primary application of the vision, but at a deeper level the sense has to do with the acceptance of persons. Peter's attitude was one of exclusivism, for association with a Gentile at a solemn meal would be defiling (Gal. 2:15). The abolishing of dietary laws was a token from God that there was no longer any barrier to keep Jews and Gentiles apart (see Eph. 2:11–18 for a later theological elaboration of this idea).

Peter's sermon is given in Acts 10:34–43. The essential Jewishness of this sermon should be noted.[2] A direct intervention of the Spirit was necessary to convince Peter that Cornelius as a Gentile had a place in God's saving mercy without conforming to Jewish rites. The sermon is important for a number of reasons. Prominent among these is that it represents the *first* offer of the gospel to the Gentile world, and so paves the way for a full-scale Gentile mission. But also it gives an outline of what the early Christians believed about the significance of Jesus' ministry, death, and triumph.[3] Not surprisingly, some have claimed that it contains a ground-plan (in vv. 37–40) of the later Gospel of Mark, which Christian tradition has associated with Peter's preaching. Addressed to a Gentile congregation (vs. 35), it received dramatic evidence of God's approval in a way few sermons do. The preacher's voice was silenced by a gracious interposition and a remarkable outpouring of the Holy Spirit. The main point to grasp lies in the phrase "even on the Gentiles" (vs. 45), which marks the novelty of grace. The description of this episode as the Gentile Pentecost is an apt one, for these events show the deeper fulfilment of what Peter had barely hinted at in 2:39.[4]

The structure of the sermon is worth close study. Peter begins by declaring that recent events have shown that there is no "most favored

---

[2] U. Wilckens, *Die Missionsreden der Apostelgeschichte* (1961), pp. 65ff., calls Peter's speech a species of catechetical instruction, not an evangelistic sermon, since he thinks Cornelius had already understood and believed the kerygma before Peter began to speak (on the basis of 10:36–38—"you know"). This interpretation is justly criticized by G. N. Stanton, *Jesus of Nazareth in New Testament Preaching*, pp. 19–26. F. Bovon notes that the wording of 11:14 ("a message by which you will be saved") shows the sermon to be evangelistic; "Tradition et Rédaction en Actes 10,1—11,18," *TZ*, 26 (1970), 42n70.

[3] Stanton concludes that "in Luke's day, reference to the life and character of Jesus was an integral part of the preaching of the early church" (*ibid.*, p. 26).

[4] G. W. H. Lampe, *The Seal of the Spirit* (1951), Ch. 5; cf. J. D. G. Dunn, *Baptism in the Holy Spirit*, pp. 80ff.; and *Jesus and the Spirit*, pp. 154f.

nation" clause in God's covenant with his people. This is what the Old Testament prophets had also taught, with their doctrine of the remnant (faithful Israelites within the larger group of the nation) and their universalistic outlook, which comprehended the Gentiles within the scope of God's mercy and care. There is no conflict between Israel's election and God's mercy to the nations; rather, it was precisely *through* his elect people that God's love was intended to reach out to the Gentiles. Israel was elect for the sake of mankind.[5] The terminal points of Jesus' ministry are marked by John's baptism (vs. 37) and the witness to the empty tomb (vs. 41).[6] He was the Messiah (vs. 38), identified as God's saving agent in his life, death, and vindication. The apostles are the accredited witnesses to all this (vv. 39,41) and the commissioned representatives of the gospel message (vs. 42), whose offer fulfils the promise of the Old Testament (vs. 43).

The effect of the preacher's words was attested by the Gentiles' use of "tongues" (vs. 46); and they received Christian baptism—not administered by Peter, however (vs. 48)—as initiation into the visible fellowship of the church. No mention is made of circumcision, and that is Luke's important point.[7]

From Acts 11:1–18 it seems that Peter's actions had come under fire, but a retelling leads to the conclusion of verse 18, which is a cordial acceptance of the significant happening. Why then did the Jewish Christians back down from this admission and later attack Peter (Gal. 2:11ff.)? Probably they were prepared to receive Cornelius and his group as an exceptional and isolated case. But the logical conclusion of the teaching in Galatians 3:27–29, with the implication of a church in which all distinctions of race were done away, was another matter. The story ends with an interim decision (vs. 18) but the matter will later be reopened as a consequence of Paul's Gentile mission.

ANTIOCH

The missionary future of the church lay with the Hellenists who had caught the vision of Stephen (11:19f.). The city of Antioch on the river Orontes in Syria was to become the locus and springboard of this new movement. Founded in 300 BC by the first ruler of the Seleucid dynasty, the city had a population that included both Greeks and veteran Jewish soldiers from Seleucus' army. It had become a center for the Jewish dispersion, and was thus ideal for the settlement of the Hellenist Christians and suitable as a launching-pad for outreach to the Greek world

---

[5] J. Skinner, *Prophecy and Religion* (1922), Ch. 2.
[6] John and Jesus are the two epochs in salvation history in H. Conzelmann, *Theology of St. Luke* (ET 1961), p. 26.
[7] J. Munck, *op. cit.*, p. 231.

(13:1ff.). It was, as G. Dix called it: "a bastion of Hellenism in the Syriac lands . . . the inevitable meeting point of the two worlds."[8] We may refer to 2 Maccabees 4 for a description of Antioch as a center of Jewish hellenization.

Nicolaus, one of the seven (Acts 6:5), was a proselyte from Antioch, the only one of the number to have his place of origin named. Of the three "prophets and teachers" (13:1) besides Saul and Barnabas, Simeon has been equated by some with Simon of Cyrene (Luke 23:26), partly because "Niger" means "black man." Lucius is *not* to be identified with the evangelist Luke, nor with the Lucius of Romans 16:21. Manaen had been well placed in Herod's entourage as the prince's "companion."

Antioch was also the site of the name-giving (Acts 11:26): the disciples were called Christians here. The designation could only have been made in a Gentile environment, since the word-ending *-ianos* in Greek represented the Latin *-ianus*. It is a title of possession (just as *Caesariani* means "Caesar's men"). This led E. J. Bickerman to the view that "Christians" means "slaves of Christ," and so it is a title of self-designation.[9] More likely, the title was given by the people of Antioch (on the supposed connection with *chrēstus* = gracious, kind), or by the city officials to identify a political group.[10] It is by this appellation that the Roman writers Suetonius, Tacitus, and Pliny refer to followers of Jesus, and it was under this name that they were later persecuted (1 Pet. 4:16). Perhaps this name marks a new dimension to the church's self-consciousness and is the beginning of the idea of a "third race," already implicit in 1 Corinthians 10:32.

THE FIRST MISSION TO ASIA

The New English Bible heads the section of Acts beginning with chapter 13 *"The Church Breaks Barriers."* This is an accurate summary of the new phase of missionary activity begun by the church at Antioch. The church's preoccupation was worship directed to Jesus as Lord when the Spirit's summons came and two men were chosen.

---

[8] G. Dix, *Jew and Greek: A Study in the Primitive Church* (1953), p. 33. On the importance of Antioch in the ancient world, see further G. Downey, *Ancient Antioch* (1963); B. M. Metzger, "Antioch-on-the-Orontes," *BA*, 11.4 (1948), 70–88, who states that "with the exception of Jerusalem, Antioch in Syria played a larger part in the life and fortunes of the early Church than any other single city of the Graeco-Roman Empire" (70).

[9] E. J. Bickerman, "The Name of Christians," *HTR*, 42 (1949), 109–24.

[10] So E. Peterson, "Christianus," *Studi e Testi 121. Miscellanea Giovanni Mercati*, 1 (1946), 355–72 (cited by Haenchen, *Acts*, pp. 367f.); cf. H. B. Mattingly, "The Origin of the Name 'Christiani,'" *JTS*, 9, n.s. (1958), 26–37. The spelling with "e" survives in the French *chrétien*. "Chrestus" was a popular pronunciation in later times (Tertullian, *Apol.* 3; Lactantius, *Inst. Div.* 4.17).

The first missionary tour is then detailed.[11] From Seleucia, the port of Antioch, they went to Salamis, the chief town of Cyprus. Christian witness was made in the Jewish synagogues, mainly (to judge from vs. 15) by Paul's seizing the opportunity for any qualified visitor to expound the Scripture in a sermon to the assembled congregation in each place. The assistance of John Mark suggests that he was a catechetical teacher, engaged in "follow-up" instruction of new converts (vs. 5).[12]

The encounter with Elymas at Paphos is a reminder that the gospel of Christ had many rivals in the ancient religious world. The lure of magic—astrology, fortune-telling, healing, exorcism—was powerful, and magicians practiced their art all over the Roman world. Magical ideas had invaded Judaism as well, chiefly through Persian sources; and Elymas was also known by the Jewish name Bar-Jesus.[13]

Sergius Paulus, the Roman proconsul, showed a remarkable openness to the Christian message (vs. 7).[14] This obviously displeased the magician, who had the wit to realize that if his master became a believer in the Christian God his services would quickly be dispensed with. This explains his obstruction (vs. 8) which, in turn, met with a forthright statement from Paul.

From this passage (13:13-41) in the Book of Acts on, the Roman name "Paul" replaces the apostle's birth name "Saul" (cf. 13:9), except in those few passages which tell again the story of his conversion (e.g., 22:7). The reason is that his missionary activity increasingly moved on to Gentile territory, where the apostle's Roman *cognomen* would be more suitable.[15] Moreover, for the first time, we read of "Paul and his company" (vs. 13). Barnabas has slipped into second place (contrast 12:25; 13:2; 13:43). Whether the new prominence given to Paul was the cause of John Mark's defection (vs. 13b), as he saw his cousin (Col. 4:10) passed over, is a matter of speculation. It is more probable that Mark had never envisaged the extent of penetration into Gentile country which emerged as Paul and the party pressed on into Asia Minor.

---

[11] See G. Ogg, *The Odyssey of Paul* (British title, *The Chronology of the Life of Paul*), Ch. 10. On the place of the first missionary tour in Acts, see P. Menoud, "Le plan des Actes des Apôtres," *NTS*, 1 (1954-55), 44ff.

[12] R. O. P. Taylor, "The Ministry of Mark," *ExpT*, 54 (1942-43), 136-38.

[13] On Elymas, see M. Simon, *Verus Israel* (1948), pp. 394ff. See also B. M. Metzger, "St. Paul and the Magicians," *Princeton Seminary Bulletin*, 38 (1944), 27-30; A. D. Nock, "Paul and the Magus," in *The Beginnings of Christianity*, Vol. 5, note XIV, pp. 164-88.

[14] On the name Sergius Paulus, see Bastiaan Van Elderen, "Some Archaeological Observations on Paul's First Missionary Journey," in *Apostolic History and the Gospel*, edd. Gasque and Martin, pp. 151-56.

[15] G. A. Harrer, "Saul who also is called Paul," *HTR*, 33 (1940), 19-33, discusses the use of the *cognomen* "Paul" and Saul's association with the Roman proconsul but concludes that the Latin "Paul" was probably his birth-name with "Saul" his *signum;* see Haenchen, *op. cit.*, pp. 399f., for other possible reasons.

The first goal of Paul's journey beyond the Taurus mountains was Antioch in Pisidia (vs. 14). Paul selects a place of strategic importance as a center and base of apostolic ministry. Pisidian Antioch was a Roman colony. Again, he makes full use of the synagogue as a sounding-board from which his message may go out. His sermon was an appeal to God's revelation under the old covenant. His chief point centers on David (vs. 22), who prefigures his greater Son, Israel's Messiah (vs. 23).[16] At the heart of the message lies the characteristic Pauline emphases on the resurrection of Jesus as God's vindication of him, and the provision of righteousness by faith, which met the demands of the law.[17]

Many Jews and proselytes were won over and were encouraged to persevere (13:42-52). To judge from the next paragraph, they came back the next week with a great crowd of interested Gentiles (vv. 44f.). Did Paul see in this sequence a divine confirmation that this was Israel's destiny and mission—to be a light for the Gentiles (vs. 47)?[18] National Israel, the Jewish people of old, represented in their synagogue officers of verse 45, had failed to seize this opportunity; the task therefore fell to the Christian apostles to accept the vocation of the servant and as "elect for the sake of mankind" to reach out to the distant peoples. So "we turn to the Gentiles" (vs. 46). This solemn announcement sounded the death-knell for Jewish exclusiveness and that selfish particularism which said, "What we have as a special privilege we want to keep to ourselves." Equally it proved a manifesto and charter of Christian liberty and the promise of a worldwide church. No longer could the Christian movement be thought of as a sect within Judaism, whatever misunderstanding their enemies might have. Acts 24:5 shows that this is what the Jews would like to have believed about the church, but having burst the cocoon, the missionary church showed itself no inert chrysalis, but a living creature, ready to fly to earth's extremities with a message and a ministry to all (vs. 47). Small wonder that the Gentiles, regarded by official Judaism as beyond the pale and hopeless, were overjoyed to receive the news of their salvation through Israel's Savior.

---

[16] On vv. 32–37 see E. Lövestam, *Son and Saviour, A Study of Acts 13, 32–37* (1961), who relates the course of the sermon up to vs. 23 to the promise given in 2 Sam. 7:6–16 (p. 10); O. Glombitza, "Akta xiii.15–41: Analyse einer lukanischen Predigt vor Juden," *NTS*, 5 (1958–59), 306–17, finds here answers to challenges posed by the Jews to Paul's assertions that Jesus is the Son of David and his Lord; that Jerusalem is the place where prophecy referring to Jesus was fulfilled; and that Jesus as high priest is set above the law as redeemer.

[17] On the exegetical problem in vs. 38 see F. F. Bruce, *The Speeches in the Acts of the Apostles* (1944), pp. 12f.

[18] Conzelmann (*Apostelgeschichte, ad loc.*) calls this *das heilsgeschichtliche Prinzip* (as seen in Acts 14:1; 16:13; 17:1,10,17; 18:4,19; 19:8). It implies an initial approach to the Jews of the Dispersion.

From Antioch the apostles moved on to Iconium (now called Konya) and a junction of several routes (Acts 14:1-7). Virulent opposition was encountered here also, stirred up by unbelieving Jews. A critical point was evidently reached when Paul learned of a concerted effort to attack him and his company (vv. 5f.). The principle of Matthew 10:23 was invoked; and they took refuge in Lystra and Derbe, where fresh scope for evangelization was given (vs. 7).[19]

Both parts of Paul's ministry at Lystra are full of interest. His healing of the crippled man recalls Peter's work at the Temple gate (3:1-10). Both apostles evidently had a presence which commanded attention and drew out the earnest hopes of the needy invalids they encountered: note the references to intense longing in 3:5 and 14:9, which was matched by a direct look from the apostles. The behavior of the crowd (vv. 11-13) was typical of the people of Lycaonia, whose district, tradition reported, had once been favored by a visit from Zeus (the king of the Greek gods) and Hermes (his messenger). Archaeological finds in that area of Asia Minor have shown that the cults of Zeus and Hermes flourished in the third century of our era and may go back earlier.[20] In fact, the priests of Zeus (cf. vs. 13) are referred to in the inscription unearthed by W. M. Calder of Manchester in 1922.

The second point of interest is Paul's speech (vv. 15-18). This brief, impromptu statement was Paul's first opportunity to address a Gentile audience; and it is important to observe the features of the Christian message it highlights. It cannot be complete in itself and was probably never finished, for Paul had not yet mentioned the distinctive elements, such as the cross and resurrection of Jesus, when he was stopped (vs. 18). The verses, therefore, contain a preamble to the gospel, and lay the foundation for it in a concise summary of "natural theology."[21]

Experiences at Lystra left a permanent mark on Paul's mind (cf. 2 Tim. 3:11) and his body, if Galatians 6:17 is interpreted as the scars of his suffering in missionary service.[22] Not for the last time did he face imminent death (vv. 19f.); and this successful attempt at rescue, as the disciples formed a ring around him, permitted him to escape and press

---

19 On the site of Derbe, see the archaeological report in Van Elderen, loc. cit., pp. 156-61.

20 W. M. Calder, "Zeus and Hermes at Lystra," Expositor, 7,10 (1910), 1-6; also "Acts 14.12," ExpT, 37 (1925-26), 528, concluding that "we know that the Lycaonian inhabitants of the Lystra valley itself associated Hermes with the supreme god in their local cult."

21 See B. Gärtner, The Areopagus Speech and Natural Revelation (1955), pp. 227f.

22 T. W. Crafer, "The Stoning of Paul at Lystra, and the Epistle to the Galatians," Expositor, 8, 6 (1913), 375-84; cf. R. P. Martin, "Mark, Brand," in NIDNTT, ed. C. Brown, Vol. 2 (1976), 572-75. For an understanding of Luke's possible purpose in the recital of Paul's sufferings, see Haenchen, op. cit., pp. 429-34.

on undeterred to the next town, Derbe. Thence, by a return circuit of the mission stations, they arrived at their base in Syrian Antioch (vv. 21–28).[23]

---

[23] Luke's purpose in reciting the details of the mission preaching of the first journey is brought out by three items in his description: (1) the presence of "signs and wonders" (14:3), (2) the witness of the Spirit in boldness (13:46; 14:3), and (3) the corroboration of the Old Testament Scripture. The evidence has parallels in the earlier chapters of Acts, thus uniting Paul's ministry in its validity with that of Peter, the *Urapostel*. It is significant that in connection with his initial evangelism Paul is called an "apostle" (14:4, 14). See A. A. Trites, *The New Testament Concept of Witness*, pp. 149–53.

CHAPTER NINE

The Jerusalem Council and Paul's Attitude to Israel

THE ISSUE AT THE COUNCIL

In approaching Acts 15 and the so-called Apostolic Council described there, we should begin with what the text has to say as we take it at face value.[1]

The immediate occasion of the council was the success of Paul's missionary journey. Jews and Jewish proselytes had been won, but—more significantly—the gospel had made a noticeable inroad into pagan territory and (chiefly in Galatia) a ready welcome to the message had been received, so much that Paul had introduced a rudimentary church organization for maintaining congregational life and growth (14:22f.). News of this had reached the Jerusalem church, where the alarm of some led to a full-scale discussion.

The "dissension and debate" (vs. 2) centered on the admissibility of Gentile believers to the church. Cornelius had clearly been a special case; and at all events, though technically a pagan, he had been halfway to becoming a Jew before his conversion to Christ. But were Gentile converts to be welcomed *en masse* the moment they were converted, or should they be gradually introduced to full Christian standing by receiving the imposition of certain Jewish rites and rituals? The chief qualification which the strict Jewish Christians were insisting upon was circumcision (15:1,5).

The danger of a divided church, split into two factions and with two headquarters, at Jerusalem and at Antioch, was present. So to settle the question a consultation was arranged. Clearly Paul and Barnabas stood for a liberal attitude, which Paul strenuously argues for in his Galatian Epistle. At the opposite end of the scale, a rigid policy was

---

[1] The importance of this episode has been observed in recent studies on Acts. For instance, H. Conzelmann (*Apostelgeschichte*, p. 81) writes: "Not by accident does the Apostolic Council come in the middle of the book. It is the great turning-point, marking the transition from the 'original church' (*Urkirche*) to the church of Luke's day." The critical issues are well displayed by K. Lake, "The Apostolic Council of Jerusalem," in *The Beginnings of Christianity*, Vol. 5, Note XVI, pp. 195–212.

adopted that Gentile converts should be turned into good Jews before they were accorded full Christian status.

At the outset, we should list certain assumptions of identification and chronology we are making here. These will be discussed in more detail in the chapter on the Galatian letter.

1. Paul's year at Antioch (11:26) was followed by his second trip to Jerusalem, and this visit is to be equated with the visit mentioned in Galatians 2:1–10 = Acts 11:27–30 (the famine-visit).

2. According to this view, Galatians is a precouncil document, and was written to churches in south Galatia.

3. It was the success of the first missionary journey that stirred up opposition from the Judaizing party within Jewish Christianity at Jerusalem and led to the defection of the Galatian Christians.

4. Therefore, the events immediately antecedent to the council, which account for its happening, were the arrival at Antioch of a Jewish group from Jerusalem (15:1), whose coming led to an acrimonious debate (vs. 2); the presence and influence at Antioch of "certain men [who] came from James" (Gal. 2:12); and bad news came from Galatia showing that the Judaizers were set on disrupting the Pauline churches.

5. The aim of these Jewish Christians was to break the mission concordat between Paul and Peter (Gal. 2:1–10), by which each apostle agreed to restrict his labors to a particular ethnic group with an understanding of parity and a mutual recognition of the legitimacy of this work of evangelization.

The matter came to a head with a decision to hold a "summit conference" and to settle some pressing issues. From the Jewish Christian standpoint, these were claims by which the offer of the gospel to non-Jews was restricted by requiring them to be circumcised before according them full Christian status. Conzelmann states the issue clearly: the problem is "not the admission of the Gentiles as such, but the terms on which they are to be received."[2] (We can only surmise that this was so, for we have no independent statement of their case.) The Judaizing Christian teachers insisted that converts from the Gentile world should receive the rite of circumcision.[3] They based this requirement on apostolic authority, evidently invoking the "pillar" apostles of Galatians 2:9 in support,[4] and buttressed it by an appeal to Scripture. Genesis 17, they argued, states that circumcision is required for every descendant of Abraham and every foreigner who enters the household. This is an "everlasting covenant" not to be revoked.

[2] Conzelmann, op. cit., p. 81.
[3] F. V. Filson, A New Testament History, pp. 214f.
[4] C. K. Barrett, "Paul and the 'Pillar' Apostles," in Studia Paulina in honorem Johannis de Zwaan (1953), pp. 1–19, argues that the unique eschatological status of James, Peter, and John implies that they were regarded as "indispensable connecting links between the historical Jesus and the community of the New Age" (p. 18).

There would also have been, on the part of these Judaizers, a secret fear that the character and ethos of the church would be changed by the mass influx of Gentile converts who were not (on Paul's terms of admission) required to be circumcised before being received as full church members. "Taking the yoke of the commandments" was a prior necessity for the proselyte to Judaism: why should this requirement be waived in the case of converts to Judaism's fulfilment in the gospel? Derogation of circumcision was construed as an attack on the divine authority of the Torah religion, and a blow struck at morality with an effect leading inevitably to an abandonment of all that Judaism stood for (implied in Acts 21:21).

Paul's reply was aimed at repelling these charges, though all through his apostolic life he would have to live down the unsavory reputation his first Gentile mission inevitably fastened on him. Some of his converts did not exactly help him (cf. Rom. 6:1ff.; 3:8—"some people slanderously charge us with saying"). Paul's position was to confront the teaching of Acts 15:5 head-on, and to seek to overthrow it. For him this restriction was an intolerable betrayal of the gospel of the grace of God, according to his (earlier) letter to the Galatians. Another serious matter, as we have noted, is the logical conclusion on the Judaizers' principle that there may well eventuate a divided church, split into two factions and with two headquarters, one at Jerusalem and the other at Antioch.[5] This possibility had already been envisioned and rejected by Paul in Galatians 3:25–29 and 4:21–31.

Much debate at the council evidently led nowhere (15:7); and Peter's statement was intended to cut through the knot by an assertion that the grace of the Lord Jesus was the sole requirement for salvation (vs. 11). Peter's rehearsal of God's dealings with him served to underscore several important convictions: that God himself had taken the initiative in the choosing and calling of Cornelius (vs. 7);[6] that the proof of his pleasure was that he gave the Holy Spirit in the same way and on the same basis as the blessing of Pentecost which inaugurated the Christian era (vv. 8f.); as there was no distinction in the gift of messianic grace, there must be no "extra" necessity which would obscure the gracious way in which God chooses to act (vv. 9,11); and, in any case, to insist on a Jewish prescription was an invitation to bondage from which Christ had set believers free (vs. 10).

If we accept the sequence of events and the order of the literature suggested above, we can conclude that Peter had profited from the rebuke administered by Paul at Antioch (Gal. 2:11–21). At that earlier

---

[5] W. Neil, *The Letter of Paul to the Galatians* (1967), p. 90.

[6] The links with Cornelius are brought out by J. R. Porter, "The 'Apostolic Decree' and Paul's Second Visit to Jerusalem," *JTS*, 47, o.s. (1946), 169–74, who sees the issue at Jerusalem as one of table-fellowship at common meals, rather than admission to the church.

time he had vacillated, first welcoming the Gentiles as brothers and sharers in a common table; but later, under pressure, "playing the Pharisee" (Gal. 2:12a) by a deliberate withdrawal and refusal to share fellowship.[7] His motivation at that time was described sadly by Paul, who observed its effect on others (Gal. 2:12).

Next it is James's turn to contribute to the discussion (15:13–21).[8] He expresses cordial acceptance of Peter's statement and adds a scriptural precedent for the thought that God intended to include the Gentiles in the assembling of his people. This is part of the missionary message of the Old Testament.

The quotation from Amos 9:11f. is taken from the Greek Old Testament and makes two points.[9] The rebuilding of David's dwelling speaks, in the first place, of God's covenant of restoration with Israel after the exile. Second, Acts 15:17 relates to "the rest of men": the Gentiles who are called by God's name. The promise is that they, too, find a place within the fold of God's people.[10] The upshot is the verdict of verse 19, which runs clearly counter to the Judaizing proposals of verses 1 and 5. Yet James wished to safeguard the Jewish position by imposing the terms of a "decree" (15:20), the terms (according to the record here and at 21:24, 25) Paul and his associates were willing to promise to convey to their Gentile churches in the Syrian province.

THE APOSTOLIC DECREE

The terms of the so-called apostolic decree are disputed, and it is hard to know what exactly is meant in 15:20 and 29. At least two views have been proposed, and the matter is made more complex by a textual uncertainty. Stated succinctly, the choice is between a ritual or a moral interpretation of the terms of the edict.[11]

---

[7] ἀφώριζεν ἑαυτόν: "he separated himself" as the Pharisees did (Vol. 1, pp. 85f.), thus indicating their right to be called "the separated ones."

[8] On James's role at the Council, see W. Schmithals, *Paul and James* (ET 1965), pp. 38ff.; J. Jervell, "James: The Defender of Paul," in *Luke and the People of God* (1972). See *NTF*, Vol. 1, p. 268.

[9] On the textual problem here, see Bruce, *The Speeches in Acts*, pp. 19f. The nub of the exegetical issue is that the Masoretic Text says that Israel will possess the land of Edom, while the LXX (quoted by James) holds out the hope that the heathen will be converted, as the rest of mankind (Adam) will seek the Lord. The confusion between the Hebrew radicals underlying the verbs "possess" ($y\bar{\imath}re\check{s}\hat{u}$) and "seek" ($yi\underline{d}re\check{s}\hat{u}$) is easy to explain, involving an addition and a transposition. Similarly the vocalization of '-$\underline{d}$-m produces either "Edom" or "Adam."

[10] N. A. Dahl, "A People for His Name (Acts xv.14)," *NTS*, 4 (1957–58), 319–27. For the logic in James's statement, see W. Michaelis, *TDNT*, 7 (ET 1971), 374f.

[11] The authorities on each side are listed by Haenchen, *Acts*, pp. 449f. Several recent studies contain full bibliographical data, esp. G. Zuntz, "An Analysis of the Report about the 'Apostolic Council,'" in his *Opuscula Selecta: Classica, Hellenistica, Christiana* (1972), pp. 216–51; M. Simon, "The Apostolic Decree and its Setting in the Ancient Church," *BJRL*, 52 (1970), 437–60; and F. F. Bruce, *New Testament History*, Ch. 22. On the textual problem see C. S. C. Williams, *Alterations to the Text of the Synoptic Gospels and Acts* (1951), pp. 72ff.

1. *Ritual.* On this understanding, the avoidance of "what is strangled" and "blood" refers to the Jewish horror of eating animal blood left in the carcass and not drained off by the *shechita* method of butchering.[12] The assumption is that most Gentiles would recognize this scruple as valid. If they wanted to have social intercourse with neighboring Jewish Christians who still respected the Levitical code, which forbade the eating of animal blood (Lev. 17:10), they would not mind abstaining from such food out of respect for Jewish sensitivities. There is precedent for this in the so-called Noachian laws, which (on the rabbinic view) were given to Noah and were binding on all Gentiles (Gen. 9:4).[13]

Paul agreed to this compromise, because the main issue for him was circumcision, and he was already used to the idea of teaching his converts to recognize Jewish feelings. "They added nothing to me" (Gal. 2:6) refers to the fact that before the council he had already conceded the point in defense of the larger principle regarding circumcision.

2. *Moral.* An alternative reading of the text follows the Western textual authorities and omits "what is strangled." It is thus possible to interpret the remaining three prohibitions as moral demands against idolatry, adultery (marriage within the forbidden family limits of Lev. 18),[14] and murder ("blood" seen as metonymy for "shedding human blood").

There are two considerations to support this view. First, in Paul's dealings with Gentile churches at Rome and Corinth he refuses to legislate formally and leaves the matter of eating idol-foods to be settled by guidance from individual conscience. He never cites the decree. In the second place, it is argued that Paul would have no scruple about accepting such elementary moral regulations for Gentile believers, whereas he was not likely to have thrown away his "fight for Galatia" already won by tamely accepting some ceremonial rules, which at best would smack of a compromise—a line he never conceived possible in Galatians.

Three recent views may be surveyed here. Zuntz regards the decree as originally directed against "the consumption of any kind of meat which from a ritualistic point of view could be regarded as polluting."[15] The argument would be strengthened if πορνεία were regarded as a later insertion. His position is supported by the contention that all three remaining terms—"idol foods," "things strangled," and "blood"—

---

[12] What constitutes *kosher* meat is still a live issue in present-day Judaism; see Rabbi Solomon D. Sassoon, *A Critical Study of Electrical Stunning and the Jewish Method of Slaughter (Shechita)* (1955). For a modern illustration of Jewish sensitivity see Saul Bellow's autobiographical *To Jerusalem and Back: A Personal Account* (1976), pp. 1–4.

[13] On these laws see G. F. Moore, *Judaism*, Vol. 1 (1946), 274f., 339.

[14] This interpretation requires understanding πορνεία as marriage within the prohibited degrees (cf. Vol. 1, p. 229; Bruce, *op. cit.*, p. 271; J. A. Fitzmyer, "The Matthean Divorce Texts and Some New Palestinian Evidence," *TS*, 37 [1976], 197–226).

[15] Zuntz, *loc. cit.*, pp. 224–29.

are most naturally taken to refer to ritual items; the view that πορνεία cannot refer to marriage within forbidden degrees of consanguinity; and the omission of the word πορνεία from the Chester Beatty papyrus, p 45. These are large assumptions, and the last two points can be disputed. In particular, the textual peculiarities of p 45 in this chapter are considerable. Nonetheless, it is worth mentioning Zuntz's demonstration that the entire verse deals with food laws (πορνεία is not so alien a notion in this context, since idolatrous meals are often associated in Jewish law with sexual difficulties). He concludes that the three clauses circumscribe the range of possibility; for such food could be unclean either by its substance (αἷμα: blood left in the carcass) or by the way of its preparation for use (πνικτόν: a strangled animal) or by having previously been offered to idols (εἰδωλόθυτον; cf. vs. 20: "the pollutions of idols").

Second, J. W. Drane has defended the thesis that Paul shifted his ground at the Council and reneged on the teaching of Gentile freedom declared in the Galatian letter. This gave rise to a Jewish Christian ascendancy—seen in 1 Corinthians—which was only checked when Paul later changed his position again and came back to a more centralist stance in writing 2 Corinthians.[16]

A. S. Geyser holds that the decree had validity only in the churches of Syria and Cilicia; and that in the other Gentile churches Paul did not use the decree but tried to convince the erring church members (the "strong" in Corinth and Rome) with arguments based on brotherly love.[17]

On balance, since the textual data in support of the moral interpretation are clearly late and it is difficult to see what justification there might be for altering a moral code into a ceremonial one, we should abide by the first view, and see in Paul's acceptance of the decree—obviously made under pressure—an illustration of his concession to necessity for the sake of the gospel (1 Cor. 9:15-23).[18] Such a conclusion raises inevitably the question of Paul's attitude to the law. Before we turn to that, let us note the sequel to the "apostolic decree."

A delegation of four is appointed to carry a letter with the terms of the "apostolic decree" from Jerusalem to Antioch (15:22-35). It was at Antioch that Christian fellowship between the two branches of the church had been disrupted by the Judaizing teachers claiming James's authority, who insisted on a separation of Jewish Christians from uncir-

---

[16] J. W. Drane, *Paul: Libertine or Legalist?* (1975). These alleged oscillations in Paul's attitude to the law seem to go beyond the evidence. In a later, popular work Drane explains this in terms of Paul's conciliatory attitudes; *Paul* (1976), pp. 54f.

[17] A. S. Geyser, "Paul, the Apostolic Decree, and the Liberals in Corinth," in *Studia Paulina*, pp. 124-38.

[18] H. Chadwick refers to Paul's "flexibility in dealing with situations requiring delicate and ingenious treatment"; "'All Things to All Men' (1 Cor. ix.22)," *NTS*, 1 (1954-55), 261-75.

cumcised Gentile believers, and brought pressure on Peter (Gal. 2:11f.). It was therefore necessary that these Judaizers be checked, that Paul and Barnabas, who had put matters right at Antioch, be vindicated by the general assembly; that independent evidence of the assembly's decision be provided, lest the Antiochians imagine Paul to be inventing all this; and that the terms of Christian fellowship practices should be spelled out clearly, so that the unity and the high moral tone of the church, which was quickly becoming the spiritual home of Gentiles converted to Christ from a world of license, immorality, and self-indulgence, should be preserved (vv. 28f.). The guidance of the Holy Spirit is acknowledged in this epoch-making decision.[19]

The "decree" was evidently well received. The happy outcome of the debate, the approval of the Holy Spirit, and the commendation of the two "prophets" charged with declaring God's mind to the congregations of Paul's churches (cf. 1 Cor. 14:3) all serve Luke's purpose by showing the idyllic conditions in the Camelot of the apostolic age.

PAUL AND THE LAW

There is much confusion in sorting out Paul's precise attitude to "the law," caused mainly by his use of the one Greek term νόμος to do the job of several concepts.[20] This confusion (as far as we are concerned) was inherited from his Jewish past, in which he learned to distinguish three aspects of law.

1. "Law" may stand for a partly moral, partly ceremonial code designed to regulate man's life before God. Paul attached value to this, including the ceremonial parts such as fasting and Temple observance (Acts 21:26ff.). Even the fateful word "circumcision" can receive a neutral treatment in a non-polemical context (1 Cor. 7:19). He expects the

---

[19] The approving of the Spirit is given again at vs. 29 in the Western text where there is the addition of "being borne along by (the) Holy Spirit." A possible reason is suggested by E. J. Epp, *The Theological Tendency of Codex Bezae Cantabrigiensis in Acts* (1966), p. 111, namely, "to counteract any legalistic overtones which might accompany the apostolic letter." A more controverted assessment of the "decree," based on Paul's negative attitude to it, is in D. R. Catchpole's discussion, "Paul, James, and the Apostolic Decree," *NTS*, 23 (1977), 428-44, on which I have drawn in "The Setting of 2 Corinthians," *TB*, 37 (1986), forthcoming.

[20] On the much ventilated topic of Paul's teaching on νόμος several recent studies contain full bibliographies: C. E. B. Cranfield, "St. Paul and the Law," *SJT*, 17 (1964), 43-68; G. E. Ladd, *A Theology of the New Testament* (1975), pp. 495-510; F. F. Bruce, "Paul and the Law of Moses," *BJRL*, 57 (1974-75), 259-79; and H.-H. Esser, "Law," in *NIDNTT*, Vol. 2, pp. 438-56; H. Räisänen, *Paul and the Law* (ET 1983); H. Hübner, *Law in Paul's Thought* (ET 1984), who traces, on exegetical grounds, a line of development and modification in Paul's concept of the law; E. P. Sanders, *Paul, the Law, and the Jewish People* (1983), who argues that Paul's critique of the law is informed by his understanding of christology and election.

Christian to fulfil the spirit of the law (Rom. 13:8,10), but with a new motive.[21]

2. "Law" may also stand for the prescriptions of the Torah in rabbinic Judaism. Under this definition, keeping the law as a means of attaining a right standing before God is misdirected and a positive evil. This attitude can only lead to a concern for merit based on pride and complacency with oneself (Phil. 3:4–9). This is the burden of Paul's attack on nomistic Pharisaism: it results in the dreadful possibility that the law's place will come between the Jew and Christ.[22] Here Torah is often almost personified and equated with a sinful power dominating the life and enticing a person away from the Lord (Rom. 7:9–25; 8:2; Gal. 3:23). In that sense, Christ is the end (τέλος) of the law—for he brings its regime over human life to an end.[23] There is a side-effect even in this: the law convicts humans of their sinful condition by showing to them how hopeless is the quest for personal knowledge of deliverance sought along this route of law-keeping. So Galatians 3:24 declares unequivocally that the law was "our tutor-custodian" as well as our jailor (3:23) to lead us to Christ.

3. The values of the law are conserved when it is seen in its God-appointed way as setting a standard for human life which can be attained only by the person-in-Christ. Paul is not arguing for jettisoning the law of which he approves (Rom. 7:12) as an ideal. The essence of his gospel is that God in Christ offers through the Spirit a dynamic by which the law may be obeyed from the heart and with the right motive (Rom. 8:4). This is the new law of the Spirit of life (Rom. 8:2; 2 Cor. 3:4–18), and following Christ means obeying his law (Gal. 6:2; 1 Cor. 9:21).[24] This is a corrective to any antinomian attitude. In that sense, "we set the law on its true base" (Rom. 3:31).

PAUL AND ISRAEL

We find the same ambivalent attitude in Paul when we consider his relationship to his nation Israel. Any classification runs the risk of being too neat and tidy, but the following positions seem to be attested.

1. Paul never renounced his Jewish heritage (Rom. 9:1–5; Phil. 3:5ff.) and never thought that the Jewish people were finally rejected

---

21 C. F. D. Moule, "Obligation in the Ethic of Paul," in *Christian History and Interpretation,* J. Knox *Festschrift,* edd. Farmer, Moule, and Niebuhr (1967), pp. 389–406. See further G. M. Styler, "The Basis of Obligation in Paul's Christology and Ethics," in *Christ and Spirit in the NT,* C. F. D. Moule *Festschrift,* edd. Lindars and Smalley (1973), pp. 175–87; P. Perkins, "Paul and Ethics," *Interpretation,* 38 (1984), 268–80.

22 This point is well established by W. D. Davies, *Paul and Rabbinic Judaism,* Ch. 8.

23 On Rom. 10:4 see Moule, *loc. cit.,* pp. 402f. NEB mg. reads: "Christ is the end of the law as a way to righteousness for everyone who has faith"; cf. NEB text and Rom. 13:10 for another meaning to be attached to τέλος.

24 C. H. Dodd, "ENNOMOS CHRISTOU," in *Studia Paulina,* pp. 96–110.

even in their unbelief (Rom. 3:1ff.; 11:1ff.).[25] We may contrast what he says in 1 Thessalonians 2:16, which is more in the form of an emotional outburst than a reasoned, sober conclusion. Or else the "Jews" of this verse are *false* Jews, as in 2 Corinthians 11:24; Galatians 2:13; Romans 2:28; Philippians 3:2.[26]

2. Yet the consequences of Jewish unbelief are serious and entail God's judgment, which falls with particular severity on the leaders, who remain blind and self-deceived (Rom. 2:17ff.; 10:3ff.; Gal. 1:6–9; 3:10; 5:4,10).

3. Not all Israel is obdurate and disobedient (Rom. 11:25). There is a token response to Paul's ministry, which he sees as part of divine providence, so that the Gentile mission may take place and this responsiveness may incite Israel to envy at the massive influx of the Gentiles. Hereby he recalls the Old Testament idea of the Gentiles thronging to Zion in the messianic era (Isa. 2:2,3). After the πλήρωμα (full tally) of the Gentiles is brought to Christ, God's purpose will be achieved in the salvation of "all Israel" (Rom. 11:26—a group presumably composed of believing Jews and Gentiles in one church, according to Eph. 2:11ff.).

4. In the interim the mission to Israel must go on (Rom. 1:16*b*) without delay. There must be no mistaking the basis of Paul's appeal—those who respond belong to the true Israel on a spiritual—not racial or national—basis (Rom. 2:28,29; Phil. 3:3). Paul bends over backwards in this appeal to secure the salvation of all who will hear (1 Cor. 9:20–22).

---

[25] See J. Munck, *Christ and Israel. An Interpretation of Romans 9–11* (ET 1967), on the ἀποβολή (casting-away by God) of Israel.

[26] This is the argument of J. Coppens, "Miscellanées bibliques, LXXX. Une diatribe antijuive dans I Thess, II, 13–16," *ETL*, 51 (1975), 90–95.

CHAPTER TEN

From Philippi to Jerusalem

In this chapter we shall look briefly at the leading features of Paul's mission from the time he left Philippi (see below, Ch. 16) to his arrival in Jerusalem, where he was greeted by James, the head of the Jerusalem *Urgemeinde* (original community of Jewish Christian believers). Our main interest will be to spotlight those features of the apostle's missionary work which form a background to an understanding of the Epistles.

THESSALONICA AND BEROEA

The apostolic band (minus Luke, who evidently stayed on at Philippi to consolidate the work there; the "we"-narrative abruptly breaks off at 16:17) moved southward, calling at Amphipolis (30 miles from Philippi) and Apollonia (27 miles further on) en route to Thessalonica (another 35 miles). The excellent Roman roads—this one was the useful *Via Egnatia*—made travel safe and speedy; and both factors were of incalculable importance for the spread of the gospel message in the early days of the church (see above, p. 22).

At Thessalonica (Acts 17:1–9) a three weeks' ministry at the local Jewish meeting-place (vs. 2) gave Paul a chance to set out the scriptural basis of his message. The reaction was true to form: some were won over to faith in Jesus as Messiah and Lord, a response which angered the Jews, who aroused the rabble against the visiting missionaries on the convenient charge that they preached a subversive message calling for disloyalty to Rome (vv. 6f.). The evidence for this accusation was the proclamation of the kingship of Jesus, which the Jews interpreted in a malicious way to mean that the Christian preachers were political agitators, offering a rival emperor to Caesar.[1]

---

[1] E. A. Judge, "St. Paul and Classical Society," *Jahrbuch für Antike und Christentum*, 15 (1972), 19–36, points out that "recently discovered inscriptions have shown that the oath of personal loyalty to Caesar ... was administered through the cities, and that it was expressed in more prescriptive terms than previously known, so that it might have been spoken of as a decree" in Acts 17:7 (p. 26). See too F. F. Bruce, *1 & 2 Thessalonians* (WBC, 1982), pp. xxiii, xxiv. Also to be noted is R. F. Collins, *Studies on the First Letter to the Thessalonians* (1984).

The authorities were not easily taken in by this specious allegation, though they did investigate the claim. Jason, at whose house the apostles were lodging, was required to give an assurance that his guests were not seditiously minded (vs. 9). To make sure, Jason agreed that the apostles should be "bound over" and prevented from speaking in Thessalonica. This explains their immediate departure for Beroea (vs. 10).

We have Paul's later comment on the turn of events which made him rather suddenly have to quit Thessalonica (1 Thess. 2:17). Possibly he would not have accepted the dismissal so tamely, but Jason had given his word to the magistrates and he would abide by that.

So he came to Beroea, sixty miles away. Here the previous pattern of his ministry was repeated. His preaching encouraged the people there to investigate the Scriptures for themselves. Not surprisingly, when this happened, "many of them . . . believed" (vs. 12). Truth personally sought out and discovered is always more vital and precious than ideas handed to us on a platter.

Meanwhile, the infant church at Thessalonica faced a good deal of hardship (see 1 Thess. 1:6; 2:14; 3:3); yet it did not cease its witness to the gospel (1 Thess. 1:8). A later reference in that letter (4:13) probably implies that persecution had caused the premature death of some believers, and the Jewish leaders, determined to crush every outcropping of the church, moved on to Beroea (vs. 13).

Paul had to face fresh opposition from the Thessalonian Jews, and felt it wise to travel on to Athens, using Silas and Timothy as his delegates to encourage the believers in the place he had been forced to flee (vs. 15). It is likely (on the basis of 1 Thess.) that Paul had to meet another kind of insinuation as well. Perhaps he had been accused of cowardice and running away from danger, or of double-dealing by staying at Thessalonica only long enough to get a money-gift from Philippi, and then quickly moving on, hoping to collect more subscriptions from rich ladies en route. So in the Thessalonian letters he seeks to vindicate his character and to account for his actions. To make matters worse, he could not come in person to Thessalonica while Jason's pledge was in force, so he sent two men as his personal representatives.

PAUL AT ATHENS

The apostle's first reaction to what he saw in Athens led to a public ministry of disputation, both in the Jewish synagogue and in the marketplace (Acts 17:16–34).[2] No record is given of his appreciation of the

---

[2] See W. A. McDonald, "Archaeology and St. Paul's Journeys in Greek Lands, Part II—Athens," *BA*, 4 (1941), 1–10. For an up-to-date report of archaeological work at Athens and its bearing on Acts 17 see C. J. Hemer, "Paul at Athens: A Topographical Note," *NTS*, 20 (1973–74), 341–50, who concludes Paul may have made his defense to a court meeting in or before a colonnade of the agora.

city's objects of beauty. What stuck in his mind was its senseless idolatry (vs. 16), a judgment called forth by the excessive religiosity of the Athenians (vs. 22) and their custom of dedicating shrines to a variety of deities (vs. 23).

His encounters with the philosophers who met him occurred in two settings. In the marketplace they overheard his preaching, which they could not understand. He kept referring to "Jesus and the resurrection" (vs. 18), which they probably misconstrued as an allusion to two deities: Jesus and his consort *Anastasis* (the Greek word for "resurrection"). Others dismissed him with the disdainful term "babbler" (literally seed-picker, a slang expression for a worthless person who picked up scraps of food in the markets). But some wished to hear more. The second scene is the Areopagus (vs. 19), a venue for the Athenian court and a meeting point for religious discussion and debate. Luke had a pretty low opinion of what usually went on there (vs. 21); and his verdict was shared by many of his contemporaries.

Paul's apologetic or defense of the faith before the Athenians is a classic statement of what later became known as "natural theology" (an earlier and shorter specimen is Acts 14:15–17). It aims at laying a foundation on which the special revelation of the gospel may be built; but no foundation is ever complete in itself and requires a superstructure to explain its *raison d'être*. Taking his text from an altar reared to an "Unknown God" (vs. 23), Paul proceeds to answer the basic question of all theology, Who is God?

His answers stress the following points: he is Maker, Lord of heaven and earth (vs. 24); he is Spirit, unimprisoned in any earthly temple (vv. 25,29); he is self-existent, in whom all creation lives (vs. 25); and he is the Creator of human beings, whose span of life and dwelling-place on earth are determined by him (vs. 26).[3] If the last phrase of verse 26 ("the boundaries of their habitation") refers to territorial ambitions, then God is also seen as Lord of history, concerned with the rise and fall of national powers. Moreover, he is the source and goal of man's spiritual life (vv. 27f.).[4] Two final attributes (vv. 30,31) are logically connected with this list. As God is one and almighty, with no visible image, all idolatry stands under his judgment, since he is a righteous Lord who summons men to repentance. As Lord of history and of the universe, it is his design to bring the world to its consummation at the final day of reckoning. The proof of this final judgment has been given in Jesus' resurrection from the dead.

---

[3] On translating and interpreting vv. 26 and 27, see M. Dibelius, *Studies in the Acts of the Apostles*, pp. 27–37.

[4] The appositeness of these statements to an audience composed of Stoics and Epicureans (see earlier, pp. 41f.) has been remarked by F. F. Bruce, *The Speeches in the Acts of the Apostles* (1944), p. 18. On the speech as a whole, see also Bruce, "Paul and the Athenians," *ExpT*, 88 (1976), 8–12, with bibliography.

Paul's hearers would have followed him in the preliminary stages of his case, but the mention of repentance (which implies sin), judgment (which involves moral responsibility), and the resurrection and return of Jesus (which ran counter to Greek ideas of immortality, union with God, and the circularity of history) was too much for most of them. Some derided (vs. 32); some deferred (vs. 32); only a few decided for the Pauline gospel (vs. 34). We may ask whether Paul failed in this situation.

PAUL AT CORINTH

Reflecting later on his ministry in this part of southern Greece, Paul called "the household of Stephanas" his first converts in Achaia (1 Cor. 16:15). Since Stephanas was a Corinthian, this suggests that no church—certainly no thriving community—was left in Athens after his departure.

Some scholars infer that on reflection Paul regretted his philosophical and cultural approach to the Athenians, and that 1 Corinthians 2:1-5 mirrors his resolution henceforth to focus his preaching on "Jesus Christ and him crucified."[5] We may doubt this inference, but it does seem clear that the initial response at Corinth was a tremendous encouragement to him, in contrast to the somewhat barren ministry in Athens. In fact, the evidence from his letters is that the church at Corinth turned out to be his main pastoral concern.

The exigencies of the situation at Corinth also may have contributed to his desire to proclaim the "simple gospel" in full reliance on the Holy Spirit (Acts 18:1-23). For Corinth was a flourishing seaport, notorious for its moral laxity and crude ways, the "Vanity Fair" of the Roman Empire. In such an unpromising setting Paul directed his ministry to both Jews and Greeks (vs. 4), and found support in two friends, Aquila and Priscilla, husband and wife, who had been forced out of Italy by an imperial edict aimed at the Jews (c. 49-50).[6] Jewish rabbis were taught a trade, so it is not surprising to read this reference to Paul's craftsmanship (vs. 3). There are a number of important features in Paul's labors at Corinth.

1. *Evangelism.* Verse 5 is best understood as "Paul began to give himself fully to the preaching of the word" once Silas and Timothy

---

[5] N. B. Stonehouse disagrees; *The Areopagus Address* (1949). The links between Paul's sermon at Athens and his teaching in Rom. 1:18-23 would support the view that Paul spoke in character when he was confronted with the Athenian audience. See also F. F. Bruce, "The Speeches in Acts—Thirty Years After," in *Reconciliation and Hope, Festschrift* for L. L. Morris, ed. R. Banks (1974); pp. 64f.; for an illuminating recent study of the twenty-five speeches, see G. A. Kennedy, *New Testament Interpretation through Rhetorical Criticism* (1984), ch. 6.

[6] Or at Christian preachers and their converts, or at both groups. Only a portion of the Jewish population may have been involved in this ban. See E. M. Smallwood, *The Jews under Roman Rule* (1976), pp. 210-16.

arrived. If they brought gifts from Macedonia (cf. 2 Cor. 11:8–9; Phil. 4:15), they probably freed him from the need to divide his time between preaching and his craft, and made a full-time ministry possible.

2. *Strategy.* A decision, following the hardened attitude of the Jews (vv. 6f.), was made to divert his energies into the channel of a mission to the Gentiles (vv. 6, 8) and to set up a rival meeting-place next door to the synagogue. Crispus' conversion, to be followed by that of many Corinthians, seems to have been a direct fruit of this bold venture.

3. *His encouragement* (vv. 9f.). In spite of some success and the strength of Christian fellowship in the work, Paul grew depressed. He needed the heartening reminder and caution of a night-time vision. The message was precisely suited to his immediate situation: "Stop being afraid, and go on speaking." A special promise of the Lord's protecting hand implies that his life was in some peril; and the assurance that his work was not to be in vain (1 Cor. 15:58) must have breathed fresh courage into his jaded spirit.

Chapter 18:12–17 gives details of the kind of opposition Paul met at Corinth (vs. 10). His policy of setting up a rival center next door to the Jewish synagogue led, not unnaturally, to this united attack on him. He was hauled before the tribunal of Gallio, who was proconsul of Achaia in 51–52.[7] In his capacity as local magistrate, Gallio heard the charge (vs. 13) but did not stay for the defendant's reply (vs. 14). He could not be bothered, verse 17 implies, even when a flagrant injustice was done before his eyes—though Luke intends the allusion to Gallio to suggest that at least he was not hostile.[8]

Paul's itinerary took him from Corinth via Ephesus to Antioch, and then back to Galatia to re-visit the churches in that province (vv. 18–23). At Ephesus he parted company with Aquila and his wife (vs. 26; cf. 1 Cor. 16:19, written from Ephesus, where he conveys a greeting from them to their friends at Corinth). The account of Paul's vow (vs. 18) is an interesting one. Based on Numbers 6:1–21, the custom of taking a Nazirite vow was followed by a person setting out on a dangerous journey. The traveler would vow not to cut his hair until the trip was completed; then he would shear his head at a ceremony of thanksgiving in the Jerusalem Temple (21:23f.). Paul's intention, once his hair was cut at Cenchreae, was not to have it cut again until he reached Jerusalem safely. Then the hair would be offered as a token of thankfulness for "journeying mercies." Probably we may understand a visit to Jerusalem in the phrase "went up" (vs. 22). This is Luke's ending of the second missionary tour, the final stage being told with breathless rapidity.[9]

---

[7] See Smallwood (*ibid.,* p. 213n35) for the dating of Gallio's entry into office in AD 51.

[8] E. Haenchen, *Acts,* p. 541.

[9] Bruce observes that "in these two verses [18:22,23] and xix.1 is compressed a journey of 1500 miles"; *The Acts of the Apostles* (1951), p. 350. This reminds us how incomplete the record in Acts is.

PAUL'S EPHESIAN MINISTRY

Paul's work at Ephesus falls into three categories—apostle (19:1-7), apologist (vv. 8-10), and miracle worker (vv. 11-20).

The Ephesian disciples who professed to be ignorant of the Holy Spirit (vs. 2) must have been Gentiles, if we take their statement literally, for Jews would have recalled the Old Testament teaching of Psalm 51:11 and Isaiah 63:10.[10] These were believers (vs. 2) who had been baptized as disciples of John the Baptist (vs. 3). Possibly the description "disciples" (vs. 1) is meant to fit this case (cf. Matt. 14:12) though it is also conceivable that they were disciples of Apollos, whose earlier life as an incomplete believer seems to have matched theirs (18:25).[11]

At all events we are clearly meant to see here the exceptional circumstances of a small group (the number is given in vs. 7 as twelve) who had believed in Christ as the coming one, heralded by John, and received a pre-Pentecostal baptism in anticipation of Messiah's coming. Their Christian knowledge and experience, while sincere and genuine, was defective. There is a transition from the anticipatory baptism of John (and Apollos?) to the fulfilment-baptism which is the norm in the gospel age. Ephesians 1:13 states the accepted sequence explicitly. The aorist participle in the Greek ("having believed") is to be construed as coincident in time with the action of the main verb. "Did you receive the Holy Spirit at the time of your believing?" (Acts 19:2) corresponds exactly to the Pauline teaching, "At the time of your believing you were sealed with the promised Holy Spirit." No interval is envisaged, and the possibility of believing without the sealing of the Spirit is not entertained. This is why the Ephesian disciples were an exceptional case. The story contains a polemic against remaining content with John's baptism and a pre-Pentecostal faith and experience. The Twelve were encouraged to submit to *Christian* baptism, which was followed by apostolic ordination and the gift of "tongues" (vs. 6).

Paul's Ephesian ministry took on the features familiar in our earlier studies of his apostolic career. Ministry in the Jewish synagogue met with opposition and defamation (vv. 8f.), which obliged him to continue on neutral ground. The lecture-hall of Tyrannus became the new meeting-point, made available to Paul during the hot midday hours from 11 a.m. to 4 p.m. (RSV mg.—a credible addition, supplied by the Western text) when the room would be unused.[12] The townspeople would

---

[10] On Acts 19:1-7 see J. D. G. Dunn, *Baptism in the Holy Spirit*, Ch. 8; J. H. E. Hull, *The Holy Spirit in the Acts of the Apostles* (1967), pp. 109-17.

[11] Käsemann, "The Disciples of John the Baptist in Ephesus," in *Essays on New Testament Themes*, pp. 136-48, comments on the argument that "disciple" always means "Christian" in Luke-Acts. C. H. H. Scobie, *John the Baptist* (1964), p. 188, refers to Luke 5:33; 7:18f., where disciples of the Pharisees and of John are mentioned. "The determining factor in the interpretation of 'disciples' in Acts 19:1 must therefore be the context, and the rest of the passage" (*ibid.*).

[12] "At 1 p.m. there were probably more people sound asleep than at 1 a.m." (Lake and Cadbury, in *Beginnings of Christianity*, Vol. 4, p. 239).

then be enjoying their meal and siesta, while Paul and his devoted followers met to present Christ's claims to any who cared to come.

Paul gained some notoriety as a worker of miracles (vs. 11). This reputation induced some itinerant Jewish magicians to capitalize on his success and to try their hand at using the name of Jesus as a formula of exorcism (vs. 13). The spiritual power released by the apostolic ministry had other beneficial effects (vv. 18–20), with a notable display of the gospel's effectiveness to counter and overcome false religion. No price was too high to obtain release from the tyranny of bad religion and crippling superstition which plagued the first-century Hellenistic world (see above, pp. 31f.), and still grips many areas of modern life in spite of the sophistication and technology of contemporary society.

After an intimation (vv. 21f.) of Paul's future plans, including the expression of his desire, which thereafter runs like a thread through the rest of Acts, to visit the imperial city Rome, the story of the dramatic opposition led by Demetrius the silversmith follows. The evidence for opposition in Ephesus is partly factual (like the story of the riot in the amphitheater), and partly inferential (e.g., the hints of a terrible danger to his life, 1 Cor. 15:32; 2 Cor. 1:8–10; cf. Phil. 1:30; 2:17; Rom. 16:3f.).

Paul's preaching was seen as a danger to the silversmiths, but Demetrius' protest may very well have been occasioned also by the social anarchy and unrest that followed the assassination of Junius Silanus in 54. The murder of this proconsul of Asia at the instigation of Agrippina may possibly have been carried out by two men who afterwards stayed on in Asia to oversee the imperial business until a successor to Silanus was appointed. G. S. Duncan makes this interesting suggestion, and thus explains the use of the plural proconsuls (vs. 38) and the fact that Paul's Roman citizenship failed to protect him from the venom of the mob and the authorities.[13]

In God's providence, however, the apostle was able to call on influential local friends (vs. 31). A moderating voice was raised by the Ephesian "town clerk" or head of the municipality (Gk. *grammateus*) (vv. 35–40). Luke relishes the irony of the situation (vs. 32), though it was no doubt an ugly scene for a time until reason prevailed (vs. 41).

PAUL'S VOYAGE TO JERUSALEM

From Ephesus Paul's journeys took him to Macedonia and then to southern Greece (Acts 20:1ff.). Later, as he faced opposition, he decided to return northwards and sail from Neapolis, the port of Philippi (vs. 6), across the Aegean to Troas on his long trip to Jerusalem (cf. vs. 3: "set sail for Syria").

[13] G. S. Duncan, *St. Paul's Ephesian Ministry* (1929), pp. 100ff. For the bearing of this possibility on the date of the prison epistles, see pp. 219f.

In a section which deals with Paul's travels we do well to dig a little below the seemingly uneventful surface, for this was an important period in his life. His visit to Macedonia (vs. 1) was evidently that mentioned in 2 Corinthians 2:12, when he halted at Troas, where he had arranged to meet Titus. This was a critical period in his apostolic service, for he had been insulted at Corinth (2 Cor. 2:5) and had written a "tearful letter" to rebuke the factious Corinthian minority who had opposed his authority. But this letter was not composed easily, as 2 Corinthians 2:4 makes clear. At Troas he was anxious to receive news of the letter's effect, but Titus failed to rendezvous with him there and he decided to cross over into Macedonia (2 Cor. 7:5–13). There good news awaited him as Titus arrived with the report that the Corinthian disturbance was over and the church had voted confidence in him. From Macedonia, he wrote 2 Corinthians, following the letter with a visit (vs. 2), during which he composed the Epistle to the Romans, which was sent out from Corinth.

The return trip, through Macedonia to Troas, brought him a further stage on his eastward journey. It was a slow voyage (compare vs. 6 with 16:11,12), with a hurried stopover at Miletus instead of a diversionary visit to Ephesus (20:16). The reason for this may have been one of time; equally, it may be that he had made things too uncomfortable for a return visit to Ephesus.[14]

Opportunity to make contact with the Ephesian churches was not altogether lost. If Paul could not come to them, they or their leaders could travel to meet him at Miletus (20:17–38). Ministers and church leaders should find special relevance and challenge in these words. Paul's address is the only example in Acts of a speech delivered by him to a Christian community. "Almost certainly Luke heard it himself, and may even have taken shorthand notes," comments F. F. Bruce.[15] Even if that estimate is too optimistic, it carries all the marks of a Pauline composition, especially when compared with the document called the Letter to the Ephesians.

The details of verses 18–21, mainly in the past, relate Paul's type of ministry in Asia. This would be well known to his hearers who, as "elders" (vs. 17) or "overseers" (vs. 28), would have special reason to be grateful for his "all-around" (vs. 20f.), if personally costly (vs. 19), ministry. "The plots of the Jews" (vs. 19) remind us of some far more

---

14 H. Conzelmann, *Die Apostelgeschichte*, pp. 114f.; and *History of Primitive Christianity*, p. 100; E. Haenchen, *Acts*, p. 588. For the collapse of Paul's credibility in the area of Asia around Ephesus and its bearing on the setting of the so-called "Letter to the Ephesians," see below, pp. 232f. Cf. R. P. Martin, *Colossians and Philemon* (NCB), pp. 31f.; Haenchen, *op. cit.*, p. 596, with reference to W. Bauer, *Orthodoxy and Heresy in Earliest Christianity* (ET 1971), pp. 233ff. See R. Jewett, *A Chronology of Paul's Life*, p. 16.

15 "The Speeches in Acts—Thirty Years After," *loc. cit.*, p. 63; cf. J. Dupont, *Le discours de Milet: Testament pastoral de saint Paul (Actes 20,18–26)* (1962); and H.-J. Michel, *Die Abschiedsrede des Paulus und die Kirche, Apg. 20,17–38* (1973).

serious danger to his life than Luke has recorded, as we observed earlier.

Verses 22-27 are in the form of an announcement of what the future holds. Paul is on his way to Jerusalem, fully alive to the perils which beset him (vv. 22f.). In fact, he does not anticipate a return to Ephesus (vs. 25). His life is forfeit, yet expendable if only the divine purpose for which he was called and chosen may be realized (vs. 24).

The concluding parts of this pastoral charge are both exhortation and example (vv. 28-38), with special relevance to the church of Luke's day. Encouragements are given in verses 28,31, and 35. He holds himself up as a model to emulate in verses 31,33, and 34. The call to vigilance and faithfulness is all the more insistent and urgent because of the attacks of heretical teachers (vv. 29f.), whose influence in the later church would become only too apparent (cf. Eph. 4:14; 1 Tim. 4:1-3; Jude; 2 Pet. 2:1-22; 1 John 4:1-6; Rev. 2:2).[15a] The saddest warning is given in the announcement that these heretics will arise "from among your own selves." They will be apostate teachers, who desert the Pauline faith and distort Christian doctrine and ethics in Roman Asia.

Chapter 21:1-14 narrates a further stage in the apostolic sea voyage from Miletus to Tyre. En route they berthed at various ports of call (vv. 1-3) until they reached Tyre on the Syrian coast. There a lengthy process of unloading the ship's cargo meant some delay (vv. 3f.), but Paul redeemed the time by making the acquaintance of Christian friends at Tyre. The church there was probably formed as a result of the missionary dispersal referred to in the story of 11:19. A warning came to Paul, possibly by some inspired utterance in the church assembly, that he should not proceed to Jerusalem (vs. 4b); but he recognized some higher constraint (20:22) impelling him onwards. The cameo in verses 5 and 6 is a touching scene, filled with tenderness and pathos. The final parting came as the two groups of Christians went their own ways: "we went on board the ship ... they returned home."

Chapter 21:7-14 again takes up the theme of prophetic warnings to Paul, this time from Agabus, a noted prophet in the Judaean churches (11:27f.). Both Paul's companions and the Caesarean church sensed the imminent danger, and Paul's refusal to follow their advice was not made lightly or in a foolhardy manner (vs. 13). Like his Master, he was answerable to the divine will of which he had an assurance (Luke 13:31-33). The church eventually accepted his firm persuasion of God's will (vs. 14)—an observation Luke wished clearly to emphasize.

Chapter 21:15-26 continues the story that brings Paul to his destination in Jerusalem. James, the Lord's brother and leader of the church in the city, gave the apostolic travelers a cautious welcome (vv. 18ff.). The response to Paul's celebration of the gospel and its success

---

[15a] All these texts are credibly related to situations in Asia Minor, following the failure of the Pauline mission in the province.

among the Gentile peoples (vs. 19) matched his enthusiasm with a sobering reflection that Paul's ministry had been a source of embarrassment, due partly to a false report (vs. 21), partly to the logical conclusion of his doctrine of salvation by faith alone.

"What then is to be done?" was a natural question, demanding some action (vs. 22) to allay Jewish suspicions that Paul was advocating a wholesale rejection of the Jewish law and its relevance to Jews who became Christians. Underlying the fear of the Jewish party was undoubtedly a healthy regard for moral standards, which occasioned the insinuation that the Pauline message led inevitably to the casting off of all moral restraints in the interests of a supposed freedom and championing of divine grace (as in Rom. 6:1ff.; Gal. 5:13)—an innuendo which dogged Paul all his missionary life.

In fact, Paul had never quarreled with the use of the law for Jewish believers (see Rom. 2:25; 3:1ff., 31; 7:12) and had never renounced his Jewish heritage (1 Cor. 7:18; 9:20; 2 Cor. 11:21ff.). It was the attempt to shackle Gentile converts with the law that called forth his loudest protest, as in Galatians, which was written directly to a Gentile Christian church in a controversial situation.

The evidence for his deep loyalty to his ancestry was provided by his acceptance of a Nazirite vow,[16] both for himself and four men whose expenses—eight pigeons and two lambs in all (referred to in vs. 24)—he paid. He is reminded of the earlier apostolic decree, made binding on the Gentile churches; and since this code (see our earlier discussion of Acts 15) did not infringe Gentile liberty in Christ, he was willing to comply (vs. 26).

There is an indirect element of pathos in the passage (21:27–39). Paul was arrested (vs. 33), and as far as the story in Acts goes, he was never again a free man. Verses 27–32 therefore tell of the apostle's last days of freedom.

Paul's fulfilment of the vow in company with four Jewish Christians (vv. 23f.) was done openly in order to serve as a notification of his ancestral loyalty. But he paid a heavy price for such notoriety. Certain Asian Jews spotted Trophimus, a Gentile from Ephesus, in his company, and drew the conclusion that Paul had taken him into the most sacred and restricted part of the Temple.[17] This was a serious breach; hence the outcry (vs. 28). The gates were shut (on the order of the Temple police chief presumably, vs. 30c; he is referred to at 4:1) to prevent further

---

[16] See H. Greeven, *TDNT*, 2, 775.

[17] This barrier kept non-Jews at a distance from the holy precinct, on pain of death. It is mentioned by Josephus, *Jewish War* 5.193f.; 6.124-6; *Ant.* 15.417; *Contra Apionem* 2.8; and Philo, *Leg. ad Gaium* 212. An inscription giving the warning notice has been discovered: see A. Deissmann, *Light from the Ancient East* (ET 1927), pp. 75f.

trouble;[18] and the Roman tribune took Paul into protective custody (vv. 32f.).

The fury of the crowd is seen both in their uncontrolled demonstration (vs. 34) and their determination to get at Paul, who was carried into the safety of the barracks on the backs of Roman soldiers (vs. 35). Claudius Lysias (23:26) was the tribune's name. He thought that he had carried off a notable prisoner (vs. 38); and before the incident closed, Paul was given a chance to speak to the angry mob, but to no avail (22:22f.). Paul was placed under arrest and eventually taken off into custody.

---

[18] J. Jeremias, *Jerusalem in the Time of Jesus* (ET 1969), pp. 209f.

CHAPTER ELEVEN

Paul en route to Rome, and the Church at Rome

Earlier we observed the importance for Luke's narrative in Acts of the last sections of the story that involve Paul's journey to Rome (see above, pp. 58ff.). Under the surface here are Luke's intentions to show how the apostle's life was at all times under divine protection, how the Roman authorities were in no way hostile, and how it was God's will for Paul to get to the Imperial City.

In what follows we shall concentrate on some points of historical detail in which the author of the book addressed to Theophilus seems to have a particular interest, then move on to consider the origin of Christianity at Rome.

FROM JERUSALEM TO ROME

1. *Paul's Removal from Jerusalem.* After his encounter with the mob and his stormy experience before the Jewish assembly, Paul must have wondered what the outcome would be. His life seemed to hang on a fragile thread, with three serious attempts on it made in two days (21:31; 22:22; 23:10). His autobiographical remark, "often near death" (2 Cor. 11:23), was no poetic expression. The Lord's encouragement was, therefore, timely and to the point (23:11).

Verses 12-15 give the inside story of a plot by fanatical Jews to put Paul out of the way once and for all. They had taken an oath and sought the ready cooperation of the religious authority. But the conspiracy was discovered by Paul's nephew—one of the rare sidelights on his family connections.

The following scene, set in the Roman garrison-house, is a drama of suspense and mystery, with hurried exchanges of information, quick decisions, and sworn secrecy (vs. 22). The name of God does not appear in the swift-flowing narrative, no moral is drawn from the drama, and the characters act and speak like the "men of the world" who might be found in any modern spy tale. Scripture does not moralize unnecessarily, nor is it tediously "pious," as though every character in

129

its story were constantly talking about religion. Yet the undertone of divine providence runs throughout; and God is there, if unseen and unrecognized, in the plans and counter-plans of enemies and friends.

The counter-plan was to abduct Paul by night from Jerusalem to Caesarea, the headquarters of Roman authority in Palestine, with a formidable bodyguard detailed to escort him to Felix, the Roman procurator there. At least, the armed guard accompanied the party to Antipatris. Thereafter the way via the coastal plain was less hazardous, and Paul was only lightly protected.[1]

Lysias wrote a covering letter (23:26–30). Some commentators, impressed by the realistic style of writing, wonder if Luke had actually seen a copy of this letter. Ehrhardt suggests that Luke quotes this letter by way of contrasting "the tumultuous way of Jewish justice with the quiet, mechanical working of Roman justice."[2] Certainly the letter bears the imprint of what a Roman official may well have said in such circumstances, including a touch of embellishment (vs. 27) designed to enhance his own reputation for prompt and decisive action. Strictly speaking, Lysias had not learned of Paul's Roman status until after the arrest, and his motive in rescuing Paul was hardly that of verse 27. He carefully omits an incident which had clearly embarrassed him (22:24–26).

2. *The Accusation Before Felix.*[3] Felix, into whose presence the apostle was ushered, had begun his term as procurator in 52. His tenure was marked by uprisings and fierce counter-measures. As a result of one such commotion and its harsh treatment by Felix he was recalled (24:27), though Nero's termination of his office in AD 58/59 was more because of Felix's incompetence than his cruelty. Yet Tacitus has a low view of him, describing him as "brutal and licentious, behaving as a tyrant but showing the mentality of a slave" (*Hist.* 5.9; cf. *Ann.* 12.54). Luke is kinder (esp. 24:22,23), but does note some basic flaws in his character (24:26,27).[4]

Chapter 24 shows us Paul through the eyes of his enemies (particularly vs. 5), and we learn something of how the earliest Christians had to contend with misrepresentation and implacable hate.

The speech of Tertullus is a delightful parody of the oratory of the second-rate Greek hired pleader; Luke must have enjoyed writing it. It begins with a high-flown compliment, and then quite suddenly subsides into the baldest colloquialism, as if the poor creature could not keep it up.[5]

---

[1] E. M. Smallwood, *The Jews Under Roman Rule* (1976), p. 276.

[2] A. Ehrhardt, *The Acts of the Apostles,* p. 113.

[3] On the legal issues in Paul's Roman trials, see A. N. Sherwin-White, *Roman Society and Roman Law in the New Testament,* Ch. 3. His discussion of the situation described in Acts 23:34f. is especially valuable. See also B. Reese, "The Apostle Paul's Exercise of his Rights as a Roman Citizen," *EQ,* 47 (1975), 138–45.

[4] On Felix see Smallwood, *op. cit.,* pp. 268–80; B. W. Henderson, *Life and Principate of the Emperor Nero* (1903), pp. 363ff.

[5] J. A. Findlay, *The Acts of the Apostles* (1934), p. 205.

Tertullus begins with a palpable exaggeration: "much peace" (vs. 2) is sharply contradicted by the series of uprisings and punitive retaliations which had plagued Felix's tenure (Josephus, *Jewish War* 2.253–63). His rhetoric distorts the facts, trying to denigrate Paul by making him no better than a messianic revolutionary (vs. 5), like the Egyptian revolutionary whom Felix, aided by Jews, had put down (21:38). His sense of justice is perverted (vv. 6b, 7, 8a—RSV mg., which many editors and commentators believe to be authentic).[6] Clearly more needs to be added to explain Paul's "arrest" by the Jews, but Tertullus glosses over any thought that the Jews were ready to lynch their enemy and puts the blame for "violence" on Lysias' head (vs. 7). He hints that there was no need for Felix to bother himself overmuch with this case; let him just release Paul for the Jews to deal with according to their law (vs. 6b).

The main intention of Paul's point-by-point defense before the procurator's tribunal is to show himself innocent of all political charges, and that the real issue between him and the Jews was a *theological* one (vv. 20f.). He contends that his visit to Jerusalem was recent enough that the facts of the case should be known to all (vs. 11). He denies all responsibility as a troublemaker at the time, for he was going about his lawful business (vv. 12,18). In any case, the men who confronted him now were not the real assailants: "Jews from Asia" were the disturbers of the peace (vv. 13,18b,19). The nub of the dispute between Paul and the Jews was a conflicting interpretation of Scripture (vv. 14f.) and a debate over theology (vs. 21). The implication was clear: he had a clear conscience over the charges of supposed agitation (vs. 16) and the matter before the procurator had no political significance. The "one thing" was a domestic affair which ought to be settled peacefully.

In the course of this brief statement Paul had indirectly made his position clear. He was and always had been a loyal Israelite (vs. 14) with a faith built on the Old Testament revelation which, as prophetic Scripture, looks beyond itself to the fulfilment of divine promises. Part of that faith is an expectation of resurrection (vv. 15,21), which was a Pharisaic tenet also. From this belief it is a short step to the central Christian article of faith: the resurrection of Jesus, which validated his messiahship as Israel's king and savior. Paul was no iconoclast; he had no taste for acting irresponsibly and upturning his ancestral beliefs (vs. 16). Quite the contrary: he had come to Jerusalem with money for Jewish Christians as a token of charitable concern and a proof of unity among the one people of God (vs. 17).[7]

Felix deferred the case. Luke describes a notable interview which brought the two men together (vv. 24,25). Felix wanted to hear

---

[6] E.g., F. F. Bruce, *Commentary on Acts* (1952), *ad loc.*; Haenchen, *Acts*, p. 653n4.
[7] On this gift, see C. H. Buck, "The Collection for the Saints," *HTR*, 43 (1950), 1–29; K. F. Nickle, *The Collection* (1966); R. P. Martin, *2 Corinthians* (WBC, 1985), pp. 256–58.

the Christian missionary speak on a vital theme; Paul, for his part, refused to fawn in front of those who had the power to set him free. The triad of "justice" (better "righteousness," in the sense of Rom. 1–4, as a divine standard by which human life is tested and condemned, and a divine offer in the gospel), "self-control," and "future judgment" was hardly calculated to make the preacher popular. These may have been "the very subjects that Felix and Drusilla most needed to hear about,"[8] but this was certainly not what they *wanted* to be reminded of. Terrified, Felix cut short the interview. Paul was given further opportunities (vs. 26b), evidently without making much of an impression on this dilettante. In any case, Felix seems not to have seen the injustice in holding in detention a blameless man (vs. 27). So much for his religious interest.[9]

3. *The Arrival of Festus and Paul's Appeal.* Porcius Festus succeeded to the office of procurator at Caesarea in AD 58/59. Virtually nothing is known of him apart from what Luke and Josephus tell us.[10] Paul's fortunes seem unchanged. Apparently hoping to keep the Jews quiet (24:27), the Roman authorities were unwilling to decide his case. A second deputation of Jews, sent from Jerusalem, had nothing new to say and repeated the old, unfounded charges (25:7). Paul simply denied any complicity (vs. 8).

Then came the decision-laden question. "Do you wish to go up to Jerusalem?" (vs. 9). The prisoner was clearly at the crossroads. To say yes would play into the hands of his accusers, suggesting that they had a case to answer and were competent to judge it. Besides, his safety was involved, and he probably suspected the planned attempt on his life (vs. 3). On the other hand, to refuse now might alienate Festus and lose the protection of Roman custody. In his deliberate reply, Paul probably used the technical phrase for the privilege to which he was entitled as a citizen of the empire: *Caesarem appello*—"I appeal to Caesar" (vs. 11).[11] This at once quashed all local proceedings and transferred his case to the imperial court of Nero in Rome, as Festus perceived in consulation with his advisors (*consiliarii*) (vs. 12). So, in a roundabout way, the divine purpose was strangely carried forward (23:11).[12]

---

[8] F. F. Bruce, *The Acts of the Apostles* (1951), p. 427.

[9] For some reasons why Felix refused to take action, see Ehrhardt, *op. cit.*, pp. 115f., and, by contrast, Haenchen, *op. cit.*, pp. 658f., 663.

[10] Ehrhardt calls him "the one honourable governor Rome ever sent to Judaea" (*op. cit.*, p. 117). Luke's characterization of Festus is both friendly and frank, depicting him as a benighted pagan, for whom there is yet hope.

[11] H. J. Cadbury's essay, "The Appeal to Caesar," *Beginnings of Christianity*, Vol. 5, Note XXVI (1933), pp. 312–19, is still fundamental, to be updated by A. N. Sherwin-White, *op. cit.*, pp. 57ff., and F. F. Bruce, *New Testament History*, pp. 339ff. See also A. H. M. Jones, *Studies in Roman Government and Law* (1960), pp. 67ff.

[12] Haenchen, *op. cit.*, p. 669.

Verses 13–22 portray a courtesy visit by Herod Agrippa II, with his sister Bernice, to the newly installed Festus. Agrippa was a somewhat influential political figure, important as a tetrarch of some districts in north Palestine and as the secular authority who appointed the high priests. His state visit gave Festus a chance to mention Paul's case (vv. 13,14), not to re-try him (which was now beyond his power, since Paul had appealed directly to the emperor), but simply to get information for the dossier to be sent to the imperial court. One cardinal Christian truth had penetrated into his mind (vs. 19), which proves that the general debate over the resurrection of the dead turned on the case of *one* particular resurrection. This special application of a principle was more than the Pharisees could believe or allow; but at least the pagan Roman had the wit to see what Paul was continually talking about.

4. *The Speech before Agrippa.* After a brief introduction deferential to "king" Agrippa, whose Jewish ancestry would give him a special sympathy with Paul's case, the apostle begins his "defense" in three sections.

a. The story of his past life is told (26:4–11). This may be summed up as "sincere, but wrong," with verse 9 as its epitome. Yet, in a strange way, the Christians were simply announcing in Messiah's resurrection (vs. 8) a special application of a tenet cherished by all good Pharisees (vv. 6f.).

b. The crisis of his conversion is indicated (vv. 12–15). His encounter with the living Lord was a judgment on his past life and a new beginning, memorably called elsewhere a new creation (2 Cor. 5:17). In the darkness of his ignorance and folly, the light of God had shone (vs. 13); and the real meaning of his persecuting zeal was made known (vv. 14f.), for in attacking his people, Saul was wounding Christ himself—a fearful possibility he never forgot (1 Cor. 8:11–13),[13] which probably became the basis of his teaching on the church as Christ's body (see 1 Cor. 12:12; cf. Eph. 1:23; 2:16; 5:23,29f.).

c. The terms of his commission are given (vv. 16–18). This account of what the Lord said to Paul is the most detailed we have, sketching the life-work of the future apostle to the Gentiles from the initial experience of personal knowledge of Christ to the establishment of Pauline churches. Notice the effect of the gospel ministry, which includes conversion, deliverance, forgiveness, and a place in the new society of Christ's people (vs. 18). All these benefits recur in Paul's writings (notably in Colossians), and suggest that Luke's resumé is based on some reliable information of what was said at the time.

When the facts are examined, Paul concluded, there is nothing anti-Jewish in the message he brought; rather, it complements and brings to fulfilment the Old Testament hope of a Messiah, humiliated

[13] Cf. J. A. T. Robinson, *The Body* (1952), pp. 55–58.

yet vindicated, the author of God's blessings to all—Jews and Gentiles (vv. 22f.).

Festus was plainly out of his depth. Much study, Qoheleth remarked, is a weariness of the flesh (Eccl. 12:12); the Roman governor pronounced it a danger to sanity (vs. 24). Paul repelled that charge by insisting that his Christian knowledge and experience were based on the opposite of "madness," namely, soberness, the possession of a right mind (cf. 2 Tim. 1:7). Christianity makes no claims which are irrational in the sense of being contrary to reason (cf. vs. 8), though there is much that is *above* human reason, and may be known only by faith.

The interchange between Paul and Agrippa (vv. 26–29) is interesting. The Christian preacher confidently appealed to what was public knowledge, and he pressed home the appeal. Agrippa eased himself off the horns of the dilemma with a facetious retort: "In short (or in such an easy way), you are trying to persuade me to play the Christian." Paul picked up the king's words: "The long and the short of it is: I wish that you and all who hear me today could *become as I am* (as opposed to "play a part"), but not as a prisoner!"[14]

Estimates of Paul's appearance before Agrippa have varied. Cadbury thinks the scene was artificially contrived by Luke to impress Theophilus.[15] But there is historical verisimilitude in the arrangement of this gala performance, which befitted the presence of a representative of Rome on a state visit. Agrippa, a suzerain prince, was a Roman citizen in high standing. Luke's motive in the account is probably rather to show how exchanges between Christians and Roman authority brought nothing adverse to the former to light. To be sure, the audience was not converted—or even favorably impressed. But the hostility is caused by Paul's religious beliefs, not his social or political philosophy.

A key notion emerges in verse 26: "This was not done in a corner." This idea, Haenchen says, "light(s) up Luke's presentation in Acts from beginning to end."[16] Christianity is a public religion, open to inspection, not wrapped in the mists of obscure legend; and in Luke's time it was a factor in world history.

5. *En route to Rome.* Commentators praise the vividness and accuracy of the narrative (27:1—28:15) of Paul's sea voyage from Palestine to Italy; it is "one of the most instructive documents for the knowledge of ancient seamanship."[17] Paul's cherished ambition to get to Rome was

---

[14] See F. F. Bruce, *The Speeches in the Acts of the Apostles* (1944), p. 25; but cf. N. Turner, *Grammatical Insights into the New Testament* (1965), pp. 97–99; Haenchen, *op. cit.*, p. 689.

[15] Cadbury, *The Book of Acts in History* (1955), p. 43.

[16] Haenchen, *op. cit.*, p. 691; M. Hengel, *Acts and the History of Early Christianity*, p. 60.

[17] H. J. Holtzmann, quoted by F. F. Bruce, *The Acts* (1951), p. 450. See James Smith, *The Voyage and Shipwreck of St. Paul* (1880). At a different level, cf. E. Haenchen, "Acta 27," in *Zeit und Geschichte: Festschrift* R. Bultmann (1964), pp. 235–54. Grounds for dismissing the story as a piece of Lukan artistry are that it can be

made good, though in circumstances he could not have relished, and by this long journey the divine promise (23:11) was realized.

Paul had traveling companions all the way; Aristarchus is named in verse 2; and Luke's presence in the party is signaled by the "we"-section beginning there. The centurion Julius showed consideration to his Christian prisoner, even permitting him to make contact with his fellow-believers at Sidon. Verse 3 probably means that he allowed Paul's friends to visit him on board before they disembarked.

Having transshipped at Myra, the party sailed on a grain ship bound for Italy. The next stage of the voyage was slow and difficult, owing to unfavorable winds and the dangerous coastal rocks. At Fair Havens Paul came forward with a suggestion (vs. 8). The inference is that the ship's captain should have anchored in the security of Fair Havens bay during the stormy season, but his advice was ignored (vs. 11), since the crew hoped to get to Phoenix to winter there (vs. 12).

The sailors were deceived into thinking that a gentle southerly wind augured well (vs. 13). Putting out from Fair Havens, the ship coasted along the shore of Crete, only suddenly to be struck by the Euraquilo, a fierce northeasterly gale sweeping down from Mount Ida in Crete, which quickly had the vessel out of control (vs. 15). The danger was that the strong waves would overwhelm the ship or smash its structure (hence the measure which was taken of undergirding the ship, vs. 17), or drive it helplessly on to the Syrtis, a dreadful whirlpool and quicksands off the North African coast. It was not the first time Paul had faced the perils of a storm (2 Cor. 11:26). From his past experience and present faith he speaks words of cheer, explanation, giving grounds for his confidence and courage, and testimony. One man's presence and faith made all the difference.

After two weeks of drifting at the mercy of the elements came the first signs that Paul's promise was true. The sailors sensed that they were nearing shore as they took soundings (vs. 28) and possibly heard the thud of breakers on the shore. Anchors were dropped to brake the vessel; and Paul again showed his leadership in preventing a party of sailors from saving their own skins at the expense of the rest (vv. 30–32). Among the crew and passenger list of 276 he stands out for his practical faith and sturdy common-sense (vs. 34). The angelic vision and the divine promise of safety were proof enough for him, and he was prepared to act upon the assurance which had come to him (vs. 34b). With his splendid example to encourage them the rest of the ship's complement took fresh heart (vv. 35f.).

---

detached stylistically from the foregoing narrative; sea stories were common in ancient literature; and Luke (since "we"-sections are artistically contrived) would have no personal knowledge of how Paul got to Rome (Conzelmann, *Apostelgeschichte,* pp. 150f.). But see R. P. C. Hanson's robust rejoinder in *SE,* 4 (1968), 315–18. See now C. J. Hemer, "First Person Narrative in Acts 27–28," *TB,* 36 (1985), 79–109, for a full discussion of the storm-scene.

The shipwreck scene is dramatically painted in the remaining verses of the chapter. The sailors severed the cables and left the anchors in the sea. At the same time, unleashing the steering-paddles and hoisting the foresail to catch a wind, they drove the ship on to the shore. The beaching operation worked. The ship struck a spit of land which jutted out where the two seas met (vs. 41, RSV mg.), and the prow became embedded in the sandbank of the promontory, while the stern was broken up by the force of the sea (vs. 41).

The soldiers' plan to kill the prisoners to prevent their escaping in the confusion of the shipwreck was thwarted—for Paul's sake, to whom everyone owed a great deal. We can only guess by what method—swimming, clutching a plank, or holding part of the ship's spar—Paul and Luke reached land.

The island on which the storm-tossed sailors found refuge was Malta[18] (a Phoenician word meaning "escape," which may lie behind Luke's wording in 28:1). Rain and cold added to their miseries, so the warmth of a fire (vs. 2) was especially appreciated, as the historian records.

The incident of the viper's sudden appearance from among the firewood Paul was helping to gather illustrates popular opinion on the island. The first reaction was to see this as a judgment on Paul, who may have been easily recognizable as a prisoner by his dress or perhaps by a chain. Since no ill effects followed, the Maltese—illustrating graphically the fickleness of human nature—changed their tune and hailed Paul as a god. Bruce draws the interesting contrast in this reversal of opinion "with the attitude of the Lycaonians in 14:11ff., who first acclaimed him as a god, and later nearly stoned him to death."[19]

The layover on Malta illustrates the dictum "one good turn deserves another." On the one hand, Publius extended to the apostle some friendly hospitality which lasted three days (vs. 7); on the other, he received the added happiness of seeing his father cured of gastric fever and dysentery following the visit and prayer of Paul (vs. 8). Paul's healing ministry became widely known, and sick folk throughout the island saw a chance to be healed by this Christian leader whom the ocean had washed up on to their beach. They showed their gratitude by the offer of gifts and ship's stores (vs. 10).

Luke does not attach any deeper spiritual significance to these incidents. Did Paul preach the gospel as he exercised a ministry of prayer and healing? Were any Maltese won for Christ? Did the apostolic party leave behind a Christian community? The record is silent; but we

---

[18] Or a Dalmatian island now called Mljet; A. Acworth, "St. Paul's Shipwreck," in *St. Paul: Traveller and Teacher*, ed. I. Bulmer-Thomas (1975), pp. 79–84. See O. F. A. Meinardus, "St. Paul Shipwrecked in Dalmatia," *BA*, 39 (1976), 145–47; but C. J. Hemer has replied to Acworth in "Euraquilo and Melita," *JTS*, n.s. 26 (1975), 100–111. See too Hemer, *TB*, 36 (1985), 79, n.1.

[19] F. F. Bruce, *The Acts of the Apostles* (1951), p. 471.

may surely believe that here was an evangelistic opportunity too good to be missed.

The Roman writer Pliny the Elder informs us that the winter season, when the seas were closed for navigable traffic, ended on February 7,[20] and we may infer that the three months' stay on the island ended about that time of the year (vs. 11). The ship in which they resumed their journey was another Alexandrian grain ship which bore as a figure-head the Heavenly Twins (Castor and Pollux, the patron saints of navigators in the ancient world).

The course led them at last to Puteoli in the Bay of Naples. In this flourishing seaport a Christian fellowship was contacted, and Paul and his company had a week with them. The last leg of the long journey brought them via the Appian Way to within sight of the Imperial City.

6. *Rome at Last.* The narrative moves to its zenith, as Bengel observed in his classic remark: "The victory of the Word of God: Paul at Rome, the climax of the Gospel, the conclusion of Acts." Paul's effort to clear himself with Jewish leaders at Rome failed, although he was able to make plain the reason for his being in Rome as a prisoner (vv. 17–20) and to testify, at a conference called for the purpose, concerning "the hope of Israel" (vs. 20) and the central theme of the gospel message (vs. 23).

As on so many previous occasions, such preaching divided his hearers into two camps (vs. 24; cf. 1 Cor. 1:18; 2 Cor. 2:15f.). The unconvinced Jews left in total disarray (vs. 25; cf. vs. 29—RSV mg.), and Paul clinched his point with a quotation from the Old Testament and with a hint of the teaching amplified in Romans 9–11 that the Gentiles have received mercy because of the disobedience of Israel (Rom. 11:30)—also a leading motif in Luke's record of how the gospel was brought from Jerusalem to Rome.

"They will listen" (vs. 28) is the final thrust of the Pauline testimony that Luke intends the reader to recognize and ponder. Israel's salvation, rejected by its national representatives and leaders, is now offered to the Gentiles, and nothing can stop the onward march of God's truth to the "ends of the earth" (1:8). Paul's "free custody," as the Romans called it (vv. 30f.),[21] gave him opportunity to do the work of an evangelist among an audience which had free access to the hired room, which was his prison-cell. The closing words "quite openly and unhindered" stress both his personal confidence and the unrestricted scope he enjoyed to proclaim the message of Christ.

---

[20] Pliny, *Natural History* 2.122; Josephus, *Jewish War* 2.203 reports that envoys from Rome to Caesarea were delayed three months during the winter season.

[21] Or *custodia militaris,* as distinct from the more severe confinement of *custodia publica.*

These two elements—the preacher's boldness and an all-embracing proclamation—are interwoven in the fabric of the history of Acts as it speaks of the good news: "It began at Jerusalem; it finishes at Rome. Here, O Church, is your model. It is your duty to keep it and to guard your deposit."[22]

THE ORIGIN OF THE CHURCH AT ROME

1. *Roman Christianity before Paul.* A debatable issue raised but not answered in the history of the early church is how the gospel first reached the Imperial City. The biblical evidence to answer this question is negligible: possible data are Acts 2:10; 18:2; Rom. 16; Heb. 13:24; 1 Pet. 5:13.[23] Early Christian tradition attests to the founding of the Roman church by Peter and Paul. Irenaeus is one source for this opinion (*Adv. Haer.* 3.3.1f.; cf. Eusebius, *HE* 6.1). Eusebius cites Dionysius, bishop of the Corinthians, to the effect that Peter and Paul "together taught in Italy" (*HE* 2.25.8; 4.23); and he also (3.25.7), quoting Gaius, a contemporary of Bishop Zephyrinus (198–217), draws attention to evidence that the two apostles were martyred in Rome: "You will find the trophies (τὰ τρόπαια) of those who founded this church" among the memorial places on the Ostian Way.[24] Increased interest in these memorial places has arisen as a result of recent excavations in and near Rome. Earlier skepticism that Peter and Paul ever set foot in Rome[25] is difficult to justify. There is a growing consensus, since the work of Duchesne and Lietzmann on the literary sources and the more recent finds considered by Toynbee and Ward Perkins, Cullmann, and D. W. O'Connor, that the bodies of the apostles were first buried at or near the place of execution in Rome and in 258, at the time of the persecution under Valerian, taken to the Christian catacombs under San Sebastiano; thence they were transferred in the fifth century to the basilicas built for this purpose by Constantine.[26]

The New Testament evidence pertaining to the establishment of

---

[22] Bengel's comment, to indicate that "the programme mapped out in i.8 has been carried through" (Bruce, *op. cit.,* p. 481).

[23] On these texts see F. F. Bruce, *New Testament History,* Ch. 29; L. E. Elliott-Binns, *The Beginnings of Western Christendom* (1948), pp. 91–100; F. J. Foakes Jackson, *Peter: Prince of Apostles* (1927), Ch. 15; G. Edmundson, *The Church in Rome in the First Century* (1913), Ch. 1 and *passim.*

[24] On this text, see J. Lowe, *Saint Peter* (1956), pp. 33ff.

[25] Cf. K. Heussi, *War Petrus im Rom?* (1927).

[26] L. Duchesne, *Origines du culte* (1925; ET *Christian Worship*[5], 1949, pp. 277ff.); H. Lietzmann, *Petrus und Paulus in Rom*[2] (1927); J. M. C. Toynbee and J. B. Ward Perkins, *The Shrine of St. Peter and the Vatican Excavations* (1956); O. Cullmann, *Peter: Disciple, Apostle and Martyr*[2] (ET 1962); D. W. O'Connor, *Peter in Rome* (1969); J. Lowe, *op. cit.,* p. 37; F. F. Bruce, *New Testament History,* pp. 348, 385–89; H. Chadwick, "St. Peter and St. Paul in Rome: The Problem of the Memoria Apostolorum ad Catacumbas," *JTS,* 8, n.s. (1957), 31–52. A. A. de Marco, *The Tomb of St. Peter* (1964), surveys the bibliography.

the church at Rome fails to make these statements conclusive. The most we can know as a certainty are the following items.

a. The letter to the Romans shows that Paul was unknown to his readers at the time of his writing. He had never visited the city then (1:13), nor did he know anything of Peter's presence in the city there, unless Romans 15:20 refers to Peter in the phrase "another man's foundation."[27]

b. It is virtually impossible that Peter should have founded the church at Rome before 49, for his activities so far as our records go were mainly based in Jerusalem. Acts 12:17 poses a well-known historical problem, but there is no compelling reason to conclude that Peter's departure to "another place" means that he left Jerusalem for Rome in 42.[28]

c. "Ambrosiaster" certifies that the early origins of the church were Jewish, which suggests that Christians returned from Jerusalem (Acts 2:10) and organized churches spontaneously. Romans 1:7 points to the existence of house-groups, for which Judge argues on the basis of Romans 16, which includes at least five sets of names in such a way as to suggest such groups.[29] The evidence in the Epistle seems to imply a decentralized form of Christianity, though the letter was intended to be read to an assembled company. This situation is to be approximately dated in the year 58.

By 64/65 the church grew to the extent that 1 Clement could speak of the martyrs under Nero as a "great number of the elect" and Tacitus wrote of "a huge crowd."[30] For later sidelights on the church at Rome, 1 Clement—a document from Rome to the church at Corinth (AD 96)—and Ignatius' To the Romans (e.g., 4:3) are to be appealed to. Both testify to the vigor and importance of the church in the Imperial City.

One further datum of the church at Rome would be available if W. Manson's theory is correct that the Letter to the Hebrews was sent to a Jewish-Christian house-church in Rome, urging them to remain loyal to their new allegiance and not to go back to the synagogue nor to be discouraged by the persecutions suffered by their banishment in 49 (Acts 18:2; cf. Heb. 10:32–34). On this reckoning, Hebrews 12:4, with its summons to courage in view of impending suffering and the prospect of martyrdom, gives an ominous foreboding of what lay ahead in 65, when fierce persecution broke out.[31]

---

[27] Edmundson, op. cit., pp. 82f.
[28] See D. W. O'Connor, op. cit., pp. 10f., for a discussion of the various theories built on Acts 12:17. Edmundson, op. cit., Ch. 3, follows Jerome's witness, postulating a stay in Antioch (47–54), prior to Peter's second visit to Rome in 54–56.
[29] E. A. Judge, The Social Pattern of Christian Groups in the First Century (1960).
[30] But see E. T. Merrill, Essays in Early Christian History (1924), pp. 100f., on Tacitus' phrase, multitudo ingens.
[31] W. Manson, The Epistle to the Hebrews (1951). This is only one way to read the evidence in Hebrews, as we shall see later (p. 353). Cf. Merrill, op. cit., pp. 114f. O.

2. *Nero's Pogrom and its Aftermath.*[32] The blow fell on Roman Christians at midnight, July 19, 64, when part of the city caught fire and ten districts (out of fourteen) were quickly ablaze. The imperial palace itself was destroyed. There were rumors that Nero was responsible for this arson and intended to destroy the city with a view to a rebuilding and beautification program. Later Roman writers point in this direction, even calling the fire "Nero's conflagration" (Pliny the Elder).[33] As the suspicion of his complicity lingered on, Nero tried to scotch the rumors by providing scapegoats, settling on the Christians in Rome, probably in the spring of 65. They were a large group, known for their anti-social attitudes, and were at this time distinct from the Jews (who were protected by Roman law as adherents of a *religio licita*). Contemporary Roman writers were contemptuous of Gentile Christians. They may have learned, through torturing some, of the Christian belief that the world would be consumed by fire (cf. 2 Pet. 3),[34] and used this to justify their fierce hostility against them. The real cause was not arson but the anti-social ways of the Christians, their "hatred of the human race."[35] Their execution for the entertainment of the callous Roman citizens in Nero's gardens was arranged, and Christians were cruelly killed.[36] 1 Clement 6 may be read for a commentary; and the impression of Rome and especially Nero as an antichrist monster remained, to be revived at the time of Domitian according to Revelation 13:11–18; 17:10f. (see below, pp. 375–77).

Cullmann, *Peter,* pp. 105f., uses the evidence of Phil. 1:12–18 to throw light on the divisions within the Roman church during Paul's captivity. But this is built on several assumptions as to the date of Philippians and a comparison with 1 Clem. 5. See R. P. Martin, *Philippians (TNTC,* 1959), p. 72.

[32] See Paul Winter, "Tacitus and Pliny," *Journal of Historical Studies* (1967), 31–40. E. T. Merrill, *op. cit.,* Ch. 4, provides a useful discussion of the texts, to be supplemented by E. Stauffer, *Christ and the Caesars* (ET 1955), Ch. 9; F. F. Bruce, *op. cit.,* pp. 378–82, 389. Also see J. A. T. Robinson, *Redating the New Testament,* pp. 221–53.

[33] *Nat. Hist.* 17.5. The phrase *"Neronis principis incendia"* may have been added later (Merrill, *op. cit.,* p. 84n1); but cf. Dio Cassius, *Hist.* 62.16.

[34] Tacitus reports that "through information furnished by them a large number were condemned." J. Stevenson, *A New Eusebius* (1957), p. 3, refers also to Rev. 18:8–10, 17f.; 19:3 (the destruction of the city by fire) for an earlier Christian belief, which may have become the ground for an accusation of arson. See Robinson, *op. cit.,* pp. 249–53, for the setting of these descriptions in Rome. Recently Z. Yavetz has suggested that neither Nero nor the Christians were the likely culprits who were guilty of setting Rome ablaze. More probably unknown enemies of the emperor—at a time when Nero's reputation was low—did the job; "Forte an Dolo Principis Tac. Ann. 15.38," in *The Ancient Historian and his Materials,* ed. B. Levick, pp. 181–97.

[35] Tacitus's explanation for the seizure of Christians is their *odium generis humani,* though Merrill may well be correct that "the primary charge before his [Nero's] court must certainly have been arson" (*op. cit.,* p. 126). Tacitus is exhibiting here his contempt for both Nero and the Christians (Yavetz, *loc. cit.,* p. 194).

[36] Nero's device backfired, and the "populace was shocked by the manner of the executions, instead of amused" (Merrill, p. 129).

At this time, under Nero, tradition has it that Peter and Paul were martyred. We shall leave the question of the exact date when this occurred and the tradition that Paul was released at the end of his two-year confinement and undertook further travels for our discussion of the Pastoral Epistles (see below, pp. 298–307).

PART FOUR

The Pauline Corpus of Letters

The words of St. Paul, said Martin Luther, are not dead words; they are living creatures, and have hands and feet.[1] Generations of Christian people would agree with this picturesque remark; and, as the Christian faith encircles the earth, Paul's words still speak to the human condition in a way that would be difficult to account for unless there was an intrinsic truth in his claim that he was uttering the words of God in the Spirit (1 Cor. 2:10–16).

It is just as evident that there is a human side to Paul's writing, since all the Epistles emerge from a social matrix of life in the early communities and are composed against a historical background. To explore that setting and to try to read the historical Paul in his first-century context is the aim of these chapters. But the task is not easy. For one thing, we have only Paul's side of the conversation, except in those few instances where he quotes from the churches' letters or alludes directly to his opponents' reported notions. Another difficulty is that Paul is not a systematic writer.[2] Among the characteristic features of his letters are emotional and pastoral outbursts—of indignation, reproof, counsel, and admonition. It requires great agility of mind to keep pace with the flow, often erratic and unexpected, of Paul's pen.

Finally, there are the cultural, linguistic, conceptual and theological barriers to be crossed as we in the twentieth century try to get on the wavelength of this man of the ancient world. To many of our contemporaries this is the problem that cannot be overcome. They see Paul as ein antik denkender Mensch, a man whose thoughts are dated by the age in which he lived. Their sentiments are captured in the words of the Pardoner in Sir David Lindsay's Three Estates:

---

[1] Quoted on the title page of Arthur S. Way, *The Letters of St. Paul*[7] (1935). John Donne said, "Wheresoever I open St. Paul's epistles I meet not words but thunder, and universal thunder, thunder that passes through the world"; quoted in M. Muggeridge and A. R. Vidler, *Paul: Envoy Extraordinary* (1972), p. 12.

[2] Dibelius' dictum, "Paul's thinking is opportunist, not systematic" (*als Gelegenheitsdenker, nicht Systematiker*), *Paul* (ET 1953), p. 40, may be recalled.

By him that bore the crown of thorn,
I would Saint Paul had never been born;
or by the claim of the contemporary British politician Lord
Boothby, who regards Paul as the archfoe of "true religion."[3] In
any case the attempt to come to terms with Paul is treated as not
worth the effort.

But we owe it to ourselves to exert our intellectual endeavor
to understand Paul even in the face of these hurdles. To recall his
influence on the great leaders of the church—Augustine, Luther,
Calvin, Wesley, Barth—is to be set on the inquiry as to what there
was about this man that has made that influence so pervasive and
so profound.[4]

Paul, as a child of his age, addressed his contemporaries.
Far more important, as prophet and apostle of the kingdom of God,
he speaks veritably to all people of every age. Here is a claim worthy
of putting to the serious test. Karl Barth continues: "If we rightly
understand ourselves, our problems are the problems of Paul; and
if we be enlightened by the brightness of his answers, those answers must be ours."[5]

[3] Lindsay is cited in A. M. Hunter, *Interpreting Paul's Gospel* (1954), p. 13. The
reference to Lord Boothby is cited from William Barclay, in *ExpT,* 78 (1966–67),
32. See also J. W. Fraser, *Jesus and Paul: Paul as Interpreter of Jesus from
Harnack to Kümmel* (1974), p. 9. For Paul as a "morbid crank," see H. J. Schoeps,
Paul (ET 1961), pp. 276f. On the broader issue of Paul's role in the eyes of
his fellow Jews see D. A. Hagner, "Paul in Modern Jewish Thought," in *Pauline
Studies. Essays Presented to F. F. Bruce,* edd. D. A. Hagner and M. J. Harris
(1980), pp. 143–65.

[4] C. K. Barrett, *A Commentary on the Second Epistle to the Corinthians* (Harper-
Black, 1973), p. vii, writes this tribute: "Like most people, I sometimes wonder if
Christianity is true; but I think I never doubt that, if it is true, it is truest in the
form it took with Paul, and after him, with such interpreters of him as Augustine,
Luther, Calvin, and Barth."

[5] K. Barth, *The Epistle to the Romans* (ET 1933), preface to the first ed., p. 1. Recall
Kierkegaard's reminder: "I have not got to listen to St. Paul because he is clever,
or even brilliantly clever; I am to bow before St. Paul because he has divine
authority" (quoted by Muggeridge and Vidler, *op. cit.,* p. 13).

CHAPTER TWELVE

Paul's Struggle for Galatia

"The Epistle to the Galatians is spiritual dynamite, and it is therefore almost impossible to handle it without explosions."[1] This striking assessment is illustrated and confirmed by the part its message played in Luther's spiritual awakening and development and in John Wesley's assurance of faith. John Bunyan claimed to have preferred Luther's commentary on Galatians to all the other books he had read except the Bible.[2] Galatians speaks powerfully to any reader who comes to it with a sympathetic understanding and a desire to enter into Paul's conflict with the Galatian agitators. But we shall appreciate its relevance more fully if we try to understand its historical setting.

WHO WERE THE GALATIANS?

The name "Galatia" (1:2) covers a wide area of Asia Minor, the region embracing modern Turkey. Γαλάται is a variant form of Κέλται; and in the context of Paul's letter it refers strictly to the inhabitants of the region around Ancyra (modern Ankara) who left Gaul in the fourth century BC and settled there shortly after 280 BC. When Amyntas, the last king of the Galatians, died in 25 BC, Augustus reorganized the kingdom as a province of the Empire under a legate, and extended the region southward.[3] At the time of Paul, Galatia reached from the northern region of Pontus around the Black Sea (see 1 Pet. 1:1) to the Mediterranean Sea. So our first question is whether churches to whom this letter is addressed (Gal. 1:2) were located in the original territory of Provincia Galatia (the North Galatian theory) or in the southern part of the province, around the Phrygian and Lycaonian cities of Pisidian

---

[1] A. Cole, *The Epistle of Paul to the Galatians* (1965), p. 11.
[2] Monica Furlong, *Puritan's Progress* (1975), p. 66.
[3] T. R. Holmes, *The Architect of the Roman Empire 27 B.C.–A.D. 14* (1931), p. 14. See also B. Levick, *Roman Colonies in Southern Asia Minor* (1967), Ch. 4 and Appendix I.

Antioch, Iconium, Lystra, and Derbe (the South Galatian theory).[4] These Galatian churches were those established in the first missionary journey (Acts 13–14); there is no independent evidence from the Acts that Paul evangelized the northern area. A brief look at the strengths and weaknesses of the opposing views will introduce us to the problem of identifying the recipients of the letter.

1. *The North Galatian Theory.* This is the traditional view; no commentator apparently thought otherwise before the eighteenth century. The main reason for the unanimity of opinion is that in the second century of our era the area of Lycaonia Galatica was detached from Galatia as it was originally and united to Cilicia to form an enlarged province. Toward the end of the third century (c. 297) the remainder of South Galatia became the province of Pisidia, with Pisidian Antioch as its capital city and Iconium as its second city. The province of Galatia was thus virtually reduced to the northern part of the area. So patristic writers read Galatians 1:2 in the sense familiar to them, and considered "Galatia" to refer to the northern tracts of the country as in their day.[5]

In more modern times (1865) the case for this identification has been made by J. B. Lightfoot.[6] He argued that Acts does not call the churches formed in the first missionary journey Galatian churches, though Luke's usage need not be the same as Paul's.[7] Lightfoot's positive arguments were as follows:

a. In Acts 16:6 and 18:23 the phrase "region of Galatia" is probably used in an ethnic sense.

b. By the time of the visits mentioned in these two references, Paul had been to Galatia twice. Evidence for this double visit is found in Galatians 4:13, especially if the alternative reading (NEB mg.) is preferred which renders τὸ πρότερον (lit. "at first") as "on the first of my two visits."

c. The temperament of the Galatian Christians harmonizes with external testimony to their "fickleness," superstition, and devotion to augury provided in Caesar's and Cicero's writings.

2. *The South Galatian View.* In the late nineteenth century the work of W. M. Ramsay provided a turning point with its proposal that the letter was sent to churches in southern Galatia.[8] He was the first to

---

[4] F. F. Bruce sets out the options in terms of the geographical data: "Galatian Problems (2): North or South Galatians?", *BJRL,* 52 (1969–70), 243–66; see now Bruce's commentary on Galatians (NIGTC, 1982), pp. 3–18. Kümmel prefers the terms "territory hypothesis" and "province hypothesis" to North and South Galatian theories respectively (*Introduction to the New Testament*[2], p. 296). See also H.-D. Betz, *Galatians* (Hermeneia, 1979).

[5] W. M. Ramsay, *The Church in the Roman Empire*[3] (1894), p. 111.

[6] J. B. Lightfoot, *St. Paul's Epistle to the Galatians* (1865), pp. 1–35.

[7] F. F. Bruce, *loc. cit.,* p. 249.

[8] *Op. cit.*; also *A Historical Commentary on St. Paul's Epistle to the Galatians* (1899). On Ramsay's contributions see W. W. Gasque, *A History of the Criticism of the Acts of the Apostles,* pp. 140f.

base his support for this understanding of the identity of the readers on a personal survey of the terrain in Asia Minor and its archaeological significance, and on a study of epigraphy and classical literature.

Up to Ramsay's time the lines of demonstration in favor of this view had been of doubtful cogency. Paul habitually uses the official Roman nomenclature for labeling the provinces, but this hardly proves anything, since the entire region would have been "Galatian" to him.[9] Paul's writing in Greek was taken as support for the southern view, but this language was widespread and would have been intelligible in at least the larger communities in the north of the province. It was said further that Paul writes of Barnabas (2:1ff.) as though he were well known to his readers, and Barnabas was in Paul's company—and in the places where Paul's churches were founded—only on the first missionary journey. But 1 Corinthians 9:6 refers to Barnabas as known in Corinth, and there is no evidence he had visited that church.

Acts 20:4 names Gaius and Timothy as representatives of the churches formed on the first mission tour,[10] and no name is given as representing the churches in the northern part of the region. But neither is the Corinthian church represented there, so not much of a case can be built on that omission. Finally, in Galatians 4:14 Paul refers autobiographically to his reception as ἄγγελος θεοῦ—"an angel/messenger of God." This is thought to reflect his being hailed as Hermes the messenger of the gods in Acts 14:11ff. Yet Paul was mobbed at Lystra, and not warmly received as Galatians 4:14 implies.

To these somewhat tenuous arguments Ramsay added more substantial considerations:

a. He appealed to the data of historical geography, in particular to Paul's mission policy of concentrating on main trade routes and centers of communication.

b. As a consequence, Ramsay maintained, it is unlikely that Paul would have been interested in the ethnic Galatian region, since there was no important road through this district.

c. The south side of the Anatolian plateau would seem to Paul to offer a more promising field for missionary service than the more uncivilized and bleak reaches of the north.

James Moffatt sought to answer this defense of the South Galatian view by asking pertinently whether Paul always followed the main trade routes and lanes.[11] If so, how did it come about that he landed in

---

[9] See E. Haenchen, *The Acts of the Apostles* (ET 1971), p. 483n2.

[10] NEB prefers (following D) "the Doberian" to "Derbaean" for Gaius in Acts 20:4, making him a Macedonian. See B. M. Metzger, *A Textual Commentary of the Greek New Testament* (1971), pp. 474f.; F. F. Bruce, *The Acts of the Apostles* (1951), *ad loc.*; A. C. Clark, *The Acts of the Apostles* (1933), pp. xlix–xl, 374–76; and C. S. C. Williams, *Alterations to the Text of the Synoptic Gospels and Acts* (1951), p. 70; but cf. E. Haenchen, *op. cit.*, pp. 52f.

[11] Moffatt, *An Introduction to the Literature of the New Testament*³ (1918), pp. 95ff.

Lystra and Derbe, which on Ramsay's own admission represented more of a "quiet backwater" than important centers of population and influence? And if choosing such a center was of first importance to Paul, Ancyra in North Galatia would well qualify as the provincial seat of Roman government, as Ramsay again was quick to grant. It was "one of the greatest and most splendid cities of Asia Minor," as he calls it.

More recent opposition to the South Galatian hypothesis has pursued lines of investigation which are not concerned with historical geography and its evidence. W. Marxsen objects that Paul's use of the names of Roman provinces provides a counter-argument to the identity of Galatia with the southern Roman region. But F. F. Bruce shows that in Paul's day "the region of Galatia" could refer to the entire province and is not restricted to ethnic Galatia, as Marxsen wished to insist. "The burden of proof lies on those who understand Γαλατία and Γαλάται in his writings in another than the provincial sense," Bruce comments.[12] Marxsen also argues that the reference of Galatians 1:21 to Paul's visits to Syria and Cilicia must, on the South Galatian view, be to the first missionary journey. But, if the South Galatian hypothesis is true, Paul must have founded churches at that time, yet there is no mention of this. Bruce replies that 1:21 may refer not to the activity of Acts 13 and 14 but to the interval between Acts 9:31 and 11:30 when Paul was active in Tarsus and Antioch, which were leading cities in the province of Syria-Cilicia.[13] Finally, Marxsen appeals to the title "Galatians" (3:1) and says that this can only be a racial term, and cannot refer to the inhabitants of a Roman administrative district. Yet no other term was viable for Paul's use, as Ramsay shows.[14]

More desperate expedients to bolster the case for the Northern Galatian theory depend on treating the Acts narrative as fictitious or at least so unreliable that no recourse can be made to it for evidence. Still, no last word of decisive proof can be spoken. F. F. Bruce's summary seems fair: "If the Epistle to the Galatians was indeed addressed to the churches of Pisidian Antioch, Iconium, Lystra and Derbe, then we have important historical, geographical, literary and epigraphic data which will provide material for its better understanding."[15]

WHEN WAS THE LETTER WRITTEN?

There is no certainty about when Paul sent this letter. Part of the difficulty lies with the identification of the readers. If they are located in

---

[12] F. F. Bruce, in *BJRL, loc. cit.,* 261ff.; cf. Marxsen, *Introduction to the New Testament* (ET 1968), p. 46.
[13] On the phrase "regions of Syria and Cilicia," see E. M. B. Green's note, *ExpT,* 71 (1959–60), 52f.
[14] W. M. Ramsay, *The Church in the Roman Empire*[5] (1897), p. 43.
[15] F. F. Bruce, in *BJRL, loc. cit.,* 266.

northern Galatia, Paul could not have written to them prior to his evangelization of that area—and Acts is silent on that, apart from the incidental references to his follow-up visits in 16:6 and 18:23.[16] But even if we accept a setting of the addressees in the southern region, it is still an open question when Paul faced difficulties within the congregations—whether directly after the close of his mission visit to them or during the later, Ephesian period of his ministry.[17]

From 4:13 we learn that when Paul wrote the letter he had been in Galatia either once or twice. The adverb τὸ πρότερον refers either to his initial evangelism ("at the first") or to a visit which was not the last one (see NEB margin). Lightfoot, as we have seen (p. 146), argued that these later visits are those referred to in Acts 16 and 18, and that the time of the letter-writing is subsequent to such visits. But even if it has the second meaning the adverb may refer only to Paul's return visits to the Galatian congregations in the latter part of the first missionary tour (Acts 14:24f.).

Galatians 1:6 expresses surprise that the Galatians have fallen away "so quickly." This can refer only to the time of the church's establishment or the pastoral visit of Acts 16:6; and the former is much more likely, because 16:6 speaks only of passing through the region of Galatia and not of a mission there. Acts 18:23 hardly fits in at all, since it speaks of Paul's strengthening the disciples and not of a work among the churches there.

The occasion of the letter would be much clearer if we could be sure of Paul's movements to and from Jerusalem. In Galatians we learn of two such visits: the first three years after his conversion and stay in Damascus (1:18–24); the second after an interval of fourteen years (2:1–10). The complicated issue is which events in Acts correspond to these visits, assuming that Luke is aware of all the significant movements of Paul and that Paul is telling in Galatians all he knows. The first assumption is doubtful, since we have other indications that the Lukan record is not comprehensive in its coverage of Paul's life (e.g., where in Acts can we fit all the data given in 2 Cor. 11:23–29?) and that Luke has been selective in putting together the elements of Paul's missionary service which he has at his disposal.[18] The second assumption is much more certain. Paul was under obligation to "tell all" about his contacts with the Jerusalem leaders, and any omission would have been

---

[16] F. F. Bruce, "Galatian Problems (4): The Date of the Epistle," *BJRL*, 54 (1972), 251.

[17] Correspondences in the use of terms and language between Gal. and Rom. and 1–2 Cor. appealed to by Lightfoot are not so compelling as is sometimes thought. See B. N. Kaye, "'To the Romans and Others' Revisited," *NovT*, 18 (1976), 37–77.

[18] J. J. Gunther argues that Luke's predilections and lack of interest in the personal relations of the major apostles dictated his silence about the events described in Gal. 2:6–9; *Paul: Messenger and Exile*, p. 33.

fatal to his credibility in the eyes of the Galatians and would almost certainly have been exploited by his enemies there. He is therefore emphatic that he is telling the (whole) truth: "In what I am writing to you, before God, I do not lie!" (1:20).

Acts records five visits of Paul to Jerusalem. Two of these came too late to be considered germane here (Acts 18:22; 21:27ff.). The other three are: Acts 9:26–30—Paul came to Jerusalem after his conversion; Acts 11:27–30—Barnabas and Paul were sent from Antioch to Jerusalem to aid the famine-stricken church there; they returned later (12:25); Acts 15:1–30—Paul was present at the "summit meeting" of Christian leaders in Jerusalem.

The most natural correspondences between the data in Galatians and in Acts would link Galatians 1:18–24 with Acts 9:26–30, and Galatians 2:1–10 with Acts 11:27–30. To be sure, in the latter case the two passages describe different purposes for Paul's journey to the holy city, but those may well have overlapped. The "famine visit" may well have given Paul and Barnabas the opportunity to consult with leaders of Jewish Christianity about the terms on which Gentiles would be admitted to the church.[19] This was a private meeting, although the record in Galatians 2 may contain in part the wording of an agreement reached between Paul and Peter; the alternation of names Cephas/Peter suggests that this is the case. "Peter" in 2:7f. is used in the more or less official transaction of the conference, whereas Paul's own telling of the story prefers "Cephas." The conference is not mentioned in Acts.[20]

Several points confirm that this is the best equation. In the first place, a discussion on the admissibility of the Gentile believers and the terms of their inclusion in the church is more appropriate *before* the first missionary journey. Galatians 2:9 reads like a statement of agreement on respective spheres of missionary service, on the strength of which Paul and Barnabas made ready to evangelize the pagan peoples of Galatia (Acts 13, 14). Also, Paul's acknowledgment that he went to Jerusalem "by revelation" (2:2) may be an allusion to the prophetic advice of Agabus in Acts 11:28 and its sequel in the church's resolve to dispatch Paul to Jerusalem. Finally, this suggested link keeps the order

---

[19] See D. R. Hall, "St. Paul and Famine Relief: A Study in Galatians 2:10," *ExpT*, 82 (1970–71), 309–11. D. R. de Lacey equates the visit of Gal. 2:1–10 with that of Acts 9:26–30, which would date the Galatian letter very shortly after the founding of the churches in South Galatia; "Paul in Jerusalem," *NTS*, 20 (1973–74), 82–86. But we must allow room (in spite of the witness of 1:6) for false teachers to have infiltrated and set to work (implied by 4:8–11,17; 5:12). R. H. Stein's endeavor to identify the visit of Gal. 2:1–10 with the council visit (Acts 15) is no more successful; "The Relationship of Galatians 2:1–10 and Acts 15:1–35: Two Neglected Arguments," *JETS*, 17 (1974), 239–42. There is no evidence to support the idea of Paul as team-leader at Jerusalem, and Stein's contention that 2:7f. presupposes a successful mission to Asia is countered if the letter was written just prior to the council.

[20] See F. F. Bruce, "Galatian Problems (5): Galatians and Christian Origins," *BJRL*, 55 (1973), 279.

of events in Acts and the Epistle in sequence, and it does not require us to admit that either author has erred or omitted anything of material importance in his account.[21]

Other attempts at suggesting a correspondence seem less successful. If the visit of Galatians 2:1–10 and the council meeting are one and the same event, Paul would have skipped over the famine visit in his account. Some scholars contend that this visit was too brief and unimportant to mention, but as we observed, Paul's very purpose here is to give a full account of his contacts with the Jerusalem leaders, which would involve enumerating his visits there. Any omission, however well intentioned or accidental, could ruin his case.[22]

Moreover, if Galatians 2 was written subsequent to the leaders' meeting, the dispute with Peter at Antioch (Gal. 2:11ff.) would have had to take place *after* the Jerusalem council. It is conceivable that Peter had vacillated or reneged on the council's decision and so needed a sharp rebuke such as Paul administered according to 2:11, but it is more likely that Acts 15 shows how Peter profited from such an encounter with Paul and arrived at his own position at the council in accord with what he learned at the Antioch meeting. Also, if Paul had occasion to administer his warning *after* the council session, it is certainly strange that he failed to mention the council's "decree" (Acts 15:19–21) which had Peter's concurrence.[22a]

It has been suggested that Acts 15 itself is a composite narrative, with two separate conferences being run together and confounded: the first—between Paul's first two missionary journeys—dealing with circumcision (identified with Gal. 2:1–10); a second conference—after the dispute between Peter and Paul—concerned with table fellowship between Jews and Gentiles (Acts 15:5–11,13–33; Gal. 2:11ff.). Paul was not present at this latter session, which is why James later has to explain to him the terms of the apostolic "edict" as though the latter had never heard of it previously (Acts 21:25). This hypothesis helps account for the introduction of the discussion on circumcision, but it has difficulty locating the council's consideration of table fellowship at a point in time prior to the confrontation in Antioch. Nor does it explain the omission of the famine visit from the Galatian narrative.

On balance, the first view given above commends itself as most satisfactory. To sum up:

1. The churches mentioned in Galatians 1:2 and 3:1 are those

---

[21] For other explanations see Kümmel, *op. cit.*, pp. 302f.

[22] Cf. J. B. Lightfoot, *Galatians*, pp. 122–27. Lightfoot's argument is used by J. A. T. Robinson (*Redating the New Testament*, pp. 38–42) in favor of equating Gal. 2 with Acts 15.

[22a] I am less disposed to argue thus in the light of Paul's increasing alienation from both the mother church and Antioch as well as his more emphatic polemical stance in regard to the Jerusalem "pillar" apostles and their emissaries in 2 Cor. 10–13. See "The Setting of 2 Corinthians," in *2 Corinthians* (WBC, 1985), pp. lii–lxiii.

formed in the course of the first missionary journey in south Galatia.

2. Galatians 4:13 refers to this initial evangelism or to Paul's return visit on his way back to the Mediterranean coastline (Acts 14:21b–23).

3. Paul's first visit to Jerusalem (Gal. 1:18) is that following his conversion (Acts 9:26). The years in Arabia and Damascus intervened between his conversion and that visit. Then, fourteen years later *than his conversion* (this is the most likely way of understanding 2:1) he went up to Jerusalem again—the famine relief visit. But see p. 97.

4. The success which attended his ministry to the Gentiles of Asia during his first missionary tour, provoking reactions from certain Jewish Christians (see the next section for discussion of who they may have been), raised questions which caused disturbance within the Galatian congregations. Paul was moved to amazement that this teaching appealed so readily to the new believers (1:6), and he wrote—probably from Syrian Antioch, possibly en route to the council—this letter to set in right perspective the issues provoked by the presence and activity of these agitators. The date is c. 48–49.[23]

WHO WERE THE TROUBLERS
OF THE GALATIANS?

Twice (1:6–9; 5:10,12) Paul makes it clear that the situation in Galatia is serious and that it has come about because of the appearance on the scene of false teachers whose aim is to unsettle the Galatian Christians. Clearly these were Christian teachers professing to proclaim the apostolic message, but their version of it was at variance with Paul's gospel.[24] It is difficult to say precisely what their teaching was.

1. The traditional view is that these were Judaizing Christians who claimed that full salvation was impossible apart from the observance of Jewish law and ritual, especially in regard to circumcision as a badge of membership within the covenant community of Israel (5:2; 6:12f.), even the new Israel (6:16). Possibly they appealed to Abraham's example (cf. Gen. 17:9–14, according to which all members of the patriarch's family, both in present and future generations, were required

---

[23] For an early date, see F. F. Bruce, *BJRL*, 54 (1972), esp. 266f.; J. W. Drane, *Paul: Libertine or Legalist?* (1975), Appendix B; William Neil, *The Letter of Paul to the Galatians* (CBC, 1967); D. Guthrie, *Galatians* (NCB, rev. 1974), pp. 27–37 (based on the South Galatian theory). On the latter point, see G. S. Duncan, *The Epistle of Paul to the Galatians* (MNTC, 1934), pp. xviii ff.; H. N. Ridderbos, *The Epistle to the Galatians* (NICNT, 1954), pp. 22f. See now C. J. Hemer, "Acts and Galatians Reconsidered," *Themelios*, 2 (1977), 81–88.

[24] Contrast A. E. Harvey, "The Opposition to Paul," *SE*, 4 (*TU* 102, 1968), 319–32, for whom Paul's concern at Galatia was occasioned by the church's behaving in ways he could not approve of. Paul objects to their following Jewish behavior-patterns (suggested by the verb ἰουδαΐζειν; 2:14), not their aberrant theological beliefs. But this position is to be questioned. See Drane, *op. cit.*, pp. 8–11. See also E. Baasland, "Persecution: A Neglected Feature in the Letter to the Galatians," *ST*, 38 (1984), 135–50.

to practice the rite as a sign of their inclusion in the "everlasting covenant" [vs. 7]). Possibly their teaching, crisply spelled out in Acts 15:1 and
5, claimed to voice the sentiments of James, the leader of the church at
Jerusalem.[25]

2. The Jewishness of these teachers cannot, however, explain
all the evidence in Paul's rebuttal of their position. Specifically, the
version of Judaism or Jewish Christianity they represented must also
have included some veneration of the "elemental spirits" or astral powers, which suggests a mixture of pagan worship (4:3,8f.);[26] an insistence
on the need to observe the "calendar," which is more probably an allusion to planetary powers or astrological signs of the zodiac than to the
Jewish festivals (4:10); and an attitude to morality which treated the
claims of ethical responsibility, both personal and corporate, as irrelevant to the Christian life and which saw no harm in indulgence and
selfishness in private and social behavior (see 5:13-26). Equally there
was a lack of concern for fellow Christians, coupled with a judgmental
attitude to others in the community (6:1-10). The desire to do justice to
these additional aspects in the Galatian situation has led to further
theories about the identification of these opponents.

3. The chief issue is how there could be in the same group of
Christian congregations both a stress on observing the law and scope for
libertine tendencies. Some explain this by arguing that the Judaism the
teachers were trying to import was a gnosticizing variety, which advocated a missionary campaign to promote circumcision as necessary for
salvation, but which sat loose to moral responsibility.[27] Others see it as

---

[25] For classic traditional statements, see F. C. Baur's celebrated essay on the
"Christ-party" in early Christianity (discussed by Gasque, *op. cit.*, pp. 27f. and H.
Harris, *The Tübingen School*, pp. 181ff.); and H. Lietzmann, *The Beginnings of the
Christian Church* (ET 1949), pp. 108ff. Stauffer identifies James's supporters with
the troublers of the Galatians (1:7; 4:17); *New Testament Theology* (ET 1955), p.
38. See R. H. Fuller, *A Critical Introduction to the New Testament* (1966), pp. 27f.,
with reference to J. Munck, *Paul and the Salvation of Mankind* (ET 1959), pp. 87ff.

[26] On τὰ στοιχεῖα τοῦ κόσμου in Gal. 4, see the commentaries, esp. H. Schlier (1949),
and A. J. Bandstra, *The Law and the Elements of the World* (1964). But E.
Schweizer, "Versöhnung des Alls: Kol 1,20," in *Jesus Christus in Historie und
Theologie*: H. Conzelmann *Festschrift*, ed. G. Strecker (1975), pp. 487-501, has
shown that the setting of τὰ στοιχεῖα is the world of astrological dualism, not
Judaism seen as a preparation for the gospel; cf. B. Reicke "The Law and This
World According to Paul," *JBL*, 70 (1951), 259ff.; and the present writer's arguments, in agreement with Schweizer, in *Colossians and Philemon* (NCB, 1974), pp.
10-14.

[27] W. Schmithals, *Paul and the Gnostics* (ET 1972), pp. 13-64. The legalism here in
view is not a Jewish-Christian variety, as J. B. Tyson says, "Paul's Opponents in
Galatia," *NovT*, 10 (1968), 241-54. His argument in respect of a Judaistic notion of
the "'Works of the Law' in Galatians," *JBL*, 92 (1973), 423-31, has been followed
by D. P. Fuller, "Paul and 'the Works of the Law,'" *WTJ*, 38 (1975), 28-42. The
hypothesis of gnostic influence in the Galatian congregation has been challenged
by R. McL. Wilson, "Gnostics—in Galatia?" *SE*, 4 (*TU* 102, 1968), 358-67; and
R. H. Fuller, *op. cit.*, p. 29.

a syncretistic type of Judaism, which gave circumcision a symbolic value.[28] A different explanation is that Paul is fighting against two quite different sets of opponents.[29] W. Lütgert divided the Galatian agitators into traditional Judaic nomists and spiritual enthusiasts inclined to a relaxed view of the moral law. Marxsen also thinks of Paul as defending his gospel on two fronts: on the one side, against a Pharisaic legalism (which he filled out with gnostic features by equating the *stoicheia* of 4:3, 9 with the law); on the other, against an antinomian tendency that led to an ethical laxity in the church. He suggests that Paul's understanding of the opponents' teaching developed from incomplete acquaintance (cf. his vagueness in 1:7; 3:1; 5:10 about the source and nature of the trouble) to fuller knowledge after he encountered similar teaching in Corinth.[30] But this line of reasoning, while novel, is speculative and not necessary.

4. The contrast between stress on freedom in Christ from the claims of the Mosaic Torah religion (5:2–6) and equal insistence on the abiding claim of "the law of Christ" (6:2) and the rule of the Spirit which allows no moral laxity (5:22–26) is so great that it may seem foolhardy to try to bring them together. But an attempt will be made to do just that.

A recent writer who has prepared the ground for a tentative suggestion is Robert Jewett.[31] He calls attention to a question often bypassed in expositions of Galatians. The promulgators of "another gospel" (1:7) evidently embarked on a rival missionary policy to win over Gentile Christians to their side and to encourage them to accept the badge of circumcision (5:2–12). But in 5:11 Paul asks rhetorically why he is still persecuted when he has long since given up preaching circumcision as a requirement for Gentiles. Later (6:11–17) he returns to the interrelation between circumcision and persecution, remarking that the Galatian troublers advocate Gentile circumcision to escape persecution but at the same time boast that the Gentile believers who accepted circumcision as a post-baptismal rite are *their* pride and joy.

The question is in what circumstances Jewish Christians would lose their traditional indifference to evangelizing Gentiles and start

---

[28] F. R. Crownfield, "The Singular Problem of Dual Galatians," *JBL,* 64 (1945), 491–500; H. Köster, "*Gnōmai Diaphoroi*: The Origin and Nature of Diversification in the History of Early Christianity," *HTR,* 58 (1965), 279–318; repr. in *Trajectories through Early Christianity* (1971), pp. 114–57 (esp. pp. 121f.).

[29] W. Lütgert, *Gesetz und Geist: Eine Untersuchung zur Vorgeschichte des Galaterbriefes* (1919); J. H. Ropes, *The Singular Problem of the Epistle to the Galatians* (1929).

[30] W. Marxsen, *op. cit.,* pp. 52–57.

[31] R. Jewett, "The Agitators and the Galatian Congregation," *NTS,* 17 (1970–71), 198–212; cf. his *Paul's Anthropological Terms* (1971), pp. 17–20, and *passim*; also B. Reicke, "Der geschichtliche Hintergrund des Apostelkonzils und der Antiochia-Episode, Gal. 2,1–14," in *Studia Paulina in honorem J. de Zwaan* (1953), pp. 172–87.

actively advocating a campaign to have Gentile Christians circumcised. The point to notice, as Jewett perceptively remarks, is that it is the Jewish Christian agitators who launched this campaign in order to avert persecution from themselves. If they were Jewish Christians who agreed with Paul up to a point, the question can be put more sharply: if they go along with Paul and abandon the ancestral custom of circumcising Gentile believers as a sign of their incorporation into the family of Abraham (3:16) and the new Israel, they will experience persecution, as Paul has. If, however, they insist on Gentile circumcision, as they evidently did, they will escape this bitter fate and make life easier for themselves (a tactic Paul calls "pleasing men" in 1:10 and refuses to adopt). But who are the opponents whose hostility they wish to neutralize?

The answer is found in the renewed activity of the Jewish Zealots in Palestine in the late 40s and early 50s. Jewish Christians were subjected to pressure to declare themselves loyal Jews at a time of a fierce nationalistic upsurge.[32] One way in which they could demonstrate their allegiance to the ancestral faith, albeit as Christians, was to dissociate themselves from lawless Gentiles; and in answer to the charge that Gentile Christians were no better than pagans, they came to insist that Paul's converts in Galatia should accept the token rite of circumcision to prove that they did belong to the Israel of God. Thus Judaizing Christians would deflect opposition from themselves and avert the wrath of Zealot-minded Jews in Judaea.

It is feasible that Gentile Christians would find this argument attractive, especially if phrases such as "the seed of Abraham" (3:16–29) and the Jerusalem which is our mother (4:26) were propaganda current in their church and introduced by these newcomers. It may well be that the promise of a place in this elect community was all that was needed to minister to their native sense of wanting to be "secure" in possessing salvation—as the Hellenistic mind conceived of salvation: a present blessed reality, an inalienable possession involving a divinization of human nature and an eschatology with no room for future judgments, rewards, and penalties, since the believer is already risen with Christ to a celestial state, even while he is here on earth.

Exactly these traits are seen in the latter section of this Epistle. The Galatian Christians, in the first flush of their new life as believers delivered from the evil age of paganism (1:4; 4:3,8) and introduced to a

---

[32] This may have begun even earlier if J. J. Gunther's arguments about the chronology of the political events of the period, the drought in Judaea and the resultant famine, and the antipathy after Stephen's death are sound, as they may well be; *Paul: Messenger and Exile*, pp. 36–43.

dynamic experience of the Spirit in miracle-power (3:3,5), were still very much captivated by Hellenistic ideas of spirit (πνεῦμα). They have recently known the vivifying experiences of new life in the Spirit (5:25) and pride themselves on the title οἱ πνευματικοί—men of Spirit (6:1; Paul is evidently ironic in his use here of their self-applied term). By receiving πνεῦμα they were being immortalized, and this confidence in a blessed state already begun has led to a blurring of ethical distinctions. They can see no harm in indulging themselves (5:19–23).

Moreover, the "Gnostic" who believed himself a man of the Spirit had no need to show concern for others. His religion was essentially personal and individualistic. So it is not surprising that the Galatians were guilty of anti-social vices (5:26—6:5) like those found at Corinth. They claim to be on the road to a final perfection already begun. Paul grants, again ironically speaking, that this may be true (3:3). But they will attain their goal only by a true corporate life "in Christ," and for this they need to be concerned for one another in a spirit of tender sympathy for the erring brother (6:1), in an attitude of mutual caring (6:2), in a disposition of lowliness (6:3f.), and in a recognition that they need the office of the (Pauline) teacher to instruct them in divine truth (6:6).

The prospect of future judgment is real, no matter what the heretical teachers say about a present entry into the heavenly Jerusalem here and now (6:7). Let the Galatians not be deluded nor reject highhandedly God's claims on their lives. Living so as only to gratify the lower nature, on the mistaken assumption that a saved spirit is all that counts, will surely reap a sad harvest (6:8).

So it is possible that Paul is contending with only one erroneous teaching afflicting the Galatian church. Judaizing Christians, anxious to divert attention from themselves and to demonstrate that they were true, patriotic Jews, were investing circumcision with a powerfully symbolic meaning. What may have been regarded as a primitive puberty custom was given a deep meaning as a rite by which Gentile believers were thought to be linked with a mythical seed of Abraham and given a status in an already realized and present heavenly kingdom, a new Israel here and now. The Spirit has introduced them to this experience in some unforgettable ways, as they are quickened and lifted into a new world by him (3:2; 5:25). At this point they draw some fatal conclusions, namely, that as members of a new race of men, they can live indulgent, self-centered, careless lives. Paul opposes all such libertinism, and he just as emphatically brings down the full weight of his biblical and theological exegetical work to crush the notion that circumcision (which was the chief contention of the false teachers) has any saving virtue as an addendum to his gospel.

THE MESSAGE OF THE LETTER

Paul is greatly moved as he writes (1:6,20; 4:12-20; 5:2,12), for so much is at stake—the very future of the gospel and the church of Jesus Christ.[33] His enemies (and he treats them as such because they are "enemies of the gospel" in his view) evidently opposed his statement of the apostolic *kerygma* and wished to undermine his authority by alleging that he was no true apostle but was dependent on the Jerusalem leaders. He must declare his apostolic authority, which springs from a commission received directly from God and has no need to be authorized by the apostles of the Jerusalem *Urgemeinde* (1:11-24). Thereafter he seeks to answer the claims of the agitators' teaching along the lines of true faith in Christ, which alone sets the sinner in right relationship with God (2:16-21), and true freedom in the Spirit, whose work in human lives releases a moral dynamic unknown by external codes and religious institutions (4:10).[34]

Yet liberty is not license. Just because the Holy Spirit delivers us from bondage to bad religion and legalistic codes, we are not invited to antinomianism or casting off all restraints (5:13). There is a true freedom in Christ which binds the Christian to a quality of life in which caring for our fellow members and the service of the community sets us free from self-centeredness (5:22—6:10).

Above all, this Epistle emphasizes the unity of the church as one body with an ongoing life stretching back to Abraham, the father of the faithful (3:6-18). There is no room for racial distinctions in this unity, for the church is made up of all believers, whether Jews or Gentiles. Nor is there any place for other barriers which separated men and women, masters and slaves, in the ancient world (3:27-29).[34a] The key to this discussion is the all-inclusiveness of God's purpose, which is gathered up in Christ. And in Christ all who belong to him find the focus of unity which transcends their natural differences. In the context Paul is answering irrefutably the gnosticizing Jewish claim that membership of the elite "true church" is open only to those who become Abraham's family in the way they prescribe. But Paul's principle has an application far wider than this, and gives to the Epistle its timeless quality.

[33] On the "broken" quality of Paul's style, matched by a careful conformity to rhetorical forms and patterns, both designed to win over his readers, see H. D. Betz, "The Literary Composition and Function of Paul's Letter to the Galatians," *NTS*, 21 (1975), 353-79. This stylistic feature is elaborated in Betz's more recent (1979) commentary. The methods used are surveyed in G. A. Kennedy, *New Testament Interpretation through Rhetorical Criticism* (1984), with some criticisms of Betz (pp. 144-52).

[34] See W. Neil, *op. cit.,* pp. 89-93. See too J. D. G. Dunn, "The New Perspective on Paul," *BJRL*, 65 (1983), 95-122.

[34a] The contrasts in 3:28 seem deliberately framed as a response to the Jewish benediction according to which the synagogue worshiper thanked God that he was not created a Gentile, a slave, or a woman (*Berakoth* 13b).

Wherever the sole sufficiency of what God has done for men and women in Christ and his cross needs to be asserted, wherever the single requirement that we are accepted by God as we accept what has been finally accomplished must be set forth, wherever life-in-Christ needs to be displayed in terms of its moral energy to set people free from self to a life of service for others, this letter will maintain its appeal.[35]

[35] On the Epistle's theology see H.-D. Betz, "Spirit, Freedom, and Law, Paul's Message to the Galatian Church," SEA, 39 (1974), 145-60; M. Barth, "The Kerygma of Galatians," Interpretation, 21 (1967), 131-46; and my effort to expound the leading themes of the epistle in simple terms in The Daily Commentary (1974), reprinted from the Bible Study Books series (1968).

CHAPTER THIRTEEN

Persecution and Parousia in the Thessalonian Letters

Acts 17:1–10 introduces us to Paul's first contact with the Thessalonians and describes his initial evangelism in that city of Macedonia (see above, pp. 118f.). The mission there was successful, with a larger response from God-fearing Greeks than from Jews (vs. 4).[1] The Jewish population, indeed, was stirred to opposition; and so fierce was the conflict that Paul and Silas had to escape by night to Beroea, some sixty miles away (17:10).

They left hurriedly, but not before their three or four weeks' ministry at the local Jewish meeting-place (vs. 2) and in Jason's home (vs. 7) had yielded some encouraging results.[2] The adherence of a group of influential women (vs. 4) may account for the self-defense Paul feels obliged to make in his correspondence: perhaps there was circulated at Thessalonica after Paul's departure the insinuation that he had stayed only long enough to have received money from wealthy ladies.

The Jews found a pretext in the apostles' assertion that Jesus was king of human lives. They distorted this to imply that Paul's message was political, and that he was advocating a treasonable opposition

---

[1] On the nature of Paul's mission preaching and the response it elicited, see 1 Thess. 1:9f., on which Harnack commented: "here we have the mission preaching in a nutshell"; quoted and critically discussed by J. Munck, "1 Thess. 1.9–10 and the Missionary Preaching of Paul," *NTS*, 9 (1962–63), 95–110; see also D. W. Kemmler, *Faith and Human Reason: A Study of Paul's Method of Preaching As Illustrated by 1–2 Thessalonians and Acts 17, 2–4* (1975).

[2] Paul's ministry there may have been more extended than seems implied by Acts 17:2, which says no more than that his preaching in the synagogue extended over three or four weeks. He may well have continued to reside in the city for a longer period. A longer stay seems required by the reference in 1 Thess. 1:8ff., according to which the Thessalonians' faith had become widely known, and the allusion in Phil. 4:16 to the sending of gifts to Paul in Thessalonica "once and again," i.e., repeatedly; see L. Morris, *NovT*, 1 (1956), 203–208; and the commentaries *ad loc.* by J. Gnilka and J.-F. Collange. On Paul's ministry there, see E. Haenchen, *The Acts of the Apostles*, pp. 511ff.

to the Roman *imperium*.[3] The authorities in this community, which the Romans had made the administrative center of Macedonia, were disturbed by this charge, but when Jason gave an assurance that his guests were not seditiously minded, Paul was permitted to go free. Jason, however, agreed that the apostles should be "bound over" and prevented from speaking in Thessalonica. Jason's pledge accounts for their immediate departure from the city and for Paul's not feeling free to revisit the city (cf. 1 Thess. 2:17f.).

The matter did not rest there. Persecution was leveled at the infant church, even when Paul's offending presence was withdrawn to Beroea. This is suggested in the first letter (1:6; 2:14; 3:3). The Thessalonians came to understand early that bearing witness in a hostile world was a responsibility laid on them as Christians, and Paul praises their zeal in evangelism (1 Thess. 1:8); but persecution inevitably followed their courageous witness. Such duress took its toll. Opposition in their city apparently led to the premature death of some believers (1 Thess. 4:13); and this bereavement raised questions of faith in the minds of the persecuted church.

Even more violent activity against the message followed. Jewish leaders, determined to crush every outcropping of the church, moved on to Beroea in pursuit of Paul (Acts 17:13). This was a time of great strain for Paul, since the coming of these Jewish agitators meant that he could no longer remain in Beroea. So he was sent by friends to Athens, leaving Timothy and Silas behind to join him later.

It is clear from 1 Thessalonians 3:1ff. that Paul's reputation was at stake in Thessalonica. He found it necessary to send Timothy there during his stay in Athens, and his mission was evidently calculated to make up for the absence of Paul himself, who could not return there while Jason's pledge was in force.[4] Timothy reported back to Paul—possibly at Athens, more likely at Corinth to where Paul had moved on—that the church was standing firm in faith (1 Thess. 3:6–10). At a personal level, Paul expresses a measure of relief that this church is still kindly disposed to him.

The picture is filled out in 1 Thessalonians 2:1–12. Either Paul

---

[3] On "the decrees of Caesar" (17:7), see A. N. Sherwin-White, *Roman Society and Roman Law in the New Testament*, pp. 51f., 100, 103; cf. E. A. Judge, "The Decrees of Caesar at Thessalonica," *RTR*, 30 (1971), 1–7; and "St. Paul and Classical Society," *Jahrbuch für Antike und Christentum*, 15 (1972), 19–36.

[4] There are problems in reconciling 1 Thess. 3:1ff. with Acts 17:14, according to which Timothy remained in Beroea and was later bidden by Paul to come quickly to him to join him in Corinth (Acts 18:5). The record in Acts passes over Timothy's meeting with Paul at Athens and has the two rendezvous in Corinth—another instance of Luke's abbreviation and telescoping of the movements of Paul and the others in his mission. See below, pp. 163f.

had been accused of cowardice and running away from danger; or else he stood under the cloud of suspicion that he had stayed at Thessalonica only long enough to receive a money gift from Philippi (Phil. 4:16). Even then, he may have been charged with avarice, as we saw, especially if the women in the congregation had supported him financially. So part of the reason for his writing lies in a desire to vindicate his character, to explain why he could not return to the city, and to justify his missionary and pastoral motives.

PAUL'S SELF-DEFENSE

The immediate occasion of the first letter, probably written around AD 50, when Timothy and Silas rejoined Paul at Corinth (Acts 18:5),[5] was to rejoice with his friends in the church at their steadfastness under trial (3:6), to strengthen their faith and to dispel certain doubts and fears that had arisen (4:11ff.; 5:1,14), and to defend himself against accusations impugning his motives and assaulting his character (2:1-12).

The last element here deserves a further comment in the light of Marxsen's reconstruction. He thinks that Paul's self-defense is directed against the Thessalonians' association of him with the character and habits of pagan "divine men" (θεῖοι ἄνδρες), who made a living in religious quackery.[6] Paul goes out of his way to renounce any connection with practices labeled "unclean" (2:3) and emphasizes that this type of religious teacher, who performed cures and gave oracles for money and to please people, is the opposite of the Christian preacher (2:4-6). He has never striven to gain the praise and flattery of others. His maintenance and support at Thessalonica were not a liability to this congregation, since he worked for his living during his stay (2:9). His character references are impeccable (2:10)—as his readers know full well.

Perhaps, too, he is on the defensive in the matter of his sufferings. Among Hellenistic religious teachers the gnostic apostle gloried in his commanding stature, his credentials as a holy man and thaumaturge, and his exemption from personal loss and suffering. Paul had already acquired a reputation for meeting trouble wherever he turned—at Philippi (2:2), Thessalonica, Beroea, and now at Corinth. To the impressionable Thessalonians who (Schmithals argues) were being infiltrated by gnostic teachers, a suffering apostle would seem to be a

---

[5] G. Ogg, *The Chronology of the Life of Paul* (US title, *The Odyssey of Paul*), pp. 104–11; J. A. T. Robinson, *Redating the New Testament*, p. 53.

[6] W. Marxsen, *Introduction to the New Testament* (ET 1968), p. 35. Hellenistic "divine men" claimed the right to be paid for their services; B. Reicke, *Diakonie, Festfreude und Zelos* (1951), pp. 243ff., 308ff.; D. Georgi, *Die Gegner des Paulus im 2. Kor.* (1964), pp. 211ff., 220ff.; both cited by E. Best, *A Commentary on the First and Second Epistles to the Thessalonians* (Harper-Black, 1972), pp. 16ff.

contradiction in terms. It fell to him, therefore, to make a defense of his apostolic ministry on this score.[7]

This reconstruction of Schmithals is suggestive, but hardly convincing. For one thing, certain verses (2:1ff., 18f.; 3:9f.) suggest that the problem in Thessalonica was not that false teaching had encroached on the scene, for Paul speaks confidently of their continuing faith and stability. The enemies of Paul and of the church are certainly Jewish (2:14–16), and there is no hint that he had to contend with the presence and influence of hostile Christians at Thessalonica.[8]

Form critical study of the letter has attempted to place its purpose in a more precise frame. According to P. Schubert the typical Pauline Epistle has six parts: prescript (opening), thanksgiving, central section or body, apostolic *parousia* (in which Paul pledges a visit by himself or his colleagues), exhortation (*paraenesis*), and closing.[9] But this regular pattern is broken in 1 Thessalonians, where a second thanksgiving is encountered at 2:13ff. H. Boers overcomes this difficulty by regarding these verses as extraneous, an anti-Jewish interpolation dating from after AD 70.[10]

The grounds for this hypothesis are that it is difficult to interpret in context the statement "and we also thank God ... for this" (vs. 13: καὶ διὰ τοῦτο καὶ ἡμεῖς εὐχαριστοῦμεν τῷ θεῷ); that what is said in these verses presupposes the fall of Jerusalem, considered to prove God's judgment on Israel; and that verses 12 and 17 go together if the intervening section is removed.[11] When this passage is removed, Boers contends, the pattern of the Epistle can be regarded as normal, and its true purpose stands revealed.

Granted that 2:1–12 has an apologetic tone, it must not be as-

---

[7] W. Schmithals understands Paul's concept of apostleship against the background of contemporary ideas, drawn from gnosticism, of the "divine apostle"; *The Office of Apostle in the Early Church* (ET 1969). He tries to prove that gnosticizing enemies of the Pauline gospel had crept into the church since Paul's departure; *Paul and the Gnostics* (ET 1972), pp. 123–218. Against this reconstruction see Best, *op. cit.*, pp. 17ff.

[8] This part of the argument would be invalid if 2:13–16 are an interpolation, as is argued by Schmithals (*op. cit.*, pp. 127ff.) and B. A. Pearson, "1 Thess. 2:13–16: A Deutero-Pauline Interpolation," *HTR*, 64 (1971), 79ff. But the arguments adduced against the section, on grounds of content and style, are by no means persuasive. See further below and a comment on 2:16 on p. 116.

[9] P. Schubert, *Form and Function of the Pauline Thanksgivings* (1939); modified by R. W. Funk, "The Apostolic *Parousia*: Form and Significance," in *Christian History and Interpretation* (J. Knox *Festschrift*), edd. Farmer, Moule, and Niebuhr (1967), pp. 249–68.

[10] H. Boers, "The Form Critical Study of Paul's Letters: 1 Thessalonians as a Case Study," *NTS*, 22 (1974–75), 140–58.

[11] For a critique of this theory see Kümmel, *Introduction*[2], p. 260; cf. his essay "Das literarische und geschichtliche Problem des ersten Thessalonicherbriefes," in *Neotestamentica et Patristica: Freundesgabe O. Cullmann* (1962), pp. 211–27, esp. pp. 218ff.; and R. Schippers, "The Pre-Synoptic Tradition in 1 Thessalonians II.13–16," *NovT*, 8 (1966), 223–34.

sumed that such apologies in ancient letters necessarily involved the sole purpose of the letter. It is more likely that a statement of apology served only to create a feeling of well-being and friendship (Gr. *philophrōnēsis*) between sender and addressee. The purpose of 1 Thessalonians must be seen elsewhere, in connection with Paul's use of the verb "to beseech" (παρακαλεῖν). C. J. Bjerkelund argues that the use of this verb in the sense of exhortation in 4:1 and 4:10b points to the heart of Paul's intention—to "spur on [the Thessalonian Christians] to a way of life pleasing to God."[12] He has already shown them warm affection in the thanksgiving portion (1:2–10), which expresses his joy over them and his satisfaction with them. Thus 4:1—5:11 stand out as a paraenetic section, just as 1:2–10 expresses the philophronetic sentiment,[13] with the apologetic section (2:1–12) and the promise of an apostolic *parousia* (2:17—3:13) supporting the Pauline offer of friendship and joy.

There are useful insights in this approach, chiefly to show how Paul's handling of the problems at Thessalonica is set within the recognized framework of ancient letter-writing conventions (cf. Demetrius, *On Style*). But Boers' reconstruction of a "normal" pattern, conformable to those conventions, is dependent on the elimination of 2:13–16 as non-Pauline. If we are not persuaded by his acceptance of Pearson's hypothesis (footnote 8), we must concede that Paul's writing to this church was more flexible. Boers himself grants at the outset of his study that "one should be careful not to assume that Paul's letters had to conform to a particular pattern"[14]—a warning his study is in danger of disregarding.

THE QUESTION OF THE OCCASION

It is possible to hold that the first letter comes from a period later than that suggested. In addition to Schmithals' argument that Paul's enemies at Thessalonica were the same gnostic Christian errorists who plagued his work in Galatia and Corinth, we may examine some other evidence.

1. The widespread public notice of the Thessalonians' faith (1:8f.; 2:14) may suggest that the church had become established since its early days. But this is not necessarily so, and an eager grasp of evangelistic opportunities could just as well be true of an infant as of a more mature congregation—perhaps more so. The section of the letter 1:5—2:12 rather suggests a church only recently founded. Paul's reiterated appeals to his first ministry among them (1:5; 2:1ff., 5, 9f.), using phrases like "you know," "remember," "you are witnesses," sound more

---

[12] C. J. Bjerkelund, *Parakalô* (1967), p. 134.
[13] Boers, *loc. cit.*, pp. 156–58.
[14] *Ibid.*, p. 142.

like fresh recollections addressed to a congregation Paul had only just left.

Still, it is possible that there had been time for the Thessalonians to write Paul a letter of inquiry. Then, our first letter may be seen as his pastoral reply to matters on which they had asked for his advice and guidance. In this way C. E. Faw explains the wording of 4:9, 13; 5:1 (cf. 5:12) with their repeated phrase "concerning . . ." this and that matter.[15]

2. The relation of 1 Thessalonians and the Acts-narrative has been called to account for some difficulties felt if the letter was written shortly after Paul's initial visit. According to Acts 17:4 and 18:5 Timothy was not with Paul at Corinth. But he appears to be sent by Paul to Thessalonica from Athens. There is some confusion here, since 1 Thessalonians 3:1f. says plainly that Paul was "alone" (μόνοι) at Athens. See the discussion in F. F. Bruce,[15a] who notes Lightfoot's explanation which postulates a return trip by Timothy from Athens to Thessalonica to see how the church was getting on; Silas, too, was charged to go on other errands to Macedonia. This accounts for Paul's solitary state at Athens which he left before the return of Timothy and Silas — and he was by himself at Corinth until he was joined by the two colleagues. Yet there is a problem with the plural μόνοι in 1 Thessalonians 3:1. Michaelis therefore argues that we should think of a later visit of Paul to Corinth, or a stopover there in 50–52, when he sent Timothy to Thessalonica.[16] The issue is how to fit exact movements into the Acts-itinerary, but we should not blithely assume that Acts gives a full and detailed account of all of Paul's movements. We simply do not know for certain the full range of Paul's movements at this time in his life. For instance, some hurried trips to Corinth alluded to in the Corinthian correspondence cannot be fitted into the itinerary in Acts.

3. A further suggestion is that Paul must have written after AD 50, because 4:13ff. requires that there had been several deaths in the congregation; and it is for this reason that the state of the departed dead is a matter of concern. But even a single reported death would have sufficed to trigger the question of the welfare of Christians who die before the *parousia*. Besides, in a time of persecution, there may indeed have been several believers who died prematurely.

THE THESSALONIANS' MISUNDERSTANDINGS

The church needed guidance and comfort in the face of persecution,

---

[15] C. E. Faw, "On the Writing of First Thessalonians," *JBL*, 71 (1952), 217–25; see too A. J. Malherbe, "Exhortation in First Thessalonians," *NovT*, 25 (1983), 238–56.

[15a] *1 and 2 Thessalonians* (WBC, 1982), pp. 60f.

[16] W. Michaelis, *Die Gefangenschaft des Paulus in Ephesus und das Itinerar des Timotheus* (1925), pp. 65ff.; and *Einleitung in das Neue Testament*[2] (1954), pp. 221–25.

which had raised the problem of theodicy. There was a need to justify to perplexed believers ways of God which appeared meaningless and thus challenged faith. There were two related questions. One was the delay of the *parousia*. Why was the Lord delaying his coming and deferring the advent of his kingdom? Meanwhile, Christians were passing from the scene in death. What would be their share in the coming kingdom? Had they lost their place? Would they be at a disadvantage because they had not survived until the promised advent? The other matter was a natural corollary of this: if Christians have to die, what is their state and what comfort may their mourning relatives have amid their sense of loss?

Paul's answers (4:13–18) strike a note of admonition (do not come to hasty conclusions about the deferment of the *parousia* or the loss inevitably suffered by the deceased) and consolation alike. The *paraenesis* is essentially one of hope, founded on the resurrection of Jesus and the future resurrection of his people. This may suggest that the root error at Thessalonica was the loss of future eschatology.[17] They based their loss of the hope that believers will be raised at the end-time on the mistaken notion that at baptism believers were raised to new life and that this "spiritual" resurrection constituted their sole hope, so that death would present a real problem.

The prospect of the *parousia* follows directly from the Lord's triumph over death. When Jesus comes—and Paul sets the advent in the framework of Jewish apocalypticism—both the living church and the departed saints will be united in the best of all bonds: they will share in Christ's presence (παρουσία). "So we shall always be with the Lord" (4:17) is one of Paul's noblest words on a dark subject. It is enough for us to know that, and for the Thessalonians that they should rest in the assurance of the union of the believer and the Lord in both life and death—a firm basis of Pauline eschatology (cf. 2 Cor. 5:1–10; Phil. 1:21).[18]

If a type of "realized" eschatology was a mistaken teaching

---

[17] This part of Schmithals' thesis (see above, p. 161) is at least a plausible reconstruction of what Paul is responding to; much more questionable is that these erroneous opinions and faulty eschatology were introduced by intruding gnostic teachers. See J. Plevnik, "The Taking Up of the Faithful and the Resurrection of the Dead in 1 Thessalonians 4:13–18," *CBQ*, 46 (1984), 274–83, on the "pattern of assumption" found in Paul's text. This argument partly answers C. L. Mearns, "Early Eschatological Development in Paul: The Evidence of I and II Thessalonians," *NTS*, 27 (1980–81), 137–57; cf. J. Gillman, "Signals of Transformation in 1 Thessalonians 4:13–18," *CBQ*, 47 (1985), 263–81, who sees the key to development in Paul's eschatological language and idiom in the transformation of believers in this life to a "spiritual body."

[18] On 2 Cor. 5:1–10 cf. two essays by M. J. Harris, "Paul's View of Death in 2 Corinthians 5:1–10," in *New Dimensions in New Testament Study*, edd. Longenecker and Tenney (1974), pp. 317–28; and "Resurrection and Immortality: Eight Theses," *Themelios*, 1 n.s. (1976), 50–55. On Phil. 1:21 see the bibliography in R. P. Martin, *Philippians* (1976), pp. 76–79, esp. P. Hoffmann, *Die Toten in Christus* (1966).

cherished in this church, it may well explain further aberrations.[19] Clearly there was a failure to apply the eschatological motif to Christian living.[20] Church members were growing slack in discipleship and unconcerned about the future (5:2–10). Paul reminds them that the Christian life is lived between the two advents and its true expression is one which reckons with the eschatological tension of "already . . . not yet." We are already "children of light and of the day," and we wait for our completed salvation at the end-time. Thus, we are called to live with self-restraint, morally alive to God's holy requirements.

The Thessalonians had forgotten this. Paul rebukes their evil and immoral ways (4:3–8), their lack of love in community (4:9–12), and their feeble grasp of the stringent ethic which should control their congregational life (5:14–16). In all this he sets before them a gentle corrective of their lives and urges them to aspire to a life pleasing to God (4:1) based on his own example.

It looks as though they took his teaching to heart—and did so in excess. By the time the second letter was composed, Paul had to bring the church back from the other end of the spectrum. There may have been extenuating circumstances to account for this distortion of the apostolic tradition.

Evidently in the short time separating the two letters, false teachers *had* arisen within the congregation (2 Thess. 2:2). Professing to be transmitters of revelations, they claimed apostolic authority. Moreover, spurious letters carrying Paul's name were being circulated and possibly his signature was being forged (cf. 3:17). The church was reacting to these pressures by adopting some fantastic conceptions about the *parousia*. The net result of the inference that "the day of the Lord has already begun" (2:2) was an abandonment of daily work and an unhealthy absorption with excited preparations for the final climax (3:6–13).

Paul's speaks out in clear terms and tones (3:14–16). Such conduct is reprehensible, yet those who are deluded should be gently won back to the right way. His recall to the apostolic traditions is the fundamental argument to which he appeals (2:15).

THE ORDER OF THE LETTERS

The traditional ordering of "First" and "Second" Thessalonians is a convenient way of identifying documents, not based on anything inherent

---

[19] Lütgert and R. Jewett postulate the presence of "enthusiastic" Christianity at Thessalonica, which involved a loss of eschatological depth. There is a useful survey in Best, *op. cit.*, pp. 16–22, concluding: "Instead therefore of looking for one definite group which Paul was attacking in Thessalonica we must see present a number of ideas from the Hellenistic atmosphere which were foreign to Christianity's Jewish cradle and which Paul had to refute."

[20] But see B. N. Kaye, "Eschatology and Ethics in 1 and 2 Thessalonians," *NovT*, 17 (1975), 47–57, who however underrates the eschatological problems occasioned by false notions.

in the text. It is popularly thought that this ranking is a matter of length: 1 Thessalonians is longer, therefore it was written first, and so placed first in canonical order. But some have suggested reversing this sequence.[21]

The heart of the problem with the traditional sequence is that not everyone finds it convincing that Paul would write a second letter so shortly after the first, which does not add much to the content of the first. But as we suggested above, if we can postulate the advent of false teachers (in 2 Thess. 2:2) and a consequent general misunderstanding of Paul's teaching soon after receipt of the first letter, the quick succession of a second would be accounted for.

1. Some maintain that the sending of Timothy from Athens to Thessalonica (1 Thess. 3:1) is better explained on the theory that our 2 Thessalonians was written first. The inference is that Timothy took our "second" letter with him, for the tone of this letter is said to be anxiety-laden and it is full of Paul's fears for a congregation under duress. The writing of the longer epistle attests to Paul's relief when Timothy returned to Corinth with a report of the good news of the church's confidence in the faith. That explains its notes of joy and assurance. But these distinctions hardly seem to be true.

2. 1 Thessalonians 2:17f. with its statement that Paul tried ἅπαξ καὶ δίς—repeatedly (lit. "once and twice," "more than once")—to revisit the church seems to sound "hollow and unreal if we maintain the orthodox order of the epistles, but become[s] full of meaning if we reverse the order."[22] But this is so only if we know exactly what was in Paul's mind as he wrote what we traditionally call 1 Thessalonians. Perhaps he *did* try repeatedly to make the journey. He does not need to mention this fact in 2 Thessalonians, because the need to justify and vindicate his conduct has passed.

3. 1 Thessalonians is held to reflect a church situation more mature than 2 Thessalonians. This is of course a subjective judgment; and it is a dubious axiom indeed that "maturity" inevitably comes later in time and grows as the months and years pass. A similar response must be made to the argument that 2 Thessalonians is more Judaic in tone and temper, whereas 1 Thessalonians is more "stately" in its eschatology. W. G. Kümmel, however, makes the cogent point that there is no suggestion in 1 Thessalonians that the faith of the church had been endangered by apocalyptic fanaticism. An earlier letter would surely have been mentioned in what we know as the first epistle.[23]

---

[21] The case for reversing the order has been attractively presented by T. W. Manson, in his chapter in *Studies in the Gospels and Epistles* (1962), pp. 259–78. Cf. also W. Kümmel, *Introduction*[2], pp. 263ff.; Best, *op. cit.*, pp. 42–45.

[22] R. Gregson, "A Solution to the Problems of the Thessalonian Epistles," *EQ*, 38 (1966), 76–80. Cf. J. C. West, "The Order of 1 and 2 Thessalonians," *JTS*, 15 o.s. (1914), 66–74.

[23] Kümmel, *op. cit.*, p. 264.

4. If we take seriously the problem raised by the transmission of two letters to the same community in a short time, we may see the difficulty eased by several more radical suggestions.

a. Harnack's suggestion is that 2 Thessalonians is directed to a Jewish-Christian minority in the church, and was sent simultaneously with 1 Thessalonians. M. Dibelius, too, argues that there were two different sets of recipients for the two letters—the first being addressed to the church leaders, the second to the entire community.[24] But neither of these hypotheses can dispel the strangeness of the suggestion that Paul sent two letters dealing with related issues to the same place and did not make a cross reference from one to the other. We may compare the situation in regard to Colossians and its references to the Laodicean epistle (though we should observe that Philemon is *not* alluded to).

b. E. Schweizer surmises that 2 Thessalonians was really addressed to Philippi, and was sent at the same time as 1 Thessalonians.[25] The single ground of support for this is found in Polycarp (*Phil.* 11:3), who quotes 2 Thessalonians 1:4 as though it referred to the Philippians. But there is a world of difference between the tone and theme of Philippians (e.g., Phil. 1:5) and 2 Thessalonians. The same negative judgment must be passed on M. Goguel's hypothesis that 2 Thessalonians was an epistle to the Beroean church.[26]

c. A final option is that the problem of interrelating the two is unreal, on the ground that 2 Thessalonians is non-Pauline. Arguing that there is a literary dependence of 2 Thessalonians on 1 Thessalonians and that the apostolic signature in 2 Thessalonians (2:2; 3:17) betrays the sign of a *falsarius* using Paul's name, W. Wrede concluded that the second epistle was spurious.[27] Other—less substantial—arguments have centered on the lack of agreement in eschatological teaching between 2 Thessalonians 2:1–12 on the one hand and 1 Thessalonians 4:13ff. and 1 Corinthians 15 on the other;[28] and the alleged moralistic teaching in 2 Thessalonians 1:5ff.; 2:12, which is contrasted

---

[24] A. Harnack, *Das Problem des zweiten Thessalonicherbriefs* (1910); M. Dibelius, *An die Thessalonicher, i, ii* (1937), pp. 57f.

[25] E. Schweizer, "Der zweite Thessalonicherbrief ein Philipperbrief?", *TZ*, 1 (1945), 90–105. This is criticized by W. Michaelis, "Der zweite Thessalonicherbrief kein Philipperbrief," *TZ*, 1 (1945), 282–86, and J. Gnilka, *Der Philipperbrief* (1968), p. 11. See further, R. P. Martin, *Philippians*, p. 12.

[26] M. Goguel, *Introduction au Nouveau Testament*, 4, 1 (1925), 335–37.

[27] W. Wrede, *Die Echtheit des zweiten Thessalonicherbriefes* (1903). Schmithals has sought to overturn Wrede's argument with the suggestion that 2 Thess. may well itself be a composite (*Letter A*: 1:1–12; 3:6–16: *Letter B*: 2:13f., 1–12, 15–17, 3:1–3(5), 17f.); and that the similarities between the two are the result of the combination of several Pauline fragments. See his *Paul and the Gnostics*; and "Die Thessalonicherbriefe als Briefkompositionen," in *Zeit und Geschichte* (Bultmann *Festschrift*) (1964), pp. 295–315. Cf. Best, *op. cit.*, pp. 31–33, 45–50, for a cogent critique.

[28] R. H. Fuller, *A Critical Introduction to the New Testament*, pp. 57f.

to the teaching in the undisputed letters.[29] W. Marxsen believes that 2 Thessalonians 2:2 reflects the presence of gnostic heresy. The church of 2 Thessalonians, he avers, is one which is afflicted by the presence of gnostic fanatics, who insist that the end has come. "Paul"—an apocalyptist who borrows the apostle's name—counters this with a scenario drawn from Jewish writings (2:3–12).[30]

But Marxsen's thesis falls down on the close linguistic connections between the two epistles.[31] And the authenticity of 2 Thessalonians was not suspected by the early canon-makers. Marcion in the second century placed it in the Pauline list. We may conclude that both letters originate from the same hand and from the same period. New situations at Thessalonica required fresh emphases, but in both documents there are common themes. These are the duty of suffering as a concomitant of the Christian life; the threat of judgment on the church's oppressors; and the reproof of the slothful and fanatics, who imagined that they were already "risen with Christ" to a celestial life on earth and were morally irresponsible on the ground that no evil could come to their "pure" spirits.

[29] H. Braun, in *ZNTW*, 44 (1952–53), 152ff.; cf. Best, *op. cit.*, pp. 51, 54.
[30] W. Marxsen, *Introduction*, pp. 37–44.
[31] See B. Rigaux, *Saint Paul: Les épîtres aux Thessaloniciens* (1956), pp. 80–94; Best, *op. cit.*, pp. 22–29, 52.

CHAPTER FOURTEEN

The Corinthian Correspondence and Its Setting

THE CHURCH AT CORINTH

"Anxiety on account of all the churches" (2 Cor. 11:28) was no idle Pauline phrase, and no church caused the apostle more stress than the community at Corinth. Before we examine the New Testament Epistles in which those conflicts are aired, let us look at the city at the time of Paul's visit and what we know of the church he founded there.[1]

First-century Corinth was the leading commercial center of southern Greece. Its favorable geographical situation contributed to this, for it was located on the isthmus connecting northern Greece with the Peloponnesus, and it boasted two harbors, Lechaeum to the west, and Cenchreae to the east. It thus became an emporium for seaborne merchandise passing in either direction, and a considerable number of roads converged on it. Sailors were able to avoid the dangerous route around the Peloponnesus; and a more northerly trip across the Aegean Sea, away from storms, was made possible.

Like most seaports throughout history Corinth took on an international reputation. There must have been considerable intermixing of races in its population; and this resulted in a variety of religious cults. Corinth's chief shrine was the temple of Aphrodite, the Greek goddess of love and life. In Corinth her cult appeared in a debased form, due to the admixture of certain Oriental influences. This meant a low moral tone and sexual perversion in a possibly attested cult of sacred prostitution.[2]

---

[1] For discussions of 1st-century Corinth see the standard commentaries of C. K. Barrett (Harper-Black, 1968 and 1973 on the two Epistles), F. F. Bruce (NCB, 1971), H. Conzelmann (*Hermeneia*, ET 1974), as well as the detailed information provided in older works such as Robertson-Plummer (ICC, 2nd ed., 1929) and J. Moffatt (MNTC, 1938). For a report of archaeological work at Corinth, see O. Broneer, "Corinth," *BA*, 14 (1951), 78–96. There is an earlier report by W. A. McDonald, "Archaeology and St. Paul's Journeys in Greek Lands (3): Corinth," *BA*, 5 (1942), 36–48. The latest account is in V. P. Furnish, *2 Corinthians* (Anchor Bible, 1984), Introduction. See too N. Papahatzis, *Ancient Corinth: The Museums of Corinth, Isthmia and Sicyon* (1977); J. Murphy-O'Connor, *St. Paul's Corinth* (1983); and the same writer's "The Corinth that Saint Paul Saw," *BA*, 47 (1984), 147–59.

[2] Strabo, *Geogr.* 8.6.20: "The Temple of Aphrodite was so rich that it owned more

From the luxury and vice of Corinth was coined the word "corinthianize" (i.e., to fornicate) as an infamous sign of the wealth and immorality for which the city was renowned in the ancient world. But Aristophanes may have invented the verb as part of Athenian disdain for the region in southern Greece during the Peloponnesian war, or else the term reflects the rivalry of Athens whose trade was jeopardized by Corinth.

In such a place, by the grace of God and the ministry of his servant Paul, a church was formed. A large proportion of its members must have been drawn from the pagan world, with its heterogeneous standards of life and conduct. Not surprisingly issues of Christian morality and behavior dominate the first Epistle; and in 2 Corinthians 6 a strong warning is issued against association with unbelievers. "Also, the tendencies to factiousness and instability have a real psychological basis in both the blend and the clash of racial character to be found in such a cosmopolitan city."[3]

A section of the church belonged to the Jewish colony, the so-called Dispersion, which was naturally represented in such a commercial center. Acts 18:1-11 tells us that the church was formed as a result of Paul's preaching in the local synagogue. Archaeologists have uncovered an inscription from a later site of this meeting-place with the words "synagogue of the Hebrews."[4] Nonetheless, it is probably correct to assume that the preponderance of the church members was Gentile, converted to Christ from a pagan milieu. These were called to be God's people in the "Vanity Fair" (or Las Vegas) of the Roman Empire.

Corinth had attained eminence as a city much earlier than Paul, owing to its commercial advantages, but it had been destroyed by the Roman conqueror L. Mummius about two hundred years before the apostle's visit. After lying in ruins for about a century, it was reconstructed by Julius Caesar in 46 BC and peopled as a Roman colony. This may account for Roman names which appear in the Corinthian letters (1 Cor. 1:14: Crispus, Gaius; 16:17: Stephanas, Fortunatus, Achaicus).

In the first century the city was heavily populated, and its place as a political and commercial center can be gauged from the Romans' having made it in 27 BC the capital city of the senatorial province of Achaia in southern Greece. And while its reputation for moral corruption made the "Corinthian life" synonymous with luxury and licentiousness, its pretensions to philosophy and literary culture made the phrase "Corinthian words" a token of polished and cultivated speech.

In this great and busy center Paul spent a year and a half or

---

than a thousand temple-slaves, courtesans, whom men and women had dedicated to the goddess." But Conzelmann, op. cit., p. 12, doubts the relevance of this description to the city of Paul's day on the ground that Strabo's reference to "prostitutes in the temple service" (of Aphrodite) is anachronistic, and Pausanias is silent on the issue.

[3] R. H. Strachan, Paul's Second Epistle to the Corinthians (MNTC, 1935), p. xiv.

[4] A. Deissmann, Light from the Ancient East (ET 1927), p. 16; J. Finegan, Light from the Ancient Past (1969), II, 360-63.

more in the course of his second missionary journey (Acts 18:11,18), having arrived in the city probably in the winter of 50/51. (As we have noted, Gallio's accession on July 1, 51, as proconsul of Achaia in southern Greece is one of the fixed points of apostolic chronology.)[5] Paul found hospitality in the home of Aquila and Priscilla, a Jewish couple who had come from Rome in 49 following the decree of Claudius (see below, p. 188), eminent for their generosity and devotion. With them he carried on his trade of tentmaking.

Beginning his ministry in the synagogue, he was soon compelled by the opposition of the Jews to seek another place of meeting, which he found in the house of Justus, a converted proselyte. There he preached the gospel, encouraged by a vision from God. Divine blessing was manifest in the conversion of his hearers and the establishment of a Christian community in spite of the Jews' attempt to invoke the civil power against him (Acts 18:4–18). The converts seem to have been drawn from the lower classes (1 Cor. 1:26–29), but not exclusively so (cf. 10:27; 11:17–34). They were not free from the prevailing tendency to intellectual pride (cf. 1:18–20; 3:18, 19; 8:1). Added to this was a proneness to sensual sin, equally characteristic of their native city (5:1–11; 6:15–18; 11:21), though there is probably a theological reason for these symptoms.

Internal evidence in the first letter in the canonical order suggests that several features marred the life of this church. There was a factious spirit which broke the church up into rival groups and showed itself in bickering which drew them to civil courts to settle their disputes (ch. 6). This party rivalry destroyed the unity of Christ's body (ch. 12) and was seen even at the Lord's table meal (11:17ff.). Also, they boasted of their "knowledge" (8:1) and "freedom" (6:12; 8:9; 10:23). These two terms have suggested to some scholars that a species of Judaeo-gnostic thought and practice had penetrated the church and influenced the thinking and conduct of some of the members.[6] Numerous signs of this heresy have been identified: the value placed on esoteric "knowledge" (gnōsis; 1:5; 8:1,7,10,11; 12:8; 13:2; 14:6)[6a]; "freedom" claimed and used in many ways;[6b] denial of a future resurrection (ch. 15; cf. 2 Tim. 2:18);

---

[5] The evidence, set forth in J. Finegan, *Handbook of Biblical Chronology* (1964), pp. 316–18, may also be construed to fix the date twelve months later (AD 52); see J. J. Gunther, *Paul: Messenger and Exile* (1972), pp. 57, 171f., and, for the earlier dating, F. F. Bruce, *New Testament History* (1969), pp. 282,298; J. A. T. Robinson, *Redating the New Testament*, pp. 31,35; and E. M. Smallwood, *Jews under Roman Rule* (1976), p. 213n35.

[6] W. Schmithals, *Gnosticism in Corinth* (ET 1971), pp. 117–285; W. Marxsen, *Introduction to the New Testament* (ET 1968), p. 75.

[6a] Cf. 2 Cor. 2:14; 4:6; 8:7; 10:5; 11:6.

[6b] To these Corinthian catchwords must be added "spiritual" (*pneumatikos*), which is found fourteen times in 1 Cor. as against four times in the other undisputed Pauline letters. Individual Corinthians evidently set themselves above the constraints of community order and control; each church member became a law to himself or herself (1 Cor. 8:9; 10:23). Another slogan was evidently the verb

high value placed on sacramental efficacy as conferring "protection" (ch. 10) with a devaluation of ethical seriousness; an importance attached to demonstrations of the Spirit (14:1ff.); the setting up of a clique of Spirit-endowed persons (14:37); strange marriage practices (ch. 7; cf. 1 Tim. 4:3); and a disavowal of interest in the earthly Jesus in a concentration on the heavenly "aeon" Christ (12:3), with a consequent passing over of the *kerygma* centered in the cross (1:18f., 23).[7] At 2:8 the christological title "Lord of glory" is probably borrowed from Paul's Corinthian opponents and turned against them as it is anchored in the cross, namely, by insisting that Jesus became Lord only by first submitting to humiliation and death.

The attractiveness of this interpretation is that it makes all the facets of the Corinthians' erroneous teaching and practice spring from a single source. However, it begs the question of whether second-century gnostic ideas appeared so early in the apostolic age (a theme we shall take up later). Some have explained the contents of the Corinthian correspondence without any recourse to gnosticizing ideas,[8] but it is more likely that at Corinth we see the beginning of that accommodation of the Christian gospel to Hellenistic mysticism which was later to blossom in the various gnostic schools. F. F. Bruce's term "incipient gnosticism" might well be flexible enough to account for the Corinthian phenomena.[9]

PAUL'S VISITS TO CORINTH

Paul's motives and movements in connection with his visits to this city form a difficult complex, but the following outline of events is likely, and we shall base our discussion of his Corinthian correspondence on this reconstruction.

1. The founding of the church (Acts 18:1ff.).
2. Paul leaves Corinth and goes to Ephesus (Acts 18:18f.).
3. He sends the Corinthians a letter, to which he refers in

"to excel" (*perisseuein*), esp. in the debate over *charismata:* see R. P. Martin, *The Spirit and the Congregation* (1984), p. 154, for references.

[7] Cf. J. M. Robinson, "Kerygma and History in the New Testament," in *Trajectories through Early Christianity* (with H. Köster, 1971), p. 34: "It would seem to be this heretical interpretation of the kerygma in terms of an already consummated eschaton for the initiated that is behind the various Corinthian excesses to which Paul addresses himself in 1 Corinthians."

[8] E.g., J. C. Hurd, Jr., *The Origin of 1 Corinthians* (1965).

[9] F. F. Bruce, *1 and 2 Corinthians*, p. 21. Cf. R. McL. Wilson, "How Gnostic were the Corinthians?", *NTS*, 19 (1972–73), 65–74; R. M. Grant, *A Historical Introduction to the New Testament* (1963), pp. 204–206, bases his conviction that "there were Gnostics at Corinth, and that Gnosticism was essentially a way of viewing the Christian gospel" on the Corinthians' claim to adopt a fully realized eschatology, drawn in part from Jewish apocalypticism. But this is challenged by D. J. Doughty, "The Presence and Future of Salvation in Corinth," *ZNTW*, 66 (1975), 61–90, who argues that the controversy at Corinth turns not on the futurity of salvation, but rather on the understanding of salvation as such (see later, pp. 408f.). See in particular A. C. Thiselton, "Realized Eschatology at Corinth," *NTS*, 24 (1977–78), 510–26; and the bibliography in Martin, *The Spirit and the Congregation* (1984).

1 Corinthians 5:9, now lost, though some scholars believe that 2 Corinthians 6:14—7:1 may be a fragment of it.[10]

4. He learns from "members of Chloe's household" (1 Cor. 1:11) that the church in Corinth is split into factions.

5. About the same time, Paul receives a letter from the Corinthians asking for his advice and guidance on certain issues affecting the ordering of worship and Christians' relations with the outside world (1 Cor. 7:1).

6. He responds to the factiousness and answers their request for advice by writing the letter we know as 1 Corinthians. This letter is taken by Titus (cf. 2 Cor. 12:18, though this verse more probably refers to the "severe letter" visit of para. 10 below), who subsequently returns to Ephesus where Paul is.

7. Timothy is sent to Corinth on a special mission (1 Cor. 4:17; 16:10).

8. In the meantime a serious crisis breaks out in Corinth, fomented by the arrival of Jewish emissaries. Paul's authority is challenged (2 Cor. 10:10; 11:23; 12:6f.). Timothy is evidently at a loss to deal with it and returns with the news to Ephesus.

9. On receiving Timothy's report, Paul pays a brief visit to Corinth, to deal with the issue in person. This he later refers to as the "painful visit" (2 Cor. 2:1). He is humiliated before the church, and has to return to Ephesus in great distress.

10. He now writes a powerful letter of remonstrance, at great cost to himself, in order to deal with the crisis (2 Cor. 2:4; 7:8). This is known as the "tearful" or the "severe letter," which is either lost or only partially preserved in 2 Corinthians 10–13. Titus is instructed to meet Paul at Troas.

11. According to the plan outlined in 1 Corinthians 16:5ff., but after some delay caused by the "intermediate visit" to Corinth (mentioned as para. 9 above), Paul leaves Ephesus for Macedonia. He comes to Troas, and cannot find Titus; so he goes on to Macedonia to intercept him (2 Cor. 2:12f.).

12. Paul meets Titus, who relates that the worst is over, and the rebellion is quelled (2 Cor. 7:6–16).

13. He writes the letter we have as 2 Corinthians, either in its entirety (in which case the last four chapters are aimed at clearing up the remaining pockets of resistance and opposition in the church) or in part (that is, what we know as chapters 1–9). This letter he sends from Macedonia through Titus, accompanied by two other brethren.

14. Paul himself reaches Corinth (Acts 20:2).

---

[10] Kümmel, *Introduction*, pp. 276f., concludes that "the 'prior letter' has simply not survived." We shall return to this question (p. 183).

CORRESPONDENCE WITH THE CHURCH AT CORINTH

From internal evidence in 1 Corinthians it is clear that that letter was written on the eve of Paul's second visit to Corinth, which he was about to pay after passing through Macedonia, having already sent Timothy in advance as his representative, apparently from Ephesus (1 Cor. 16:8–10). This plan links up with what we read in Acts 20:1f., that at the close of a three-year stay at Ephesus Paul visited Greece. It appears that almost immediately before he left Ephesus he sent Timothy before him to Macedonia (19:21–23). There are other indications in the first Corinthian letter that it was written while the apostle was at Ephesus (16:19; cf. Acts 18:18f.; also 1 Cor. 15:32).

Although we can fairly certainly place the writing of 1 Corinthians at this point in Paul's missionary career, it is difficult to fix a more precise time of composition. 1 Corinthians 16:8 shows that he wrote shortly before a feast of Pentecost, which we may place early in May of 54/55. We infer, too, from 16:1f. that the collection at Corinth for the poor believers in Jerusalem had not yet been started. In 2 Corinthians 8:10 and 9:2 he writes that the Corinthians began the collection "last year." As McNeile and Williams say, "the relation between the dates of the two epistles depends upon this phrase."[11] It is clear that 2 Corinthians was written from Macedonia after Paul had left Ephesus. Eager to learn the results of the visit by Titus to Corinth to enforce the apostle's views and gauge the response to his severe letter, Paul had no heart to embrace the opportunity to preach at Troas when his emissary did not show up there. Finally they met in Macedonia. Titus brought the good news that Paul's letter had done its work well, producing in the Corinthians a repentant sorrow. His joy at learning that the crisis was over is the immediate occasion of what we know as 2 Corinthians.

> He had been racked with fear that they might defy his authority by refusing to listen to the pleadings and to follow the directions in his sorrowful letter. His relief was unbounded when he heard from Titus that they had accepted his letter in the right spirit, and had shown their penitence by dealing strongly—almost too strongly—with the offender. And he at once wrote this letter. It was not a moment for dealing with Christian doctrine or Church practice; the letter is simply a pouring out of the man himself.[12]

Whereas the contents of 1 Corinthians fall into well-defined sections, corresponding largely to the matters on which the church had written to Paul for advice (several of which we shall take up in Part Seven), in 2 Corinthians the flow of Paul's writing is erratic and less

[11] A. H. McNeile-C. S. C. Williams, *An Introduction to the Study of the New Testament*[2] (1953), p. 133; but see Kümmel, *op. cit.,* p. 282; Gunther, *Paul,* p. 77.
[12] A. H. McNeile-C. S. C. Williams, *op. cit.,* p. 138; see also C. K. Barrett, "Titus," in *Neotestamentica et Semitica* (M. Black *Festschrift*), edd. E. E. Ellis and M. Wilcox (1969), pp. 1–14. This is the traditional view. But the issues are more complex, as I have tried to set out in some detail in *2 Corinthians* (WBC, 1985), pp. xxxiv-lii.

well-ordered, especially in the first seven chapters. Before we come to grips with some critical problems of the letter, it will be necessary to set down an analysis of the contents and to say something about its values.

AN ANALYSIS OF 2 CORINTHIANS

Introduction (1:1–11): notes of salutation (vv. 1,2) and thanksgiving (vv. 3–11).

I. *Paul justifies his conduct toward the Corinthians* (1:12—7:16).

A. *The question of Paul's journeys to Corinth* (1:12—2:13): Paul has changed his voyage plans and has consequently been accused of vacillation. He defends himself by explaining that he wants to spare both of them fresh pain like that of the "painful visit" (see below). He explains his movements from Troas to Macedonia, where Titus had brought him news.

B. *First defense of the apostolic ministry* (2:14—7:4).

1. *The faithfulness of the apostle* (2:14—3:6): the Christian apostle is the "aroma of Christ to God among those who are being saved." He has confidence in the message he proclaims and needs no "letters of recommendation." Believers who respond to the gospel are living letters, proving the validity of the new covenant applied by the Holy Spirit to their hearts.

2. *The superiority of the apostle in the new covenant* (3:7—4:6): this excellence of the new covenant is contrasted with the Mosaic order.

3. *The weaknesses and sufferings of the apostle* (4:7—5:10).

   a. *His present experiences* (4:7-12) bearing about in his body the dying of Jesus in a "passion-mysticism."

   b. *His future hope* (4:13—5:10) in the resurrection of Christ.

4. *The apostle as ambassador and servant of God* (5:11—6:10): a blend of doctrine (5:11—6:1) and practice (6:2-10) in an exposition of the gospel of God's reconciliation.

5. *Double conclusion* (6:11—7:4): "our heart is open to you: open to us your heart completely." In the middle of this passage is inserted an exhortation not to associate with unbelievers (6:14—7:1).

C. *Again, Paul's journeys* (7:5-16): the long digression on apostolic ministry is followed by a return to personal issues, taking up the thread of 2:12. Titus had brought him good news, gladdening his heart.

II. *The collection for the Jerusalem church* (8:1—9:15).

A. *Recommendations for the collection and delegates* (ch. 8): the Macedonian churches have been generous. In the collection that Titus has begun to organize at Corinth, let the Corinthians imitate

this Macedonian generosity and, above all, the example of the Lord. One's extra resources should meet the needs of the poor. Three brothers sent by Paul are commended warmly to the Corinthians.
B. *A second recommendation* (ch. 9): the collections would have to be organized promptly to prove to the Macedonians that Paul's estimate of the Corinthians' zeal was correct. One who gives liberally receives liberally from God. Present service is turned to the glory of the gospel and cements the love between Gentile and Jewish elements in the church.

III. *Polemical argument and defense* (10:1—13:10).
A. *Paul defends himself against personal accusations* (ch. 10): Paul clears himself of the charge of cowardice (vs. 6) and points out to those who deny his legitimate apostolic ministry [12a] that the Lord himself has authorized him.
B. *Paul's self-eulogy* (11:1—12:18): Paul regrets the need to speak thus of himself, but it is for the Corinthians' sake and the gospel's. He is in no way inferior to the "super-apostles"; indeed, he is more disinterested than they. There follows (11:21—12:18) his autobiography, his *apologia pro vita sua*. He enumerates his claims, works, sufferings, extraordinary gifts from God, and, at the same time, his weaknesses, especially his "thorn in the flesh." In a final touch of irony he clears himself and his colleagues of any suspicion of covetousness: they had never cost the Corinthians any money!
C. *Final notices* (12:19—13:10): the apostle fears that the third visit will be a time for stern measures. He issues a last call for the church to reform its life and expresses his confidence in them.

Conclusion (13:11-13): final appeal and greetings, ending with the trinitarian formula of apostolic prayer.

[12a] This is the chief concern of the four-chapter letter (10–13), which has the appearance of a separate composition written in response to a fresh incursion of opponents at Corinth (11:4). They build on the accusations mentioned in the earlier correspondence (e.g., 2:17; 3:5f.) but carry their insinuation that Paul is no true apostle — not even a Christian person (10:7) — much farther. Hence chs. 10–13 are marked by an unparalleled vehemence and the use of rhetorical forms (see G. A. Kennedy, *New Testament through Rhetorical Criticism* [1984], ch. 4) unusual for Paul. See the epochal contributions of E. Käsemann, *Die Legitimität des Apostels* (as on p. 187); H.-D. Betz, *Der Apostel Paulus und die sokratische Tradition* (1972); and the forthcoming studies of P. Marshall and C. B. Forbes, referred to in my *2 Corinthians* (WBC, 1985).

On this understanding chs. 10–13 are in the right sequence, but are a later composition addressed to a new, threatening situation that arose directly out of the presence of emissaries, branded in 11:13-15 in an unmeasured way. Only the onset of a new danger, in my view, explains the highly charged language forms in these four chapters, best read as a "Fool's Speech" (see J. Zmijewski, *Der Stil der paulinischen "Narrenrede"* [1978]).

LITERARY PROBLEMS IN 2 CORINTHIANS

Bearing in mind that the bulk of 2 Corinthians is related to Paul's relief at the Corinthians' change of attitude, we may now address ourselves to some more complex literary details.

1. *The "Painful Visit."* In 2 Corinthians (if we think of the letter as a unity as it stands in our Bible), Paul made up his mind to visit Corinth twice—once immediately, crossing directly by sea from Ephesus, and then again after going from there to Macedonia (1:15f.). The first of these visits was made; but the second was not because the first was so painful that Paul could not bring himself to go a second time (1:23; 2:1). That a second visit, unrecorded in Acts, is required is confirmed in 12:14 and 13:1f., which speak of "the third time" he proposes to come to Corinth.

Paul's visits to the city, therefore, may be tabulated thus:

a. A first visit (Acts 18:1–11) was made in the course of Paul's second missionary journey.

b. A second visit (the so-called painful visit) followed when Paul heard adverse reports subsequent to the sending of 1 Corinthians. He decided to pay this visit, which was a painful and humiliating experience for him. Following this he quickly returned to Ephesus and sent to Corinth a letter, written "out of much affliction and anguish of heart" (2 Cor. 2:4) in an attempt to rectify the matter. This is often referred to as the "tearful" or "severe letter." From Titus, the bearer of the severe letter, whom he met in Macedonia, he heard improved news and, as we have seen, his relief occasioned the writing of 2 Corinthians.

c. He spent the next winter at Corinth, fulfilling the promise of 2 Corinthians 12:14 and 13:1f., which explicitly allude to a third visit (Acts 20:2).

Can we trace the "severe letter" which follows the second, sorrowful visit to Corinth? Along with that question comes, for many modern scholars, a doubt: can the *whole* of 2 Corinthians be regarded as expressing satisfaction that the church has acted favorably to the apostle for which response the apostle expresses his relief? In Kümmel's words, "the question [is] whether 1–9 and 10–13 could have been parts of the same letter."[13] These two matters are really quite separate, but they are matched in the modern assumption that part of the "severe letter" may survive in 2 Corinthians 10–13, which (it is held) do not really belong in a letter of thanksgiving and congratulation.

2. *The "Severe Letter."* Some have proposed that this may be canonical 1 Corinthians. It is suggested that the matters in Paul's first letter which caused grief to the Corinthians were his reproaches of their lax discipline and disorderly conduct (esp. chs. 5,6,11). But this identification is rejected by most scholars because Paul's language describing

---

[13] Kümmel, *op. cit.*, p. 290.

his state of mind while writing it (2 Cor. 2:4) is thought to be extravagant if 1 Corinthians is in mind. However, it is at least possible that his words give a flashback to his subjective reactions while he was writing the first letter though he had managed to conceal his feelings.

J. Moffatt objects that 1 Corinthians is permeated by a spirit of calm, practical discussion. Its occasional outbursts of emotional tension (e.g., in ch. 5,6) could not have caused Paul even a momentary twinge of compunction. The language in 2 Corinthians 2:4 and 7:8 is too definite to be explained as the mere recollection of one or two isolated sentences in an epistle of the size and general character of 1 Corinthians. Moffatt also criticizes the view (held by J. Denney among others) that the offender referred to in 2 Corinthians 2:5–8 and 7:12 is the same as the incestuous person of 1 Corinthians 5:1.[14]

A second conjecture as to the identity of the "severe letter" is that the letter in question—minus its beginning—is preserved in 2 Corinthians 10–13. This is a widely held modern theory, first proposed in 1870 by A. Hausrath,[15] who maintained a double thesis—first that 2 Corinthians 10–13 form a separate letter, mutilated at the beginning; and second that this letter is identical with that letter written with tears (*Tränenbrief*), spoken of in 2 Corinthians 2:4. On what does this view rest?

a. *The change of tone between chapters 1–9 and 10–13.* In the former part Paul writes with considerable relief at what he has heard of the change of attitude on the part of the Corinthians. Hostility is absent; friendly relations seem to have been restored. But (so it is held) the latter chapters are "written in remonstrance, anger, satire, and self-defence."[16] The claim that these two sections are incongruous was made as early as 1776 by Semler, who detached 12:14—13:14 as a later epistle and thought of chapter 9 as a separate "note," written independently of the Corinthian letters.

Would the apostle, having expressed his happiness over the success of an earlier and more severe letter and having given some hint of his regret after writing the severe letter, close his epistle with such unparalleled invective in self-defense as is found in 2 Corinthians 10–13? The contrast between the two hypothetical sections of 2 Corin-

---

[14] J. Moffatt, *Introduction to the Literature of the New Testament*[3], pp. 119, 122n. For Denney, see *The Second Epistle to the Corinthians* (1894), pp. 2f.; to be reckoned among those making the same identification is A. M. G. Stephenson, "A Defence of the Integrity of 2 Corinthians," in *The Authorship and Integrity of the New Testament* (1965), pp. 82–97; and "Partition Theories on 2 Corinthians," *SE*, 2 (1964), 639ff. Moffatt argues against the identity of the person in 2 Cor. 7:12 with the sinner of 1 Cor. 5 on the ground that Paul would not have dealt so lightly with the offense of the incestuous person.

[15] A. Hausrath, *Der Vier-Capitel Brief des Paulus an die Korinther* (1870). The best English advocate of the view is J. H. Kennedy, *The Second and Third Epistles of St. Paul to the Corinthians* (1900). One of the clearest statements of the case for partitioning the letter is K. Lake, *The Earlier Epistles of Paul*[2] (1930), pp. 144ff.

[16] McNeile-Williams, *op. cit.*, p. 139.

thians must not be overstated, however. There are evidences in chapters 1–7 of the opposition to Paul which still persisted.[17] In 1:17f. he argues strongly in self-defense; while in 2:6 he speaks of the offender as being punished by the majority, implying that there was a minority who did not agree with Paul's authoritative pronouncement on the case. Also, 2:17 and 4:2–5 advert to those who vexed the apostle's soul by their lack of fidelity to the true gospel, and in 5:12f. we read of their attitude to Paul himself. These evidences suffice to show that chapters 1–7 do not give the impression that the Corinthians are now *wholly* on the side of Paul. His relief is occasioned by the responses of the majority, which was a big step forward, but he must still deal with the more dangerous minority; and it is possible that Paul commends the majority in the first part of the letter, before turning his severe words of rebuke to the still recalcitrant minority in the closing chapters.

b. *Differing references to the apostle's visits*. There are, according to K. Lake, three pairs of passages to support the contention that chapters 10–13 precede chapters 1–7.[18] These are:

I	II
10:6	2:9
13:2	1:23
13:10	2:3

It is evident that the references in the latter part of the Epistle (our column I) are all forward-looking, whereas those in the earlier section (column II) are all in the past. If the sequential order of these parts is reversed, i.e., if column I precedes column II in time, both groups of references could refer to the same visit.

Lake's argument is ingenious but not conclusive. In comparing 13:2 with 1:23 we should note that in 1:23 Paul is concluding his explanation of his altered plans following his painful visit, while 13:2 refers to his intended severity towards those who are still recalcitrant and might, with good reason, look ahead to the visit he anticipates paying from Macedonia. It is the apostle's hope in 13:10 that on this next visit he will not have to use sharpness, but this is the same hope expressed in 2:3; the difference is that in the earlier reference he thinks back to the expression of sentiment in an earlier letter, while in 13:10 he contemplates the effect of the present letter on the Corinthians. There is no obvious reason for placing 10:6 before 2:9, since the context of the latter does not suggest that their obedience was now complete. If, however, in 2:9 the

---

[17] See Stephenson, *op. cit.*, pp. 87ff.; W. H. Bates, "The Integrity of II Corinthians," *NTS*, 12 (1965–66), 56–69; J. L. Price, "Aspects of Paul's Theology and their Bearing on Literary Problems of Second Corinthians," in *Studies in the History and Text of the New Testament: Festschrift* for K. W. Clark (1967), p. 100.

[18] K. Lake, *op. cit.*, pp. 159f.; see also F. F. Bruce, *1 and 2 Corinthians*, pp. 166–70; D. Guthrie, *New Testament Introduction*[3], pp. 433ff.

apostle is saying that in his former letter he was seeking proof of their obedience, it is reasonable to assume that the answer he received was not one hundred per cent, and he still looks forward to its completion in 10:6.

c. *Differing attitudes towards self-commendation.* It is alleged that two irreconcilable—almost schizophrenic[19]—attitudes to self-commendation are found in 2 Corinthians: in 3:1 the apostle deprecates it; in chapters 10–13 he is at great pains to engage in it. In 5:12 he asserts, "We are not commending ourselves to you again." Since both 3:1 and 5:12 use the word "again," it is an attractive suggestion that Paul is thinking of the wording of chs. 10–13 sent at an earlier date.

But 3:1 clearly alludes to the practice of some of Paul's Corinthian opponents to arm themselves with letters of commendation, to which Paul himself strongly objects. Indeed, he sees no need for such letters: the Corinthians themselves are his commendation. The same thought is present in 5:12. In chapters 10–13, however, Paul is addressing those who still oppose him and dispute his credentials. For them a different approach was clearly necessary.

On these three grounds, if their plausibility is granted, the Epistle is regarded as a hypothetical fusion of two separate pieces of correspondence. In addition to our remarks above, however, there are other considerations which make it doubtful or at least not proved.

In the first place, if the hypothesis is true, an explanation is needed for Paul's mention (12:18) of Titus' previous visit.[20] Obviously, if chapters 10–13 constitute the "severe letter," this visit could not have been the occasion on which Titus conveyed the severe letter; yet the language is more naturally read as referring to the time when he took the severe letter and, having reported the changed conditions to the apostle, was sent back with 2 Corinthians (cf. 8:16f.).

Second, it seems likely from 2:1ff., and 7:12 that the reason for the severe letter was the wrongdoing of some individual.[21] Yet there is no mention of this in chapters 10–13. The explanation that this omission can be accounted for by supposing that such a reference was contained in that part of the severe letter which is no longer extant—either accidentally lost or purposely suppressed while the offender was still living—is very feeble.

Finally, we may note that there is no manuscript authority for dividing the Epistle into two parts. It is asked, "Can we suppose that interpolations so serious as to amount . . . to the formation of an entire Epistle out of heterogeneous fragments—or even the interpolation of any one of the passages in question [6:14—7:1; 8–9; 10–13]—can have taken place without leaving so much as a ripple upon the stream of

---

[19] The description of R. P. C. Hanson, *Second Corinthians* (1954), p. 20.
[20] As Kümmel, *op. cit.*, p. 290, observes.
[21] See C. K. Barrett, "HO ADIKĒSAS (2 Cor. 7,12)," in *Verborum Veritas: Festschrift for G. Stählin* (1970), pp. 149ff., on the identity of this individual.

textual tradition?"[22] Moreover, the partition theory requires an extraordinary weaving together of two separate epistles; each only partially preserved; one missing its close, the other its beginning; the two truncated fragments happening to join together to make a single epistle with the appearance of a whole.

There is a third answer to the question of the identity of the severe letter: that it is no longer extant. Since the *entire* letter mentioned in 1 Corinthians 5:9 has certainly been lost (see earlier, p. 174), there is strong presumption in favor of the view that other correspondence between Paul and the Corinthians has also been lost. This view faces fewer difficulties than the other views, though it leaves us without any data for reconstructing the subject-matter of the letter. One can assume that it contained nothing of sufficient general interest to warrant its preservation or that it was suppressed or destroyed because it dealt with some personal opponent of the apostle (2 Cor. 2:5ff.).

We must nevertheless account for the obvious change of tone at the end of 2 Corinthians 9 which J. Héring has likened to the sudden onset of a storm after a clear sky and calm weather.[23] H. Lietzmann proposed a solution in the psychology of the apostle. He imagined that a bout of insomnia caused Paul to adopt a different tone on the day when he came to write chapter 10. Though it may be difficult to take this idea seriously,[24] it does lead on to a second possibility—that the writing of 2 Corinthians took many days, and a distinct time-interval lapsed between the writing of chapters 9 and 10. Possibly more disquieting news reached Paul as he was in the course of his letter, and this inflamed his wrath against the "false apostles" who were none other, in his eyes, than "ministers of Satan" (11:13–15). In any case, Paul's literary manner includes the phenomenon of abrupt digressions. Finally, if we are correct that after addressing the majority in chapters 1–9 Paul directs his attack to a still unsubdued vociferous minority in the church, this change of theme would quite naturally call forth a different emotional reaction. Lietzmann-Kümmel find the explanation in the apostle's change of intention:

> In 2 Corinthians 1–9 Paul has spoken only to the church: now [in chapter 10] he is dealing with his opponents against whom his anger is flaring up, and

---

[22] A. Robertson, in *Hastings' Dictionary of the Bible* (1898), I, 497, supported by R. V. G. Tasker, *The Second Epistle of Paul to the Corinthians* (1958), p. 25. Not much weight can be attached to this part of the argument, however; see C. K. Barrett, *First Corinthians* (1968), pp. 14f.; and J. J. Gunther, *Paul*, pp. 74f., has offered some possible reasons to account for the lack of manuscript evidence.

[23] J. Héring, *La seconde épître de s. Paul aux Corinthiens* (1958), p. 11. For some possible explanations see Kümmel, *op. cit.*, p. 291n27.

[24] H. Lietzmann-W. G. Kümmel, *An die Korinther I–II*[3] (HzNT, 1923), p. 138. The suggestion is hardly a scientific "explanation" (*Erklärung*), and is rightly dismissed by Moffatt, *op. cit.*, p. 123.

with it all kinds of things about the church that he had kept back in chapters 1-9 are coming out again.[25]

3. *The Problem of 2 Corinthians 6:14—7:1.* The unity of 2 Corinthians, on the suppositions above, is defended by several Anglo-Saxon scholars; and also by a number of continental scholars whose outlook is by no means conservative.[26] Yet there is one outstanding problem still remaining. It has been strongly claimed by many scholars, some of whom have otherwise defended the unity of the Epistle, that this section in 2 Corinthians breaks the connection of thought, and may therefore be regarded as an interpolated fragment from another genuine epistle.[27] Since it deals with the problem of the believers' relationships with unbelievers, and since the apostle says in 1 Corinthians 5:9, "I wrote to you in my letter not to associate with immoral men," it is an attractive hypothesis that the 2 Corinthians passage is in mind. Moreover, 1 Corinthians 5:10f. shows clearly that Paul's advice had been misunderstood, and it is at least conceivable that some might have concluded from 2 Corinthians 6:14—7:1 that he wrote advising believers to have nothing to do with unbelievers. Furthermore, 6:13 gives an excellent introduction to 7:2, and removing 6:14—7:1 improves the flow of the argument.

Yet before concluding that the section must be an interpolation, the investigator must be satisfied that this is not another example of the apostle's tendency to digress.[28] The change from 6:13 to 6:14 is abrupt, and the tone differs from the preceding sections. Such a digression would be unpardonable in a treatise, but the same rigid literary rules cannot be applied to letter-writing. If Paul composed the letter in stages over a length of time,[29] one of his breaks may have come here, and he may have taken up a new theme on resuming the letter. Such an explanation would seem more satisfactory than trying to find an unnatural connection with the preceding context.

On the other hand, if the section does really go back to the letter referred to in 1 Corinthians 5:9, how do we explain its present position

---

[25] H. Lietzmann-W. G. Kümmel, *op. cit.*, p. 139 (my translation); cf. A. Wikenhauser, *New Testament Introduction* (ET 1958), pp. 397f.; J. Munck,*Paul and the Salvation of Mankind*, p. 171.

[26] British scholars besides Stephenson, Bates, and Bruce, mentioned above, include D. Guthrie, *op. cit.*, pp. 121-30; R. V. G. Tasker, *op. cit.*, pp. 20-25, P. E. Hughes, *Paul's Second Epistle to the Corinthians* (1962), pp. xxiff. W. G. Kümmel, *op. cit.*, p. 292, concludes: "Looking at the whole question, the best assumption is that II Cor. as handed down in the tradition forms an originally unified letter."

[27] D. Guthrie, *op. cit.*, pp. 425f.; see also R. H. Fuller, *A Critical Introduction to the New Testament*, pp. 41f.; R. M. Grant, *A Historical Introduction to the New Testament*, p. 181; T. W. Manson, "The Corinthian Correspondence," in *Studies in the Gospels and Epistles*, ed. M. Black (1962), p. 220; J. C. Hurd, *op. cit.*, pp. 235-37 (bibliography).

[28] See E. Stange, "Diktierpausen in den Paulusbriefen," *ZNTW*, 18 (1917-18), 115f.

[29] See other suggestions by G. Bornkamm, "The History of the Origin of the So-Called Second Letter to the Corinthians," *NTS*, 8 (1961-62), 258-64.

in 2 Corinthians? It is difficult to believe that anyone would intention-
ally place it here, and the only recourse is therefore to suppose that it got
there accidentally.[29a] But this idea is difficult to sustain in the absence
of any supporting manuscript evidence, particularly as it involves the
insertion of a fragment in the middle of an existing manuscript, and
there is no break in the textual tradition to encourage this view. The
scantiness of our present knowledge of the preservation of the Pauline
Epistles, however, allows for such a hypothesis, and recent studies of the
origin of this passage in the light of the Qumran scrolls have added
further testimony to the idea that this is an independent Pauline—or
non-Pauline—fragment which has become attached loosely to this part
of 2 Corinthians.[30]

FEATURES OF THE EPISTLE

From the analysis of the Epistle's contents and its literary composition
we can now extract its main emphasis and teaching. The first part of the
letter reflects what must have been one of the most distressing experiences of Paul's life. He had been personally opposed and insulted by a
group in the church at Corinth, which "taunted him with the insignifi-
cance of his presence (10:10), and charged him with making promises
which he did not fulfil, with arrogantly asserting authority which he did
not possess."[31] *To* this fractious group he wrote, first, the severe letter;
and *about* this group (on the assumption of the unity of the Epistle) he
wrote the later section of 2 Corinthians.

1. He relates his experience in these humiliating circumstances
and also in the course of his recent apostolic trials in Asia Minor. He had
almost despaired of his life and seemed completely dejected; yet he had
come to a new awareness of God's presence and power and was led to
trust him more fully (4:8–10 is a poignant expression of this).

2. He claims over against his detractors that he has those very
credentials they challenged and denied to him. The call of God in his
own soul, the living proof of his ministry in the changed lives of those
converted under that ministry, the "signs of an apostle": all this ac-
credits him as truly a servant of God. His detractors made a threefold
assault on him: they attacked his person, his teaching, and his character. Paul conducts his defense along these three lines: for the first attack, see 10:1,10; 11:6; and Paul's reply in 10:7; 13:4; for the second
assault, see 10:12–18; 11:7–12; 12:13; 11:4; 2:17; which he answers in

---

[29a] But see G. D. Fee's attempt to relate the section to the problem of idol meats in
1 Cor. ("I Corinthians vi.14–vii.1 and Food Offered to Idols," *NTS,* 23 [1976–77],
140–61). The drawback to this suggestion is, as Fee grants, that idol meats are not
specifically mentioned either in this passage or its immediate context.

[30] J. A. Fitzmyer, "Qumran and the Interpolated Paragraph in 2 Cor. 6:14—7:1,"
CBQ, 23 (1961), 271–80; J. Gnilka, "2 Cor. 6:14—7:1 in the Light of the Qumran
Texts and the Testaments of the Twelve Patriarchs," in *Paul and Qumran,* ed. J.
Murphy-O'Connor (1968), pp. 48–68. Cf. J. J. Gunther, *St. Paul's Opponents and
their Background* (1973), pp. 308–13.

[31] F. B. Clogg, *An Introduction to the New Testament*[3] (1948), p. 39.

2:17; 4:2,5; 10:12–18; 11:1–4; 11:22–30; 12:1–12; and for the third insinuation against his character, see 1:15–17; 10:9–11; 11:16–19; 12:16–19; and Paul's defense in 3:1–6; 10:18; 1:15–24; 12:14–18; 7:2–4; 5:13; 11:16–19.

Notice the grounds on which Paul was attacked: fickleness (1:17f.,23), pride and boasting (3:1), obscurity in preaching (4:3), weakness (10:10), rudeness of speech (11:6), being a mean person (4:7–10; 10:10; 12:7–10), dishonesty (12:16–19), unsoundness of mind (5:13; 11:16–19; 12:6), and lack of apostolic standing (11:5; 12:12).

3. Finally, the emphasis falls on an appeal for generosity on the part of the Corinthians. Chapters 8 and 9 relate to this theme. Those at strife among themselves at Corinth had to look further afield to the needs of the church outside, especially the poor "saints" at Jerusalem. The supreme model is that of the incarnate Lord (8:9).

Above all, 2 Corinthians is a very human document, opening a window into the inner life of the apostle. R. H. Strachan's words are a tribute to this feature:

> The letter is an artless and unconsciously autobiographical description of the ways in which Paul was accustomed to meet slander and calumny, physical danger and bodily suffering, disloyalty and ingratitude, from those for whom he had given of his best, the disillusionment and disappointment that invaded his spirit from time to time.[32]

The personal element obviously comes to the fore often in this Epistle, and this accounts for one of its outstanding values.

> Here Paul is a minister of Christ, and a man among men; none the less so truly human because he was so spiritual. What would hurt us, hurt him; and nerves affected him, as they affect us. The whole Epistle pulsates with emotion. "It enables us, as it were, to lay our hands upon his breast, and feel the very throbbings of his heart." His feelings oscillate between the extremes of satisfaction and indignation: "explanation, defence, protestation, appeal, reproach, invective, threatening, with a vein of subduing pathos blended with the most subtle irony" runs through the whole.[33]

The Epistle has many lessons to teach us. We should be ready to forgive (2:10), grateful for good news (2:13,14, 7:6), courageous and hopeful (4:8–10), recognizing that affliction leads to glory (4:16–18). There should be true ambition for the Christian (5:9). We should see that life contains paradoxes (6:10). There should be a concern for poor church members (chs. 8–9). We should not be eager to defend ourselves against the attacks of others, but there are times when it is right and necessary to do so (chs. 10–11). We should be glad to suffer if God wills (12:8–10). We should be strictly honest (8:16–22; 12:17,18).

PAUL AND POLEMICAL ISSUES AT CORINTH

Finally, let us isolate three special issues in Paul's relations with the Corinthian church.

---

[32] R. H. Strachan, *op. cit.,* p. xxix. His section on 2 Cor. as "A Human Document" (pp. xxix–xxxviii) is worth reading.

[33] W. G. Scroggie, *Know Your Bible,* II (n.d.), 140f.

1. *Rival Parties at Corinth.*[34] An ugly feature of church life in Corinth was how the community split into factions. Part of this was accepted by Paul (1 Cor. 11:19; though this may be ironical), but in the main he sternly criticized the divisions as a blow to the unity of the church and a betrayal of the gospel (1 Cor. 1:10ff.).

The nature of the groups referred to presents a problem (cf. 1 Cor. 1:12; 3:4,5,22; 4:6; 1 Clem. 47:3: "with true inspiration he [Paul] charged you concerning himself and Cephas and Apollos, because even then you had made yourselves partisans"). The names of the apostles and Apollos suggest that the Corinthians were claiming special attachment to these leaders by placing them on the level of pagan mystagogues, with whom the initiate in the Hellenistic mystery religions felt at one in a special way (cf. the reference to baptism in 1 Cor. 1:13f.). More obscure is the allusion to the Christ-party (1:12). Was this a radical Judaizing group; or a clique of "enthusiasts," men of the Spirit, *illuminati* who claimed a special, direct descent from Jesus; or libertines who wanted to be free from any apostolic authority; or Judaeo-Christian gnostics?[35] Perhaps the phrase is a scribal addition, drawn from 2 Corinthians 10:7.

We should note that the groups mentioned are not really schisms or heresies: all attend the same liturgical meeting. Rather it is a matter of diverse tendencies which make use (possibly in a wrongful way) of the apostles' names.[36]

2. *Paul's Apostolate.* From 2 Corinthians we learn that Paul had more serious problems on his hands than the existence of rival groups at Corinth.[37] His spirited defense of his true apostolic ministry was occasioned by challenges he faced from those who claimed to be true apostles and denigrated Paul's office and status by branding it no true apostleship. He directs his argument against these "apostles" (11:5,13,23; 12:11), who made some clearly defined claims for themselves, among them that they were a privileged people of God (11:22f.) and that they worked miracles in the power of the Spirit (11:13ff.; 12:12). What they preached was a rival gospel to Paul's, based on a Christology at odds with his (11:3f.).[38] They exploited the Corinthians (11:20).

---

[34] See N. A. Dahl, "Paul and the Church at Corinth according to 1 Corinthians 1:10—4:21," in *Christian History and Interpretation,* edd. Farmer, Moule, Niebuhr, pp. 313–35, for a review of the various viewpoints, going back to F. C. Baur's seminal essay "The Christ-Party in the Corinthian Church."

[35] W. Schmithals, *Gnosticism in Corinth,* pp. 117ff., considers the various possibilities before championing the last-named suggestion.

[36] Cf. Munck, *op. cit.,* p. 139; Héring, *First Corinthians* (ET 1962), p. 4.

[37] J. M. Robinson, *op. cit.,* pp. 59ff., concludes that in 2 Cor. "Paul was primarily confronted by a distorting transmission of traditions about Jesus as a glorious miracle worker, and he replied, with an ironic presentation of himself within that succession, to document the invalidity of such a scope for the traditions; and by repudiating such knowledge of Jesus." For a similar conclusion, see R. H. Fuller, *op. cit.,* pp. 49f. See now P. W. Barnett, "Opposition in Corinth," *JSNT,* 22 (1984), 3–17; R. Bultmann, *The Second Letter to the Corinthians* (ET 1985), *passim.*

[38] W. Schmithals, *op. cit.,* pp. 124–35, views this teaching in the light of 1 Cor. 12:3;

Paul's characterization of them has suggested to some that these men were a type of Hellenistic miracle-worker-preacher common in the early Christian centuries—and Paul's lack of credentials showed up poorly in contrast to these men, who boasted of their superiority and success.[39] Paul's reply is to deny that this style of life and ministry proves anything in Christian service. He has his own qualifications, quite unlike those claimed by his opponents (12:12).[40] His marks of success are found in a catalog of suffering, privation, physical weakness (11:23ff.; 12:1ff.). These "superlative apostles" (11:5) have cut themselves off from the message of the cross of Jesus by their over-emphasis on power and brilliant performance (see 13:4). Paul comes back to the cross "side" of the *kerygma* in a sustained argument for weakness-as-strength.

3. *Paul and the Collection.*[41] 1 Corinthians 16:1ff. and 2 Corinthians 8–9 are important treatments of this theme, which is a part of Paul's concern for the church at Jerusalem. Clearly this task occupied a central place in Paul's missionary and ecumenical strategy as a promise to the pillar apostles (Gal. 2:10), a proof to the Jewish Christians in Jerusalem of the concern of the Gentile congregations (2 Cor. 9:13f.), and an effective reply to Judaizers who charged Paul with disloyalty to the mother church and (by implication) to the Old Testament heritage of the gospel.

---

but see J. M. Robinson, *op. cit.,* p. 61 and note. See for a full statement R. P. Martin, "The Setting of 2 Corinthians," *TB,* 37 (1986), forthcoming.

[39] D. Georgi, *Die Gegner des Paulus im 2. Korintherbrief* (1964); J.-F. Collange, *Enigmes de la deuxième épître de Paul aux Corinthiens* (1972), pp. 320–24. Against this see D. W. Oostendorp, *Another Jesus: A Gospel of Jewish-Christian Superiority in II Corinthians* (1967), who maintains that Paul's opponents were Jewish Christians who stressed the supremacy of Israel and advocated the "Jewish-Christian superiority" of the original apostles, the law of Moses, and the Jewish heritage of the gospel. Also defending this general position is C. K. Barrett, *Commentary on the Second Epistle to the Corinthians* (1973), pp. 28–30 and *passim*; "PSEUDAPOSTOLOI (2 Cor. 11,13)," in *Mélanges B. Rigaux,* edd. A. Descamps and R. P. André (1970), pp. 377–96; and "Paul's Opponents in II Corinthians," *NTS,* 17 (1970–71), 233–54, where Barrett distinguishes between the "super-apostles" of the Jerusalem church and "false apostles" who came to Corinth, perhaps claiming to be representatives of the "pillar apostles" in Jerusalem.

[40] The thrust of E. Käsemann's essay, "Die Legitimität des Apostels: Eine Untersuchung zu II. Korinther, 10–13," *ZNTW,* 41 (1942), pp. 33–71, was to establish that at the center of the debate between Paul and the "super-apostles" at Corinth was the question of which style of life is the true and valid credential of an apostle. See C. K. Barrett, *The Signs of an Apostle* (1970); and his *Commentary* on 2 Cor., p. 30. Barrett's articles are now reprinted as his *Essays on Paul* (1982).

[41] See K. F. Nickle, *The Collection* (1966). Ivor H. Jones has shown how the theme of the "collection for the saints," suggesting that the Christian social responsibility is life-in-partnership, pervades chs. 1–9; *The Contemporary Cross* (1973). H.-D. Betz, *2 Corinthians 8 and 9* (Hermeneia, 1985), has offered a detailed commentary on "the two administrative letters" of chs. 8 and 9 and has refurbished in a new way J. J. Semler's hypothesis (1776) that the chapters are two separate letters. Betz calls in the aid of rhetorical criticism and proposes a suggestive life-setting of these two distinctive chapters. For a comment written before Betz's work appeared see my *2 Corinthians* (WBC, 1985), pp. 249f.; and cf. G. A. Kennedy, *New Testament Interpretation through Rhetorical Criticism* (1984), p. 92.

CHAPTER FIFTEEN

Paul's Missionary Manifesto in Romans

THE FOUNDING OF THE CHURCH AT ROME

It is one of the ironies of history that (as we saw earlier) the origins of the Christian church which was to become the most important in the world are wrapped in obscurity. What we do know is that, when Paul sent his letter to this community of Roman Christians the church there had already been in existence for some time. He praises their faith and remarks that it is well known throughout the world (1:8). He had not yet visited the city (1:10), in spite of his efforts to do so (1:13; cf. 15:14–23).

We may speculate that Roman Jews present in Jerusalem on Pentecost (Acts 2:10) returned to their home with the good news. And if Romans 16:7 refers to the composition of the church at Rome, we may identify Andronicus and Junias, who were Christians before Paul came on the scene, as leaders who preached and taught the gospel in the capital city of the Empire.

Our first certain knowledge of Roman Christianity comes from what Suetonius (*Life of Claudius* 25.4) tells us about the edict of Emperor Claudius (AD 49). "Because the Jews of Rome were indulging in constant riots at the instigation of Chrestus," he writes, "Claudius expelled them" (see also Dio Cassius, *Hist.* 60.6). This decree of expulsion (*relegatio*) is to be differentiated from *deportatio*, which could involve the confiscation of property, according to Dio.[1]

No fewer than thirteen synagogues in Rome ministered to a Jewish population of between forty and fifty thousand (out of a total population between 700,000 and one million). Early Christian authorities suggest that one of these synagogues was a Jewish Christian one, and it is here that we should probably find the origin of Roman Christianity. By AD 65 (at the time of Nero's persecution) both Tacitus (*Ann.* 15.44) and 1 Clement (6:1) could speak of the martyrs as forming a

---

[1] For a full discussion see F. F. Bruce, *New Testament History*, Ch. 23; and "Christianity under Claudius," *BJRL*, 44 (1962), 309–26.

considerable group, "an immense number of the elect."[2] Some have inferred that we should think of several house congregations as comprising the "saints" at Rome (1:7), and even that part of Paul's purpose in writing was to cement relations between the rival groups meeting in many places in the city.[3]

If the church at Rome began on a Jewish foundation, Paul clearly thought of it as predominantly Gentile (1:13; 11:13,19–22, 25,28). If we may appeal to chapter 16, several names given there are of emancipated slaves and freedmen, and at the other end of the social scale there is at least one aristocratic family in the "household of Aristobulus" (16:10), i.e., a member of Herod's family. But see later, p. 195.

THE PURPOSES OF THE LETTER

Paul wrote this letter shortly after the death of Claudius and the accession of Nero in 54, when the edict of the former had just ceased to be operative. We may trace the most obvious reason for the letter in the following suggestions.

1. Paul had reached a turning-point in his life. Chapters 14–16, especially 15:22–29, make it clear that with Paul's missionary work in the east now concluded (15:19,23) he is turning to face new opportunities in the west. He projects a trip to Spain and wishes to secure the full support of the church in Rome for this venture. He believes that they can materially assist his plans for this new missionary enterprise. As Marxsen contends, Paul speaks of his travel plans only incidentally, so that they cannot be regarded as *the* theme of the letter; but there is at least a subsidiary purpose in what Paul discusses in chapter 15.[4]

In any case Paul must first go to Jerusalem with the "collection for the saints" gathered in from the Gentile congregations. He enlists

[2] E. T. Merrill, *Essays in Early Christian History* (1924), pp. 100ff., thinks that Tacitus' number is inflated.

[3] P. S. Minear, *The Obedience of Faith: The Purposes of Paul in the Epistle to the Romans* (1971), pp. 7, 43f. E. A. Judge and G. S. R. Thomas, "The Origin of the Church at Rome: A New Solution," *RTR*, 26 (1966), 81ff., propose that Christians arriving later in Rome had been converted elsewhere and were thus unwilling to merge with other groups that had similarly migrated to Rome. This was compounded by Jewish-Gentile problems, and Paul is writing to urge the formation of a united church. Since there was as yet no united community, the word ἐκκλησία is missing in the prescript and appears only in ch. 16. G. Klein, "Der Abfassungszweck des Römerbriefes," in *Rekonstruktion und Interpretation* (1969), pp. 129ff., has argued that Paul wrote in order to offer to this group of believers his apostolic authority, and thereby to confer the status of ἐκκλησία on them. But Paul does write to them by way of reminder (15:15) as though they were regarded as renowned in the world (1:5; 15:14ff.) and their faith was genuine; cf. H.-W. Bartsch, "The Concept of Faith in Paul's Letter to the Romans," *BR*, 13 (1968), 44. See also W. S. Campbell, "Why Did Paul Write Romans?", *ExpT*, 85 (1974), 264–69; and "Some Recent Literature on Paul's Letter to the Romans," *BT*, 25.2 (May 1975), 25–32. See, too, G. Klein in *IDB, Supp. Vol.* (1976), 752–54.

[4] W. Marxsen, *Introduction to the New Testament*, p. 92; cf. Campbell, in *ExpT*, *loc. cit.*, 265.

the prayers of his readers that this venture may be concluded satisfactorily (15:31) with the money safely delivered to its destination. Then he will feel free to head west. Marxsen and Minear suggest that Paul mentions the visit to Jerusalem as a prelude to his coming to Rome because he is facing the same situation in both places.[5] In order to assure himself a good hearing among the Jewish Christian groups in Rome, he shows his personal concern for the mother church in Jerusalem. Matthew Black adds that since there were close links between Jewish believers in Jerusalem and in Rome, Paul would want to state the substance of his gospel, especially regarding the Jewish law and its true fulfilment, to both classes of readers in the capital of Judaism no less than in the capital of the Empire.[6]

2. It was during a winter's respite in Corinth (Acts 20:2–6), waiting for the return of spring and the possibility of traveling to Jerusalem for the Passover, that Paul composed this Epistle, most likely in 58. He did not know what dangers being in Jerusalem would entail (they are hinted at in 15:31; see Acts 20:3), nor did he have any assurance that his presence at Jerusalem would be welcome. So he compiled this document as his "last will and testament,"[7] ensuring that, even if he never reached Rome or even Jerusalem, there would be a record of his gospel to be sent to the western outpost of the church, for Christians to whom he was apparently something of a stranger.

The Epistle to the Romans is to be read as Paul's "theological self-confession . . . which arose out of a concrete necessity of his missionary work,"[8] and as his summing up of the gospel to the Gentile world as he had proclaimed and applied it. It is therefore to be classified as "epistolary catechesis," instruction in Christian belief and life in the form of a letter, patterned after the Jewish literary style.[9]

The letter is catechetical: it gives the substance of Paul's teaching used for the training of new converts. It is also argumentative: it contains the substance, set in a debating style, of material used in Paul's encounter with Jews in the synagogue. These combined features make the letter unique in Paul's correspondence with the churches. To be sure, it is a real letter, with addressees who are named, meant to meet the needs of a real-life, not imaginary, congregation; but much of the argument is cast in a formal style of exposition. Frequently Paul engages in polemic with Jewish and heretical opponents. Evidence for the former polemic is seen in Paul's question-and-answer treatment of several

---

[5] W. Marxsen, op. cit., p. 93; P. S. Minear, op. cit., p. 5.
[6] M. Black, Romans (NCB, 1973), p. 23n2.
[7] G. Bornkamm, "Der Römerbrief als Testament des Paulus," Geschichte und Glaube, II (Collected Essays IV) (1971), 120ff.; ET in Australian Biblical Review, 11 (1963), 2–14. See his Paul (ET 1969), pp. 88–96.
[8] W. G. Kümmel, Introduction[1] (ET 1966), p. 221.
[9] O. Michel, Der Brief an die Römer[10] (1955), p. 5; cf. M. Black, op. cit., p. 18.

themes.[10] His overcoming opponents with the repeated thrust "by no means" (μὴ γένοιτο; 3:4,6,31; 6:2,15; 7:13; 9:14; 11:1,11) illustrates how he refutes false premises and conclusions in his enemies' arguments. Stoic rhetorical features, e.g., diatribe, are also present,[11] but Paul's debating style is more obviously linked with that of Hellenistic Judaism.

3. The church at Rome sorely needed this statement of Pauline *kerygma* and *didache*.[12] Serious difficulties within the congregation(s) there (Rom. 16:17–20) make a letter of warning and admonition necessary. Even if chapter 16 ought not to be admitted as evidence on this matter (see below), it is still clear that in chapters 14 and 15 a divided church and painful divergencies within the life of the community, disfiguring the image of the body of Christ, are in view. P. S. Minear professes to find no fewer than five different groups of people—with differing emphases—in the Roman church, diverging over questions of dietary problems and the use of holy days.[13] The "strong" and the "weak" represent the extremes of entrenched positions, and several other groups represent differing mediating convictions as to whether Christians should or should not use certain foods and treat every day as the Lord's gift to his people. Minear's is probably too neat a classification, but the existence of rival groups in the church is undoubted, and Paul writes in a pastoral spirit to set matters right. The issues in these two chapters were not marginal, though to make them determinative of the entire letter[14] is to exaggerate their importance.

4. A much more central concern of Paul's was to ensure the Gentiles' freedom in the gospel but at the same time to maintain their sense of indebtedness to Israel. So he reproduces specimen arguments for and expositions of his theological position concerning the way of

---

[10] J. Jeremias, "Zur Gedankenführung in den paulinischen Briefen," in *Studia Paulina* (J. de Zwaan *Festschrift*) (1953), pp. 146–51; cf. Black, *op. cit.*, pp. 29f.

[11] Cf. R. Bultmann, *Der Stil der paulinischen Predigt und die kynisch-stoische Diatribe* (1910). He maintains that the best examples of *diatribe* are seen in Epictetus' *Discourses* (see earlier, pp. 42ff.).

[12] On the Roman situation as a factor in the purpose of the Epistle, see Kümmel, *Introduction*², p. 314; W. S. Campbell, *ExpT, loc. cit.*, 268ff. Various points of view on this question are represented in R. Jewett, "Major Impulses in the Theological Interpretation of Romans since Barth," *Interpretation*, 34 (1980), 17–31; cf. Campbell's later essay, "The Romans Debate," *JSNT*, 10 (1981), 19–28. See too J. C. Beker, *Paul the Apostle* (²1984), pp. 59–93, on the Jewish dialogical setting of the epistle, now supported by S. K. Stowers, *The Diatribe and Paul's Letter to the Romans* (1981), who redefines diatribe as a pedagogical tool used by teachers to correct their students and refute their lapses in logic, though in a constructive way.
See too R. Jewett, "Romans as an Ambassadorial Letter," *Interpretation*, 36 (1982), 5–20; F. F. Bruce, "The Romans Debate — Continued," *BJRL*, 64 (1982), 334–59.

[13] Minear, *op. cit.*, pp. 8–15.

[14] K. H. Schelkle, "Römische Kirche im Römerbrief: zur Geschichte und Auslegungsgeschichte," *ZKT*, 81 (1959), 393–404.

salvation by divine grace, to be received by faith, without observance of the law as a merit-conferring system. Yet the true purpose of the Old Testament revelation runs through this treatment, and Paul is concerned to set the law on its proper base (3:31).[15] He does this to convince the multiracial Roman church that only on that basis is there a future for Christianity. Perhaps he sensed intuitively the vast and strategic importance of the church at the heart of the Empire (see Acts 19:21; 23:11). He wanted this church to have no doubts that this was the gospel God had so signally honored for him and for the Gentile mission in the east, and that this was the gospel they, too, should embrace without demur.

For Jewish Christians, however, the place of national Israel was an enigma. So Paul moves, with the same logic that guided him in chapters 1-8, to consider in chapters 9-11 Israel's past heritage, present unbelief, and future hope. And since for Paul the Christian life is practical and social, he draws out the implications of his exposition in chapters 1-8 with a series of discussions in chapters 12-15 on the Christian life in the church and the world.[16]

THE PLAN OF THE LETTER

The Epistle to the Romans is constructed according to a threefold division. Its central "theme" is the offer and outworking of God's salvation, foretold in the Old Testament and culminating in Jesus Christ, now embracing all people, extended, on the basis of faith, to believing Jews and Gentiles, and expressed in a life of obedience and love. How Paul discusses this overall theme has occasioned much debate.

It is traditional to see three main divisions in the entire Epistle (not including the exordium—1:1-15—and conclusion—15:30—16:27). Paul wrestles with three basic questions: How can sinful man be set right with God? What is the significance of Israel in history? What are the practical evidences of the outworking of Christian life and character? As far as the first main question is concerned, Protestant exegesis has typically traced Paul's exposition of "righteousness by faith" as follows:

—man's condemnation (1:18—3:20);
—the believer's justification (3:21—5:11);
—the Christian's sanctification (6:1—8:11);
—the final glorification (8:12-30).

Ch. 1:16f. sets the stage for the overall theme; and 5:12-21 is an excursus on Adam-Christ typology.

In a study hailed by Matthew Black[17] as "the most influential" recent work on the structure of Romans, A. Feuillet has modified the

---

[15] Cf. J. D. Wood, "The Purpose of Romans," *EQ*, 40 (1968), 211-19.
[16] On ch. 16 and its separate status see below, pp. 194f.
[17] M. Black, *op. cit.*, p. 25.

above scheme in several important ways.[18] He views the "saving design" of God as the theme running through the whole Epistle, at least as far as 15:13. Individuals, Israel, and the church are all brought into the prosecution of God's plan of salvation. This makes obsolete the older division of the Epistle, according to which Paul's gospel is contained in chapters 1–8; chapters 9–11 are treated as a diversion; and chapters 12–15 are demoted to the level of a loosely connected section of exhortation and moral instruction. Instead, the one theme of divine salvation offered to all men in Christ through faith is seen throughout.

A second insight of Feuillet has to do with the importance of Habakkuk 2:4 (quoted in 1:17) for Paul's single question, How is God's righteousness manifested in a world of rebellion?[19] The prophet's "He-who-through-faith-is-righteous" shall live" is likely always to be in the apostle's mind. Hence the first eight chapters are best subdivided according to the scheme: 1:17—5:11 (How are sinners justified? By grace through faith); and 5:12—8:39 (How are they brought over from death to life? By union with the last Adam).

One advantage of this method of treating Paul's exposition is that it makes God's judgment preparatory to his vindicating activity, not an end in itself. Furthermore, it respects the way that the justification-language is contained in 1:17—5:11 and thereafter gives way to terms that describe the consequences of being set right with God (cf. 8:30,33).[19a] Finally, it allows the two Adams contrast to function as an integral part of the argument, not as a mere interlude. Thus, the social nature of God's saving activity in the gospel of justification is highlighted: by a soteriological act of divine grace the believing Christian enters the company of those who belong to a new world set right with God's eschatological purpose.[20]

[18] A. Feuillet, "Le plan salvifique de Dieu d'après l'épître aux Romains: essai sur la structure littéraire de l'épître et sa significance théologique," *RB*, 57 (1950), 336–87, 489–529.

[19] See A. Feuillet, "La citation de Habacuc II.4 et les huits premiers chapîtres de l'épître aux Romains," *NTS*, 6 (1959–60), 52–80. See R. M. Moody, "The Habakkuk Citation in Romans," *ExpT*, 92 (1981), 205–8.

[19a] See C. E. B. Cranfield, *The Epistle to the Romans*, II (ICC, 1979), p. 438, n.4; and J. A. Fitzmyer, "Reconciliation in Pauline Theology," in *No Famine in the Land*, edd. J. W. Flanagan and A. W. Robinson (1975), pp. 162–67 (now reprinted in his *To Advance the Gospel. NT Studies* [1981], ch. 7). See too R. P. Martin, *Reconciliation*, pp. 127–54, for a recent option on setting the epistle in a Pauline life-situation, which W. S. Campbell has favored (see his review in *Theology*, 86 [1983], 302). In regard to particulars see S. K. Williams, "'The Righteousness of God' in Romans," *JBL*, 99 (1980), 241–90.

[20] On the eschatological dimension of justification see my *Philippians* (1976), p. 132, which refers to Käsemann's important discussion of "righteousness," which is seen as God's activity more than his attribute. The exhibition of divine righteousness at the cross of Christ (cf. Rom. 3:21–26) is not so much a *forensic* act as a *soteriological* one, by which God puts men into right relationship with himself by introducing a new aeon and by cleansing them of sin so that they may share that age which is the eschatological promise of the future brought into the present. See E. Käsemann, *Perspectives on Paul* (ET 1971), pp. 60–78; D. Hill, *Greek Words and Hebrew Meanings* (1967), pp. 82–162. But Käsemann's position is criticized by Klein, *IDB, Supp. Vol.*, 750–52. See later, pp. 420f.

To summarize the newer understanding of the structure and groundplan of this Epistle, let us turn briefly to several isolated points.

1. There are three sets of contrasts in chapters 1–8. First, man's unrighteousness is portrayed as a foil for the divine righteousness (1:18—5:11); second, man in Adam is offset by man in Christ (5:12—6:23); and, third, the law kills whereas the Spirit makes alive (ch. 7–8).

2. The groundplan of the Epistle is set by 1:16–17. This, as we have noted, is the apostle's citation of Habakkuk 2:4. This one sentence encapsulates the Pauline gospel with its notes of "the just" (1:18—5:11); "by faith" (ch. 6–8: Israel's destiny is linked to a believing remnant [11:5] that presages a universal church [11:26,32]); and "shall live" (ch. 12–15).

3. Much of Paul's thought is shaped along trinitarian lines. The Father purposes both to condemn and to save; the Son's obedience and righteousness lay the foundation of justification; and the Spirit's new life imparts a dynamic for victory over sin and death and a new social life-style in the church and society.

4. The main themes of the letter are salvation by faith, the life of the Christian believer, the destiny of Israel, and the obligations of the Christian—which are all set in a cosmic or social framework.[21]

TEXTUAL PROBLEMS[22]

The chief textual question is whether Romans as we have it is a complete whole, composed by the apostle at one time, or whether Paul or some other author has had his writing incorporated at an earlier or later date. The problem arises from four pieces of evidence.

1. A short form of Romans was in circulation during the second and third centuries. There are manuscripts, represented in particular by Marcion's *Apostolikon,* which ended with 14:23 or ch. 15. He probably expunged chapter 15 because of its references to the Old Testament (15:4).

2. The Epistle as we now read it has various endings: "The God of peace be with you all. Amen" (15:33); "The grace of our Lord Jesus Christ be with you all. Amen" (16:24, which RSV, following the best manuscripts, omits); "To the only wise God be glory for evermore through Jesus Christ! Amen" (16:27).

3. In the shorter recension the doxology which appears in English versions at 16:25–27 (the so-called "wandering doxology") is found at the close of chapter 14 (so the Vulgate texts). Some manuscripts insert it at the close of both chapters 14 and 16. Some have doubted its genuineness because it is not written in Paul's usual style.

[21] M. Black, *op. cit.,* p. 26. This cosmic background to Paul's entire argument in the letter is the *leitmotif* of E. Käsemann's commentary (ET 1980), which is rich in theological perceptions and is matched by U. Wilckens's edition in the Evangelischkatholischer Kommentar series (1978).

[22] For a review of the data, with a full bibliography, see C. E. B. Cranfield, *The Epistle to the Romans,* I (1975), 5–11.

4. The personal greetings of chapter 16 are considered inappropriate given the fact that Paul was a comparative stranger to the Roman church.[23] It is suggested that this list suits rather the church at Ephesus. Included in the list are Aquila and Priscilla, who left Rome for Corinth in 49, then moved to Ephesus. It is, of course, possible that they had returned to Rome between the writing of 1 Corinthians and Romans; still, 26 names is a surprisingly large number of greetings for a community Paul had never visited.

These objections clearly call for some explanation. The solution of the textual problem is probably that the heretic Marcion (who flourished at Rome 144–166) deliberately expunged the last two chapters because chapter 15 gave Judaism a preparatory function in the furtherance of the gospel. Moreover, chapter 15 has at least five quotations from the Old Testament; and chapter 16 was of no importance to Marcion's views one way or the other. It is also possible that Marcion's shortened text can be explained by his having found the text already mutilated, which may account for the presence of 16:25–27 after 14:23 and 15:33 in some traditions as well as after 16:23.

As for chapter 16, it can be argued that the list of 26 names was appropriate considering Paul's intention was to create as many contacts as possible. And one might contend that Rome would have been as likely a home for Paul's friends as Ephesus, even apart from the hypothesis of Ephesus as the origin of many of the Pauline Epistles.[24] Yet there is no denying the strength of the claim that the list of names is that of the significant church of Ephesus.

T. W. Manson accepts 1:1—15:33 as Paul's letter to Rome in its original form, rounded off by the addition of the doxology, 16:25–27.[25] This is the text of p 46, the oldest available copy of Romans. Chapter 16 contains, on Manson's view, items that connect it with Ephesus and the letter as we now have it is a version which found its way into the archives of the Ephesian church. A third version (1:1—14:23 + 16:25–27), he suggested, was sent to other Pauline churches (e.g., in Syria).

From this reconstruction Manson went on to maintain that Romans was originally conceived not as a pastoral letter intended for Christians at Rome but a summing up of the position reached by Paul and his friends at the end of the long controversy reflected in Galatians, 1 and 2 Corinthians, and Philippians. Romans is best understood as a

[23] Cf. R. H. Fuller, A Critical Introduction, p. 51; also J. I. H. McDonald, "Was Romans XVI a Separate Letter?", NTS, 16 (1969–70), 369–72; K. P. Donfried, "A Short Note on Romans 16," JBL, 89 (1970), 44ff. Klein, ibid., 752, champions an Ephesian provenance of ch. 16.

[24] Cf. C. H. Dodd, The Epistle to the Romans (1932), pp. xvii–xxiv.

[25] T. W. Manson, "St. Paul's Letter to the Romans—and Others," repr. in Studies in the Gospels and Epistles, ed. M. Black (1962), pp. 225–41. But see M. J. Suggs, "The Word is Near You: Rom. X:10 within the Purpose of the Letter," in Christian History and Interpretation (1967), p. 295; R. H. Fuller, op. cit., p. 53; B. N. Kaye, "'To the Romans and Others' Revisited," NovT, 18 (1976), 37–77.

Gentile charter of freedom over against the Judaizers, though its immediate occasion was to prepare the way for Paul's visit to Rome from where the next westward phase of the Gentile mission would be launched. This suggestion of Manson's explains the reason for and relevance of the Epistle's transmission to other centers of Pauline Christianity as well as Rome. On its face value this view has most to commend it.[26]

---

[26] Residual problems are mentioned by Cranfield, op. cit., pp. 9–11. He prefers to accept that Paul wrote 1:1—16:23 to the church in Rome. Romans 16:25–27 presents problems of its own, not least because of the un-Pauline style and content (cf. W. Schmithals, "The False Teachers of Romans 16:17–20," in Paul and the Gnostics, pp. 219ff., who relates these warnings to the Asia Minor scene, described in Colossians and Ephesians). See, however, F. F. Bruce's defense, The Epistle of Paul to the Romans (1963, ²1985), p. 282; and the recent full discussion, concluding "that Rom. 1–16 preserves the original extent of Paul's letter" (p. 95), offered by H. Gamble, Jr., The Textual History of the Letter to the Romans (1977).

CHAPTER SIXTEEN

Paul and His Converts at Philippi[1]

THE CHURCH AT PHILIPPI

1. *The City.* Paul's intention to enter the Roman province of Asia in the course of his second missionary journey was momentarily checked. He therefore took the road northwards to Pisidian Antioch, crossed the Sultan Dagh mountain range, and continued north until he and his party reached the borders of Bithynia, a senatorial province in northwest Asia Minor (Acts 16:6).

As he tried to enter Bithynia via the north road to Nicomedia, he was once more thwarted, with the result that he turned westwards, coming down to the coast at Troas, where the apostolic party stopped. Here Paul received a night vision in which the invitation came to him: "Come over to Macedonia and help us" (Acts 16:9). Responding immediately to this summons, Paul sailed directly to Samothrace. Since sea travel along this coastline was often delayed by unfavorable winds, Luke's mention of direct and speedy journeys is probably meant to indicate divine approval. From there he sailed to Neapolis (modern Kavalla), the port for Philippi, which lay eight miles inland on the Roman road, *via Egnatia.*

The Lukan description of Philippi in Acts 16:12 is noticeably full. The city is called "the leading city of the district of Macedonia, and a Roman colony." The translation of this, however, is difficult and the Greek text underlying it is uncertain.[2] We shall have to be content with a general equivalent: Philippi, says Luke, was "first city of its region" and, more importantly, it was a Roman colony.

The history of the site where Philippi now stands goes back to the fourth century BC. About 360 BC Philip II of Macedon took it from

---

[1] Parts of this chapter draw with permission on three of my published studies of the Philippian letter: in *The New Bible Dictionary* (1962), pp. 985–88; the Tyndale Commentary (1959, rewritten 1986) and New Century Bible Commentary (1976, rev. 1980 with Supplementary Bibliography, 1975–79). See too F. F. Bruce, *Philippians* (Good News Commentary, 1983); and G. F. Hawthorne, *Philippians* (WBC, 1983).

[2] The issues are handled deftly by A. N. Sherwin-White, *Roman Society and Roman Law in the New Testament,* pp. 93ff.

197

the Thracians. He gave the town its name—Philip's city—fortified it and exploited its mineral wealth (Strabo, *Geogr.* vii, frag. 34). Nearly two centuries later, under Aemilius Paulus, it was transferred to the Roman Empire, but its distance from the port of Neapolis prevented it from achieving much importance, and Roman administration settled in Amphipolis (Acts 17:1). In 42 BC Philippi was the scene of the battle between the republican forces of Brutus and Cassius and the imperial armies of Octavian and Antony. Strabo tells us that Roman veterans from Octavian's victorious army settled there (*Geogr.* vii, frag. 41), enlarging the small settlement. There was a further intake of soldiers into the new Roman colony after the defeat of Antony and Cleopatra at Actium by Octavian in 31 BC.

The civic dignity of Philippi as a Roman *colonia* (attested by an inscription found in its ruins) is important for the background of the Epistle. Of all the benefits of the status conferred by Octavian Augustus, which included the use of Roman law in local affairs and sometimes exemption from tribute and taxation, the most coveted was the *ius Italicum,* the privilege "by which the whole legal position of the colonists in respect of ownership, transfer of land, payment of taxes, local administration, and law, became the same as if they were upon Italian soil; as, in fact, by a legal fiction, they were."[3] The *ius Italicum* accounts for the presence of Roman officials in the city.

No doubt Luke took such pains to describe in detail the technical status of the city and the part played by the Roman administrators in the accusation and release of the Christian missionaries because Paul's adventures in Philippi can only be understood in the light of the special circumstances of the indictment brought against him. Equally notable is the special character of the charge against him and the Romans' refusal to accept the accusation.[3a] Even when Paul is unjustly beaten, they are compelled to apologize and request that he leave the city. That explains his determination not to go until he had received a full apology (Acts 16:35–39). Much was at stake for Paul's future contact with Roman officialdom, and he sensed the importance of leaving Philippi with the record set straight. The charges leveled against the apostles were unfounded, and the Romans had to admit that they made a mistake in beating and detaining Roman citizens (Paul, Silas) when their case had not been heard (Acts 16:37).

2. *Religion in Philippi.* The special nature of the opposition Paul encountered at Philippi is brought out by some recent discussion. This was the first clash between Christians and non-Jewish authorities. Paul had been involved in religious riots at Pisidian Antioch and Iconium, but this was the first formal indictment before municipal magistrates

---

[3] H. J. Cadbury, in *The Beginnings of Christianity,* Vol. 4 (1933), p. 190.
[3a] See D. R. Schwartz, "The Accusation and the Accusers at Philippi (Acts 16:20–21)," *Biblica,* 65 (1984), 357–63.

(Acts 16:20). The charge was twofold: causing a disturbance and attempting to introduce an alien religion (16:21).

This accusation is worth following up as background to the setting of Paul's Epistle. It seems clear, in the first place, that Roman patriotism was strongly influential at Philippi. To be sure, the owners of the possessed slave-girl were probably looking for no more than a way to safeguard their commercial interest when they invoked the principle of incompatibility, according to which a Roman citizen could not practice a cult not publicly sanctioned by the state. This restriction was overlooked if the practice was not socially unacceptable, that is, immoral or subversive. Since no such charge was brought against the apostles we are led to suspect that the real allegation lay in their being Jews.

The anti-Semitic flavor of the charge may have been brought about by recent events in the Roman world. In AD 49, as we have seen, Claudius had taken steps to discourage the spread of Judaism. Perhaps there is a further hint of Philippian intolerance of alien sects in the banning of the Jews to a place outside the gate. Hence Lydia and her band met "by the riverside" (16:13). Animosity against the Jews at Philippi may also account for the continuing hatred of the infant Christian church, in view of its close link with these Jewish women (cf. Acts 16:40). From the letter (1:28–30; 2:15) we learn of the hostility and persecution the church continued to endure, presumably from the pagan world. Paul's call to stand firm is renewed time and again (1:27; 2:16; 4:1); and the church is assured of the apostle's ongoing interest and confidence as it shares with him in the grace of God given to his people undergoing trial (1:7).

The religious environment which surrounded the Philippian church can be seen vividly from a reading of the letter in the light of archaeological and historical study. The climate was that of syncretism. The Greek and Roman pantheon of the gods had merged with cultic worship imported from the east, and this fusion was imposed onto a background of the local Thracian indigenous religion. Above all, there was the imperial cult, seen in the existing monuments from the city. Inscriptions mention priests of the deified emperor and his genius: Julius, Augustus, Claudia; and monuments were erected to his gifts of peace (*Quies Augusta*) and victory (*Victoria Augusta*).

3. *Paul's Visits.* The year of Paul's arrival has been estimated at anywhere between 49 and 52. Scholarly opinion on the historical value of the graphic stories of Acts 16:11–40 varies considerably. All agree that the narratives are wonderfully vivid, but at that point agreement stops.

For some the stories simply betray Luke's artistry as a storyteller. Their verisimilitude is part of the literary form, embodying legendary elements to arrest attention and drive home his point. One commentator writes: "Luke has reported this story (involving an exorcism, a conversion of the jailer, a release from prison) with the full array of Hellenistic narrative art, so that the glory of Paul beams brightly."[4] At the other extreme, Ramsay found in the account of Paul's Philippian ministry a sign of Luke's own civic pride, assuming that he was the "man of Macedonia" and that he was encouraging Paul to visit his native city.[5] The "we"-section opens at Acts 16:10 and breaks off at 16:40, suggesting that Luke stayed behind in what was his home town. Intimate details of civic status (16:12), the local officials (16:20,38), and the frequent earthquakes in that area were all taken by Ramsay to be hallmarks of an eyewitness narrator with a personal involvement in the scenes he depicted and described.

Perhaps the truth lies in a middle ground. A. N. Sherwin-White has thrown light on the essential veracity of Luke's account, while admitting that there are outstanding problems, such as the textual difficulties at 16:12, and that the nomenclature of στρατηγοί ("magistrates") in verse 20 is not quite the correct designation.[6] We should note with Haenchen[7] how Luke has pieced together different materials into a unified narrative, but for an overall description of the first mission preaching on non-Asian soil and its effects we may appeal to this passage. What Paul writes in 1 Thessalonians 2:2 (cf. Phil. 1:30) confirms that the mission here was a time of conflict for him and that he underwent some humiliation as he was haled before the rulers (ἄρχοντες, corresponding to the Latin aediles) at the market place (ἀγορά) and put into jail.

Also ringing true in the Acts narrative is the way its first conversion story centers on a group of women proselytes. We know that the Jewish faith appealed to women and also that in Macedonia, of all the Greek provinces, the status and importance of these women was well known. Tarn and Griffith write:

> If Macedonia produced perhaps the most competent group of men the world had yet seen, the women were in all respects the men's counterparts; they played a large part in affairs, received envoys and obtained concessions for them from their husbands, built temples, founded cities, engaged mercenaries, commanded armies, held fortresses, and acted on occasion as regents or even co-rulers.[8]

The presence of women members of the congregation at Philippi is attested in the Epistle at 4:2,3.[9]

---

[4] E. Haenchen, *The Acts of the Apostles*, p. 504.
[5] W. M. Ramsay, *St. Paul the Traveller and Roman Citizen* (1908), pp. 206–26.
[6] A. N. Sherwin-White, *op. cit.*, pp. 92f.
[7] Haenchen, *op. cit.*, p. 503.
[8] W. W. Tarn and G. T. Griffith, *Hellenistic Civilisation*[3] (1952), pp. 98f. On the status of women proselytes in the Dispersion, see J. N. Sevenster, *The Roots of Pagan Anti-Semitism in the Ancient World* (1975), pp. 198ff.
[9] On this see W. D. Thomas, "The Place of Women in the Church at Philippi," *ExpT*, 83 (1971–72), 117ff.

What we know of the religious climate and political sensitivity in Philippi accords with the story of the ventriloquist slave girl in the grip of the spirit of divination (16:16). Her declaration that the Christian missionaries are heralds of the "most high God" probably referred to the supreme god of a syncretistic cult. The Philippian jailer, too, acts in a typical way as a soldier who knows what is at stake if the prisoners manage to escape and who prefers death to a loss of honor and the inevitable disgrace of the penalty he will receive for his lapse of duty (16:27). When we add in the detail of Paul's response to the current pro-Roman feeling (16:37) and see that many verses in the Epistle presuppose exactly that pride and obligation which marked out Roman colonists (e.g., 1:27; 2:15; 3:20; 4:8) we may well believe that the historical narrative in Acts 16 is firmly founded on fact and not spun out of Luke's imaginative reconstruction.

Beyond dispute is that after Paul's initial evangelism in the city a church was founded in circumstances that left an indelible mark on Paul's mind. He is able to look back on the "first day" when God's good work began in his converts' lives (1:3-6). He had come to see the significance of the penetration of his message into the Roman world as it turned in the direction of the Imperial City, and so can call his first visit "the beginning of the gospel" (4:15). Since that day he has had contact with the church there from time to time.

Acts mentions a return visit to Philippi (20:1-6 refers to two such visits). The prospect of a visit in this period is alluded to in 1 Corinthians 16:5; and to judge from 2 Corinthians 7:5 (cf. 2:13) one of these was far from pleasant, since Paul was in the midst of the Corinthian crisis. Cordial relations with the Macedonian churches were maintained throughout this bleak time in the apostle's life, and he was impressed by their generosity and sincerity (2 Cor. 8:1ff.), boasting of them to other churches. The tribute in 2 Corinthians 8:2 is reflected in Polycarp's letter to the Philippians 11:3 and in the Marcionite prologue to the Epistle: "The Philippians are Macedonians. They persevered in faith after they had accepted the word of truth and they did not receive false prophets. The apostle praises them writing to them from Rome in prison by Epaphroditus." Of them, as of no other church, he writes: "Brethren whom I love and long for, my joy and crown . . . my beloved" (4:1; cf. 1 Thess. 2:19).

THE OCCASION OF THE LETTER

1. The most obvious reason for the letter is Paul's situation as a prisoner and his desire to commend his colleagues Timothy and Epaphroditus to the church. Paul writes as though he wanted to prepare the way for the coming of these men, and particularly to disarm any criticism which might be raised against Epaphroditus (cf. 2:23ff.).

2. There is also a note of appreciation for the Philippians' gift, to which he alludes in several places.[10] This gift had evidently come through Epaphroditus, and Paul gratefully acknowledges both the gift and the presence of their messenger (2:25).

3. Epaphroditus had clearly brought news of the outbreak of various troubles at Philippi, especially the disturbing news of disunity within the ranks of the church members. This is clear from 2:2-4,14 and 4:2, where the disputants are named, and perhaps 1:27. Paul gently reproaches them and recalls them to agreement in the Lord.

4. Another source of confusion seems to have been the existence and influence in the fellowship of a "perfectionist" group. There is no direct mention of such an opinion, but the way in which the apostle writes in chapter 3 endorses the verdict that "it can hardly be doubted that Paul here deals with a question which was warmly discussed in the Philippian church."[11] The reason for such dissension has been vigorously debated in recent studies, as we shall see (pp. 205ff.).

5. The Christian cause at Philippi seems to have been the object of persecution and attack from the outside world. There is definite mention of the church's "opponents" (1:28) and a scathing description of the society in which the church was called upon to live and bear witness to Christ (2:15). Hence the repeated call to stand fast (1:27; 4:1). A ministry of encouragement may be a further reason for Paul's writing, though Lohmeyer's interpretation of the entire Epistle as a "tract for martyrs" is somewhat extreme.[12]

WHERE WAS PAUL A PRISONER?

From the Acts-record of Paul's life we know of only three imprisonments (16:23-40; 21:32—26:32, 28:30), during one of which this letter was supposedly written (Phil. 1:7,13,14,16, KJV). Obviously it was not written during the first imprisonment—at Philippi—and it seems at first sight that the choice is a simple one between his captivity at Caesarea and the two-year detention at Rome.

1. *The Caesarean hypothesis.* This view goes back to 1799, when it was propounded by H. E. G. Paulus of Jena. Support for it came later from Lohmeyer, but on the whole scholars have not been attracted to it. The suggestion has several points in its favor (most recently, brought out by J. J. Gunther and J. A. T. Robinson),[13] but there are some counterbalancing difficulties. The custody of Acts 23:35 does not suggest the

---

[10] 1:3,5; 4:10,14ff. For the meaning of 1:3 as expressing Paul's thanks, see P. T. O'Brien, "Thanksgiving and the Gospel in Paul," *NTS*, 21 (1974-75), 151f.

[11] E. F. Scott, "Philippians," in *Interpreter's Bible*, Vol. 11 (1955), p. 11.

[12] E. Lohmeyer, *Der Brief an die Philipper* (1956), pp. 6f.

[13] J. J. Gunther, *Paul: Messenger and Exile* (1972), pp. 98-120; J. A. T. Robinson, *Redating the New Testament*, pp. 57-80 (Philippians is dated in the spring of 58).

imminent martyrdom which Lohmeyer takes as the controlling theme of the entire letter. Nor does the size and type of the Christian community at the place of his captivity tally with that we know of the church at Caesarea (Phil. 1:12ff.);[14] and the apostle was at the time of the Caesarean imprisonment consumed by his desire to visit Rome, but of this there is not a hint in Philippians; rather, he looks forward to a return visit to Philippi (2:24ff.).

2. *The Roman hypothesis.* An alternative proposal is that the letter was written and dispatched during Paul's Roman captivity; this traditional view has considerable evidence in its favor. The allusions to the *praetorium* (1:13) and to "Caesar's household" (4:22) correspond to the historical detail of the Roman detention, whatever the precise meaning of the terms may be.[15] The gravity of the charge and impending verdict (1:20ff.; 2:17; 3:11) suggests that Paul is on trial for his life in the highest judicial court, from which there can be no appeal. Had it been a provincial court whose judgment Paul was awaiting, he would still be holding a "trump card" (in C. H. Dodd's phrase)[16] which could quash an unfavorable local verdict and transfer his case to Rome. That he does not appear to have recourse to this is presumptive evidence that he has already so appealed, and that the appeal has brought him to the Imperial City.

Furthermore, the church at Rome would correspond in size and influence to the references in 1:12ff., which point to a Christian fellowship of considerable importance. The length of Paul's Roman imprisonment was sufficient, according to the proponents of this view, to allow for the journeys mentioned or implied by the letter, though this is a matter of debate. Finally, indirect witness to the Roman provenance of the Epistle comes in the Marcionite prologue, which says, "The apostle praises them from Rome in prison by Epaphroditus."

Certain difficulties about this time-honored view have made some modern scholars hesitate. Deissmann was apparently the first to formulate these doubts.[17] In the first place, he argued that journeys to and from the place of captivity imply that the place cannot have been far from Philippi. On the Roman hypothesis it is difficult to fit "those enormous journeys," as he called them, into the two years mentioned as the duration of the Roman imprisonment.

Moreover, the situation reflected in the letter, with its foreboding of imminent martyrdom, hardly corresponds with the comparative

---

[14] J. Moffatt, *An Introduction to the Literature of the New Testament*[3] (1918), p. 169.
[15] On the question of "praetorium," see B. Reicke, "Caesarea, Rome, and the Captivity Letters," in *Apostolic History and the Gospel,* edd. Gasque and Martin, p. 283.
[16] C. H. Dodd, *New Testament Studies* (1953), p. 103.
[17] A. Deissmann, "Zur ephesinischen Gefangenschaft des Apostels Paulus," in *Anatolian Studies: Presented to Sir W. M. Ramsay,* edd. W. H. Buckler and W. M. Calder (1923), pp. 121–27.

freedom and relaxed atmosphere of Acts 28:30f. If the letter came out of that detention, it is clearly necessary to postulate an unfavorable development in the apostle's relations with the authorities which led to a change for the worse in his conditions and prospects.

A final criticism of the traditional theory is Paul's hope expressed in Philippians 2:24 that if he is set free he can visit the Philippians again and take up his missionary and pastoral work there. We know from Romans 15:23,24,28 that at that time he considered his missionary work in the east completed and was setting his face to the west, notably to Spain.[18] If the letter emanates from Rome (if it is later than the writing of Rom. 15), we must assume that a new situation had arisen which led him to revise his plans. This is not unthinkable, as we know from his movements at Corinth, but it does show that the Roman view is not entirely free from weaknesses.

3. *The Ephesian hypothesis.* In place of the Roman dating some have proposed that it was written during an Ephesian captivity. Evidence for such an imprisonment is only inferential, but those who support it find that locating the letter in this period of Paul's life eases difficulties the Roman theory encounters. The intended revisit to Philippi is that recorded in Acts 20:1-6, and Timothy's movements also tally with the record of Acts. W. Michaelis, who has consistently championed the Ephesian origin of this Epistle, shows how the movements mentioned both in Acts and in Philippians fit together like the pieces of a jigsaw puzzle.[19] The shorter distance between Philippi and Ephesus makes the journeys more within the bounds of likelihood. There is inscriptional evidence that would satisfy the requirement of 1:13 and 4:22: Ephesus was the center of the imperial administration in Asia, and there would have been a *praetorium* there.

The immediate difficulty with this novel theory is its speculative character, for the Ephesian imprisonment cannot be proved from a direct source, although there is much which might be considered indirect attestation of it, especially in 1 and 2 Corinthians. In Dibelius's words, it "rests on mere supposition."[20] Furthermore, there is in Philippians no mention of a matter which must have filled the apostle's mind at that time—the collection for the churches in Judaea.[21] Finally, the Ephesian

---

[18] See J. Knox, "Romans 15:14-33 and Paul's Conception of his Apostolic Mission," *JBL*, 83 (1964), 1-11.

[19] W. Michaelis, *Einleitung in das Neue Testament*[2] (1954), pp. 208f. But see P. N. Harrison's challenge—"The Pastoral Epistles and Duncan's Ephesian Theory," *NTS*, 2 (1955-56), 250-61—to G. S. Duncan's defense of the Ephesian origin of the letter; *St. Paul's Ephesian Ministry* (1929), summarized in his article in *ExpT*, 67 (1955-56), 163-66.

[20] M. Dibelius, *An die Philipper* (1937), p. 98. But see later, pp. 219ff.

[21] J. Schmid, *Zeit und Ort der paulinischen Gefangenschaftsbriefe* (1931), p. 114, calls this a "chief argument" against dating in the Asian period of Paul's life; cf. J. A. T. Robinson, *op. cit.*, p. 59.

hypothesis does not explain why Paul, if he were in jeopardy at Ephesus, did not use his right as a Roman citizen to extricate himself by an appeal to the Emperor. Of this possibility there is no mention in the letter. But there may well be a historical reason for this, to do with the social disturbances and breakdown of order at Ephesus (see pp. 124, 220).

Our conclusion will be disappointing for those who hope for a firm answer. Recent discussion of this issue has run into an impasse. The evidence, we feel, is finely balanced, and a final decision is not possible. Other factors enter the picture, to do with questions of the letter's unity, the trustworthiness of Acts, and above all the identity of the schismatic teachers, referred to in 1:12–18, and Paul's opponents in ch. 3.[22]

PROBLEMS IN CHAPTER 3

There is no substantive evidence for thinking that this Epistle is a compilation (though some scholars appeal to Polycarp, *Phil*. 3:2). It must be on internal evidence that the unity is assailed, and in particular this is done on two grounds. First, verses such as 1:27,28 are warnings against opponents in which the danger is largely hypothetical and vague, but in 3:2ff. there is description of an acute danger whose form Paul knows well. The inference is that 3:2—4:3 is an interpolated letter. But one may ask whether the dangers are comparable. Is it not that 1:28 refers to persecution from outside the church, whereas 3:2ff. describe a heresy that impinges on the church's inner life?

A second argument for the composite nature points to 4:10–20, where Paul is saying thanks for the money gifts he has received from the Philippians via Epaphroditus. But it is strange that he should have waited so long in his letter to say this word, especially since Epaphroditus has been mentioned earlier (2:25). So the inference is that 4:10–

---

[22] Those who accept the traditional view do so with caution; e.g., J. L. Houlden, *Paul's Letters from Prison* (1970), p. 42, who faults Duncan's case for Ephesian origin as too dependent on Acts and attempting to "rescue" historical data in the Pastorals (see also below, pp. 300–307). Other points in favor of Ephesian origin are the hypothesis that it is a composite of several fragments from Paul's debates at Ephesus; so Schmithals, *Paul and the Gnostics* (ET 1972), pp. 65–122; G. Bornkamm, "Der Philipperbrief als paulinische Briefsammlung," in *Neotestamentica et Patristica* (1962), pp. 192–202; J. Gnilka, *Der Philipperbrief* (1968), pp. 23–25; its affinities with 2 Cor., esp. the case against sectarian opponents in 2 Cor. 10–13; so Schmithals, *Gnosticism in Corinth* (ET 1971), pp. 135ff.; R. H. Fuller, *A Critical Introduction to the New Testament* (1966), p. 35; J.-F. Collange, *L'épître de Saint Paul aux Philippiens* (1973), ad 3:18ff.; and *Enigmes de la deuxième épître de Paul aux Corinthiens* (1972), pp. 320–24; and the identity of the rival preachers in Phil. 1:12–18, taken to be "divine men," itinerant propagandists located in Ephesus; so R. Jewett, "Conflicting Movements in the Early Church as Reflected in Philippians," *NovT*, 12 (1970), 362–90. On the contrary, G. B. Caird, *Paul's Letters from Prison* (1976), pp. 2–6, concludes that the "balance of probability rests with Rome."

20 form a separate letter presumably earlier than the main verses and sent in immediate response to the gift. But does he not as early as 1:3,5 acknowledge this gift in an oblique way?[23]

Chapter 3 offers a teaser. What is its purpose? Who are the enemies Paul has in mind? Three prior issues are posed by J. Gnilka: What is the true circumcision? In what does the true knowledge of Christ consist? Is perfection (according to these heretical teachers) attainable already in this life?[24] The issue is of some importance and is worthy of a separate treatment.

Identifying those who form the butt of Paul's attack in chapter 3 is fraught with special difficulty. For one thing Paul does not specifically place an identity-label on his opponents, and seems content to assume that his readers will know who they are. They are on the horizon as he writes, so we should not regard their presence or influence at Philippi as entrenched (3:2). But the language Paul uses suggests a very real and dangerous threat. The most we have to go on is his descriptive language in reference to their character and teaching (3:2,18f.).

Assuming that chapter 3 is an integral part of the letter, not a fragment from some earlier letter to the Philippians or an independent composition somehow inserted in our canonical letter, we have to determine whether the enemies of Paul in chapter 3 are related to those mentioned in 1:28, and whether the "dogs," "evil-workers," and "mutilators of the flesh" (3:2) are the same as the "enemies of the cross" (3:18).

Despite the reference to destruction (ἀπώλεια) in both 1:28 and 3:19, there seems to be no connection between the adversaries of 1:28 and the false teachers of chapter 3. Probably the opposition in 1:27-30 came from the pagan world, and Paul's emotional reaction to the enemies of the cross (3:18) is less likely to be in regard to the world's indifference and persecution of believers than directed against misguided Christians who perverted his message.

The more complicated issue is whether the danger from those referred to in 3:2, which Paul answers with the long debate of 3:3-16, is part of the problem which evokes the warning given at 3:17ff. Is Paul confronting a single opposition, with several facets (Jewish nomism or gnosticizing ideas in 3:2, 6-8; a perfectionist tendency in 3:12-16; libertinism in 3:18f.) or does he switch the defense of his gospel against a Jewish or Jewish Christian rival understanding of religion in the earlier part of the chapter to a defense against Gentile perversions of "free grace?"[25]

Two questions therefore press for an answer: Are Paul's criti-

---

[23] R. P. Martin, *Philippians* (1976), pp. 63f.
[24] J. Gnilka, *op. cit.*, pp. 212f.
[25] No fewer than eighteen suggestions of the identity of Paul's enemies are listed by J. J. Gunther, *St. Paul's Opponents and their Background* (1973), p. 2.

cisms directed to the same persons throughout the chapter? Who are the Philippian sectarians and what is their relation to the congregation? These two questions are at the center of the recent debate in Philippian studies. Elsewhere I have provided a full survey of the discussion, so it will be enough here to set down some conclusions.[26]

1. Schmithals' argument that Paul has in his sights a single-front opposition (of Judaeo-gnostics) at Philippi fails to convince.[27] We are left with the assumption that the apostle has different opponents in mind in the early part of chapter 3 and the section that begins at 3:18. The residual problem is the transition made in 3:10–16 between one section, which rebuffs Judaizing nomists, and the other, addressed to gnosticizing libertines. The answer derives from a study of the reaction of the Philippian church to the sectarian influences that threatened it.

2. At 3:2ff. we may detect the presence of Jewish Christian opponents who have all the marks of the men who resisted the Pauline mission at Corinth (in 2 Cor. 10–13).[28] They were characterized by a triumphalist understanding of the Christian life removed from suffering and defeat. Nor does Paul withhold the charge that they led the Corinthian congregation into immoral ways (2 Cor. 12:20f.), while at the same time they were proud of their Jewish inheritance as expressed in circumcision.

It is possible to argue that this type of person appeared at Philippi and that chapter 3 was written against such individuals. They appear to be Jewish nationalists *par excellence*. The reasons for their insistence on circumcision as a badge of national identity may link them with the Jewish Christians in Judaea who were caught in a political struggle to reassert their loyal ethnic status, as in the situation apparent in Galatia (cf. Chapter 12, note 31, above).

The appeal to Gentile congregations in Galatia, Corinth, and now Philippi was one that made much of membership in the true Israel (secured by the acceptance of circumcision) and the attainment of true *gnosis*. In the background lies a false claim to perfectionism, occasioned in turn by a denial of the future hope of the *parousia*. Hence Paul's trenchant denial of a present perfection and his equally insistent stress on a coming *parousia* (3:20f.).

3. R. Jewett finds the heart of the alien message brought by

---

[26] R. P. Martin, *Philippians* (1976), pp. 22–36.

[27] W. Schmithals, *Paul and the Gnostics*, pp. 82ff.

[28] D. Georgi, *Die Gegner des Paulus im 2. Korintherbrief* (1964); J. Gnilka, *op. cit.*, pp. 211–18; and "Die antipaulinische Mission im Philippi," *BZ*, 9 n.f. (1965), 258–76; and R. Jewett, in *NovT, loc. cit.* But see G. Baumbach, "Die Frage nach den Irrlehrern in Philippi," *Kairos*, 13 (1971), 252–66; N. Hyldahl, *Loven og Troen: En analyse af Filipperbrevets tredie kapitel* (1968), who sees in the "dogs" (vs. 2) non-Christian Jews and in vv. 18f. pagans who persecute the church. Therefore ch. 3 does not (in his view) polemicize against heretics at all. (This conclusion is drawn from his English summary.)

these teachers in their offer of perfection.[29] I would modify this by adding that they were evidently claiming that the Christian could know a life exempt from hardship, strife, and loss, since he was already a pneumatic person, raised with Christ to a heavenly life on earth.

This proposition is countered by Paul. His letter to the Philippians was written to teach that suffering is to be expected. When it comes it is God's good will that permits it (1:28-30), just as Paul's prison experience is a sign, not of his false apostleship, but of its God-given authenticity (1:12-18). Furthermore, Paul says, final perfection is a hope to be grasped in the future. The Christian life is like a race demanding exertion and concentrated effort (3:12-15). This is a counterblast to gnosticizing quietism based on the false assumption of a past resurrection and a blissful state of present immortality. Finally, the apostle's point is that the hope of the *parousia* (3:20f.), with its pledge of the resurrection to new life, bears on ethical concerns in this life. Paul finds the genius of the Christian life in an outworking of personal and social relationships under the lordship of Christ (2:1-15). He came to that lordship along a road of suffering and costly obedience; the church can expect to do no less.

[29] R. Jewett, *loc. cit.*, p. 387.

CHAPTER SEVENTEEN

Crisis at Colossae[1]

THE CITY AND PEOPLE OF COLOSSAE

Colossae lay in the valley of the Lycus River, a tributary of the Maeander, in the southern part of ancient Phrygia (western Turkey). Situated on a main trade route from Ephesus to the east, it is referred to by ancient historians in their descriptions of the military movements of Xerxes and Cyrus. Its commercial importance was largely as an emporium of the weaving industry. Wool, gathered from sheep which grazed on the slopes of the Lycus Valley, was dyed; and the name of the city was given to a particular color (*colossinus*) of dyed wool (Strabo, *Geogr.* 12.8.16; Pliny, *Hist. Nat.* 21.51).

In Roman times the city's neighbors, Laodicea and Hierapolis, expanded and grew more prosperous, while the commercial and social importance of Colossae declined. What effect this depression might have had on the Colossian townspeople, or the Christians among them, we have no means of knowing. It does seem certain that, in Lightfoot's words, "Colossae was the least important church to which any epistle of St Paul is addressed."[2]

When Paul wrote to the Christians in Colossae, the city's population consisted mainly of indigenous Phrygian and Greek settlers. But Josephus (*Ant.* 12.147–53) records that Antiochus III in the early part of the second century BC had brought two thousand Jews from Mesopotamia and Babylon and settled them in Lydia and Phrygia. Colossae in Paul's day was thus a cosmopolitan city.

We can appreciate something of the Jewish influence which prevailed there since the immigration of the second century BC. Grave

---

[1] Parts of this chapter draw with permission on two of my published studies of the Colossian letter: the New Century Bible Commentary (1974, rev. 1981 with a Supplementary Bibliography [1974–81]) and the more popular treatment in *Colossians: the Church's Lord and the Christian's Liberty* (1972). Of fundamental significance for study of the Epistle is E. Lohse, *Colossians and Philemon* (Hermeneia, 1971). Also important are P. T. O'Brien, *Colossians and Philemon* (WBC, 1982); and E. Schweizer, *The Letter to the Colossians* (ET 1982). For the archaeology of the region see Sherman E. Johnson, "Laodicea and its Neighbors," *BA*, 13.1 (1950), 1–18.

[2] J. B. Lightfoot, *Commentary* (1879), p. 16.

inscriptions at Hierapolis show how well Jews had become part of the Asian culture. In 62/61 BC an order of the Roman governor Flaccus forbade Phrygian Jews from sending twenty pounds of gold from the region of Laodicea as part of the Jerusalem temple tax (Cicero, *Pro Flacco* 28.68); and this has led to the calculation that there was a Jewish male population of 11,000 in Laodicea.

The religious scene in Phrygia was one in which several characteristic elements were known to have been present. The cult of Cybele, the great mother-goddess of Asia, flourished. Strabo says that all Phrygia worshiped her. Along with ecstatic celebrations ascetic practices were also part of this religion, and it has been suggested that Paul's allusion to "severity of the body" (2:23) and circumcision (2:11) refer to initiatory rites and mutilation practices familiar from this cult.

In an atmosphere of syncretism other cults were easily merged with existing religious ceremonies. The worship of Isis was widespread in the world of Paul's day; and the oracle shrine of Apollo at Claros records an inscription which contains the same verb as occurs in Paul's text (2:18) used of the Colossian "mystery" (cf. Apuleius, *Met.* 11:23). The influence of syncretistic Judaism in Asia Minor is possibly seen in the cult of Mēn Ascaenus who was, according to Strabo, the chief god of Pisidian Antioch. The ritual was immensely popular during the empire and offered a healing cult with a strong element of enthusiastic personal religion.[3]

Though a full treatment of the enigmatic Greek phrase τὰ στοιχεῖα τοῦ κόσμου (2:8,20)—"the elemental spirits of the universe," as RSV renders—is not possible here,[4] we may note that the manifestations of the four simple "elements" of which the ancients thought the universe to be composed, fire, earth, water and air, were treated by the religion of Mithraism as divinities. This process of deification probably originated with Iranian (Persian) sources.[5] Inscriptions which depict the Mithraic conflict and victory often portray the characters wearing Phrygian caps. This is part of the evidence which shows that Iranian cosmology and astrology were linked with the redemption-mystery of the religion of Mithras and came early to Asia Minor. This, too, was in the background of the religious life of the Colossians when Paul wrote to them.

Lähnemann's summary is concise: the Judaism in the towns of the Lycus Valley was set in a Hellenistic cultural mix in which the

  [3] J. Ferguson, *The Religions of the Roman Empire* (1970), p. 217. The Claros text is discussed fully by M. Dibelius, "The Isis Initiation in Apuleius," *Conflict at Colossae*, edd. F. O. Francis and W. A. Meeks (1973), pp. 61–121.

  [4] See esp. J. Blinzler, "Lexikalisches zu dem Terminus *ta stoicheia tou kosmou* bei Paulus," *Analecta Biblica*, 17–18 (1963), 429–43; as well as the commentaries *ad loc.*

  [5] F. Cumont, *The Mysteries of Mithra* (1956); cf. H. D. Betz, "The Mithras Inscriptions of Santa Prisca and the New Testament," *NovT*, 10 (1968), 62–80.

rigorism of Phrygian religion was joined with Iranian religious elements and with characteristics of a wisdom-teaching taken from the
mystery cults.[6] Against this background we must see the rise of the
teaching which came to assault the church at Colossae. As we shall
observe, the nature of the teaching is composite, partly Jewish, inter-
mingled with ideas from the world of Hellenistic religious philosophy
and mysticism. Colossae was a cultural center where this syncretism
might well have been expected.

THE CHURCH AT COLOSSAE

The Christian gospel was introduced to Colossae during Paul's ministry
in Ephesus. According to Acts 19:10 the result of Paul's preaching
ministry in the capital city of proconsular Asia was that "the whole
population of the province of Asia, both Jews and pagans, heard the
word of the Lord" (NEB). This description must mean that, while he was
based in Ephesus during a period of two or three years (cf. 20:31), and
"at the zenith of his labours,"[7] he sent out his representatives to carry
the message to outlying cities and districts in the province. The Epistle
to the Colossians itself affirms that Paul was not personally responsible
for evangelistic work in the Lycus Valley region eighty miles or so from
Ephesus. In two places (1:4; 2:1) there are indications that Paul had not,
at the time of writing, visited the church or any Christian communities
in the area including Laodicea. His hope to meet them personally may
have been realized later, if the hope expressed in Philemon 22 was
fulfilled.

The most likely person to have carried the good news of Christ to
Colossae was Epaphras. He was probably a native of that city (cf. 4:12)
and stood in a special relation to the believers there as well as to the
apostle (4:13). Tribute is paid to him (1:7) as a "faithful minister of
Christ" who as Paul's personal delegate had evidently evangelized the
Lycus Valley district and later had come to visit Paul in his captivity.
Whether voluntarily or not, he had shared Paul's imprisonment (Phm.
23), and so was not free to return to the congregation when the letter
was sent. Tychicus was commissioned to carry the letter and bring news
of the apostle's prison experience and encouragement to the Colossian
church in the face of the detention of Epaphras, their pastor, from whom
they had "heard and understood the grace of God in truth" (1:6f.). Other
members of the Colossian church included Philemon and his family
(Phm. 1,2) including Archippus (4:17) and his fugitive slave Onesimus
(4:9; Phm. 11) who is to be welcomed as a fellow-believer and new church
member (Phm. 16,17).

6   J. Lähnemann, Der Kolosserbrief (1971), p. 104.
7   E. Haenchen, The Acts of the Apostles (ET 1971), p. 558.

When Epaphras came to seek Paul in his imprisonment, he was able to report that the Colossian church was responding well to apostolic instruction, both in growth (1:6) and in determination to stand firm in the faith (2:5–7). The tenor of these verses and others has suggested to some interpreters that the Colossian church was a young community, only recently established at the time of Paul's writing to them. Whether this inference is correct or not, it is a matter of some consequence to envisage the situation in the Colossian church which led to Paul's writing to them.

This raises several questions which are still being actively debated. Epaphras brought Paul news of a threat to the church's faith, which called for the apostle's intervention, couched in the plain warnings of 2:4,8, and 16. The first question is, Is the nature of this false teaching such as would appeal to a newly-formed church? Then, what can we say about the speculative and practical issues involved in this Colossian "heresy"? Another matter is the dating of the Epistle, settled in part by the answer to the question of where Paul was in captivity (4:3,18). But there is also the matter of the Epistle's genuineness, since if the false teaching is patently later than Paul's time or if his answers presuppose a line of reasoning which is different from what we know of his theology in the accepted Epistles, then the inference will be that Colossians comes out of a post-Pauline era.

These issues are not all of equal importance. For understanding the letter, far more depends on what we make of the nature of the Colossian errorists' teaching than on the location of Paul's imprisonment and the Epistle's date and authenticity.

THE THREAT TO FAITH AND THE COLOSSIAN CRISIS

The church at Colossae was being exposed, perhaps quite unconsciously, to a false teaching which Paul regarded as a denial of the gospel Epaphras had brought to them. The occasion of his letter may be traced in part to the presence of this threat and the need to rebut the error at the heart of what Paul describes as a strange aberration of the apostolic *kerygma*. Nowhere does Paul explicitly define this teaching, so that its chief features can be detected only by piecing together and interpreting his counter-arguments. There are, however, some crucial passages where he seems to be actually quoting the slogans and watchwords of the cult. These citations enable us to sketch a rough picture of the teaching against which Paul sets his face. The verses in question are:

> 1:19—for in him all the fulness of God was pleased to dwell
> 2:18—insisting on self-abasement and worship of angels
> 2:21—"do not handle, do not taste, do not touch"
> 2:23—rigor of devotion and self-abasement and severity to the body.

Also, the allusions to "elemental spirits of the universe" (2:8,20) pick up terms which seem to be advocated as an important part of the strange theosophical cult.

Even from this short list we can see that the threat to apostolic faith and life was both academic and practical. Part of the teaching centered on the question of the meaning of religion. Ira Howerth's description of religion aptly exposes the core of the problem: "the effective desire to be in right relations with the Power manifesting itself in the universe."[8] The answer suggested in the incubus which the teachers at Colossae were laying on the church ran along these lines—if we assume that their interpretation of the universe was gnosticizing: God's fulness is distributed throughout a series of emanations from the divine, stretching from heaven to earth. These "aeons" or offshoots of deity must be venerated and homage paid to them as "elemental spirits" or angels or gods inhabiting the stars. They rule human destiny and control human life. Entrance to the divine realm is in their keeping.[9] Christ is one of them among many.

The other question was intensely practical. How may a person prepare for a vision of heavenly realities as part of his rite of passage into a knowledge of the divine mysteries? The reply was by a rigorous discipline of asceticism and self-denial. Abstinence, especially from food and drink; observance of initiatory and purificatory rites; and possibly a life of celibacy and mortification of the human body (2:21,23)—such were the exercises and taboos prescribed as part of the regimen to be accepted if one were ever to gain "fulness of life."

Phrygia was fertile ground for the germination and luxuriant growth of strange religious practices. The synagogues had a reputation for laxity and openness to speculation drifting in from the Hellenistic world. The Colossian church seems to have been a place where the free-thinking Judaism of the Dispersion and the speculative ideas of Greek mystery-religion were in close contact. Out of that interchange and fusion came a syncretism both theologically novel (bringing Christ into a hierarchy and a system) and ethically conditioned (advocating a rigorous discipline and an ecstatic visionary reward). On both counts it is in Paul's eyes a deadly danger to the young church.

M. D. Hooker's suggestion that Paul's letter was occasioned only by the need to warn the Christians against "the pressures of the pagan environment," but that no actual "false teachers" are in mind, is not convincing.[10] Her case is based on the absence of any clear reference in

---

[8] W. W. Fowler, *The Religious Experience of the Roman People* (1911), p. 8, gives this citation, without reference.

[9] For the precariousness of human life and happiness in later Hellenistic religion, see above, pp. 31ff. On the phrase "elements of the universe," see H.-H. Esser, "Law," in *NIDNTT,* ed. C. Brown, 2 (1976), 451–53.

[10] M. D. Hooker, "Were There False Teachers in Colossae?", in *Christ and Spirit in the New Testament,* edd. Lindars and Smalley, pp. 315–32. Further on the nature

Colossians to the supposed error and the fact that Paul does not seem distressed. But several verses do look as though they contain actual quotations of the heretical slogans (1:19; 2:18,21,23; and *stoicheia* in 2:8,20). And it should be borne in mind that the Colossian church was not the direct pastoral responsibility of Paul (1:7f.; 2:1; 4:12), and the role of pastoral care fell to Epaphras, his representative. Paul regards this church at a distance (cf. 2:5) and makes the apostolic traditions (2:6f.) the center of his appeal. Finally, the troublemakers who may have emerged from inside the fellowship (2:18f.) are surely very clearly identified in 2:8,16,18—which are personalized allusions to a definite danger.

PAUL'S RESPONSE

1. *Paul's main emphasis is on his christological teaching.* For him the chief danger in this Colossian aberration is that it cuts one off from union with Christ, the church's head (2:19), and so from the source of spiritual life and access to God. The polemical setting explains Paul's insistence on the cosmic and reconciling role of the church's Lord, especially in the impressive diptych of 1:15–20. Here the two sides of Christ's office are fully described. He is both cosmic agent in creation (1:15–17) and the reconciler through whom God restores harmony between himself and his creation (1:18–20). No loophole is left for any aeon to intrude between God and Christ on the one hand, or between Christ and the world and the church on the other. In him (and not in any spirit or angel or other intelligence) the totality of the divine fulness dwells, at the pleasure of God (1:19). This encourages the security of the church, which is assured thereby of fulness of life in him (2:9f.).

So comprehensive is his reconciling work that it includes even those alien powers the Hellenistic world thought of as hostile. The risen Lord is both their creator and ruler. He engineered their coming into being (1:16) in the beginning; and by his victory over death he has taken his place as "the head" or ruler over all cosmic forces, angelic and demonic (2:10). In the new beginning marked by his resurrection, he takes his rank as the preeminent one (1:18), having gained the victory over all the evil powers which first-century man most feared (2:15).

of the Colossian error, cf. *Conflict at Colossae*, edd. F. O. Francis and W. A. Meeks (1973); A. Bandstra, "Did the Colossian Errorists Need a Mediator?" in *New Dimensions in New Testament Study*, edd. Longenecker and Tenney, pp. 329–43; and the essays in *RE*, 70.4 (1973). For applications of Paul's teaching in rebuttal of the Colossian error, see R. S. Barbour, "Salvation and Cosmology: the Setting of the Epistle to the Colossians," *SJT*, 20 (1967), 257–71; J. S. Stewart, "A First-Century Heresy and its Modern Counterpart," *SJT*, 23 (1970), 420–36. See too E. Schweizer's application of the Epistle's message on Christ, the way of salvation, and its ethical concerns in *Der Brief an die Kolosser* (1976), pp. 215–23; J. C. O'Neill, "The Source of Christology in Colossians," *NTS*, 26 (1979), 87–100; and J.-N. Aletti, *Colossiens 1, 15–20. Genre et exégèse du texte* (1981).

Paradoxically, the syncretistic theological teachers not only demoted Jesus Christ from his pinnacle as God's image and Son; they seem to have doubted the reality of his humanity also. This was part of their general understanding of God and the world: God was remote and inaccessible except through a long chain of intermediaries. Jesus Christ was one of these, but he was sufficiently related to God to share the divine abhorrence of direct contact with matter. To the gnostic mind God was pure spirit, and the world stood over against him as something alien and despicable. The character of God as creator was imperiled, and redemption was expressed in terms of an ascent of the soul to the higher world. Bound up with this attitude to the present world was a devaluation of human history and a denial that any serious value was to be attached to Jesus' death.

Paul attacks this situation on several fronts. He is emphatic on the historical reality of Jesus' incarnation (1:22; 2:9,11). He locates redemption in the cross where his blood was shed (1:20) after his experience of suffering (1:24). The cosmic work of Christ is thus grounded in historical existence, since the aim of his reconciliation was to unite heaven and earth (1:20). Any teacher who denies a real incarnation and a factual redemption in the interests of a mythical schema is branded as the victim of his own delusion (2:18).

2. In taking up these positions *Paul's appeal is made to apostolic tradition*, which is set in antithesis to "human tradition" (2:8,22). The key verses here are 2:6 and 7. Paul is reflecting on the past experience of the readers' Christian standing. From Epaphras they had learned of God's grace (1:7); he had come to their city as Paul's proxy and missioner. What he taught was the "gospel," and this was certified as "the word of truth" (1:5); that is, it carried the ring of truth as a God-given message. The Colossians had accepted it as such and had been drawn to "faith in Christ Jesus" (1:4).

Paul can therefore express his deep gratitude to God for this ready reception and cordial acceptance of the saving word. Now (in 2:6) he recalls this in the statement that the Christ they had received as Lord was the Christ of apostolic proclamation. It was no human tradition they had assented to; rather they had been "taught" the true word and had begun to build their lives on Christ, to take root in the soil of divine truth and to bear fruit in Christian living (1:6). They had come to know God's grace "as it really is" (1:6), not in reliance on any human tradition.

3. *Paul's final rejoinder is conveyed in essentially practical terms*. He addresses himself to the effect of the cultists' regimen on daily living. The Colossian propagandists made much of dietary taboos and ascetic practices. Paul sees these as a threat to the Christian's charter of freedom in Christ, already secured in him by his death and risen life. The call he sounds is one to a new quality of Christian living, unencum-

bered by false inhibitions and man-made regulations (2:22). These prescriptions and rules belong to the shadows (2:17). Why remain in the
dismal twilight of fear and uncertainty when the sun is high in the sky,
filling the world with light? Seek a life which draws on Christ's own
risen power (3:1–3), as those who share an inheritance in light (1:12)
with all God's people, since you have died with him to those agents of
demonic powers which tried to get rid of him on the cross (2:20). Have no
dealings with their taboos, for their authority has been broken once-
for-all. And do not compromise or forfeit your Christian liberty (2:8) by
surrendering to a specious philosophy and a religion which can only be
branded as man-made and therefore fake (2:23).

For Paul the essence of "religion" is Christ, and the mainspring
of morality is a death-and-resurrection experience (signified in a believing response in baptism) in which the old nature dies to self and sin, and
the new nature is received as a gift from God (2:11–13; 3:9–12). That new
humanity, which is Christ living in his body the church, provides both
the sphere in which Christian morality is defined and also the motive
power by which Christians are able to live together in the one family of
God. This has been called the *koinōnia* motive,[11] on the ground that
Paul's ethical norms are found by following the call, "Act as members of
Christ's body." His counsels in chapter 3 include a teaching on the true
self-discipline as well as a much fuller statement of what life is to be like
among Christian men and women in their church relations and in contemporary society, who are called into the "one body" (3:15) with love
giving coherence to all the ethical qualities which characterize that new
life-style (3:14f.).

THE PLACE OF PAUL'S IMPRISONMENT

Of the four so-called Prison Epistles (Eph., Phil., Col., Phm.) three stand
together. Colossians (4:7f.) and Ephesians (6:21f.) speak of Tychicus as
bearer, and there are indications of "the most extensive verbal contact"
between the two letters at this point.[12] Moreover, Tychicus had as his
companion on the journey to the Lycus Valley Onesimus, who is mentioned in the note to Philemon as returning at what is presumably the
same time (Phm. 12), so that brief "covering letter" is brought into the
same orbit as Colossians-Ephesians. The place of Archippus adds a confirming feature. He is addressed in Colossians 4:17 and also in the list of
recipients in Philemon 2.

On the other hand, there is nothing in Philippians to suggest a
dating at the time of these other Epistles, if we are to judge from the
memoranda of proper names and travel plans. Furthermore, Paul's fu-

---

[11] A. M. Hunter, *Interpreting Paul's Gospel* (1954), pp. 104, 118.
[12] See M. Dibelius-H. Greeven, *An die Kolosser* (1953), p. 99.

ture, as reflected in Philippians, was full of uncertainty and anxious foreboding. His life was in the balance (1:20ff.,30; 2:17) and he had no way of predicting which way the decision would go, though he hoped for a release on theological grounds (2:24) rather than trusting to any favorable turn in his legal position as a prisoner. Indeed, on the latter score, he can contemplate his fate as a martyr for Christ (1:21; 2:17).

The other three Prison Epistles show none of this apprehensiveness and alarm for the future. The tone of Colossians is calm and even; there is nothing to compare with the perturbation of spirit suggested in Philippians. If these two letters belong to the same captivity, Paul's situation must have worsened considerably between the two letters, suggesting that, if the imprisonment is identified with the one recorded in Acts 28:30, Colossians (but not Philippians) may well belong to the earlier phase of the two-year detention at Rome. This is the traditional view.

1. *Roman Imprisonment.* The basis for the identification of Paul's place of confinement with Rome appears to be laid as early as the time of Eusebius, who records that Paul was brought to Rome and that "Aristarchus was with him, whom also somewhere in his epistles he suitably calls a fellow-prisoner" (*HE* 2.22.1). The passage mentioned is Colossians 4:10, which matches the reference in Acts 27:2. Paul's confinement in Rome "without restraint" (Eusebius' term, borrowed from Acts 28:30) suggests a freedom which would make practicable both letter-writing (possibly requiring the presence of a scribe: see 4:18) and the companionship of friends (4:7-17). These names link up with similar lists in Philemon (23,24) and bring into the picture Onesimus, the fugitive slave who had sought asylum with Paul. It is argued that a runaway slave, fearful of being caught and punished, would seek the anonymity of the Imperial City, in whose shadows he could safely disappear from public notice.

No other imprisonment recorded in Acts seems a viable alternative. At Philippi (Acts 16:23-40) he was in the jail for one night only. A setting at Caesarea (Acts 23:33—26:32), where he was imprisoned for two years, must face the difficulties enumerated in the following section.[13]

2. *Caesarean Imprisonment.* The case for this has never been strong, although its advocates in recent years have included some weighty names.[14] The main evidence on the positive side is the presence at Paul's side in Caesarea of several Hellenistic Christians (which matches the data in Phm. 23f.; Col. 1:7; 4:7-14). This is the inference

---

[13] See also A. Wikenhauser, *New Testament Introduction* (ET 1958), p. 418.
[14] Cf. E. Lohmeyer, *Kommentar* (1964 ed.), pp. 14f.; W. G. Kümmel, *Introduction*², pp. 347f.; B. Reicke, "Caesarea, Rome, and the Captivity Epistles," in *Apostolic History and the Gospel*, edd. Gasque and Martin, pp. 277-82; J. J. Gunther, *Paul: Messenger and Exile*, pp. 98-112; J. A. T. Robinson, *Redating the NT*, pp. 65ff.

Reicke draws from Acts 20:4, 16 (cf. 24:23). It is likely that Onesimus would have sought Paul's protection in such congenial company. Reicke further suggests that Paul intended to visit Colossae on his way as a prisoner to Rome, once he had appealed to Caesar. Other data appealed to are more tenuous, namely that Philemon 9*b*—"now also a prisoner"—indicates that Paul had been arrested only shortly before and so considers his imprisonment to be a new situation. In fact, he had been arrested in Jerusalem and later transferred to Caesarea where he spent two years (59–61). More recently Reicke has argued that since Colossae was destroyed by earthquake in 60–61, Paul's captivity must be dated before then.[15]

But such a small city as Caesarea could hardly have been the home of active missionary work requiring the presence of a number of Paul's Gentile helpers (Col. 4:3,11), as Kümmel grants, tacitly admitting that Caesarea "cannot be said to have been the center of vigorous Christian propaganda" as in Colossians 4:3,4,11, where Paul has freedom to speak.[16] Lohse, for whom the question is really academic, since he finds the Epistle to reflect a post-Pauline situation, accepts this criticism of the Caesarean theory but attaches little importance to it since, in his view, Paul's captivity is described in idealized terms as what the author regarded as a "typical picture."[17] Nor is there any hint in Acts that Paul contemplated an early release once he had asked for his case to be remitted to Rome.

3. *Doubts over a Roman captivity dating.*

a. The distance between Colossae and the place of Paul's imprisonment is a factor to be reckoned with, since certain journeys have been made prior to the letter (Epaphras and Onesimus have come to Paul) and others are contemplated (Tychicus and Onesimus will return). Is it likely that these journeys across land and sea, some 1200 miles one way, would have been envisaged as casually as Paul refers to them?

b. Would Onesimus have risked his safety and been able to evade the watchful eye of the police throughout such a long voyage from Colossae to the Imperial City in order to bury himself in Rome?

c. If Epaphras (Phm. 23) has been arrested and is a prisoner in Paul's cell at Rome (though Paul's word is συναιχμάλωτος, fellow prisoner of war, not δέσμιος, the normal word for prisoner; however, see Col. 1:7) on what ground was action taken against him in this pre-Neronian period? The same goes for Aristarchus (Col. 4:10), who is also called "my fellow-prisoner."

d. If Paul's hopes for release from prison are granted, he is expecting to visit Colossae (Phm. 22). But this entails a revision of his

---

[15] B. Reicke, "The Historical Setting of Colossians," *RE*, 70.4 (1973), 429–32.

[16] Kümmel, *op. cit.*, p. 347; cf. J. Moffatt, *Introduction to the Literature of the New Testament*[3] (1918), p. 169.

[17] E. Lohse, *Colossians and Philemon*, p. 167.

earlier resolve to turn his face westwards to Spain (Rom. 15:28) in the conviction that his missionary and pastoral work in the eastern Mediterranean was completed (Rom. 15:23f.). While we must allow room for a change of plans, it must be noted that if Colossians comes out of Rome, a shift of missionary strategy is required. This is a substantial argument against locating Paul's imprisonment in either Caesarea or Rome. Implicit also in this reading of Paul's plans for the future is the acceptance of the tradition (which derives from Eusebius, HE 2.22.2f.) that Paul was released after the two years of detainment in Rome, which is by no means certain, as G. Ogg has shown.[18]

Furthermore, Paul's hopes for early release (implied in Phm. 22) are to be followed by a journey to Colossae; but "prepare a guest room for me" is a strange request if a mammoth sea and land trip were required before he could reach Philemon's home.

4. *An Ephesian detention.* Do some of the so-called Prison Epistles come out of a confinement in Ephesus? One of the fullest discussions of this possibility is given by G. S. Duncan.[19] The enforced confinement of Paul at or near Ephesus is an inference to be drawn from a number of lines of evidence.

a. 1 Corinthians 15:32 speaks of Paul's enduring a life-and-death struggle at Ephesus. This puzzling verse is best taken to mean that Paul was exposed to the danger of being condemned to the arena and that if his enemies had had their way he would have perished, but that he was delivered from this fate, perhaps—but not necessarily—by his Roman citizenship.[20] Romans 16:3f. speaks of Paul's exposure to peril and his rescue by Prisca and Aquila. And Romans 16:7 mentions his fellow-prisoners. It is very possible that Romans 16 was written to the church at Ephesus (see above, pp. 195f.).

b. There are some extra-biblical traditions, whose value may be limited, but whose bearing on this hypothesis should not be passed over. A local tradition mentions a watchtower in Ephesus known as Paul's Prison. In the Marcionite prologue to Colossians is the ascription: "The apostle already a captive writes to them from Ephesus" (*apostolus iam ligatus scribit eis ab Epheso*). There is also an apocryphal story of Paul and the lion in the Ephesian arena.[21]

c. Evidence of imprisonments other than those recorded in Acts is forthcoming in 2 Corinthians 11:23, and Clement of Rome (AD 96)

---

[18] G. Ogg, *The Odyssey of Paul,* Ch. 21.

[19] G. S. Duncan, *St. Paul's Ephesian Ministry* (1929).

[20] G. Kehnscherper, "Der Apostel Paulus als römischer Bürger," *SE,* 2 (TU 87) (1964), 411–40; R. E. Osborne, "Paul and the Wild Beasts," *JBL,* 85 (1966), 225–30; A. J. Malherbe, "The Beasts at Ephesus," *JBL,* 87 (1968), 71–80. 2 Cor. 1:8–10 may relate to the same crisis or a later one, perhaps in an outlying part of the Asian province; cf. Duncan, *op. cit.,* Ch. 14.

[21] See the "Acts of Paul," in *New Testament Apocrypha,* ed. W. Schneemelcher, II (ET 1965), pp. 369ff., 387ff.

mentions seven imprisonments. Moreover, several passages in the extant Corinthian letters which *ex hypothesi* come out of a period of Paul's conflict in Ephesus are suggestive of his deep troubles (1 Cor. 4:9–13; 15:32; 2 Cor. 1:8–10; 4:8–12; 6:4f.; 11:23–25).

If we grant the possibility of such a captivity, it is reasonable to test whether we can place Colossians more satisfactorily during Paul's extended stay at or near Ephesus, from the fall of 54 to the late summer of 57. Whether we can be more precise in dating Paul's enforced disengagement from active missionary work in Asia depends on a number of other factors.

The most imaginative reconstruction is that of Duncan, who attributes Paul's imprisonment directly to the Demetrius riot (Acts 19:23–41), connected with the festival in honor of the goddess Artemis, probably in late spring, AD 57. This would link up with the notice in 1 Corinthians 16:8; in AD 57 Pentecost fell in May. The presence of a crowd of people in Ephesus would give Paul a real opportunity for mission work, and he may have this "wide door" in view in 1 Corinthians 16:9. If Demetrius forestalled Paul's exploiting of the opportunity to preach against Artemis (Acts 19:26f.), and the riot occurred before the festival, Paul's plea in Colossians 4:3,4 (using the same imagery of an open door) expresses a deep and poignant meaning and explains his discomfort at being in confinement at a crucial season of the year.

If this identification is a guide to Paul's time in prison or at least under restraint, another historical factor may be involved: the social anarchy which followed the assassination of Junius Silanus, the proconsul of Asia, in October 54, and lasted for several years. According to Tacitus (*Annals* 13.33) Publius Celer, one of the assassins, remained in the province until 57. It may well be that in a time of confusion Paul's Roman citizenship and standing were ignored as the authorities yielded to popular pressure and placed him in custody. This type of custody—a form of *custodia militaris* similar to his confinement in Rome—would explain the paradox of his alluding to his "bonds" (4:18) while enjoying comparative freedom of social intercourse.[22] It also throws some light on his prospect of early release (in Phm. 22) and his concern that Tychicus and Onesimus will inform his friends at Colossae of what has transpired at Ephesus (4:7,9)—a hint that there may have been a new anticipation of immediate release.

Let us enumerate the arguments for setting the Epistle to the Colossians in the period of Paul's Ephesian ministry.

First, the proximity of Ephesus to Colossae is a decided point in favor of this hypothesis. Onesimus is just as likely to have sought refuge in metropolitan Ephesus as in far-away Rome.

---

[22] Cf. G. Edmundson, *The Church in Rome*, pp. 98f.

He would make for the nearest town.... He would want to go far, but Ephesus, of which he must have known and heard not a little, would surely be his limit. He could go the whole distance by foot. He would not need to be at the expense or risk the exposure of embarking on board a ship. He would have been more or less familiar by hearsay with Ephesus, the greatest city of Asia, while none of his fellows are likely ever to have been in Rome.[23]

Second, the request made in Philemon 22 is more realistic on this theory, since Paul's captivity, while short and sharp, had none of the legal indictments of his arrests in Jerusalem, Caesarea, or Rome. He can therefore await with confidence his release once his Roman citizenship is known (as in his experience at Philippi) or social order in the province is restored.

Third, the personnel surrounding Paul in his confinement are satisfactorily accounted for on the Ephesian theory. As C. R. Bowen concludes:

Of the ten companions of Paul named in these letters, four (Timothy [Acts 19:22], Aristarchus [Acts 19:29], Tychicus [Acts 20:4, 21:29], Luke [from Acts 19:21 the narrative proceeds with more attention to detail which may denote Luke's presence at Ephesus during the final stages of Paul's ministry there]) seem quite certainly to have been in Ephesus with Paul, three (Epaphroditus, Epaphras, Onesimus) could have been there much easier than in Rome, the other three could have been there as easily as in Rome, while for no one of the ten is there *any evidence* (save inference from these letters) *that he was in Rome,* at least in Paul's time.[24]

Fourth, Bowen has offered as an independent support his impression from the text of Colossians that the city had only recently been evangelized when Paul wrote.[25] If so, this would be additional support for locating the letter in the period between Acts 19:10 and Paul's subsequent imprisonment in the region around Ephesus.

Counter-arguments to this hypothesis based on the development of Paul's theological themes are not conclusive. We cannot categorically say that the christological and ecclesiological thinking developed in this Epistle was possible only at the end of Paul's life. Any enforced interruption of his missionary activity, particularly while the church was threatened by false teaching, would have set his mind to work; and his "prison Christology" in Colossians is a plausible extension of his earlier thought in 1 Corinthians.[26]

A. F. J. Klijn has indicated that the only argument against an "earlier" dating of this Epistle is the fact that the letter states in 1:6,23

[23] B. W. Robinson, "An Ephesian Imprisonment of Paul," *JBL,* 29 (1910), 184.
[24] C. R. Bowen, "Are Paul's Letters from Ephesus?" *AJT,* 24 (1920), 112–35, 277–87.
[25] C. R. Bowen, "The Original Form of Paul's Letter to the Colossians," *JBL,* 43 (1924), 177–206.
[26] F. F. Bruce, "St. Paul in Rome (3): The Epistle to the Colossians," *BJRL,* 48 (1965–66), 280.

that the gospel has been preached in the whole world.[27] But clearly this is a polemical statement, intended to show the universality of his proclamation in contrast to the heretics' esoteric message. Probably he has more than his own personal ministry in mind; this statement attests the genuineness of the apostolic preaching in general and is his way of rebutting the cultists' claim. Besides, if these verses were not literally true in AD 54–57, how could they be validated only a few years later on a Caesarean or a Roman imprisonment dating?

Some have concluded on this ground that the Epistle emanated from a period well after Paul's death and represents his disciples' apology in his name.[28] While this understanding of a "Pauline" composition can be defended for an encyclical, impersonal Epistle of catholic proportions like Ephesians, which holds up Paul's ministry to some sort of veneration (Eph. 3:1–5), it is hardly justified on exegetical grounds for Colossians, an Epistle which does not even give Paul the title of apostle after 1:1 and is addressed to a congregation with closely defined needs.[29]

Our verdict is that this apostolic letter belongs to that tumultuous period of Paul's life represented in Acts 19–20, when for a brief space his missionary labors were interrupted by an enforced spell as a *détenu* near Ephesus. Epaphras came to bring him news of troubles on the horizon at Colossae. Our Epistle is Paul's reply. His answer, couched in epistolary form, met a species of false teaching which was increasingly to afflict the church in future years. The Pauline gospel and Greek thought (in a Hellenistic-Jewish dress) were here engaged in a struggle; and the letter to the Colossians "thus represents the first confrontation of Christianity with a trend against which it was to be forced to defend itself for centuries to come."[30]

---

[27] A. F. J. Klijn, *An Introduction to the New Testament* (1967), p. 116.

[28] E. Lohse, *op. cit.*, p. 167; E. Käsemann, *Essays on New Testament Themes* (ET 1964), pp. 166f. Cf. R. P. Martin, *Colossians and Philemon*, pp. 32–40.

[29] It might be argued that 1:15–20 and 2:13–15 are not authentically Pauline; cf. R. P. Martin, "An Early Christian Hymn," *EQ*, 36 (1964), 195–205; and "Reconciliation and Forgiveness in the Letter to the Colossians," in *Reconciliation and Hope*, ed. R. Banks (1974), pp. 116–24.

[30] Klijn, *op. cit.*, p. 117. On the later fortunes of Pauline Christianity in Roman Asia, see Martin, *Colossians and Philemon*, pp. 31f.

CHAPTER EIGHTEEN

Christ and the Church in the Ephesian Epistle

THE PURPOSE OF EPHESIANS[1]

No part of the New Testament has a more contemporary relevance than Ephesians.[1a] Its importance as a timely message to the modern church has been recognized by both Protestant and Roman Catholic scholars at a time when a divided Christendom seeks to find common ground by participating in a joint study of the Scripture. The doctrine of Christ and the church is the central ecumenical issue of our day, and no New Testament document speaks more relevantly to this theme.

At a different level, academic interest focuses on this Epistle. Long-debated questions of authorship and authenticity are set in the context of some newer concerns.[2] Does Ephesians represent a later development of Christian thinking on the vital topics of Christology and ecclesiology? Do these features of the letter place it in a period after Paul's lifetime and in the time of an "incipient catholicism"?

The decisive matter in the modern debate is the setting of the Epistle in the stream of early Christianity.[3] Does it belong to the closing years of Paul's ministry at Rome and represent "St. Paul's spiritual testament to the Church"[4]—the final summing up of the apostle's life's work and thought? If so, we should look on the Epistle as "the crown of Paulinism," in C. H. Dodd's phrase.[5] But other scholars are in general

---

1 For a response to this chapter see D. J. Rowston, "Changes in Biblical Interpretation Today: The Example of Ephesians," *BTB*, 9 (1979), 121–25.

1a Neil Alexander, "The Epistle for Today," in *Biblical Studies: Essays in Honour of William Barclay*, edd. J. R. McKay and J. F. Miller (1976), pp. 99–118.

2 I have referred to these in the *Broadman Bible Commentary*, Vol. 11: *2 Corinthians-Philemon* (1971), p. 125.

3 See E. Käsemann, "Ephesians and Acts," in *Studies in Luke-Acts* (Schubert Festschrift), edd. L. E. Keck and J. L. Martyn (1968), pp. 288–97; H. Chadwick, "Die Absicht des Epheserbriefes," *ZNTW*, 51 (1960), 145–53; K. M. Fischer, *Tendenz und Absicht des Epheserbriefes* (1973); C. L. Mitton, *Ephesians* (1976), pp. 25–32. V. Subilia, *The Problem of Catholicism* (ET 1964), pp. 104–20, raises problems with the teaching of Ephesians on the "whole Christ" (*totus Christus*).

4 J. N. Sanders, in *Studies in Ephesians*, ed. F. L. Cross (1956), p. 16.

5 C. H. Dodd, in *Abingdon Bible Commentary* (1929), pp. 1224f.; cf. Mitton, *op. cit.*, p. 2.

convinced that, on grounds of vocabulary, style, and content, the letter does not come from Paul's hand.[6] Moreover, it contains a body of developed doctrine, which they see as placing it in a later period than Paul's lifetime, at a time when the church was growing in self-consciousness as an institutional organization. Features these scholars appeal to as indications of a later dating and life-setting are the waning of the eschatological emphases in Ephesians, the highly structured doctrine of the ministry, in which Paul's apostleship is venerated, the near-metaphysical significance given the teaching on the church as Christ's body, and the moralizing tendency in the realm of Christian ethics.[7]

To anticipate our conclusion, the truth would seem to lie between these polarities. Elsewhere I have suggested that it was Luke who published this letter under the apostle's aegis, either during his final imprisonment or after his death (see below, pp. 230ff.). He gathered a compendium of Paul's teaching on the theme of Christ-in-his-church and added a number of liturgical elements (prayers, hymns, confessions of faith) of the worshiping life of the apostolic communities with which he was familiar. His purpose was to show the nature of the church and the Christian life to those who came to Christ from a pagan heritage and environment, and to remind the Gentile Christians that Paul's theology of salvation-history never disowned the Jewish background out of which the now predominantly Gentile church came.

We may well imagine what prompted this manifesto when we study closely its chief emphases. The author stresses the requirement that the call of the Christian life is one to the highest levels of morality, both personal and social (4:17ff.; 5:3,5,12). He insists that Gentile believers who enjoy rich privileges as members of the "one body in Christ" can never deny the Jewish heritage of the gospel without severing that gospel from its historical roots. Hence, the Epistle's insistence (2:11f.) that the messianic hope meets all the needs of its Gentile readers (3:6). Though they were converted to Christ later in time than their Jewish brethren (1:12f.), they are neither inferior nor independent on that account. Rather, the privilege they now have binds them indissolubly to

---

[6] We shall return to the matter below, pp. 227ff. For a resumé of the arguments see C. L. Mitton, *The Epistle to the Ephesians: Its Authorship, Origin and Purpose* (1951), pp. 7-24; and his New Century Bible commentary, pp. 4-6. See also D. E. Nineham, in *Studies in Ephesians*, pp. 21-35, and E. J. Goodspeed, *The Meaning of Ephesians* (1933). The case against Pauline authorship *on these grounds* is not unanswerable; cf. D. Guthrie, *New Testament Introduction*[3] (1970), pp. 482ff.; M. Barth, *Ephesians* (2 vols., 1974); A. van Roon, *The Authenticity of Ephesians* (1974); see also H. J. Cadbury, "The Dilemma of Ephesians," *NTS*, 5 (1958–59), 91–102; J. A. T. Robinson, *Redating the New Testament*, pp. 62–64.

[7] W. G. Kümmel, *Introduction to the New Testament*[2] (ET 1975), pp. 360ff.; see also the works cited in n. 3 above; on the teaching in Eph. on apostleship and ministry, see esp. H. Merklein, *Das kirchliche Amt nach dem Epheserbrief* (1973); R. Schnackenburg, "Christus, Geist und Gemeinde (Ephes. 4:1–16)," in *Christ and Spirit in the New Testament*, pp. 279–96.

their Jewish fellow-believers. Both groups share in the Holy Spirit of messianic promise (1:13; 4:30).

Apparently the Gentile Christians to whom the letter is addressed, who were streaming into the church, were adopting an easy-going moral code on the basis of a perverted understanding of Paul's stress on salvation by faith alone and free grace (cf. Rom. 3:5–8,31; 6:1ff.). Church history is replete with evidence that the line from Paul's emphasis to antinomian indifference is a short one; a compelling spokesman for this error from contemporary fiction is the Reverend Mr. Kruppenbach in John Updike's novel *Rabbit, Run*: "Make no mistake. There is nothing but Christ for us. All the rest, all this decency and busyness is nothing. It is the Devil's work."

At the same time these Gentile believers were boasting that they were independent of Israel, and they were becoming intolerant of their Jewish Christian brothers and forgetful of the Jewish past of salvation-history (cf. Rom. 11:13ff.).

This Epistle effectively checks both wrong-headed notions, by displaying the true meaning of Christ's relationship to the church. He is its head and Lord. He requires loyal obedience and service; he is the bridegroom who is seeking a pure bride. He is both Israel's Messiah and the Gentiles' hope, so uniting in himself a new people, both Jews and Gentiles. To be sure, these distinctive features of the letter are not unique to Ephesians, and Paul's disciple has faithfully utilized and conveyed the substance of his master's teaching. But he has angled it so as to refute some erroneous doctrine and practice. The significance of the letter will be enhanced if we see it as a magnificent statement of "Christ-in-his-church," presented and applied in such a fashion that false ideas and wrong ethical conclusions are rebutted.

FEATURES OF THE LETTER

1. Except for the next-to-the-last paragraph (6:21f.) the argument and appeal of the document are strangely impersonal and indirect. Not that the apostolic author writes as a detached observer, interested in his readers' problems and needs only at a distance. On the contrary, he expresses great concern that they not succumb to false teachers (4:14) nor surrender their ethical ideals by listening to those who would lead them astray (5:6). He rejoices to be assured of their Christian standing (1:15f.) and knows that their faith is well-founded (4:20). A mark of his confidence in them is that he uses material in which Paul solicits their prayers on his behalf (6:19f.) as a true spokesman for Paul's teaching (the call to prayer in 6:19f. is based on Col. 4:3f., just as the two places where Paul's name is mentioned—1:1; 3:1—seem to derive from comparable sections in Col.—1:1; 1:23b—and echo the authentic voice of Paul).

Yet it remains true that the writer's relationship with his

readers is far from intimate. In this way Ephesians contrasts with Galatians and Philippians, in which personal features are pronounced and persistent; and there are differences from the tone of Colossians, which is traditionally linked with Ephesians as a companion document. The author of Ephesians has heard of his readers' Christian profession through indirect channels (1:15) and knows that it is only thus that they have heard of Paul's apostolic ministry for the Gentiles (3:1f.). His bond with his readers is that of an author to the recipients of his letter (3:4), rather than one of firsthand acquaintance. Warm interest in the readers (visible in Col. 1:7f.; 2:5–16; 4:12) is missing from Ephesians. Indeed, though it would be an exaggeration to say that the more Colossians is defended as authentically Pauline, the less likely it is that Ephesians came *directly* from the same hand, that dictum puts an emphasis on very real contrasts between the two documents; at the same time we recognize the close links that do exist between the two letters.

2. It is a good question whether we are correct to speak of Ephesians as a letter at all. R. H. Fuller remarks that the document "is really a tract dressed up in epistolary form."[8] Literary usage—both choice of words and employment of a studied style—mark out this Epistle as unusual in the Pauline literature.

There are 38 words in Ephesians which do not appear again in the New Testament; and 44 additional words which are not used in the other writings attributed to Paul. The stylistic peculiarities are even more noticeable. Erasmus was the first to call attention to the long, ponderous sentences (1:3–10,15–23); the many relative clauses; the profusion of abstract nouns; the use of parallel phrases and clauses in close apposition (4:12f.); the piling up of synonyms connected together by the use of the genitive case (1:19); and the common use of prepositions, especially "in" (see 1:3ff.).[9] All these traits seem far removed from the style of a pastoral letter addressed to the church at Ephesus by the apostle Paul, whose letter-writing habits are known to us from his other Epistles and include the use of rhetorical questions and a pointed, direct approach (e.g., in Galatians).

3. That leads to our next question. Is Ephesians addressed to the church at Ephesus? It is difficult to believe that Paul would write in an impersonal and indirect way to a Christian fellowship among whom he had lived and labored a long time (Acts 19:10; 20:17–38). Clearly this "letter" is no ordinary pastoral address to a specific congregation or group of churches. This is confirmed by the textual uncertainty of 1:1. The words "at Ephesus" are lacking in the leading manuscripts and the

---

[8] R. H. Fuller, *A Critical Introduction to the New Testament* (1966), p. 66.
[9] J. A. Allan, "The 'in Christ' Formula in Ephesians," *NTS*, 5 (1958–59), 54–62; see too C. F. D. Moule, *The Origins of Christology* (1977), pp. 62f., on the "in Christ" form in Ephesians. For the wider issues see A. G. Patzia's Introduction (pp. 102–22) to his Good News Commentary on Ephesians (1984).

important Greek papyrus p 46 (AD 200).[10] Moreover, early Christian writers endorse the view that "at Ephesus" was not found in the earliest texts.

Two suggestions have been offered to explain this textual irregularity. One is that the book did not originally have a place-name or a particular intended readership but was composed as a general tract or essay. A second-century scribe supplied "at Ephesus" to bring the document, which later Christians claimed as a Pauline composition, into conformity with the other Pauline letters to the churches of the first-century world. But while the letter reads more like a sermon than a pastoral letter to a church with specific needs, the author does have a certain group of persons in mind and uses the second person of the verbs (e.g., 5:3ff.). A second, more likely hypothesis, then, is that this document was composed as a circular letter to the churches in a wide region. Asia Minor is the most probable location of these churches, in view of the letter's affinities with Colossians. It was either carried from one place to another in the area by a courier or (in view of the later textual authority for the place-name of Ephesus) left by the author with a blank space in the superscription, to be filled in on each copy given to a particular church. There are some difficulties with this reconstruction,[11] but on balance it seems to be the most plausible view.

The judgment that the Epistle is an encyclical addressed to the Gentile churches in Asia (3:1), akin to the Johannine Epistles, which also have the Asia Minor churches in view, helps to account for the style, which is influenced by a liturgical and catechetical strain. Directly personal allusions are not expected in a document described more accurately as an exalted prose-poem on the theme of Christ in his church than as a pastoral letter sent to meet the needs of a particular local congregation. The author breaks out into an elevated meditation on the great themes which fill his mind—God's purpose in Christ, his fulness in Christ, Christ's fulness in the church which is his body. Concepts like these lift him onto a plane of rapture and contemplation betrayed in his language. His rare terms may well be drawn from the worship of the (Asian) churches. His style, with its prolific use of relative pronouns, its participial constructions, and its fulsomeness of expression, clearly resembles that of a typical early Christian liturgy into which reports of Paul's pastoral instruction have been fitted.

AUTHORSHIP

As was said earlier, the question of authorship is complex and much debated.

1. Evidence from the letter itself (1:1; 3:1) and from the church fathers (Irenaeus, Clement of Alexandria, Tertullian) supports the tra-

---

[10] M. Santer, "The Text of Ephesians 1.1," *NTS*, 15 (1968–69), 247–48. See too E. Best, "Ephesians I, 1," in *Text and Interpretation. Festschrift for Matthew Black*, edd. E. Best and R. McL. Wilson (1979), pp. 29–41.

[11] Cf. G. Zuntz, *The Text of the Epistles* (1953), p. 228.

ditional view that this Epistle came from Paul's hand. Solid defenses of that tradition have been made by Ernst Percy and A. van Roon, as well as by writers of articles appearing in recent dictionaries.[12] These scholars argue that unusual vocabulary and exceptional style are no impediments to authenticity and can be explained by the special circumstances of the nature of the document. Nothing in the letter points indubitably to a period later than the mid-60s, and there are points of contact between Ephesians and the earlier Pauline correspondence. It should be recognized that both Percy and van Roon must make certain concessions in their defense of tradition, especially regarding the peculiar style of Ephesians over against the chief Pauline Epistles. Percy grants that Paul had access to liturgical materials drawn from the worshiping life of the churches; van Roon postulates the active influence of the scribe or scribes who wrote down Paul's thoughts and drew on a common stock of stereotyped expressions and traditional matters.

F. F. Bruce argues that ideas stated in outline in the earlier Epistles are developed and continued here. On this view, the letter was written during Paul's imprisonment in Rome, c. AD 62; and in the light of its points of similarity with Colossians (esp. 6:21f. = Col. 4:7ff.), it seems clear that both letters were circulated together.[13]

Bruce's statement of the position that this Epistle represents the quintessence of Paul's teaching on a variety of themes is one of the fullest, and it is worth a summary. His contribution was written "to show that this document in large measure sums up the leading themes of the Pauline epistles, and at the same time the central motive of Paul's ministry as apostle to the Gentiles." In all, Ephesians embodies "the pith of Paul's teaching," which is not to be found in justification by faith or the *parousia* of Christ. Both aspects of Paul's gospel, he concedes, are only marginally represented in the letter.

Instead, prominent place is accorded to the doctrine of the Holy Spirit (1:13, 14; 4:30, which are related to 2 Cor. 1:22 and Rom. 8:23). The unity of the church in 4:4 is believed to emerge from Paul's statement in 1 Corinthians 12:13, but its emphasis universalizes the church doctrine. Christian conversion is dramatized in Ephesians 5:14, which is set in the context of 5:7-14, and it is a baptismal setting that best explains the call, as in Romans 6:4. We pause to observe, however, the change of emphasis, so that baptism in Romans is eschatologically oriented as the start of a new life in Christ, whereas in Ephesians 2:1-10

---

[12] E. Percy, *Die Probleme der Kolosser- und Epheserbriefe* (1946), esp. pp. 445–48. The strengths and weaknesses of Percy's case are assessed by J. C. Kirby, *Ephesians, Baptism and Pentecost* (1968), pp. 18–40; and C. L. Mitton, *Ephesians* (1976), pp. 10f. See also A. van Roon, *op. cit.*, esp. pp. 438ff. Representative of conservative statements is G. W. Barker, "Ephesians," in *Zondervan Pictorial Encyclopedia of the Bible*, ed. M. C. Tenney (1975), II, 316–24.

[13] F. F. Bruce, "St. Paul in Rome (4): The Epistle to the Ephesians," *BJRL*, 49 (1967), 303ff.; see also G. B. Caird, *Paul's Letters from Prison* (1976), pp. 11ff.

salvation is already completed and perfect.

Teaching on the bringing together of Jews and Gentiles, which is classically described in Ephesians 2:14ff., had earlier been portrayed as a divine "secret" (Col. 1:26f.), even if the earlier Epistles do not embrace the cosmic agencies so obviously as in Ephesians 3:9–11.

The vivid presentation in Ephesians 4:8–10 of the victorious Christ who gave gifts to his church is linked with Romans 1:3f.; 10:6, while the "descent" of Christ is related to his incarnation, not a harrowing of hell. Yet it cannot be without significance that it is only in Luke-Acts and Ephesians that the enthronement of the risen one is intimately associated with the gift of the Spirit.

Finally, F. F. Bruce suggestively asks where Paul's instruction of "God's wisdom in a mystery" (1 Cor. 2:7) may be found. The answer is in this Ephesian Epistle. The interesting thing is that Paul in 1 Corinthians 2 is opposing a false *gnosis,* using the terms current in the Corinthian error; and it is precisely the same task that is pursued—but at a deeper level, with more concentration on the cosmic significance of Christ and the transcendental status of the church and a more vivid sensibility of demonic forces and universal reconciliation—in the letter to the Ephesians.

F. F. Bruce's essay is a notable illustration of scholarly interpreters of Ephesians who see it as Paul's "final masterpiece," the summation of his apostolic labors as a missionary thinker. These writers, like G. B. Caird, accept the traditional ascription of the document to Paul, maintain that the "whole tenor of its composition" is truly Paul's and that no imitator could have risen to such noble heights of thought and expression. They are candidly aware of residual problems in that Ephesians, as Caird grants, "is curiously unlike the other Pauline letters." The dissimilarity comes chiefly in the areas of style and theological content. Both features, however, are accounted for by (1) allowing that arguments from style are inconclusive, and (2) conceding that, at the end of his life, with time for reflection that was his during his Roman imprisonment, Paul's mind became more expansive, his idioms more intricate, his vocabulary usage more wide-ranging, using concepts and terms unparalleled elsewhere, and—as Caird puts it, in a remarkable insight into Paul's inner life—his genius stretched to the limit.

2. Other commentators believe that the way the main ideas of Ephesians are handled betrays a distinct shift from the authentically Pauline manner of statement and presentation. M. Bouttier remarks that the tension between Jew and Gentile is overcome in Ephesians; and salvation, which in Paul has an eschatological character, appears as already achieved in Ephesians.[14] Even words which are common to both

---

[14] M. Bouttier, "L'horizon catholique de l'épître aux Éphésiens," in *L'Evangile Hier et Aujourd'hui* (Leenhardt *Festschrift*) (1968), pp. 28ff.

the earlier authentic Epistles and Ephesians are not used in the latter in the same sense—for example, "fulness," "mystery," οἰκονομία ("stewardship" or "economy"), "giving thanks," "inheritance."[15] "Head" in Colossians 2:19 refers to Christ's headship over the church, whereas in Ephesians 1:22f. the headship of Christ is over all cosmic powers, though this reasoning is less secure in view of passages where the "head-body" metaphor is used both in Colossians (1:18) and Ephesians (4:15f.; 5:23).[16] More cogent items suggested against Pauline authorship are the treatment of Paul's apostleship, the use of the term for "Gentiles," and the teaching on the ministry.[17]

3. In seeking to evaluate these rival positions, we recognize that substantial external evidence supports the traditional view of Pauline authorship, which is maintained by a solid body of opinion today, as we have seen. However, we should give due weight to the difficulties that arise when we examine the evidence of the letter itself.

A third possibility, then, is that the teaching of this Epistle is Pauline, but its compilation and publication were entrusted by the apostle to a disciple-colleague and amanuensis. This is not to say that some compiler masqueraded as Paul or wrote with any intention of deceiving his readers. The author is faithfully representing the apostle and adapting his teaching to the present situation in so self-conscious a way that he can claim Paul's name and authority for it since it derives from what Paul taught *in the ultimate sense.* He shares the same Spirit that inspired his master. Note, too, that Paul's use of a secretary is attested in Romans 16:22. One suggestion is that Paul left Tychicus to put together this Ephesian Epistle.[18]

Our proposal of Luke as the one who gave the document its final form takes account of various links between the Gospel and Acts and this Epistle.[19] Of the 44 words found in Ephesians but not in Paul's generally acknowledged writings, 25 are used in Luke-Acts. Significant among these are the following:

> *agnoia* (4:18; Acts 3:17; 17:30); only elsewhere in 1 Peter 1:14.
> *anienai* (6:9; Acts 16:26; 27:40); only elsewhere in Hebrews 13:5.
> *apeilē* (6:9; Acts 4:17—variant—29; 9:1); not elsewhere.

---

[15] See the data discussed in Mitton, *Ephesians* (1976), pp. 11–15; on "inheritance" see P. L. Hammer, "A Comparison of *klēronomía* in Paul and Ephesians," *JBL,* 79 (1960), 267–72.

[16] G. B. Caird (*op. cit.,* p. 15) has drawn attention to this, but his explanations of other differences are not so successful.

[17] Cf. F. W. Beare, in *The Interpreter's Bible,* 11 (1953), 599a.

[18] G. H. P. Thompson, in *Cambridge Bible Commentary* (1967), pp. 17–19. Others who have suggested Tychicus include C. L. Mitton, both in his 1951 treatise (pp. 27,268) and his 1976 commentary (p. 230); and M. Goguel, *Introduction au Nouveau Testament,* 4.2 (1923–26), 474f., who thought of Tychicus as the author of a first draft, subsequently edited by Paul.

[19] R. P. Martin, "An Epistle in Search of a Life-Setting," *ExpT,* 79 (1968), 296–302.

hosiotēs (coupled with *dikaiosynē* in 4:24; Luke 1:75); not
  elsewhere.
panoplia (6:11,13; Luke 11:22); not elsewhere.
politeia (2:12; Acts 22:28); not elsewhere.
synkathizein (2:6; Luke 22:55); not elsewhere.
to sōtērion (6:17; Luke 2:30; 3:6; Acts 28:28); not elsewhere.
phronēsis (1:8; Luke 1:17); not elsewhere.
charitoun (1:6; Luke 1:28); not elsewhere.
cheiropoiētos (2:11; Acts 7:48—variant—17:24); only elsewhere
  in Hebrews 9:11,24; Mark 14:58.

We may observe some other points of connection: persons as the
object of *eudokia* (divine favor) (Eph. 1:5; Luke 2:14); the ascension of
Jesus (Eph. 1:20; 4:8,10; Luke 24:51—variant—and Acts 1:9); the contrast "dead... alive" (Eph. 2:5; Luke 15:24); the term "excess" for debauchery (Eph. 5:18; Luke 15:13); the idea of "knowing the will of God"
(Eph. 5:17; 6:6; Luke 12:47); and metaphors for preparedness (Eph. 6:14;
Luke 12:35). The closest parallels between a single section from Luke's
writing and Ephesians are with Acts 20:17–38:

Ephesians	Acts 20
1:11	vs. 27
3:2,7; 4:11,12	vs. 24
1:6,7,14	vs. 28
1:11,14	vs. 32
4:11	vv. 28, 29
4:2	vs. 19
1:15	vs. 21
1:18	vs. 32

C. L. Mitton has raised some objections to this suggestion.[20] He
asks, for example, why the writing of Acts shows no knowledge of Paul's
letters, whereas Ephesians is written in full knowledge of them. The
answer may be the different genre of the two writings, one πράξεις; the
other a liturgical-epistolary sermon. The speeches in Acts, however,
could be the vehicle to express Pauline theology and this might offer
comparative material with Ephesians. Is it not suggestive that the one
speech in Acts directed to a Christian audience (Acts 20: Paul's address
to the Ephesian leaders) is precisely the part of Acts that *is* full of echoes
that are heard in the Epistle to the Ephesians? Finally, as to the dating
of the latter work—on the assumption that Luke had a hand in compiling the Pauline materials—Mitton finds a suggested time "during
Paul's final imprisonment" impossibly early. This may be so, but not for
the reason given. Mitton wants to argue that the composition of Ephe-

---

[20] C. L. Mitton, *Ephesians*, p. 17; see also C. K. Barrett, "Acts and the Pauline
Corpus," *ExpT*, 87 (1976), 2–5.

sians requires the assembling of the Pauline letters into a corpus. But, if Luke as the putative author of both Acts and Ephesians was also a travel companion of Paul and contemporary with the apostle during the time he sent out his letters, this would give him first-hand acquaintance with Paul's thought as expressed in those Epistles, and it could account for the use he has made of such data in putting together the document called Ephesians by using Paul's epistolary matter and stamping it with his own *Tendenz*.

Even more important than our hypothesis concerning the *final* authorship of Ephesians, however, is the question of the ruling purpose of the letter and its relevance to the situation in the Gentile churches of Asia Minor immediately after Paul's death. The suggestion that we are reading thoughts that were originally Paul's, now expressed in words of a faithful Paulinist follower, would account for at least four problematic features: its differences of style from the "capital Epistles" of Galatians, Romans, Corinthians, and Philippians, which has been recognized by all since the Renaissance;[21] its portrayal of Paul's apostleship as all-authoritative and unique (3:1-12) in a way quite different from, say, 1 Corinthians 3:5-11; unparalleled emphases such as the use of perfect tenses in chapter 2 (salvation regarded as already accomplished) and the absence of eschatological "reserve," suggesting that the expectation of Christ's imminent *parousia* has waned (3:20f. is clear evidence of this);[22] and, above all, the concept of one body in Christ as of a multiracial, transnational society in which old distinctions are obliterated and the future of the church on earth is assured.[23] This would explain the teaching on ecclesiastical offices in chapter 4 and the use of liturgical passages to reinforce the exhortation.

We may finally appeal to what may be called the Asia Minor situation. W. Bauer, in his *Orthodoxy and Heresy in Earliest Christianity*, has shown that Pauline Christianity never really took hold in Roman Asia. There is evidence for this in the Pastorals (e.g. 2 Tim. 1:15). Further data are the disappearance of some Pauline churches such as Colossae by the time of Ignatius and Paul's lack of influence on the Johannine school.

---

21   This is true even if doubts are still present over the hypothesis of a liturgical origin of Ephesians, as advocated by J. C. Kirby, *op. cit.*, and J. P. Sampley, *"And the Two Shall Become One Flesh": A Study of Traditions in Ephesians 5:21-23* (1971). See Mitton, *Ephesians*, pp. 22-24.

22   Noted by Ch. Masson, *L'épître aux Ephésiens* (1953), p. 199. But see also M. Barth, "Die Parusie im Epheserbrief, Epheser 4,13," in *Neues Testament und Geschichte: Festschrift O. Cullmann* (1972), pp. 239-50, and his *Commentary*, in the Anchor Bible series (1974) (Vol. 2, pp. 484-87), who wishes to find a "movement to the end-time" in the verb *katantaō*, as in Matt. 25:1,6; 1 Thess. 4:17, which have cognate nouns. But the object of the verb in Eph. 4:13 tells against this interpretation and the verb in Paul is "always metaphorical" (W. Mundle, *NIDNTT*, 1 [1975], 325).

23   M. Barth, "Conversion and Conversation: Israel and the Church in Paul's Epistle to the Ephesians," *Interpretation*, 17 (1963), 3-24; B. M. Metzger, "Paul's Vision of the Church," *Theology Today*, 6 (1949-50), 49-63.

I suggest that we may see Ephesians as a last ditch stand by a well-known representative of Paul in his final attempt to regain Asia for the Pauline gospel by publishing an assemblage of Pauline teaching slanted to achieve several goals: to magnify Paul's person as apostle to the Gentiles; to check a landslide to gnosticizing Christianity; and to establish a footing for the Gentile churches in the history of salvation. Since the validity of this argument rests on how accurately the evidence of the Epistle has been assessed, we turn now to a study of the main concerns of the letter.

THE CENTRAL IDEAS OF EPHESIANS

1. Addressed to a perilous situation, this document is full of Christian instruction of great importance. The author is gripped by what is virtually a single theme. As a true disciple and follower of the great apostle in whose name he writes, he marvels at the grace of God which has brought into being a united church. In this Christian society Jews and Gentiles find their true place (2:11-22).[24] The unity of this universal society, which is nothing less than Christ's body (1:23; 3:6; 4:4; 5:30), is his great concern (4:3ff.). He starts from the premise of "one new man" (2:15) in which a new humanity has been created by God through Christ's reconciling work on the cross (2:16).[25] By this achievement in relating man-as-a-sinner to God, Christ has brought Jews and Gentiles into God's family (1:5; 2:19; 4:6; 5:1) as brothers. The coming into existence of this one family, in which all barriers of race, culture, and social status are broken down, is the wonder which fills his vision. The earlier Pauline teaching of Galatians 3:28 and 29 and 1 Corinthians 12:12 and 13 is now filled out and its lessons drawn and applied.[26]

---

[24] Cf. H. Merklein, "Zur Tradition und Komposition von Eph. 2, 14-28," *BZ*, n.f. 17 (1973), 79-102; G. Giavini, "La structure littéraire d'Eph. 2, 11-22," *NTS*, 16 (1969-70), 209-11; K. E. Bailey, *Poet and Peasant* (1976), p. 63, arranges Eph. 2:11-22 in a chiasmus.

[25] On this reconciling work, see the note on Eph. 2:14 by F. D. Coggan, *ExpT*, 53 (1941-42), 242.

[26] On Eph.'s extension of the Pauline teaching on the church, see J. L. Houlden, "Christ and Church in Ephesians," *SE*, 6 (*TU* 112, 1973), 267-73, who argues that the author of Eph. looks at the church as existing in its own right (271f.), consequently downplaying the Pauline teaching on mystical union between Christ and the believer (Rom. 6:1-11; Col. 1:27; 2:12; 3:3), which was perhaps becoming exaggerated in the post-Pauline period. J. E. Crouch argues that the *Haustafeln* (formalized ethical teaching to control the way various relationships within society were to be maintained) in Eph. 5 (which in turn extend the Pauline version in Col. 3:18—4:1) denote a conscious bid to correct the misunderstanding of Gal. 3:27-29 as calling for revolution in the case of women's and slaves' status in the church and society. Paul responds in the *Haustafel* of Col. 3 that no such emancipation is implied and reverts to the Torah-teaching, confirmed in Hellenistic Judaism, that keeps the social order intact. The version in Ephesians marks a further insistence, in the name of Pauline "orthodoxy," that false enthusiasm (seen among Corinthian women) is to be refused. See Crouch, *The Origin and Intention of the Colossian Haustafel*, p. 151; R. P. Martin, "Haustafeln," *NIDNTT*, 3 (1978).

2. But a new slant put on the apostolic teaching marks a novel phase of development in the doctrine of the church. One factor is the way Christ and his church are regarded as a single entity. The head-body metaphor which is familiar to us from the earlier Pauline letters takes on a new dimension, in that the head becomes inseparable from the body. In 1 Corinthians 12 Paul had insisted on the indivisibility of the body, which is made up of many members (cf. Rom. 12:4f.). But in Ephesians the head and the body are inextricably united and interdependent (1:22f.; 4:15f.; 5:30).

3. Another important slant on the nature of the church is in the attribution to it of a sort of transcendental status.[27] The church shares the heavenly life of its exalted Lord even now (1:22; 2:6; 5:27), and the distinctive features of the church in Ephesians are akin to those classically stated in the creed, "I believe in one holy, catholic, apostolic church." There is a timeless, idealistic quality to what is said about the church's life, more in line with what the people ought to be than what they actually are.

4. Yet the Epistle recognizes that the church lives an empirical life in this world and that its members face pressing dangers. They are counseled against allowing pre-Christian moral standards to decide and control their present conduct (4:17ff.).[28] They are put on guard against pagan teachers who would undermine the Christian ethic they had accepted as part of their new life in Christ (5:3ff.). Baptism is appealed to as a dramatic summons to arouse the readers from moral stupor and a call to walk in the light of holy living (5:14).[29]

References to the seductions of those who were leading the readers astray with empty words (5:6) and causing them to be tossed about by crafty dealings (4:14) suggest that a type of gnostic teaching was present.[30] Basic to the gnostic world-view was a dualism which

---

[27] H. Chadwick, in ZNTW, loc. cit., 149; cf. Subilia, op. cit., who focuses on the christological difficulty encountered in such an exalted dimension that is accorded to the church.

[28] Cf. J. Gnilka, "Paränetische Traditionen im Epheserbrief," in Mélanges B. Rigaux (1970), pp. 397–410.

[29] B. Noack, "Das Zitat in Eph. 5,14," ST, 5 (1952), 52–64, on the eschatological motif as applied to baptism, and my brief comment on this essay, "Aspects of Worship in the New Testament Church," VE, 2 (1963), p. 30.

[30] The contributions to this theme are diverse, among them F. Mussner, Christus, das All und die Kirche: Studien zur Theologie des Epheserbriefes (1955); Kümmel, Introduction², pp. 364f.; E. Käsemann, loc. cit.; P. Pokorný, Der Epheserbrief und die Gnosis (1965); "Somá Christoú im Epheserbrief," EvTh, 20 (1960), 456–64; H. Schlier, Der Brief an die Epheser (1957); C. L. Mitton, Ephesians, pp. 20f.; as well as the observations in R. McL. Wilson, Gnosis and the New Testament (1968), Ch. 2, and E. M. Yamauchi, Pre-Christian Gnosticism (1973), pp. 47–49. H. F. Weiss, "Gnostische Motive und antignostische Polemik im Kolosser- und Epheserbrief," in Gnosis und das Neues Testament, ed. K.-W. Tröger (1973), pp. 311–24, gives some differing emphases. On dualism in particular, see A. T. Lincoln, "A Re-Examination of 'the Heavenlies' in Ephesians," NTS, 19 (1972–73), 468–83.

drove a wedge between God and his creation, regarding the latter as alien and insinuating that one could safely ignore the claims of morality. The strange paradox, attested in second-century gnosticism, is that both libertinism and asceticism are logical consequences of the principle that God is remote from matter and unconcerned about what one does with physical life. One may either indulge bodily appetites without restraint or treat bodily instincts with contempt.

The author warns against a cluster of evil practices (5:3,5,12) and argues for resistance to the pull of degrading influences (2:3). He is equally concerned to defend the value and dignity of marriage against those who, from false ascetic motives (cf. 1 Cor. 7; 1 Tim. 4:3), would depreciate the marital state.[31] His real answer to these false notions and practices is to deny outright the dualistic basis of the teaching. This denial is carried through by an insistent statement of the church's heavenly origin and earthly existence. The incarnation of Christ and the elevation of redeemed humanity are two powerful facts to which he appeals for his conclusion that heaven and earth have been brought together into harmony (1:10).[32]

This same concept of cosmic unity effectively challenges and overturns the gnostic tenet that humanity is held in the grip of a relentless and pitiless fate. The answer to this element in Hellenistic religion is found in the eternal purpose of God, whose will embraces those very cosmic powers—the aeons—which first-century man most feared (3:11). The divine plan in Christ was that these spiritual beings, which Greek astral religion thought of as holding person's lives in thrall, have lost their hold on men and women (3:9f.). For God has raised his Son from death's domain and placed under his feet the entire universe, including these cosmic agencies (1:21ff.). He has exalted the church, too, above these powers and so lifted Christians beyond the range of cosmic tyranny and bad religion (1:22; 2:1-10; 5:8,14,27).[33]

---

[31] See J. P. Sampley, op. cit., pp. 160f.; R. A. Batey, "Jewish Gnosticism and the 'Hieros Gamos' of Ephesians 5, 21–33," NTS, 10 (1963–64), 121–27; and "The mia sarx Union of Christ and the Church," NTS, 13 (1966–67), 270–81. Eph. 5 is in this regard in some tension with Paul's teaching in 1 Cor. 7 where the eschatological motif (vv. 26,29,31) controls the recommendation of the unmarried state (vv. 7f.,26f.,29). The awareness that "the world, as it is now, will not last much longer" (7:31, TEV) has dimmed in Ephesians, though, to be sure, in 1 Corinthians, there is nothing like the negative attitude to the marital state taken in the gnostic literature (e.g. Acts of Thomas, 12–14).

[32] H. Odeberg, The View of the Universe in the Epistle to the Ephesians (1934), p. 8; Martin, in ExpT, 79 (1968), 299. See also N. A. Dahl, "Cosmic Dimensions and Religious Knowledge (Eph. 3:18)," in Jesus und Paulus: Kümmel Festschrift; edd. E. E. Ellis and E. Grässer (1975), pp. 57–75.

[33] The empirical church, described in this letter, is caught in an ambivalent position. Already exalted in union with the triumphant Lord (1:22f.), it is called to contend against demonic agencies whose habitat is in those same "heavenly regions" (6:12). H. Bietenhard, Die himmlische Welt im Urchristentum und Spätjudentum (1951), p. 211n1, remarks that "Eph. 6.12 is the only place in the New Testament

Christ's victory through God's raising him from death is at the very heart of the theology and cosmology of the Epistle. But the question presses, How do believers come to share in this conquest over evil powers? The New Testament answer is that in baptism they "put off" the old nature (4:22ff.) and so die to the rule of these malevolent powers (Col. 2:20). At that time they "put on" the new man with his Christlike qualities. This explains the hinge (represented by the baptismal chant of 5:14) on which Paul's practical and hortatory counsels turn (5:3ff.) and the admonitions he addresses to his readers to be renewed in the image of the new Adam (4:17ff.).

The experience of baptism (in 5:26) marks the start of a new life of holiness to which this Epistle summons its readers. The author warns them to shun the specious doctrines of gnostic libertinism with its disparagement of the body, and he calls them (6:10ff.) to stand courageously against the evil powers ranged against them, for victory over the foes of the church will come only as Christians are diligent in the use of the armor God has provided and prove the reality of their conversion and baptism by standing firm in the Lord.

5. In summary this Epistle teaches the cardinal doctrine of the God who is all-powerful and all-wise in his loving design for the world. Christians, sharing the risen life of Christ, are raised above the pitiless control of cosmic forces which would treat them as playthings of "fate" or "luck." They are lifted onto a high plane of noble living, which opposes all that is sensual and debasing. The conflict they engage in is a sign of the reality of their new life, begun in the conversion-baptism experience.

The church is the historical witness to God's renewing purpose. Originally centered on Israel, a nation elect for the sake of mankind, that purpose now embraces the Gentile peoples. Both races find their focal point of harmony and understanding in the creation of a new society, "one new man" (2:15), which is neither Jew nor Greek but Christian. Here is the clear articulation and enlargement of Paul's thought in 1 Corinthians 10:32 and the foundation of the later Christian claim that the church forms a "third race" of men who, reconciled to God through Christ, are united in a new way to realize a new society of men and women and to be a microcosm of God's ultimate design for a broken and sinful race.[34]

---

where the sky is described as the residence of evil spirits"; and even E. Percy, *op. cit.*, p. 258, who maintains Paul's authorship, concedes how unusual is the teaching of 2:2 and 6:12 as being the only places in Paul where the believers struggle against demonic *powers* (pl.). Elsewhere in Paul Satan alone is mentioned as the seducer of the church; he never uses "devil" of man's adversary. Cf. C. R. Schoonhoven, *The Wrath of Heaven* (1966), pp. 59ff.

[34] See the fascinating treatment of Ephesians from this angle by J. A. Mackay, *God's Order* (1953).

CONCLUSION

We can now summarize the leading issues in this document as we examine some points of disputed exegesis.

1. Much is made of the *person of Christ*, which is unfolded on a cosmic scale as he is described as the agent of God's eternal plan.[35] The key term here is οἰκονομία (1:10, etc.). Christ fulfils his role as the one through whom the divine purpose is realized. That purpose embraces both angelic intelligences (3:9) and human beings in time (1:12f.). Chapter 1:3–10 uses the expression ἀνακεφαλαιοῦσθαι ("to sum up") to denote this cosmic dimension of Christ's place in God's redemptive scheme and also his work of reconciliation of mankind to God (2:16). God's plan is "to bring all creation together, everything in heaven and on earth, with Christ as head" (1:10, TEV).[36]

The background here seems to be an implicit denial of this universal scope of reconciliation and may be traced to some gnosticizing separation of God from his universe.

2. The direct result of reconciliation is the *emergence of one church*,[37] dignified here by language not found elsewhere in the New Testament, though there are some antecedents: the church is Christ's body (1:23),[38] Christ's building (2:20–22), and Christ's bride (5:25ff.). The exegetical issue is whether this terminology is purely metaphorical (the church is "like" a body—so 1 Cor. 12) or whether it is metaphysical in any way—is the idea of Christ without a body as monstrous a thought as a headless body or a bodiless head? Arguments on both sides can be found, and the matter is hard to resolve in a clear-cut way.

At all events, Ephesians clearly envisages a universal church, free from local restrictions and already glorified with the glory now bestowed on the head (1:21 is connected logically to 2:1ff.). Yet there is an empirical application in the ethical calls to a people who are in danger of slipping into loose moral ways (4:17ff.; 5:3ff.). The Epistle is not just a treatise on the nature of the church *coram Deo*; its life in the world is very much in view also.

The treatment of the church's nature as a new people of God, composed of believing Jews and Gentiles, indicates how several prob-

---

[35] D. E. H. Whiteley, "Christology," in *Studies in Ephesians*, ed. F. L. Cross (1956), pp. 51 63; W. Diedei, "Das Geheimnis des Christus nach dem Epheserbrief," *TZ*, 11 (1955), 329–43.

[36] M. Barth's survey (*Ephesians*, Anchor Bible, Vol. 1, pp. 86–92) on the meanings of the verb is especially valuable.

[37] L. Fendt, "Die Kirche des Epheserbriefs," *TLZ*, 77 (1952), 147–50; E. Best, *One Body in Christ* (1955); C. Colpe, "Zur Leib-Christi-Vorstellung im Epheserbrief," in *Judentum, Urchristentum, Kirche: Festschrift* J. Jeremias (1960), pp. 172–87. See too G. Howard, "The Head-Body Metaphor of Ephesians," *NTS*, 20 (1974), 350–56.

[38] See *NBD*², *s.v.* "fulness," and R. Yates, "A Re-examination of Ephesians 1²³," *ExpT*, 83 (1972), 146–51, and G. Howard, *loc. cit.*, 351–54.

lems in early Christianity were resolved. When this Epistle was written, the place of national Israel was settled. Israel has a future within the one body of Christ; Gentiles who imagine an independence from Israel are firmly put in their place. There is no salvation without the Old Testament; the *heilsgeschichtlich* scheme is utilized to show the fulfilment of God's age-old plan now realized in Christ.[39]

3. The *place of Paul*, as the minister *par excellence* of this gospel and God's chosen exponent of his plan for one church, stands out clearly (3:1–13). He takes on this role by virtue of his calling as the apostle to the Gentiles and his suffering on their behalf. He straddles both ethnic groups, Jews and non-Jews, and cancels out the distinction. His insight (3:4) has historically brought the church into being, and this insight must be preserved for posterity (6:19f.). Only on this foundation (2:20; contrast 1 Cor. 3:11) can the church survive and witness in the world.[40]

In a word, the message of this magisterial Epistle is that *God's ancient plan to have one people (uniting the witness of both Old Testament and New Testament) is made good in the gospel of a universal and cosmic Lord, proclaimed by the apostle to the Gentiles.* The Epistle to the Ephesians, in our understanding, adds considerably to our appreciation of Paul's ministry since it represents and embodies not only the substance of the apostle's missionary message, but the development and extension of that message to a new set of conditions. Ephesians, with its clearly discerned distinctives, adds a superstructure to the Pauline kerygmatic base, and permits us to see how Paul's ministry became authoritative and normative in the period following his martyrdom. Thus our knowledge of the historical Paul is enhanced by this inspired reinterpretation of how his teaching was seen to be apposite in situations that, while they may have been embryonic in his lifetime, became fully grown after his death, as anticipated in Acts 20:28–30. There is a comparable case with 2 Peter when it is viewed as embodying "the testament of Peter" designed for a subsequent time in the church's life (see below, pp. 383–88).

---

[39] See M. Barth, "Conversion and Conversation," *loc. cit.*, which represents one understanding of the purpose of how the epistle handles the tension between Israel and the church. Another viewpoint is given in R. P. Martin, *Reconciliation*, ch. 9: "Pauline Theology in a New Situation, Reconciliation and Unity in Ephesians," esp. pp. 159–66.

[40] On the image in Eph. 2:20*b*, see R. J. McKelvey, "Christ the Cornerstone," *NTS*, 8 (1961–62), 352–59.

PART FIVE

Special Issues in the Pauline Corpus

Not all the questions raised by our reading of Paul's letters are addressed, let alone solved, by a study of their historical and contextual background. The reader may well be curious to know how Paul's letters compare with other letters of his contemporary world. Did Paul draw on previous materials as well as follow existing models in his letter-writing habits? When letters were conveyed to the churches, was there any interchange of these documents? What is known about how the letters were preserved in the archives and handed on to posterity? When did Paul's letters become objects of study and close scrutiny? When the first attempts at canon-making were begun, how soon was recognition given to Paul's letters? Was it accorded to all of them at once?

Finally, the student is bound to ask about the authority of Paul's letters in today's church.

It is to these issues that we address the bulk of these pages, with final chapters devoted to some controversial matters regarding the Pastoral Epistles, the consideration of some social concerns in Paul, and alleged "gnostic motifs" in Paul's writings.

CHAPTER NINETEEN

Paul the Letter-Writer

While the art of letter-writing is almost as old as writing itself, the use of letters as vehicles of communication in early Christianity is distinctive, with no real precedent in the Old Testament or Jewish literature.[1] For all the formal characteristics that letters in the apostolic writing share with their counterparts in Hellenism, there are features that brand the former as a unique creation. "In the letters we confront the linguistic newness and creativity of the primitive Christian movement as nowhere else."[2]

CONTEMPORARY BACKGROUND

There were several factors that encouraged letter-writing in the world of the first century.

1. The expansion of Greek culture that followed Alexander's meteoric rise and pervasive influence[3] brought with it a need to keep the lines of communication open across the geographical extremities of his empire. Trading facilities required verbal contact by written documents. The increase of interest in schooling and learning promoted and ensured the availability of a body of scribes who could undertake this task.

2. "Open letters," addressed to a wide constituency, served as part of the propaganda media for the later Roman authority. A case in point is the letters of Sallust (86–34 BC), written in the last decade of his life, after his return to Rome from Numidia, when he had amassed a fortune. These carried all manner of news items throughout the Empire. Government bulletins would be placed on public display, as the first-century counterpart to newspaper announcements and TV "public service" features. The Greek verb for such a "posted announcement" is commandeered by Paul in a religious context (Gal. 3:1).

---

[1] E. J. Goodspeed, *The Formation of the New Testament* (1926), p. 25.
[2] W. G. Doty, *Letters in Primitive Christianity* (1973), p. 77; cf. R. L. Archer, "The Epistolary Form in the New Testament," *ExpT*, 63 (1951–52), 296–98.
[3] See *NTF*, 1, 53–55. More recent is R. L. Fox, *Alexander the Great* (1975). I am indebted in this section to Doty, *op. cit.*, and the literature cited there. See too N. A. Dahl, *IDB, Supp. Vol.* (1976), 538–41.

3. The most prolific letter-writer in terms of number of extant pieces is Cicero (106–43 BC). One estimate is that 931 of his published letters have survived. What makes Cicero especially interesting for our purpose is the way he wrote for two quite separate audiences. As he himself puts it: "You see, I have one way of writing what I think will be read by those only to whom I address my letter [private correspondence], and another way of writing what I think will be read by many [public letters]" (*Ep. ad Familiares* 15.21.4). This distinction is of obvious value in the debate over whether Paul's letters to the churches were private or semi-private or whether he deliberately intended a public audience at all times.

We also know that Cicero feared that letters might be intercepted or diverted to the wrong persons, and used against him by his political enemies. To the proconsul of Cilicia he wrote: "My letters are not of the kind that I can entrust them in a casual way to anyone. Whenever I can get hold of trustworthy men into whose hands I can properly put them, I shall not fail to do so" (*Ep. ad Familiares* 1.7.1). He might also commit parts of what he wanted to say to a courier, who could be relied on to transmit by word of mouth the more delicate items of opinion and judgment in a context where the political ramifications of leaked information might be explosive.[4] Paul, for different reasons, was also alert to the dangers of forgery (2 Thess. 2:2; 3:17), and he alludes to oral instructions that accompanied the letters he handed over to his representatives (e.g., 1 Cor. 4:17).

4. The clear distinction between a personal note and a letter intended for a wider readership is important. Many letters, recorded on papyri and ostraca, may be classified as belonging to the worlds of commerce and trade—business letters, invoices, receipts, bills. There were also many official letters—legal decisions and military communiqués, for example. In contrast to these were public letters, written mainly for ideological or propaganda purposes. Isocrates (436–338 BC) is credited as the first person to use the letter as a way to influence public opinion. "Letters to the editor" in the national and local press form the modern parallels to this practice; and there is some common ground here with the purpose that motivated New Testament letter-writers. They too wrote with a desire to persuade and encourage their readers.

5. Another specimen of ancient letter-writing that bears on our study here is the "nonreal letter." The form of this writing is epistolary, but the contents seem directed at no particular situation or constituency. The so-called "church letters" or "general letters" of Peter and John in the New Testament may fall into this category, but an encyclical document like Ephesians may also be classified here, since these "fictitious"

---

[4] T. A. Dorey, ed., *Cicero* (1965), esp. the chapter "Cicero the Man" by J. P. V. D. Balsdon. Cicero's sixteen books *Ad Familiares* have been edited by D. R. Shackleton Bailey in two volumes (1981).

letters often gathered into a compendium the substance of a mentor's teaching and were published by his students and disciples in his name. The collected teachings of philosophers like Plato or the Sophists, gathered to meet public curiosity, "were considered legitimate extensions of the original writer's own works."[5]

6. Finally, some have distinguished a type of letter that had pretensions to literary style and dealt with an elevated subject-matter. This is the "letter-essay," termed "the epistle" by Deissmann in his well-known classification of the New Testament literature.[6] Deissmann argued that the Pauline compositions, by contrast, should be classified as letters of a private character, *ad hoc* writings intended for the limited readership of their immediate addressees.

Deissmann's attempt is generally conceded to have failed.[7] Neither Paul's most tender writings (e.g., Philippians) nor his most individualistic (e.g., Philemon) may rightly be called "letters" in Deissmann's sense. Recent studies have marshalled impressive evidence that Paul and the other letter-writers of the New Testament (especially the author of Hebrews) wrote well-constructed letters in a carefully thought-out manner and according to accepted canons of letter-writing technique.

PAUL'S ARTISTRY

Earlier studies by W. M. Ramsay and Johannes Weiss drew attention to the literary elements in Paul's writings.[8] Weiss maintained that Paul's letters were not creations of the moment, composed on the run, but give evidence of careful and long-pondered thought, differentiating them from the improvisations that constituted an ordinary letter of the Hellenistic period.

1. Recent studies have extended the pioneering work of Ramsay and Weiss. Examples of technically developed rhetorical forms such as chiasmus have been noted by J. Jeremias. Especially in letters such as Romans, the artistic arrangements of Paul's arguments and discussions

---

[5] Doty, *op. cit.*, p. 7.

[6] A. Deissmann, *Light from the Ancient East* (1927); *Bible Studies*[2] (1903), pp. 1–59; *Paul* (1926), pp. 8ff.

[7] W. G. Doty, "The Classification of Epistolary Literature," *CBQ*, 31 (1969), 185ff.

[8] W. M. Ramsay, *The Teaching of Paul in Terms of the Present Day*[2] (1914), pp. 412–47; J. Weiss, *History of Primitive Christianity*, Vol. 1 (ET 1937), pp. 399–421, esp. p. 400 on Paul's rhetorical style. Even in Philemon Paul uses "an elegant method of expression which is not at all the language of every-day life" (p. 405). See E. A. Judge, "Paul's Boasting in Relation to Contemporary Professional Practice," *Australian Biblical Review*, 16 (1968), 37–50: Paul could write "passages which by style and content belong to [his] struggle with rhetorically trained opponents for the support of his rhetorically fastidious converts" (48). Of special interest is the discussion of Paul's rhetorical language in 2 Corinthians (see P. Marshall, "Enmity and other Social Conventions in Paul's Relations with the Corinthians," forthcoming in the series Wissenschaftliche Untersuchungen zum Neuen Testament and elsewhere (see G. A. Kennedy, *New Testament Interpretation through Rhetorical Criticism* [1984]).

have become prominent.[9] But even the simplest and most touching of them—letters of consolation (see above, p. 47), complaint, even love letters—are set in a format. The author's name is followed by that of the recipient, and occasionally the name of a secretary and/or messenger is inserted. Then comes a standardized greeting (χαίρειν). The main body of the letter states the business in matter-of-fact terms. The closing greeting takes the place of a signature. In many papyri the final salutation is in a hand different from the rest of the letter. This suggests that the author dictated the letter to a scribe, reviewed the contents before dispatch, corrected where necessary, and endorsed the letter by adding his own final greeting as a quasi-signature.

Otto Roller has argued that, in keeping with the contemporary practice, the New Testament writers never dictated letters verbatim.[10] Such a process would have been incredibly slow and labored,[11] since Roller discounted the use of shorthand, which was in use among the Romans from the time of the first century BC and among the Greeks even earlier. On Roller's hypothesis, the letter-writer would employ an amanuensis, to whom he would give not his words to be recorded verbatim but his ideas. The scribe would gain the general sense of the sender's intention, go away and compose the letter, and return it for approval.

Roller found evidence for his thesis in Romans 16:22, where it is said that Tertius "wrote" the letter, and 1 Peter 5:12, which attributes to Silvanus/Silas the composition of this document credited to Peter. The assumption is that in Christian circles the amanuenses were themselves Christians, and therefore they would be trusted faithfully to report their master's thoughts in words he would approve of. This process, it is maintained, accounts for the informal conversational style of the writings. The immediacy of the writer—say, Paul in Galatians—comes through because the scribe has so fully conveyed the substance of Paul's heated statements down to the biting irony and fierce invective (e.g., Gal. 5:12). Galatians is especially interesting; its postscript (6:11ff.) looks on the face of it as though Paul, having dictated the main body of the letter, finished by taking up the reed pen himself. Similarly in 2 Thessalonians 3:17 we read of Paul's own personal signature coming at the close of a letter he presumably has had another person (perhaps Silvanus or Timothy; 1:1) write for him.

Not all parts of Roller's position have escaped criticism,[12] but the

---

[9] J. Jeremias, "Zur Gedankenführung in den paulinischen Briefen," *Studia Paulina*, edd. Sevenster and van Unnik, pp. 146ff. See N. Turner, *A Grammar of New Testament Greek*, Vol. 4: *Style* (1976), Ch. 6.

[10] O. Roller, *Das Formular der paulinischen Briefe* (1933).

[11] To the contrary S. Lyonnet has demonstrated the speed of dictation: "De arte litteras exarandi apud antiquos," *Verbum Domini*, 34 (1956), 1–11.

[12] See W. G. Kümmel, *Introduction*², p. 251; cf. C. F. D. Moule, in *BJRL*, 47 (1965), 449; B. Rigaux, *The Letters of St. Paul* (ET 1968), pp. 117ff.

use of a scribe does confirm that Paul was consciously and deliberately composing a document that he intended to represent his own authority and whose impact would be strengthened by the witness of his colleagues, who are invariably mentioned with his name in the opening section or prescript.

2. The layout of the letter conforms to a set pattern, at least in its main outline.

a. The opening salutation, expressed by the colorless "greeting" in many contemporary letters (cf. Acts 15:23; 23:26; James 1:1), is enriched by Paul's "grace and peace," terms that combine the characteristic Greek and Hebrew ideas that run through Paul's gospel.

b. The thanksgiving, which in the papyri expresses hope for the readers' health and happiness, is given a deeper significance in Paul: it introduces the cause for which thanks to God are offered and paves the way for "the vital theme of the letter," called the "epistolary situation."[13] Modeled on the Hebrew *berākāh* or "blessing" of God, Christian adaptation has shifted the emphasis from blessing to thanksgiving for the mercies seen in the new age of salvation and the new life at work among the congregations (obvious examples are Eph. 1:3ff.; 1 Pet. 1:3ff.). The eschatological motif is frequently sounded, and this too serves to celebrate the arrival of the new age of redemption to be consummated at the *parousia* of Christ (cf. 1 Cor. 1:7; Phil. 1:10f.; Col. 1:5; 1 Pet. 1:7).

Schubert related the thanksgiving period to exhortation and a didactic purpose. Other studies have stressed the liturgical setting of these thanksgiving sequences, as though Paul were anxious to make himself at one with the congregations by sharing in liturgical prayers of thanks and intercession. Rigaux proposes that Paul customarily began his congregational preaching with an expression of thanksgiving and this pattern slid over into his correspondence.[14]

There is surely no need to choose one of these explanations to the exclusion of the others. Paul was versatile enough that his tributes of thankfulness would serve many purposes.

c. The body of the letter opens with a formula of request, appeal, or injunction. Sanders sees the purport of this as "to introduce new material, to change the subject of discussion, or when the argument takes a new tack."[15] Another suggestion is that Paul is deliberately courting good relations with his friends by this device. This feature is prominent and important in Hellenistic letters—establishing and ex-

[13] P. Schubert, *Form and Function of the Pauline Thanksgivings* (1939), pp. 71–82.
[14] B. Rigaux, *op. cit.*, pp. 120–22; cf. L. G. Champion, *Benedictions and Doxologies in the Epistles of Paul* (1934).
[15] J. T. Sanders, "The Transition from Opening Epistolary Thanksgiving to Body in the Letters of the Pauline Corpus," *JBL*, 81 (1962), 348–62; cf. H. Boers, "The Form-Critical Study of Paul's Letters. 1 Thessalonians as a Case Study," *NTS*, 22 (1975–76), 140–58; T. Y. Mullins, "Petition as a Literary Form," *NovT*, 5 (1962), 46–54.

pressing a "friendly relationship" (*philophronēsis*) between two persons.[16] The evidence of Philemon 4–10 is noteworthy.

A formula of "disclosure" is found in expressions such as "I want you to know" or "I would not have you to be ignorant," repeated often in Paul's writing.[16a] An alternative to this—and sometimes its accompaniment—is an effusion of joy, as Paul picks up the mood of congratulation over the success of his work (Phil. 1:3–6; 1 Thess. 1:2–10) and the spiritual vitality and confidence of his congregations (Col. 1:3–8). In Paul's letter to the Galatians a note of astonishment is struck, with a device that is paralleled in the papyri, where the writer is disappointed that his correspondent has failed to write. In Paul's case, of course, the amazement is at their desertion of the gospel he brought to them (1:6)—in contrast to the optimism expressed elsewhere (1 Thess. 1:4f.; 2 Thess. 1:3f.).

The argument in the main body of the letter combines theoretical and practical matters, as we saw in our consideration of the Corinthian letters, Philippians, and 1 Thessalonians. Galatians is perhaps the most carefully structured of the Epistles, falling into two sections of exposition (chs. 1–4) and exhortation (*paraenesis*) (chs. 5–6).[17] Romans also conforms to this general pattern—the two sections are chapters 1–8 and 12–15, with the intervening chapters seen as integral to Paul's purpose in setting forth the nature of salvation history.

A couple of other items in Paul suggest a set pattern: the promise of an apostolic *parousia*, by which he holds out the prospect of a visit to the community (e.g., Rom. 1:10; 15:22ff.; 1 Cor. 4:21; 11:34; Phil. 2:24; Phm. 22),[18] and a section often called a "travelogue"—Paul, unable to visit in the immediate future, plans to send one of his apostolic team as his representative (e.g., Timothy, Phil. 2:19–24; 1 Cor. 4:17; Tychicus, Col. 4:7f. = Eph. 6:21f.).[19]

---

[16] Based on Demetrius, *On Style*, who remarks that letters should be an expression of "friendly feeling" (*philophronēsis*) between sender and recipient. Paul's method of securing good relations is partly that of his defense of the proclamation, an apostolic apology akin to Socrates' defense (cf. H. D. Betz, *Der Apostel Paulus und die sokratische Tradition* [1972]; see Boers, *loc. cit.*, 153). See now S. N. Olson, "Epistolary Uses of Expressions of Self-Confidence," *JBL*, 103 (1984), 585–97; and his "Pauline Expressions of Confidence in his Addressees," *CBQ*, 47 (1985), 282–95.

[16a] T. Y. Mullins, "Disclosure: A Literary Form in the New Testament," *NovT*, 7 (1964), 44–50.

[17] H. D. Betz, "The Literary Composition and Function of Paul's Letter to the Galatians," *NTS*, 21 (1974–75), 353–79, finds a much more complex structure in the Galatian letter, suggesting that it carries all the rhetorical marks of an "apologetic letter."

[18] R. W. Funk, *Language, Hermeneutic and Word of God* (1966), pp. 264–70; "The Apostolic *Parousia*: Form and Significance," in *Christian History and Interpretation* (1967), edd. Farmer, Moule, and Niebuhr, pp. 249–68; J. L. White, *The Form and Function of the Body of the Greek Letter* (1972), pp. 97–108. Cf. Boers, *op. cit.*, 145f.

[19] R. W. Funk, "The Apostolic *Parousia*," *loc. cit.*

d. The closing sections of the Pauline letters are given over to greetings, doxology, and benedictions.[20] The doxologies and benedictions, like the opening thanksgivings, incorporate liturgical specimens and suggest that the true "atmosphere" in which Paul wrote and expected his letters to be read was that of the church at worship. It has been suggested that 1 Corinthians 16:20–24 forms not only the close of the letter but marks the transition to a worship service, set in a eucharistic gathering, at which the letter would be read out.[21] The public reading of Paul's letters is mentioned in 1 Thessalonians 5:27 and implied in Philemon 2; and the call to circulate them among other communities is sounded in Colossians 4:16.

CONCLUSION

What emerges from this picture of Paul the letter-writer is that he had a lively sense of community with the congregations and thought of himself as "present in the spirit" with them at worship (Col. 2:5). The contribution that his letters would make to their liturgical life as well as to the strengthening of their faith and the practice of their discipline is further evidence that he took his letters to be an extension of his person, a means of conveying apostolic authority, and a vivid realization of the closeness of the bond that united apostle and congregation.

These letters, which played the role of mediating that presence—both Paul's closeness with the church, and the church's nearness to him (vividly seen in 1 Cor. 5:1–13)—cannot have been ephemeral pieces of correspondence, dashed off and dispatched in a casual manner. Rather they form a vital link connecting Paul and his churches. There is ample evidence that he viewed his letters as charged with apostolic "power." Even his enemies conceded that (2 Cor. 10:10). By such writings he demonstrated and conveyed all the moral persuasion he intended to bring to bear on his Christian readers and on his opponents.[22]

---

[20] Champion, op. cit.; cf. Rigaux, op. cit., pp. 131–33; T. Y. Mullins, "Benediction as a New Testament Form," Andrews University Seminary Studies, 15 (1977), 59–64.

[21] For criticism of this view, see C. F. D. Moule, "A Reconsideration of the Context of Maranatha," NTS, 6 (1959–60), 307–10; M. Black, "The Maranatha Invocation and Jude 14, 15 (1 Enoch 1:9)," in Christ and Spirit in the New Testament (1973), pp. 189–96.

[22] M. L. Stirewalt, "Paul's Evaluation of Letter-Writing," in Search the Scriptures (Festschrift R. T. Stamm), edd. J. M. Myers et al. (1969), pp. 179–96; J. L. White, "Saint Paul and the Apostolic Letter Tradition," CBQ, 45 (1983), 433–44.

CHAPTER TWENTY

Paul and His Predecessors

One of the firmest conclusions of the modern study of the New Testament, especially the Epistles and the Apocalypse, is that much of what we read today in our Bibles had a previous history of composition prior to being incorporated into the documents. So it is possible to investigate our present documents and probe beneath the surface to explore the twilight zone of Christian thought and life between Pentecost and the writing of the Pauline Epistles, which were the earliest parts of the New Testament to be written.

Also, since Paul used earlier material in his letters and wove these already-existing sections into his writings, it is wrong to regard him as a sort of spiritual Columbus who voyaged across uncharted seas where none before him had sailed or to treat him as a lone pioneer who blazed a trail across the terrain of early Christianity.[1] True, Paul is looked on in the surviving documents as a special person, chosen by the heavenly Lord and summoned to exercise an apostolic ministry as the result of a direct call from heaven (see his own witness in Gal. 1:11–17 and the tributes paid him in Acts 9:15f.; Eph. 3:1–12; 1 Tim. 2:7; 2 Pet. 3:15f.). But he did not spend his life or exercise his labors as a recluse, cut off from other Christians. Nor did he live and write in splendid isolation from fellow-preachers in the Christian mission. His first contacts after his conversion were with the churches in Damascus and Jerusalem (Acts 9:19,26); later he is found at work in the fellowship at Tarsus and Antioch (Acts 11:25–30; 13:1f.)—all prior to the missionary

---

[1] The most readable account is A. M. Hunter, *Paul and his Predecessors*[2] (1961). Other useful studies are O. Cullmann, "The Tradition," in *The Early Church* (ET 1956), Ch. 4; H. N. Ridderbos, *Paul and Jesus* (1958); L. Goppelt, "Tradition nach Paulus," *Kerygma und Dogma*, 4 (1958), 213–33; K. Wegenast, *Das Verständnis der Tradition bei Paulus und in den Deuteropaulinen* (1962). P. Fannon, "The Influence of Tradition in St. Paul," *SE*, 4 (TU 102) (1968), 292–307; and J. W. Fraser, *Jesus and Paul: Paul as Interpreter of Jesus from Harnack to Kümmel* (1974), Ch. 5, bring the discussion up to date. There is full survey of the material in Bultmann, *Theology of the New Testament*, 1 (ET 1952), Ch. 3. P. Gächter correctly criticizes the view of Paul as "a parachutist, equipped and ready for action, dropping out of the sky"; *Petrus und seine Zeit* (1958), p. 338. See too M. Barth, "Traditions in Ephesians," *NTS*, 30 (1984), 3–25.

journeys that led to the founding and pastoral care of churches (2 Cor. 11:28). In Romans 16 he pays tribute to his helpers and colleagues who were "in Christ" (i.e., Christian believers) before him (vs. 7), and whom he valued as co-workers.

SOURCES

To investigate the data already in existence in the churches, we need to look closely at the New Testament Epistles and apply to them the methods of literary and stylistic analysis practiced in form criticism as it has been applied to the Gospels (cf. *NTF,* 1, 132ff.). Several criteria concerning the style, language, and form have been devised. Applied to the epistolary literature these help isolate material the New Testament authors were borrowing and taking over as they composed their Epistles. To ascertain such traditional—mainly credal—elements the most reliable criteria are as follows:[2]

1. Citations from other writings of a traditional character are not usually and expressly acknowledged by the New Testament writers. 1 Corinthians 15:3-7 is an exception; Paul explicitly says that he has "received" (by tradition) certain items in a credal list and is handing them on to his readers. His Greek verbs, παραλαμβάνειν and παραδιδόναι, are technical expressions for this kind of transmission and correspond to the rabbinic verbs *qibbēl* and *māsār.* (See too 1 Cor. 11:23f.; Phil. 4:9; Col. 2:6 for other uses of the verb "to receive" in this sense.)[3]

2. Credal elements may be seen in the text by the presence of such introductory words as "deliver," "believe," "confess" (1 Cor. 15:3f.; Rom. 10:9; 1 Thess. 4:14). The clearest illustration is the introduction to 1 Timothy 3:16: "Great indeed, *we confess,* is the mystery of our religion."

3. Often contextual dislocations point to the insertion of a confessional or hymnic passage. Colossians 1:15-20 is introduced by a relative pronoun which fastens it like a pendant on to the preceding section (1:12-14) with little syntactical or contextual connection. The readers are not mentioned in verses 15-20, but they reappear in verse 21 which is linked with verse 14 in the introduction to the hypothetical quoted material. (Similarly with Philippians 2:6-11 and 1 Timothy 3:16.) In the latter case it is the relative pronoun which leads into the creed which follows. Revelation 1:4 fits only awkwardly in the context and has no syntactical relation with the surrounding text.

4. Unusual linguistic usage in a phrase or expression is a

---

[2] See E. Stauffer, *New Testament Theology* (ET 1955), Appendix III; O. Cullmann, *The Earliest Christian Confessions* (ET 1949), p. 20; J. N. D. Kelly, *Early Christian Creeds*[3] (1972), Ch. 1.

[3] B. Gerhardsson, *Memory and Manuscript* (1961), pp. 288ff.

telltale mark of its being an inserted confessional text. The most obvious instance is 1 Corinthians 16:22 where μαρανα θα simply puts into Greek letters the Aramaic watchword *mārānâ tâ,* "our Lord, come!"—a formula of invocation to the risen Lord to be present either in the eucharist or at his *parousia.* The same is true of terms like Amen, Abba, and Hallelujah, all of which are borrowed from the church at worship.

  5. The validity of an appeal to a poetic or metrical style has been variously assessed in recent study. Some scholars claim to detect the presence of rhythm behind the choice of certain words involving contrived syllabic lengths and stresses (e.g., Col. 1:15–20).[4] More likely evidence comes from stylistic tests which show an antithetical or anaphoral style. Certain rhetorical devices, such as words ending with similar vowel sounds (*homoioteleuton*), are seen or heard in 1 Timothy 3:16. More elaborate devices such as chiasmus (a crisscrossing of meaning caused by the positioning of terms to form a pattern *a-b : b-a*) are seen in liturgical texts as Colossians 1:15–20. An elevated, even monumental, style is attained in poetic passages through the choice of rare words, ceremonial terms, sonorous expressions, and heavily weighted theological statements. One example which contains much of this style is Philippians 2:6–11; and 1 Corinthians 13 is widely recognized as an independent poem dedicated to love.

  6. There are several passages in the Epistles and the Apocalypse which may be set down in lines and stanzas. Colossians 1:15–20, Philippians 2:6–11, and 1 Timothy 3:16 have been mentioned, and there are various arrangements to display the texts in versified form. Ephesians 5:14 is a clear illustration of a three-line chant whose baptismal origin is very likely:

> Awake, O sleeper!
> Arise from the dead,
> And Christ will dawn upon you.

This passage will be discussed in some detail later (see pp. 262f.).

  7. A final test has to do with the content of material whose confessional or liturgical or catechetical origin is suggested by the other tests. Often such passages are concerned to express and expound central kerygmatic truths about the person of Christ or his work of salvation. They state in succinct and memorable form the elemental parts of salvation-history, tracing the career of the Savior from his pre-existent relationship to God and the cosmos, through his incarnation and sacrifice in death, to his present position as Lord of all creation and object of worship and obedience. One of the clearest specimens of a succinct compendium of christological and soteriological teaching is Hebrews 1:1–4.

---

 [4] Ch. Masson, *L'épître de saint Paul aux Colossiens* (1950), *ad loc.*; cf. R. P. Martin, *Colossians and Philemon* (NCB, 1974), pp. 61–66.

There are longer formulations in John 1:1-18, if we are prepared to see underlying the present text a christological hymn made up of verses 1-5, 9-12, 14, and 16; and in Philippians 2:6-11. 1 Timothy 3:16 expresses succinctly the work of redemption in terms of uniting heaven and earth in a cosmic reconciliation. This is a characteristic feature of the christological hymns (see later, pp. 267f.).[5]

With this summary of the methods by which traditional material may be seen in existing documents we may classify the results.

PRE-PAULINE CATECHESIS

Catechesis is material used in training new converts and preparing them for baptism and later admission to the church's fellowship through Christian instruction.[6] Certain parts of the Epistles, mainly in Paul's writings, give evidence that they were first used in this way. We may subdivide the evidence as follows:

1. *Kerygmatic elements*. 1 Corinthians 15:3ff. is a statement of Christian faith which Paul quotes as a frontispiece to the argument for Christ's resurrection. He admits that this is not his own formulation, but he received it, presumably from his Christian predecessors. Much importance was attached to this statement, and Paul hands it on as part of his training of the Corinthians in the faith shared by all believers (1 Cor. 15:11). The substance is:

> that Christ died for our sins
>> in accordance with the scriptures;
> that he was buried;
> that he was raised on the third day
>> in accordance with the scriptures;
> that he appeared to Cephas [Peter],
>> then to the Twelve.

We notice straightway the telltale marks which stamp it as a credal formulary. The fourfold "that" (ὅτι) introduces each member of the creed (in vv. 3,4,5). The vocabulary is unusual, containing some rare

---

[5] On the literary structure of early hymns and the significance of their content, see G. Schille, *Frühchristliche Hymnen* (1962); R. Deichgräber, *Gotteshymnus und Christushymnus in der frühen Christenheit* (1967); J. T. Sanders, *The New Testament Christological Hymns* (1971); K. Wengst, *Christologische Formeln und Lieder des Urchristentums* (1972); and O. Hofius, *Der Christushymnus Philipper 2,6-11. Untersuchungen zu Gestalt und Aussage eines urchristlichen Psalms* (1976).

[6] A. Seeberg, *Der Katechismus der Urchristenheit* (1903), is still valuable; cf. P. Carrington, *The Primitive Christian Catechism* (1940). Both works, however, are severely criticized by J. E. Crouch, *The Origin and Intention of the Colossian Haustafel* (1972), pp. 13ff. See too R. P. Martin, "Virtue," in *NIDNTT*, III (1978), 928-32, on the Household Codes, to be supplemented by E. Schweizer, "Traditional Ethical Patterns in the Pauline and Post-Pauline Letters," in *Text and Interpretation*, edd. E. Best and R. McL. Wilson (1979), pp. 195-209; D. L. Balch, *Let Wives be Submissive: The Domestic Code in 1 Peter* (1981); and C. Osiek, *What Are They Saying About the Social Setting of the New Testament?* (1984), ch. 6.

terms and expressions Paul never employs again. The preface informs us that Paul "received" what follows as part of the instruction he had known, no doubt, in the early days of his discipleship, possibly through his contacts with the church at Damascus, Jerusalem, and Antioch. From verse 11 it seems clear that what Paul is citing was the shared possession of a wide range of church leaders.

Recent studies have shown the importance of this pre-Pauline passage. While some maintain that this is a summary of beliefs held by Greek-speaking churches, which Paul learned when he came into touch with these communities, notably at Antioch,[7] the case for tracing this fragment, seen as the earliest Christian confession and statement of the atonement, to the Jerusalem church has been impressively argued.[8] The important features here are the stress placed on the redemptive work of Christ, the appeal to the Old Testament (notably Isaiah 53), and the coherence of this statement with what Paul later expanded into a full-blown theologoumenon of redemption in Romans 1-8.

Although not so complex, the other evidence drawn from Romans (4:25; 10:9) places the emphasis in the same place, as Ridderbos shows. The two-member creeds insist on both the death of Jesus for sin and his resurrection, which assures the believer that his acceptance with God is a confident reality. It is not difficult to see in these verses specimens of elemental instruction based on the cross and triumph of Jesus which formed the substance of the good news taught to young Christians as expressing the faith they held and by which they were in turn sustained.

2. *Liturgical context.* The learning of the faith was promoted in an atmosphere of the church's worship. A good example of the likelihood that teaching on the atonement wrought by the Lord would be handed on and applied in the context of the church's liturgical life is 1 Corinthians 11:23ff.

The "interpreting words" in the institution of the Lord's Supper at Corinth are designed to convey powerful reminders to Christians sharing the communion (1 Cor. 10:16) of the body of Christ offered for them, and the blood by which the new covenant was sealed. J. Jeremias has demonstrated that these eucharistic formulas are traditional, built on a Semitic *Urtext* found in Mark. Paul was the transmitter of a liturgi-

---

[7] H. Conzelmann, "Zur Analyse der Bekenntnisformel 1 Kor. 15:3-5," *EvTh,* 25 (1965), 1-11; ET in *Interpretation,* 20 (1966), 20-30; also his *Hermeneia* commentary on *1 Corinthians* (1975), pp. 251-54. Cf. B. Klappert, "Zur Frage des semitischen oder griechischen Urtextes von 1 Kor. XV.3-5," *NTS,* 13 (1966-67), 168-73; and I. Howard Marshall, *The Origins of New Testament Christology* (1976), pp. 93f.

[8] J. Jeremias, *The Eucharistic Words of Jesus*[2] (ET 1966), pp. 95f., 101-105; "Artikelloses Χριστός: Zur Ursprache von 1 Cor. 15,3b-5," *ZNTW,* 57 (1966), 211-15; B. Gerhardsson, *op. cit.,* pp. 296ff.; H. N. Ridderbos, "The Earliest Confession of the Atonement in Paul," in *Reconciliation and Hope,* ed. R. Banks, pp. 76-89.

cal tradition he had inherited from his predecessors in the church.[9] To be sure, there are fresh elements in Paul's eucharistic doctrine marking his creative adaptation of the tradition, but it is an already existing tradition which he used as his basis; and in that pre-Pauline form it is clear that the Lord's Supper language is already defined as redemptive, soteriological, and covenantal. Paul makes some of the teaching explicit and adds correctives to certain false notions in the Corinthians' understanding and practice of the rite.

3. *"Words of the Lord"* were current in the early church. Although there is no explicit reference to the Galilean setting of the Gospel tradition,[10] in several places sayings of Christ found in the Synoptic Gospels seem to be in the background of the apostle's teaching (the clearest cases are 1 Cor. 7:10; 9:14; cf. 1 Tim. 5:18).[11]

In addition, allusions are made to a "word of the Lord" which may or may not relate to sayings of Jesus that circulated in the oral period but never found a place in the written Gospels. A Pauline example is 1 Thessalonians 4:15, and there are other instances in the apocryphal literature. A more probable example of this "floating" tradition is Acts 20:35, which expressly makes reference to Jesus' words. *Verba Christi,* "words of Christ," are also to be found in 1 Peter, as recent study has shown.[12]

4. *Attestation at baptism.* In the later church the ceremony of baptism included the "handing over" of a creed and its attestation by the candidate. Examples of this part of the initiation come from Justin Martyr (100–165), Irenaeus (130–200) and Hippolytus of Rome (c. 215). The practice—though not in any formal sense, yet with a confession monumental in its simplicity and brevity—goes back to apostolic times. The basic creed is the sentence "Jesus is Lord" (Rom. 10:9; 1 Cor. 12:3); earlier formulations may have been made in terms of "Jesus is the Messiah" (Mark 8:29; Acts 9:22). By the time of Paul's mission preaching the emphasis was being placed on the relevance of Jesus' lordship to the Gentile congregations, and the messianic confession was already on the way out. Paul's preaching was in terms of "Christ Jesus as Lord" (2 Cor. 4:5), and his congregations were encouraged to make this attestation (Col. 2:6).

---

9 Jeremias, *Eucharistic Words,* pp. 164ff.; see D. L. Dungan, *The Sayings of Jesus in the Churches of Paul* (1971).

10 Reasons for this omission are suggested in R. P. Martin, *Mark: Evangelist and Theologian* (1974), pp. 156–60; cf. H. W. Kuhn, "Der irdische Jesus bei Paulus," *ZThK,* 67 (1970), 295–320, who drives a wedge between Paul and his gnostic opponents who *did* rely on a tradition of the Lord's words. Paul, on the contrary, has recourse to the Spirit (1 Cor. 7:40).

11 For a recent discussion, see G. N. Stanton, *Jesus of Nazareth in New Testament Preaching* (1974), pp. 86–116; and for maximal value placed on the verbal links between Jesus' and Paul's teaching, see J. W. Fraser, *op. cit.,* Ch. 6.

12 R. H. Gundry, "'Verba Christi' in 1 Peter," *NTS,* 13 (1966–67), 336ff.; and "Further *Verba* on *Verba Christi* in 1 Peter," *Biblica,* 55 (1974), 211–32; in response to E. Best, "1 Peter and the Gospel Tradition," *NTS,* 16 (1969–70), 95ff.

In Acts 8:35–38 and 16:33 we read of baptisms in which the neophyte was called on to attest his faith. The Ethiopian did so in terms of "I believe that Jesus Christ is the Son of God" (8:37, RSV mg.; the Western text reading may well reflect primitive practice). The Philippian jailer evidently answered the call, "Put your trust in Jesus as Lord, and you will be saved, you and your household" (16:31) with an appropriate response just prior to his receiving baptism and instruction.

Ephesians 5:25f. may also be mentioned here, if the correct translation of the phrase "the washing of water with the word" means that baptism was accompanied by recitation by the person baptized of a formula acknowledging publicly Jesus as Lord.

5. *Catechetical instruction* is seen in Paul's frequent reference to "the traditions" (παραδόσεις). The chief texts are 1 Corinthians 11:2; 2 Thessalonians 2:15; 3:6; cf. 1 Thessalonians 4:1; Philippians 4:9.

The most interesting texts, such as 1 Thessalonians 4:1–9 and 1 Peter 1:13–22, look as though they originally formed part of an early Christian holiness code, setting forth the church of Jesus Christ as a "neo-levitical community," a designation coined by Carrington and Selwyn in view of the use made of the Holiness Code in Leviticus 17–20 and the stress on Christian discipline as involving abstinence from immorality practiced in the surrounding society.[13] There is a corresponding positive side with repeated calls to peace and brotherhood in love within the church.

Another distinctive feature of catechesis is the pattern of social behavior required of believers. It contained several traits, of which the best attested are: "putting off" the old evil nature, "putting on" the new nature as Christians identify with the corporate life of the new society in the church, "being subject" to the prevailing civic authorities, and "standing fast" in the faith when there is testing ahead (Col. 3:8—4:2; 1 Pet. 2:11—4:2; James 1:21; on which see below, pp. 309f.).

The transmission of such teaching—evidenced not only by the phrase "to hand on" but also by Paul's admission that what he taught was common knowledge in the churches (e.g., Rom. 6:3; 1 Thess. 5:2)—is thought to have taken place in a baptismal setting. The chief argument for this is the use often made of the series of contrasts ("light"/ "darkness"; the old way of life replaced by the new, as in Eph. 5:3–20) such as would be fitting in a dramatic experience of renunciation and new life betokened in baptism.

6. *The Old Testament.* Clearly the Scriptures of the old covenant were treated in different ways according to the intentions and predilections of the various New Testament writers. Dodd's findings here have largely stood the test of critical scrutiny:[14]

---

[13] P. Carrington, *op. cit.*; E. G. Selwyn, *The First Epistle of Peter* (1946), pp. 369ff., 459f.

[14] C. H. Dodd, *According to the Scriptures* (1952); cf. F. F. Bruce, *This is That* (US

a. The quotation of passages from the Old Testament gives evidence of a certain method of biblical study which had early established itself as part of the equipment of evangelists and teachers.

b. This method included the selection of certain large blocks of Old Testament writing, chiefly Isaiah, Jeremiah, certain minor prophets (e.g., Hab., Zech.), and the Psalms. These were understood as *wholes* rather than as quarries for isolated, independent proof-texts.

c. The relevant Scriptures were understood and interpreted according to intelligible and consistent principles, mainly concerned to explicate the plan and purpose of God, now seen to be fulfilled in the events of the gospel.

d. This common substance of the Old Testament is shared by the main New Testament contributors (Paul, Peter, Hebrews, the Fourth Evangelist), and it forms the substratum of their Christian theology in line with the consentient witness that God's salvation was wrought "in accordance with the scriptures."

To this exposition, of which we have given only a skeletal outline, may be added the evidence from Qumran.[15] The common item linking Bible interpretation among the people of the Dead Sea Scrolls and the teachers of the New Testament is the way in which both groups wrestle with "mysteries."

The "Teacher of righteousness" in the Qumran community evidently interpreted the prophets of the Old Testament according to well-attested principles: that God revealed his purpose to the prophets, but the exact significance of such a revelation could only be known at the time when the prophecy was made good; that the time of fulfilment was the end-time; and that the end-time, for the community, is now. Prophecy is being fulfilled before their eyes, and the office of the righteous Teacher is to show the relevance of ancient Scripture, considered as a mystery, to the day in which he and his contemporaries at Qumran lived.

This line of investigation is carried over into the New Testament church and applied to selected passages bearing on the understanding of the present. The church lived in the days of God's new order, and its teachers and preachers consistently appealed to the Old Testament witness to the coming rule of God and the establishment of his final purpose. This witness was centered in Christ. The most important difference between biblical interpretation at Qumran and in the early church was how the latter saw Scripture as pointing to the person of

---

title: *New Testament Development of Old Testament Themes*) (1968); R. N. Longenecker, *Biblical Exegesis in the Apostolic Period* (1975).

[15] See *NTF*, Vol. 1, pp. 88f.; F. F. Bruce, *Biblical Exegesis in the Qumran Texts* (1959); and the important observations of J. A. Sanders, "From Isaiah 61 to Luke 4," in *Christianity, Judaism and Other Greco-Roman Cults: Festschrift* M. Smith, ed. J. Neusner, Part One (1975), with reference to the work of K. Elliger and B. J. Roberts, pp. 94f.

Jesus Christ, primarily because Jesus himself claimed to be the one who fulfilled the old covenant's promises and hopes. T. W. Manson sees Jesus' treatment of the Old Testament as "based on two things: a profound understanding of the essential teaching of the Hebrew Scriptures and a sure judgment of his own contemporary situation."[16]

One further feature of biblical interpretation in the New Testament church may be noted—the piecing together of widely separated Scriptures that have terms in common and features that are parts of a united pattern. The result has been called unitive exegesis.[17] It is also attested in the rabbinic literature (the so-called *gezērāh šāwāh* principle or "argument by analogy") and at Qumran, and it gives a coherence and supplies a common theme seen to be running through the New Testament interpreters of the saving events of the gospel.[18]

PRE-PAULINE HYMNS

That the Christian gospel brought with it an outburst of hymnody and praise to God is not surprising, as A. B. Macdonald has pointed out: "We should expect that a movement which released so much emotion, and loyalty, and enthusiasm, would find expression in Song." After citing from church history cases of religious awakening and showing that these have been accompanied by outbursts of song, he goes on: "So it would have been strange indeed if the Church had remained songless in that first glorious dawn when the light from Christ came breaking across the horizons, making all things new."[19]

Encouragement for the task of locating New Testament cultic songs comes from the direct biblical evidence that in the worship of the New Testament churches, at least those of Pauline foundation, psalms of praise were sung. The oldest allusion is found in 1 Corinthians 14, where Paul writes: "When you come together each one has a hymn, a lesson, a revelation, a tongue, or an interpretation" (vs. 26). Looking forward to this is verse 15: "I will sing with the spirit and I will sing with the mind also." Verses 13-16 seem to indicate that "the speaking with tongues"—*glossolalia*—expressed itself in the form of an inspired hymnic prayer. Verse 15 sets praying and singing side by side; and it is apparent from the phrasing that both activities were thought of as directly inspired by the Spirit and were consequently highly valued. Verse 16 explicates the preceding verse by replacing "praying" and "singing psalms" with "blessing in the Spirit," which is then called "giving thanks" (εὐχαριστία); and this new terminology is continued in verse 17.

---

[16] T. W. Manson, "The Old Testament in the Teaching of Jesus," *BJRL*, 34 (1951-52), 332.

[17] F. F. Bruce, *Tradition: Old and New* (1970), p. 80.

[18] See J. Jeremias, "Zur Gedankenführung in den paulinischen Briefen," in *Studia Paulina*, pp. 149ff., for an example from Rom. 4:1-12.

[19] A. B. Macdonald, *Christian Worship in the Primitive Church* (1934), p. 112.

From this development in the apostle's discussion it may be concluded that the ψαλμός of 14:26 was in the nature of an ecstatically inspired hymn of thanksgiving to God, as the worshiper is caught up in an emotion of ecstasy and pours forth his praise in blessing God. Paul, while recognizing this type of utterance as a product of the Spirit's activity (note the admission of vs. 18: "I thank God I speak in tongues more than you all," with a possible pun on εὐχαριστεῖν), places the emphasis more on the praying and "hymning" with the mind.[20]

Two similar verses from Colossians and Ephesians provide additional insight:

Let the word of Christ dwell in you richly, as you teach and admonish one another in all wisdom, and as you sing psalms and hymns and spiritual songs with thankfulness in your hearts to God (Col. 3:16).

Addressing one another in psalms and hymns and spiritual songs, singing and making melody to the Lord with all your heart, always and for everything giving thanks (Eph. 5:19f.).

It is doubtful whether firm distinctions between "psalms," "hymns," and "songs of the Spirit" can be drawn; and recent scholars have been unwilling to delimit the exact scope of the three terms.[21] The epithet πνευματικός (spiritual) may be taken to extend to all the terms. Whatever the different emphases suggested by the use of three separate terms, it is the Spirit who stirs the worshiper and directs his thought and emotion in lyrical praise. The inspiration of the Spirit is matched by the subject-matter of the hymns, and this feature marks out Christian from pagan hymns. "The content of the primitive Christian hymns which have been handed down to us is not, therefore, subjective effusions of the emotions but they express in clear-cut sentences praise for the saving activity of God in Christ."[22] The manifold terminology indicates that many aspects of this redeeming act called forth Christian adoration in various ways. This is apparently what Schlier means: "Spontaneous accumulation [of terms] would signify the fulness of song in the worship."[23] The common motif running through the variety of liturgical expressions is thanksgiving to God (εὐχαριστοῦντες, Col. 3:17; Eph. 5:20 with a subtle difference of meaning in the two verses, as mentioned previously, p. 230).

From these verses we may sketch the form and content of the psalmody of the primitive Christian churches. The characteristic note is spontaneous praise expressing thanksgiving to God. There is no sugges-

---

[20] See J. M. Robinson, "Die Hodajot-Formel in Gebet und Hymnus des Frühchristentums," in *Apophoreta: Festschrift* E. Haenchen (1964), pp. 194–235; J. D. G. Dunn, *Jesus and the Spirit* (1975), pp. 227ff., 238f., 242ff.

[21] See G. Delling, *TDNT*, 8 (1972), 498–503.

[22] G. Delling, *Worship in the New Testament* (ET 1962), pp. 87f. This accounts for their character as confessions of faith.

[23] H. Schlier, *Die Verkündigung im Gottesdienst der Kirche* (1953), p. 39.

tion of a stereotyped pattern, except that in the Corinthian assembly the "psalm of praise" is placed at the head of the list. Unpredictable spontaneity under the immediate afflatus of the Spirit seems to have been the distinctive characteristic. There is no mention of the use of musical instruments, which is not surprising if we picture the believers as men and women drawn from the poorer strata of society and meeting clandestinely.[24] The "making melody" (ψάλλοντες, Eph. 5:19) is "in the heart."

These early "inspired odes" would no doubt be of little lasting value, and their contents would be quickly forgotten. There is evidence that, partly under Pauline influence, the flow of spontaneous utterances of this type was checked, and a more formal, stylized pattern of worship emerged, leading to the church manuals and service-books of the second century on.[25] But the texts just quoted do testify to the existence of early Christian hymns; and this evidence raises the question whether any traces of such material remain in the documents of the New Testament period. The existence of "traditional" forms shared by Paul and his converts suggests that we should seek in what comes from his hand traces of hymnic material which belong to this common stock of the nascent church.

1. *Hymns, confessions, and creeds.* Recent studies have shown the importance attached to congregational confessions in the worship of the early church. As believers assembled for worship and were reminded of all God had accomplished on their behalf, they would break forth in a formula of grateful acknowledgment at once confessing their praise and appreciation, expressing their faith, and responding to God's call in resolute action.[26]

A second feature of Christian confession has been noted in modern study. It was in the sacraments that the church could most clearly see and hear the nature of all God had achieved. In an objective form the kernel of the gospel would be revealed and make its appeal to the gathered company. Both gospel ordinances powerfully conveyed the reality of God's redeeming action in Christ. Baptism depicted the inner meaning of what God had done and how people were brought within the sphere of the gospel's saving influence (Rom. 6:4ff.; Col. 2:12ff.; 3:1ff.; cf.

---

[24] On music in early worship, see W. S. Smith, *Musical Aspects of the New Testament* (1962).

[25] See J. M. Robinson, *op. cit.*, summarized in Martin, *Worship in the Early Church*[2] (1975), pp. 135–40.

[26] On the Near Eastern enthronement ceremonial as context for the doxological side to Christian worship, see the references in R. P. Martin, *Carmen Christi* (1967), pp. 263f. R. Deichgräber (*Gotteshymnus und Christushymnus*, pp. 188ff.) wants to relate New Testament hymns to a paraenetic setting, as if they were preserved because of their hortatory function. But this use is clearly secondary to the "confessional" purpose of the hymns. The ethical application lies rather in the affirmation of living under Christ's lordship. *Carmen Christi* (1967); rev. ed. 1983, with special reference to M. Hengel, "Hymn and Christology," in *Studia Biblica 1978*, III. JSNT Supplement, series 3 [1980], 173–97.

Gal. 3:27; Eph. 5:25ff.; Titus 3:5–7). It is not difficult to imagine that it was at a service of baptism that the newly awakened Christian would wish to make some definite verbal response to the message he had heard and accepted (Eph. 5:14). And there is evidence that this is precisely how confessions of faith were made; and how confessions grew into creeds. At the Lord's table, too, the declaration was made of all that the Lord's death involved (1 Cor. 11:26), after the pattern of the Jewish recital (in the *Haggādāh*, a noun derived from the Hebrew verb *higgîḏ*, "to declare") of God's redemption of the fathers from Egyptian bondage. H. Lietzmann has argued with cogency that confessions of Christ find their natural setting in the eucharistic prayers which gave meaning to the rite.[26a]

We must be careful when generalizing about New Testament worship, for there is a great deal of diversity in early Christianity, and it would be a mistake to think that the patterns we see in Pauline mission church settings (1 Thessalonians, 1 Corinthians, perhaps Phil. 3:3) were standard everywhere. Diversity is seen in the growing trends to institutionalism in the Pastorals, the appeals in Hebrews, the bulwarks against heresy in Ephesians. Johannine Christianity may well represent a protest against a stifling formalism, in the name of a personal communion with God in Christ which is detached from holy places (John 4:21–24) and sacramental rites (John 6). Nevertheless, it is worth noting that the general impression we get from what we know of worship at Corinth is one of spontaneous and uninhibited freedom. Chapters 10–14 of 1 Corinthians present us with a series of cameos of the church at worship in that city. The main characteristic seems to have been variety. Each member made his or her contribution to the pattern of worship, all of it ideally drawing the minds and emotions of the worshipers to the redeeming acts of God. The believers would give expression to these deep sentiments in praise, hymn, prayer, *glossolalia*, and confession; and with the interpreting word given to them by one member who had the *charisma* of teaching, they would be in a right frame of mind to meet at the table.

The term "confession" is thus to be explained as the jubilant response of the fellowship sharing in acts that remind them of—and in a sense take them up into—the saving activity of God in Christ. At least one fragment of confessional material has survived in its original Aramaic form—the invocation *mārānâ ṯâ*: "our Lord, come." It has been proposed that this prayer belongs to the congregational worship of the primitive church at Jerusalem in those post-Pentecostal days when the Nazoraeans met for "the apostles' instruction, fellowship, the breaking of bread, and the prayers" (Acts 2:42–47).

It is hard to draw a firm line between responses properly called

[26a] H. Lietzmann, "Symbolstudien VIII–XII," *ZNTW,* 23 (1923), 265.

confessions and those which took on a poetic and hymnic form. R. Bultmann, commenting on 1 Peter 3:18–22, makes a rough distinction we may use:

> Is the original text a hymn or a creed? We cannot always sharply distinguish between the two; for the style and language and construction may be the same in both cases. We know too little about the cultic praxis of the early churches to say just how far cultic doxology, confession and hymn were separated from one another. In general, however, we can say that a confession in the strict sense, and particularly a baptismal creed, was relatively short. Originally it would have consisted in a simple "Jesus Christ is Lord" (Rom. 10:9), or in a short sentence like the Western text of Acts 8:37: "I believe that Jesus Christ is the Son of God." Gradually this confession became extended. Christ was characterized by descriptions of his person and his saving work, until that confession of him took precedence over the confession of God.... Compared with the relatively brief creeds, the hymns must have had a wider range—for instance Philippians 2:5ff.; Colossians 1:15–20 and the Odes of Solomon....[27]

Bultmann mentions in this paragraph some of the main credal forms scholars have detected and classified. Let us now look more closely at distinctive features that mark out the various kinds of hymns in the New Testament.

2. *Criteria for ascertaining confessions and hymns.* When it comes to the question of the detection in the New Testament of hymn-forms (as distinct from credal statements) the evidence is more difficult to assess. The boundaries between the two types of cultic formulations are, as we have noted, not finely drawn; but the following criteria may be appealed to:

a. The clearest sign that a hymn-like passage is being quoted is that a relative clause marks its opening, and is continued by the use of participles in preference to main verbs. Instances of this occur in Philippians 2:6ff.; Colossians 1:15ff.; 1 Timothy 3:16; 1 Peter 1:20 (participles); 2:23ff.; 3:18ff. (participles). In certain of these texts there is intentional antithesis, with two clauses set side by side. The usual shorthand expression for this contrast is flesh/spirit (σάρξ/πνεῦμα). The formulation takes up the twin themes of the humiliation and exaltation of Christ (cf. 2 Cor. 5:16 for the symbol). Romans 1:3f. also contains this antithesis.

b. The antithetic style is only one of the rhetorical devices tending to give a rhythmical quality to the verses. There is the use of anaphora and epiphora (i.e., the beginning and ending of the words are composed of the same vowel sounds, thus imparting a rough rhyme and assonance). Examples of this are in Colossians 1:15–20 (especially if we accept the elaborate analysis of Masson, who introduces the element of

[27] R. Bultmann, "Bekenntnis- und Liedfragmente im ersten Petrusbrief," *Coniectanea Neotestamentica,* 11 (1947), 9; my translation.

metrical quantity) and in Philippians 2:6–11 (according to the equally complex analysis of G. Gander).[28]

c. Other stylistic criteria are gradation (1 Tim. 3:16; cf. Rom. 8:29f.; 10:13–15); couplets called *parallelismus membrorum*,[28a] both antithetical (Rom. 1:3,4; 1 Tim. 3:16; 2 Tim. 2:8) and synonymous (Eph. 5:14; Rom. 10:9; 1 Cor. 15:39–41,53–55); positioning words in such a way that lines and strophes may be arranged (Phil. 2:6ff.; Col. 1:15ff.; 1 Tim. 3:16; John 1:1–14), and even a verse-form may be detected (Eph. 5:14, where a division into three lines produces a swinging trochaic rhythm, with *homoioteleuton* in the first two lines).

d. The language test may show the presence of rare terms, in some instances *hapax legomena* as far as the authors are concerned, which produce an elevated, ceremonial, hieratic style. Perhaps the words in question were selected because of their syllabic length and case-ending, with a view to producing the right number of stresses in the line and the correct vowel at the end of the line (cf. Phil. 2:6ff.; Col. 1:15ff.; 1 Cor. 13:1ff.; 11:23ff.; 1 Tim. 3:16). The artistic structure, rhythmic style, and stately bearing stand out all the more clearly in vivid contrast to the narrative prose of the surrounding verses.

e. Introductory formulas are sometimes a telltale mark (e.g., Eph. 5:14—διὸ λέγει; Phil. 2:5—ὃ καὶ ἐν Χριστῷ Ἰησοῦ; 1 Pet. 2:6—περιέχει ἐν γραφῇ; 2 Tim. 2:11—πιστὸς ὁ λόγος).

f. A final criterion, of recent date, is of debatable validity.[29] A number of scholars have identified gnostic motifs in early Christian literature; and in the most important places where these motifs are seen the structure of the passages is hymnlike—not only in the canonical New Testament, but also in the Apostolic Fathers (e.g., Ignatius) and the gnostic literature of the second and third centuries (e.g., Acts of Thomas, the Gospel of Truth, Odes of Solomon). Some of the traits are uniform in all the documents (e.g., the descent of Christ into Hades, his victory over evil spirits). Where these doctrines are mentioned or alluded to, it is argued, the passage is likely to be in the literary form of a hymn (Phil. 2:6–11; Col. 1:15ff.; 1 Tim. 3:16; 1 Pet. 3:18ff.; and certain hymnic portions of Hebrews which, it is claimed, utilize the framework of the gnostic redemption-myth).

3. *The classification of New Testament hymns.* The most obvious distinction here is that between Jewish-Christian canticles in the New Testament and distinctively Christian compositions. This method of division cannot be applied in a hard and fast way; but it will provide a

[28] Masson, *L'épître aux Colossiens* (1950), p. 105; G. Gander, "L'hymne de la Passion" (unpublished dissertation, Geneva, 1939).
[28a] See O. Linton, "Le *parallelismus membrorum* dans le Nouveau Testament," *Mélanges bibliques. Hommage au R. P. B. Rigaux* (1970), pp. 489–507.
[29] See J. T. Sanders, *The New Testament Christological Hymns*, pp. 96–98.

starting point for classifying the various hymnic forms in the New Testament. Among Jewish hymns which the early believers took over and
modified to suit their own purposes we may include the Lukan canticles
(1:46–55, 68–79; 2:14, 29–32); Jewish-Christian fragments (Rom.
11:33–36; 1 Tim. 1:17) and certain liturgical forms like "Amen," "Hallelujah," "Hosanna," "Abba," and "Marana tha"; and the hymnic forms
of the Apocalypse, certain sections of which draw directly from the liturgical vocabulary of the Hellenistic synagogues (e.g., 4:8,11; 11:17f.; 14:7;
15:3f.) while other parts contain distinctively Christian versicles (e.g.,
5:9f., 12; 12:10–12; 19:1ff.).

For hymns which are original Christian creations, we suggest a
fourfold classification—with the qualification that it is not possible to
categorize the New Testament hymns into a rigid pattern: any one
hymn may be classified in more than one way. The four families of
distinctive Christian hymn compositions which bear witness to the new
age that dawned with the coming of the Lord Jesus Christ are sacramental, meditative, confessional, and christological.

a. Under the heading of *sacramental hymns,* the following texts
may be placed: Ephesians 5:14; Titus 3:4–7; Romans 6:1–11; and Ephesians 2:19–22. Ephesians 5:14 is generally recognized as the clearest
New Testament witness to the existence of Christian hymns in the
primitive church. There are some good grounds for this confidence.

The introductory formula διὸ λέγει (RSV, "therefore it is said")
reads as though it were added expressly to prepare for the citation of a
hymn. Furthermore the verse naturally divides into three lines on
stylistic grounds. A. M. Hunter has called attention to the "swinging
trochaic rhythm in the Greek, and homoioteleuton in the first two lines"
of the triplet.[30] There is a formal correspondence between this call to
arousal and activity and the religious chants in the Attis cult in the
Hellenistic mysteries. And the most suitable *Sitz im Leben* for the verse
would be the cultic life of the early church.

The verse contains an invocational appeal summoning the
Christian to action and at the same time offering the promise of divine
favor. The first two lines are a rousing call to moral activity; the third
line is the accompanying promise:

διὸ λέγει·

ἔγειρε, ὁ καθεύδων
καὶ ἀνάστα ἐκ τῶν νεκρῶν
καὶ ἐπιφαύσει σοι ὁ Χριστός.

This may be reproduced in translation as:

Therefore it is said:

[30] A. M. Hunter, *Paul and His Predecessors*[2], p. 39.

Awake, O sleeper,
From the grave arise.
The light of Christ upon you will dawn.

In view of the stirring exhortation in the verse and the combination of metaphors applied to the spiritual life of the Christian (sleep, death, light), the most natural event to associate it with is Christian baptism. These lines would then, it is surmised, form the chant accompanying the baptismal action. The verbs ἔγειρε, ἀνάστα, and ἐπιφαύσει are common in a baptismal context, and in the primitive church baptism was frequently known as "enlightenment" (φωτισμός). The rising of the convert from the death of sin to union with the living Lord is represented by the sacrament of initiation. The solemnity of the occasion—especially if there are eschatological overtones in the hymn[31]—would fix the verse indelibly on the mind and heart of the neophyte as he emerged from the baptismal water. If this is a correct explanation, it is easy to see how the author of the letter could quote it as something well-known to his readers, and introduce it quite naturally in his ethical counsels as a challenging call to that newness of life into which his readers were first introduced at baptism.

     b. We may classify the following as *hymn-like meditations*: Ephesians 1:3–14; Romans 8:31–39; 1 Corinthians 13. These passages are marked by a highly rhetorical style, elevated and stately language, and a concern with profound theological and ethical themes. But it would be rash to say that they are to be identified as Christian hymns, used in divine service, unless we are willing (as some are) to give the name "hymn" to any New Testament passage of poetic and lyrical structure.

     c. There is more justification for the title *confessional hymn* for 1 Timothy 6:11–16 and 2 Timothy 2:11–13. There is no agreement on the exact setting of the first passage. Timothy is reminded of "the good confession" he has made "in the presence of many witnesses" (vs. 12), and is charged "to keep the commandment unstained and free from reproach" (vs. 14). This confession and vow may be the promises given in baptism, or an ordination vow, or an arraignment at court. The hymnic form of the passage is most apparent in verses 15f., where the rhythmical (even rhyming) language, the elevated style, and the presence of some unusual expressions seem clearly to point to the incorporating by the author of some traditional, hymnic material, possibly borrowed from the Hellenistic *Diaspora*. "As often, so here, the thought of the apostle comes to rest only in the worship of God. . . . He prays in solemn lan-

---

[31] B. Noack, "Das Zitat in Eph. 5,14," *ST,* 5 (1952), 52–64. He wants to take the language of awakening and arousal as literal; thus "only the second advent of the Lord can be meant. . . . The hymn is concerned with the resurrection of the dead at the *parousia* and is an eschatological hymn whose words, strictly speaking, have not yet sounded out, but will do so first at Doomsday" (62); my translation.

guage with the words of a well-known doxology, which is associated with the prayer-forms of the hellenistic synagogues."[32]

2 Timothy 2:11–13 has all the marks of an independent hymn the author has taken over. It is prefaced by the introductory formula "The saying is sure,"[33] and is built up of four couplets to form a unified poem on the theme of martyrdom.

> If we have died (with him),
>   we shall also live (with him);
> if we endure,
>   we shall also reign (with him);
> if we deny (him),
>   he also will deny us;
> if we are faithless,
>   he remains faithful;
> For he cannot deny himself.

It is not universally agreed that all three verses are to be included in the hymn. B. S. Easton maintains that the "faithful saying" extends only to verse 12a on the ground that the first two sets of couplets have a rhythm and assonance not continued in the later verses.[34] But verse 13a does have an obvious and carefully worded contrast. Verse 13b may conceivably be the comment of the author on the hymn's last line.

The hymn is written as a tribute to the martyr's endurance and vindication, although some recent commentators have sought to anchor it in a baptismal setting, on the assumption that the "dying with Christ" motif is linked with Pauline teaching in Romans 6:1ff. The two themes of baptism and the prospect of martyrdom are closely allied, for "endurance of suffering for Christ is a natural outcome of dying with Christ in baptism."[35]

d. From considering these snatches of Christian hymnody we go on to examine some outstanding christological passages in the New Testament, giving special attention to those places in the literature where traces not only of hymns but of *hymns to Christ* have been detected. Not surprisingly, the material in this category is rich and full, for when Christians think and write about their Lord, their thoughts naturally tend to be expressed in lyrical and worshipful terms. Religious speech tends to be poetic in form; and meditation on the person and place of Jesus Christ in the church's life and in the experience of the believer is not expressed in a cold, calculating way, but becomes rhapsodic and ornate. The borderline between prayer, creed, and hymn becomes difficult to fix precisely.

Illustrations of these points may be sought and discovered in

---

[32] J. Jeremias, *Die Briefe an Timotheus und Titus* (1953), p. 39; my translation.

[33] On the "sure sayings" see G. W. Knight, *The Faithful Sayings in the Pastorals* (1968).

[34] B. S. Easton, *The Pastoral Epistles* (1948), *ad loc.*

[35] G. R. Beasley-Murray, *Baptism in the New Testament* (1962), p. 208.

those sections of the apostolic literature which have been classified as both "christological" and "hymnic." The most notable examples are Philippians 2:6–11; Colossians 1:15–20; 1 Timothy 3:16; Hebrews 1:3; and parts of 1 Peter. Of these we shall consider three.

Philippians 2:6–11. This is one of the most powerful christological portions in the New Testament. It portrays the drama of Christ's glory with the Father, his abasement and obedience on earth, even to the death of the cross, and his exaltation to God's presence and cosmic triumph and lordship, which all the spiritual powers confess.

There are various suggestions as to how these lines should be arranged. Analyses into a six-stanza or three-verse hymn are widely accepted, though it is possible that in its original form the Philippians psalm consisted of a series of couplets and was an early tribute to Christ's divine person. Paul incorporated it into his letter and drew out the important teaching by the insertion of certain interpreting words and phrases, especially the phrase "even the death of the cross" (vs. 8). The pre-Pauline verses, set in antiphonal form, may well have read as follows. The apostle's additions are placed in brackets.

> Although he was in the divine form,
> He did not think equality with God a thing to be grasped;
>
> But surrendered his rank,
> And took the role of a servant;
>
> Becoming like the rest of mankind,
> And appearing in a human role;
>
> He humbled himself,
> In an obedience that went so far as to die
> [even death on a cross].
>
> For this, God raised him to the highest honor,
> And conferred upon him the highest rank of all;
>
> That, at Jesus' name every knee should bow,
> [of every being in heaven, on earth, and under the earth]
> And every tongue should own that "Jesus Christ is Lord"
> [to the glory of God, the Father].[36]

Colossians 1:15–20. As early as 1913 the German scholar E.

---

[36] For bibliography on these verses up to 1975 see R. P. Martin, *Philippians* (NCB, 1976), pp. 90–102, 109–116; see also G. B. Caird, *Paul's Letters from Prison* (1976), pp. 100–104, 118–124; J. Murphy-O'Connor, "Christological Anthropology in Phil. II, 6–11," *RB,* 83 (1976), 25–50. See too R. P. Martin, *ExpT,* 94 (1983), 132–36; *Carmen Christi,*[2] p. xxi.

J. D. G. Dunn, *Christology in the Making* (1980), esp. pp. 114–28, has placed some question marks behind the idea of preexistence in the traditional interpretation of Phil. 2:5–11, to which several contributors in *Christ the Lord. Festschrift for D. Guthrie,* ed. H. H. Rowdon (1982), have responded. See Dunn's rejoinder in *ExpT,* 95 (1984), 295–99.

Norden had arranged these verses into a hymnic form and detected certain liturgical traits. His analysis produced the following:[37]

STROPHE A

Who is the image of the unseen God, the first-born of all
     creation,
For in him were created all things in heaven and on earth;
[Seen and unseen,
Whether Thrones or Dominions
Or Powers or Rulers]
All things through him and for him have been created;
And he himself is before all things,
And all things in him cohere,
And he himself is the head of the body, [the church].

STROPHE B

Who is the beginning, the first-born from the dead,
That he might become in all things himself pre-eminent;
For in him all the fulness (of God) chose to dwell,
And through him to reconcile all things to him,
[Making peace by the blood of his cross
Through him], [whether things on earth
Or things in heaven].

Apparently the two stanzas cover two subjects: Christ and creation (vv. 15–18a) and Christ and the church (vv. 18b–20). Later analytical studies have improved on this twofold division by suggesting an intermediate strophe (vv. 17–18a) which acts as a bridge linking the first (vv. 15f.) and the third (vv. 18b–20). A pre-Pauline draft of the hymn has been detected; and Paul's additions (bracketed) are seen as his way of emphasizing certain truths which the original hymn was in danger of either omitting or obscuring, such as redemption through atonement and the universality of Christ's reconciling work. In particular Paul has introduced the "church" into the presentation of what was originally a tribute to Christ and his cosmic body.

The two parts are comparable in a number of ways and certain stylistic peculiarities are present which cannot be there by chance, for example, the repetition of words and phrases in the two main stanzas. In some cases the words are repeated in exactly the same position in each stanza. A. M. Hunter has observed that three pairs of lines are precisely correspondent in the main parts of the hymn. The vocabulary also is

[37] E. Norden, *Agnostos Theos* (1913, repr. 1956), p. 252. For a summarizing statement and evaluation of recent study see R. P. Martin, *Colossians and Philemon* (NCB, 1974), pp. 55–66; see also P. Benoit, "L'hymne christologique de Col. 1,15–20. Jugement critique sur l'état des recherches," in *Judaism and Other Greco-Roman Cults*, pp. 226–63.

unusual; and the whole "betrays the hand of an exacting composer,"[38] who penned this noble tribute to exhibit the primacy of Christ in creation and redemption. Paul uses an already existing hymn in which Christ is portrayed as lord of the universe and redeemer of the church to refute an incipient gnosticism which denied the Lord's supremacy and uniqueness as mediator between God and man. This is not the last time in Christian history when God's people have been kept from error and prevented from lapsing into heresy because they have been recalled to the robust teaching of the traditional hymns of the faith.

Hebrews 1:3. As a final example of what may be adduced as New Testament odes to Christ, we may cite Hebrews 1:3:

> Who reflects the glory of God,
> And bears the very stamp of his nature,
> Upholding all things by the word of his power.
> When he had made purification for sins,
> He sat down at the right hand of the majesty on high.

Again the tell-tale marks of style are evident (more so in the King James Version)—the use of the introductory relative pronoun ("who") and participles ("being, upholding, had purged") and the elevated, ceremonial style, of which Norden writes: "It is instructive to notice how this style is the best among New Testament authors."[39] The vocabulary too is rare and there is a splendid climax in the sonorous ending of verse 3. By the three-fold test of theological content, stylistic construction, and unusual vocabulary, we may confidently assess this verse to be a Christ-hymn.

Conclusion. Our study of the literary form and christological content of these Christ-hymns leads to the following conclusions. The Lord of the church is depicted in a "cosmological" role in the double sense of that adjective. First, his preexistence and pretemporal activity are made the frontispiece of the hymns. From the divine order in which he eternally is, he "comes down" as the incarnate one in an epiphany. Then, at the conclusion of his earthly life he takes his place in God's presence, receiving the universal homage and acclamation of the cosmic spirit-powers that confess his lordship. His saving work brings together the two orders of existence (the celestial and the terrestrial), and his reconciliation is described in a cosmic setting. The hymns are essentially *soteriological*, setting forth the person of Christ in relation to his work, but ethical application follows directly: believers who sing the hymns are encouraged to live under the lordship of Christ in the fellowship of his kingdom.

---

[38] A. M. Hunter, *op. cit.*, p. 125.
[39] E. Norden, *op. cit.*, p. 386.

Inasmuch as Christ accomplished what God alone can do—in particular the pacification of the hostile powers of the universe—and had taken his place on his Father's throne (Rev. 3:21; 5:1-14) as the divinely appointed *Cosmocrat* and judge of all history, it was a short step for the early Christians to set him *in loco Dei* (in the place of God) in their cultic worship. From this point of conviction that "Jesus Christ is Lord to the glory of God the Father" (Phil. 2:11) the line runs on to the Bithynian Christians' "hymn to Christ as to God"; and to the *Te Deum*: "Thou art the King of glory, O Christ; Thou art the everlasting Son of the Father."[40]

PRE-PAULINE STATEMENTS OF FAITH

1. *The church as a believing, preaching, and confessing community*. What evidence is there in the New Testament scripture of credal and confessional forms? Clearly no full-scale creed in the sense of "a fixed formula summarizing the essential articles of (the Christian) religion and enjoying the sanction of ecclesiastical authority"[41] is found in the New Testament. Later creeds are couched in a different language and style. But that does not imply that the New Testament church was unconcerned about the doctrinal significance of the message believed and proclaimed. Far from it. The church of the New Testament is already a believing, preaching, and confessing community of men and women. This implies the existence and influence of a body of authoritative doctrine (although embryonic in matters such as belief in the Trinity), which was the given and shared possession of those who formed the nascent Christian communities in the world of the Roman Empire. What Paul declared about the resurrection must have been true about the main tenets of the faith which were cherished and proclaimed: "Whether then it was I or they [the other apostles], so we preach and so you believed" (1 Cor. 15:11).

Only on the assumption of a corpus of doctrine accepted as authoritative and binding can we explain the Christian consciousness of the church as a distinct entity in the world, over against the Jews and Gentiles (1 Cor. 10:32). Only thus can we grasp the church's missionary zeal in proclaiming the gospel, which was not offered as a tentative suggestion to be entertained along with other attractive possibilities but as God's unique truth, without rival or peer, demanding a full and unreserved commitment (see Gal. 1:8f.; 1 Cor. 15:1; 1 Thess. 2:13). The reason for the imperious call of the gospel, which will brook no rivalry, is given in Acts 4:12 and 2 Cor. 11:4: there is only one Savior and Lord.

Furthermore, only on the ground of the possession of a clearly

---

[40] For further discussion of early Christian hymns see R. P. Martin, "Aspects of Worship in the New Testament Church," *Vox Evangelica*, 2 (1963), 6–32; *IDB, Supp. Vol.* (1976), 556f.

[41] J. N. D. Kelly, *Early Christian Creeds*[3] (1972), p. 1.

defined body of gospel truth can we account for the believers' organizing themselves into communities with a definite cultus (a practiced religious devotion drawing men and women into a society of worshipers or devotees), a standard of belief (2 Cor. 9:13; Phil. 1:27), and a precise membership, from which defaulters and "heretics" could be, and in fact were, excommunicated (e.g., 1 Cor. 5:3–5; 1 Tim. 1:19f.; 2 John 9f.) and in which disciplinary measures were exercised (2 Cor. 2:5–11). If the early church had been a society of freethinkers, with everyone at liberty to believe what he thought acceptable and to live as he pleased, with no guiding lines of doctrine and ethical behavior patterns, the New Testament letters would be far different from what they are. "The truth of the gospel" was clearly a doctrinal standard to be jealously preserved (see Gal. 2:14), and the "law of Christ" (Gal. 6:2; 1 Cor. 9:21) was a moral directive to be honored and obeyed.[42]

Let us examine the evidence, to see whether these forms may be located and note the circumstances in which they arose.

2. *The church's preaching and teaching.* In New Testament times, a corpus of distinctive doctrine was held as a sacred deposit from God. The references to such a web of saving truth are set forth with a fulness of description and variety of details, although the evidence must not be pressed too far. Note how many terms were used by the early Christians for this:

> "the apostles' teaching" (Acts 2:42)
> "the word of life" (Phil. 2:16)
> "the standard of teaching" (Rom. 6:17)
> "the words of faith and good doctrine" (1 Tim. 4:6)
> "the pattern of sound words" (2 Tim. 1:13)
> "sound teaching" (2 Tim. 4:3; Titus 1:9)

Then there are considerable allusions to "the faith" (Phil. 1:27; Eph. 4:5; Col. 2:6f.; 1 Tim. 6:20f.); "the truth" (Col. 1:5; 2 Thess. 2:13; 2 Tim. 2:18,25; 4:4); "the apostolic traditions" (1 Cor. 11:2; 15:1ff.; Gal. 1:9; Col. 2:6; 1 Thess. 4:1; 2 Thess. 2:15); and the "gospel" (Rom. 2:16; 16:25; 1 Cor. 15:1ff.; Phil. 1:7,27).

a. This doctrinal formulation is to be held fast, especially in time of doubt when the tendency to apostasy and denial of the faith is marked. It is not surprising that the call to stand fast in the faith and to hold firm to its teaching sounds through the Epistle to the Hebrews, since that letter was addressed as a "word of exhortation" (Heb. 13:22) to a community of Christians in danger of relapsing into their pre-Christian or, more likely, of following aberrant ways (3:6,14; 4:14; 10:23). The same background of Christians menaced by false ideas or

---

[42] The precise definition to be attached to "law" is debated. See C. H. Dodd, "ENNOMOS CHRISTOU," in *More New Testament Studies* (1968), pp. 134–48; D. L. Dungan, *Sayings of Jesus in the Churches of Paul*; J. W. Fraser, *Jesus and Paul*, pp. 100, 112f.

heretical tendencies is present in Jude 3 and 20 and 1 John 2:18–23.

Certain expressions of the apostolic faith were designed specifically to refute false doctrines which were raising their head. At Corinth Paul had to deal with a wrong-headed notion of the resurrection (1 Cor. 15:3–5,12,35f.); and in the Pauline church situations in Asia Minor docetism cast doubt on the reality of the Lord's incarnation and passion "in the flesh," considering it only an "appearance" in human form.[43] The Elder John met this subtle heresy with an insistence on a real incarnation and a veritable humanity which Christ assumed (see 1 John 4:2f.; 2 John 7); and he did so in a language which has a credal ring about it.

b. The deposit of the faith is to be cherished and handed on to the succeeding generation of believers (2 Tim. 2:2), as the apostolic writers themselves had received it from their predecessors in the faith and ultimately from the Lord himself (1 Cor. 11:23; prob. Gal. 4:14). Oscar Cullmann shows how "from the Lord" in the Corinthians passage is especially important, for it refers back to

> Christ as the One who stands, not only at the beginning, but also behind the transmission of the tradition, that is, the One who is at work *in* it. "From the Lord" can mean a direct receiving from the Lord, without it being necessary to think of a vision or of excluding middle men through whom the Lord imparts the *paradosis* (tradition).... The Apostles are these middle men and ... their reality as Apostles lies in their being bearers of direct revelation.[44]

That Paul saw himself as the receiver of an authoritative tradition concerning the Lord's Supper, solemnly bound to transmit this truth to others, is clear from the terms he uses. As we saw, the verbs "I received" and "I delivered unto you" are equivalent to rabbinic expressions for receiving and transmitting a piece of authoritative teaching (see above, p. 249). This tradition of "holy words" forms a continuous link between the apostolic age and the succeeding generations of those who came after the apostles. The expression in 2 Timothy 2:2 illustrates the connection: "What you have heard from me before many witnesses [cf. 1 Tim. 6:12] entrust to faithful men who will be able to teach others also," as does also the statement in 1 Clement 44 (c. AD 90–100) which speaks of "other eminent men" and "other approved men," who were appointed to succeed the ministry of the apostles and their associates.

c. This body of doctrine is referred to in certain contexts as material that is to be utilized in the public proclamation of the Christian message (e.g., Phil. 2:16; 2 Tim. 2:15). The most celebrated credal passage which contains the crystalization of apostolic teaching on the basic elements of the gospel is 1 Corinthians 15:3–5 (see above, p. 251).

---

[43] As in the Colossian heresy, which seemed to imply a docetic denial of Jesus' true humanity; on Col. 2:9 cf. R. P. Martin, *Colossians: The Church's Lord and the Christian's Liberty* (1972), pp. 7f., 75.

[44] O. Cullmann, "*Kyrios* As Designation for the Oral Tradition concerning Jesus," *SJT*, 3 (1950), 189.

3. *The church's worship*. Vernon H. Neufeld has closely inspected the New Testament confessions of faith and concluded that the earliest form of Christian witness may be taken back into the period of the gospel record and to the disciples' confession that Jesus is the Christ (Mark 8:29).[45] Jesus' messiahship was a live issue in the period of the Acts of the Apostles and the Christian mission to the Jews of the Dispersion. Not surprisingly, the confession "Jesus is the Messiah" is found as a major theme in the early days of the New Testament church (e.g., Acts 2:36; 3:20; 5:42; 8:5; 9:22). Since this exact confession runs through the Gospel of John, Neufeld argues that this gospel (at least in its first draft, we should add) is to be placed in the early stages of the growth of the New Testament literature. The title "Christ" features in the call of Peter in Acts 2:38, which is also connected with a baptismal scene.

As the church moved out into a Gentile environment, the debate concerning messiahship became irrelevant. In Paul's dealings with the Gentile churches of the Roman Empire the messianic status of Jesus is of secondary concern. "In the epistles Paul never says 'Jesus is the Christ'. . . . He never seems to have laid much stress on teaching the Gentiles the meaning of the name."[46] The appropriate appellation is Lord; and this, for him, is the vital thing. "If you confess with your lips that Jesus is Lord . . . you will be saved" (Rom. 10:9); "For we preach not ourselves but Christ Jesus as Lord" (2 Cor. 4:5); "No one can say, 'Jesus is Lord' except by the Holy Spirit" (1 Cor. 12:3).

The confession "Jesus Christ is Lord" may be placed in the setting of the church's worshiping life. We have seen that it is a fitting formula by which the new convert testified to faith in Christ; and the record in the Acts of the Apostles demonstrates that conversion and baptism were regarded as the inside and outside of the same experience. Acts 2:37f. speaks of both the inquiry, "What shall we do?" and the apostle's directive, "Repent, and be baptized every one of you in the name of Jesus Christ." Here is a scene when the initial confession of the lordship of Christ (see Acts 2:36: "God has made him both Lord and Christ") was most appropriate and in order. Let us look at some other places where this initial answer to the gospel's call is very closely related to submission to the baptismal rite.

a. *Acts 8:35–38* is of considerable interest because the important Western textual tradition preserves the actual terms in which the confession was made. After verse 37 are the words (RSV mg.): "And Philip said, 'If you believe with all your heart, you may [be baptized].' And he replied, 'I believe that Jesus Christ is the Son of God.'" Then follows the record of the eunuch's baptism at the hands of Philip the

---

[45] V. H. Neufeld, *The Earliest Christian Confessions* (1963).
[46] N. A. Dahl, "Die Messianität Jesu bei Paulus," in *Studia Paulina*, p. 94; ET, "The Messiahship of Jesus in Paul," in *The Crucified Messiah and Other Essays* (1974), p. 46. See too M. Hengel, "'Christos' in Paul," *Between Jesus and Paul* (ET 1983), ch. 4.

evangelist. Quite possibly this addition represents the earliest form of a baptismal creed.[47] At the baptism of converts some inquiry would be made as to faith in Christ, and a simple confession and attestation of belief and allegiance to him called for. The dialogue between the evangelist and the newly awakened believer in Acts 8 mirrors what must often have happened before the administration of the ordinance; and the later history of baptismal practice confirms this evidence.[48]

b. *Acts 16:31–33* is a cameo of the conversion of the Philippian jailer and his household, with the result that, having believed in God with all his household and family, he was baptized in response to the apostle's call: "Put your trust in the Lord Jesus [or, in Jesus as Lord], and you will be saved, you and your household."

c. *Ephesians 5:25f.* may be mentioned here, following C. A. Anderson Scott's translation of the Pauline words: "Christ also loved the church, and gave himself up for her, that he might consecrate her after cleansing in the water-bath [of baptism] together with the Formula."[49] "The Formula" (lit. "saying") evidently means the public acknowledgment by the persons to be baptized of Jesus as Lord.

d. In *Philippians 2:11* Paul quotes the confessional acclamation: "Jesus Christ is Lord." As noted before, this cry comes as the climax of the hymnic adoration of the cosmic Christ as all creatures throughout the universe bow down and submit to his dominion. A modern study of the passage by J. Jervell has sought to place this hymn and its closing acclamation in a baptismal context.[50]

The cogency of this ingenious argument depends on one's acceptance of certain assumptions Jervell makes: that the confession of Christ's lordship refers primarily to the submission of the evil spirit-forces which assent to his victory over them and their consequent defeat; that the mention of the "name" links up with other references to the calling of Christ's name over the convert in baptism; and that the term "form" is to be equated in meaning with "image." We may therefore bring into the discussion those texts in which the image of Christ is said to be formed and seen in the believer (esp. Phil. 3:10,21; 2 Cor. 3:18; Rom. 8:29; Gal. 4:19). Jervell then argues that it was by union with Christ in baptism that the image of Christ began to take shape within the Christian (as in Rom. 6:3–5; Gal. 5:24; Col. 2:12).

The final line of reasoning runs as follows. The confession of Jesus Christ as Lord by the convert may well have betokened for him the passing from the domain of the spirit-powers by which his old life was controlled (cf. Gal. 4:3–9; 1 Cor. 12:2) into the liberty and joy of the

[47] J. N. D. Kelly, *op. cit.*, p. 16.
[48] P. T. Fuhrmann, *An Introduction to the Great Creeds of the Church* (1960), pp. 15–18.
[49] C. A. A. Scott, *Christianity According to St. Paul* (1932), p. 119.
[50] J. Jervell, *Imago Dei: Gen. 1.26f. im Spätjudentum, in der Gnosis und in den paulinischen Briefen* (1960), pp. 206–209.

gospel (see Rom. 8:15,21,38f.; Gal. 5:1ff.; Col. 1:12f.; 2:8–15). The old life, like the old nature, was put away; and the new convert put on Christ, the new man in whose image he was renewed and reborn (Eph. 4:22–24; Col. 3:9–12). By submitting to the act of baptism into Christ he is called to live out the life of his Lord as he becomes conformed to that image. Thus Christ "takes shape" (Gal. 4:19) in him from the very moment of conversion-baptism; and the hymn which powerfully sets the person of Christ as the image of God and his victory and exaltation may well have been sung at the service of baptism when the church is reminded of the need to live out the life of that Lord, who is the conqueror of all the foes that menaced first-century people and held them in bondage to fear and the lower nature.

If the Philippians 2 hymn may be placed in such a setting, it would provide one more endorsement of the general view that the affirmation "Jesus Christ is Lord" belongs to the cultic life of the early Christians as they engaged in their worship of the sovereign master of their lives and of the universe.

4. *The church's witness against paganism.* The early church was called to live its life and maintain its testimony in tumultuous times. From the first, threats of persecution are seen clearly in all their intensity; later we read that Christians were hauled before Jewish authorities and Roman officials and required to attest their allegiance to Jesus Christ. Therefore, the Christian confessions are shaped by their emerging in a time of conflict and duress.

The prototype of these statements of belief goes back to the tradition of the Lord's own *credo* before the Sanhedrin at his trial (Mark 14:61f.; 15:2). The apostle makes allusion to this in reminding Timothy of "Christ Jesus, who before Pontius Pilate witnessed a good confession," in a passage which reproduces "the substance of a primitive baptismal creed."[51] The point is the need to stand firm in the face of opposition, even as the Lord Jesus, when arraigned before his earthly judges, both Jewish and Roman, bore witness to a "noble confession." The call to such a confession had already been hinted in Jesus' own words in Matthew 10:32f.

The arraignment of Christians before Jewish tribunals was chiefly of an incidental character, and the punishment they received was occasioned largely by hysterical outbursts of indignation and wrath. Such a circumstance would hardly leave room for a formal declaration of belief. But as the church came into collision with the Roman authorities, the questions which the Romans asked were such as to elicit careful statements of the faith.

Oscar Cullmann has theorized that the formulation of early creeds was controlled partly by the apologetic needs of the church facing

---

[51] J. N. D. Kelly, *The Pastoral Epistles* (1963), p. 143, referring to 1 Tim. 6:13.

the hostile pagan world.[52] Haled before the Roman magistrate and required to attest their supreme loyalty to Christ, the Christians confessed, "Jesus Christ is Lord," not Caesar. This is the historical background of Acts 17:5–10; 18:12–17. Cullmann suggests the same setting for 1 Corinthians 12:3. True Christians, inspired by the Spirit, whose help is promised (Matt. 10:19f.), will never curse Christ (and say, "Jesus is anathema"), but will attest "Jesus as Lord," as Polycarp and the later martyrs did. The *Martyrdom of Polycarp,* written as an eyewitness account of the bishop of Smyrna in the early years of the second century, is a moving document of the aged man's refusal to swear allegiance to Caesar by saying "Lord Caesar" (8.2) and thereby deny his Lord Christ (9.3).

While the evidence from Polycarp's martyrdom looks parallel to the wording of 1 Corinthians 12:3, it is doubtful that Cullmann's suggestion can be sustained, for there is no hint of Roman persecution in 1 Corinthians. It is more plausible that the background is the readmission of apostate Christians to the synagogue, when the declaration required would be "Jesus is accursed" (in the sense of Deut. 21:23)—and therefore no true Messiah—in reversal of the Christian confession, "Jesus is Lord." W. Schmithals offers another, more cogent possibility—that the call to "anathematize Jesus" is made by gnosticizing Corinthian enthusiasts, who thus vent their disdain for the human Jesus in exalting the heavenly aeon Christ.[53] Paul's rebuttal is to insist that a true confession of the historical Jesus as Lord is the only sure hallmark of the Spirit's inspiration and presence.

Still, the point Cullmann makes is valid: the early Christians, struggling against both Jews and Gentiles, expressed the gist of what distinguished them by simple formulas of confession. And in the later church this led to the class of persons known as "confessors" who were called on to attest their allegiance to Christ as well as the "martyrs" who sealed that testimony with their blood.

5. *The range of the early creeds.* The confessions of the New Testament extend from the simple "Jesus is Lord" to the detailed summaries of 1 Corinthians 15:3–5; Romans 1:3f.; 4:24f.; 8:34; Philippians 2:6–11; 1 Timothy 3:16; 1 Peter 3:18–22. As confessions of Christ, they comprehend the various aspects of his person (both pre-existent and incarnate), his mission (death, burial, descent into the underworld of Hades), and his victory and exalted status and role as intercessor and Lord of all.

There are also binitarian creeds which unite the Father and the

---

[52] O. Cullmann, *The Earliest Christian Confessions,* pp. 28ff.

[53] W. Schmithals, *Gnosticism in Corinth* (ET 1971), pp. 124–35; similarly N. Brox, "ANATHEMA IĒSOUS (1 Kor. 12,3)," *BZ,* 12 n.f. (1968), 103–11. But cf. E. Fascher, "Die Korintherbriefe und die Gnosis," in *Gnosis und das Neues Testament,* ed. K.-W. Tröger (1973), pp. 281–91.

Son (1 Cor. 8:6; 1 Tim. 2:5f.). Nor should we overlook the implicit trinitarian fragments such as Matthew 28:19; 2 Corinthians 1:21f.; 13:14; 1 Corinthians 6:11; 12:4f. There are also those verses which are shaped in a triadic scheme, which set out the "division of work" of the trinity—the Father who sends, the Son who is sent, and the Spirit who applies the work of salvation (see Gal. 3:11-14; 4:4f.; 1 Peter 1:2; Heb. 10:29). Here are the raw materials of the later fully developed trinitarian creeds which bid us praise:

> Glory to the Father,
> Glory to the Son.
> And to thee, blest Spirit,
> While all ages run.[54]

---

[54] For a consideration of the relevance of New Testament hymns and creeds to the churches' liturgical practice, see R. P. Martin, *The Worship of God: Some Theological, Pastoral, and Practical Reflections* (1982), chs. 4, 6.

CHAPTER TWENTY-ONE

The Authority of Paul's Letters: Apostleship, Tradition, and the Canon

According to C. F. Evans, there are three related technical problems for one who wishes to understand the Pauline letters: "their formation into a corpus, their unity and authenticity, and their chronology."[1] Having considered the bulk of this literature, we now ask, How did Paul's letters, by construction and intent "occasional letters," become accepted by the church as authoritative Scripture? There are really two issues here: how did a letter written to a local congregation (say, Philippi) become known to and then claimed as the property of other Christian groups in the Mediterranean world? and how did Paul's separate letters, written to scattered groups, become collected into a corpus and recognized by the church in such a way as to exercise influence on it? The data for answering these questions are inadequate for a final solution, and we can only venture some guesses.

PAUL AS A LETTER-WRITER

Earlier we discussed Paul's letters in general—their genre, format, and purpose (see above, pp. 8–13, 245–47). In looking at the individual Epistles, we have learned several facts which complicate the picture. For instance, we know that Paul wrote some letters that did not survive: not all of his Corinthian correspondence is preserved nor the so-called "letter to the Laodiceans" (Col. 4:16). We suspect that in some instances at least existing first drafts of letters may have been editorially supplemented (Rom. 16; Eph. 1:1; 2 Cor. 6:14—7:1; chs. 10–13). More extreme theories have been proposed, involving the insertion of scribal glosses from the margin and longer interpolations.[1a] The danger here is that the modern editor may fall into the error of Marcion, abbreviating New Testament books according to his liking, making everything "snip-shape."

---

[1] C. F. Evans, *The Cambridge History of the Bible*, Vol. 1, edd. P. R. Ackroyd and C. F. Evans (1970), p. 239.

[1a] J. C. O'Neill, *Paul's Letter to the Romans* (1975), is the latest, extreme example of this theory.

We know that Paul invariably had his eye set on the local scene in his churches. His chief motivation in writing was pastoral, as an apostle of the risen Lord. Only in special cases did he seem to have the universal society of Christ's church in his sights (as in parts of Romans and in Ephesians; the latter being best considered as an encyclical from a Pauline circle of disciples). We learn from this that many of the problems with which he wrestles were peculiar to the local churches (e.g., *glossolalia* and marriage questions at Corinth), and that he can distinguish between the Lord's commands and his own counsel (1 Cor. 7:6,25,40) relative to a given situation.[2] At the same time he writes in full awareness of his calling as Christ's special messenger (ἀπόστολος) and "teacher of the Gentiles" (as he is called in 1 Tim. 2:7).

1. Some conclusions may be drawn from the above data.

a. Some of the Pauline correspondence was evidently treated as ephemeral and allowed to sink into oblivion or even purposely destroyed (e.g., the "tearful letter" to Corinth and, quite conceivably, the letter to the Laodiceans, referred to in Col. 4:16, perhaps as a result of the slide of that church into apostasy, as predicted in Rev. 3:16).

b. Other parts of his correspondence were highly treasured and placed in the local archives of his congregations.

c. Still other pieces were circulated among the churches, partly on the recommendation of Paul himself (Col. 4:16), like letters from the Jerusalem Jewish hierarchy to the Diaspora synagogues.

d. By the time of the writing of 2 Peter 3:15f. Paul was recognized as a writer of Scripture on a par with "other scriptures." Outside the canon Ignatius could speak of Paul as one who gave commands to the churches and expected to be obeyed (*Romans* 4:3; cf. 1 Clement 5). The Scillitan martyrs, AD 180, refer to the contents of their box as "the Epistles of Paul a righteous man."[3]

2. In the crucial period between 1 Clement (c. AD 96)[4] and the drawing up of Marcion's canon (AD 140–150) there is no clear picture of development. 1 Clement at best knows only four Pauline letters; Marcion has ten; while Polycarp can refer (apparently but not certainly) to two Philippian letters. By AD 200[5] the Muratorian canon, which is evidence for the corpus accepted in Rome, has seven Pauline letters written to the churches that represent the universal church in the world, with letters sent to individuals—Philemon, Titus, and two to

---

[2] On this issue see D. L. Dungan, *The Sayings of Jesus in the Churches of Paul* (1971).

[3] L. E. Elliott-Binns, *The Beginnings of Western Christendom* (1948), pp. 149, 213.

[4] Most scholars hold this date for the epistle, but J. A. T. Robinson, *Redating the New Testament*, pp. 327ff., wants to bring it forward to early in AD 69/70.

[5] The text of Canon Muratori is given in Hennecke-Schneemelcher, *New Testament Apocrypha*, Vol. 1 (ET 1963), pp. 43–45. See A. C. Sundberg, "Canon Muratori: A Fourth Century List," *HTR*, 66 (1973), 1–41, for the position that the Muratorian canon is probably a fourth-century Eastern list, not a Roman product, to be dated c. AD 200. See also "The Bible Canon and the Christian Doctrine of Inspiration,"

Timothy—valued as concerned with ecclesiastical discipline. Spurious letters, such as the letter to the Laodiceans which is recognized by Marcion, are to be refused. For Egypt at the same time, p 46 witnesses to a list of ten books including Hebrews.

Several theories have been proposed to account for the growing acceptance of Paul's writings in the early church:

a. One hypothesis is that Paul's letters were preserved, valued, and instinctively recognized as authoritative Scripture, so that by the time of Polycarp (to give one example) in AD 110–117[6] they are the object of study and the instruments of faith (*Phil.* 3.2).

b. As an alternative explanation some have maintained that there was no circulation of the letters for a while; then, somewhat spontaneously, the idea was born that they should be grouped into a corpus.

Both of these views encounter difficulties explaining how some letters were allowed to perish, and why Christian writers before Marcion showed very little appreciation of the Pauline *gospel* within the "Pauline corpus."[7]

c. E. J. Goodspeed proposed that there was a danger that Paul would be forgotten in the decades subsequent to his death.[8] Only with the publication of Acts (c. AD 80–90) did his memory revive, and there was an awakening of interest in him. A key figure in Goodspeed's imaginative reconstruction of early Christian history is an unknown Paulinist in the Lycus Valley, who knew Colossians and Philemon and used them as the basis for a collection, following the topography of Paul's travels in Acts. In favor of this view is the omission of Colossae from the Acts' record, suggesting that the first compiler of the Pauline canon began from there with the letter to this otherwise unknown city. Later, Goodspeed accepted John Knox's view that this Paulinist was Onesimus, though still later adherents of this general hypothesis have opted for Tychicus.[9]

Interpretation, 29 (1975), 352–71, an issue that also contains D. L. Dungan's serviceable overview of recent study on the New Testament canon (pp. 339–51). But cf. Kümmel's negative attitude to Sundberg's hypothesis (*Introduction*[2], pp. 492f.). See too D. A. Hagner, *The Use of the Old and New Testaments in Clement of Rome* (1973), pp. 314–31.

[6] Or earlier, if 2 Peter (3:15f.; cf. 1:20) is earlier than the second century (see Chapter 29 below). If P. N. Harrison's division of Polycarp's extant letter is correct, the major part of that letter is from the fourth decade of the second century. See *Polycarp's Two Epistles to the Philippians* (1936).

[7] T. F. Torrance, *The Doctrine of Grace in the Apostolic Fathers* (1948), shows how little grasp there was of this in the late first and early second centuries.

[8] E. J. Goodspeed, *The Meaning of Ephesians* (1933); cf. C. L. Mitton, *Ephesians* (NCB, 1976), pp. 7ff., 25–27.

[9] J. Knox, *Philemon Among the Letters of Paul*[2] (1959); cf. R. P. Martin, *Colossians and Philemon* (NCB, 1974), pp. 144–52. For Tychicus, see Mitton, *op. cit.,* p. 230; an earlier suggestion was made by W. L. Knox, *St. Paul and the Church of the Gentiles* (1938), p. 203.

This understanding of the situation does have some problems. It accords a lot of weight to the publication of Acts, and it underrates the possibility of exchange of letters between the Pauline churches. Connected with it is a questionable theory that Ephesians was written to introduce the Pauline corpus.[10] But it does account for the neglect of Paul immediately following his martyrdom, which is perhaps less strange than one might think if Paul's gospel was soon exposed to two powerful influences, a re-Judaizing and an acute Hellenization.

The question of how and when Paul's letters found general acceptance cannot be understood, much less answered, apart from the larger frame of Paul's claim to authority, the apostolate, and the use of tradition. In the remainder of this chapter we shall place these matters in a wider setting.

AUTHORITY, TRADITION, AND CANONICITY[11]

1. *Authority in the Early Church.* All Christians acknowledge by profession the supreme authority of Jesus Christ, the head of the church and the savior of his body (Eph. 5:23). Not surprisingly, the earliest confession of faith known in the New Testament church proclaims this unrivaled lordship of Christ, both in personal allegiance (Rom. 10:9; 1 Cor. 12:3; cf. Acts 8:37—RSV mg.) and in his cosmic authority over all created things (Phil. 2:9–11; Rom. 14:9; Rev. 5:6–14). Included in the scope of this dominion is his control of his people, the church, which holds the central place within the whole *regnum Christi*, as O. Cullmann has shown.[12]

How was this authority exercised? How was the will of the risen Christ made known to the church in apostolic times? We may point to some data in the literature of the New Testament church. The Gospel narratives portray Jesus as an authoritative teacher whose word was "with power" (ἐξουσία) (Mark 1:22; Luke 4:32). Jesus himself claimed to speak and act with decisive authority (Matt. 7:24–27), in such matters as his right to forgive sins (Mark 2:10), to cast out demons (Mark 1:27), and to oppose the venerable Jewish Torah in the antitheses of the Sermon on the Mount (Matt. 5:17ff.). Käsemann elucidates the force of the oft-repeated assertion ἐγὼ δὲ λέγω ὑμῖν ("But I say to you"): these words,

---

[10] See M. Barth, *Ephesians* (Anchor Bible, 1974) and G. B. Caird, *Paul's Letters from Prison* (1976), pp. 22–27.

[11] What follows draws on my article in *EQ*, 40 (1968), 66–82, where fuller documentation may be found.

[12] O. Cullmann, "The Kingship of Christ and the Church in the New Testament," in *The Early Church* (ET 1956), pp. 105–37. C. F. D. Moule, *The Birth of the New Testament* (1966), p. 9, finds the common element in the New Testament to be "devotion to the person of Jesus Christ—the historical Jesus acknowledged as Messiah and Lord."

for which there are no Jewish parallels, embody a claim to an authority which rivals and challenges that of Moses.[13]

Two other less-well-attested features of Jesus' ministry are nevertheless significant for appreciating his authority in the early church, especially in its controversy with the Jews and its growing self-awareness as Messiah's people. E. Stauffer claims that the formula I AM (ἐγώ εἰμί) is an allusion to the divine name (expressed in the Hebrew form 'ʾnî hûʾ), and is therefore an overt ascription of deity to the Johannine Christ.[14] Secondly, Jesus claimed at his trial to be the rightful occupant of the place at God's right hand in heaven (Mark 14:62), and so to fulfil Psalm 110:1 and, perhaps even more audaciously, Daniel 7:9–14.[15]

The unique authority thus displayed made the early church aware that they were living in the age of Messiah's rule. The exaltation and kingship of Jesus confirmed what was true if hidden in his earthly life, namely that he had come to be Israel's Messiah and king, and was now exalted as head of the new people of God. His presence was known to his followers, who were called by his name, as they assembled in worship, particularly at his table, where they shared a common meal in remembrance of him. Moreover, his Spirit, promised before his bodily presence was withdrawn, had come to recall to them what they needed to remember of his earthly ministry (John 14:16–18,26). That Spirit was actively at work in many ways, empowering their witness (e.g., Acts 1:8) and guiding their corporate and individual life. Acts 16:7 refers to "the Spirit of Jesus" as restraining the missionaries from entering the territory of Pontus-Bithynia. That phrase is unique in New Testament literature, but it shows eloquently how close was the association between the exalted Lord and the Spirit (cf. 2 Cor. 3:17). In Acts 21:11 Agabus prefaces his admonition to Paul with "Thus says the Holy Spirit," words which surely recall the Old Testament prophetic authorization placed before the oracle, "Thus speaks Yahweh" (nᵉûm Yhwh). This shows how divine guidance was attributed to the same Spirit who moved Israel's prophets.

The mention of Agabus calls attention to early Christian prophecy as a medium through which the risen Lord communicated his mind to the church.[16] An earlier reference to Agabus (11:28) showed him similarly as one especially gifted by the Spirit to predict the great famine in Judaea. Perhaps Philip's daughters (Acts 21:9) had the same gift. The use of προφητεύειν in 1 Corinthians 11 and 14, however, dem-

---

[13] E. Käsemann, "The Problem of the Historical Jesus," in *Essays on New Testament Themes* (ET 1964), pp. 37f.

[14] E. Stauffer, *Jesus and His Story* (ET 1960), pp. 149–59; D. Daube, *The New Testament and Rabbinic Judaism* (1956), pp. 325–29.

[15] On Dan. 7:9 see B. Lindars, "The Apocalyptic Myth and the Death of Christ," *BJRL*, 57 (1975), 366–87.

[16] E. E. Ellis, "The Role of the Christian Prophet in Acts," in *Apostolic History and the Gospel*, edd. Gasque and Martin, pp. 55–67.

onstrates that predictiveness was not the only concern of the prophet's ministry. The immediate interest of the prophets at Corinth was a revelation of God's will for the church, according to the formal definition of the prophetic ministry in 1 Corinthians 14:3, which gives priority to the work of upbuilding as the Lord's purposes for the church are achieved. The blend of prediction and a timely contemporary message is seen in the letters of Revelation 2 and 3, where the risen Christ is addressing his people through the prophet John (Rev. 1:3; 22:7—"the words of this prophecy"), who in turn is inspired by the Spirit (Rev. 2:7, etc.).

The New Testament church thus lived in conscious awareness of the unseen yet real lordship of the risen Jesus, made known to it by the Spirit's presence and leadership. The Spirit himself conveyed that presence by uniting believers in communion (κοινωνία) with the Lord and with one another, and by inspiring the words and writing of prophets who claimed inspiration on the basis of Old Testament precedent.

As to the further content of early Christian oracles, several suggestions have been made bearing on Gospel passages (e.g., Luke 11:49–51) and apocalyptic oracles (Mark 13) as well as "sentences of holy law" in the Epistles.[17] The chief source is the literature produced by the apostles and those who claimed an intimate association with the apostles either as their personal coadjutors (e.g., Mark and Luke) or as members of their circle (e.g., the authors of Ephesians and 2 Peter).

2. *Pseudonymity*. The matter of the authorship of Ephesians and 2 Peter (see also pp. 227–33 and 383–88) raises the disputed issue of pseudonymity, which we do well to discuss at this point.[18] K. Aland makes some important theoretical judgments on the subject. He stresses how pseudonymity—if it is granted—does not lessen the authority of the message attributed to the apostolic author whose aegis is claimed. On the contrary, it is enhanced, since the writer believed that he shared in

---

[17] See D. Hill, "On the Evidence for the Creative Role of Christian Prophets," *NTS*, 20 (1973–74), 262–74; on Luke 11:49–51, see E. E. Ellis, in *Luke* (NCB², 1972), pp. 171–74; this pericope is traced to a Christian prophet or group of prophets who transmitted the oracle from the exalted Jesus or interpreted and applied a saying of his pre-resurrection ministry in reference to the siege of Jerusalem. Hence it is an authoritative "word of the Lord," and so "authentic" in that situation. On "Sentences of Holy Law in the New Testament," see Käsemann's essay by that title, in *New Testament Questions of Today* (ET 1969), pp. 66–81. See the far-ranging discussion of these themes in D. E. Aune, *Prophecy in Early Christianity and the Ancient Mediterranean World* (1983).

[18] The sharp edges of the debate are exposed in the essays by K. Aland and D. Guthrie, reprinted in *The Authorship and Integrity of the New Testament* (1965), pp. 1–13, 14–39. The issues are also posed by E. J. Goodspeed, *New Chapters in New Testament Study* (1937), Ch. 7: "Pseudonymity and Pseudepigraphy in Early Christian Literature." An especially helpful discussion is B. M. Ahern, "Who Wrote the Pauline Epistles?" in *Contemporary New Testament Studies*, ed. M. R. Ryan (1963); repr. in *The Bible Today*, 1 (1964), 754–60. See also M. Rist, "Pseudepigraphy and the Early Christians," in *Studies in New Testament and Early Christian Literature*, ed. D. E. Aune (1972), pp. 75–91; B. M. Metzger, "Literary Forgeries and Canonical Pseudepigrapha," *JBL*, 91 (1972), 3–24; J. A. T. Robinson, *op. cit.*, pp. 186f.

the same inspiration of the Spirit as his apostolic mentor, and he did not pretend to be his rival or substitute. The use of the apostle's name is thus an appeal to high authority, and the claiming of the venerable name is an index of humility on the writer's part and an acknowledgment of the apostolic credentials of what he (faithfully) recorded.

K. Koch cautions that "the designation 'pseudonymous' should be used only with reservation." The disciple may be using the name of his master because the latter was thought to be still living in heaven and therefore his influence was effective in the present. The use of an honored name (say, Paul's) becomes tantamount to ascribing the writing to God or the heavenly *Kyrios*.[19]

If this explanation of what is usually referred to as pseudonymity fails to satisfy those who insist on taking literary attributions at their face-value (e.g., Eph. 1:1; 3:1; 2 Pet. 1:1,18), there are other data to be considered. For example, the oracles of the Hebrew prophets were most likely assembled by the prophets' followers (cf. Isa. 8:16), who took responsibility for publishing these directly inspired utterances under their masters' names. Yet the composition was not the prophets'; rather it was their pupils who felt able to employ the prophets' names at the head of the recorded oracles (Isa. 1:1).

At another level, the rigid conservative demand that literary attributions be ascribed to the authors explicitly mentioned founders on the question of the authorship of Ecclesiastes, which appears internally designated as Solomon's work (1:1,12). Even E. J. Young concedes that a later writer (c. 450 BC) has "placed his words in the mouth of Solomon, thus employing a literary device for conveying his message." Criteria of "language and diction" (says Young) date Ecclesiastes in the fifth century BC.[20] While the time-span is certainly not comparable in the case of Ephesians and 2 Peter, the grounds for a later, post-apostolic dating are the same as Young appeals to, at least in the estimation of some critics. Finally, that authorship in the Bible is not rigidly fixed is seen from Mark 1:2f., where a composite quotation drawn from Isaiah, Malachi, and Exodus 23:20 is indiscriminately ascribed to "Isaiah the prophet" (cf. Heb. 2:6 for a professed uncertainty in authorship).

3. *The Apostolate in the New Testament Church.* Here we touch on the most important locus of authority in the primitive church: the apostolate. Ἀπόστολος occurs 79 times in the New Testament, and is obviously a key term in early Christianity. From the linguistic researches of K. H. Rengstorf, we can form a fairly clear picture of what this term meant in the New Testament period. In the words of J. N. Geldenhuys, who has harvested the gains of Rengstorf's work, the apostles of Jesus were chosen by him "to act as His authoritative representa-

---

[19] K. Koch, in *IDB, Supp. Vol.* (1976), pp. 712–14.
[20] E. J. Young, *Introduction to the Old Testament* (1949), p. 340; cited by Harry R. Boer, *Above the Battle?* (1977), p. 48.

tives through whom He was to lay the foundations of His church." This description equally fits Paul, whose consciousness of being an apostle "is essentially determined by his encounter with Jesus on the Damascus road."[21]

This consciousness was apparently unshared by any other in the church apart from those who belonged to the original apostolate. There are only four cases of Paul's using ἀπόστολος of persons other than himself and the Twelve (2 Cor. 8:23; Phil. 2:25; Rom. 16:7; Gal. 1:19), and in each the text is either irrelevant to this discussion or the use is non-technical, as in the instance of James, the Lord's brother (see below, p. 359). The conclusion seems valid that, in the exact and unique sense of the term "apostle," referring to one directly commissioned by the risen Lord as his special messenger and personal representative, only Jesus' original apostles and Paul were appointed to the office. Indirect confirmation of this conclusion is found in the way Matthias was elected (Acts 1:15ff.), in Paul's claim to have seen the risen Christ (1 Cor. 9:1), in the apostolic witness in Ephesians 2:20; 3:7ff.; 4:11, and explicitly in Revelation 21:14, which describes how the foundations of the city wall in the heavenly Jerusalem are inscribed with the names of the twelve apostles of the Lamb.

We may agree with T. W. Manson that this apostolic function was exercised once for all and in a way which was not transmissible.[22] But what was this precise function? We may note how the apostolate and the *kerygma* are closely associated in the New Testament literature. Indeed, it would not be too much to affirm that "apostleship"—ἀποστολή (Acts 1:25; 1 Cor. 9:2; Rom. 1:5; Gal. 2:8)—is a part of the κήρυγμα in the sense that apostolic witness to the risen Lord and fulfilment of his charge to them to make the gospel known are part of the commission they have received. (The stories of Paul's conversion, esp. Acts 26, accentuate this call and commission.) The uniqueness of the apostolate, however, is not to be sought in terms of witness and preaching, for many saw him (1 Cor. 15:6f.), and the company of New Testament preachers extends far beyond the Twelve and Paul (e.g., Phil. 1:12ff.). Rather, it is in connection with the exercise of authority in the churches—in particular, the custodianship of the traditions, whether oral or written—that we must see their originality.

Paul believed his ministry to be clothed with an authority none

---

[21] Rengstorf, cited by J. N. Geldenhuys, *Supreme Authority* (1953), pp. 46ff.; see also J. A. Kirk, "Apostleship since Rengstorf: Towards a Synthesis," *NTS*, 21 (1974–75), 249–64. W. Schmithals, *The Office of Apostle in the Early Church* (ET 1969), argues that "apostle" is a creation of the Hellenistic church. See later, p. 359. See also the recent discussion by C. G. Kruse, *New Testament Foundations of Ministry* (1983), of New Testament apostleship; cf. J. Jervell, "The Signs of an Apostle," in his *The Unknown Paul* (ET 1984), ch. 5. Of fundamental significance are J. H. Schütz, *Paul and the Anatomy of Apostolic Authority* (1975); and B. Holmberg, *Paul and Power. The Structure of Authority in the Primitive Church as Reflected in the Pauline Epistles* (1978, 1980).

[22] T. W. Manson, *The Church's Ministry* (1948), p. 51.

should gainsay.[23] 2 Thessalonians 3:4,6 speak of his "commanding" the Thessalonian church, and he speaks even more forcefully in dealing with the recalcitrant group at Corinth (2 Cor. 10:8; 13:10; cf. 1 Cor. 4:21; 5:3ff.). On this basis he can hold himself forth as a pattern to be accepted and imitated (1 Cor. 4:15ff.; 11:1; 1 Thess. 1:6).[24]

In particular Paul expects that his writings will be received as binding for the moral decisions his readers are called on to make, as well as determinative for the acceptance of the gospel message over against its spurious rivals (Gal. 1:6–12; 2 Cor. 11:4ff.). The measure of concurrence his words are entitled to receive comes from the fact that he speaks on the authority and in the name of the risen Lord (1 Thess. 2:13).

That the Pauline letters were treated with such respect is shown by the witness of the later church. 2 Peter 3:15f. is a familiar New Testament attestation of their authority, also seen in such apostolic fathers as Clement of Rome: "Take up the epistle of the blessed Paul the apostle," who is distinguished from Apollos as "a man approved in their sight" (1 Clem. 47); Ignatius: "I do not think myself competent . . . to give you orders like an apostle" (*Trallians* 3.3); "I do not command you, as Peter and Paul did. They were apostles, I am a prisoner" (*Rom.* 4:3); and Polycarp: "For neither am I, nor is any other like unto me, able to follow the wisdom of the blessed and glorious Paul. . . . If you look diligently [at the letters he wrote to you], you shall be able to be built up unto the faith given to you" (*Phil.* 3). It cannot be without significance that Paul himself expected his congregations to read his letters in public worship (1 Thess. 5:27) and that these letters would be passed around the churches (Col. 4:16) with a view to their acceptance as authoritative literature (cf. 1 Cor. 14:37), written by one who claimed the Spirit's insight and inspiration (1 Cor. 7:40).

So much for the Pauline writing which has survived, later to become canonical "Scripture." Some of his writings, as we have noted, were lost, and fourth-century attempts to remedy the deficiency and enrich the Pauline canon, as in the so-called third letter to the Corinthians, produced only tendentious specimens.[25] What about the apostolic "traditions" which existed in oral form in the Pauline churches and are attested in references found in the apostolic Fathers and later Christian writers? Here we may cite 1 Clement 7:2: "Let us come to the glorious and venerable rule (κανών) of our tradition"; the *Epistle to*

---

[23] See J. H. Schütz, *Paul and the Anatomy of Apostolic Authority* (1975), who traces Paul's authority to his function as proclaimer rather than to his office as apostle.
[24] *Ibid.*, pp. 226–32; cf. W. P. De Boer, *The Imitation of Paul* (1962).
[25] For the pseudepigraphical "Letter to the Laodiceans," see Hennecke-Schneemelcher, *op. cit.*, Vol. 2 (ET 1965), pp. 128ff. "Third Corinthians" is part of the *Acta Pauli*, written to ward off gnostic influence (*ibid.*, pp. 34, 326, 341, 374ff.). On these see D. Guthrie, "Acts and Epistles in Apocryphal Writing," in *Apostolic History and the Gospel*, pp. 328–45, 330–34, 341–43.

Diognetus 11:6, which speaks of the "tradition of the apostles." The idea is prominent in Irenaeus (παράδοσις, Latin *traditio,* 30 times; παραδιδόναι, Latin *tradere,* 14 times), Tertullian, for whom *tradere* has rich overtones, chiefly in his writings against Marcion, and in Clement and Origen. "Tradition(s)" is a term attested in the New Testament; and to an examination of its usage there we now turn.

4. *Tradition: the New Testament Evidence.*[26] Among the various usages of the verb παραδιδόναι (from *paradidōmi,* I hand over) the relevant one for our purpose is that in which the verb has as its object some allusion to teaching. The use of the noun παράδοσις in the New Testament is in line with this verbal connotation, for "tradition" is used in the New Testament only of *what* is transmitted, not of the *act* of transmitting. Our attention, therefore, is drawn to references to the content of the tradition.

Of the thirteen places where παράδοσις occurs, nine refer to rabbinic practice and the scribal tradition, which had been elevated to authority above the law itself. This "tradition of the elders" Jesus condemned (Matt. 15:2,3,6; Mark 7:3,5,8,9; cf. Gal. 1:14). The point at issue is well described by Büchsel:

> The Pharisees regarded unwritten tradition as no less binding than the Law.... The Sadducees rejected it (Joseph, *Ant.* 13.297). So did Jesus. He agreed with the Pharisees that the good demanded of men is obedience to God's commandment. As He saw it, however, men could not add to this commandment, since they were too seriously in conflict with God.[27]

"Tradition" is also used in a good sense. In these New Testament passages (1 Cor. 11:2; 2 Thess. 2:15; 3:6) it denotes Christian practices rather than Christian teaching, although other verses have reference to some body of truth without specifying exactly what this is (cf. Rom. 6:17; 2 Pet. 2:21; Jude 3,20). Presumably the latter existed in oral form, although the parallelism of διὰ λόγου and δι᾽ ἐπιστολῆς ἡμῶν is to be noticed in 2 Thessalonians 2:15. These two phrases pinpoint the vexing problem of this discussion: how far, if at all, did there develop a relation between oral tradition and written authority in the early centuries of the church? Is it valid to speak of two sources of authority, with apostolic oral teaching surviving side by side with apostolic writings which later became recognized as canonical Scripture?

Two other important passages bear on the ultimate source of Christian tradition. 1 Corinthians 11:23 contains the key term παρέδωκα coupled with the complementary verb παρέλαβον. What Paul had received he saw as his duty to pass on to others. The origin of this

---

[26] On tradition see F. F. Bruce, *Tradition: Old and New* (1970); "Scripture and Tradition in the New Testament," in *Holy Book and Holy Tradition,* edd. Bruce and Rupp (1968), pp. 68–93; also G. E. Ladd, "Revelation and Tradition in Paul," *Apostolic History and the Gospel,* pp. 223–30; and *A Theology of the New Testament* (1974), Ch. 28.

[27] F. Büchsel, in *TDNT,* 2 (1964), 172.

paradosis is given as ἀπὸ τοῦ κυρίου, which apparently means that he is acknowledging the mediation of the church in the transmission of the tradition, with the living Christ as the one who stands behind it and is actively at work in it. So "the *Kyrios* appears as the content of the *paradosis,* but he is at one and the same time its *content and its author.*"[28]

The reference in 1 Corinthians 11 has to do with the setting of the Lord's Supper, which is taken back to the Upper Room and the dominical words of interpretation over the bread and wine (cf. Chapter 20 above). Later, in 1 Corinthians 15, the associated verbs ("delivered," "received," vv. 3ff.) are again brought together in an early Jewish-Christian creedlike formulation. This statement is clearly detachable from its immediate context. Full of semitic echoes and undertones, it lays bare the skeleton of what is perhaps the first Christian confession of faith. It is invested with special importance by the introductory verse 2: it is by adherence to the saving truth, which confesses Christ crucified, buried, and risen, that the salvation of the church is assured.

R. P. C. Hanson has drawn attention to the varied content of early tradition in the New Testament church. He isolates three elements: moral rules to regulate Christian ethical and church practice (1 Cor. 11:2; 2 Thess. 3:6; Rom. 6:17; Phil. 4:9; Col. 2:6); a summary of the Christian message, expressed as a formula of faith and combining the facts of the life of Jesus and their theological significance (1 Cor. 15:3ff.); and at least one specimen of a single narrative from the earthly life of Jesus (1 Cor. 11:23).[29]

The ultimate source of the authority of tradition may be traced back to the Lord, who first set the process in motion and is active at every stage in its continuance. The solemn reminder echoed in the phrase ἀπὸ τοῦ κυρίου (1 Cor. 11:23) explains the importance of handing on the tradition in its entirety. In 1 Corinthians 15, τίνι λόγῳ εὐηγγελισάμην (vs. 2) and the carefully arranged formal structure of verses 3ff. have been regarded as evidence of the care taken over the actual *words* used in this statement of essential christological and soteriological teaching.[30] The immediate background of this apparently careful preservation of precise terms has been found in the rabbinic method of transmission.[31] Yet W. D. Davies has shown (in reference to 1 Cor. 11:23ff.) that, in Paul's method of delivery, the emphasis falls not on the actual words spoken by Jesus but on the gist of those words as interpreted by the apostle in his dealings with the Corinthian community.[32]

[28] O. Cullmann, "The Tradition," in *The Early Church*, p. 68.
[29] R. P. C. Hanson, *Tradition in the Early Church* (1962), p. 11.
[30] C. H. Dodd, *The Apostolic Preaching and its Developments* (1936), p. 13, stresses this.
[31] B. Gerhardsson, *Memory and Manuscript* (1961), pp. 294–300.
[32] W. D. Davies, *Paul and Rabbinic Judaism*² (1955), pp. 248ff.

It should not be inferred, however, that Paul had an unwarranted right to adapt and modify the original tradition received "from the Lord." There is a second way the traditions he passed on were clothed with authority: the status and privilege of the apostolate. Bultmann has shown the close connection in the New Testament between tradition and apostleship.[33] The passages which deal with tradition also contain statements of the Pauline apostolic authority. Clearly in 1 Corinthians 11:23 the introductory ἐγώ is not slipped in accidentally, but has a purpose within the context of passing on the eucharistic tradition. Cullmann writes:

> The reason why he does so ... is that it was vital, in opposition to the false conception of the Lord's Supper current at Corinth, to stress the dignity of his apostolic office as bearer of the correct tradition.[34]

In other, less specific passages (cf. 1 Cor. 15:2; Phil. 4:9; 1 Thess. 2:13f.; 1 Cor. 4:17; 7:10; 14:37f.), the same reason for the authority of the tradition holds good. Paul can appeal to his readers for a full acceptance of the tradition and their obedience to it on the ground that he is, *as apostle,* "the legitimate and authorized mediator of the paradosis of Christ."[35]

The conclusion may be stated that in the New Testament church "tradition" stood for principles and precepts of Christian living, partly doctrinal but chiefly practical (cf. 1 Cor. 7, 11, and 14 for well-known examples of areas of dispute and disorder). Paul addressed himself to these matters, sometimes by writing to the churches (2 Thess. 2:15; 3:14; cf. 1 Thess. 4:9; 5:1, 27; 1 Cor. 4:6 [?]; Col. 4:16), sometimes by word of mouth (1 Cor. 11:2; 1 Thess. 2:4; 4:1f.; 2 Thess. 2:15; 3:6) or personal presence (1 Cor. 11:34; cf. 4:21; 2 Cor. 13:1); sometimes by example (1 Thess. 2:10f.; Phil. 4:9). The "charges" (παραγγελίαι) he gave them and the quality of his life displayed before them were not only effective reminders of what the Christian fellowship should be and do, but were enforced by his apostolic standing.

So Paul was able to appeal to "traditions" as divinely authorized because they proceeded from the exalted Lord, who was present with his people and solicitous for their highest well-being as they lived their life "in Christ." He could cite himself and his fellow-apostles as examples of the embodiment of what "living by the tradition" meant (1 Cor. 11:1; Phil. 4:9). He could claim his authorization as an apostle (cf. 2 Tim. 2) by the sufferings he had endured (Rom. 15:18; 2 Cor. 12:12) and by his insight into the mind of Christ (1 Cor. 2:16) as a possessor of the Spirit (1 Cor. 7:40) and by his election to the high office of apostle (Gal. 1:1, 15f.; cf. Eph. 2:19f.; 3:7f.). He could confidently lay claim to "the authority which the Lord has given me for building up" (2 Cor. 13:10).

[33] R. Bultmann, *Theology of the New Testament,* 1, 59f.
[34] O. Cullmann, *The Early Church,* p. 73.
[35] *Ibid.,* p. 74.

5. *Authority: Jesus and Paul.* So far we have been concerned to trace and pinpoint the locus of authority in the church of the New Testament period. The scheme apparent from the New Testament records is as follows.

Jesus in his earthly ministry was viewed as possessing messianic authority. This dignity was subsequently understood in the early Jerusalem church and became the substance of post-Pentecostal preaching (e.g., Acts 2:36; cf. Rom. 1:3f.),[36] which looked back to God's raising Jesus from the dead and installing him as head of the messianic community. Paul, accepting the further enlargement of Messiah's status made possible in Hellenistic-Jewish thought, which is represented by the preaching of Stephen and his school (cf. Acts 7:56ff.; 11:19–21), carried the range of Messiah's cosmic authority still further and drew out the implications of the exaltation of Jesus and its application for the entire cosmos.[37] Hence Paul's favorite designation for Jesus is "Lord" (χύριος), to which he gives a new connotation not emphasized previously. The early references to *Kyrios* were found mainly in a liturgical context and (if we include the witness of Acts) in connection with the church's mission to the Hellenists. Paul uses the title to reinforce his ethical appeals and to show what type of practical conduct is fitting for those who acknowledge the lordship of the church's Head. Thus Paul's "Kyriology" accentuates and spells out "the authority to whom men are accountable for their every decision."[38]

As far as Paul is concerned, the Lord's authority is embodied in and mediated by two means. First of all, there is the personal presence of Paul himself and the authority he claims as Christ's delegate. He has a most realistic understanding of what his presence can mean to the congregation, and he regards himself as almost tangibly real to them as they assemble for worship and congregational discipline (1 Cor. 5:5; cf. 4:21—"Shall I come to you?"; 1 Cor. 14:34; 2 Cor. 13:1; Col. 2:5). His enemies, seeking to cast doubt on the legitimacy of his apostolic authority,[39] can only point to the unimpressive nature of his personal presence (2 Cor. 10:10), but Paul retorts that the *viva vox* of his presence is the same as his admittedly effective letters (vs. 11).

[36] Romans 1:3f. in its final form may be a Hellenistic-Jewish formula of christological faith; K. Wengst, *Christologische Formeln und Lieder des Urchristentums* (1972), pp. 112ff. But it is almost certainly constructed of primitive material; see J. D. G. Dunn, "Jesus—Flesh and Spirit: An Exposition of Romans 1. 3–4," *JTS*, 24 n.s. (1973), 40–68; H. Schlier, "Zu Röm. 1,3f.," in *Neues Testament und Geschichte: Festschrift* O. Cullmann (1972), p. 213, who suggests a version of the earlier form. M. Hengel, *The Son of God* (ET 1976), pp. 59–66, relates it to the exaltation of the Son of man.

[37] For a specimen of a new expansion of Christ's domain to include the spirit-world, see Phil. 2:6–11 as a pre-Pauline tribute to the heavenly *Kyrios.*

[38] W. Kramer, *Christ, Lord, Son of God* (ET 1966), pp. 169ff.: sec. 47.

[39] E. Käsemann, "Die Legitimität des Apostels," *ZNTW*, 41 (1942), 33–71; cf. C. K. Barrett, *The Second Epistle to the Corinthians* (1973), p. 266 and *passim.* R. P. Martin, *2 Corinthians* (WBC, 1985), seeks to survey the more recent debate.

This last reference points to the other aspect of Paul's apostolic authority: his letters, sent as extensions of his pastoral and didactic ministry to complement his apostolic work in fulfilment of his God-given task. Though occasioned by the needs of the congregations, Paul's letters, once composed and sent, constituted the literary deposit of his apostolic influence. Only on this assumption can we explain the authoritativeness of what he writes, the expectancy he cherishes that their contents will be heeded, and the future he assures for them by requiring them to be preserved and circulated among the churches.

The apostle's person, with his living presence and voice transmitting the traditions as the embodiment of the *Kyrios,* and the apostle's writing (thought of as his *alter ego*[39a])—these were the two effective means by which the heavenly Lord's authority was known in the Pauline communities. Polycarp sums it up: "When he was among you in the presence of the men of that time he taught accurately ... and also when he was absent he wrote letter(s) ..." *(Phil.* 3:2).

With the close of the apostolic age, the question arose immediately: how was the apostolic authority to be handed on in concrete and permanent form?

6. *The Growth of the Canon.* How the later church grappled with these problems is not exactly clear. Many historical and theological factors were involved in the establishment of the canon of New Testament Scripture. The usual reasons for the composition of the Gospels are relevant here: the expansion of the church and its geographical distribution throughout the Graeco-Roman world[40] and the delay in the *parousia* made Christians become increasingly aware of their commission to carry the gospel to the uttermost bounds as a prelude to the Lord's return. The death of eyewitnesses and the gradual disappearance of the original apostolic witness led to a desire to conserve this testimony in easily identifiable and permanent form—another motive behind the composition of the Gospels (certainly so in the cases of Mark and the Fourth Gospel; hence the traditions of their Petrine and Johannine authorization). Papias, who records this tradition, according to Eusebius *(HE* 3.39), was as late as the fourth decade of the second century still optimistic about being directly in touch with an eyewitness report: "for I did not suppose that information from books would help me so much as the words of a living and surviving voice." There was also the need to check an incipient docetism by stressing the full humanity of the Lord.[41]

The church of the sub-apostolic period inherited from the New Testament era, particularly from Jesus himself, a deep respect for the

[39a] See B. Holmberg, *Paul and Power,* pp. 82f.
[40] Cf. E. E. Ellis, "New Directions in Form Criticism," in *Jesus Christus in Historie und Theologie: Festschrift* H. Conzelmann, ed. G. Strecker (1975), p. 306.
[41] Cf. *NTF,* Vol. 1, pp. 126f., 221ff.; J. L. Houlden, *The Pastoral Epistles* (1976), p. 37.

Old Testament. Jesus found direction for his messianic ministry in the pages of the Old Testament, and the apostolic preaching was undergirded by an appeal to "the law and the prophets" (Rom. 3:21), which bore testimony to the gospel events and their saving significance. The church took over this attitude, usually in a restrained fashion but occasionally lapsing into fanciful allegory and strained typological exegesis (e.g., *The Epistle of Barnabas*).

The growth of canonical authority was slow and sporadic. Not until AD 367—the date of Athanasius' 39th Festal letter[42]—did the church agree on the exact limits of the New Testament canon. Athanasius designated three classes of Christian literature: the collection of Holy Scripture (κανών); rejected books (ἀπόκρυφα); and wholesome books which may be used in baptismal instruction. A number of historical circumstances led to this fixing of the canon. Undoubtedly the chief impulse came from the challenge of Marcion, whose version of Christianity denied all connection with the Old Testament. Earlier heresies, like docetism, had been checked by a recital of the evangelical facts, drawn mainly from quasi-credal formulas (as in Ignatius' replies to docetic influences among his correspondents). What was new in Marcion's heresy was his appeal to his own canon, consisting of a mutilated version of the Gospel of Luke and ten Epistles of Paul. Whether Marcion chose his canonical books out of a larger number then available or whether he was the first to advocate the notion of a fixed canon at all is not known. What seems clear is that his canon "scarcely provided the occasion for the church's formation of its canon, but the fact that Marcion had already established the canonical authority of Paul ... strengthened the tendency" to delimit Holy Scripture.[43]

Hard on the heels of Marcion's threat came refined and complicated forms of gnosticism. These gnostics took over the orthodox canon, but appealed to a secret tradition which they claimed went back directly to the apostles. Anti-gnostic writers in the church (mainly Irenaeus) countered that there was no such tradition and that the gnostics' esoteric teaching was contrary to the message of the apostles. Observe the basis of Irenaeus's stand against the gnostics: in effect, he says that one can discover what Jesus Christ taught either in the written Scriptures or in the public preaching of those churches which rest on apostolic foundation (a side-glance at Marcionite conventicles and Montanist groups in Phrygia; *Adv. Haer.* 3.1.1). The apostolic doctrine to which Irenaeus appeals is, as R. P. C. Hanson concludes, "not the doctrine taught by the men who are successors of the apostles, whatever they

---

[42] For events leading up to this date, see K. L. Carroll, "Toward a Commonly Received New Testament," *BJRL*, 44 (1962), 327–49.

[43] W. G. Kümmel, *Introduction to the New Testament*², pp. 487f.

teach, but the doctrine of the essentially apostolic book, the New Testament."[44]

The test of apostolicity for books which the church subsequently admitted as canonical may be interpreted in several ways. Obviously not all the New Testament literature can claim direct apostolic authorship; and not all books ascribed to an apostolic circle retained a permanent place in the canon (e.g., Clement of Alexandria treated as apostolic the Apocalypse of Peter, 1 Clement, and the *Didache*). Further complicating any straightforward theory of canonicity are differences of opinion between the Christian East and West; changes of attitude regarding certain books (e.g., the exclusion of the *Shepherd of Hermas* and the adoption of books previously suspected—Hebrews and 2 Peter); and differing understanding of "oral traditions."[45]

The Council of Trent (1546) settled the question for the Roman Catholic Church by declaring the entire Old Testament and New Testament books in the Vulgate to be canonical. Canonicity was treated as equivalent to apostolicity by ascribing Hebrews to Paul and James to the Lord's brother. Luther's norm turned on the peculiarly oscillating meaning he gave to "apostolic." Sometimes the term stands for "apostolic authorship"; more characteristic, perhaps, is his definition as that which "has apostolic quality."[46]

> The proper touchstone by which to criticize all books is to see whether they treat of Christ or not (*ob sie Christum treiben oder nicht*). Whatever does not teach Christ is not apostolic, even if Peter or Paul teaches it; on the other hand, whatever preaches Christ (*was Christum predigt*), that is apostolic, even if it is done by someone like Judas, Annas, Pilate, or Herod (*Preface to James*).

By this criterion—what treats of Christ—Luther constructed "a canon within the canon," rejecting four of the seven writings disputed in antiquity (Hebrews, James, Jude and the Apocalypse) and regarding them as inferior to "the really certain chief books of the New Testament," because only these "clearly and purely present Christ to me" (*mir Christum hell und rein dargeben*). Opinion will vary as to whether the application of Luther's norm in eliminating the four books mentioned is right, even if we agree with Kümmel that, in view of the gradual and irregular evolution of the canon, for us today the final criterion must be that "the books of the New Testament are canonical in the full sense

[44] R. P. C. Hanson, *op. cit.*, p. 168.
[45] See A. Souter-C. S. C. Williams, *The Canon of the New Testament*[2] (1954); more recently, R. M. Grant, *The Formation of the New Testament* (1965); and in the *Cambridge History of the Bible*, 1 (1970), 284–308; C. S. C. Williams in *ibid.*, 2 (1969), 42–53; and H. von Campenhausen, *The Formation of the Christian Bible* (ET 1972).
[46] Kümmel, *op. cit.*, p. 505.

insofar as they make audible the witness to God's historical act of redemption in Christ in such a way that it can be promulgated by preaching."[47]

Kümmel's statement follows the principle enunciated by Ignatius, who took as his basic authority "the gospel." In his letter to Smyrna, he wrote, "Give heed to the prophets and especially to the gospel, in which the Passion has been revealed to us and the Resurrection has been accomplished" (7.2; cf. *Philadelphians* 8.2, which anchors the gospel in the Lord's death and resurrection).

This Lutheran conclusion that canonicity and thus authority are determined by the kerygmatic nature of Scripture's content may be contrasted with two rival views. The one, taken by Cullmann, is that the apostolic rule of faith has a parallel place with the New Testament in its witness to Christ. On the other hand is the classical Roman Catholic acceptance of "oral tradition" "with equal affection and reverence of piety," articulated in Session IV of the Council of Trent. The Tridentine doctrine of tradition, which juxtaposed a secondary authority alongside Scripture by holding that the canon must be interpreted and modified by "the sense which the Holy Mother Church has held and holds," clearly opposes what the early church believed about the place of tradition. It is open to criticism on a number of grounds; for example, there is no evidence from early Christianity of an independent tradition held to be on a par with Scripture; and tradition regulates praxis, not doctrine.[48] This is being increasingly recognized by post-Vatican II Catholic scholars, many of whom prefer to speak of "streams" of tradition rather than "sources."

Yves Congar has proposed a modification of the usually accepted Roman Catholic view.[49] He denies that there are orally transmitted "truths of faith" which have survived, and maintains that "tradition" today is not a rival or parallel source of canonical authority but another way (*une autre manière*) of complementarily communicating the truths of Scripture. Tradition is a *midrash* on the text of Scripture, which is available in the church only in an interpreted form. Fact and interpretation go hand in hand; and such "midrashic" activity is the Holy Spirit's way of preserving "alive" the original deposit of the faith (the παραθήκη of the Pastoral Epistles). Congar appeals to "an unwritten part of the tradition of the apostles" which survived the fixing of the canon and continued as a court of doctrinal and ecclesiastical appeal into the time of the Apologists and Fathers and made a chief point in the argument of Athanasius and Basil in the fourth century.

---

[47] *Ibid.*, p. 510.
[48] R. P. C. Hanson, *op. cit.*, p. 238.
[49] Y. M.-J. Congar, *Tradition and Traditions* (ET 1967), pp. 64f.

R. P. C. Hanson has pointed to the weaknesses in Congar's position.[50]

a. The analogy of *Torah-midrash* is calamitous. To confuse and commingle Scripture and ecclesiastical tradition is to abandon the one objective check on the church's doctrine and life. "Every attempt to exalt the authority of the Church at the expense of that of Holy Scripture is not only illogical but suicidal" (A. L. Lilley, cited by Hanson), because then the church is shut in with itself and, when it speaks on the authority of Scripture, hears only the echo of its own voice.

b. The elevation of tradition to parity with Scripture subverts the canon, and (as Hanson pointedly says) "ends by putting the whole possibility of revelation in jeopardy."

c. Historical evidence does not show that the third-century fathers believed in the validity of this unwritten apostolic norm. To the contrary, "none of the fathers [in the earlier period] . . . imagined that the Bible and the Church's interpretation together formed one indistinguishable whole. . . . Irenaeus could hold that the Church's teaching was equivalent to the contents of Scripture; he did not believe that revelation consisted of the Church's interpretation of Scripture *in addition to* the contents of Scripture. . . . There is something almost ludicrous in the fact that Congar can find more references to an unwritten tradition among the fathers of the fourth and fifth centuries . . . than among those of the second and third."

The case against Congar's theory is compelling. To quote Hanson once more: "The Church has always interpreted the Gospel, and always will do so, sometimes with more success and sometimes with less. But the interpretation is not the Gospel, and never can be." The notion of a tandem relation between Scripture and tradition is false because it denies the place of the church and ecclesiastical customs rightfully "under the judgment-power of the word."

7. *Conclusion.* To inquiries about the authority of the New Testament for today, evangelicals have usually invoked the Reformers' appeal to the binding and normative quality of "Scripture alone." Yet the claim *sola scriptura* may be misunderstood; and it is wrongly conceived if it implies a static, mechanical view of inspiration and a doctrine of textual and extraneous inerrancy,[51] if it forgets that we cannot willy-

---

[50] Hanson, *op. cit.*, pp. 239–45.

[51] The term "extraneous inerrancy" may be elucidated by reference to a recent helpful distinction between what Scripture *teaches*—for which the evangelical will want to assert complete trustworthiness and infallibility (i.e., the teaching will not mislead)—and what Scripture *touches* as incidental to its function as revelatory of God's purpose in redemption—for which "inerrancy" cannot be claimed in the same way. Cf. E. E. Ellis, "The Authority of Scripture: Critical Judgments in Biblical Perspective," *EQ*, 39 (1967), 196–204. The teacher of New Testament

nilly recapture apostolic Christianity and retroject ourselves into the halcyon days of the primitive church, nor overleap the centuries as though nothing of value had transpired in two millennia of Christian history.

Sola scriptura means that the literary deposits of the New Testament era—the period of *Heilsgeschichte*[52]—are, by divine providence and inspiration, uniquely authoritative in all matters of faith and practice and in those matters of lasting and essential value, that is, matters which bear directly on our understanding and communication of the *kerygma* and its implementation. This final phrase is significant as over against the view that the Word-of-God character of Pauline Scripture is exclusively christological or exhaustively soteriological (Luther's well-known position). We would want to include the response to Paul's *kerygma* and its outworking in personal life, social behavior and concerns for the family of mankind. As Hanson phrases it, for us the New Testament "has become ... the successor of the apostles."[53]

We cannot, therefore, appeal to the New Testament for justification of *every* church practice adopted today. Nor is all the church polity and custom of the New Testament period obligatory for the modern church. The test of what is mandatory and what is optional (and indeed of what is to be discarded) is straightforward, although we are often slow to see it and apply it. The question is, Can this article of belief, rite, custom, or piece of ecclesiastical polity be shown to be an essential part of the *kerygma,* and does it outwardly express it? "Essential apostolic practice," writes S. F. Winward, "is the *kerygma* in action, whether in personal or corporate conduct, in worship or in the sacraments."[54] By the application of this test the living church is assured of the guidance of the Holy Spirit, who leads us into a deepening apprehension of God's truth for his people, encapsulated in the gospel, and places a check on any extraneous outgrowth and malformation of belief and practice within

---

Scripture is under an obligation to clarify the guidelines within which he or she pursues the exegetical and hermeneutical task, or to state the reason why it is believed that no such guidelines are possible. See further the concluding section of this chapter.

[52] See G. Wainwright, "The New Testament as Canon," *SJT,* 28 (1975), 551–71, on the centrality of the christological witness in the New Testament canon: "The proper attitude of the Christian with regard to the New Testament canon will be one of gratitude to the early Church—and, ultimately, to the providence of God— for providing the indispensable materials" for the search into the historical reality of Jesus of Nazareth who is now "proclaimed and confessed as 'Lord'" (560). The lordship of Jesus Christ is, as we saw, *the* central message of the New Testament literature (see n. 12 above). *Sola scriptura* is carefully defined by B. Ramm in *Biblical Authority,* ed. J. B. Rogers (1977), pp. 109–23.

[53] R. P. C. Hanson, *op. cit.,* p. 236.

[54] S. F. Winward, "Scripture, Tradition, and Baptism," in *Christian Baptism,* ed. A. Gilmore (1959), p. 51.

the Christian society.[55] So our custom and traditions must be brought to the bar of apostolic tradition, embodied in the Scripture, which in turn is centered on Christ and his saving work. Only in this way does the church become and remain *ecclesia semper reformanda,* "the church always in need of being reformed."

BIBLICAL AUTHORITY TODAY

Four aspects of this theme—with reference here to Paul's letters—call for brief comment: the nature of Scripture, its intention, the legitimacy of criticism, and the meaning of exegesis.

1. The New Testament is rightly perceived by the Christian as having a Word-of-God character because it is to be looked on and obeyed as God's word expressed in and conveyed by human words.[56] On the one side, we encounter in any human work problems of interpretation, and these are too numerous to ignore or overlook. They arise when we face translation uncertainties (e.g., in Paul, 1 Cor. 4:6; 1 Thess. 4:4–6; 1 Tim. 2:15), or a text that has so suffered in transmission that the "original" is beyond recovery today (Eph. 1:1). In other cases, difficulties come about with the genre or literary format of the writings: the presence of interpolated or quoted material in 1 Corinthians and Philippians 2 would greatly affect the meaning today since we would have to distinguish the meaning of the interpolated data *before* their insertion and the meaning they have acquired by being used in the apostolic literature.[57] More problems occur because of historical disparities (e.g., in reconciling Paul's movements in Acts with Galatians), cultural limitations (the veiling of women's heads in 1 Cor. 11), and cosmological descriptions (Phil. 2:10 speaks of demons in subterranean regions, but exactly where are

---

55 "Testing the spirits" (1 John 4:2f.) is relevant here. Wainwright (*loc. cit.*) gives an instance of the importance of this criterion when the claims of the African Kimbanguist church are under scrutiny. See M.-L. Martin, *Kimbangu. An African Prophet and His Church* (1976); W. J. Hollenweger, *Pentecost Between Black and White* (1974).

56 G. E. Ladd's formulation; *The New Testament and Criticism* (1967), Chapter 1.

57 In 1 Cor. 6 and 7 the issue is whether Paul is reproducing verbatim (as in the modern device of using quotation marks) what the Corinthians were saying about liberty and marriage; if so, what follows directly will be his corrective comment appended to the citation. With Phil. 2:6–11 the matter is more delicate, since it has to be shown that the putative *Vorlage* or original hymn has been taken over, added to, and so adapted to Paul's purpose in quoting it. Several scholars dispute this process—e.g., most recently G. B. Caird, *Paul's Letters from Prison* (1976), p. 104—but there are some cogent arguments to demonstrate its existence; cf. R. P. Martin, *Carmen Christi* (1967), p. 287, citing G. R. Beasley-Murray in *Peake's Commentary*[2] (1962), p. 986, that it is "necessary to distinguish between the intention of the hymn and the meaning it would have had for the apostle." Not least is the argument that the same procedure can be traced elsewhere in Paul, notably at Col. 1:15–20 (*Carmen Christi* [1967; rev. ed. 1983]), p. 287 (cf. pp. xii-xix, xxxiv).

they?).[58] All these items come readily to the surface in our study of the Pauline writings, and it is no service to God's truth to pretend they do not exist.

Nonetheless, on the other hand, it may fairly be maintained that these data belong to the incidental penumbra of Paul's thought, and do not touch the central issues of his teaching.[59] In spite of these limitations we must affirm that New Testament Scripture as an entirety is, by divine providence and inspiration—since clearly Paul and the other writers claimed to be men of the Spirit (1 Cor. 2:12f.,16; 7:40; 14:37f.)— God's message to his people in as clear a manner as to ensure the communication of his will in accordance with Scripture's purpose set forth in 2 Timothy 3:16,17.[60]

2. This brings us to the intention of Paul's letters as sacred writing. From his own disclosures (and his letters are wonderfully revealing of the man) we have no doubt that Paul ties in the purpose of his ministry, both oral and written, with conveying the true knowledge of God. This God is the one who saves his people and pledges to bring them indefectibly to his kingdom, of which life in the fellowship of the church here and now is a foretaste and a preparation. To the extent that this purpose is unfolded and applied in the various biblical books they stand as infallible and uniquely trustworthy. They will not fail in their purpose, nor will they mislead or deceive any who seek the truth about God.

The primary witness of Scripture as a totality is to God's incarnate Word, Jesus Christ, in whom this gracious purpose is actualized and spelled out. Like the other New Testament writers, Paul makes it clear that the Old Testament points to him, both negatively (cf. Heb. 8:13) and positively (e.g., 1 Cor. 10). The documents both contain and are the indispensable record of what the first believers and witnesses found to be true in their experience. The normative value of Scripture derives from its witness to Christ and to the quality of life that springs directly from a relationship, both personal and corporate, with him.

3. Since God has been pleased to make himself known in historical events—the Exodus, the exile, the incarnation, the resurrection, the coming of the Spirit and the birth of the church—it follows that we owe it to the scriptural record to investigate to the full the data of its histori-

---

[58] See my chapter in *New Testament Interpretation* (1977), ed. I. H. Marshall.

[59] A. Harnack calls attention to what is recognized by all readers of Paul: side by side with "words of Divine mercy and loving-kindness" we read such mundane items of information as, "My cloak I left at Troas" (*The Origin of the New Testament* [ET 1925], p. 43).

[60] In God's providence we would include his overruling human circumstances concerning the writers' heredity and training and their insight into and expression of divine reality; the supply of sufficient knowledge of the biblical languages and their cognates; and the preservation of the text in its overall integrity in spite of earthly vicissitudes, such as the hazards that caused textual variants; M. R. Austin, "How Biblical is the 'The Inspiration of Scripture'?" *ExpT*, 93 (1981), 75–79.

cal setting.[61] To that extent the gospel stands or falls with its claim to be historically grounded. Yet all interpretation of historical data depends on who does the interpreting. The canonical nature of Scripture derives from an emerging consensus that the interpretation of Jesus Christ and his mission, in both his earthly life and the church, has a unique status. It establishes an authoritative and binding norm by which all other forms of Christian faith and life may be tested. In the New Testament itself this is already begun, as spurious and alien notions are exposed and judged by the criteria of the person and place of the Lord of the church and the new life of love that derives from him.[62]

4. Exegesis is the explanation of the thrust and force of a given passage in the overall context of its setting and historical significance. It starts with the milieu in which the passage is set and requires us to interrogate the text and so to ask its "scope" in the light of the response it makes to Jesus Christ who, within the same hermeneutical circle (or better, spiral), is known and confessed as Lord and Savior.[63] Yet the unique character of Scripture is such that as we interrogate it and subject it to analysis (with all the scientific disciplines at our disposal), it interrogates us and speaks its own words to test our lives. This is the work of the Spirit who by his "internal testimony" "re-inspires" the word and makes the New Testament, including Paul's letters—from one angle part of an ancient book of miscellaneous religious, social and cultural documents of a bygone era—the living word of God to his church in every age.

---

61 On the legitimacy, indeed the necessity, of the historical-critical method, see further R. G. Cavin, "Is Biblical Criticism Morally Permissible?", *SBT*, 6.2 (1976), 29–32.

62 These criteria are phrased more fully by J. D. G. Dunn, *Jesus and the Spirit*, pp. 293ff., as the test of the kerygmatic tradition (the earthly Jesus is the exalted Lord); the test of love (the *agapē* of 1 Cor. 13); and the requirement of upbuilding (1 Cor. 14). See the illustrations culled in R. P. Martin, *The Worship of God*, pp. 191–94, in the light of the coherence of the New Testament churches' praxis of worship and its underlying theology (pp. 194–208).

63 On the "hermeneutical circle" see also R. S. Barbour, *Traditio-Historical Criticism of the Gospels* (1972), p. 19; G. Wainwright, *loc. cit.*, 559–61; J. I. Packer, "Biblical Authority, Hermeneutics and Inerrancy," in *Jerusalem and Athens: Festschrift Cornelius Van Til*, ed. E. R. Geehan (1971), pp. 146ff.

CHAPTER TWENTY-TWO

The Place of the Pastorals
and the Close of Paul's Life

The historical notice in Acts 28:30f. describes Paul's two years in Rome as a period of *libera custodia* ("free custody"). Luke does not tell us what happened at the close of that two-year period. Are there in the Acts of the Apostles any indications of what subsequently befell the apostle? Do the Epistles attributed to him throw any light on his later history? What is the historical worth of the extra-canonical tradition in this matter? Unfortunately the sources of information do not speak with a common voice on these questions.

TWO ALTERNATIVES

1. On the traditional view, Luke's purpose was served when he had brought Paul to the Imperial City. There he ended his narrative, and it is an open question whether he even knew of Paul's life subsequent to what he records in Acts 28.

a. Clearly if the case had gone by default and Paul was released at the end of two years, it would have fit in with Luke's interest *vis-à-vis* Theophilus (Acts 1:1; Luke 1:1–4) to have shown by this narrative that the Roman court had no case against the most illustrious Christian leader of the early 60s. Yet even within the earlier narrative of Acts there are dark hints that Paul's fate would be sealed by his visit to Rome, especially the references in 20:4—21:15.[1] But these are no more than inferences.

b. The evidence from the Epistles is also ambiguous. If Philippians dates from the Roman captivity, we know that Paul was hopeful about his release and planning a subsequent visit to Macedonia (1:26; 2:24). But to argue thus is to assume the very thing to be proved, namely that Paul was anticipating his release from prison in Rome. The same

---

[1] On Acts 20:25–29 as a type of "farewell speech," see J. Munck, "Discours d'adieu dans le Nouveau Testament et dans la littérature biblique," *Aux sources de la tradition chrétienne: Mélanges M. Goguel* (1950), pp. 155–70.

problem arises with the evidence of Colossians and Philemon (Phm. 22): again we cannot be certain about the locale of Paul's imprisonment or the date on which he hoped for release. Romans 15:28f. suggest that Paul did not plan to return to the eastern circuit but venture westward to Spain.[2] Whether he ever realized this ambition is open to question, and we have no evidence from his own hand.

c. Later Christian writers have been understood to state that Paul's mission did include a Spanish visit. 1 Clement 5:6f. states of Paul: "After he had taught the whole world righteousness and had come to the limits of the west and had testified before rulers he was taken away from this world."[3] The following note is contained in *Actus Petri Vercellenses*: "And Paul fasted for three days and asked the Lord what was best for him, and he had a vision and the Lord said to him: Paul, stand up and become a physician to those who are in Spain [by going to them] in person."[4] The Muratorian Canon (*c.* 200) explains that Luke omits some details from the Acts, including "Paul's departure from the city [of Rome] for Spain." Finally, Eusebius records: "Having therefore made his defense at that time the apostle again journeyed on the ministry of preaching and after he had set foot for the second time in the same city [Rome] he was perfected by his martyrdom. While still in bonds, he composed his second Epistle to Timothy, mentioning both his former defense and also his imminent perfecting" (*HE* 2.22.2f.). This is the most explicit allusion to a release from Rome (based on 2 Tim. 4:16f.) and Paul's subsequent re-arrest and trial, which eventuated in his death. On this evidence, we can construct the following chart of events at the close of Paul's life:

AD 62–64 is the traditionally accepted date for the two-year release, if the Jews failed to bring charges against him.[5]

---

[2] J. Knox, "Romans 15:14–33 and Paul's Conception of his Apostolic Mission," *JBL*, 83 (1964), 1–11.

[3] Since 1 Clement was written in Rome, the phrase "limits of the west" has been taken to imply an extension of Paul's ministry in the far western Mediterranean region. So W. G. Kümmel, *Introduction*[2], p. 377, and earlier, W. K. Lowther Clarke, *The First Epistle of Clement to the Corinthians* (1937), pp. 89f. To the contrary, P. N. Harrison, *The Problem of the Pastoral Epistles* (1921), pp. 107f., places the location in Rome. To his chief argument that Paul's martyrdom is evidently located in the same place as Peter's in 1 Clement 5:3,4, we may add the lexical point that the wording of 1 Clement 5:7 has a parallel in Psalms of Solomon 17:12 where the text speaks of the "west," i.e., Rome, to which Pompey banished Aristobulus and his family. The later allusions to a Spanish visit become then inferences from Romans 15:24,28. A more drastic solution, that Paul had earlier abandoned the prospect of a Spanish mission, is suggested by A. Schlatter, *The Church in the New Testament Period* (ET 1955), p. 236, and accepted by D. Guthrie, *The Pastoral Epistles* (1957), p. 21.

[4] Cf. Hennecke-Schneemelcher, *New Testament Apocrypha*, 2, 279f.

[5] See H. J. Cadbury, "Roman Law and the Trial of Paul," *Beginnings of Christianity*, Vol. 5, Note XXVI, pp. 297ff.; L. P. Pherigo, "Paul's Life After the Close of Acts," *JBL*, 70 (1951), 271–84. J. J. Gunther, *Paul: Messenger and Exile*, Ch. 6, suggests that Paul was tried and sentenced to *relegatio*, or voluntary exile (to Spain?). Then

AD 64–67/68. During this time Paul has freedom for missionary work either in the east (the Philippian letter promises a visit to Macedonia) or west (the projected visit to Spain).

AD 67/68. His re-arrest and death are set in the time of Nero's pogrom, which Eusebius dates near the close of Nero's life; with this Jerome agrees (*De vir.* 11.5). But this late dating seems impossible (see below), and we have to conclude that the exact time of Paul's death is uncertain.

2. An alternative reconstruction has been proposed on the basis of other evidence. 1 Clement 6 speaks of Christian martyrs at Rome in such a way as to fit the description of Tacitus that it was during Nero's outbreak in 64/65 that Paul and Peter perished.[6] This line of reasoning denies that Paul was released at the close of the two-year imprisonment of Acts 28 and makes impossible any further ministry after the close of Acts. The inference is that when the Roman authorities decided in 64/65 to proceed against Christians, they immediately dealt with Paul's case, passed judgment on him, and had him beheaded. There is a considerable body of opinion to endorse this view.[7]

3. There is a further possibility mentioned by J. J. Gunther. This reconstruction implies that Paul's two-year detention in Acts ended with his voluntary banishment to the extreme part of the Empire (Spain). Since this was a mild punishment, he would be free to engage in missionary work. On learning that Christians were being blamed for Nero's conflagration in AD 64, he returned to the Imperial City, was rearrested and martyred. The points in favor of this hypothesis are (1) it gives Paul a limited time of freedom, whether in the west (as Gunther suggests) or in the east, since *relegatio,* or exile, left the person free to go where he chose, and (2) it permits us to accommodate the travel plans in such verses as 1 Timothy 1:3, Titus 3:12, prior to his second imprisonment when he called for Timothy to come to him at Rome (2 Tim. 4:9, 11, 21). The evidence of 2 Timothy 1:17 must be given its due weight.

THE PASTORAL EPISTLES

The addressees of these letters are known to us from both Acts and Paul's church letters. As Paul's faithful travel-companions, they seem to

---

it becomes possible to maintain that after two years in Rome (AD 60–62) Paul suffered two years in (missionary) exile. In AD 64, on hearing of the fire at Rome, he returned to the city, was arrested again and executed.

[6] Later Christian writers speak uniformly of this; see E. T. Merrill, *Essays in Early Christian History,* Ch. 4.

[7] H. J. Cadbury, *op. cit.,* p. 338, is spokesman for many historians: "Certainly no other evidence that we possess is authoritative enough to disprove that as a matter of fact the two years in Rome was followed by the Apostle's crown of martyrdom." See too O. Cullmann, *Peter*[2] (1962), pp. 87–98, with reference to Lietzmann and von Campenhausen.

have been allotted special spheres of labor: Timothy in the Macedonian churches (cf. Phil. 2:19); Titus in the church at Corinth.[8] It is not surprising, then, that both men received positions of leadership in the Pauline churches, at Ephesus and Crete respectively, and that Paul should wish to write to them in a way that fit their needs as church leaders, offering directives for new congregations on matters of controlling, guiding, and instructing their members. False doctrine is shown to be a particular menace, and the pastors are called to be alert and active in rebutting it.

However, though these letters also speak of obvious Pauline themes and contain a number of personal names known to us from Acts and other Pauline letters (e.g., Luke, Mark, Aquila, Prisca), doubts have been raised about the setting of the Epistles at the close of Paul's ministry in Acts. We may briefly enumerate these doubts.

1. The language and style of the letters have been taken to conflict with what is preserved in the undisputed letters of Paul. Unusual terms (e.g., "sober," "religious," "appearing") are found here but not elsewhere in Paul; and typical Pauline terms (e.g., "covenant," "righteousness by faith," "boast," "effect") do not appear here; some grammatical connectives, which are familiar from the earlier Pauline Epistles, are omitted in the Pastorals.[9] We must, however, recall the nature of these letters, their address to a special clientele for a particular purpose which may explain several linguistic peculiarities; and there are undoubted examples of verses which have a Pauline ring.

The use of an amanuensis has also been appealed to in this connection. The most likely candidate for this role is Luke, in view of the close parallels in language, concepts, and teaching between Acts and the Pastorals.[10] Kelly's designation of the writer as a secretary who "may

---

[8] C. K. Barrett, "Titus," in *Neotestamentica et Semitica*, edd. Ellis and Wilcox, pp. 1-14.

[9] See B. S. Easton. *The Pastoral Epistles* (1948), pp. 171-237. The standard work is still Harrison, *op. cit.*; cf. his later *Paulines and Pastorals* (1964); K. Grayston and G. Herdan, "The Authorship of the Pastorals in the Light of Statistical Linguistics," *NTS*, 6 (1959-60), 1-15; D. Guthrie, *The Pastoral Epistles*, pp. 212-28; B. M. Metzger, "A Reconsideration of Certain Arguments Against the Pauline Authorship of the Pastoral Epistles," *ExpT*, 70 (1958-59), 91-94, who calls attention to "certain basic limitations . . . involved in the statistical analysis of literary vocabulary"; and E. E. Ellis, "The Authorship of the Pastorals," in his *Paul and His Recent Interpreters* (1961), pp. 49-57.

[10] First suggested by H. A. Schott, *Isagoge historico-critica in libros Novi Foederis sacros* (1830), pp. 324f.; more recently cf. C. F. D. Moule, "The Problem of the Pastoral Epistles: A Reappraisal," *BJRL*, 47 (1965), 430-52; A. Strobel, "Schreiben des Lukas?" *NTS*, 15 (1968-69), 191-200; Kümmel, *op. cit.*, p. 374n24; and for a useful conspectus of the data see J. L. Houlden, *The Pastoral Epistles* (1976), pp. 23-26. On Luke's credentials see further M. A. Siotis, "Luke the Evangelist As St. Paul's Collaborator," in *Neues Testament und Geschichte*, edd. H. Baltensweiler and B. Reicke (1972), pp. 105-11. For criticism of the Lukan thesis see N. Brox, "Lukas als Verfasser der Pastoralbriefe?" *JAC*, 13 (1970), 62-77. However, there are 34 non-Pauline Lukan words found in the Pastorals (N. Turner, *A Grammar of New Testament Greek*, Vol. 4, p. 104).

have been a Hellenistic Jewish Christian, a man skilled in rabbinical lore and at the same time a master of the higher *koinē*"[11] would chime in with what is known of the author of Luke-Acts (and Ephesians?). Tychicus, Jeremias's suggestion,[12] is too shadowy a character in early Christianity.

Whether the particular identification of Luke can be proved or not is not quite the point. What seems a reasonable hypothesis to test is whether Luke-Acts, the Pastorals, and Ephesians belong, in Houlden's words, "to the same milieu, both in the history of the early Christian church and in the world of thought of their time."[13] Houlden, however, wishes to locate that milieu in the middle of the second century, a conclusion by no means required by what the three documents mentioned have in common. A setting much earlier would be just as feasible. Guthrie's statement that "it is open to question whether Paul would have allowed such freedom" to an amanuensis that would otherwise account for the stylistic and conceptual peculiarities in the Pastorals[14] is too negative, once we recall that considerable freedom was allowable (see pp. 243ff.) and remember the obvious links between Luke's account in Acts and the vocabulary and ideas of the Pastorals. Luke's suggested compilation of Paul's teaching has been argued by F. J. Badcock in a little-known book.[14a] His careful discussion begins by remarking that Paul thought out his letters beforehand and made notes of the headings, leading ideas, and paragraph themes. Doubtless, Paul kept notes or memoranda of such communications (cf. 2 Tim. 4:13) as well as collections of hymnic or confessional passages, as we see in 1 Timothy 3:16, 2 Timothy 2:11-13. These Pauline *scripta* may have included statements on church order and organization suitable for the setting up of a regular ministerial office at a time when the church entered a period of growth and organizational solidity.

From what we know of Paul's letter-writing habits, his quick, staccato-like method of speaking when under pressure (e.g., Phil. 1:22f.), would leave only the outline to be filled in by a trusted, sympathetic scribe, such as Tertius (Rom. 16:22). Badcock proposes three stages in

---

[11] J. N. D. Kelly, *The Pastoral Epistles* (Harper-Black, 1963), p. 27. E. F. Harrison, *Introduction to the New Testament* (1964), p. 342, opts for Luke as amanuensis. This case has been strengthened by S. G. Wilson's full discussion, *Luke and the Pastoral Epistles* (1979), who concludes that "given a choice between Paul and Luke as the author of the Pastorals, Luke is the far more likely candidate" — a bold statement, and not guiltless of being a *non sequitur*. Nonetheless there *is* a case to be made for Lukan authorship, not least the evidence of Luke's ostensible purpose in seeking to cope with the problems of second-generation Christianity; see R. P. Martin, *The Worship of God* (1982), pp. 202–5; cf. J. D. G. Dunn, "Models of Christian Community in the New Testament," in *Strange Gifts? A Guide to Charismatic Renewal*, edd. D. Martin and P. Mullen (1984), ch. 1, esp. pp. 11–13, for "a second generation perspective" (p. 12).

[12] J. Jeremias, *Die Briefe an Timotheus und Titus* (1953), p. 8.

[13] Houlden, *op. cit.*, p. 26.

[14] Guthrie, *op. cit.*, p. 48.

[14a] F. J. Badcock, *The Pauline Epistles* (1937), Ch. 6.

the procedure by which the letters were produced, on their human side: the original notes, the transcript, and the fair copy.

Some of the "fair copies" have perished, e.g., in the Corinthian correspondence (1 Cor. 5:9), and Paul's transcripts may have been lost at sea (Acts 27). The original notes would be lightly regarded, once the fair copy was made or else retained by the amanuensis for his own interest's sake.

Suppose that Tertius kept a set of Paul's "notes" on which Romans was based; the notes would have neither particles, prepositions, or even pronouns, and be written in an abbreviated form.

Let us imagine that this same procedure was followed in the case of the Pastorals. The original "notes" were destined for Timothy and Titus to aid them in their work as leaders at Ephesus and Crete, and items that are recognized as personal memoranda, travel notes, and intimate reflections formed the substance of those apostolic communications. Later the "notes" were edited by being written up and set in a form that made them more readable. To these statements of Paul's teaching were added materials such as hymns and credal forms, based on what was common property in the Pauline churches. The completed wholes, compiled by a man such as Luke who was Paul's companion in Rome (2 Tim. 4:11), were later available to be sent off to churches in Asia and Crete at a time when there was need to reinforce the Pauline emissaries who were wrestling with false teaching and also needing special reminders of what the apostle had taught. The call "to instruct" and "to remember" is a frequent one in these Epistles (1 Tim. 4:6,11; 6:2,20; 2 Tim. 2:7f.; 3:14).

Badcock in this volume, hailed as "conservative-revolutionary," has an elaborate set of proposals for dating the Pastorals in the time of Paul's Ephesian and Caesarean period. It is, however, his verdict on authorship that interests us here. He concludes:

> There is nothing in the wording which may not belong to the apostolic period, though they (the letters) have been edited from notes made by St. Paul's amanuensis, and as regards this epistle (1 Tim.) possibly by St. Luke.

This theory would account for the use made of material that P. N. Harrison regarded as Paul's own "notes,"[15] entrusted to a man who utilized them in his own way—hence the linguistic phenomena.[16] Yet he is more than a copyist, and because of this special service he rendered Houlden's criticism that no reference to a scribe is found in these letters is deflected.[17]

2. The church and its ministries are emphasized, and it is ar-

---

[15] Isolated by P. N. Harrison, op. cit. (1921), pp. 115ff. as Titus 3:12–15; 2 Tim. 1:16–18; 3:10f.; 4:1,2a,5b–8,16–19,21b,22a; cf. N. Brox, "Zu den persönlichen Notizen der Pastoralbriefe," BZ, 13 (1969), 76–94.

[16] Cf. C. K. Barrett, The Pastoral Epistles (1963), p. 7, on the distinction between a passive secretary and an author.

[17] Houlden, op. cit., pp. 21f.

gued that such descriptions betray a period of organization and development. "The pillar and bulwark of the truth" (1 Tim. 3:15) is perhaps a formal definition of the church which applies not only to 1 Timothy but also the other letters in this corpus. Leadership must be carefully selected and watched: bishops, deacons, deaconesses (1 Tim. 3), along with elders, play a prominent role. There is a regular manner of ordination including the laying on of hands by Paul, the pastor, and the elders. The custodianship of "healthy doctrine" is one of the prime responsibilities of the pastor.

Yet this developed church organization and leadership is not unprepared for, and Paul evidently anticipated the need for pastoral oversight in the churches.

a. Acts 14:23 mentions Paul's concern for ministerial oversight on the Jewish pattern of "elders" ($z^e q\bar{e}n\hat{i}m$). Acts 20:17 and 28 apparently equate "elders" and "overseers/bishops." There is a Jewish precedent in the office of $m^e baqq\bar{e}r$ (camp superintendent at Qumran) according to the Dead Sea Scrolls.[18]

b. The singular "bishop" in 1 Timothy 3:1 does not indicate the existence of a system of monarchical episcopate, which was clear in Ignatius' day; the term here is a generic one.[19]

c. The Pauline churches (Phil. 1:1)[20] and the congregations mirrored in extra-canonical literature (*Didache* 15) know a type of church leadership similar in form and arrangement to that in the Pastorals.

3. The type of heresy attacked in these letters suggests to some scholars a second-century situation.[21] 1 Timothy 6:20 refers to "contradictions," *antitheseis*, the title of a book written by Marcion. But this identification can hardly be sustained, for Paul has his eye on Jewish aberrations, which would place him, if anything, alongside Marcion. In fact, the Jewishness of the false notions suggests an early period (1 Tim. 1:4; Titus 3:9). The false teachers are clearly Jews in Titus 1:10,14, though there is a gnosticizing element in their refusal to accept marriage (1 Tim. 4:3), their asceticism (1 Tim. 4:3f.) and their disdain of matter (Titus 1:15). Further the "wordiness" of the debate suggests a type of Jewish-Christian dispute (1 Tim. 6:4; 2 Tim. 2:14; Titus 1:11).[22]

[18] J. N. D. Kelly, *op. cit.*, pp. 73f., referring to 1QS 6:10f., 19ff.; CD 13:7–16; 14:8–12.
[19] As Kümmel, *Introduction*[2], p. 381, allows, with reference to H. von Campenhausen, *Ecclesiastical Authority and Spiritual Power in the Church of the First Three Centuries* (ET 1969), pp. 106ff.
[20] For the discussion see R. P. Martin, *Philippians* (NCB, 1976), p. 62.
[21] J. N. D. Kelly, *op. cit.*, pp. 10–12.
[22] R. J. Karris, "The Background and Significance of the Polemic of the Pastoral Epistles," *JBL*, 92 (1973), 549–64. The links between the Pastorals and the refutation of the charismatic, prophetic, women-oriented movement later known as Montanism have been exploited by J. M. Ford, "A Note on Proto-Montanism in the Pastoral Epistles," *NTS*, 17 (1970–71), 338–46; see further D. F. Wright, "Why were the Montanists Condemned?" *Themelios*, 2 n.s. (1976), 15–22. But the center of the debate with the errorists is found more in the realm of a false understanding of eschatological salvation: see W. L. Lane, "1 Timothy iv. 1–3. An Early Instance of Over-Realized Eschatology?" *NTS*, 11 (1964–65), 164–67.

Attempts to date the Pastorals later than AD 96 founder on their attestation in 1 Clement, published in that year. The persecutions spoken of in these letters (1 Tim. 6:13; 2 Tim. 2:9; 3:11f.; 4:16–18; Tit. 2:3) reflect a situation earlier than Domitian (AD 90), who launched an attack on the church in Asia.

4. The more difficult problem is the chronological one. How do we fit the Pastorals into the framework of the events narrated in Acts?[23] If the Eusebian chronology is put in doubt, how are these letters to be related to Paul's missionary career? Either we say we know so little about his life from his situation in Acts 28 to his death that we should make room for the Pastorals in that segment of his ministry, or we try to accommodate the Pastorals into his earlier ministry of Acts 20ff.[24] Alternatively, the Pastorals have been treated (as most German scholars do) as pseudonymous, with no claim to historical veracity and reflecting a post-Pauline "early catholic" period of the church.[25] A third possibility, which seeks to explain the unusual features of the letters and yet gives due weight to their intimate association with the apostle, is that they are the final work of a disciple of Paul, dated in the period after Paul's martyrdom. In one sense, the message of these documents is clearly affected by their historical setting; at a deeper level they speak to Christ's servants in every age, especially when doctrinal laxity and

---

[23] Already recognized by J. V. Bartlet, "The Historical Setting of the Pastoral Epistles," *The Expositor*, 7th ser., 5 (1913), 28–36 (on the problem), 161–67 (on language and style), 256–63 (religious content) and 325–47 (on the historical setting).

[24] For the former see F. J. Badcock, *op. cit.*, and C. F. D. Moule, *loc. cit.*; for the latter J. J. Gunther's reconstruction (*op. cit.*, pp. 107–20) may be mentioned. J. A. T. Robinson, *Redating the New Testament*, pp. 67–77, also wishes to place Paul's defense in 2 Tim. 4 during his imprisonment at Caesarea. But while there are several suggestive points of contact between the Pastorals and Acts, the chief obstacle is 2 Tim. 1:16f.: Onesiphorus "when he arrived in Rome searched for me eagerly and found me." The exegesis that would make a hiatus between "arrived in Rome" and "found me" (in Caesarea) is not convincing. Also in this group of interpreters are P. N. Harrison, *The Problem of the Pastoral Epistles*, pp. 115ff.; and "The Authorship of the Pastoral Epistles," *ExpT*, 67 (1955), 77–81; against Harrison's reconstruction, see Guthrie, *op. cit.*, pp. 21ff.; Moule, *loc. cit.*, 433f.; cf. also G. S. Duncan, *St. Paul's Ephesian Ministry* (1929), pp. 184–216; this in turn is critically handled by Harrison, "The Pastoral Epistles and Duncan's Ephesian Theory," *NTS*, 2 (1955–56), 250–61. One of the first ambitious attempts to date the letters between the closing of the Ephesian ministry and the last voyage to Judaea was by J. V. Bartlet, *loc. cit.*; but at the conclusion of these essays he reverts to the traditional placing of the imprisonment in Rome and places the composition of the Pastorals there.

[25] See M. Dibelius-H. Conzelmann, *The Pastoral Epistles* (ET 1972; *Hermeneia*), pp. 1–10. J. L. Houlden looks sympathetically on H. von Campenhausen's theory that Polycarp of Smyrna (died AD 155 or later) may be the author of these documents; see the latter's *Polykarp von Smyrna und die Pastoralbriefe* (1951); and *Ecclesiastical Authority and Spiritual Power in the Church of the First Three Centuries*, pp. 106–19. The argument turns mainly on the plausibility of reading the Pastorals as though the monarchical episcopacy were already in operation, and the bishop and the elders were the professional holders of an established office. But this is contrary to what we have seen as evidence for an earlier dating.

stress prevail. We would thus value these documents for the light they cast on the closing years of Paul's ministry and by extension on a situation that arose in the Pauline churches and appreciate them as indicating how a devoted Paulinist (Luke or someone else) used his master's teaching and example to confront situations that were embryonic in Paul's lifetime which Paul had foreseen and which emerged in the Aegean region in the time immediately following his death as already envisaged in Acts 20:29-32 in Paul's address to the Ephesian church leaders.

PAUL THE PASTOR

This short corpus of letters carries the *imprimatur* of Paul's authority and reveals his character as *pastor pastorum,* a leader who provides for continuing leadership in the churches. The compiler—whether Luke (as some believe) or not—had access to materials that go back to Paul's own statements of his faith and life (e.g., 1 Tim. 1:11, 12–16; 2 Tim. 1:3,11f., 15–18; 3:10), to the apostle's prison experiences (2 Tim. 4:6–8), and to travel-notes relating to his Asian ministry (2 Tim. 4:9–21). These he incorporated to display Paul's deep concern for the churches. Timothy and Titus embody a type of diocesan leadership, in Ephesus and Crete respectively. The writer consciously recalls Timothy's youth in Derbe, Lystra, and Iconium (2 Tim. 3:10f.; cf. Acts 16:1–3), his family connections (2 Tim. 1:5; 3:15), and his knowledge of Paul's ministry (2 Tim. 2:2).

Both pastors were facing problems that emerged out of a tense situation. False prophets are already on the scene (1 Tim. 1:19f.; 2 Tim. 2:17; 3:13) and the tendencies to division within the church are pronounced (Titus 3:10f.; 2 Tim. 3:8f.). Both men are puzzled over these inroads of falsehood. Paul's teaching is made the touchstone for what must be maintained in the face of heterodox doctrine (1 Tim. 1:4f.) and practice (Titus 3:8,14). The source of authority, as a kind of "rule of faith," lies in credal statements (the "faithful sayings"), baptismal confessions (e.g., 2 Tim. 2:11–13), and hymnic fragments (1 Tim. 3:16), as well as the "Rules of the Household" (1 Tim. 6:1f.; Titus 2:9f.) and the inspired "sacred writings" of the Septuagint (2 Tim. 3:16f.), though this term may extend more widely to cover dominical sayings, such as 1 Timothy 5:18 (Luke 10:7).

The church is evidently entering a period of institutional stability and organizational fixity. There are both assets and dangers inherent in this situation. The gains of the past had to be conserved and the encroachments of upstart teachings resisted, lest they tear down the edifice of the church life that is slowly rising and becoming consolidated. Succeeding generations of believers needed the continuity with the past, and Paul is invoked as one of the links in an unbroken chain of teachers and leaders (2 Tim. 2:2; cf. 1 Clem. 44). Regulations regarding the selection, appointment, credentials, and ordaining of church officers (1 Tim. 3; 5:17–25) are meant to be taken seriously. Pastoral problems concerning widows and church discipline (1 Tim. 5:3ff.) evidence this concern to preserve the church in good order within the social framework.

There were attendant hazards, too. Only too obvious were the dangers that formalization of teaching and the overlay of institutional forms would place a suffocating blanket over the free enthusiasm of the charismatically oriented church and check the uninhibited freedom of the Spirit in worship, service, and activity—as can be seen from later church history. These pastoral directives avoid this danger and point to a middle course. There have to be institutional patterns and rules, as the church settles down in the period when Paul's personal presence is no longer there to guide it on an *ad hoc* basis (1 Cor. 11:34). Paul had envisioned this need. The legacy of his teaching remains in the data on which the writer of these letters can draw faithfully and apply to new circumstances, representing his mentor's mind by recalling his status and authority as "teacher of the Gentiles" (1 Tim. 2:7). That this exponent of Paul's teaching has so remarkably captured the master's outlook is seen above all in the refusal he records to quench the Spirit (2 Tim. 1:7) and his insistence that formalism in religion is a betrayal of the Pauline gospel (2 Tim. 3:5). The middle line between dead and barren orthodoxy and unbridled enthusiasm marks this distinctive of the gospel preached by Paul as it related to a later period;[26] and as such it remains normative to challenge and guide us today.

---

[26] The period is called "The Emergence of the Institutional Church"—a phrase taken as the chapter heading to the Pastorals by Barker-Lane-Michaels, *The New Testament Speaks* (1969), p. 235. See too A. T. Hanson, *The Pastoral Epistles* (NCB, 1982), who denies Pauline authorship, and G. D. Fee, *1 and 2 Timothy, Titus* (Good News Commentary, 1984), who offers a recent defense of the traditional view and is interesting in that he sees the key to the letters (at least 1 Timothy) in Paul's polemic against elders who were leading the congregations astray; on the broader issues of a post-Pauline attribution, see A. G. Patzia, "The Deutero-Pauline Hypothesis: An Attempt at Clarification," *EQ*, 52 (1980), 27–42. This important essay has distinct bearing on the themes of our earlier Chapter 18 as well as the present one.

CHAPTER TWENTY-THREE

Church and State in the New Testament

In the first three parts of this chapter we shall investigate Paul's understanding of the Roman state and the social nature of the Christian life; then move on to some wider questions about the state in New Testament times.

ROMANS 13

1. A strictly historical interpretation of this passage to verse 7 begins with a reminder that this Epistle was written after Claudius' decree had been revoked, and expelled Jews (and Jewish Christians) were returning to Rome and to the church there (see further above, pp. 188f.). They had been dismissed by imperial decree for squabbling with Gentile believers, and they had returned to find the church much different from the one they had left nine years earlier. They were "weak," full of scruples about diet and the observance of holy days (Rom. 14:1–23; 15:1–16), in contrast to the "strong" Pauline Christians, who took a relaxed attitude to controverted issues and practices. On this view, Paul is warning the two factions not to allow their differences to lead to open antagonism. This could probably be construed as conduct disloyal to the Empire and call forth another imperial edict. Hence the summons of obedience to the state is sounded as a piece of practical accommodation to the contemporary situation.

2. O. Cullmann is the chief spokesman for the view that in addition to the primary reference to civil authorities in the text, there is a secondary allusion to angelic powers standing behind and acting through those human social institutions.[1] His main arguments involve the lexical evidence (the plural form of *exousia*, "powers," in 13:1, clearly signifies invisible angelic powers elsewhere in Paul) and the contempo-

---

[1] O. Cullmann, *Christ and Time* (ET 1962), pp. 194ff.; *The State in the New Testament* (ET 1957), pp. 95ff., building on M. Dibelius, *Die Geisterwelt im Glauben des Paulus* (1909), who subsequently abandoned this interpretation.

rary idea, both Jewish and pagan, that invisible forces were at work behind the visible phenomena. Thus Cullmann can bring together the positive attitude to the state in Romans 13 with a negative stance in Revelation. The powers of evil have been subdued by Christ, yet they are held on a long tether and "have the illusion that they are releasing themselves from their bond with Christ while in reality, by this striving which here and there appears, they only show once more their original demonic character; they cannot, however, actually set themselves free."[2] They are like a bull in a net, to use the illustration of P. T. Forsyth in the same context.[3] If we reject Cullmann's view, we are left with the historical consideration that Paul wrote before the Neronian persecution, which was the beginning of the official hostility to the church, later to become a policy of declared antagonism.

EPHESIANS 4-6

These three chapters exemplify the use made by the New Testament writers (Paul, Peter, James) of the so-called "household codes" (Haustafeln), which were familiar patterns of domestic and social behavior in the Graeco-Roman world. The pioneer study of these was by K. Weidinger, who traced them to Stoic origins.[4] Included are lists of vices and virtues and appeals to several members of the household (fathers, wives, husbands, children, slaves, masters). The Jewish background, however, should not be overlooked and many of the parallels from Stoic moral philosophy (e.g., in Phil. 4) have a counterpart also in Diaspora Judaism (perhaps under Hellenistic influence).[5] The Dead Sea Scrolls also contain interesting sidelights on the New Testament ethical instructions, as recent investigators have observed.[6]

[2] Cullmann, *Christ and Time*, p. 198.
[3] P. T. Forsyth, *The Glorious Gospel*, p. 7, cited by J. S. Stewart, *A Faith to Proclaim* (1953), pp. 96f. C. K. Barrett, *The Epistle to the Romans* (Harper-Black, 1957) *ad loc.*, opposes Cullmann; F.-J. Leenhardt, *The Epistle to the Romans* (ET 1961), pp. 328f., is also critical of Cullmann. G. B. Caird, *Principalities and Powers* (1956), pp. 22ff., allows that Paul may be speaking ambiguously, but insists that Cullmann is wrong to deny God's activity in the state. Other useful surveys of the problem are C. E. B. Cranfield, "Some Observations on Romans 13:1-7," *NTS*, 6 (1959-60), 241-49; A. Strobel, "Zum Verständnis von Römer 13," *ZNTW*, 47 (1956), 67-93. C. D. Morrison, *The Powers that Be* (1960), offers a full-scale response in support of Cullmann's position. M. Black, *Romans* (1973), pp. 158-63 has a good bibliography, to which may be added J. H. Yoder, *The Politics of Jesus* (1972), Ch. 10.
[4] K. Weidinger, *Die Haustafeln* (1928), on which see W. K. L. Clarke, *New Testament Problems* (1929), pp. 157-60; see further J. E. Crouch, *The Origin and Intention of the Colossian Haustafel* (1972); R. P. Martin, "Virtue," *NIDNTT*, III (1978), 928-32; G. E. Cannon, *The Use of Traditional Materials in Colossians* (1983), esp. ch. 4: "Traditional Paraenetic Materials: The Household Code."
[5] As Lohmeyer pointed out in his commentary on Phil. 4:8ff.; see Martin, *Philippians* (NCB, 1976), pp. 157ff.
[6] S. Wibbing, *Die Tugend- und Lasterkataloge im Neuen Testament* (1959); see too W. Lillie, "The Pauline House-tables," *ExpT*, 86 (1975), 179-83.

The most informative study is that by P. Carrington, *The Primitive Christian Catechism.*[7] Features found in Ephesians 4-6 are:

1. New creation/new birth as a ground for new behavior patterns.

2. *Deponentes*—put off former practices, belonging to your old life.

3. *Abstinentes*—steer clear of evils around you in the pagan world.

4. *Subiecti*—a subordinationist code by which the attitudes of the Christian to society, the church at worship, and the family are regulated in a kind of "chain of command" or hierarchy of authority.

5. *Vigilate*—duties of watchfulness and prayer.

6. *State*—stand when faced with the testing of persecution.

Since Carrington's time, a significant advance has been made in the study of the social background of early Christian "station-codes." The most illuminating is that by J. E. Crouch. After surveying the possibilities, he concludes that Hellenistic Jewish propaganda materials, used in the Dispersion, played a significant role in the way the New Testament codes were written. But "borrowing"—to express indebtedness—is an inadequate term, since the material in the Epistles is after all a *Christian* adaptation and so a new creation to meet current needs.[7a]

CHRISTIANITY AND SLAVERY IN PHILEMON

1. *Occasion and purpose.* This is the shortest of the letters in the Pauline corpus, consisting of only 335 words in the original Greek. It is the only example in the extant Pauline correspondence of what may be termed a personal note, although both E. Lohmeyer and Théo Preiss have argued that the opening, which associates Timothy with Paul and links Philemon to an entire church that assembled in his house, shows that the document is an "epistle," intended for a public hearing. This is confirmed by verse 9, in which the translation "Paul an ambassador" (πρεσβευτής) is to be preferred to "Paul, an old man." In short, this brief Epistle is to be seen not so much as a private letter from Paul as an individual (*Privatmann*) but as an apostolic letter about a personal matter (so U. Wickert) or "a letter to a church, embodying . . . a letter to an individual" (J. Knox). But it remains true that the individual in question (Philemon) is seen as a member of the corporate fellowship of Christians, all of whom have an interest in his decision.

---

[7] P. Carrington, *The Primitive Christian Catechism* (1940), summarized by A. M. Hunter, *Paul and his Predecessors*[2], pp. 128f.; E. G. Selwyn, *First Peter*[2] (1947), pp. 367ff.

[7a] Crouch, *op. cit.,* p. 147. Cf. D. Schroeder, *IDB, Supp. Vol.* (1976), 546f.; E. Schweizer, *Colossians* (ET 1982), "Excursus: The Household Rules," pp. 213-20.

The occasion of the letter may be inferred from its contents, even though some details are obscure. A slave named Onesimus had wronged his owner Philemon, a Christian living at Colossae (cf. the names in vv. 1,2 with Col. 4:9,17), and had run off. Somehow Onesimus had come into contact with Paul, either as a fellow prisoner or because he had sought refuge in Paul's company. In the latter event, he might have benefited from the Athenian law, widespread throughout the Empire, by which a runaway slave could seek asylum in the home of a friend at the family altar. This may illumine Onesimus' desire to seek Paul's protection, though it is difficult to explain verse 13 in view of the further requirement that a delinquent slave must be sold if he refused to return to his former owner.

It is usually assumed that the offense of Onesimus was to have stolen money and absconded (vs. 18). As Roman law required that whoever gave hospitality to a runaway slave was liable to the master for the value of each day's work lost, Paul's promise to stand guarantor (vs. 19) may be an assurance that he will make up the amount incurred by Onesimus' absence from work. We may quote from a letter dated AD 298 which bears on this background:

> Aurelius Sarapammon, called Didymus... to Aurelius.... I appoint you by this my instruction as my representative to journey to the most illustrious Alexandria and search for my slave called... aged about 35 years, with whom you too are acquainted...; and when you find him you are to deliver him up, having the same powers as I should have myself, if present, to... imprison him, chastise him, and to make an accusation before the proper authorities against those who harboured him, and demand satisfaction.[8]

Perhaps Onesimus had come on an errand to Paul and overstayed his time.

In any event, the primary purpose of this letter is to ensure that Philemon will receive back his delinquent slave, although some scholars think Paul was asking Philemon for Onesimus to be returned to him and allowed permanently to remain at his side. Verse 21 carries an undertone of hope that Philemon will agree to the manumission of the slave. The methods by which a slave could gain freedom were familiar; it was common to deposit money in a temple and for the priests of that particular god to officiate in the purchase of freedom. What walls remain of the temple of Apollo at Delphi are covered with the names of slaves whom the god has set free.

To show forgiveness to a criminal slave who had escaped, however, was a revolutionary thought in contrast with the contemporary treatment of runaway slaves for whom punishment could be brutal—imprisonment, flogging, even crucifixion. An extant papyrus from the

---

[8] Grenfell and Hunt, edd., *The Oxyrhynchus Papyri*, 14 (1920), 70–72.

mid-second century BC gives the text of a warrant for the arrest of a slave on the run.[9] Rewards are offered to anyone who finds him and brings him back or who can give information as to his whereabouts. An even higher reward is promised to an informant who says that the slave is lodging with a private person; then not only would the slave be returned but the person who harbored him could be prosecuted and held liable for the loss of the slave's work incurred by his absence from his master.

Against such a background Paul's bold request is carefully prepared for by his approach of gentle language (vv. 8f.) with its tones of entreaty, and leads to an appeal to Philemon's willing cooperation and consent (vs. 14) and the promise to accept any liability he may have incurred (vs. 19).

But the letter does not stay on the surface of a simple request for a slave's life on humane grounds. A good illustration of a plea for clemency on a humanitarian level is seen in the younger Pliny's letters to a certain Sabinianus (Ep. 9.21,24). He intercedes for a young freedman who has sought refuge in Pliny's home and is full of fear at the prospect of his master's wrath. Pliny grants the master's right to be angry but tries to steer Sabinianus in the direction of clemency (mansuetudo), a Stoic virtue, because of the deserter's repentance, amendment of life, and request to be forgiven. Sabinianus is entreated to be benevolent and to forbear his anger, which has been justly aroused. The tenor of Pliny's letter is quite different from Paul's, and the contents are obviously not the same. Paul says nothing about Philemon's "right" to exact vengeance nor does he even contemplate that Onesimus will be punished. This omission militates against the view that Colossians 3:25 is a covert allusion to the case of Onesimus and Philemon: "the man who wrongs will be paid back for the wrong he has done."

Running through Paul's appeal is the current of Christian compassion (vs. 12) and the powerful reminder that Philemon himself is already in debt to Paul (vs. 19b), owing his very salvation under God to the apostle's preaching of the gospel. The characteristic notes are "for love's sake" (vs. 9), "refresh my heart in Christ" (vs. 20), and receiving the truant slave "as you would receive me" (vs. 17). The request ends with a parting shot (vs. 21) that Philemon will go beyond the limit of Paul's desire; and this appeal is reinforced by the prospect of the apostle's visit (vs. 22), surely meant seriously, not (as has been proposed) "in a playful way," or as a "mere jest." Paul genuinely hoped that the idea of his coming would spur Philemon to a ready acceptance of what was asked of him. There is every reason to believe that Philemon did respond; otherwise the letter would not have been preserved at Colossae.

---

[9] For the text see C. F. D. Moule, *Commentary on Colossians and Philemon* (1957), pp. 34–37.

2. *Historical significance.* Paul's letter to Philemon throws unusual light on the Christian conscience regarding the institution of slavery in the ancient world, and so complements and corrects what we find in the so-called *Haustafeln* in the other New Testament Epistles (esp. Col. 3:22—4:1; Eph. 6:5-9; cf. 1 Cor. 7:21-23; 1 Tim. 6:1f.; Titus 2:9f.; 1 Pet. 2:18-21). From these traditional teaching patterns Paul draws the framework of his instruction, but he injects a moralistic tone with his reminders that the slaves are "serving Christ," that the owner has a "master in heaven," God, who deals impartially, and that both slave and owner are bond-servants of Christ. From that last position it is a short step to a relativizing of slavery so that it becomes indifferent (1 Cor. 7:20-24) and has lost its sting (Gal. 3:28; Col. 3:11)—at least insofar as slaves and masters are members of the one household of Christian faith.

a. The striking feature of this Epistle is brought out by Bruce: that it "brings us into an atmosphere in which the institution could only wilt and die."[10] Paul's statement of verse 16 is the Magna Carta of true emancipation and human dignity even if it is true that "the word 'emancipation' seems to be trembling on his lips, and yet he does not once utter it."[11] It is sometimes alleged that since the New Testament never explicitly condemns slavery it is defective at a crucial point. But part of the answer to this is that Paul does not advocate a social philosophy which countenances revolution and violence. Given the social structures of the Roman Empire of Paul's day, slavery could have been overthrown only by violent means; and the apostle will be no party to class hatred or violent methods (cf. Rom. 12:17-21). W. Bousset's assessment is worth quoting: "Christianity would have sunk beyond hope of recovery along with such revolutionary attempts; it might have brought on a new slave rising and been crushed along with it. The time was not ripe for this solution of such difficult questions."[12]

b. Paul's approach to Philemon was voluntaristic, leaving him to settle the matter by an appeal to his conscience. Though Paul could have ordered him to act, he preferred to allow Philemon to respond with a measure of spontaneity and self-determination. What mattered was to secure Philemon's willing consent, not in perfunctory compliance but because he saw his duty as Paul wished him to see it. This "technique of Christian co-operation"[13] was based on the common share both had in the

[10] F. F. Bruce, "St. Paul in Rome (2): The Epistle to Philemon," *BJRL*, 48 (1965-66), 90.
[11] J. B. Lightfoot, *Commentary on Philemon* (1879), p. 321.
[12] W. Bousset, *Die Schriften des Neuen Testaments*, Vol. 2 (1929), p. 101. Crouch's comment is worth pondering: "The struggle against the social order in the name of love becomes in reality a perversion of love when it is clear that the struggle can only lead to suffering for one's neighbor" (*op. cit.*, pp. 106f.).
[13] L. S. Thornton, *The Common Life in the Body of Christ* (1950), p. 39.

realities of the faith and their common life as members of the one body. This feature, represented both in Paul's attitude to Onesimus as a child and a brother (there is no condescending paternalism in Paul's references) and his relations with Philemon as a joint-sharer in the Christian faith and experience, lifts Paul's appeal above the humanitarianism seen in contemporary Stoicism. Paul's conviction is not based on a common humanity shared by slave and master; rather, he writes to a fellow-Christian about a slave who is a fellow-Christian. He employs a Stoic term in verse 8—"what is required" or "fitting"—but quickly modifies it to his own ends.

The note to Philemon, then, while ostensibly about the treatment to be given a law-breaking slave by his master, is more properly thought of as a witness to "life in Christ." Its "teaching" is more about how the Christian life is to be lived in a social context. It aims to construct a "network of new situations and the circuit of new relations which constitute the life in Christ, the life of the Church"[14] and to set the particular issue of Philemon's treatment of Onesimus in that network. The apostolic attitude to slavery as an institution is nowhere defined and, at best, has to be extrapolated from his teaching on the life of Christian believers.

c. Another aspect of this small Epistle has to do with the important place it holds in the reconstruction of Paul's correspondence as adopted by several scholars.[15]

Knox offers two identifications which, if accepted, would modify our understanding of this letter and enlarge our picture of apostolic Christianity. First, he contends that the slave-owner was Archippus, and Philemon was the one whose services Paul sought to enlist in an attempt to persuade Archippus to have compassion on Onesimus. Second, he believes that Onesimus was set free to return as Paul's aide, and later became a second-century bishop of Ephesus. This identification is attested (says Knox) by Ignatius, who in his letter to the Ephesians shows that he had read Philemon and used the same play on words as Paul uses in verse 20. Ignatius writes: "May I always have profit from you (ὀναίμην ὑμῶν), if I am worthy" (*Eph.* 2:2). On this basis, Knox maintains that Onesimus, now a church leader, was responsible for the collection and publication of the Pauline Epistles, including the one to Philemon, in which he had such a personal stake.

Critical opinion on these two hypotheses has not been too favorable. Moule rightly objects that Philemon's name at the head of the list of persons addressed (vs. 1) seems "fatal to the theory that Archippus is primarily the one addressed."[16] Another criticism is of Knox's use of

---

[14] Théo Preiss, "Life in Christ and Social Ethics in the Epistle to Philemon," in *Life in Christ* (ET 1954), p. 41.
[15] For references see J. Knox, *Philemon Among the Letters of Paul*² (1959).
[16] C. F. D. Moule, *Colossians und Philemon*, pp. 16f.

Colossians 4:17. He identifies Archippus' "ministry" as obeying Paul's recommendation and accepting Onesimus, but this is by no means obvious; and the verb Paul uses—*'fulfil* the ministry"—is an active word (so Moule) and the service Archippus had "received" is more probably something which had been "handed on" to him by tradition. Moreover, the delicacy of Paul's appeal in the Epistle to Philemon would be lost if he gave a blunt order to the slave-owner in Colossians 4:17.

A more fundamental difficulty is the inferential nature of the relationship between Philemon and Archippus, for which there is no evidence. The verdict of Dibelius and Greeven is to the point: "Speculation about Archippus' position in Philemon's household is idle."[17] Greeven concentrates further on Knox's translation of verse 10, which is taken to mean that Paul is asking for Onesimus to be permitted to remain; and on Knox's identification of the "letter from Laodicea" (Col. 4:16) with Philemon. The hypothesis is that this "letter from Laodicea" was sent first to Philemon as overseer of the churches in the Lycus Valley, who lived at Laodicea, the main town in the region. Paul wrote to him first of all so that his influence could be brought to bear on Archippus in Colossae. In this way, it is claimed, we can do full justice to Paul's prepositional phrase: "the letter *from* (ἐκ) Laodicea." But no such meaning is required, as we have observed (see earlier, p. 277); and Greeven produces several reasons why this letter to the Laodiceans has not survived.

Bruce is sympathetic to Knox's second point regarding Onesimus, but unpersuaded by his treatment of Archippus. He concedes that the identification of the ex-slave with the Onesimus mentioned by Ignatius as "a man of inexpressible love and your bishop" (*Eph.* 1:3) is possible. However, it may be that this identification stretches the long arm of coincidence too far. A more cautious view is Lightfoot's that the later bishop of Ephesus took the name of Paul's friend. Lightfoot mentions another Onesimus, to whom Melito, bishop of Sardis half a century later still, dedicated his volume of Old Testament extracts (Eusebius *HE* 4.26.13f.). The practice of revering "Onesimus" by taking his name—perhaps because of its symbolic meaning—is not unique.

Even on this moderating view it seems clear that Onesimus was set free and became a prominent figure in the Colossian church. Only then would a later bishop wish to accept his name (if he does have Paul's convert in mind) as a mark of honor. As P. N. Harrison notes, after setting down the views of Knox and Lightfoot, "In either case, St. Paul's letter to Philemon must in fact have produced its desired effect."[18]

We should not fail to note how this Epistle opens a window into Paul's character. He is the true man who is also an apostle, as Chrysostom aptly comments, full of sympathy and concern for a person in dis-

---

[17] M. Dibelius-H. Greeven, *An die Kolosser, Epheser, und Philemon* (1953), p. 103.
[18] P. N. Harrison, "Onesimus and Philemon," *ATR*, 32 (1950), 293.

tress and willing to do all in his power to help, even at some cost (vs. 19). Each of the parties involved was called on to do something difficult: Paul, to deprive himself of Onesimus' service and company; Onesimus, to return to his master whom he had wronged; Philemon, to forgive. As Scott says, "each of the three [is to do] what he was called upon to do as a Christian."[19] Moreover, Paul so identifies himself with both the slave and his master that he can fulfil the office of mediator and meaningfully represent both parties. Our knowledge of Paul would be much poorer had this slender document not been preserved.

THE STATE IN THE NEW TESTAMENT

In discussing this topic we shall be touching on a question often posed in connection with the first Jewish war and fall of Jerusalem (AD 66-70): how far is the New Testament literature historically conditioned? Literature dated prior to that time would reflect a different attitude to the Roman state and the Jewish nation from that taken up after the Jewish war and its outcome.[20] Not that the various writers of New Testament Scripture are in hopeless disagreement about the stance Christians ought to take to the state, but their answers do vary according to historical circumstances, and these were not always the same within the time the New Testament was written. We may isolate four blocks of teaching: Jesus in the Gospels, Paul in Romans, Peter in 1 Peter 2-4, and the Revelation of John. But it is one thing to set down the texts; it is more problematical to try to fit them together into anything like a developing pattern.

1. *The State as a Divine Agency.*

a. *Jesus and Roman authority.* From the little we have in the Gospel tradition it seems clear that Jesus accepted the jurisdiction of Rome and was content to live under it. He called neither for revolt nor for emigration into the wilderness. The appeals of John the Baptist his forerunner (Luke 3:10-18) and of Jesus himself are to be understood historically in terms of the positive and practical summons they gave not to do what the Zealots wanted and the Sadducees feared. Jesus' teaching was in line with the Pharisees' belief that the issue should be left in the hands of God, who would bring in the kingdom in his own time and way. He proclaimed the nearness of that reign of God as a spiritual reality to be entered by the commitment of discipleship and trustful

---

[19] C. A. A. Scott, *St. Paul—Man and Teacher* (1936), p. 59.
[20] This is so despite J. A. T. Robinson's bold attempt to place the entire New Testament literature in the time before AD 70; *Redating the New Testament* (1976). Indeed, the divergencies within the literature relating to the Christians' attitude to Rome perhaps go a long way to making Robinson's thesis untenable. On the "shock wave" caused by the destruction of Jerusalem and the Temple, see N. Perrin, *The New Testament: An Introduction* (1974; rev. by D. C. Duling, 1982), pp. 40f., though he overemphasizes the importance of the event.

obedience to God as rightful king, but without denying that this was compatible with living under Roman rule (*NTF*, Vol. 1, 95–97).

Mark 12:13–17, the familiar question about paying tribute to Caesar, is a puzzling pericope, but of great value for understanding Jesus' mind. The traditional view is that he distinguished between the two kingdoms and stated that there was no conflict of loyalties between them. In Schmid's words: "While paying the tax imposed by the emperor, one can still give to God what belongs to him, namely, unreserved personal dedication. . . . The enemies find that they cannot accuse Jesus, either of being a friend of Rome and a traitor to his people—thereby destroying his reputation—or of being a rebel against Rome."[21] S. G. F. Brandon, however, uses this account as the linch-pin of his theory that Mark has redacted an original story which proclaimed Jesus as fervent supporter of the Zealots who refused to endorse the tribute-money as part of his general stance of revolt against the occupying Roman power in God's land.[22] Writing in Rome in the aftermath of Titus' victory, Mark altered the story to soften this declaration and thereby to show that Christians are not to be charged with the sort of sedition that brought Judaism to its knees before the Roman legions.

Brandon has few followers in this piece of interesting speculation. He makes much of the idea of Jesus as a patriot who could never have been silent in the face of Roman militarism and its possession of Palestine, God's land. But it is just as conceivable that Jesus was a patriot more of the order of Jeremiah than Nahum, and that his advice was no more a counsel of betrayal than the misunderstood oracles of Jeremiah who advised against resistance to the Babylonians.[22a]

b. *Paul in Romans 13* followed the Gospel tradition, seeing no incompatibility between devotion to God and loyalty to the Roman state, "the powers that be." How far what he said must be seen against the background of Claudius' expulsion of Jews "on account of continual quarreling at the instigation of Chrestus" is, as we have seen, hard to determine, but it surely bore on this statement of praise of the Roman authorities.

Moreover, Paul's attitude harmonizes with his own experience throughout his travels in the Roman world. Everywhere he had encountered the helpful and just side of the Roman government.[23] Acts 18:17 means on this reckoning that Gallio "is commended for his impartiality,

---

[21] J. Schmid, *The Gospel According to Mark* (ET 1968), pp. 220f.

[22] On Brandon's works see Martin, *Mark: Evangelist and Theologian*, pp. 75–79; further M. Hengel, *Was Jesus a Revolutionist?* (ET 1971); A. Richardson *The Political Christ* (1974); and C. F. D. Moule and E. Bammel, edd., *Jesus and the Politics of his Day* (1984).

[22a] Prophetic spirits can equally cherish a fervent patriotic loyalty to their country, as in the modern example of the Russian martyr Georgi Vins, *Three Generations of Suffering* (1976).

[23] 2 Thess. 2:6f. is often taken to refer directly to the Roman authorities who restrain evil tendencies in society; see C. H. Giblin, *The Threat to Faith* (1967).

not blamed for his indifference to spiritual matters."[24] Paul writes from the standpoint of a Roman citizen within the Empire, which was pledged to protect and uphold his rights through the judicial process. No wonder he sees it as altogether praiseworthy that the powers of Rome be respected and preserved, for his own work and the general progress of the gospel were immensely aided by all that Rome and the *Pax Romana* stood for.[23a]

c. *First Peter* echoes the same admonitions. The writer issues a call to submission and a reminder that the governing powers are part of God's providence for the maintenance of good order in society (2:13-17). Chapter 4 speaks of persecutions which are hard to identify. Presumably (if the letter is a unity—see below, pp. 339f., 346) the persecuting agency is not the state but the local populace, from whose wrath the state may well be expected to protect Christians. This may be a sign of an early date for the Epistle, as we shall observe when we examine it in its setting.

2. *The State as Persecutor.* In the 60s the church saw the state put on a new face in its attitude to Christians. Till then, Rome had viewed Christianity as a species of Judaism, and the church came under the sheltering umbrella of Judaism's status as *religio licita,* a religion permitted to exist by law within the pluralist tolerance of the Empire. But with the separation of church and synagogue (leading to initial breaches in AD 66-70) Rome withdrew that legal protection. Nero in AD 64/65 capitalized on the unprotected status of Christians, and harried them at Rome as anti-social sedition-mongers (see above, pp. 140f.). Luke combats this reputation for political involvement in his two books, and Peter voices warnings that Christians in Pontus should allow no ground for this suspicion (1 Pet. 2:15; 4:16).

The Revelation to John is a sustained piece of hortatory moral teaching (*Mahnrede*), cast in apocalyptic guise which certifies that the future lies with the cause of Christ, not the persecuting Roman power, and encourages afflicted believers to submit to their present trials by faithful confession, suffering, and martyrdom. Again no call to revolution is issued, even though the evil forces of the Dragon, the Beast, and the false prophet are tyrannical and anti-Christ.[25] The cry is for the vindication of the martyrs (Rev. 6:10) before God more than for personal vengeance, even if the final collapse of anti-Christian forces in the Em-

---

[23a] See M. Hengel, *Christ and Power* (1977), pp. 34f.

[24] F. F. Bruce, *The Acts of the Apostles* (1952), p. 348; and *New Testament History,* pp. 298-300. Bruce comments further: "The mere fact that Gallio refused to take up the case against Paul may reasonably be held to have facilitated the spread of Christianity during the last years of Claudius and the earlier years of his successor"; "Christianity under Claudius," *BJRL,* 44 (1962), 325f.

[25] H. M. Gale, "Paul's View of the State,"*Interpretation,* 6 (1952), 409-14, is germane here, for there are parts of Paul's teaching that suggest a teaching on the way the state can become demonic when it aspires to absolute authority (cf. 2 Thess. 2:1-12).

pire is fervently hoped for and is spoken of as having happened (Rev. 18:16—19:3).

3. *The State as Cultural Pace-Setter*. How far does the New Testament share in the culture-patterns of its milieu? There is little material to press into service for answering this query, but we can risk some generalizations.

a. The chief factor in the mentality and spirituality of New Testament people is the Jewish heritage with which they begin to formulate the gospel for society. This implies a distinct attitude to the arts, literature, recreation, work, and learning in general.

b. Paul and the author of Hebrews stand out as equal members of the larger world of Hellenistic society, the one through his connection with Tarsus and Hellenistic Judaism, the other through Philo and the Alexandrian tradition. Yet both writers are Jews at heart, however much they are open to the influences of the Graeco-Roman world around them. To a lesser extent, the authors of the Third and Fourth Gospels show an awareness of the extra-Palestinian outreach of the gospel, and their style is appreciative of cultural interests in a non-religious sense. Luke, in particular, keeps an eye on appealing to Theophilus throughout. He shows obvious versatility in combining a familiarity with rabbinic tradition (e.g., in the speeches in Acts) and a wider acquaintance with Roman administration and courtly ethos (e.g., Acts 24–26).

c. The polarization of Christianity and culture is still several decades in the future at the time the canon closes. There is as yet nothing of the tension we find in the two extremes represented by Justin (*c.* 150) and Tertullian (*c.* 200).[26] The former affirms that "those who live according to reason are Christians, even though they are accounted atheists. Such were Socrates and Heraclitus" (*Apol.* 1.46.1–4). The latter opposes this liberalism in his familiar question: "What is there in common between Athens and Jerusalem? Between the Academy and the Church?" (*De praescr. haer.* 7). In a large measure this difference can be accounted for by the opposite backgrounds of these two men; and the issue at stake includes the nature of Christian conversion and the sense in which the gospel was continuous with contemporary culture or marked a clean break with it.[27]

---

[26] On the apologists (esp. Tertullian) see K. Aland, "The Relation Between Church and State in Early Times," *JTS,* 19 n.s. (1968), 115–27.

[27] On the ancient setting of the term "conversion" see A. D. Nock, *Conversion* (1933); on the gospel and culture see further H. R. Niebuhr, *Christ and Culture* (1950). See too M. Hengel, *Christ and Power,* pp. 38f., for Christian attitudes to social institutions; also W. A. Meeks, "The Social Context of Pauline Theology," *Interpretation,* 36 (1982), 266–77, and his *The First Urban Christians* (1983). Also G. Theissen, *The Social Setting of Pauline Christianity* (ET 1982).

CHAPTER TWENTY-FOUR

Gnostic Motifs in Paul

Two technical terms which figure prominently in recent discussion of the New Testament are "gnosticism" and "early catholicism." In this chapter we shall sketch, in bold strokes, the former; and in chapter 29 we shall use the Epistles of Jude and Second Peter as a test-case for understanding the latter.

THE GNOSTIC MYTH

Gnosis is a descriptive title for an attitude to life and interpretation of human existence expressed in certain literary sources in antiquity.[1] By nature and composition *gnosis* (this word is preferable to "gnosticism," which may suggest something formalized and rigid)[2] is syncretistic, drawing into a common orbit ideas from Greek thought and Oriental cosmology and mythology, "from the highest philosophical mysticism to the lowest forms of magic."[3] Its basis is expressed in terms of human bondage and liberation. The soul is held captive by matter and placed under the tyranny of outside cosmic forces alien to its true life. Release comes in self-knowledge (hence the name) and an awakening to the real meaning and dimension of life. Hence the gnostic literature is punctuated with calls to become self-aware and arouse oneself from sleep, lethargy, and subservience to alien forces in the universe.[4]

---

[1] The starting point defined by H. Jonas, *The Gnostic Religion* (ET 1958), p. 80. He emphasizes its fundamental dualism, by which God and the world were separated and treated as mutually hostile, and its doctrine of man as fallen and enslaved, yet who can be saved only by *gnōsis*—esoteric knowledge.

[2] Much confusion would have been avoided if this terminological distinction had been observed. R. Bultmann, *Theology of the New Testament*, Vol. 1, §15: "Gnostic Motifs," speaks of *gnōsis* where the ET renders "gnosticism"; cf. R. McL. Wilson, *Gnosis and the New Testament* (1968), pp. 8f., on the importance of using terms clearly either descriptively or derivatively.

[3] R. McL. Wilson, *The Gnostic Problem* (1958), p. 69.

[4] See, e.g., the *Poimandres* tract of the Hermetic literature; repr. in C. K. Barrett, *The New Testament Background: Selected Documents,* pp. 80–90; and R. M. Grant, ed., *Gnosticism: An Anthology* (1961), pp. 211–19.

This existential summons is set in the framework of a myth, a dramatic story of the descent to this world of a heavenly figure who becomes enmeshed in matter and darkness.[5] He is successful in his mission, which is partly revelatory—he announces himself as emissary of the high God—and partly redemptive—he gathers a body of persons enlightened with special, saving knowledge, who allow his call to activate the sparks of light in their mortal bodies and are thereby set free from matter and cosmic fears. The leading figure in this drama, referred to as "original man,"[6] returns to heaven as a "redeemed redeemer," thereby opening a way as forerunner by which his followers at death may in turn follow. Part of this return is through daemonic regions in the sub-lunar atmosphere and they need to *know* (again the name derived from the verb γινώσκειν) the secret formulas which constitute the passwords on their upward flight-path. The purpose of this heavenward flight is to assemble all those whose individual sparks of light may be united to form a composite whole. This marks the end of the world. The judgment follows, and the darkened world returns to its original chaos.

Man in this present world is a picture of homelessness and fear, yearning for absorption into the divine. His body, composed of matter, prevents the sparks of light from being released and winging their way to God. But when the call of the revealer-redeemer comes, his liberation begins and the devotee shows disregard for the physical body either by denial of its appetites or an abandonment to them. Either way the body is treated as irrelevant, and indeed this present world has no abiding significance. We may spell out a few fundamental notions for the gnostic understanding of man and his redemption:

1. The body is like a prison (σῶμα-σῆμα is the Orphic tag).[7]

2. The true self is capable of being aroused.

3. Redemption is a private affair between the soul and God. There is no community aspect to the gnostic religion and no cultus.

4. There is a fundamental dualism by which God and the world are pitted against each other, the one alien to the other.

5. Much is made of astrology. The stars are seen as hostile forces in the universe, the habitat of spirit-forces whose laws of necessity

[5] The account of this "myth" in W. Schmithals, *Gnosticism in Corinth*, pp. 32ff., supplements the older presentations of W. Manson, *Jesus the Messiah* (1943), pp. 174ff.; S. Mowinckel, *He that Cometh* (ET 1956), pp. 420ff. For critical scrutiny see M. Black, "The Pauline Doctrine of the Second Adam," *SJT*, 7 (1954), 177f.; J. M. Creed, "The Heavenly Man," *JTS*, 26 o.s. (1925), 113–36; R. McL. Wilson, *The Gnostic Problem*, pp. 218ff.; E. M. Yamauchi, *Pre-Christian Gnosticism* (1973), pp. 39–43, 163ff.; F. F. Bruce, "Myth and History," in *History, Criticism and Faith*, ed. C. Brown (1976), pp. 79–100. See now for an up-to-date report E. M. Yamauchi, "Pre-Christian Gnosticism, the New Testament and Nag Hammadi in Recent Debate," *Themelios*, 10 (1984), 22–27.

[6] See C. H. Kraeling, *Anthropos and Son of Man. A Study in the Religious Syncretism of the Hellenistic Orient* (1927).

[7] F. C. Burkitt, *Church and Gnosis* (1932), pp. 33ff. The phrase is picked up in Plato, *Gorgias* 493A.

(ἀνάγκη) and determination (εἱμαρμένη) control human life and make it a plaything of luck (τύχη) and fate (see above, pp. 31f.).

6. The meaninglessness of life in this world follows directly from all this. That explains man's great need. Modern expositions of ancient gnosticism find the most suitable term in *Daseinsverständnis* ("understanding of human existence"), which is Martin Heidegger's term for modern man's plight.

DEMYTHOLOGIZING AND GNOSTICISM

Bultmann's enterprise of "demythologizing" the New Testament begins with the assumption that Paul in particular shared the gnostic world-view as a Hellenistic Jew.[8] When he became a Christian, he faced the need to make his message intelligible to Greek congregations. Demythologizing enters the picture at this juncture. Bultmann sees this process as a hermeneutical tool by the use of which it can be shown that "what Paul intended to say" (his phrase) is relevant to modern man (who is made in the image of Heidegger). But this aspect of Bultmann's thought is not our immediate concern, for we are more interested in Bultmann as a student of Paul and the *kerygma*.

It is not difficult to see how the myth of the redeemer outlined above could be discerned in the background of Paul's message, especially in his letters to Corinth, Galatia, and Colossae. For W. Schmithals the presence of gnosticizing Christians was the immediate problem at Corinth, where the heretics were promoting a cult of a heavenly aeon Christ distinct from the human Jesus of the gospel tradition (1 Cor. 12:3) and imagining themselves as already risen with Christ into a new life here and now.

This notion of a gnosticizing group at Corinth becomes for Schmithals an Ariadne's thread running through the entire labyrinthine correspondence with this church. We are led hereby to an understanding of many of the problems of the church there. The resurrection belief of certain Corinthians was based on the premise that the only acceptable eschatology was a realized one (1 Cor. 15:12), and the experience of the kingdom was also related to the here and now (1 Cor. 4:8). This, too, explains the strange marriage customs at Corinth (1 Cor. 7), where celibacy and spiritual marriage were practiced on the assumption that Christians were living in the new order in which earthly ordinances did not apply. Conversely, some gnostics in the church struck out on the other line, disregarding all moral distinctions (1 Cor. 5), sitting loose to moral demands (1 Cor. 6,10) in preference to the enjoyment of

---

[8] Similarly, Bultmann understands the Fourth Gospel as the evangelist's attempt to refute the gnostic redeemer myth, while at the same time he shares its presuppositions of a dualistic universe and a revealer-redeemer *persona; The Gospel of John* (ET 1971).

ecstatic experiences (1 Cor. 14:12). Paul's reply denied at its base this teaching of a realized kingdom and emphasized the "eschatological reserve" of the so-called "not yet" element that awaits fulfilment in the future kingdom of God. At the same time, he underscored the ethical implications of the Christian life and the cross "side" of the *kerygma* (1 Cor. 1,2; 2 Cor. 4).

What occurred among the Hellenistic Christians at Corinth was perhaps the most ambitious attempt to turn a Pauline church into a gnostic conventicle, according to Schmithals' reconstruction of the data. But not everyone is persuaded that this reading of the evidence is correct.[9] C. K. Barrett maintains that Paul's opponents in the church were liberal Jews who acted as agents for the conservative Jewish Christian pillar apostles in Jerusalem.[10] Even those who continue to associate the Corinthian false teachers with a gnostic world-view are cautious about giving a technical sense to the term "gnostic."[11] The assumptions that underlie Schmithals' presentation have been negatively assessed by Yamauchi.[12]

For Paul's alleged indebtedness to the gnostic myth of a saved Savior, we refer to Bultmann's treatment of "gnostic motifs."[13] The chief themes he appeals to are dualistic references to Satan (2 Cor. 4:4; cf. Eph. 2:2) and evil angels (in Col., Eph., 1 Cor. 15), setting up the contrast between darkness and light; the fall of creation (Rom. 8:20ff.), with the consequence that man becomes enslaved (Gal. 4:3,9); Christ's achievement of deliverance in terms of his involvement in man's lot (especially Phil. 2:6–11) and his return to the realm of light (Eph. 4:8–10) after his victory over the evil powers (Col. 2:15). Henceforth it is Christ who fills the *plērōma* (the inter-space of the universe between the high God and mankind) and makes access to God possible.

GNOSIS IN THE NEW TESTAMENT

We may now summarize the evidence for gnostic elements in the New Testament and assess these.

[9] J. C. Hurd, Jr., *The Origin of 1 Corinthians* (1965), explains the Epistle without recourse to gnostics; see earlier, p. 173; and D. J. Doughty, "The Presence and Future of Salvation in Corinth," *ZNTW*, 66 (1975), 61–90. H. E. W. Turner, *The Pattern of Christian Truth* (1954), p. 69, suggested that the background to the freewheeling morality at Corinth was that of life in any seaport. But see the cogent position advocated by A. C. Thiselton, "Realized Eschatology at Corinth," *NTS*, 24 (1977–78), 510–26.

[10] C. K. Barrett, "Paul's Opponents in II Corinthians," *NTS*, 17 (1971), 233–54; and "PSEUDAPOSTOLOI (2 Cor. 11,13)," in *Mélanges B. Rigaux*, pp. 377–96.

[11] E.g., H. Conzelmann, *An Outline of the Theology of the New Testament* (ET 1969), pp. 187ff.; and "On the Analysis of the Confessional Formula in 1 Corinthians 15:3–5," *Interpretation*, 20 (1966), 24; and B. A. Pearson, *The Pneumatikos-Psychikos Terminology in 1 Corinthians* (1973).

[12] E. M. Yamauchi, *Pre-Christian Gnosticism*, pp. 39ff.

[13] R. Bultmann, *Theology of the New Testament*, Vol. 1, pp. 164ff.; for the implications of this discussion see his "New Testament and Mythology," in *Kerygma and Myth*, ed. H.-W. Bartsch (ET 1953), pp. 1–16.

1. We have to reckon with the possibility that Paul was using the language and terminology of his opponents, who may well have been infected with a syncretistic type of religion in which Christianity of the Pauline type was one ingredient.[14] This seems clearly the case in his controversy with the Corinthian deviationists and in the polemical Epistle to the Colossians (and may underlie Phil. 3 and Ephesians, too). But he insists in his Christology and soteriology on many aspects which are not gnostic. Central here is the historical Jesus, who became truly incarnate and lived a human life (Rom. 8:3; Phil. 2:7 safeguard the divine nature),[15] died a veritable death on the cross (Phil. 2:8, perhaps Paul's addition to an earlier statement which did not accentuate the cross enough; cf. Col. 1:20, appending the idea that "peace" is made "by the blood of his cross"), and whose factual resurrection points forward to a future resurrection for his people (1 Cor. 15). These seem to be important "non-gnostic motifs" to be set alongside Bultmann's exposition.[16]

2. Evidence for direct connections between second-century classical gnostic systems of Marcion (c. AD 140 in Rome), Valentinus (135–160), Basilides (120–145), and the first-century church is debatable. The central issue is one of priority: which came first, gnosticism or primitive Christianity? Obviously, the New Testament antedates the classical gnostic systems, but the question is really whether the gnostic world-view is a pre-Christian and independent phenomenon and whether the New Testament could have been decisively influenced by it. Two further comments may be made. First, Harnack's famous discussion enshrining the dictum that later gnosticism represented an "acute Hellenization of Christianity" is one-sided and ignores the roots of gnosticism in the Judaism of the Greek world, as R. M. Grant argues.[17] Second, evidence

---

[14] See R. Bultmann, *Primitive Christianity in its Contemporary Setting* (ET 1956), pp. 175ff. The reverse procedure set in later as second-century Gnostics transposed Paul's writings to fit into their systems, as E. H. Pagels, *The Gnostic Paul* (1975), has shown.

[15] I have discussed the apparent docetic tendency in these verses in *Carmen Christi: Phil. 2:5–11* (1967), pp. 202ff.

[16] Critics of Bultmann's use of gnostic terminology to interpret Paul's message (e.g., in *Primitive Christianity*, pp. 180–208) have faulted him for overlooking those elements in Paul's gospel that are not the product of syncretism; cf., e.g., A. Richardson, *An Introduction to the Theology of the New Testament* (1958), pp. 141–44, based on a determined effort to stay within the framework of biblical historicality (p. 143); and M. Hengel, *The Son of God* (ET 1976), p. 90, expressing the uniqueness of the eschatological saving event in Jesus.

[17] A. Harnack, *History of Dogma*, 1 (ET 1897), 226; cf. F. C. Burkitt, *op. cit.*, pp. 27f., who thought of the second-century gnostic teachers as Christians who wished to make the message acceptable to and understood by their contemporaries. See, by contrast, R. M. Grant, *Gnosticism and Early Christianity* (1959), esp. in the light of recent discoveries from the ancient world of Jewish sectarianism (see Wilson, *Gnosis and the New Testament*, Ch. 1). For a counter-position see H. Jonas, "Response to G. Quispel," in *The Bible and Modern Scholarship*, ed. J. P. Hyatt (1965), pp. 279–93. On the general question, see *The Origins of Gnosticism.* Messina Colloquium, ed. U. Bianchi (1967); and *Gnosis und das Neues Testament*, ed. K.-W. Tröger (1973).

from the Nag Hammadi texts in Upper Egypt gives the impression of a syncretistic religious philosophy current in a milieu contemporary with, yet uninfluenced by, the New Testament writings (especially the *Apocalypse of Adam* from Codex V of the texts).[18] So the question of gnosticism as a pre-Christian phenomenon is wide open—though this does not directly settle the bigger concern of dependence.[19]

3. There is a danger in this discussion of fitting the New Testament to a Procrustean bed of modern philosophy, too readily finding a direct link between the Hellenistic man and "existential" man of the twentieth century. Bultmann's case rests partly on what he envisages his "modern man" to be. He never seems to be an "ordinary Christian" (as J. Munck says against Bultmann),[20] but rather a composite man constructed from elements drawn from Augustine, Luther, Kierkegaard, and Heidegger.

[18] On this text, see G. W. MacRae, "The Coptic Gnostic Apocalypse of Adam," *Heythrop Journal*, 6 (1965), 27ff., who sees here a redemption myth unaffected by the Christian story of Jesus; R. McL. Wilson, *Gnosis and the New Testament*, pp. 138f., who believes the text betrays dependence on the New Testament; Yamauchi, *op. cit.*, pp. 107–15, who similarly doubts whether the document refers to non-Christian and pre-Christian gnosticism. On the wider issues see J. M. Robinson, "The Coptic Gnostic Library Today," *NTS*, 14 (1968–69), 356–401. The texts are available in English in *The Nag Hammadi Library*, ed. J. M. Robinson (1977).

[19] The historical question is discussed at length by Yamauchi, *op. cit.*, who concludes that we have no extant evidence yet to hand of gnostic texts anterior to the New Testament, a judgment that would not command universal acceptance. Cf. R. Bergmeier, "Quellen vorchristlicher Gnosis?" in *Tradition und Glaube: Festschrift K. G. Kuhn* (1971), pp. 200–20. Yet an admission of evidence for pre-Christian gnosis in no way settles the matter of whether the New Testament was decisively influenced by or dependent on these thought-forms. And even then, it is moot whether Paul and John shared the vocabulary and ideological concepts current in their day as a way of communicating with their contemporaries or as a device of taking over the slogans and watchwords of opponents in the churches and filling them with a new distinctive content.

[20] J. Munck, "The New Testament and Gnosticism," in *Current Issues in New Testament Interpretation*, edd. G. F. Snyder and W. Klassen (1962), pp. 224–38.

PART SIX

Other New Testament Writings

As there were brave men before Agamemnon, so there were Christians before Paul came on the scene. As contemporaries and immediate successors they flourished as church leaders in the apostolic communities. Some of their names we know from Paul himself—Apollos, Barnabas, Aquila, Priscilla, Peter. There are other names known from the Acts of the Apostles, like Timothy. But it is remarkable that little evidence survives that gives independent attestation of these names. Instead we have to place a higher value on what does survive in the epistolary writings of the New Testament even if tantalizing issues of authorship and provenance still haunt the inquirer and promise no final solution.

There are several blocks of epistolary literature outside the Pauline library. First, there is a document associated with the apostle Peter. Second, an anonymous document, called the Epistle to the Hebrews, reflects some special circumstances of its origin and its readership, who were presumably Jewish-Christians of the Dispersion. Also in this tradition, though ostensibly set on a Palestinian stage, is the letter attributed to James. Third, there are parts of the New Testament linked with the name of "John." Whether he is the apostle, son of Zebedee, or a disciple of his also called John and surnamed "the Elder," is an open question. He writes several letters to deal with theological, practical, and ecclesiastical concerns in the churches of his constituency. The Apocalypse, as its name implies, belongs to a different literary genre, and was written by a person also called John to encourage and sustain the faith of persecuted Christians in Roman Asia. Finally the letters called 2 Peter and Jude enable us in the final chapter of this part to look at trends in early Christianity as it moved into institutionalization and a more intense struggle with heresy. The term applied to this period is "early catholicism," to distinguish it from the age of the apostles.

CHAPTER TWENTY-FIVE

Christianity According to First Peter

TITLE AND ATTESTATION

Since the eighteenth century the letters of James, Jude, First and Second Peter, and First, Second and Third John have been designated Catholic Epistles. The term "catholic," meaning universal, suggests that these letters were directed to the Christian church as a whole, not to specific congregations or to certain individuals.

Early Christian references to this block of New Testament literature are interesting. Eusebius, for example, records that "Themiso [a heretic]... ventured to write a catholic letter (καθολικὴν ... ἐπιστολήν) in imitation of the apostle" (*HE* 5.18.5). He also speaks of "John the apostle, whose are the Gospel according to John and the Catholic Epistle" (7.25.7) and "the Epistle of Jude... which is one of the seven Catholic Epistles" (2.23.25).

In the case of First Peter, however, the designation is less appropriate, since the definite geographical area of the first recipients is given (1:1), and they are referred to throughout as a group of Christian congregations facing a set of specific circumstances, marked off from the rest of Christendom scattered through the ancient world (5:9).

These first readers lived in Pontus and Bithynia, on the coast of the Black Sea, at the northeast end of the world of New Testament times, in a district later known to us from the correspondence between the emperor Trajan and the governor Pliny (AD 111–112).[1]

Eusebius places the letter among the ὁμολογούμενα, the acknowledged parts of the New Testament canon of his day (*HE* 3.25.1–3). There is no suggestion that its authenticity was ever challenged in the early church. The first witness to its authorship comes in 2 Peter 3:1, though this identification is open to doubt, since the addressees of the

---

[1] On this correspondence see E. C. Kennedy, *Martial and Pliny* (1952) *ad* 10.96; further on the establishment of Christianity in Asia, see B. H. Streeter, *The Primitive Church* (1929), Ch. 4.

two Epistles are not the same.[2] Valuable attestation for it comes in 1 Clement and in Polycarp, who quotes from it several times in his *Letter to the Philippians*. But there is no explicit ascription of the document to the apostle Peter until Irenaeus (*c*. AD 185) (*Adv. Haer.* 4.9.2; 4.16.5; 5.7.2).

AUTHORSHIP

1. The internal evidence offers presumptive witness to apostolic authorship (1:1; 5:1). The writer claims to be an eyewitness of the Lord's passion and possibly his resurrection and/or transfiguration, which he sees as a foretaste of the glory of his *parousia*. In E. G. Selwyn's words, the "impression of eyewitness runs through the Epistle, and gives it a distinctive character."[3] There are impressive correspondences between Peter's language in Acts and in this Epistle:[4]

a. The character of God as the impartial judge is described by the Greek ά-προσωπολήμπτης, sometimes rendered by the English phrase "no respecter of persons," which is found in Acts 10:34 and 1 Peter 1:17 (with slight grammatical variation). The term is, however, a common one in other contexts (Rom. 2:11; Col. 3:25; James 2:1, 9; Polycarp, *Phil.* 6.1).

b. What has been called the "stoneship" of Christ[5] is attested by Acts 4:10f. and 1 Peter 2:7f., both of which draw on Psalm 118:22. Although the Pauline literature also appeals to this Scripture proof-text on Christ as the rejected and exalted stone (Rom. 9:32f.; Eph. 2:20), the reference is not so explicitly to Psalm 118 as in these two sections in Acts and 1 Peter.[6]

c. The centrality of the Lord's "name" in Acts and 1 Peter cannot be accidental. The idiom is Semitic—"name" standing for the person involved. But the association of "name" with persecution (see below, p. 333) in both Acts and 1 Peter is striking. This comes to the fore in Acts 3:6,16; 4:10,12; 5:41; 10:43, all of which have Peter playing a distinct role, and in the epistle at 4:14,16.

d. Peter's speech in Acts 3:18,24 sets great store by how God has

---

[2] Th. Zahn, *Introduction to the New Testament*, Vol. 2 (ET 1909), p. 202; cf. J. A. T. Robinson, *Redating the New Testament*, p. 195. In *Can We Trust the New Testament?* (1977), p. 67, Robinson suggests that 2 Pet. 3:1 refers to Jude's Epistle.

[3] E. G. Selwyn, *The First Epistle of St. Peter* (1946), p. 28.

[4] *Ibid.*, pp. 33–36.

[5] A. M. Hunter, *Paul and his Predecessors*[2], pp. 62,87. The expression alludes to Cyprian's collection of biblical references under the rubric "*quod idem et lapis dictus sit*"—"that he is also called a stone" (*Testimonies* 2.16).

[6] C. L. Mitton, *The Epistle to the Ephesians* (1951), Ch. 17, maintains that the author of 1 Peter had read Ephesians, but the correspondences are none too close, and the hypothesis of a common fund of tradition on which several New Testament authors (including Luke) drew is more favorably regarded. See E. G. Selwyn, *op. cit.*, additional note E, and pp. 461f.

fulfilled the Old Testament prophecies in sending the Messiah. An identical position in regard to messianic prophecy is taken in 1 Peter 1:10–12.

There are some further items of common interest which unite the Peter of the Gospel story and the author of our letter. Of these the following are the most noteworthy.[7]

a. The allusion to the "testing of faith" (1:7) naturally suggests a reference to the apostle's own experience in Luke 22:31.

b. His own recovery and re-commissioning (implied in the four-fold Gospel tradition) may be read in his poignant words of 5:10.

c. The shepherd-sheep picture (2:25; 5:2ff.) recalls a similar depiction in both the synoptic (Mark 14:27f.) and Johannine accounts (John 21:15ff.), with special application to Peter (Mark 16:7).

d. Praise of humility as necessary for Christian experience and living is present in both the explicit teaching of the Epistle (5:5) and the dramatic action-parable of the Fourth Gospel (John 13:1ff.), in which Peter is the interlocutor. The Greek verb "to clothe" (ἐγκομβοῦσθαι, in 5:5) calls to mind a person attiring himself in a garment tied to his body, reminiscent of Jesus' wrapping the towel used by slaves around himself before washing the disciples' feet.[8] This incidental detail suggests that Peter is consciously reminiscing in his later writing.

F. W. Beare argues against Selwyn's inferences on the ground that John 21 has influenced the writer of 1 Peter, who has read the Fourth Gospel and stands consciously under its influence. He sees the links of common languages and common ideas as literary not personal.[9]

Beare denies that 2:21–25 is evidence of a personal reminiscence; he sees here a writer "whose knowledge of the Passion is literary and theological . . . since it is framed wholly in phrases of the Second Isaiah and the Apostle Paul; there is not a shred of personal reminiscence."[10] The explanation, drawing on Old Testament prophecy, must face the question of what impulse prompted the writer to cite the servant passage (only rarely attested in the New Testament) if not a conscious recall of Jesus' bearing as a harmless lamb led to the slaughter. That Paul makes so little use of the servant of God prophecy in Isaiah 53

---

[7] For a full discussion see R. H. Gundry, "'Verba Christi' in 1 Peter," NTS, 13 (1966–67), 336–50 (esp. 345ff.); and E. Best's reply, "1 Peter and the Gospel Tradition," NTS, 16 (1969–70), 95–113, denying that parallels with the Gospel logia require the thesis of Petrine reminiscences. See in turn Gundry, "Further Verba on Verba Christi in First Peter," Biblica, 55 (1974), 211–32; he concludes that 1 Peter was dictated by Peter in Rome and is "peppered with frequent allusions to dominical sayings and incidents which were both authentic and possessive of special interest to him."

[8] Cf. the happy rendering of TEV: "Put on the apron of humility, to serve one another." On the history of the word see J. N. D. Kelly, A Commentary on the Epistles of Peter and Jude (Harper-Black, 1969), p. 206.

[9] F. W. Beare, The First Epistle of Peter[3] (1970), p. 191.

[10] Ibid. Cf. E. Best, loc. cit.; and 1 Peter (NCB, 1971), p. 54.

suggests that the author of 1 Peter is not indebted to him at this point.

2. On a broader front, we may ask on what grounds Petrine authorship is denied.

a. The similarities of language between this Epistle and the Pauline literature have been observed. Ephesians is especially important here, in view of the close parallels between the two documents. C. L. Mitton sought to place Ephesians later than 1 Peter because of its alleged dependence on it. More recent study has remarked that the common matter relates mainly to liturgical interest (e.g., 1 Pet. 1:3ff.; Eph. 1:3ff.) and that the closeness of the parallels may best be accounted for by the access of both writers to a common fund of liturgical and catechetical material.[11]

b. The literary style of 1 Peter has led some to hesitate to attribute it to a Galilean fisherman. It is undeniable that some of the vocabulary is classical.[12] The Old Testament is cited in the Septuagint version. Could one known to be an "uneducated common man" (Acts 4:13) have written in the style and manner of these chapters? Two points may be made in connection with this doubt. First, C. H. Dodd suggests that Acts 4:13 probably indicates no more than that Peter and John were unversed in rabbinic lore; the Greek terms there, he submits, represent the rabbinic *bôr w^ehedîyôt,* meaning that the apostles were ignorant of Torah in the eyes of official Judaism.[13] They say nothing about the apostles' cultural background or linguistic expertise. Hence, Beare's verdict that the apostles were "not merely 'unlearned,' but actually 'illiterate'" is surely an exaggeration.[14] Second, O. Cullmann has argued that Peter's village of Bethsaida (John 1:44) was cosmopolitan and open to cultural influences which may well have equipped him for the task of letter-composition.[15]

Moreover, the polished literary format and style of this document could be attributed to the work of an amanuensis. The Epistle itself, it is proposed, says as much in 5:12: "By Silvanus, a faithful brother as I regard him, I have written briefly to you." E. G. Selwyn uses this text to defend the idea that Silvanus was the real author of the letter.[16] He argues that Silvanus (= Silas, referred to in Acts) wrote out Peter's teaching and couched it in his own language and terminology.

However, the argument for Silvanus as amanuensis is not clearcut, since its proponents find a connection between 1 Peter and 1 Thes-

---

[11] C. L. Mitton, *op. cit.* J. Coutts, "Ephesians I. 3–14 and 1 Peter I. 3–12," *NTS,* 3 (1956–57), 115–27, finds traces of a common liturgical prayer (baptismal) underlying these passages. See too E. Best, *Commentary,* pp. 28–36.

[12] Cf. McNeile-Williams, *Introduction to the Study of the New Testament*[2], p. 220n1; W. C. van Unnik, "A Classical Parallel to 1 Peter ii.14 and 20," *NTS,* 2 (1955–56), 198–202, concludes that the terminology here is derived from Greek sources.

[13] C. H. Dodd, *The Interpretation of the Fourth Gospel* (1953), p. 82n.

[14] F. W. Beare, *Commentary,* p. 47.

[15] O. Cullmann, *The New Testament* (1968), p. 99.

[16] E. G. Selwyn, *op. cit.,* pp. 9–17, 369–84.

salonians, which is also attributed, at least in part, to Silas.[17] But this embarrasses more than aids the case; and B. Rigaux, commenting on 1 Thessalonians, notes that "the appeal to Silvanus is in vain ... since words, grammar, phrases and ideas are Paul's."[18] F. W. Beare goes on to consider one further point, namely, "the character of the teaching, most conspicuously ... the meagreness of the references to the doctrine of the Spirit."[19] But this objection is by no means realistic, as we shall see when we examine the leading theological ideas in 1 Peter, one of which is precisely the teaching on the Holy Spirit.

c. It is stressed that the scantiness of references to Jesus' earthly life in 1 Peter does not comport with what we would expect of the reminiscences of the chief of the apostles. But this argument not only overlooks such allusions as there are (see above), but also seems to assume that what the author is intending to do is give his memoirs in letter form. For the purpose of his writing, however, at least on the surface, we may mention what he says in 5:12: "exhorting and declaring that this is the true grace of God; stand fast in it."

d. The nature of the persecutions reflects a time later than the apostolic age, it is claimed. F. W. Beare builds much of his case on this, arguing that 4:12-16 can only mean that Christians were being accused of a political charge and were suffering *propter nomen* ("on account of the name" of Christ) as sedition-mongers and enemies of the state.[20] If this interpretation is correct, we should look for a time when Christians were openly branded as a political group subversive of the Roman state. Emperors who showed hostility to the church were Nero (65), Vespasian (died 79), Domitian (81-96), and Trajan (111-112).[21]

Beare maintains that the only one on this list whose enmity tallies with the evidence in 1 Peter is Trajan. Pliny's correspondence in AD 111-112 (*Ep.* 10.97) shows that Christians in Pontus-Bithynia were being accused of "crimes adhering to the name" (*flagitia cohaerentia nomini*) of Christian, which looks as though it matches precisely 4:14-16. This is a neat link, and Beare exploits the correspondence to the full. But there are some serious doubts.[22]

In the first place, there is nothing in 1 Peter to indicate an

[17] *Ibid.*, pp. 14ff., 369ff.
[18] Cf. the review of Selwyn by W. L. Knox, in *Theology*, 49 (1946), 342-46; B. Rigaux, *L'épîtres aux Thessaloniciens* (1956), p. 107. J. N. D. Kelly, *op. cit.*, pp. 214-16, is more optimistic in regarding Silvanus as the drafter of the Petrine epistle The role of a revising editor of Peter's first draft is amply illustrated by N. Turner, *A Grammar of New Testament Greek*, Vol. 4 (1976), Ch. 10.
[19] F. W. Beare, *op. cit.*, p. 47.
[20] *Ibid.*, pp. 28-34. See J. Knox, "Pliny and 1 Peter," *JBL*, 72 (1953), 187-89.
[21] There is a useful survey of the options in Best, *Commentary*, pp. 39-42.
[22] Notice the link between the Pliny-Trajan correspondence and what Tacitus remarks about Nero's persecutions (*Ann.* 15.44). G. Edmundson (*The Church in Rome*, p. 139n1) comments, "The Rescript of Trajan merely confirmed in writing the practice, which had subsisted since the time of Nero, of treating the very name of Christian as a crime against the State."

official state persecution as a settled policy. After reviewing the evidence of the letter itself, J. N. D. Kelly concludes that because "there is no evidence for any very extensive persecution initiated by the government in the 1st or early 2nd centuries," there is no reason to quarrel with:

> the impression which the letter as a whole conveys ... not of juridical prosecutions by the government (these seem ruled out by the references themselves, by the statement that the ill-treatment is world-wide [see below], and by the respect shown to the emperor), but of an atmosphere of suspicion, hostility and brutality on the part of the local population which may easily land Christians in trouble with the police.[23]

Second, there is no explicit reference to official inquiry or torture, such as was practiced in Pontus-Bithynia in Pliny's time.[24] The descriptions of the trials his readers were suffering (1:6), ill-treatment meted out to them (3:13–17), and the "fiery ordeal" (4:12–19) suggest that the hardships are private and confined to the area,

> originating in the hostility of the surrounding population. The technical terms for official persecution (diōgmos, etc.) are noticeably absent, nor is there any unambiguous mention of formal accusation (katēgoria), much less of imprisonment or execution.[25]

Third, if we take 5:9 seriously, the sufferings of the readers of this Epistle are part of the general attitude shown to Christians everywhere. This is rightly regarded by Kelly as crucial. The troubles are in no way exceptional, but have their counterpart in other places. Local outburst of mob violence may well explain these pinpricks (suggested by 4:1–4).

3. We may now venture a conclusion concerning the Epistle's authorship and provenance. In the next section we shall note the letter's composition, which embodies a good deal of liturgical matter drawn from the common literary materials of the early church (e.g., 2:4ff. is related literarily to Rom. 9:33). And, as we noted, there is specific evidence of the use of a scribe and (possibly) an editor in 5:12. Also, the unspecific description of the persecutions is in keeping with a setting in the 60s before the Neronian outbreak at Rome in which Peter and Paul perished (AD 64/65). If the Epistle of 1 Peter was published with Peter's personal authorization and as representing his own apostolic teaching, a date in the earlier part of the seventh decade is required. This seems very probable.

The place of publication was almost certainly Rome. This is the most plausible explanation of "Babylon" in 5:13 (cf. Rev. 14:8; 16:19;

---

[23] J. N. D. Kelly, op. cit., pp. 10, 29.
[24] A. N. Sherwin-White, "The Early Persecutions and Roman Law Again," JTS, 3 n.s. (1952), 199–213.
[25] Kelly, op. cit., p. 10.

17:5; 18:2; 2 Esdr. 3:1ff.; Sibyll. Or. 5.143). Alternative suggestions are not persuasive.

a. A location in the literal Babylon is championed by R. G. Heard, who calls attention to Josephus' remark on the large number of Jewish communities there (*Ant.* 15.14f.),[26] but Josephus' evidence is doubtful, and there is no positive confirmation that Babylon did not fall in disrepair and ruin.

b. C. F. D. Moule gives a symbolic interpretation to the name "Babylon," arguing that the place name draws a simple parallel with ancient Babylon as the place to which God's people in the Old Testament were exiled.[27]

c. The most ambitious alternative is that of M.-E. Boismard, who opts for Antioch in Syria, on the grounds that the teaching of the "descent into Hades" was established early in the churches of Syria; and that the title "Christian" is found in those places in Acts which speak of the church in Syria (11:26; 26:28), and 1 Peter provides the remaining New Testament reference to the title (4:16). Also, the *Apostolic Tradition* of Hippolytus has a Syrian background, and reflects the language of the Epistle of Peter.[28] But the absence of influence by 1 Peter on Ignatius of Antioch is a telling counter-objection, and its closest literary affinities are clearly with 1 Clement, which is an indubitable pointer to Rome.[29]

We may conclude that, given the apostolic authorship whether direct or indirect, the Roman origin of this Epistle stands without serious challenge.[30]

COMPOSITION OF FIRST PETER[31]

Modern study of 1 Peter has concentrated on its literary structure as part of a more general interest in the form criticism of the Epistles. The

---

[26] R. G. Heard, *An Introduction to the New Testament* (1950), p. 171.
[27] C. F. D. Moule, "The Nature and Purpose of 1 Peter," *NTS*, 3 (1956–57), 1–11.
[28] M.-E. Boismard, "Une liturgie baptismale dans la Prima Petri," *RB*, 63 (1956), 182–208; 64 (1957), 161–83; cf. his *Quatre hymnes baptismales dans la première épître de Pierre* (1961).
[29] Kelly, *op. cit.,* p. 33; cf. Selwyn, *op. cit.,* p. 37.
[30] E. Dinkler, "Die Petrus-Rom Frage," *ThR*, 25 (1959), 189–230; 289–335; 27 (1961), 33–64. But see C.-H. Hunzinger, "Babylon als Deckname für Rom und die Datierung des 1. Petrusbriefes," in *Gottes Wort und Gottes Land · Festschrift* H.-W. Hertzberg (1965), pp. 67–77, who again emphasizes the Jewish apocalyptic character of the name Babylon.
[31] This section draws on my essay "The Composition of 1 Peter in Recent Study," *Vox Evangelica,* 1 (1962), 29–42. More recent discussions are E. Best, *Commentary,* pp. 20–28; K. Wengst, *Christologische Formeln und Lieder des Urchristentums* (1972), pp. 83–86, 161–64; J. T. Sanders, *The New Testament Christological Hymns* (1971), pp. 17f.; O. S. Brooks, "1 Peter 3:21—The Clue to the Literary Structure of the Epistle," *NovT,* 16 (1974), 290–305.

intention in this discipline is to investigate the literary deposits putatively embedded in the New Testament letters with a view to discovering the religious and theological situation out of which these pre-epistolary traditions have emerged. Such situations (exposed in a way corresponding to the exercise of tracking *Sitze im Leben* in the canonical Gospels) are mainly cultic, sacramental, and paraenetic (i.e., relating to the church's instruction of Christians and giving warnings and encouragements to believers in their personal and social life).

There are three chief ways in which the literary composition and cultic setting of 1 Peter have been viewed.

1. *The form-analytical approach.* The traditional position accepts 1 Peter as a letter written by a single individual to various Christian communities in Asia. This view does not preclude the insertion into it of fragments of hymns, creeds, or confessions, or even snatches of sermonic material. Such insertions vary in purpose according to the immediate concern of the writer; and the appearance of such material in 1 Peter would not be unique, as it seems fairly clear that Paul has incorporated previously existing fragments into his letters (see above, pp. 248ff.).

An illustration of this is 1 Peter 2:4–8, about which Selwyn concludes that an early Christian hymn or rhythmical prayer, common to both Peter and Paul (in Rom. 9:33), underlies these verses.[32] Selwyn analyzes a hymn of seven lines, covering verses 6–8. This analysis differs from H. Windisch's arrangement, which produces from verses 1–10 "a hymn of the holy destiny of Christianity, in four strophes, 1–3, 4f., 6–8, and 9f."[33] Selwyn justly criticizes this as using the term "hymn" too widely, for there is nothing hymnic or lyrical about verses 4 and 5.

A strong reason for believing that a Christian adaptation of certain Old Testament passages has produced a cultic psalm is the phrase περιέχει ἐν γραφῇ (vs. 6), which Selwyn takes to mean "in writing" (comparing Sirach 44:5). This could very well be taken to mean "as it is contained in the hymn," making the or introductory formula equivalent to that in Ephesians 5:14.[34]

In 1 Peter as a whole, Windisch treats the following sections as hymnic.

a. *1:3–12* is described as an *Eingangshymnus,* or introductory hymn, made up of five 7- or 5-line strophes, joined together by relative pronouns. The likelihood that the letter opens with a lengthy prayer, introduced by a solemn blessing (vs. 3)—after the manner of the Jewish

[32] E. G. Selwyn, *op. cit.,* pp. 268–77; see J. H. Elliott, *The Elect and the Holy* (1966); E. Best, "1 Peter II.4–10—A Reconsideration," *NovT,* 11 (1969), 270–93.

[33] H. Windisch-H. Preisker, *Die katholischen Briefe*[3] (1951), p. 58.

[34] Possibly also in Phil. 2:5, if E. Lohmeyer, *Kyrios Jesus* (1928), p. 13, is correct that "which is also in Christ Jesus" is "a sort of formula of citation."

bᵉrākôṯ—is becoming increasingly acceptable in view of research showing that the letters of the apostles were intended to be read in public worship.

b. *2:21–25* is designated "the second Christ-hymn." Apparently, from a cross reference to 1:18–21, Windisch wishes to include the earlier passage as a hymn addressed to Christ. There is little to support this suggestion on a strict interpretation of the term "hymn." The language is admittedly cultic and exalted, and the setting of 1:20 as a "two-member Christ-text" is possible; but it would be precarious to postulate that it owed its origin to a separate hymn of which it is a fragment.

c. *3:18–22* is regarded by Windisch as a baptismal hymn to Christ in four strophes. The exhortation in 3:13–17 is continued in 4:1, though perhaps not all of 3:18ff. belongs to the hymn. Windisch gives no formal analysis, and it is not certain whether he means that Peter was quoting from a hymn familiar in the church in 3:18–22 or whether he was led by certain associations spontaneously to break into verse-form himself. Bultmann, whose discussion builds on Windisch, holds that the author had before him an actual quotation in the passages under consideration.[35]

At all events, it is clear that the *whole* of 3:18–22 is not a quotation. The writer has commented on an existing text, whether a hymn or a creed. This is the novel contribution Bultmann's essay makes. Not only does he wish to isolate certain parts of the letter and identify them as hymnic or confessional; he holds that the author of the document known as 1 Peter had before him a series of credal or hymnlike forms on which he has commented by means of certain glosses. The role of the author in these passages is that of glossator.

The reconstructed whole of the original version of 1:20; 2:21–24; and 3:18ff., before the glossator "spoiled" the simple symmetry, looked like this:

> (? I believe in the Lord Jesus Christ,)
> Foreknown before the world's foundation,⎱
> But manifested at the end of the times: ⎰
>
> Who suffered once for sins,⎱
> To bring us to God: ⎰
> Put to death in the flesh, ⎱
> But made alive in the spirit,⎰
> in which he also preached to the imprisoned spirits;
> (But) having gone into heaven he sat at the right hand of God,⎰
> Angels and authorities and powers under his control.

---

[35] R. Bultmann, "Bekenntnis- und Liedfragmente im ersten Petrusbrief," *Coniectanea Neotestamentica*, 11 (1947), 1–14.

What are we to make of this form-critical experiment? There has been little serious attempt to pronounce on Bultmann's reconstruction.[36] The main opposition to Bultmann here comes from J. Jeremias and E. Lohse, both of whom accuse him of the same thing.[37] The price he pays for securing a completely balanced and nicely arranged text is too high. His alterations are too unrestrained and unwarranted, especially when he tears asunder verses 19 and 20ff. And even this recasting of the material fails to produce the desired result of a completely symmetrical arrangement, as we may see by noting the inordinate length of verse 22. Furthermore Bultmann's explanation of verses 20ff. in terms of the gnostic redemption myth is unnecessary. The summary judgment is "not convincing" (Lohse); and his joining together of 1:20 and 3:18ff. is pronounced by Jeremias "extremely unlikely"; C. E. B. Cranfield says exactly the same.[38]

Somewhat more convincing is the proposal of S. E. Johnson that 3:18-22 is organically connected with the opening verses of chapter 4.[39] He sees the text as an example of chiasmus on a large scale: the argument proceeds from the example of Christ's passion and resurrection in 3:18f. to a statement of what happened in the early days of human history as a type of present salvation. Then the author returns, at 3:20*b*, point by point, through the antitype of Christian baptism, concluding with a statement of what Christ has accomplished by his death and resurrection in 4:6. Johnson sets all this out perhaps too neatly, but his approach has the merit of leaving the text unmanipulated in the interests of the theory—which cannot be said of Bultmann.

2. *1 Peter as a baptismal document.* A second theory sees 1 Peter as a baptismal document. In the words of Windisch: "The bulk of the letter, 1:3—4:12, corresponds with a baptismal response."

The connection of the letter with the rite of baptism is universally attested, especially in the light of 3:18ff. J. N. D. Kelly speaks for many New Testament and liturgical scholars when he comments that this text "reads like a part-paraphrase and part-quotation of an instruction preparatory to baptism. The insertion in verses 20ff. of a short account of the meaning of the sacrament bears this out."[40] But different attitudes may be taken to this general fact. Some writers regard the references to the rite as incidental, as in many other places in the New Testament, especially in the Pauline corpus. They see the letter essen-

---

[36] Preisker accepts his conclusions without discussion. R. Leivestad, *Christ the Conqueror* (1954), p. 177, regards the analysis as "quite plausible"; similarly E. Schweizer, *Erniedrigung und Erhöhung*[1] (1955), pp. 104f.

[37] J. Jeremias, "Zwischen Karfreitag und Ostern," *ZNTW*, 42 (1949), 195ff.; E. Lohse, "Paränese und Kerygma im 1 Petrusbrief," *ZNTW*, 45 (1954), 86-89.

[38] C. E. B. Cranfield, "The Interpretation of 1 Peter iii.19 and iv.6," *ExpT*, 69 (1958), 369; J. N. D. Kelly, *Commentary*, p. 147.

[39] S. E. Johnson, "The Preaching to the Dead," *JBL*, 79 (1960), 48-51.

[40] J. N. D. Kelly, *Early Christian Creeds*[3] (1972), p. 18.

tially as a message of encouragement, written to harassed or persecuted believers, as 5:12 makes plain. The allusions to baptism are more or less extraneous to the main drift of the Epistle.[41]

But a novel hypothesis was proposed by R. Perdelwitz in 1911, and accepted by B. H. Streeter, who added some more speculation of his own.[42] The linchpin of this theory is that the letter has a clear break at 4:11. No one has marshaled the arguments for this more clearly than Perdelwitz. He notes the following:

a. The descriptions of the sufferings of Christians are understood as "present" in 4:12, whereas in the earlier part of the letter (1:6; 3:13,14,17), they are "hypothetical." Verses 3:17 and 4:19 bring out the contrast forcefully.

b. Similarly, the concept of joy is offered as a present reality in 1:6,8, but in 4:12ff. it lies in the future.

c. The "Amen" of 4:11 is not surprising when we note that the connection between 4:11 and 4:12 is "faint and appendix-like"; and there is a complete change of situation between what is future and present.

d. The assumption that 1 Peter contains two separate parts makes sense of "briefly" in 5:12: the phrase "have written *briefly*" could hardly be used of the complete whole, some 1675 words.

Later scholars have found confirmation of this hypothesis in the lack of genuinely epistolary characteristics in 1:3—4:11. It lacks reference to places and people. The style is polished and balanced, with long measured sentences; the impressive opening in 1:3ff. is matched by an equally impressive conclusion with doxology and Amen. On the other hand, Beare argues that the section from 4:12 to 5:14 "breathes an entirely different atmosphere. The style is direct and simple. There are no carefully constructed periods or nicely balanced rhythms and antitheses; ... it has the quick and nervous language of a letter written in haste and under tension."

The most plausible identification of the *Sitz im Leben* of the earlier homiletical document would be a baptismal setting. There are many signs, as Perdelwitz observed, that the address was given to a group of recently baptized neophytes. The converts in mind are those living in the first flush of Christian experience. Their joy is undaunted and exuberant (1:8); and 2:1ff. is a clear description of the first stages of their faith and incorporation into Christ and his people. "As a scarlet thread the particle 'now' runs through all the statements of the author," says Perdelwitz. And this is an important factor in the interpretation of 3:21: "Baptism *now* saves you." One of the most impressive arguments for the origin of 1 Peter as a baptismal sermon is the evidence of the use

---

[41] Cf. Selwyn, *op. cit.*; Lohse, *loc. cit.*; Moule, *Worship in the New Testament* (1961), p. 58; W. Bieder, *Die Vorstellung von der Höllenfahrt Jesu Christi* (1949).

[42] R. Perdelwitz, *Die Mysterienreligionen und das Problem des 1. Petrusbriefes* (1911); B. H. Streeter, *op. cit.*, pp. 122ff.

of catechetical forms discernible in the earlier part of the Epistle.

It would seem that this is as far as we can go in placing the document in the worshiping life of the early communities of believers. But let us examine two closely allied views which take the discussion of the *Sitz im Leben* considerably further.

3. *1 Peter as a baptismal liturgy.* Here we may bracket together the views of H. Preisker and F. L. Cross, the latter springing from the former, though in the final analysis we may ask whether or not they are mutually exclusive.[43]

H. Preisker's notable revision of Windisch's commentary is his proposal that 1 Peter is not simply the report of a baptismal service or the incorporation of baptismal material into a genuinely epistolary form, but the transcript of an actual baptismal service in progress at the time of writing, an eyewitness account of the rite in all its stages, embodying the contributions of those taking part. Thus he gives it the name of "the oldest document of a primitive Christian divine service." The great and unanswered question is how such a thing ever got mixed up, without explanation, in a document purporting to be a letter from a single person to churches in Asia.[44] This is surely the gaping hole in this hypothesis. Preisker's analysis has been summarized often,[45] and we shall mention here only those points on which criticism has fastened.

One of his main points involves discrimination of verb tenses. In 1:3–21 the thought of sanctification is future, but at 1:22f. it is taken as something fully achieved. Therefore, he boldly concludes that "between 1:21 and 1:22 the act of baptism occurs," but it was not reported openly because it belongs to the *disciplina arcani* (secret traditions) of the church. This looks suspiciously like a device to avoid an obvious criticism of the theory! Even so, the text hardly supports the theory. The present participles must be taken as anticipating the future privileges of the baptizands being addressed; but as Beare says, "it seems quite arbitrary to neglect the aorist ἀναγεννήσας (1:3) and to treat the present participle (in 1:5) as a future." A rigid division of chapter 1 into the two tenses of future (looking forward to baptismal act) and past (in recognition of what it has accomplished) will not hold.

Another supporting beam in Preisker's reconstruction is that 1 Peter contains "separate, self-contained sections, laid side by side, without transitions, each with its own stylistic peculiarities." Thus he can report, as though he himself had been present at the baptism, who it is that says what. Characters flit across the stage in a bewildering array. When the neophytes have been baptized they take a brief vow

---

[43] For Cross, see his *1 Peter—A Paschal Liturgy* (1954).

[44] See Moule, *loc. cit.,* 4.

[45] C. E. B. Cranfield, *First Peter* (1959), *ad loc.*; A. M. Stibbs-A. F. Walls, *First Epistle General of Peter* (1959), pp. 59f.; see also S. I. Buse, "Baptism in Other New Testament Writings," in *Christian Baptism,* ed. A. Gilmore (1959), pp. 171ff.

(ἐπευχή) (1:22–25), but the three-strophe hymn of 2:1–10 is sung by a Spirit-possessed individual; whereas a "new preacher stands up in the community" at 2:11 and delivers an exhortation which culminates in a hymn to Christ (2:21–24). Here Preisker accepts without demur Bultmann's conclusion that the author of this hymn has taken over a previously existing hymn. But this raises a difficulty. Are we to think of the hymn as coming spontaneously to the lips of the congregation (cf. 1 Cor. 14) or are they reciting with adaptation something traditionally known in the church?

At 3:13 the style changes and another figure—an "apocalyptic preacher"—comes forward to give an eschatological word as his contribution to the proceedings. This extends to 4:7a. The remaining verses to 4:11 are the final prayer for the baptismal service. To account for the rest of the document Preisker holds that the whole congregation is then brought in for a concluding service, including an eschatological address (4:12–19) and an exhortation to the elders and young people. Finally the church is treated to a piece of didactic instruction (*Mahnrede*) from the presbyter, rounded off by a concluding blessing from another presbyter who (says Beare drily) has evidently been sitting in the corner all the time. (Perhaps, if we may advance a speculation in this field where it is free for all, he is the transcriber of the proceedings and the ghost-writer of 1:3—4:11.)

Arguments from linguistic style are notoriously uncertain, as C. F. D. Moule reminds us in another connection.[46] The one place where Preisker brings forward some objective criteria (his attempt, on stylistic grounds, to posit a "common authorship" of 2:11—3:12 and the *paraklēsis* of 5:1–9) is far from persuasive. That there are differences of style we may freely grant; it is quite another thing to use these differences to assign various strands to putative speakers (with Preisker) or (as Lohse proposes) to allocate them to different provenances. With Beare it is better to say that in the author of 1 Peter we have a writer who evinces "the variations of a good prose stylist" and at the same time give due weight to the possibility that he has incorporated fragments of hymns and confessions which may have been the common property of the cultus of the early churches. But anything resembling a patchwork, as Preisker and Lohse suggest, seems to be imposing a theory on the evidence. This conclusion, offered by F. W. Beare, best explains the literary phenomena of 1 Peter:

> Rather than the direct use of fragments of a liturgy, the evidence seems to me to indicate a sermon developed along lines suggested by the structure of the liturgy, perhaps with an occasional outright quotation of familiar credal formulas, but as a rule freely expressed in the writer's own words and style.[47]

---

[46] C. F. D. Moule, *The Epistles to the Colossians and Philemon* (1957), pp. 61f.
[47] F. W. Beare, *op. cit.*, p. 202.

The booklet *1 Peter—A Paschal Liturgy*, by F. L. Cross, depends much on Preisker's hypothesis and seeks to improve on it in one important respect. Agreeing that 1:3—4:11 is a baptismal liturgy reporting an actual baptism in progress, Cross believes that we can more precisely date the baptism as the celebrant's part in the Easter baptismal service. The new features of his explanation are suppositions on the basis laid by the German commentator. His chief support is the notion that the key to much of the imagery of 1 Peter is the Easter celebration of the primitive church, and he traces many Easter (or Paschal) motifs in the language of the letter.

The typology of the Exodus pervades much of the text (e.g., 1:18f.) and in many of the allusions in 1:3-21 the background is clearly that of the Passover. Similarly, in 2:9f., the language is borrowed directly from Exodus 19:4f., which describes the giving of the Torah, by which the Exodus deliverance was completed. The "paschal theology," as Cross calls it, is summarized in the exordium of verses 3-12, which embodies the whole meaning of the Easter message. This assumption is obviously fundamental to the Cross hypothesis.[48]

By skilfully blending conclusions he has reached or adopted Cross states his final verdict, that 1 Peter 1:3—4:11 is a liturgical document. He confesses to embarrassment about the remainder of the letter from 4:12 on. He thinks Preisker's suggestion that it contains an address to the whole company when assembled lacks conviction, but he has nothing to offer to fill this lacuna. Here we may state a methodological principle: any literary theory which is left with 4:12 to 5:14 on its hands as a kind of inconvenient surd is *ipso facto* under a cloud of suspicion.

As far as the structure of the baptismal formula is concerned, Cross makes a few alterations to Preisker's analysis. In the main, these modifications involve attributing an author to the principal sections of the document; and it is the role of the celebrant which dominates the scene in Cross's reconstruction. Thus it is apparent that Cross has virtually fathered a new hypothesis altogether. He places all the addresses in one mouth and ignores many of the hymns which earlier scholars had confidently classified. The result is that the "baptismal liturgy" theory has gone—if by that we mean the record of a service in progress. Instead, we have (as Wand puts it) "not so much the liturgy itself as the Bishop's running commentary on the liturgy."[49]

It is a serious weakness in the baptismal liturgy theory that its advocates are thus divided over how the text should be apportioned to the different participants in the cultic rite. Both Preisker's and Cross's

---

[48] T. C. G. Thorton, "1 Peter, A Paschal Liturgy?", *JTS*, 12 n.s. (1961), 14–26 assails this supposition; for a contrary view see A. R. C. Leaney, "1 Peter and the Passover: An Interpretation," *NTS*, 10 (1963–64), 238–51; see also E. Best, *Commentary*, p. 23.

[49] J. C. Wand, "Lessons of First Peter: A Survey of Recent Interpretation," *Interpretation*, 9 (1955), 388.

arrangement have to meet the objection voiced by Moule. It is difficult to imagine, he comments,

> how a liturgy-homily, shorn of its rubrics . . . but with its changing tenses and broken sequences all retained, could have been hastily dressed up as a letter and sent off (without a word of explanation) to Christians who had not witnessed its original setting.[50]

The upshot of Moule's thorough examination of the Preisker-Cross hypothesis is that alternative explanations can be provided for all the evidence which they bring forward in support. The final judgment on this stimulating proposal must thus be "not proven."

4. We may summarize our discussion with some concluding remarks:

a. The epistolary form of 1 Peter must be our fixed starting point; and only the strongest reasons will compel us to regard it as other than what it purports to be—an apostolic letter.

b. There is ample precedent in the *corpus Paulinum* for the embodiment in a genuine letter of catechetical and cultic material. With the research of Seeberg, Carrington, and Selwyn into the former, and Hunter, Cullmann, and Lohmeyer into the latter (see above, pp. 251ff.), the incorporation by the New Testament writers of *paraenesis,* psalms and hymns of Christian worship, and rudimentary confessions of faith into their literature may be taken as demonstrated. The rite of initiation by baptism was the occasion when much of this material was used, transmitted to the convert. This accounts for liturgical terms, exalted hieratic language, and lyrical turns of expression in 1 Peter. But we must be content to say that a connection with the baptismal rite is evident and to explain much of the liturgical data as the borrowing of material from such a service. The borrowing, however, may be unconscious and indirect, and the material has passed through the mind of the author, who has thereby made it his very own.

c. On this basis it may be possible to avoid giving too prominent a place to those verses which seem to require the letter's partitioning. If liturgical forms are incorporated, some of the cogency of the view that there is a break at 4:11 is destroyed, especially if Nauck has proved his point that there is no need to think of a change in the type of distress which had come upon the church in the two parts of the Epistle. The case for the letter's unity is still arguable.[51]

d. In fine, the issue of the literary origins of 1 Peter is stated in G. W. H. Lampe's words:

> That 1 Peter makes much use of baptismal material and is concerned with baptism is generally agreed. It remains an open question whether it is a

---

[50] C. F. D. Moule, *loc. cit.,* p. 4.
[51] W. Nauck, "Freude im Leiden," *ZNTW,* 46 (1955), 80; W. J. Dalton, *Christ's Proclamation to the Spirits* (1965), also vindicates the Epistle's unity.

genuine epistle, or whether it is indeed a liturgy embodied in a kind of letter.[52]

The evidence is such that the second alternative is not imperative, and the peculiarities of the letter may be explained by the use of a special source. 1 Peter stands as a genuine letter including two baptismal homilies, one delivered before and the other after the rite.[53]

THEOLOGICAL THEMES IN 1 PETER

Probably no other document in the New Testament is so theological as 1 Peter, if we understand "theological" in the strict sense as teaching about God. The author's mind "begins from and returns constantly to the thought of God as Creator, Father, and Judge, as the One whose will determines all that comes to pass, who shapes the destiny and determines the actions of those whom He has chosen for His own, who sustains them through the sufferings which He sends to test them, and who at the last will vindicate them and reward them eternally."[54] This is a noble statement, and its assertions are amply justified.

Not that our Epistle has little or nothing to say about the other cardinal Christian doctrines, but its emphasis does fall on the character and action of God who is the Holy One (1:15), the Father (1:17), the Creator (4:19), and Judge (4:5). Faith is directed to him (1:21; 3:18) through the mediation of Christ his Son.

Jesus Christ is pictured against an Old Testament background as the true paschal Lamb (1:19) and Servant of Yahweh (2:22ff.). The twin poles of his existence are his sufferings and death (2:23ff.) and his exaltation (1:3,21; 3:18–22). Peter accentuates the sufferings of the Lord as a prelude to his death on the cross, partly to show that his death was real, partly to make the exemplary point that he is akin to his readers, who were in the throes of suffering for their faith in Christ.

The value of Christ's death is stated in terms of access to God. Also his sacrifice supplies a motive power for Christians to follow in Christ's steps and be dedicated to God. His ascension is reported after a reference to that mysterious period, *triduum mortis* (three days of death), in which the events of 3:19 and 4:6 are set. Most likely this refers to Christ's role as the new Enoch, visiting the underworld and announcing the fate of wicked super-beings, thereby assuring the church that their regime was ended and their dominion broken.[55] The chief point in favor of this interpretation is that it gives an immediate moral applica-

---

[52] G. W. H. Lampe, "Evidence in the New Testament for Early Creeds, Catechisms and Liturgy," *ExpT,* 71 (1960), 361.
[53] See O. S. Brooks, *loc. cit.,* 304f.
[54] F. W. Beare, *Commentary*[3], p. 52.
[55] On these profound themes, see B. Reicke, *The Disobedient Spirits and Christian Baptism: A Study of 1 Peter III.19 and its Context* (1946); W. J. Dalton, *op. cit.*

tion to the persecuted Christian community to whom Peter is writing.

At present Christ is the Lord (3:15) whose *parousia* is shortly to be expected (1:7,13; 4:13; 5:1). The hope of an imminent end-time motivates the author (4:7) and gives his ethical teachings a distinctive eschatological color.[56] This seems clearly to reflect a life situation in the apostolic age.

F. W. Beare argues that 1 Peter is removed from the apostolic era on account of a singular absence of the doctrine of the Holy Spirit. He comments, "The active presence of the Spirit has fallen into eclipse ... in First Peter." But the case is not so cogent, since there are four references to the Spirit (1:2,11,12; 4:14), all of which seem to betray an early date.[57] Another test case for dating is the use of the *'ebed Yahweh* figure from Isaiah 53 in 2:22-24 (and 1:19?). This anchors the Epistle's teaching in primitive not later Christianity, for there is reason to believe that this title for Jesus was short-lived in the early church.[58]

Much of the teaching described above fits into a time of consolidation, suggesting a statement of the Christian faith for new believers of Gentile origin. This is confirmed by their geographical address (1:1). The readers are unknown to Peter, who marks himself off from the preachers in the area (1:12). They have only recently been evangelized (2:2) and baptized (3:21)—unless these texts fit into a baptismal service on which 1 Peter is the running commentary. That they were Gentiles seems clear from 1:14, 2:10-12, and 4:3, though we may hesitate long before accepting Perdelwitz's notion that Peter's readers were former adherents of a Hellenistic mystery-cult who were familiar with the taurobolium (bath in a bull's blood) or with the cult of Cybele or Isis (on the basis of 1:3f.).[59]

ETHICAL ADMONITIONS IN 1 PETER

To get to the root of Peter's moral instruction to his readers, we must come to some firm conclusions concerning setting and format.

---

[56] Best, *Commentary*, p. 46; J. R. Michaels, "Eschatology in 1 Peter iii.17," *NTS*, 13 (1966–67), 394–401, interprets the hope as an imminent vindication by God in the eschatological sense: those who suffer for the sake of righteousness will be honored at the last judgment and will escape divine wrath, even if they have now to endure human wrath. The *parenesis* is thus lifted on to an eschatological plane. See also R. Russell, "Eschatology and Ethics in 1 Peter," *EQ*, 47 (1975), 78–84.

[57] This conclusion is endorsed by P. E. Davies, "Primitive Christology in 1 Peter," in *Festschrift to Honor F. Wilbur Gingrich*, edd. E. H. Barth and R. E. Cocroft (1972), pp. 115–22. He argues that "1 Peter provide[s] us with early material of a basic character on which to base a study of the Christology of the earliest Christian church," though he overlooks the teaching on Christ's pre-existence in 1:20.

[58] O. Cullmann, *Peter: Disciple, Apostle, Martyr*[2] (ET 1962), pp. 66–70.

[59] R. Perdelwitz, *op. cit.*; see Kelly, *Commentary*, p. 44. On the reconstruction of initiation rites in the mystery religions and their alleged relevance to early church sacraments see G. Wagner, *Pauline Baptism and the Pagan Mysteries* (ET 1967).

Recent study has veered in the direction of regarding the references to "persecutions" in the letter (seen to be a truly epistolary composition) as relating to some local outburst of opposition more than to an official state policy.[60] In this event it is more correct to regard Peter's call to a good conscience and steadfastness under provocation as part of his general counsel for the Christian life,[61] spoken of as a "tribulation" (as in Acts 14:22), than to see this as part of an "interim ethic" addressed to a church caught in the grip of a tyrannical government. Kelly notes how the author's purpose is seen as one of sustaining and encouraging the Asian Christians whose "troubles are the ever-felt background of every paragraph."[62] He identifies two aspects of this moral theology as significant: the strongly eschatological perspective in which he places the experiences of his readers, and the emphasis on exemplary behavior which characterizes the Epistle.

The literary question turns, as we have seen, on the possibility of a break at 4:11. Moule uses this to account for the change in verb tense and in tone from a more placid mood to a more fearful one in the later chapters.[63] Kelly has criticized this reasoning on linguistic and contextual grounds, and has argued that the entire letter is shot through with the persecution-motif, which is to be understood as the hostile treatment to be expected by minority groups living in a pagan environment. This element pervades the letter and gives it the character of a persecution tract, offering encouragement and guidance to Christians in the socially determined slave-group who were undergoing the threat of serious reprisals on account of their faith. We may add to this the evidence that they seem to be newly won converts, and on that account persecution and deprivation would be all the harder to understand and to bear.

Peter's advice may be set down in the following summary statements.

1. The Christian life is centered in hope (1:3), and sustained by faith in a God whose purposes are known in Christ (1:21). This is Peter's starting-point and the cardinal principle of his theology, both doctrinal and practical.

2. The call to self-control (1:13) is meant to issue in a display of the qualities of Christian living which will make it attractive to others in the pagan world of society around the believers (1:18; 2:11,16).[64] Even

---

[60] E. G. Selwyn, "The Persecutions in 1 Peter," *Bulletin of SNTS*, 1–3 (1950–52), 39–50; cf. J. N. D. Kelly, *Commentary*, pp. 28–32.

[61] W. C. van Unnik, "The Teaching of Good Works in 1 Peter," *NTS*, 1 (1954–55), 92–110; and "Christianity According to 1 Peter," *ExpT*, 68 (1956–57), 79–83.

[62] Kelly, *Commentary*, p. 25.

[63] C. F. D. Moule, *loc. cit.*, 10f.

[64] W. C. van Unnik, "The Critique of Paganism in 1 Peter 1:18," *Neotestamentica et Semitica*, edd. Ellis and Wilcox, pp. 129–42.

when they are unjustly provoked and harassed, Christians should be courteous and patient (3:8–17). Slaves who are maltreated without cause would be especially open to the temptation to fight back (2:18ff.).

3. The Christians' attitude to the ruling authorities is set down in 2:13ff., with a warning (4:15ff.) directed against those who would commit anti-social acts.

4. Humility is a Christian grace (3:8; 5:5ff.) which is to characterize God's people both in the outside world and in the church. In the latter sphere this summons to lowliness eminently befits those who aspire to ecclesiastical office. For church leaders need a reminder that their office is one of service not dictatorship (5:1–5).[65]

5. The summons to endurance (4:7,19; 5:8–11) fastens on a typical New Testament grace applicable specifically in a time of testing (cf. Mark 13 and parallels). If the terminology is somewhat different, clearly the admonitions to patience, persistence, and prayerful vigilance are common to this stratum of New Testament ethical teaching. Ironically, this doggedness (ὑπομονή) and refusal to give in under trial and prove unfaithful was misunderstood by the Roman magistrates when Christians were arraigned on charges of sedition; and their attitude came to be regarded as stubbornness and inflexible obstinacy (Latin, *pertinacia et inflexibilis obstinatio*) (see above, p. 49). The Christians' right attitude in these circumstances is classically expressed in 3:15f.: "Always be prepared to make a defense to any one who calls you to account for the hope that is in you, yet do it with gentleness and reverence; and keep your conscience clear."[66]

The message of this Epistle is more distinctive, J. H. Elliott argues, than the mere application of ethical *paraenesis* to particular problems. He pleads for recognition of a distinctive Petrine expression of Christianity in the New Testament, a well-attested type of Christian belief and piety, not just a footnote to Paul but something with an independent existence. New Testament Christianity is thus seen as richer and more multiform than we often credit it with being.[67]

---

[65] J. H. Elliott, "Ministry and Church Order in the NT: A Traditio-Historical Analysis (1 Pt. 5,1–5 and par.)," *CBQ*, 32 (1970), 367–91.

[66] This admonition was later misunderstood, as D. L. Stockton, *"Christianos ad Leonem,"* in *The Ancient Historian and His Materials,* ed. B. Levick (1975), pp. 208–11, makes clear.

[67] J. H. Elliott, "The Rehabilitation of an Exegetical Step-Child: 1 Peter in Recent Research," *JBL,* 95 (1976), 243–54. The latest developments in the study of 1 Peter, initiated by L. Goppelt's commentary (in the Evangelisch-Katholischer Kommentar series, 1978) and extended by J. H. Elliott's *Home for the Homeless. A Sociological Exegesis of 1 Peter, its Situation and Strategy* (1981) and D. L. Balch's *Let Wives be Submissive: The Domestic Code in 1 Peter* (1981), are rehearsed in my contribution to "Peter," "1 Peter," in *ISBE,* III (1986), 807–15. See too J. H. Elliott's essay, "Salutation and Exhortation to Christian Behavior on the basis of God's Blessing (1:1–2:10)," in *RE,* 79.3 (1982), 415–25.

CHAPTER TWENTY-SIX

The Pilgrim People of God in the Epistle to the Hebrews

IS HEBREWS A LETTER?

As we approach this document, which on literary grounds stands in a class of its own in the New Testament library, some account of its distinctive features should first be given. Details of its style and contents may be listed as follows.

1. The high literary quality of Hebrews is seen in such features as the careful construction of its sentences and the elegant diction, especially in the exordium (1:1–4) with its sonorous adverbs.[1] The author uses a rhetorical style (11:32) more suited to the spoken word than to the written.[2] He calls his composition a "word of exhortation" (13:22) and he refers to the spoken utterance (2:5; 8:1; 9:5). Yet in 13:22 he uses the verb "I have sent" (ἐπέστειλα), which suggests a written communication—which is of course what we have before us.

2. The Old Testament is used often in full quotation (especially Ps. 110 and Jer. 31) and frequently appealed to as an authority (29 actual citations and about 70 allusory references have been counted).[3]

3. The Jewish cultus is used as a foil for the Christian gospel.

---

[1] See J. Swetnam, "On the Literary Genre of the 'Epistle' to the Hebrews," *NovT*, 11 (1969), 261–69; O. Michel, *Der Brief an die Hebraer* (1949), pp. 1–9; J. C. McCullough, "Some Recent Developments in Research on the Epistle to the Hebrews," *Irish Biblical Studies*, 2 (1980), 141–65; 3 (1981), 28–45.

[2] See J. Moffatt, *The Epistle to the Hebrews* (1924), §3: Style and Diction. Of the author he writes: "He has an art of words, which is more than an unconscious sense of rhythm. He has the style of a trained speaker" (p. lxiv). "Hebrews begins as a sermon and ends as an epistle" neatly sums up the stylistic features, according to N. Turner, *A Grammar of New Testament Greek*, Vol. 4 (1976), p. 113. "The literary genre of Hebrews is that of an exhorting sermon" (D. A. Hagner, *Hebrews*, Good New Commentary [1983], p. xxiii).

[3] S. Kistemaker, *The Psalm Citations in the Epistle to the Hebrews* (1961); K. J. Thomas, "The Old Testament Citations in Hebrews," *NTS*, 11 (1965), 303–25; G. Howard, "Hebrews and the Old Testament Quotations," *NovT*, 10 (1968), 208–16; G. R. Hughes, *Hebrews and Hermeneutics* (1979); J. M. McCullough, "The Old Testament Quotations in Hebrews," *NTS*, 26 (1980), 363–79.

The entire treatment gives the impression of being an interpretative commentary on Old Testament and Jewish religion, but the author is more interested in establishing an academic point of theology than in drawing attention to some contemporary setting. The tabernacle of the wilderness wanderings rather than the Jerusalem Temple is his chief illustration.

4. His chief emphasis falls on the finality of the new order in Christ, adumbrations of which are already in the Old Testament (Heb. 8; Jer. 31).[4]

5. The Christology of Hebrews is rich and varied, using twenty titles and names of Jesus, of which the favorite terms are "Son" (twelve times) and "priest-king."[5]

6. The eschatological perspective is both present (1:2; 6:5) and futurist (9:28; 10:37).[6] The experience of Christian salvation is already enjoyed by the reader, yet its consummation lies in the future.

7. Interjected into the theoretical discussion are five passionate appeals. These are scattered throughout the treatise, not gathered—as is usual in Paul—in the second part of the Epistle. The use of the hortative mood of the verb is noteworthy (e.g., 4:1, 14; 10:22; 12:28). These give a practical thrust to the argument and confirm the assertion and description of a "word of exhortation" in 13:22. Παράκλησις is the key-term on this practical level; and κρεῖσσον—an adverb meaning "better," implying a definite contrast between two realities—is important on the doctrinal plane of discussion (see 1:4; 6:9; 7:7,19,22; 8:6; 9:23; 10:34; 11:16,35,40). On 7:19 ("The law made nothing perfect; on the other hand, a better hope is introduced, through which we draw near to God"),

4 This feature is recognized by all the commentators; e.g., C. Spicq, *L'épître aux Hébreux* (1952); J. Héring, *L'épître aux Hébreux* (1954); H. W. Montefiore, *A Commentary on the Epistle to the Hebrews* (1964); F. F. Bruce, *Commentary on the Epistle to the Hebrews* (1964). See further three essays of Bruce: "Recent Literature on the Epistle to the Hebrews," *Themelios*, 3 (1966), 31–36; "Hebrews in Recent Study," *ExpT*, 80 (1968–69), 260–64; and "The Kerygma of Hebrews," *Interpretation*, 23 (1969), 3–19; R. Jewett, *Letter to Pilgrims: A Commentary on the Epistle to the Hebrews* (1981); and D. A. Hagner, *Hebrews* (1983), pp. xxiif., xxviii.
5 See especially V. Taylor, *The Names of Jesus* (1954), p. 57; and *The Person of Christ in New Testament Teaching* (1958), p. 93. For his role as priest, see O. Cullmann, *The Christology of the New Testament* (ET 1959), pp. 89–107, whose important and lucid discussions are supplemented by more recent studies that reflect the discoveries at Qumran (11Q Melch). See J. A. Fitzmyer, "Further Light on Melchizedek from Qumran Cave 11," *JBL*, 86 (1967), 25–41; M. de Jonge and A. S. van der Woude, "11Q Melchizedek and the New Testament," *NTS*, 12 (1965–66), 301–26; D. E. Aune, "A Note on Jesus' Messianic Consciousness and 11Q Melchizedek," *EQ*, 45 (1973), 161–65; I. W. Batdorf, "Hebrews and Qumran: Old Methods and New Directions." in *Festschrift to Honor F. Wilbur Gingrich*, edd. E. H. Barth and R. E. Cocroft (1972), pp. 16–35; A. Vanhoye, *Our Priest is Christ. The Doctrine of the Epistle to the Hebrews* (1977).
6 C. K. Barrett, "The Eschatology of the Epistle to the Hebrews," in *The Background of the New Testament and its Eschatology (Festschrift* C. H. Dodd), edd. W. D. Davies and D. Daube (1956), pp. 363–93; A. Feuillet, "Les points de vue nouveaux dans l'eschatologie de l'épître aux Hébreux," *SE*, 2 (*TU* 87) (1964), 369–87.

A. B. Bruce comments that this forms "the dogmatic centre of the Epistle."[7]

8. The closing section (13:23-25) contains an epistolary conclusion.[8] The reason for this appendix-like ending has been variously assessed. Among the options are:

a. It is a genuine part of the letter, written by the author to show that he belonged to the Pauline circle.[9]

b. It was added by the author as a device to create the impression of "Paulinity."[10]

c. It is genuine, but not intended to claim any connection with Paul.

d. It was added by a later hand prior to the letter's inclusion in the canon.[11]

To sum up: if Hebrews is called an Epistle, it must be in Deissmann's sense of the word, that is, a public document intended for wide circulation throughout an area, composed as a conscious literary effort.[12] But in view of style and vocabulary, perhaps it is more properly called a written sermon, or a collection of sermons brought together in a single treatise.[13] Bornkamm has recently argued for its liturgical character, so we may offer a precise if tentative definition of Hebrews as a baptismal homily in view of the special language it employs and its reiterated appeal to stimulate the readers' progress in the Christian life.[14] But we must look first at the destination of the Epistle before reaching a final verdict on its purpose.

TO WHOM WAS IT SENT?

1. The traditional view is that this document was intended as a warning to Hebrew Christians who were in danger of apostatizing by slipping back into their ancestral faith. They had been disowned by their fellow-Jews (10:32ff.), and were wistfully looking back on their

---

[7] A. B. Bruce, *The Epistle to the Hebrews: The First Apology for Christianity* (1899), p. 271.

[8] For a survey of the problems of Heb. 13, see F. V. Filson, *Yesterday: A Study of Hebrews in the Light of Chapter 13* (1967); cf. C. Spicq, "L'authenticité du chapitre XIII de l'épître aux Hébreux," *Coniectanea Neotestamentica,* 11 (1947), 226-36.

[9] T. W. Manson, "The Problem of the Epistle to the Hebrews," in *Studies in the Gospels and Epistles,* ed. M. Black (1962), pp. 246f.

[10] Or even that Paul himself wrote 13:23-25, with the news of Timothy's release, which was appended to a letter composed by Timothy; J. D. Legg, "Our Brother Timothy: A Suggested Solution to the Problem of the Authorship of the Epistle to the Hebrews," *EQ,* 40 (1968), 220-23.

[11] W. Marxsen, *Introduction to the New Testament,* p. 218. Perhaps the chapter was assembled from Pauline materials; cf. E. D. Jones, "The Authorship of Hebrews xiii," *ExpT,* 46 (1935), 562-67; but see R. V. G. Tasker, "The Integrity of the Epistle to the Hebrews," *ExpT,* 47 (1935-36), 136-38.

[12] A. Deissmann, *Light from the Ancient East,* p. 243.

[13] E. Dinkler, "The Letter to the Hebrews," *IDB,* 2 (1969), 572.

[14] G. Bornkamm, "Das Bekenntnis im Hebräerbrief," in *Studien zu Antike und Christentum* (1959), pp. 188-203.

past traditions in the fear that they might have been mistaken when they embraced the messianic faith. Moreover, persecution and the delay of the *parousia* were posing problems of faith. Hence the need which the letter seeks to meet. This line of interpretation was taken by B. F. Westcott, who placed the recipients in Jerusalem or more generally in Palestine.[15]

2. Another view goes to the opposite end of the spectrum, identifying the readers as Gentiles, assuming that the title "To the Hebrews," which was in any case added later, is a misnomer.[16] The danger was that of lapsing into irreligion and atheism (as 3:12 and 10:26 are believed to assert).

3. Numerous theories offer variations on the traditional identification. The proponents of these views fault the identity of the Hebrews as Palestinian Jews because of strong evidence that the type of Jewish faith stressed in the document is Hellenistic and heterodox, not rabbinical. Spicq identifies the special type of Judaism with a group of priests mentioned in Acts 6:7.[17] Yadin thinks in terms of a group of Qumran members now scattered throughout the world.[18] W. Manson suggests Hellenistic Jews in Italy (13:24), whom the school of Stephen sought to reach.[19]

4. T. W. Manson's theory locates the readers in the Lycus Valley because of the links of terminology between Colossians and Hebrews.[20] The trouble with this is that Hebrews was known early at Rome,

---

[15] B. F. Westcott, *The Epistle to the Hebrews* (1892), pp. xxxv–xlii.

[16] F. D. V. Narborough, *The Epistle to the Hebrews* (1930), pp. 20–27, sees the background as gnosticism in Asia Minor; cf. Moffatt, *op. cit.*, pp. xxvif.; Kümmel, *Introduction*[2], pp. 399f. The title "To Hebrews" is first found in Tertullian, *De Pudicitia* 20.

[17] C. Spicq, "L'épître aux Hébreux, Apollos, Jean-Baptiste, les Hellénistes et Qumrân," *Revue de Qumrân*, 1.3 (1959), 365–90. Apollos is seen as the link with the ex-Essene priests (Acts 6:7), whose version of Christianity included an animus to the Temple (Acts 6:13f.).

[18] Y. Yadin, "The Dead Sea Scrolls and the Epistle to the Hebrews," in *Scripta Hierosolymitana*, 4, edd. C. Rabin and Y. Yadin (1958), pp. 36–55. Yadin builds on Spicq's observations about the polemic of the letter against the levitical priesthood; but the absence of a polemic against the Qumran expectation of a priestly Messiah is noted by F. F. Bruce, "'To the Hebrews' or 'To the Essenes,'" *NTS*, 9 (1963), 217–32. On the question whether Heb. 7 is opposed to the Qumran notion of Melchizedek as a "heavenly redemption figure," see the references in note 5 above; F. L. Horton, *The Melchizedek Tradition. A Critical Examination of the Sources to the Fifth Century A.D. in the Epistle to the Hebrews* (1976), pp. 163–68, returns a negative verdict.

[19] W. Manson, *The Epistle to Hebrews* (1951), Ch. 2; C. F. D. Moule, *The Birth of the New Testament* (1962), p. 76, relates the Epistle to Stephen himself.

[20] The connection with the Colossian letter was made by Narborough, *op. cit.*, pp. 22ff. T. W. Manson, *op. cit.*, pp. 242–58, wrote independently and further supported the authorship of Apollos, entitling the document: "The Epistle of Apollos to the Churches of the Lycus Valley." The case for Apollos' authorship has been attractively presented by H. W. Montefiore, *op. cit.*, pp. 23–28, but his thesis of a destination at Corinth is less cogent. The links between Col. 1:18 and Heb. 1:6 are established by L. R. Helyer, "The *Prototokos* Title in Hebrews," *SBT*, 6.2 (1976), 3–28.

whereas Colossians was directed to Christians in Asia Minor. Still, this suggestion is promising in view of the close tie between the false teaching presupposed in the two documents, particularly the elements of mediation between man and God, an astrological interest, especially in reference to the angel powers, a dualistic world-view, the observance of Jewish ceremonies (assuming that Col. 2:16–19 relates to Jewish rituals),[21] and the influence of ascetic practices. These correspondences (if valid) would help us to pinpoint the setting of many of the doctrinal and polemical texts in Hebrews.

DOCTRINAL TEACHING AND APPEAL

The points of interest here have to do with the person and work of Christ. The dangers facing the church are reflected in the emphases this Epistle makes.

1. Hebrews is remarkable for its heavy concentration on the humanity of "Jesus" (a favorite name, appearing ten times in the Epistle, often placed at the end of sentences to form a climax), and it teaches a veritable incarnation.[22] This is in conscious opposition to docetism which denied a real incarnation on the heretical ground that the material is alien to the divine. So this Epistle highlights the Christology of a Son who is truly human (2:14), genuinely tempted (4:15; 2:17f.), faithful unto death (13:12; 3:2), and obedient through suffering (5:7–9). "The attribution of learning through suffering to the Son of God was a daring paradox for Hellenistic thought, where it was axiomatic that God is impassible."[23] H. R. Mackintosh rightly concludes: "Nowhere in the New Testament is the humanity of Christ set forth so movingly."[24]

2. The assertion of the finality of Christ is made over against the claims of angel worship (1:4; 2:5), and a possible veneration of Melchizedek as an eschatological redemptive figure who both made atonement and was then exalted to the heights to inaugurate a new age by putting down hostile forces. There is a statement of Jesus' cosmic role as Lord of creation and ruler of the universe. No intermediary is permitted

---

[21] On this point see R. P. Martin, *Colossians and Philemon* (1974), pp. 90ff.; on recent studies that find common gnostic elements in Colossians and Hebrews, see *ibid.*, pp. 16ff.

[22] V. Taylor, *The Person of Christ*, p. 91; R. Williamson, "The Incarnation of the Logos in Hebrews," *ExpT*, 95 (1983), 4–8; P. Ellingworth, "'Like the Son of God': Form and Content in Hebrews 7, 1–10," *Biblica*, 64 (1983), 255–62. The examples in the letter are 2:9; 3:1; 4:14; 12:1, 2.

[23] H. W. Montefiore, *op. cit.*, p. 99.

[24] H. R. Mackintosh, *The Doctrine of the Person of Jesus Christ*² (1913), p. 79. The background of 5:7-10 in Gethsemane should be noted. On the translation and exegesis of the passage see O. Cullmann, *The Christology of the New Testament*, pp. 95–98; M. Rissi, "Die Menschlichkeit Jesu nach Hebr. 5, 7–8," *ThZ*, 11 (1955), 28–45; J. Jeremias, "Hebr. 5, 7–10," *ZNTW*, 44 (1952–53), 107–11; R. E. Omark, "The Saving of the Savior," *Interpretation*, 12 (1958), 39–51; G. Braumann, "Hebr. 5, 7–10," *ZNTW*, 51 (1960), 278–80; G. Bornkamm, "Sohnschaft und Leiden," in *Judentum, Urchristentum, Kirche: Festschrift* J. Jeremias (1960), pp. 188–98.

between Christ and God. A comparative study can be made of the Christology of Colossians 1:15-20 and Hebrews 1:1-14, in which common indebtedness to the Philonic thought of the Logos as a cosmic mediator and to Jewish wisdom concepts may be observed.[25]

3. There are warnings voiced against Jewish dietary laws (13:9) at the conclusion of the massive argument of chapters 5-10 that Jesus' priesthood surpasses and supersedes that of the Levitical office. The author exposes the folly of clinging to these Jewish rituals now that the sun has risen to dispel the shadows (8:5,13) and the final work of atonement and sacrifice has been achieved (9:24ff.). This once-for-all accomplishment antiquates the Jewish system of special events and observances (cf. Col. 2:16); and the readers are called to act on this message.

4. The futurist note in eschatology (9:28) and the reminder of a coming day (10:25) are warnings that Christ will reappear as Judge. This teaching attacks a false confidence in automatic moral security coupled with spiritual laxity (3:12—4:2). The thought is parallel with the idea of the church as a people who live "between the times" of Christ's two advents, and this type of eschatological attitude controls the ethical and ecclesiastical elements in the letter.

A CALL TO THE PILGRIM PEOPLE OF GOD[26]

In several areas the practical admonitions of Hebrews relate to historical and pastoral situations, but in interpreting these we are hampered by uncertainty as to the precise dating of the letter. The citation of Hebrews in 1 Clement (AD 96) places the letter in the first century, but assigning a precise date in the earlier decades is a problem. Those who affirm that the Temple was still standing at the time the writer constructed his argument obviously date the Epistle before AD 70.[27] But the use of the tabernacle imagery tells against this, even if it says nothing about the Epistle being post-AD 70. The allusions in 10:32ff. refer to persecutions; but are these to be identified with Nero's attacks on Christians (AD 64)? The experiences suffered are relegated to the

25 Narborough, *op. cit.*, pp. 17-20; C. Spicq surveys Philonic parallels, *RB*, 56 (1949), 542-72; and 57 (1950), 212-42. R. Williamson, *Philo and the Epistle to the Hebrews* (1970), offers negative assessments of the Epistle's indebtedness to Philo.
26 E. Käsemann's monograph, *Das wandernde Gottesvolk. Eine Untersuchung zum Hebräerbrief*[2] (1957), has had a decisive influence on most recent studies. It is now available in English (ET 1984) as the *The Wandering People of God. An Investigation of the Letter to the Hebrews* See also W. C. Johnsson, "The Pilgrimage Motif in the Book of Hebrews," *JBL*, 97 (1978), 239-51.
27 T. W. Manson, *op. cit.*, pp. 251f.; W. Manson, *op. cit.*, pp. 43f.; J. A. T. Robinson, *Redating the New Testament*, pp. 200-204; the main point is left unresolved, namely, that even after AD 70, Judaism did continue to exist and the author is dealing with a viable alternative to Christianity. 1 Clem. 41.2 speaks as though the Temple sacrifices were still being offered in AD 96, and Josephus, *Ant.* 3.224-57 (AD 93) writes of the sacrificial system in the present tense. See Lightfoot's *The Apostolic Fathers* 1,2 (1889), 124f.

past ("former days"),[28] and the Epistle may be twenty years later on. The current persecutions in 12:3f. seem to be more "pinpricks" than settled hostility.[29]

In seeking to place the letter in a suitable life-setting, then, we are driven to more general considerations. In the first place, 2:3 sets the readers' lives clearly in the third generation of Christianity, the so-called "sub-apostolic" age. Only the memory of the first and second generations of believers is left to the readers (13:7).[30] There are further indications that the Christians addressed in the document are believers of long standing, in danger of growing weary in the Christian race (3:12f.; 5:11—6:8; 10:35f.; 12:12f.; this is the obvious background to 2:1f. and 12:1f.). There seems to be a tendency to settle down in the world and forget the eschatological dimension of salvation. Hence the readers are reminded that while the new age of incorporation into Christ began at baptism (6:4f.), the promise of final salvation is still held out before them (9:28) as they live *zwischen den Zeiten,* "between the times," in the interim separating the two advents of Christ.

The readers of Hebrews are open to the seductive influences that beset them on the ethical plane. Here again, the picture of the internal life of this community confirms the suggestion that these Christians belong to third-generation Christianity, when the institutional church with its sacramental life and ministerial leaders was coming under fire. It would be instructive to read a sample of the non-canonical literature here to get the flavor of this period (c. AD 80–100). We may instance the *Didache,* 1 Clement, and (somewhat later) Ignatius and Barnabas.

1. *Ethical concerns.* The church situation of the readers evoked the exhortations which punctuate the writer's appeal. We may isolate three features of the church situation confronted in the letter.

a. The "strange teachings" of 13:9 are based partly on a reversion to Jewish food-laws. Possibly this verse indicates the presence of a type of evil practice condemned in Revelation 2:14,20, where the association between food and idolatry and immorality is close; and the warnings of Colossians 2:16,21f.; 1 Timothy 1:6ff.; 4:3; and Titus 1:13f. may fit into the same general scheme. All these texts relate to church situations in Asia Minor except the last, if we take the geographical allusions in Titus 1:5,12 at face value.

b. Problems of perverted sex relationships seem to be the theme

---

[28] This tells against Robinson's date of AD 67, seeing the document written to a group of Jewish Christians in the church at Rome.

[29] The term is from R. H. Fuller, *A Critical Introduction to the New Testament,* p. 148.

[30] These verses (2:3; 13:7) militate against ascription of authorship to any *direct* "apostolic" figure (Stephen, Barnabas, Apollos), though the teaching of any of these men (or women, if we introduce Prisca as Apollos' teacher; Acts 18:26) may well have been preserved in the document. A succinct statement of the case for Apollos is A. M. Hunter, "Apollos the Alexandrian," in *Biblical Studies: Essays in Honour of William Barclay,* pp. 155f.

of the warning given in 13:4, a situation reflected equally in the gnostic disdain of marriage attacked in 1 Timothy 4:3 as well as Ephesians 5:23ff. (see above, p. 235). A good illustration of this low view of the marriage state is in Ignatius, *Polycarp* 5, who also wrote against a gnostic tendency.

    c. General moral laxity characterizes at least part of the community (12:16), and there is a reluctance to face the rigors of Christian discipleship (12:3ff.). This raises the question of the severity of the author in his dealing with post-baptismal sin and his pessimism about a second repentance (6:4–9; 10:26ff.).[31] Note the type of sin under scrutiny here and how the author hedges about his warnings. Perhaps this explains why, even if his final word is one of encouragement and hope (6:9; 10:39), the dullness and sluggishness of his readers requires a stern face on his part. Early Christian writers found this teaching hard to accept.[32] Hence the delay in receiving Hebrews into the church's canon, a negative attitude shown on other grounds, too. Indeed, until the fourth century only Tertullian and Novatian in the west refer to the Epistle, and many later writers either ignore it or express doubts about its authorship or canonicity—perhaps from anti-Jewish prejudice.

    2. *Apostasy and discipline in Hebrews.* The problem is difficult here, because the verses in question have entered into dogmatic theology, which tends to color the interpreter's judgment. It requires some effort to get back to the historical and pastoral situation in a pre-dogmatic period.[33]

    The call of this Epistle is addressed to a world-weary and discontented church (drawn from a constituency in the Judaism of the Dispersion), in danger of lapsing into irreligion and false teaching as well as into a sub-Christian morality, partly through neglect (2:1–3; 10:24), partly through disillusionment over the non-arrival of the *parousia* (10:35ff.),[34] and partly through listening to heretical teachers (13:9). But the emphasis always falls on the voluntary nature of all this (e.g., 10:26: notice the adverb "willingly"). It should not have happened, and the fate of the apostates and heretics who persist in it is as certain as that which overtook the covenant people in the wilderness (3:16ff.). Hence the call

---

[31] The striking verb "to crucify afresh" (6:6) has been linked with the *Quo Vadis* legend in the apocryphal *Acts of Peter* 35 (Robinson, *op. cit.,* p. 214). The common element is the danger of apostasy under trial, but against this link-up neither Heb. 6 nor 10 refers to state or official persecutions, and 12:4 suggests that the community had not been called on to suffer the extreme penalty of martyrdom.

[32] W. Telfer, *The Forgiveness of Sins* (1959).

[33] See I. H. Marshall, *Kept by the Power of God* (1969); H. Conzelmann's treatment, *Outline of the Theology of the New Testament* (ET 1969), pp. 289ff., is instructive at this point.

[34] Hab. 2:3f. (based on LXX) are cited in 10:35–39 to assure the readers that the coming one will come; he will not delay. Therefore they should live by faith(fulness) and gain the reward. See A. Strobel, *Untersuchungen zum eschatologischen Verzögerungsproblem* (1961), pp. 79–83.

to repentance—with the warning that there can be no hope for the obdurate while they persist in hardening their heart (cf. Rev. 2:21).

The writer deals with the pressing needs in a number of ways.

a. He capitalizes on the teaching of the true ecclesiology of the church portrayed as the pilgrim or new people of God. The point of Hebrews 11 is that God's people are sustained by "faith." This is not (as for Paul) "faith that justifies and saves"—*fides justificans et salvificans*—but an existential attitude which keeps the believer in step with God along life's road.[35] The church is not a company of the elect, already saved and destined for eternity, but a journeying people, on the road, not yet having reached the homeland.

b. Sin is therefore seen as dragging of one's feet, and apostasy is like a falling out of the race (4:1); hence the writer's great fear is of a failure to reach the heavenly city (13:14), which to the vision of faith (11:1) already exists (12:12–28).[36] The key term is ὑπομονή (12:1), defined as a dogged determination not to quit the contest.

c. For the pilgrim people under the old covenant God provided manna; for his church he offers the sacramental life of the new altar (9:1–14,20; 10:19f.; esp. 13:10),[37] and the better lustration (10:22). Baptism and the eucharist are the pilgrims' support and sustenance (13:15) for their journey.

d. Leadership in the church is an effective antidote to heresy (13:7,17,24; for "rulers" cf. 1 Clem. 1:3; 21:6), as is the baptismal "confession" (3:1; 4:14; 10:23), which needs to be held firm in time of testing. These statements of accepted teaching will safeguard the readers against all novelty and the aberrations being inculcated in the congregation to which the letter is sent.

e. The "imitation of Christ" motif is used to good effect.[38] As the human Jesus, he suffered, was tested, learned obedience, and endured to

---

[35] E. Gässer, *Der Glaube im Hebräerbrief* (1965), p. 197, calls faith in Heb. a *"Haltung"*; O. Michel writes: "Heb represents an independent tradition of teaching" in regard to the meaning of "faith" (πίστις); see *NIDNTT*, 1, ed. C. Brown (1975), 604. G. Dautzenberg, "Der Glaube im Hebräerbrief," *BZ*, n.f. 17 (1973), 161–77, stresses that faith in Hebrews is not directed to Jesus, but to God (6:1; 11:6; cf. 10:36; ch. 11; 12:1f.). Jesus is seen as the exemplar of faith in God and the one who did his will (10:36–39). This type of Christology is absent from Paul. The author of Hebrews uses it to enforce a call to discipleship (cf. Rissi, *loc. cit.*, 45).

[36] See U. Luck, "Himmlisches und irdisches Geschehen im Hebräerbrief," *NovT*, 6 (1963), 192–215.

[37] R. Williamson, "The Eucharist and the Epistle to the Hebrews," *NTS*, 21 (1974–75), 300–12; cf. his "Hebrews and Doctrine," *ExpT*, 81 (1969–70), 371–76. On 13:10, see F. V. Filson, *op. cit.*, pp. 48–54, who opposes the eucharistic interpretation, as does Williamson. But J. Swetnam, "'The Greater and More Perfect Tent,'" *Biblica*, 47 (1966), 91–106; and P. Andriessen, "L'eucharistie dans l'épître aux Héb," *NRT*, 3 (1972), 269–77, are more confident about finding allusions to the Lord's Supper in these verses.

[38] Hauck, in *TDNT*, 4 (1967), 588, points out that Paul never uses the verb *hypomenein* (persevere) for the patient sufferings of Jesus.

the end; now he is crowned with honor (2:9f.). "Follow him" (12:2) is the author's clarion call.

3. *Warning against false teaching.* Hebrews is best understood as a polemical writing. The author, whom we may identify as a church teacher and pastor in the third generation of apostolic Christianity, draws freely on the liturgical, cultic, and confessional elements of the church's corporate life. His chief target is a species of heretical, gnosticizing Judaism, infected with Hellenistic ideas and presenting a powerful attraction to Jewish converts, who had entered the church from the world of Diaspora Judaism.[39] This helps to account for some of the salient features in the author's apology for his version of the Christian gospel and its emphases on Jesus' true humanity and veritable incarnation (chs. 1,2,5), which suggests a conscious opposition to incipient docetism; on the finality of Christ, which is set over against angel-worship (1:4; 2:5) as well as the Jewish cultus; on the church as an eschatological pilgrim people on the way to the final city, which suggests that this community has lost the sense of "eschatological tension" because of its wrongheaded notion that the believer is already raised to full life in God and that there is no other future hope held out to him; and finally on the sacramental life of a church that was fast becoming institutionalized. This church was gifted with leaders and possessed a structure (ch. 13) that incorporated a set "confession of faith" (ὁμολογία). This points in the direction of a counter-thrust against false ideas. By this appeal such false notions and practices are thereby refuted as novel and upstart.[40]

---

[39] I. W. Batdorf, "Hebrews and Qumran," *loc. cit.*, pp. 33-35, offers a partial corrective to Käsemann's use (*op. cit.*, pp. 98ff.; ET 156ff.) of such verses as 6:19f. and 10:20 as signs of the influence of the gnostic "redeemed redeemer" who acts as "leader" (2:10; 12:2) to deliver men who were held victim to demonic powers (2:14f.). On the contrary, Hebrews seems to oppose the gnostic myth in the ways indicated above.

[40] See O. Cullmann, *Christology of the New Testament*, pp. 103f., for a fine exposition of the leading motifs of the document, of which 13:8 is a good summary and epitome, since it stresses the past, present, and future aspects of Christ's saving work.

CHAPTER TWENTY-SEVEN

The Epistle of James and Jewish Christianity

The opening sentence of this Epistle names the author as "James, a servant of God and of the Lord Jesus Christ." Aside from 2:1 this text is the only verse in the entire letter with a distinctively Christian flavor—which has led to speculation that this is a Christian edition of a work originally Jewish. A. Meyer suggested that the "riddle" of this letter was solved by treating it as an allegorical commentary on Genesis 49. But there is no reason to regard James 1:1 and 2:1 as later interpolations into the text.[1] This Epistle provides the only example of a purely Greek preface, using the Hellenistic verb χαίρειν, in the New Testament—with the important exception of Acts 15:23 (cf. 23:26).

AUTHORSHIP

The James who wrote the Epistle has been taken traditionally as the Lord's brother, though no fewer than six persons in the New Testament church are named James.[2] Even if this Epistle is not directly from the hand of Jesus' brother, it makes its appeal to his authority.[3] What do we know of James from sources historical or legendary?

1. It is not easy to piece together how the Lord's brother came to

---

[1] A. Meyer, *Das Rätsel des Jakobusbriefes* (1930). Nor is there justification for L. E. Elliott-Binns's theory, *Galilean Christianity* (1956), pp. 47f., that 1:1 was added to turn a homily into a letter. The word-play on "greeting" (*chairein*) and "joy" (*charan*, in 1:2) suggests the author intended a close link between the two verses. The Epistle does show signs of being a series of separate paraenetic tracts, loosely connected; and its genre is not that of a pastoral letter sent to a group of churches; cf. F. O. Francis, "The Form and Function of the Opening and Closing Paragraphs of James and 1 John," *ZNTW*, 61 (1970), 110–26.

[2] (1) Son of Zebedee (Mark 1:19 par.; Acts 1:13; 12:2); (2) son of Alphaeus (Mark 3:18; Acts 1:13); (3) James the less (Mark 15:40); (4) father of Judas (Acts 1:13; Luke 6:16); (5) brother of Jesus (Mark 6:3; Acts 12:17; 15:13; 21:18; Gal. 1:19; 2:9,12; 1 Cor. 15:7); (6) brother of Jude (Jude 1). The James ("Jacob" in RSV) of Matt. 1:15f. is not included. See J. J. Gunther, "The Family of Jesus," *EQ*, 46 (1974), 25–41.

[3] As W. G. Kümmel observes; *Introduction*², p. 412. For a recent consideration of "James and the Church of Jerusalem" see F. F. Bruce, *Peter, Stephen, James and John. Studies in Early Non-Pauline Christianity* (1980) (British title, *Men and Movements in the Primitive Church* [1979]), ch. 3.

be regarded as head of the Jerusalem church. The abrupt introduction of James in the Acts-narrative may be without significance, but Brandon may be correct that Luke passes quickly over the question of how James became head of the Jerusalem church because he was embarrassed by these episodes and (less probably, it seems to me) because he was out of sympathy with what James stood for.[4] By the time Acts was published, the Jerusalem church had perished; thus, Luke would probably not want to divert his readers' attention to James, since his purpose was to highlight the Pauline mission and its potential for the future. Possibly with the imprisonment of Peter (Acts 12) James stepped into the breach and stayed there when Peter, on his release, went to "another place" (Acts 12:17). At all events, at the Jerusalem council (Acts 15) James was a chief spokesman, and this status accords with what we find in Acts 21:18 and Galatians 2:9,12, where he is numbered among the "pillar" apostles. Whether James was regarded as an apostle in the early church depends partly on the exegesis of 1 Corinthians 15:7. J. B. Lightfoot thinks he was on the strength of the risen Lord's appearance to him,[5] but the majority of recent interpreters deny this. W. Schmithals writes, "Paul limits the assertion that he has seen no apostle besides Peter, by leaving room for the possibility that one could, if need be, count James among the apostles—something he was not himself accustomed to doing—whom he had also seen," thus accounting for the studied ambiguity of Paul's language here.[6]

James rose to some eminence in the Jerusalem community, establishing a sort of caliphate as the leading member of the holy family. If we rightly classify him as an apostle, then he joined Peter as a missionary to the Jews (Gal. 2:9), though this title is a misnomer, especially if Schmithals is correct that ἀπόστολος was coined among Hellenistic Christians and refers to evangelism outside the Palestinian sector of the church.

Like the rest of the original Twelve, the destiny of James is shrouded in obscurity. Why the early church failed to preserve clear evidence of the mission and martyrdom of its earliest leaders is an unsolved mystery. Christian imagination has offered some details in the way of legendary embellishments. A considerable body of stories about James exists, in part reading back into the Gospel period, in part trying to fill lacunae in the record. In the gnostic Gospel of Thomas (Logion 12), Jesus predicts James's preeminence and caliphate status in response to the disciples' question of who will take over when he is gone: "In the place to which you have gone, you will go to James the just, for whose

[4] S. G. F. Brandon, "The Death of James the Just: A New Interpretation," in Studies in Mysticism and Religion Presented to Gershom G. Scholem (1967), p. 60.

[5] J. B. Lightfoot, The Epistle to the Galatians (1887), pp. 95f.

[6] W. Schmithals, The Office of Apostle in the Early Church (ET 1969), pp. 64f.

sake heaven and earth came into being."[7] This tribute seems to derive from the second-century apocryphal *Gospel According to the Hebrews*, in which the post-resurrection appearance of Jesus to his brother dispels his unbelief: "My brother, eat your bread, for the Son of man has risen from those who sleep."[8]

As to the precise status of James in the church and the manner of his death, there are conflicting accounts. Eusebius (*HE* 2.23) quotes Hegesippus for information as to James's piety and priestly status. The latter is almost certainly an historical fiction contrived so as to make possible the drawing up of a succession list, in imitation of that of the Jewish high priests.[9] Eusebius accepts this expedient and makes James the first *episcopos* in Jerusalem. There was a public debate between the scribes and James in 62, at the conclusion of which James made a messianic confession about the exalted Son of man and the Jewish authorities had him stoned.

Josephus gives a different version by noting the political implications. He states (*Ant.* 20.197–203) that Ananus the high priest wished to clear the Jews of any suspicion of sedition with the incoming of a new procurator Albinus (in succession to Festus, AD 62). So Ananus "convened a council of judges and brought before it James, the brother of the so-called Christ . . . and handed them over to be stoned on the charge of having broken the law."[10]

The effect of James's death was notable, and the Jewish Christians in Jerusalem were grievously stricken. This may explain their ready acceptance of the oracle advising them to flee to Pella, on the east side of Jordan (Eusebius, *HE* 3.5.3). This was the immediate antecedent of the first Jewish war in 66; and the escape to Pella had the effect of

---

[7] See B. Gärtner, *The Theology of the Gospel of Thomas* (ET 1961), pp. 56f., who remarks that this may be evidence of the way in which Jewish-Christian ideas became fitted into a gnostic system.

[8] F. F. Bruce, *New Testament History,* p. 350. The reference is preserved in Jerome, *De viris illustribus 2.*

[9] S. G. F. Brandon, *loc. cit.,* attempts to find a political reason for James's association with the lower priesthood and protest against the Sadducean aristocracy. On the Epistle as the record of James's teaching set against the background of his concern for the unjustly treated lower clergy after AD 59, when they were deprived of their income, and his protest against the Zealot resort to violence in opposition to the high priestly authority, see R. P. Martin, "The Life-Setting of the Epistle of James in the Light of Jewish History," in the William S. LaSor *Festschrift,* ed. Gary A. Tuttle (1978). For the historical value of the data from Hegesippus, see B. Reicke, *The New Testament Era,* p. 215. A parallel view of the *Sitz im Leben* of James is taken by P. H. Davids, *Commentary on James* (NIGTC, 1982), pp. 28–34, esp. pp. 33f. See too his essay "Theological Perspectives on the Epistle of James," *JETS,* 23 (1980), 97–103.

[10] *Ant.* 20.200 refers to the "law," apparently not the Torah (since the Pharisees lament James's death) nor the Roman law. Possibly it reflects Paul's alleged introduction of Greeks into the Temple (Acts 21:27–29), with James's friendly attitude to Paul interpreted as an act of disloyalty to Ananus' patriotism. Paul's sensitivity to the political situation in Judaea in these years may well underlie several references in his letters. See pp. 154f.

isolating Jewish Christians from Judaism. Tradition also places a migration of Palestinian Christians—including Mary, Jesus' mother, and John the beloved disciple—to Asia at this time.

With this background we return to the question of the author of the letter.

2. If we could be certain about the writer's identity, it would be easier to locate the Epistle in the stream of earliest Christianity.[11] But certain question marks have been set against the identification of James with the "brother of the Lord" (Gal. 1:19; 2:9,12). In particular, we may observe the following:

a. The Greek style, mirroring the higher *koinē* language, is consciously literary. Its fluent and elegant style would appeal to readers living in the Greek world. Doubts have been raised as to whether a Galilean Jew could have composed in this ornate way, and a likely hypothesis in the face of these is that a disciple, a Hellenistic Jew conversant with the Septuagint and the Wisdom literature (whose features are prominent in the treatise), served as final redactor. "James the just" may well be seen as standing behind the document; indeed, he may be the "righteous man" of 5:6,16.[12] Others have argued that it is not beyond the bounds of possibility that a first-century Palestinian Jewish Christian was capable of writing Greek with such skill—though whether knowing Greek in a bilingual setting in the Roman provinces would produce such elegance (e.g., turns of phrase like "the cycle of nature"; 3:6) is another question.[13] It should be noted further that the Septuagint is cited in the Old Testament references; and there are 63 words here (45 in LXX) not found elsewhere in the New Testament literature.

b. The characterization of the "perfect law of freedom" (1:25) does not seem to square with James's attitude recorded in Acts and Galatians, which suggest a more legalistic frame of mind—though James was not among Paul's Judaizing opponents (Acts 21:18-26), however uneasy he may have felt. The opponents who "came from James" (Gal. 2:12) may have used his name, but there is no firm connection between their teaching and his.[14] Furthermore, tradition has held that although James was closely tied in with Judaism, he died because the Jews found fault with what seemed to them a too-liberal attitude to the law (Josephus, *Ant.* 20.200). But, as we observed above (n. 10), this inference is disputable.

---

[11] J. A. T. Robinson, *Redating the New Testament*, p. 118, refers to James as "one of those apparently timeless documents that could be dated almost anywhere"; still, if historical circumstances that match its content can be plausibly suggested, the message will be thereby illuminated.

[12] See H. J. Schoeps, "Jacobus ὁ δίκαιος καὶ 'Ωβλίας," *Biblica*, 24 (1943), 398–403.

[13] On the issue of James's capability to compose in Greek see J. N. Sevenster, *Do You Know Greek? How Much Greek Could the First Jewish Christians have Known?* (1968), pp. 3–21; A. W. Argyle, "Greek Among the Jews of Palestine in New Testament Times," *NTS*, 20 (1973-74), 87–89; J. A. T. Robinson, *op. cit.*, pp. 132ff.

[14] See Robinson, *op. cit.*, pp. 130f.

c. No personal recollections of the home and family at Nazareth appear. But the tone and purpose of this letter do not call for such autobiographical or personal writing.[15] There are some points of contact between the ethical teaching of the Epistle and the Gospel tradition, especially in regard to the Sermon on the Mount, as commentators have noted.[16]

d. W. Marxsen makes much of the situation reflected in 2:14–26, which (he says) is only conceivable in a post-Pauline period, when Paul's relaxed attitude to morality and his teaching (Rom. 3:28) on justification by faith *alone* (note the word μόνον in James 2:24) have come in for critical inspection.[17] The root of the trouble lies in a changed sense of the term "faith." For Paul faith is trust and obedience, showing itself in love (Gal. 5:6). But in James a perversion of the Pauline position has appeared, understanding faith in terms of intellectual acceptance and acknowledgment of doctrines (2:19), and James writes polemically to controvert and correct. Marxsen believes that James only made matters worse, for instead of appealing to the true Pauline statement, James so exalts "works" as to end up with "an isolated ethics, a pure nominalism."[18]

But this ingenious interpretation falls down on the fact that already in Judaism the question of how a person is made right with God was debated.[19] It is equally possible to maintain that Paul is replying to James as vice versa.[20] Besides there is a possible historical setting for this controversy in James's self-defense that his association with Paul did not implicate him in some of the excesses of Paul's intemperate disciples (according to Romans 3 and 6). Something of this fear is echoed in Acts 21:21–24. One of the surest ways to neutralize this fear, felt in the politically sensitive atmosphere of Jerusalem, would have been to stress the importance of works as an evidence of true faith.

---

[15] The literary genre of James may well account for the singular absence of any reference to the Lord's death and resurrection (except at 2:1). E. M. Sidebottom, *Commentary* (NCB, 1967), notes "the impression of an almost pre-crucifixion discipleship" (p. 14).

[16] J. B. Mayor, *The Epistle of James*[3] (1910), pp. lxiif.; Sidebottom, *op. cit.*, pp. 8–11. The setting of the document in agrarian Palestinian life is well established; see J. H. Ropes, *St. James* (1916), pp. 295–97; D. Y. Hadidian, "Palestinian Pictures in the Epistle of James," *ExpT*, 63 (1951–52), 227f. From another angle, by relating James's "wisdom" to the Holy Spirit, as in Jewish literature, J. A. Kirk sets the argument for a Palestinian origin of the letter on a firm base. See his "The Meaning of Wisdom in James," *NTS*, 16 (1969–70), 24–38.

[17] W. Marxsen, *Introduction to the New Testament*, pp. 226–31.

[18] *Ibid.*, p. 230. Marxsen's term is *Nominismus*, which is better rendered "nomism," i.e., salvation by legalistic obedience.

[19] See J. Jeremias, "Paul and James," *ExpT*, 66 (1954–55), 368–71.

[20] J. A. T. Robinson, *op. cit.*, pp. 127f., drawing on J. B. Mayor, *op. cit.*, p. xcviii, who insists that Paul's argument in Rom. 4:2–5 reads more intelligibly as an answer to James than the occasion of James's later corrective comment.

e. One historical problem is less easily disposed of: the slow acceptance of this letter into the church's canon.[21] In fact the attestation of the document is unknown in the church until the time of Origen, later than 200. How can we explain this reluctance if the letter was believed to have come from the hand of the member of the holy family? R. V. G. Tasker argues that apostolic figures were accorded more authority than teachers in the early church, and that this letter had a limited circulation and appeal. When it was brought to the notice of the church at large, it was received as from James, the Lord's brother, and one whom Paul described (Gal. 1:19) as an apostle.[22]

LIFE-SETTING

If authorship by James (the man of Gal. 1:19; 1 Cor. 15:7; Acts 12:17; 15:13; 21:18) is accepted, the date of the Epistle is prior to 62, when he was executed by the Jews. An interesting sidelight is that, according to one tradition, James showed considerable sympathy for the claims of the lower clergy who may well have been identified with the Zealot call to violence. This letter devotes much space to sympathy for the poor and opposition to the rich (2:1–9; 5:1–6); at the same time, some parts read like a conscious counterblast to the Zealot manifesto (1:20; 2:8,13; 3:13–18; 4:1–4).[23]

Most who accept the traditional view date James in the 50s and see it as a counterattack on a travesty of Paul's teaching (already faced by Paul in Rom. 6:1ff.), or as a specimen of Galilean Christianity otherwise not directly attested in the New Testament.[24] Robinson dates it in 47–48, placing it before the Apostolic Council (49) and thus also earlier than Paul's pastoral problems having to do with faith and works.[25]

If a post-Pauline dating seems more feasible, James must refer to some Christian teacher of that name (not necessarily a pseudonym for the Lord's brother). It is possible to picture a church situation which would make this Epistle germane. Massey H. Shepherd, Jr., has anchored the Epistle firmly in a known *Sitz im Leben*: he takes Matthew's Gospel as the basis for much of James's moral teaching and sees both documents as emanating from Syria in the latter part of the first cen-

---

[21] See Kümmel, *Introduction*[2], pp. 405f.; Guthrie, *Introduction*[3], pp. 736–39.

[22] R. V. G. Tasker, *The General Epistle of James* (1956), p. 19. J. A. T. Robinson, *op. cit.*, p. 132 finds reasons other than that of disputed authorship to explain the suspicion that was engendered in the early church.

[23] M. J. Townsend, "James 4.1–4: A Warning against Zealotry?", *ExpT*, 87 (1975–76), 211–13.

[24] L. E. Elliott-Binns, *Galilean Christianity*, who follows E. Lohmeyer's attempt to distinguish a Galilean version of the gospel from one centered in Jerusalem.

[25] J. A. T. Robinson, *op. cit.*, p. 138.

tury or later.[26] If we may take this thesis a step further, on the ground that Matthew's Gospel speaks to a situation where Gentile Christians were resisting the claims of the moral law and were seeking to break free from the Jewish incubus of the faith, then the Epistle is another way of recalling the church to its moral responsibility, ecclesiastical moorings, and respect for the perfect law (cf. Matt. 5:17-20).[27]

C. L. Mitton is content to treat the letter as a collection of teaching from James of Jerusalem. His positive contribution is the suggestion of a suitable occasion for the letter. He imagines that in Jerusalem James received Jewish Christians from the Dispersion when they came "up to town" at festival time. Because they appreciated his teaching, they importuned him to copy down his words so that they could take back a specimen to their home churches.[28]

This is ingenious, but it sounds a little too modern. In its favor is the recent consensus that James is not an Epistle (in the regular sense of the term) but an assortment of exhortations (there are sixty verbal imperatives in 108 verses) loosely strung together. There is no ostensible pattern, so the description "a written sermon" says more about the idea of what a sermon should be than about a logical presentation of the matter.[29] Much of the material has an Old Testament and Jewish setting, though this may be conscious imitation rather than suggesting a primitive setting in Jewish-Christianity.

CONCLUSION

The nearest companion document to James is the extra-canonical *Didache*. Both pieces of literature serve a useful purpose, in showing how the gospel was applied in a non-urban community (in Syria?); and whatever the uncertain historical details of the origin of both treatises, their writing and acceptance indicate how the gospel came to be moralized in over-reaction against the Pauline *kerygma* with its Christology and its

[26] M. H. Shepherd, Jr., "The Epistle of James and the Gospel of Matthew," *JBL*, 75 (1956), 40–51, but placing James in the 2nd century. On common elements in Matthew and James, see A. Feuillet, "Le sens du mot Parusie dans l'évangile de Matthieu," in *The Background of the New Testament and its Eschatology*, edd. Davies and Daube, pp. 261–80.

[27] For a suggested origin of Matthew's Gospel in the post-Pauline period as a response to excesses in the Gentile churches, see R. P. Martin, "St. Matthew's Gospel in Recent Study," *ExpT*, 80 (1968–69), 132–36; and *NTF*, Vol. 1, pp. 231f.

[28] C. L. Mitton, *The Epistle of James* (1966), p. 9. Other recent commentators represent diverse opinions. B. Reicke, *James, Peter, and Jude* (1963), puts the work in Domitian's reign, *c.* AD 90, insisting that it is practically impossible that the Epistle is pre-Pauline (pp. 5f.). M. Dibelius and H. Greeven, *James* (1976), say no more than that the internal evidence and ethos of the letter point to second- or third-generation Christianity, and suggest that James must not be placed too late in the 2nd century. They offer an approximate time span of AD 80–130 (pp. 45ff.).

[29] But see P. B. R. Forbes, "The Structure of the Epistle of James," *EQ*, 44 (1972), 147–53.

emphasis on "new life in the risen Christ." Nonetheless, we cannot afford to dismiss the Epistle with a negative assessment. It takes its place in Scripture as a warning to any whose practice contradicts the gospel he preaches and professes to believe. James's attack on this problem was non-Pauline, to be sure, but it may well be that if the Epistle was written *ad hominem*—by the author's consciously adopting the stance of his readers and speaking to their condition in a way they could and v ould appreciate—some justification may be found for E. Thurneysen's startling contention that "James preaches Jesus Christ, His cross and resurrection, the power of forgiveness and the obedience of faith, and nothing else; but he preaches this in his own peculiar way."[30]

---

[30] Quoted by C. E. B. Cranfield, "The Message of James," *SJT*, 18 (1965), 182–93, 338–45, from whom this application is taken.

CHAPTER TWENTY-EIGHT

The Literature Published in Asia Minor

The literature associated with the name of "John," three Epistles and the Apocalypse, apparently emanating from Asia Minor, is a distinctive body of Christian writing. The Epistles and Revelation belong to different literary genres, and obvious disparities of style and authorship have been noted since Dionysius of Alexandria (AD 264/65; cf. Eusebius, *HE* 7.25). Still, there is considerable justification for assigning these New Testament books to a common geographical and cultural region. There is unanimous witness in early Christian writers to link John with Ephesus and Asia Minor and to suggest that his Gospel was published there. Eusebius reports the tradition that Asia was allotted to John when the church was scattered from its homeland at the outbreak of the Jewish rebellion in 66 (*HE* 3.1.1). Johannine Christianity is presupposed in the Apocalypse, and several terms and ideas are common to the Gospel, Epistles, and Revelation. The letters to the churches in Revelation 1–3 further associate that book with Asia Minor. The false teaching in these Johannine communities, as well as in those of the Epistles, has parallels in Colossians (Ephesians) and the letters to Timothy. Finally, the first evidence for the use of 1 John comes from Smyrna (Polycarp, *Phil.* 7, alluding to 1 Jn. 4:2–4; 2:18, 22; 2 Jn. 7).[1]

Even within 1, 2, and 3 John there are puzzling issues about literary origins, purpose, and situational context, the last aspect being the most important.

THE JOHANNINE LETTERS

1. *Authorship.* The closest ties of the Johannine Epistles are clearly with the Gospel of John, and most interpreters share the conviction that both Gospel and Epistles emanate from the same church situation and from the same source. C. H. Dodd argued on the strength of linguistic differences (Aramaisms in the Gospel are absent from the Epistles) and change of theological emphases (e.g., the eschatology of

---

[1] Not all critics are disposed to question a common authorship of all five Johannine specimens; see Robinson, *Redating the New Testament*, pp. 255f., 291f.

the Gospel is mainly a realized one, in which the possession of eternal life is a present reality; the Epistles offer a futurist hope) that the two sets of works came from diverse hands.[2]

Since Dodd, other arguments have been adduced in favor of separate authorship for the Gospel and the Epistles. H. Conzelmann argues that there is a shift in the use of ἀρχή, which in the Gospel refers to the preexistence of the divine Logos, whereas in the First Epistle it is used adverbially (2:7; cf. 2 John 6) to denote the beginning of the tradition.[3] But 1 John 1:1 and 2:13 *are* personal references. G. Klein developed this argument along the lines of seeing in 1 John the beginnings of a church tradition.[4] Bultmann also maintains that the Gospel of John and 1 John are directed against different fronts. The former confronts the non-Christian "world"; the Epistle opposes the false teachers who have arisen to challenge Johannine orthodoxy. The point of contact is that the author of 1 John had the Gospel before him, and used it to defend his position *vis-à-vis* the heretics.[5] Finally, D. M. Smith has proposed that the hypothesis of a Johannine school or set of churches which redacted and promoted the tradition emanating from "John" (see *NTF*, Vol. 1, pp. 276f.) makes the case for multiple authorship all the stronger. He points to the importance of respecting and accounting for the theological and stylistic differences between the Gospel and the Epistles.[6]

To the extent that this latest phase of Johannine study is on the right track, the older arguments in support of common authorship[7] should be reexamined, to see whether significant changes of emphasis and content in the documents may not reflect the use of the Gospel in the hands of a Johannine editor who was responsible for the Epistles.

2. *Literary associations.* Apart from the identification of the author, we must still determine the sequence of composition of Gospel and Epistles. Part of the answer to this rests on finding a suitable purpose for the Epistles. J. A. T. Robinson regards the Epistles as supplying a corrective to a misunderstanding of the Gospel on the part of gnosticizing Christians within Greek-speaking Judaism.[8] But many other scholars reverse the order of publication, so that the Epistles form a first draft of Johannine Christianity later supplemented by the Gospel.

---

[2] C. H. Dodd, "The First Epistle of John and the Fourth Gospel," *BJRL*, 21 (1937), 129–56; and *The Johannine Epistles* (1946), pp. xlvii–lvi. See N. Turner, *A Grammar of New Testament Greek*, Vol. 4 (1976), pp. 132–34.

[3] H. Conzelmann, "Was von Anfang war," in *Neutestamentliche Studien für Bultmann* (1954), pp. 194–201.

[4] G. Klein, "Das wahre Licht scheint schon," *ZTK*, 68 (1971), 261–326.

[5] R. Bultmann, *The Johannine Epistles* (ET 1973).

[6] D. M. Smith, "Johannine Christianity: Some Reflections on its Character and Delineation," *NTS*, 21 (1974–75), 222–48.

[7] Mentioned with approval by McNeile-Williams, *Introduction*[2], p. 305; J. A. T. Robinson, *op. cit.*, pp. 288f.

[8] J. A. T. Robinson, "The Destination and Purpose of the Johannine Epistles," in *Twelve New Testament Studies* (1962), pp. 126–38; cf. *Redating the New Testament*, p. 285; Bultmann, *op. cit.*, p. 1, who also believes that the Epistles came later

Another view holds that the question is irrelevant and the Epistles formed a "companion document" (*Begleitungsschrift*) sent out to accompany and interpret the Gospel.[9]

The literary format of 1 John is also a puzzle.[10] Clearly the purpose is pastoral, though the letter is encyclical and general. It is the only New Testament document without a single personal name nor does it quote from the Old Testament (except the allusion to Cain—the one biblical figure mentioned—in 3:12), though the writing stands in an Old Testament tradition and confronts a specific situation by offering both an answer to and a refutation of discernible problems in Asia Minor.

The moralistic and hortatory tone of much of the letter also suggests a baptismal context, as the material belongs to the type of instruction given to new converts ("little children," as they are called in 2:1,12; 3:18; 4:4; 5:21; cf. 2:13,18; 3:2,10). W. Nauck has theorized that 1 John is a baptismal-catechetical document. He points in particular to 1 John 5:8; "the Spirit, the water, and the blood" he sees as answering to the three stages of Christian initiation—reception of the Spirit, baptism and first communion.[11]

---

than the Gospel. Robinson now holds that the first editor of the Fourth Gospel antedated the Epistles (AD 60–65), but that the final form of the Gospel, with prologue and epilogue, is to be dated soon after AD 65. He leans on F. L. Cribbs, "A Reassessment of the Date of Origin and the Destination of the Gospel of John," *JBL*, 89 (1970), 38–55, for support of a dating of John's Gospel in its first draft in the late 50s or early 60s, and locates its place of publication in Jerusalem/Judaea.

[9] But see B. Vawter, "The Johannine Epistles," in *The Jerome Biblical Commentary*, edd. R. E. Brown, J. A. Fitzmyer, and R. E. Murphy (1968), p. 405. See too F. F. Bruce, *The Epistles of John* (1970), pp. 25ff.

[10] B. F. Westcott, *The Epistles of St. John*³ (1892, repr. 1966), p. xlvi; see R. Law, *The Tests of Life: A Study of the First Epistle of St. John* (1909), esp. pp. 2–21, for one of the deservedly best-known treatments. A useful survey is P. R. Jones, "A Structural Analysis of 1 John," *RE*, 67 (1970), 433ff. One of the simplest divisions is suggested by A. Feuillet, "Etude structurale de la première épître de saint Jean," in *Neues Testament und Geschichte: Cullmann Festschrift* (1972), pp. 307–28: 1:5—2:29 (communion with God who is light); 3:1—5:12 (communion with God who is love). Recent scholarship has focused on the unity of the Epistle, specifically whether the author has redacted an original *Vorlage*. For the view that this source was Christian see Bultmann, *op. cit.*; O. Piper, "1 John and the Didache of the Primitive Church," *JBL*, 66 (1947), 437–51; W. Nauck, *Die Tradition und der Charakter des ersten Johannesbriefes* (1957); for the view that it was Jewish see J. C. O'Neill, *The Puzzle of John* (1966). Some theories along these lines are more ingenious than convincing; cf. P. J. Thompson, "Psalm 119: A Possible Clue to the Structure of the First Epistle of John," *SE*, 2 (TU 87) (1961), 487–92. There has been a shift of emphasis away from sources to the letter as a whole; see E. Haenchen, "Neuere Literatur zu den Johbr.," *TR*, 26 (1960), 1–42, 267–92. See the latest work on the letters by I. H. Marshall, *The Epistles of John* (NICNT, 1978); R. E. Brown, *The Epistles of John* (Anchor Bible, 1982); S. S. Smalley, *1, 2, 3 John* (WBC, 1984); and K. Grayston, *The Johannine Epistles* (NCB, 1984).

[11] Nauck, *op. cit.*, pp. 147–82. He relates "spirit" (πνεῦμα) to the rite of anointing, held to be the means for imparting the Spirit (cf. 2:20,27). It is more likely that R. Schnackenburg, *Die Johannesbriefe* (1953), p. 234, is correct in seeing in πνεῦμα the life-giving power that flows through the sacramental action of baptism and eucharist. Cf. T. W. Manson, "Entry into Membership in the Early Church," *JTS*, 48 o.s. (1947), 25–33.

3. *Purpose.* J. A. T. Robinson's case for the relation between Gospel and Epistles is attractive. As we have noted, he sees the Gospel as an evangelistic book addressed to Greek-speaking Diaspora Jews and the Epistles as messages of assurance to believers "in a situation where they are in grave danger of being shaken from their belief in what they had accepted."[12] The author's programmatic statement comes at 5:13: "I write this to you who believe in the name of the Son of God, that you may know that you have eternal life."[13] This thesis is confirmed by the heavy concentration of words for "knowledge," "assurance," and the like.[14]

4. *The Situation.* We may piece together information scattered throughout the letters into a composite picture of the "grave danger" facing these Asia Minor churches in the final decade of the first century.[15] Heretical teachers have arisen (2:18f.,26; 3:7), whom the author labels "false prophets" (4:1) and "anti-Christ" (i.e., counterfeit Christ; 2:18; cf. 4:3). Christians are called to distinguish the truth from the spurious claims being bandied about. Though these false teachers have been unmasked (4:4) and expelled (2:19), their influence remains.

The claims of the false teachers are seen in sentences that begin: "if any one says. . . ." The following picture emerges from the data:

a. They have boasted of their knowledge of God (2:4; 4:8), love of God (4:20), and fellowship with him (1:6; 2:6,9). All the time, John insists, they are living a lie.

b. They have claimed unique spiritual experience (4:1f.) and they have prided themselves on these in an immoral way (1:8,10). The presence and influence of an antinomian ethic and a disregard of moral distinctions seem clear.

c. They have taught a docetic Christology (4:2), which denies true humanity to Christ and in some way they have cast doubt on the redemptive power of his death. They have denied his messiahship (2:22ff.) and his being the unique Son of God (4:15; 5:5,10f.).

---

[12] *Twelve New Testament Studies,* p. 127. For consideration of Robinson's thesis, see J. W. Bowker, "The Origin and Purpose of St. John's Gospel," *NTS,* 11 (1964–65), 398–408.

[13] Cf. Robinson, *Redating the New Testament,* p. 290; J. R. W. Stott, *The Epistles of John* (1964), pp. 41, 184f.; Bultmann, *op. cit.,* p. 83; Schnackenburg, *op. cit.,* p. 244.

[14] Cf. Stott, *op. cit.,* p. 50; Schnackenburg, *op. cit.,* p. 244.

[15] As we have seen, this dating depends on the prior question of the date of the Fourth Gospel; see *NTF,* Vol. 1, pp. 281f. The maturation of the Johannine tradition—if that is how we are to view the process underlying these documents—would require several decades; see D. M. Smith, *loc. cit.* The data in 1 John for identifying the opponents are given in most commentaries; we may mention four additional essays: H. S. Songer, "The Life Situation of the Johannine Epistles," *RE,* 67 (1970), 399–409; Frank Stagg, "Orthodoxy and Orthopraxy in the Johannine Epistles," *ibid.,* 423–32; K. Weiss, "Orthodoxie und Heterodoxie im 1. Johannesbrief," *ZNTW,* 58 (1967), 247–55; and "Die Gnosis im Hintergrund und im Spiegel der Johannesbriefe," in *Gnosis und das Neue Testament* (1973), pp. 341–56.

d. Antinomian attitudes are painfully obvious in their false sense of superiority to the commandments (2:4; 3:7,10) and their exclusivist, selfish actions (3:10ff.,17; 4:20).

Attempts to pinpoint this heresy as that of Cerinthus are based on 5:6, which is taken to be a tacit denial of his refusal to believe in Jesus' full humanity.[16] There is an interesting variant, known to Tertullian and Irenaeus, of 4:3: *qui solvit Iesum* (λύει for μὴ ὁμολογεῖ): "every spirit that severs or annuls (rather than "does not confess") Jesus is not from God," a sentiment of Cerinthus.[17] Some of these motifs are clear in 2 John also. This is especially so in verse 9 with its "progressivism," and a desire to abandon apostolic teaching.[18]

John's counter-argument is the necessity of right faith in Christ, true God and true man, and the inescapable connection between faith and proper conduct. Hence there are blocks of ethical teaching in 1:5— 2:7; 3:4–24; 5:1-3, 16–21.

5. *The problem in 3 John*. The struggle here is one of church order. The main characters in this vivid story are a Christian named Gaius, who had evidently become a believer through the "Elder" (vs. 4), and Diotrephes, who domineers over the congregation (vs. 9) and opposes the Elder. It is difficult on this evidence to equate the Elder with the Apostle John, especially since early tradition knows of a separate person surnamed the Elder.[19] Exactly how Diotrephes tried to assert his authority is not clear. Harnack thought that we have here the same tension as in the *Didache* (11–13,15) between an old provincial missionary situation (Diotrephes representing an independent type of prophetic ministry) and a more institutionalized order of ministry (the Elder speaks for the monarchical bishop who wields authority).[20] W. Bauer thinks of Diotrephes as a gnostic teacher.[21] Käsemann ties this letter

---

[16] Stott, *op. cit.*, pp. 46ff.; Robinson, *Twelve New Testament Studies*, pp. 134–36; A. E. Brooke, *The Johannine Epistles* (1912), p. xlv. Recent opinion is less certain; cf. Robinson, *Redating the New Testament*, p. 286n., with reference to Schnackenburg, *op. cit.*, pp. 13–20; and Kümmel, *Introduction*[2], pp. 441f. See also Songer, *loc. cit.*, pp. 405f. But see R. McL. Wilson, *Gnosis and the New Testament* (1968), p. 40. On the question in general see E. Schwartz, "Johannes und Kerinthus,"*ZNTW*, 15 (1914), 210–19. R. E. Brown, *The Community of the Beloved Disciple* (1979), p. 105, finds John's teaching to be directed against the enemies of Ignatius with their docetic christology. See the helpful note on "terms" used to fix the identity of John's opponents in Smalley's commentary, p. xxv, and for the link between the Johannine letters and the Fourth Gospel, see Smalley, *John: Evangelist and Interpreter* (1978), pp. 147f.

[17] The textual evidence is surveyed by Brooke, *op. cit.*, pp. 111–14. The witness is clearly late.

[18] 2 John is best read as an "attempt of an early Christian leader to stem the rising tide of Christian gnostic thought in the early part of the second century," if the internal evidence of the Epistle matches that of Ignatius' rebuttal of docetic teaching. So R. C. Briggs, "Contemporary Study of the Johannine Epistles," *RE*, 67 (1970), 421. Cf. J. L. Houlden, *The Johannine Epistles* (1973), pp. 4ff.

[19] *NTF*, Vol. 1, pp. 277f.; cf. G. Bornkamm, *TDNT*, 6 (1969), 672n125.

[20] Harnack, "Über den dritten Johannesbrief," *TU*, 15, 3b (1897). E. Haenchen has appraised this view in his survey of recent literature; *TR*, 26 (1960), 270f.

[21] W. Bauer, *Orthodoxy and Heresy in Earliest Christianity* (ET 1971), p. 93.

into a general understanding of the Johannine literature (including the Gospel) as semi-heretical, and emanating from a conventicle-type sect tinged with gnosticism.[22] On this view Diotrephes becomes the representative of orthodoxy as a monarchical bishop. But this view is bizarre, and the reversal of roles by which "John" has become a gnosticizing Christian, and a "simple presbyter" at that, and Diotrephes a spokesman for orthodox Christianity, has not met with much acceptance.[23]

More probable is the traditional reading of the text, which sets the Elder as the custodian and bearer of apostolic authority in conscious opposition to Diotrephes, who had aspired to ecclesiastical eminence, and was claiming dictatorial powers of excommunication from the church. "John" opposes this action with a reliance on the "truth," just as Paul faced his opponents in Corinth.[24]

THE APOCALYPSE

1. *Its genre.* No New Testament book demands more introductory background on the part of its modern readers than this one. G. B. Caird imagines "the untutored reader" coming to the end of the book "with the question 'What on earth is this all about?'"[25] A clue to the problem is the self-designation of the book as "Apocalypse" (1:1; 22:6).[26] Equally important is the title "prophecy" (22:7-19; cf. 1:3; 10:11; 19:10). Old Testament passages which exhibit the features of the apocalyptic

---

22 E. Käsemann, *The Testament of Jesus* (ET 1968); cf. *NTF*, Vol. 1, p. 276; on 3 John see Käsemann, "Ketzer und Zeuge," *ZThK*, 48 (1951), 292-311. But see Bauer, *op. cit.*, p. 308, for a modification of Käsemann's position.

23 The error in Käsemann's designation ("Ketzer und Zeuge," *loc. cit.*, p. 311) of "John" as a "simple presbyter" is pointed out by H. von Campenhausen, *Ecclesiastical Authority and Spiritual Power in the Church of the First Three Centuries* (ET 1969), p. 121. Guthrie, *Introduction*,[3] p. 898, cites several scholars who disagree with Käsemann; Bultmann (*The Johannine Epistles*, p. 101) disdains Käsemann's earlier views as "simply fanciful" (*phantastisch*); see also G. Bornkamm, in *TDNT*, 6 (1969), 671n121. Diotrephes "may only have been a successful ecclesiastical demagogue" in T. W. Manson's estimate (*The Church's Ministry* [1948], p. 61).

24 H. von Campenhausen, *op. cit.*, p. 123. On what is implied by this appeal to the "truth" (3 John 3,4,8,12) see R. Schnackenburg, "Zum Begriff der Wahrheit in den beiden kleinen Johannesbriefen," *BZ*, 11 (1967), 253-58. For the various ways the Elder responded to false ideas, see I. H. Marshall, "Orthodoxy and Heresy in Earlier Christianity," *Themelios*, 2 n.s. (1979), 9. See now C. K. Barrett, *Church, Ministry and Sacraments* (1985), pp. 46, 82, on the contact between the elder and Diotrephes.

25 G. B. Caird, *A Commentary on the Revelation of St. John the Divine* (1966), p. 1; his is a recent work that admirably fulfils its aim of providing the needed introductory background; other commentaries of considerable value are by R. H. Charles (1920), G. E. Ladd (1972), and G. R. Beasley-Murray (1974). Special mention should be made of Caird's series, "On Deciphering the Book of Revelation," *ExpT*, 74 (1962-63), 13-15, 51-53, 82-84, 103-105.

26 For this term, see *NTF*, Vol. 1, pp. 103-7; D. S. Russell, *The Method and Message of Jewish Apocalyptic* (1964); K. Koch, *The Rediscovery of Apocalyptic* (ET 1972); P. D. Hanson, *The Dawn of Apocalyptic* (1975). For orientation to this kind of literature, see J. Barr, "Jewish Apocalyptic in Recent Scholarly Study," *BJRL*, 58 (1975), 9-35; F. F. Bruce, "A Reappraisal of Jewish Apocalyptic Literature," *RE*, 72 (1975), 305-15; J. Lambrecht, "The Book of Revelation and Apocalyptic in the NT," *ETL*, 55 (1979), 391-97.

genre include Isaiah 24–27; 56–66; Zechariah 9–14; Joel 2–3; and many passages in Ezekiel (including 1:26, a vision picked up in Rev. 4).[27] There are also specimens of apocalyptic in non-canonical Jewish literature. Of first importance, however, as a key to the background of Revelation is the canonical Book of Daniel, especially chapters 7–12.[28]

Revelation is both like and unlike its apocalyptic predecessors.[29] It shares a religious attitude to history, in which the believer sees God's purposes as leading up to a grand climax and supernatural intervention. It makes similar use of the literary categories of vision, symbolism (especially in numbers and colors), and parable. Animal forms stand for persons and natural phenomena pictorialize events, though the identifications are not always one-for-one correspondences, as though every animal or insect had a human counterpart in history.[30] The root idea of apocalyptic is a dualism of two ages, according to which this age is one of wickedness and persecution for the saints of God and the next age is one of triumph and vindication. The turning point comes in a sudden dramatic intervention by God, who has been silently working out his purposes up to that time. Finally, the message of apocalyptists and seers is one of consolation and hope, offering a theodicy, a justification of the ways of God to men. The seer expresses the assurance that all is safe in God's hands in spite of the present stress, and the end is certain as history unfolds along its predetermined course in establishing God's rule in the new world order.

Yet the canonical Book of Revelation stands apart from its predecessors in the apocalyptic library in several ways. First of all, the vehicle of this Apocalypse is not a figure from the remote past (like Enoch or Moses), but John, who is known to his readers as their contemporary and fellow-sufferer (1:1,4,9; 22:8). Second, the introductory letters (chs. 2–3) and the epistolary conclusion (22:6–21) give the appearance of a personal message to the local churches of Asia; this document was intended to be read to those churches (1:3 RSV; 22:18). In particular, 22:6, with its claim to endorse the seer's inspiration (traced back to 19:10) as a true prophet, and 22:18f., which form a kind of canonization formula, are parts of this final appeal to the churches not to refuse the message.[31] "It is imperative that that word be delivered in its integrity to those for whom it was intended."[32]

[27] See A. Vanhoye, "L'utilisation du livre d'Ezéchiel dans l'Apocalypse," *Biblica*, 43 (1962), 436–76.
[28] J. Cambier, "Les images de l'A.T. dans l'Apocalypse de S. Jean," *NRT*, 87 (1955), 113–22; R. H. Preston and A. T. Hanson, *Revelation of St. John the Divine* (1949), pp. 34–42, summarize the extent of the indebtedness of John to the Old Testament.
[29] Cf. D. S. Russell, *op. cit.*, p. 35; L. Morris, *Apocalyptic* (1973).
[30] For a ludicrous—yet tragic—application of the "locusts" (Rev. 9:7–11,15) to the Beatles and the Sharon Tate-LaBianca slayings in 1969, see Vincent Bugliosi and Curt Gentry, *Helter Skelter* (1975), pp. 321–29.
[31] Cf. A. Farrer, *The Revelation* (1964), p. 224; G. von Rad, *Old Testament Theology*, 1 (ET 1962), 221ff.
[32] G. R. Beasley-Murray, *Commentary*, p. 347.

Another difference from Jewish apocalyptic is the way John achieves his purpose of consolation. The book contains a call to endurance (13:10; 14:12), yet John's pastoral counsel is offered not so much as a philosophy of history (common in Jewish apocalypses) as an assertion of the present reality of God's kingdom and the assurance of an imminent *parousia* of Christ (22:7,12,20). John's visions are of heavenly realities (4:1, etc.), but they are directly related to earthly events. To borrow a phrase of the Reverend Jesse Jackson, his "seeing" is not with eyesight but with insight; not *with* the eyes but *through* them, as William Blake wrote in "The Everlasting Gospel":

This life's five windows of the soul
Distorts the Heavens from pole to pole,
And lead you to believe a lie
When you see with, not thro', the eye.

In the words of E. Fiorenza: "John's primary concern is to give a prophetic interpretation of the present situation of the Christian community."[33]

However much Revelation may share the external and internal aspects of the structure, idiom, and message of its Old Testament and Judaic counterparts, even at times (e.g., ch. 12) borrowing from age-old pan-religious myths, at the heart of its message is the Christian affirmation of God's sovereignty at work in Christ as Lord of history. It is a thoroughly Christian book, especially, as Russell notes, in the place it gives to Jesus the Messiah as the meaning and end of all human history.[34] It is free of flights of fancy and irrelevant speculation. A pastoral purpose dominates; the historical situation of the churches stands in the forefront of John's purpose. No matter how much his messages were to have a timeless significance—and may well prove meaningful at the end of the age—Revelation stands in contrast to 1 Enoch 1:2: "Enoch ... saw the vision of the Holy One in the heavens, which the angels showed me, and from them I heard everything, and from them I understood as I saw, but not for this generation, but for a remote one which is for to come."

2. *Its historical setting.* The thought-world of the seer embraces heaven and earth;[35] indeed, his task is precisely to show the reality of

[33] E. Fiorenza, "The Eschatology and Composition of the Apocalypse," *CBQ*, 30 (1968), 558f.
[34] D. S. Russell, *op. cit.*, p. 35; cf. J. Kallas, "The Apocalypse: An Apocalyptic Book?" *JBL*, 86 (1967), 69–80; G. R. Beasley-Murray, *op. cit.*, pp. 18f., 191–97; and "How Christian is the Book of Revelation?" in *Reconciliation and Hope*, ed. R. Banks, pp. 275–84, concluding that "the Apocalypse takes its place as the crown of biblical eschatology."
[35] What Helmut Thielicke says of heaven could well be applied to the meaning of the Apocalypse's use of a two- or three-tiered universe: it "is not a space overhead to which we lift our eyes, it is the background, the all-encompassing Lordship of God within which we stand." See also P. S. Minear, "The Cosmology of the Apocalypse," in *The New Testament in Current Interpretation: Festschrift* O. Piper (1962), pp. 23–37; A. Yarbro Collins, "Dating the Apocalypse of John," *Biblical Research*, 26 (1981), 33–45.

this interrelation between the two realms and to correlate the divine world, where God is manifestly and undeniably sovereign (attested by the many Christian hymns sung by the angelic chorus), with the world of the Roman emperors, where man is at his most defiant and hostile.[36] Church and Empire are locked in an apparently unequal struggle, but John points to the ultimate issues of this conflict; the immediate struggle (Rome vs. the church) adumbrates the larger scene of a cosmic engagement (the devil vs. God).

The front of the stage is peopled with characters from the contemporary world. The churches in Asia Minor are already tasting bitter opposition from false teaching within and violent persecution from imperial and local forces without. Rome is the "beast" (13:1ff.), the "harlot" (17:1ff.), a persecutor (2:13) aided by the Jews (2:9ff.). More serious danger looms (3:10; 6:11; 7:9f.; 15:2), and the prospect of martyrdom is a real one (12:10f.; 14:13; 20:4,6). The immediate dangers arise from the cult of emperor worship (13:4f.) as wavering Christians are caught in a difficult situation in places such as Ephesus and Pergamum.[37] They are being pressured by the imperial priesthood (the "false prophet" of 13:11–18; 16:13; 19:20; 20:10) to deny their faith and compromise their allegiance to Jesus Christ as sole Lord.

3. *The time of composition.* Irenaeus says of the Revelation that "it was seen (ἑωράθη) not long ago, at the close of Domitian's principate" (Eusebius, *HE* 3.18.3; repeated in 5.8.6).[38] While not unanimous, early Christian evidence is powerfully in favor of a dating in the time of Domitian, *c.* 96; as F. J. A. Hort says, "If external tradition alone could decide, there would be a clear preponderance for Domitian."[39]

That dating supposedly fits in well with what Suetonius (*Dom.* 13) records of Domitian's claim to be worshiped as "our lord and God" (*Dominus ac deus noster*). Such a claim would provide the occasion for an outbreak of persecution, especially in Asia. Under Domitian Ephesus had received a new temple dedicated to the Roman emperor.[40] The situation is believed to be reflected in John's description of the monster rising from the abyss (13:1–10) and the accompanying monster from the earth (13:11ff.), the latter symbolizing the *commune Asiae* or provincial council, formed by delegates from leading cities in Roman Asia, who controlled the imperial cult. It is this body that had authorized the building

---

[36] Cf. J. J. O'Rourke, "The Hymns of the Apocalypse," *CBQ,* 30 (1968), 399–409.
[37] The local color and historical background to Rev. 1–3 are supplied by W. M. Ramsay, *The Letters to the Seven Churches of Asia* (1904); W. Barclay, *Letters to the Seven Churches* (1957); and P. Wood, "Local Knowledge in the Letters of the Apocalypse," *ExpT,* 73 (1961–62), 263f.
[38] The translation is disputed by F. H. Chase, "The Date of the Apocalypse: the Evidence of Irenaeus," *JTS,* 8 o.s. (1907), 431–35, who wishes to make John the subject of the verb "was seen." But this alternative rendering is unlikely.
[39] F. J. A. Hort, *The Apocalypse of St. John I–III* (1908), pp. xx.
[40] B. Reicke, *The New Testament Era,* p. 279, gives the details.

of a statue to the Emperor (Augustus). All his successors, with the exception of Claudius and Vespasian, claimed divine honors, but it was left to Domitian to make an explicit bid for divine titles in his lifetime; and it was in Asia that these claims were readily acknowledged and acted on. "In the days of Domitian, the final step was taken and *Caesar worship became compulsory.*"[41]

Several other lines of reasoning have been advanced for dating it in Domitian's time. The contrast with 1 Peter is worth noting: the Epistle knows of and reflects local outbursts of opposition, even if worldwide in scope (1 Pet. 5:9), but by the time of the Apocalypse the Roman state has assumed a demonic character. Much Christian blood has been shed in martyrdom (16:6; 17:6; 20:4; cf. 2:13; 7:14; 12:11; 14:13). Also, the recovery of Laodicea, which was destroyed by an earthquake in AD 60–61, is well enough underway for a tribute to their self-sufficiency (3:17) to be plausible. This suggests—though of course does not prove—a setting in a later decade than the 60s.

Moffatt points to Revelation 6:6 where in famine conditions "the olive and the vine" are yet to be spared. This he takes to be a "local allusion to Domitian's futile attempt (in AD 92) to check the cultivation of the vine in the Ionian provinces."[42] Also, there is a graphic picture in Revelation 8:8 of a "burning mountain" that falls into the sea, which in turn becomes blood and the grave of men and fish (vs. 9). This may be drawn from apocalyptic imagery where fallen angels resemble "stars like burning mountains" (1 Enoch 18:13; cf. Sibyll. Or. 5.158). But there may be a historical allusion to the eruption of Mount Vesuvius, which in August 79 emptied itself into the Bay of Naples and destroyed Pompeii and Herculaneum.

R. H. Charles gives as a reason for placing this book in Domitian's age the fact that "the Nero-redivivus myth" appears explicitly and implicitly in the text (chs. 13, 17; cf. 11:7) and that cannot be earlier than Domitian's time.[43] He detects several phases of the legend that Nero (who committed suicide in AD 68) had not in fact died, but was hiding in the east from where he would return at the head of Parthian armies. Charles argues that by the time alluded to in 17:8 the expectation of Nero's return had been abandoned, and Nero was identified with the demon from the abyss, a Jewish anti-God figure. So the transforming of *Nero redivivus* from a historical myth involving a returning emperor (17:12f.,17) to an incarnation of evil in a demonic monster (as in 17:8) is a sure sign of a later time—specifically, in Domitian's reign.

Revelation 17:7–11 is a much-controverted passage; it is here that the vision of the whore and the monster (ch. 13) is interpreted. The "seven hills" (17:9) on which the woman sits clearly represent imperial

---

[41] W. Barclay, *op. cit.*, p. 33; his italics.
[42] J. Moffatt, *Introduction*, p. 507.
[43] R. H. Charles, *Commentary*, Vol. 1, pp. xcvff.

Rome, a city set on seven hills and celebrating her enclosure every year in the festival of *septimontium* (Suetonius, *Dom.* 4). But who are the seven kings (vs. 10)?

There are many ways of calculating the lists of emperors, assuming that the apocalyptist intended a clear identification with persons in history and was not indulging in mere symbolism.[44] J. A. T. Robinson seems successfully to have shown, on the contrary, that since the *Nero redivivus* myth is attested in the book and Nero's name best fits the cryptogram of 13:18, it is difficult to deny some historical reference and one which was intended to be well understood.[45] The key figure is the sixth emperor, who is reigning at the time of writing (17:10).

a. If we commence with Julius Caesar, the sixth emperor is Nero; and B. W. Henderson (to whom Robinson refers) argues that this chapter reads best as written at the end of 68 when Nero fell and his expected return (9:14–16; 16:12) was a real fear. He then interprets 18:17f. to refer to the burning of Rome in AD 64.[46]

b. Another interpretation of the succession list sees the five kings as Claudius, Nero, Galba, Otho, and Vitellius (there were four emperors in quick succession in 69). The present emperor is Domitian, but acting in his capacity as nominee in AD 69–70. In June, however, he left Rome, to be followed as ruler by Vespasian, who is the one referred to cryptically as "not yet come" (17:10), that is, not yet arrived in Rome. He will rule only for a short while, since "the eighth" (*Nero redivivus*) will quickly return and put an end to him by consigning him to perdition.[47] The advantage of this view is that it gives color to the vivid descriptions of chapter 18 as depicting the sack of the capital in 69; the weakness is that it begins the count with Claudius for no compelling reason. And, following Charles, we note the development of the *Nero redivivus* story, so that antichrist is more demonic than human.

c. We come back then to the more generally accepted view. There is good ground for commencing the list of emperors with Augustus (so Tacitus, *Ann.* 1.1; *Hist.* 1.1); and it is feasible to omit the three in AD 69, who were upstarts more than duly appointed rulers. The sixth name is Vespasian whose son Titus reigned only briefly (AD 79–81). We might opt for the dating in Vespasian's reign, except that he is not called a persecutor of the church (Eusebius, *HE* 3.17), whereas John's narrative presupposes "an intense experience of Christian suffering at the hands of the imperial authorities."[48]

The remaining solution is to regard Domitian as clearly depicted

---

[44] G. R. Beasley-Murray, *Commentary*, p. 257.
[45] J. A. T. Robinson, *Redating the New Testament*, p. 245.
[46] B. W. Henderson, *The Life and Principate of the Emperor Nero* (1903), pp. 439–43.
[47] G. Edmundson, *The Church in Rome* (1913), pp. 175f.; noted by Robinson, *op. cit.*, p. 250.
[48] Robinson, *op. cit.*, p. 231.

in 17:11 but as the human agent who foreshadows the monster. John is writing as an exile in his reign (Eusebius, *HE* 3.17,18) and describes the fall of the emperor ("the beast that was and is not") as though it had already occurred in a form of the prophetic perfect. There are still residual problems with this understanding, but on balance it remains the least unsatisfactory amid a welter of contending hypotheses.[49]

Pinpointing the life-setting of Revelation as a document composed and published to encourage and warn Christians in Asia Minor in the last decade of the first century is tolerably easy, even if some unresolved questions are left, as we have seen. The more trying question is how this book is to be understood in the life of the church. Its primary purpose was to offer hope and comfort and strength to persecuted believers in the assurance of Christ's past victory (1:18), present rule (1:5f.; 5:5–10), and imminent *parousia* (1:7; 22:7,10,20). But what are its subsidiary purposes? What truths about God's control of history and Christ's final triumph may we glean from it? Let us pass under review the chief ways this book has been understood.

4. *Methods of interpretation.* There are four ways of making sense of this book's message, interpreting its numbers, colors, and symbolic events.[50]

a. *Preterist.* The greater part of the predictions were fulfilled in the early years of the Christian church. Revelation is a tract for the days in which John and his first readers lived. They had the key to its interpretation, now largely denied to us. Since we cannot place ourselves back in the first-century setting, our appreciation of this book is severely handicapped.

b. *Continuous historical.* The book presents a series of cameos which fit together to form a continuous history of the church (in prophetic style) from the apostolic age up to the present day—and beyond, to the end of the era. This hermeneutical tool led the Reformers to their assurance that chapters 17 and 18 pointed indubitably to the Rome of the medieval papacy.

c. *Futurist.* The message of the book is relegated to the final generation of Christians on earth. Only the "last days" will fully disclose

---

49 The device of hypothetical "fictitious antedating," as A. Feuillet calls it, is well known in apocalyptic writing; *The Apocalypse* (ET 1965), pp. 92f.

50 The options are surveyed by M. C. Tenney, *Interpreting Revelation* (1957), Chapters 13 and 14; G. E. Ladd, *op. cit.*, pp. 10–12; and, most clearly and cogently, by W. Milligan, *The Revelation of St. John* (1886), pp. 139–60. On the related question of the structure of the book, the issue is whether the narration is continuous or whether the author employs the literary device of synchronous parallelism by telling events, then later recapitulating them in a new way. For the latter line of approach to the book, which has much to commend it, see W. Hendriksen, *More than Conquerors*[4] (1947); M. Wilcock, *I Saw Heaven Opened* (1975). On the more technical side, E. Fiorenza, "The Eschatology and Composition of the Apocalypse," *loc. cit.*, 537–69, has produced a convincing schema analyzing diagrammatically the flow of the chapters.

what Revelation has to say; in that sense, this biblical book will become the property of the future church, and is not directed to our situation unless we can show cause to believe that we are the final generation.

d. *Idealist or poetic.* This view is badly named if it leads to the conclusion that the Apocalypse is simply a stringing together of imaginary scenes or fictitious situations for the sake of histrionic effect. On the idealist interpretation, it is better regarded as a pictorial unfolding of the great principles of good and evil in conflict through all ages until the dénouement in God's final victory and the ushering in of the eternal state.

There is a measure of truth in each of the above captions. Perhaps a synthesis of them is feasible. History is the arena of the fulfilment of God's purpose throughout its long haul, and yet there is reason—from here and elsewhere in the New Testament—to believe that at the end-time there will be a critical summing up of the features distinguishing the present age of conflict between the church and anti-God forces in the world. At that climax, evil will be decisively overthrown, and God's final rule will be established.

Such a comprehensive interpretation focuses rightly on the first-century situation in the churches of Asia Minor as providing the *Sitz im Leben* for most, if not all, of the allusions in the entire treatise. This is in line with the author's intent in the prologue (1:1-3,11,19) and epilogue (22:18-21). It also allows room for the possibility that an immediate first-century fulfilment does not eliminate the chance of further fulfilments in the subsequent history of the world and the church. And it respects the biblical assertion that the conflict between God and evil is not an eternally unresolved metaphysical dualism, but will be settled in the end with the triumph of God and the establishment of his rule in his world. History "will have a worthy conclusion."[51]

Recent studies have drawn attention to the contribution that the Apocalypse makes to our understanding of history and eschatology in the New Testament. It is worthwhile to point to the two emphases which have to be kept in tension. The Apocalypse illustrates once more the coincidence of realized and futurist eschatology pervading the New Testament, which Christian theology ignores at its peril.

> Christianity must always maintain a realized and a futurist eschatology in balance, if never in equipoise. In neglecting the latter it either shuts its eyes to the tragic realities of our continuing warfare or, alternatively, harbours utopian illusions of the possibility of their disappearance from the earthly scene. But in neglecting the former, it is failing to understand the specific character, the promise and opportunities, of the years of grace.[52]

---

[51] R. Niebuhr, *The Nature and Destiny of Man,* Vol. 2 (1943), Ch. 10: "The End of History."

[52] J. Baillie, *Belief in Progress* (1950), p. 207.

5. *The message of the book for the church.* There are two levels here. On the historical plane, we can trace the words of consolation and hope to the early persecuted communities. This message is picked up by most modern scholarly commentators: "That is its main purpose: to comfort the militant church in its struggle against the forces of evil."[53]

We may also observe how this message comes home to the church in our day with the same assurance that God is working his purpose out, and controlling the historical process through reversal, setback, and advance to the ultimate confrontation which will usher in the Day of Christ and the new order of his rule, once evil has been finally overthrown. The symbolic language of the book should not blind us to this reality. The language and scenes are part of the first-century *Weltbild* (world picture) but the *Weltanschauung* (the way of looking at life in God's world) is the expression of faith not tied to the former.

No other New Testament book proclaims the sovereignty and rule of God in so eloquent, if so bewildering, a way. Yet divine power is conditioned by love: the lion is also the lamb (5:5f.).[54] Finally, Revelation bids us see through the historical clash between the church and the emperor cult of Domitian's time to the real engagement between God and the Dragon (again a mythological concept for personified evil, the devil, but no less real as typifying evil in the cosmos, on that account). So better than two planes, we should prefer to speak of a double vision, as in Mark 13, where the historical fall of Jerusalem provides the immediate foreground behind which the eye of faith can perceive the larger judgment of God.

---

[53] W. Hendriksen, *op. cit.*, p. 11.
[54] "He is triumphant through *self*-sacrifice" (Preston and Hanson, *op. cit.*, p. 32). T. Holtz, *Die Christologie der Apokalypse* (1971), has surveyed the field more comprehensively. Cf. also F. Bovon, "Le Christ de l'Apocalypse," *Revue de Théologie et Philosophie*, 22 (1973), 72–80.

CHAPTER TWENTY-NINE

Early Catholicism and 2 Peter-Jude

EARLY CATHOLICISM

1. *Definition*. The term "early catholicism" (German *Früh-katholizismus*) requires some clarification. It goes back to F. C. Baur in the nineteenth century, but it has taken on a special nuance in contemporary discussion, chiefly because of its employment in 1950 by Vielhauer in a programmatic essay which concluded that Luke-Acts "no longer stands within earliest Christianity, but in the nascent early catholic church."[1] Marshall, after lucidly summarizing the contributions of Käsemann, Conzelmann, Lohse, and Wegenast to the discussion, concludes: "The expression 'early Catholicism' refers to a situation in which primitive apocalyptic expectation has been weakened, and the Church as an institution with an organized ministry and sacraments has begun to replace the Word as the means of salvation."[2]

In the above discussion the data drawn from Acts are combined with the Pastoral Epistles, Ephesians, Jude, and 2 Peter to form a composite picture of Christian theology and church life in the period between Paul and the emergence of the "catholic" church in the mid-second century. What features mark the growth of this institution of the church (a picture allegedly taken from the later New Testament books and supplemented from the Apostolic Fathers)?

---

[1] J. H. Elliott, "A Catholic Gospel: Reflections on 'Early Catholicism' in the New Testament," *CBQ*, 31 (1969), 213, attributes it to Baur; others claim it was first used by W. Heitmüller or E. Troeltsch; see K. H. Neufeld, " 'Frühkatholizismus'—Idee und Begriff," *ZKT*, 94 (1972), 1–28. E. Käsemann was probably the first to use the term in the recent debate (in 1949); cf. "Paul and Early Catholicism," in *New Testament Questions of Today* (ET 1969), p. 236n1. See also I. H. Marshall, " 'Early Catholicism' in the New Testament," in *New Dimensions in New Testament Study*, edd. Longenecker and Tenney, p. 221n17; Ph. Vielhauer, "On the 'Paulinism' of Acts," in *Studies in Luke-Acts*: Paul Schubert *Festschrift*, edd. Keck and Martyn (1966), pp. 33–50, esp. p. 49; and E. Käsemann, "New Testament Questions of Today," *loc. cit.*, pp. 1–22.

[2] Marshall, *op. cit.*, pp. 222f.; cf. E. Lohse, "Apokalyptik und Christologie," *ZNTW*, 62 (1971), 48–67.

a. The organization of the church and ministry has become developed and structured, with the charismatic, Spirit-controlled order giving way to a regular hierarchical and monepiscopal institution of the ministry.

b. The understanding of the faith has been transformed from an outgoing response to the gospel call to the possession of articles of religion which form a once-for-all deposit to be preserved intact and handed on. The term πίστις loses its eschatological and existential character and signifies a "virtue" among other qualities of the moral life (as in 2 Pet. 1:5–7; Jude 3,20).[3]

c. The boundaries of the canon are set inevitably by the later church's collecting apostolic writings and thereby erecting a "formal principle" of canonical authority (sola scriptura) as a bulwark against gnosticism (which claimed a secret tradition from the apostles) and Montanism (which relied on a direct illumination and continuous revelation from the Spirit).[4]

d. The character of the gospel is changed by these new features. Christian doctrine is objectified and so thereby a church of beati possidentes, who rejoice in their "orthodoxy," replaces the earlier Christian charismatic groups, in which the sense of living in the fresh dawn of the fulfilment in the new age is strong. The gospel is construed as a "new law" to be obeyed. There is a growing distinction between clergy and laity (as in 1 Clement), and tendencies to sacramentalism appear (evidenced by Ignatius). The unity of the church becomes itself an article of belief.

What brought about this transmutation of earlier New Testament Christianity? E. Käsemann answers this in one phrase: the deferment of the parousia.[5] The promise of an imminent second coming of Christ and of a cataclysmic end to the age failed to materialize, with two consequences. First, the prospect of "church history," which pledges the church to an indefinite period of time on the earth, meant a loss of the existential dimension to the gospel; and a "formal principle" (sola scriptura) was accepted in place of a "material principle" (justification by faith) in the debate over canonicity. In other words, the issue turned on which books were treated as authoritative, but not by the presence or absence of teaching on God's justification of the ungodly. Luke, as the "theologian of salvation history" (see above, p. 55) and "the first historian," is held responsible for this slide from the primitive Christian

---

[3] H. Conzelmann, An Outline of the Theology of the New Testament (ET 1969), pp. 289ff. On Jude 3, 20, see K. H. Schelkle, "Spätapostolische Briefe als frühkatholisches Zeugnis," in Neutestamentliche Aufsätze: Festschrift J. Schmid (1963), p. 226.

[4] Cf. E. Käsemann, "The New Testament Canon and the Unity of the Church," in Essays on New Testament Themes (ET 1964), p. 103. See earlier, p. 290.

[5] E. Käsemann, "Paul and Early Catholicism," in New Testament Questions of Today, pp. 236f.; against this see L. Morris, "Luke and Early Catholicism," WJT, 35 (1973), 121–36.

apocalyptic understanding of the church's role, associated with Paul.[6]

Second, Käsemann's criterion "by grace alone, by faith alone," enshrined in the teaching of the "justification of sinners," demotes the catholic elements in the New Testament to a lower level of importance so that the Pauline evangelical substance, seen in Romans and Galatians, may shine in clearer light. In that sense, early catholicism marks a departure from the apostolic faith.

2. *Some criticisms.* A number of critical remarks may be offered on this enterprise of finding "early catholic" elements in the New Testament.

a. We may first inquire whether this analysis of the texts is factually correct. Is it true that the Pastorals, Ephesians, and 2 Peter contain no reference to the apostolic gospel? We may freely grant that the formulation of the *kerygma* has changed in these parts of the New Testament. This change in formal expression, vocabulary, and mode of statement is indeed related to new situations in the later Pauline or even post-Pauline period. But this does not entail a change in substance, as can be seen from studies which have shown the essential oneness of the apostolic and post-Pauline *kerygma,* which is centered in Jesus Christ crucified and risen as the ground of salvation. The inroad of false teaching, reflected in such documents as the Pastorals and Ephesians, led the Pauline writer to express Paul's teaching in a new way; but it is Paul's mind he is expressing, not some inferior substitute passed off as Paul's. The same line may be taken in regard to 2 Peter, if we are correct in viewing it as a testament of the apostle conveyed through a member of his "school."

J. W. Drane argues that the "distinction between the 'early catholic' church and the 'apostolic' church is not so marked as is often supposed."[7] Käsemann has insisted, on the basis of verses like 2 Peter 1:4, that there is "a relapse of Christianity into Hellenistic dualism," in which the world is evil *per se* and communion with God confers a divine nature.[8] Michael Green counters that the distinctions made by the writer here are moral and eschatological, not metaphysically dualistic.[9]

b. It may be remarked in general that setting up a criterion and judging all else by a failure to approximate to it brings about an ever-present danger of subjectivism. Hence H. Diem has charged that Käsemann transforms the gospel from an event to a doctrine. He argues that because it is an event of history it must go through transformations relative to new situations and contingencies.[10]

---

[6] Käsemann, *ibid.,* pp. 241ff.

[7] J. W. Drane, "Tradition, Law and Ethics in Pauline Theology," *NovT,* 16 (1974), 165–78.

[8] E. Käsemann, "An Apologia for Primitive Christian Eschatology," in *Essays on New Testament Themes,* pp. 169–95, esp. 179ff.

[9] E. M. B. Green, *2 Peter Reconsidered* (1961), pp. 24f.

[10] H. Diem, *Dogmatics* (ET 1959), pp. 229–34.

c. A final allegation is that pressed home by J. H. Elliott and I. H. Marshall. They charge that Käsemann fails to see the totality of the gospel, which includes those parts of Scripture for which he has little use. For Elliott, "evangelical" can be too narrowly defined and he opts for a larger content which will embrace the so-called "catholic" elements in such matters as church order and discipline.[11] In Marshall's critique, the so-called "catholic" elements detected by Käsemann form "essential constituent element(s) of the Gospel."[12] Similarly, Hans Küng pleads for the necessity of both evangelical concentration and catholic comprehensiveness, while conceding that we must give prior place to the "original testimonies" (the Gospels and Paul) over the derived witnesses (e.g., 2 Peter). Käsemann, he says, is "more biblical than the Bible, more New Testament-minded than the New Testament, more evangelical than the Gospel, more Pauline than Paul."[13]

2 PETER-JUDE

The problem of the authorship of 2 Peter is notoriously complex. The document professes to be written by "Simon Peter, a servant and apostle of Jesus Christ" (1:1). The author claims that he was an eyewitness of the Lord's transfiguration (1:16-18), though he uses the plural verb form: "*we were* eyewitnesses," as if to emphasize the apostolic nature of his testimony against those who followed man-made myths whereas he uses the singular when he is obviously referring to himself as an individual (3:1). He attests a relationship to Paul, his "beloved brother" (3:15), that appears to put his own authority on the same level as that of the apostle to the Gentiles. Indeed, these are the two parts of 2 Peter that "compel us to believe that he intended himself to be regarded as Peter."[14]

Robinson examines these passages and concludes from them that there is nothing that would require a dating after the death of

---

[11] J. H. Elliott, *loc. cit.*

[12] I. H. Marshall, *loc. cit.*, pp. 230f.

[13] H. Küng, "Der frühkatholizismus als kontroverstheologisches Problem" (in *Das Neue Testament als Kanon* [1970], 175-204), which appears in ET in *The Living Church* (1963), pp. 268ff. C. H. Talbert, "Shifting Sands: The Recent Study of the Gospel of Luke," *Interpretation*, 30 (1976), 381-95, wants to distinguish two types of early catholicism: normative (in continuity with primitive Christianity) and non-normative (where the data are legalistic, sacramental, and clerical). This distinction, of course, assumes that we can so arrange the evidence of, say, Acts or Ephesians–a very subjective procedure.

[14] E. M. B. Green, *op. cit.*, p. 36. See the counterarguments of R. J. Bauckham's discussion (*Jude, 2 Peter* [WBC, 1983], pp. 327-30), which concludes that the author may have had some personal connection with Peter but not as a disciple. He was a senior member of the circle of church leaders at Rome when he wrote the letter as a "testament of Peter" in the 80s, and his link with Peter may have gone back to the 60s. There is some evidence that Linus as Peter's "successor" in early Roman bishop lists could be a candidate for authorship of 2 Peter (*op. cit.*, pp. 160f.).

Peter.[15] The parallel which some have found between 2 Peter 1:12–18 and the second-century Apocalypse of Peter, which elaborates the synoptic account of the appearance of Moses and Elijah on the Mount of Transfiguration,[16] he considers not proven. And he points out that even J. B. Mayor, who argues for the pseudonymity of the Epistle, grants that "the manner in which St. Paul is spoken of seems to me just what we should have expected from his brother Apostle." Mayor adds that "this does not of course prove the genuineness of the present letter."[17]

Certain other arguments for Petrine authorship are not so compelling, as Green admits. The appeal to words such as δελεάζω (entice, catch with a bait; 2:14,18) and ἀρνοῦμαι (deny; 2:1) as pointers to the presence of the fisherman who denied his Lord may indeed merit Green's concession that they are perhaps "fanciful."[18] The relationship with Paul—if securely grounded by 3:15f.—would require us to associate the writer with Paul at a time when the bulk of his extant epistolary correspondence was read, known, and highly regarded as "Scripture." If our author is Peter, this places the Epistle at the close of the lives of both apostles (cf. 1:13ff.), and also suggests that Peter had read "the majority of Paul's letters within a few months of their being written."[19] But while Paul's letters were widely regarded, since he required that they be circulated to nearby churches (Col. 4:16; 1 Thess. 5:27), there is little evidence that they received authoritative status prior to his death.[19a] To maintain, as Green does,[20] that 2 Peter 3:16 charges false teachers with misrepresenting Paul and that this was no new thing is not quite accurate. The charge in the text is that they are undermining Paul *as a writer of sacred Scripture*. And that requires a setting in a later period corresponding to the church's developing attitude to Paul's writings.[21]

The upshot is that, while the document gives the appearance of being "written in the form of a testament of Peter,"[22] there is no strict requirement to take it as written personally by Peter the apostle or published prior to AD 64/65, when (tradition has it) Peter perished as a Roman martyr. Indeed, there are several strong positive arguments for dating the Epistle after Peter's time. One of these is the use made of Jude's Epistle, itself to be dated after AD 70. We may set down the parallels in tabular form:

[15] J. A. T. Robinson, *Redating the New Testament,* pp. 175–84.
[16] Hennecke-Schneemelcher, edd., *New Testament Apocrypha,* Vol. 2, pp. 668–83.
[17] J. B. Mayor, *Jude and II Peter* (1907), pp. 164ff.
[18] Green, *op. cit.,* pp. 13,36.
[19] *Ibid.,* p. 30.
[19a] See R. P. Meye, "Canon of the New Testament," *ISBE,* I (1979), 603: "2 Peter assumes a familiar, and perhaps considerable (cf. 3:16, 'all') collection of Pauline letters."
[20] *Ibid.,* pp. 25f. But see his Tyndale commentary (1968), pp. 28ff., for another view.
[21] O. Cullmann, *The New Testament* (ET 1968), p. 106; his identification of 2 Pet. 3:16 with Marcion is a guess.
[22] W. G. Kümmel, *Introduction*[2], p. 430.

Jude	2 Peter
4	2:1-3
5	2:5
6,7	2:4,6
8,9	2:10,11
10	2:12
11-12a	2:15,13
12b-13	2:17
16	2:18
17	3:2
18	3:3

A telltale indication of the direction of indebtedness is Jude 12b-13 = 2 Peter 2:17, where "wandering stars" are consigned to the "gloom of darkness"—a mixed metaphor in Jude improved by the author of Peter by likening the false teachers to "clouds and mists" destined to disappear in the darkness. But other arguments are cumulative.[23]

Another reason for post-Petrine dating has to do with the Hellenistic coloring of the language of the Epistle (e.g., 1:3,4,16). Among the terms mentioned here are "divine power" (*theia dynamis*), "divine nature" (*theia physis*), "glory and excellence" (*doxa kai aretē*), "piety" or "religion" (*eusebeia*), and "eyewitness" (*epoptēs*).[24] Others have sought to date the Epistle in terms of the onset of heretical tendencies which it reflects—in particular antinomian laxity (2:1-22) and the denial of the imminence of the *parousia* (3:1-7).

The strong language used in 2:1 of those who sponsor "destructive heresies" may point to a form of Simonian gnosticism which, according to Irenaeus (*Adv. Haer.* 1.23.3f.), advocated antinomianism, made proud claims, and reviled the angels. Simon Magus (Acts 8) was looked upon as the archetype of false teaching and the father of gnosticism in the early church; and Peter was his great antagonist. There is no *direct* confrontation with the later heresy here, but there may well have been an earlier version of what later blossomed into the teaching known to Irenaeus. It may be that the invectives in Jude and 2 Peter depend on a tract of anti-heretical teaching that Peter earlier—or perhaps his followers—had drawn up.[25]

---

[23] See Guthrie, *Introduction*[3], pp. 920-22, though he prefers an open verdict; also Moffatt, *Introduction*, pp. 348-52; Mayor, *op. cit.*, p. xxv. Cullmann, *The New Testament*, pp. 102-105, suggests that Jude 14f. quotes 1 Enoch 1:9 and so is prior to Jamnia (AD 90) when the rabbis excluded apocryphal books; 2 Peter has then eliminated this reference in deference to the rabbinic decision.

[24] Kümmel, *Introduction*, p. 432; cf. also B. Reicke, *Peter and Jude* (1964), pp. 146f.; Moffatt, *Introduction*, pp. 360f.; P. Wendland, *Die hellenistische-römische Kultur*[2] (1912), pp. 368f.; J. Chaine, *Les épîtres catholiques* (1939), pp. 13-18, 24-26.

[25] G. W. Barker, W. L. Lane, and J. R. Michaels, *The New Testament Speaks* (1969), pp. 356-58. For what is known of Simon and the later teaching linked with his

J. A. T. Robinson concedes, after a full discussion of the arguments, including the problematical references to "your apostles" in 3:1f. (which most take to reflect the post-apostolic age in a way similar to the witness of Eph. 2:20; 3:5) and to "the fathers" in 3:4 (used presumably of the first generation of Christian believers), that "these passages do not prove a first-century date." He adds "but they do not prove a second-century either."[26] Yet the evidence has to lean one way or the other, and in this field of inquiry "prove" is too strong a term. It is a question of the balance of probability. In any case, there is another possibility: the data may support a dating of 2 Peter in the decades after AD 65, but not necessarily in the second century.

So the central issue is that of pseudonymity, as Robinson admits. Would a later *falsarius* pass off the document in the name of the apostle Peter with the intention of misleading his readers? The case of the spurious letters circulating in Paul's name (2 Thess. 2:2; 3:17) clearly was seen in this light. But this objection hardly touches the issue if the author wrote the document to embody the apostle's teaching and had no intention of deceiving his readers. The writer of 2 Peter is no impostor. Then, we can at least explain why the author mentions Paul in brotherly terms and yet appears to be uninfluenced by his theology,[27] for it is a mark of his faithfulness in reproducing Peter's teaching that he does not show indebtedness to Paul,[28] and his calling Paul as a witness to his side would further strengthen his claim to be representing his master's mind since both Paul and Peter were, in his day, known to be apostolic figures of repute (Ignatius, *Romans* 4.3, later on mentions the two apostolic names together).

Barker, Lane, and Michaels write: "Posthumous publication in Peter's name does not necessarily imply any intent to deceive. If the tradition behind Second Peter is genuinely Petrine, then the only kind of compiler of the material who might be guilty of deception would be one who presumptuously signed *his own* name to the apostle's teaching."[29] (The same conclusion stands in regard to the origin of Ephesians and the Pastorals.)

If the apostolic authorship of the letter is open to question, the

---

name, see R. P. Casey, "Simon Magus," in *Beginnings of Christianity*, Vol. 5, Note XIII, pp. 151–63; J. Daniélou, *The Theology of Jewish Christianity* (ET 1964), pp. 72–74, 210 (which quotes Irenaeus on Simon's role to correct the angelic powers; cf. 2 Pet. 2:10–12). "The way of Balaam" (2:15) has links with Balaam in Rev. 2:14, and H. J. Schoeps, *Aus frühchristliche Zeit* (1950), pp. 249–54, has suggested that this name may represent Simon. But K. Beyschlag, *Simon Magus und die christliche Gnosis* (1974), argues that the teaching linked with Simon's name is a second-century phenomenon and not the precursor of Christian gnosticism.

26 J. A. T. Robinson, *op. cit.*, p. 184.
27 *Ibid.*, p. 189.
28 Assuming that he could understand his teaching—a difficulty raised in 3:16. See A. E. Barnett, *Paul Becomes a Literary Influence* (1941), pp. 222–28.
29 Barker-Lane-Michaels, *op. cit.*, p. 352; their italics.

strength of its appeal rests on its apostolic authority. It is a true witness to Peter's apostolic teaching, couched in the language and idiom and addressing situations of a later time. This view is in tune with what we know of the slow and cautious reception of 2 Peter into the canon. It was poorly attested in the second century. Eusebius placed the book among those in dispute (*antilegomena*) and considered it spurious (*HE* 3.3.4). This judgment was forcefully expressed by Didymus of Alexandria (died 398), who ranked it as a forgery and not canonical, although his witness is equivocal.

The fortunes of the book vary in different geographical regions of the church. The Alexandrian church accepted it *c*. 200. The Antioch-Constantinople axis disputed it until 400, with some acceptance—e.g., Firmilian, a pupil and friend of Origen, who was the first to mention it and to regard it as "acknowledged but disputed" (Eusebius, *HE* 6.25.8). It was never received with authority among the Syrian churches. In the west Hippolytus knew it, but Irenaeus, Tertullian, and Cyprian did not, and it does not appear in the Muratorian Canon. It found acceptance in the west from *c*. 370–380. The stylistic differences between the two letters played a role in Jerome's explanation of why it was "rejected by the majority" (*De viris ill.* 1).[30]

As a matter of fact the two documents linked with Peter do have ties in language and content.[31] The statistical count shows 1 Peter with a distinctive vocabulary of 543 words and 2 Peter with 399; yet there are 153 words common to both.[32] There are, however, obvious differences in terminology. For instance, 2 Peter uses *parousia* where 1 Peter has *apocalypse* for the Lord's coming in power. There are also differences in content for common ideas: the flood is used in 1 Peter 3:20f. as a type of baptism but in 2 Peter 2:5 and 3:5-7 as a figure of cosmic destruction. Also there is a difference in use of the Old Testament. 2 Peter cites or alludes to the Old Testament in five verses, all having parallels with Jude; 1 Peter quotes the Old Testament 31 times, often extensively and explicitly (e.g., 1:24; 2:6ff.; 3:10-12).

This paradox of dissimilarity of style, yet points of contact in the wording, would give added support to the contention that a scribe, himself a devoted student of Peter's earlier writing, has been at work in assembling and publishing, in his master's name, a testament of that teaching in response to pressing needs in the church.

30 The difficulties the Epistle had achieving acceptance is regarded by Barker-Lane-Michaels (*ibid.*, p. 358) as the most important reason why it is difficult to attribute 2 Peter directly to Peter. Cf. Guthrie, *op. cit.*, p. 847, who overcomes the problem by suggesting that the letter was sent to a restricted destination.
31 G. H. Boobyer, "The Indebtedness of 2 Peter to 1 Peter," in *New Testament Essays in Memory of T. W. Manson*, ed. A. J. B. Higgins (1959), pp. 34-53; Green, *op. cit.*, pp. 11-23.
32 A. E. Simms, "Second Peter and the Apocalypse of Peter," *Expositor*, 5th ser., 8 (1893), 460-71.

A life-setting in a later decade seems required by the nature of the false doctrine and ethical problems that loom large on the scene.[33] The author can therefore draw on what he knows and cherishes of his mentor's teaching, yet give it a special depth and dimension appropriate to the new situation. To take one example, in the address reported in Acts 3:12 Peter uses εὐσέβεια (piety) of the apostles' character. The same noun and adjective recur in 2 Peter four times (1:3,6f.; 2:9; 3:11), but the meaning is not quite the same in the two documents. In the Pastorals (where it is common) and also in 2 Peter, εὐσέβεια carries more the nuance of "religion" than the possession of a personal moral quality.[34] So it is suggested that the disciple in Peter's circle is indebted to his master, but he has filled the term with a fresh content that was more appropriate to his later age and the needs of his community.

The conclusion is that in 2 Peter we are faced with a later expression of the apostolic gospel, extended and modified to counter the problems raised by the inroad of a gnosticizing antinomianism.[35] The writer builds his case on the deposit of apostolic teaching he has inherited and applies it to his own day. Yet it is apostolic truth and, to that extent, Peter's name and aegis can be claimed for it.[36]

---

[33] Those associated with the deferment of the Lord's *parousia* are the clearest instance (3:3ff.). The lapse of time and the passing of at least one generation of believers are creating problems (contrast the still-imminent prospect of Christ's coming in 1 Pet. 4:7,17; 5:4). The closest parallel to the disillusion reflected in 2 Pet. 3 is 1 Clement 23:3f., where it is reaffirmed that "he shall come quickly and will not delay" (cf. Heb. 10:37). This parallel is important for fixing the life-setting of 2 Peter; cf. O. Knoch, *Die eschatologische Konzeption des 1. Klementsbriefes* (1959), pp. 134f., 139f., 147–51, 179–81. On the general question, see S. S. Smalley, "The Delay of the Parousia," *JBL*, 83 (1964), 41–56; C. H. Talbert, "II Peter and the Delay of the Parousia," *VC*, 20 (1966), 137–45.

[34] For parallels with the language of the Pastorals (1 Tim. 2:2; 3:16; 4:7,8; 6:3,5,6,11; 2 Tim. 3:5; Titus 1:1), see E. M. Sidebottom, *James, Jude and 2 Peter* (1967), pp. 97f.

[35] K. H. Schelkle, *Die Petrusbriefe, Der Judasbrief* (1964), p. 178, identifies the false teaching as both gnosis and moral libertinism.

[36] Note the observation that pseudonyms in the New Testament never introduce novelty; they invariably hark back to the apostolic teaching as authoritative (see B. E. Beck, *Reading in the New Testament Today* [1978], p. 54).

PART SEVEN

The Sum of the Matter

In this final part we attempt to see how our previous studies serve as an aid to exegesis. There are several reasons for our choice of three passages from 1 Corinthians for this purpose. Problems in the congregation at Corinth resulted from pressures exerted on that community of Hellenistic Christians living in a pagan society. Our knowledge of the social, cultural, and religious background which has been before us in several chapters will help us get the feel of life in a cosmopolitan center such as Corinth.

But the prime source of the mischief that made the Corinthian church so distressful to Paul was undoubtedly theological-ethical. The church members had imbibed certain notions which affected their thinking about the nature of their life in Christ, the style of living that should be theirs as members of their society, and the prospect of what lay ahead. These ideas—to Paul so wrong-headed and aberrant—needed correction. Paul is not slow to remonstrate forcefully with some identifiable errors, and he is at pains to teach the elementary truths that God would have a distinctive and morally unblemished church as his witness in the world. Moreover, the Christian life, grounded on what God has done in a past deliverance from evil and is continuing to accomplish in purifying human lives, always has an awareness of unattained completeness. No doubt some Corinthians supposed that they had reached a blissful nirvana here and now; and this explains their ethical indifference. Paul has to hold out the hope of a future salvation, when at the "resurrection of the body" they will be called to give an account of their deeds in the body.

Above all, Paul shines out in these chapters as a wise pastor and spiritual director. He is charged with the care and nurture of his people. Though there was every inducement for him to write off this congregation as hopelessly immature and incorrigible, he persisted. The basis of his pastoral instruction is carefully laid, and so the letter has much to teach us in the vastly different setting of living the Christian life in the contemporary world and counseling believers today to be God's family and Christ's servants.

The notes that follow are intended to help students to grapple with Paul's words in the Greek. Grammatical and syntactical forms are identified and explained; commentaries and lexical studies are pressed into service; and the chief issues of exegesis are spotlighted. But the main emphasis falls on encouraging the readers to work out the meaning for themselves; and this accounts for the ending of more than one sentence with a question mark.

As a concluding chapter, which forms the Epilogue to both volumes of New Testament foundations, an attempt is made to bring it all together in a constructive statement of what these twenty-seven books are saying as their chief message, in the author's estimation.

Abbreviations Used in the Exegetical Notes

AG—Walter Bauer, trans. by W. Arndt and F. W. Gingrich, *A Greek-English Lexicon of the New Testament* (1957).

Alford—Henry Alford, *The Greek Testament* (Vol. II, 1958).

Barrett—C. K. Barrett, *The First Epistle to the Corinthians (Harper-Black New Testament Commentaries,* 1968).

BDF—F. Blass and A. Debrunner, trans. by R. W. Funk, *A Greek Grammar of the New Testament* (1961).

Bruce—F. F. Bruce, *1 and 2 Corinthians* (New Century Bible, 1971).

BSGNT—*Bible Society Greek New Testament* (2nd ed., 1968).

Bultmann—Rudolf Bultmann, trans. by Kendrick Grobel, *Theology of the New Testament* (Vol. I, 1951).

Calvin—John Calvin, trans. by John W. Fraser, *The First Epistle of Paul the Apostle to the Corinthians (Calvin's New Testament Commentaries,* 1960).

Conzelmann—Hans Conzelmann, trans. by James W. Leitch, *1 Corinthians* (Hermeneia, 1975).

Davies—W. D. Davies, *Paul and Rabbinic Judaism*[2] (1955).

DM—H. E. Dana and J. R. Mantey, *A Manual Grammar of the Greek New Testament* (1955).

Furnish—Victor Furnish, *Theology and Ethics in Paul* (1968).

Grosheide—F. W. Grosheide, *Commentary on The First Epistle to the Corinthians* (New International Commentary/New London Commentary, 1953).

Gundry—Robert H. Gundry, *Soma in Biblical Theology* (1976).

Héring—Jean Héring, *The First Epistle of St. Paul to the Corinthians* (1962).

HNTG—William Sanford LaSor, *Handbook of New Testament Greek* (Vol. II, 1973).

Hodge—Charles Hodge, *Commentary on the First Epistle to the Corinthians* (1965).

IDB—ed. George A. Buttrick, *The Interpreter's Dictionary of the Bible* (4 vols., 1962).

Kümmel—Werner Georg Kümmel, trans. by John E. Steely, *The Theology of the New Testament* (1973).

Ladd—George E. Ladd, *A Theology of the New Testament* (1974).

Lietzmann-Kümmel—H. Lietzmann and W. G. Kümmel, *An die Korinther*[4] (Handbuch zum Neuen Testament, 1949).

Metzger—Bruce M. Metzger, *A Textual Commentary on the Greek New Testament* (1971).

Morris—Leon Morris, *The First Epistle of Paul to the Corinthians* (Tyndale New Testament Commentary, 1958).

Moule—C. F. D. Moule, *An Idiom-Book of New Testament Greek* (2nd ed., 1968).

Moulton—James H. Moulton, *A Grammar of New Testament Greek* (3 vols., 1908–63).

Parry—R. St. John Parry, *First Corinthians* (Cambridge Greek Testament for Schools and Colleges, 1957).

RP—A. Robertson and A. Plummer, *The First Epistle of Paul to the Corinthians* (International Critical Commentary, 1914).

Strack-Billerbeck—Hermann L. Strack and Paul Billerbeck, *Kommentar zum Neuen Testament aus Talmud und Midrasch* (3 vols., 1969).

TDNT—edd. Gerhard Kittel and Gerhard Friedrich, trans. by Geoffrey W. Bromiley, *Theological Dictionary of the New Testament* (10 vols., 1964–76).

CHAPTER THIRTY

The Nature of the Christian Life
(1 Corinthians 5:6–8)

THE LARGER CONTEXT

In 1 Corinthians 5:1–5 Paul has reprimanded the church at Corinth for being "puffed up" (πεφυσιωμένοι; cf. 4:6,18f.; 8:1; 13:4) rather than mournful over the fact that one of their members is guilty of immorality ("fornication," Bruce, p. 53). A man is sexually involved with his stepmother (Héring, p. 34), an offense condemned by both Jewish and Roman morals (see Conzelmann, p. 96, and Barrett, p. 21, for the Jewish and Roman evidence). Since the church has not removed the offender from its midst (vs. 2), Paul has judged and will recommend that in "a solemn act of excommunication at a special meeting of the church" (Bruce, p. 54) the offender is to "be handed over to Satan for the destruction of the flesh that the spirit might be saved on the day of the Lord" (vs. 5 recalls Acts 5:1ff.; 2 Cor. 12:7; 1 Tim. 1:20).

NOTES

verse 6

Οὐ καλὸν τὸ καύχημα ὑμῶν—Is there a difference in meaning between καλός and ἀγαθός (W. Grundmann, in TDNT, 3,538,539)? Bruce, p. 55, distinguishes καύχημα, the ground of boasting, from καύχησις, the act of boasting; but Bultmann, in TDNT, 3,649n35, shows that the distinction is not strictly observed. What are they boasting about (cf. 5:1f.)? Is this a concrete instance of where the Corinthian slogan that "all things are lawful" (6:12; 10:23) led? For the view of sexuality behind this boasting, see Barrett, p. 19; and contrast the asceticism of 1 Cor. 7 (Bruce, p. 66). On the theological significance of boasting for Paul see Bultmann, in TDNT, 3,648–52.

οὐκ οἴδατε ὅτι—In questions does οὐ(κ) expect a negative or positive answer (DM, p. 264)? Οἴδατε (perf. act. ind. 2 pl.) inflects as a 2nd perfect of the hypothetical εἴδω, "I see." But it is always translated as the present tense of "know" (I have seen = I know). Does ὅτι mean "that" (indirect discourse, HNTG §37.821) or "because" (causal clause, HNTG §37.5321)?

μιϰρὰ ζύμη ὅλον τὸ φύραμα ζυμοῖ—ζύμη = "yeast, leaven" (AG, p. 340; H. Windisch, in TDNT, 2,902). It is the subject of what verb? The circumflex accent in ζυμοῖ alerts us that it is not a masc. pl. noun but a contract verb: ζυμο + ει = ζυμοῖ (HNTG §24.4112), "it ferments or leavens" (AG, p. 340). φύραμα: "that which is mixed or kneaded, (a lump or batch of) dough" (AG, p. 877); it is a 3rd decl. neut. noun (nom. and acc. case of neuter nouns always look the same). Ὅλον: 2nd decl., agreeing with φύραμα. When used with an article it is always in the predicate position (Moulton III, p. 199).

For the proverb see Conzelmann, p. 98; Bruce, p. 56; cf. Gal. 5:9. Barrett, p. 127, gives a possible Jewish source; a secular Greek proverb to the same effect is cited in 1 Cor. 15:33. The meaning in this context seems to be "the *single* case has the result of defiling the whole community" (Conzelmann, p. 98). See "Leaven" in IDB, 3, 105, for the symbolical significance of leaven in the Old and New Testaments, and why it has this significance; cf. TDNT, 2,902–906; C. L. Mitton, "Leaven," *ExpT*, 84 (1972–73), 339–42. The reference to the Passover in the next verse shows that Paul's thought about leaven springs from Old Testament texts such as Exod. 12:14–20.

verse 7

ἐϰϰαθάρατε τὴν παλαιὰν ζύμην—ἐϰϰαθάρατε: from ἐϰϰαθαίρω, "clean out, cleanse" (AG, p. 239). See HNTG paradigm V-4e on liquid verbs. For parsing note the "α" theme vowel; the "σ" tense sign drops out after ϱ, λ, and ν. What does the absence of an augment tell us about the mood?

What does the "old leaven" refer to (cf. vs. 8)? E.g., "evil influences" (Barrett, p. 128); "each knows the plague-spot in himself" (RP, 102); "remnants of the former pagan period" (Grosheide, p. 125); "not the man but the crime attaching to their character as a church" (Alford, p. 507). Conzelmann (p. 98) notes that "leaven is in actual fact old dough. But the catchword παλαιός is hardly derived from the figure itself. What is in mind is . . . the antithesis of the old and new man, Rom. 6:6; 7:6; Col. 3:9; Eph. 4:22, etc." What is the logical relation between the imperative of v. 7a and v. 6?

For understanding Paul's allusion, Héring's summary (p. 36) of details of the Jewish passover is helpful: "(1) In the night of 13/14 Nisan [March-April] and in the morning of the 14th, the house had to be cleaned out carefully to remove every trace of leavened bread which in this instance was regarded as containing a principle of contagious impurity [Exod. 12:15]. (2) The Passover bread has to be ἄζυμος, i.e.

without leaven." See also Strack-Billerbeck 3,359f.; J. Jeremias, *Eucharistic Words of Jesus*[2] (1966), pp. 59f. For the application to the Christian Eucharist, see R. P. Martin, *Worship in the Early Church*[2] (1975), pp. 125f.

ἵνα ἦτε νέον φύραμα—ἵνα introduces what kind of adverbial clause (HNTG §37.5421)? It is followed regularly by the subjunctive mood, here of εἰμί. Paul's metaphor does not seem to be exact: "clean out" pictures the church as the house of Exod. 12:15, but here the church is pictured as a new lump of dough (Conzelmann, p. 98). "The first batch of dough from which new bread is made is . . . completely unleavened [after the cleaning out of Exod. 12:15], a new lump. That is what they should be by virtue of their turning to Christ—'a new creation' (2 C. 5.17)" (Bruce, p. 56).

καθώς ἐστε ἄζυμοι—Note that καθώς can have a causal sense, translated "since" (AG, p. 392,3). "The community for which Christ was sacrificed as the paschal lamb is called the unleavened dough. This expresses the fact that to be in Christ is to be already in the fulfilled Passover" (Jeremias, in TDNT, 5,901).

What is the relationship between the imperative ("clean out the old leaven") and the indicative ("you are unleavened")? A thoughtful answer to this question is essential for a proper understanding of New Testament ethics. For a discussion of the relation between the indicative and imperative in Pauline theology and ethics see Ladd, pp. 524f.; Kümmel, pp. 224–28; Bultmann, pp. 332f.; Furnish, pp. 224–27. This tension "is a reflection of the fundamental theological substructure of the whole of Pauline thinking: the tension between the two ages" (Ladd, p. 524). Against the misleading RSV translation "as you *really* are unleavened," see Bruce, p. 56. For other New Testament passages where imperative and indicative are similarly related see Rom. 6:11–14,19; Col. 3:1–14. The meaning is: "Be *de facto* what you are *de jure*; be really what you are ideally in the purpose of God" (Bruce, p. 56).

καὶ γὰρ τὸ πάσχα ἡμῶν ἐτύθη Χριστός—What kind of clause does the postpositive (HNTG §30.3611) γάρ introduce (HNTG §37.531)? Πάσχα = "Passover, passover lamb, passover meal" (AG, pp. 638f.); it is an indeclinable noun. For ἐτύθη isolate the morphemes: ἐ - τύ - θη. The augment and θη tell us it is aor. pass. indic. 3rd sing. The present stem is not τύω but θύω ("sacrifice, kill in a ritualistic way as *kosher*"). *Theta* dissimilates to *tau* when the next syllable begins with *theta* (HNTG §13.242).

Does the γάρ connect with ἐστε ἄζυμοι (Morris, p. 90), or with ἐκκαθάρατε (Hodge, p. 87) or with both (Barrett, p. 128; RP, p. 102)? What is the function of the *kai* (Conzelmann, p. 94n13)? The comparison of Christ to the paschal lamb was part of a tradition in the early church (cf. 1 Pet. 1:19; John 1:29,36; 19:36; Rev. 5:6,9,12; 12:11). According to Jeremias (TDNT, 5,900) the link goes back to Jesus' own interpretation of his death (Mark 14:22-24). Conzelmann disputes this origin of the tradition (p. 99n50). "It is plain that in the primitive church the sequence of events comprising the Passover, the Exodus and Israel's wilderness wanderings ... provided a pictorial pattern for the narrating of the Christian salvation-story (see especially 10.1–11)" (Bruce, pp. 56f.).

verse 8

ὥστε ἑορτάζωμεν—Ὥστε may introduce independent clauses: "therefore, for this reason" (AG, p. 908,1b). Ἑορτάζω = "celebrate a festival" (AG, p. 279), is found only here in the New Testament. What kind of subjunctive is it (HNTG §31.332)?

"The Passover meal was followed by the seven-day *ḥǎgîgāh* or festival of unleavened bread (Ex. 23:15; 34:18; Dt. 16:3f. etc.)" (Bruce, p. 57). RP, p. 103, quotes Godet: "Our passover feast is not for a week, but for a lifetime."

μὴ ἐν ζύμῃ παλαιᾷ μηδὲ ἐν ζύμῃ κακίας καὶ πονηρίας—Μή rather than οὐ is used with subjunctives. Κακία ("badness, faultiness, depravity, wickedness"—AG, p. 397) and πονηρία ("wickedness, baseness, maliciousness, sinfulness"—AG, p. 697) are genitives of apposition (Alford, p. 508; HNTG §35.3112). Apparently the phrase introduced by μηδέ defines "old leaven" more specifically (Barrett, p. 129). Don't confuse πονηρία and πορνεία.

ἀλλ᾽ ἐν ἀζύμοις εἰλικρινείας καὶ ἀληθείας—Ἀλλά drops the final α before words beginning with a vowel. The plural of ἄζυμος ("unleavened bread") is due to the fact that the bread was in the form of numerous flat cakes (AG, p. 19,1; cf. Exod. 12:8,15; Heb. *maṣṣôṭ*). Εἰλικρίνεια = "sincerity, purity of motive" (AG, p. 221; F. Büchsel, TDNT, 2,397).

"Here the consciousness is expressed that Christians form a 'New' Israel—they are the real people of God and the whole Christian Life, because of the crucified Christ, can be thought of as a Passover festival of joy" (Davies, p. 105).

THE STRUCTURE OF THE ARGUMENT

The foundation stone of the argument is that Christ, our passover lamb, has been sacrificed (vs. 7d). This is the ground (hence the γάρ) for the assertion that the new people of God are *de jure* a new, pure lump of dough (vs. 7c). This indicative is in turn the ground (causal καθώς) for the imperative: "clean out the old leaven and be a new lump" (vs. 7a,b). This imperative is repeated and defined more specifically in vs. 8: "clean out wickedness and evil, and be sincere and truthful." Verse 6 is an additional ground for the church's cleaning out of all evil from its midst.

Thus the foundation stone of the argument is the death of Christ and the capstone is the appeal to walk in newness of life.

Why does Paul choose to stress the need for "sincerity and truth" when the sin that gave rise to this discussion was open sexual immorality? The reason appears to be that the Corinthians not only failed to deal with the offender, but by condoning this action were actually proud of their indifference to morality. This seems to confirm the idea that some Corinthian Christians had accepted gnostic teaching with its looseness of moral standards, particularly in the matter of sex relations, on the ground that no bodily indulgence could harm their "pure" spirit. Paul's response is to show how "sincerity and truth" affect all life's relationships.

The passage, therefore, gives an important insight into *the nature of the Christian life* in Paul's teaching.

CHAPTER THIRTY-ONE

The Claims of the New Life in Christ
(1 Corinthians 6:12–20)

THE LARGER CONTEXT

In 1 Corinthians 6:1–8 Paul leaves the matter of sexual morality and treats another issue perhaps brought to his mind by the reference to "judging those inside the church" in 5:12. The issue in 6:1–8 is the lawsuits between Christians which are being brought into court before pagan judges. Paul regrets that such disputes exist (vv. 7–8), but if they are inevitable, believers should use one of their own members to settle them (vs. 5).

  Then Paul goes on to give a catalogue of types of evildoers who will not enter the kingdom of God (vv. 9–11). Once the Corinthians were such as these but now they have been washed, sanctified, and justified (vs. 11). The connection with 6:1–8 is the link between ἀδικέω in vv. 7–8 and ἄδικοι in vs. 9: that brother is "wronging" brother leads Paul to warn "wrongdoers" of their fate.

  The inclusion of "fornicators" in the list of vs. 9 leads Paul back again to the theme of sexual immorality in 6:12–20. Whereas in 5:1–8 he dealt with a concrete case, now he deals with a principle by which some Corinthians seem to be living (Barrett, p. 144).

NOTES

verse 12

Πάντα μοι ἔξεστιν—ἔξεστιν: impersonal verb, 3rd sing. of the unused ἔξειμι, "it is permitted; it is possible; it is proper" (AG, p. 274). RSV puts these words in quotation marks because most scholars agree (including older ones such as Calvin, p. 128) that Paul is quoting a maxim which the Corinthians used to justify their immorality. See earlier, p. 295. Alford (p. 516) insists they "are the bona fide words of the apostle himself, not, as some have understood them, the saying of an opponent cited by him." There could be truth in both interpretations if the Corinthians had taken the slogan from Paul's own teaching and misused it (Conzelmann, p. 109; Barrett, p. 145). This slogan, also found in 10:23, is part of the evidence for seeing an "incipient gnosticism" or a "gnosticizing party" at Corinth. Irenaeus says of the Gnostics, "These men, while they boast of Jesus as being their Master, do in fact emulate the philosophy of Epicurus and the indifference of the Cynics" (*Adv. Haer.* 2.32.3). On the question of Gnosticism in Corinth, see W. Schmithals' book by that name and R. McL. Wilson's qualifications in *Gnosis and the New Testament*, pp. 51–55; and "How Gnostic were the Corinthians?" *NTS*, 19 (1972–73), 65–74. See earlier, pp. 172f., 322f. In context "all things are lawful for me" means "that they abused their liberty to such an extent that they stretched it to include fornication" (Calvin, p. 128).

ἀλλ᾽ οὐ πάντα συμφέρει—συμφέρω = "bring together, help, be advantageous or profitable or useful" (AG, p. 787). Cf. 10:23; 12:7; 2 Cor. 8:10; 12:1. Paul does not directly deny the slogan, but inserts his own qualification, the meaning of which is shown in 10:23 and 12:7. Note the link between συμφέρω and οἰκοδομέω and ἀγάπη in 10:23 and 8:1. Love governs the use of freedom (cf. Gal. 5:13; Barrett, p. 145). Conzelmann (p. 109n6&11) maintains that Paul is using Stoic terminology in his qualification of the Corinthian slogan.

ἀλλ᾽ οὐκ ἐγὼ ἐξουσιασθήσομαι ὑπό τινος—Note the emphatic ἐγώ. Ἐξουσιασθήσομαι: the morpheme -θησ- is a certain clue for parsing. Do not construe the "ε" as an augment. The verb is ἐξουσιάζω = "to have the right or power for something or over someone" (AG, p. 278). For this class of verb (stem ending in "ζ") see HNTG §24.251ff. and Paradigm V-4a. Would you construe τινος as neuter or masculine?

"To use things indifferent so that they become by habit indispensable is the very negation of freedom: indulgence of passions as indifferent leads to slavery to the passions" (Parry, p. 101). "Licence is not more but less than liberty" (Barrett, p. 146).

verse 13
τὰ βρώματα τῇ κοιλίᾳ, καὶ ἡ κοιλία τοῖς βρώμασιν· ὁ δὲ θεὸς καὶ ταύτην καὶ ταῦτα καταργήσει—Τὸ βρῶμα = "food" (AG, p. 147). Κοιλία = "belly, stomach, womb" (AG, p. 438). The antecedents of ταύτην and ταῦτα can be identified by the fact that one is fem. sing. and one is neut. pl. We must either supply the verb "are" and "is" in the first two clauses or translate them like exclamations: "Foods for the belly and the belly for foods!" What kind of datives are κοιλίᾳ and βρώμασιν (HNTG §35.3233)? The verb of the third clause is καταργέω = "make ineffective, powerless; abolish, wipe out, set aside" (AG, p. 418). On "contract verbs" see HNTG Paradigm V-1b. The "σ" tense sign with no augment and the ending -ει can only be one tense.

Barrett (p. 146) and Bruce (pp. 62f.) view these three clauses as part

of the rationale presented by the "gnosticizing party" ("spiritual libertines," Moffatt, p. 69) for their freedom from any food laws. Why does
the RSV not include, "God will abolish both" in quotation marks? Paul
does not seem to deny the validity of the argument "as far as food laws
are concerned" (Barrett, p. 147). The transiency of food and digestion
does relativize food laws: cf. 8:8; Rom. 14:17; Mark 7:18f. But see
Gundry's argument (pp. 55f.) that Paul denies "that the mortal body
in any of its parts is unimportant."

Paul mentions food in a context relating mainly to fornication because "he knew that for some of them the corollary held good: 'sexual
relations for the body and the body for sexual relations'" (Bruce, pp.
62f.). Since "there is no resurrection" of the body (15:12), then "nothing concerning corporeal life is of any importance for the spiritual life
and for the destiny of the soul. This is why even debauchery and other
carnal excesses cannot defile the spirit, which alone inherits the
Kingdom" (Héring, p. 44). So went the gnostic argument. But Paul
denies the validity of it in what follows.

τὸ δὲ σῶμα οὐ τῇ πορνείᾳ ἀλλὰ τῷ κυρίῳ, καὶ ὁ κύριος τῷ σώματι—The
corollary to vs. 13a is not "the body for fornication and fornication for
the body!" but rather "the body for the Lord and the Lord for the
body!" "Belly and eating, yes; but not, body and fornication" (Barrett,
p. 147).

Is not the stomach part of the body so that Paul could have said, "the
stomach for the Lord and the Lord for the stomach!"? Does the adver-
sative δὲ mean that Paul sees a contrast between the stomach and the
body (RP, p. 123) or does it mean "*despite* the physical nature and
ultimate destruction of the present body, it *nevertheless* is meant for
the Lord rather than for immorality" (Gundry, p. 55)? With this question the much larger issue of the meaning of σῶμα in Pauline anthropology is raised. Bultmann (pp. 194f.) has been extremely influential here in arguing that "*sōma* = self, person" or "your body means
you." He has been followed in this by many scholars: Moule, p. 197;
Morris, p. 100 ("body is the whole personality, man as person meant
for God"); Barrett, p. 147 ("the *body* is myself"); Conzelmann, p. 110
("I am *sōma* inasmuch as I am not a 'thing' but enter a relationship");
Ladd, p. 464 ("Man, his person as a whole, can be denoted by *sōma*").

Gundry's book deals this interpretation an extremely powerful
blow. His conclusion is that in neither the Pauline Epistles, nor the
literature of the New Testament outside those Epistles, nor the LXX,
nor extra-biblical ancient Greek literature, does the definition "whole
person" find convincing support. "The *sōma* may *represent* the whole
person simply because the *sōma* lives in union with the soul/spirit.
But *sōma* does not *mean* 'whole person,' because its use is designed to
call attention to the physical object which is the body of the person
rather than the whole personality. Where used of whole people, *sōma*

directs attention to their bodies, not to the wholeness of their being"
(pp. 79f.). On our verse Gundry offers four arguments why no contrast
is intended between stomach and body. The point is the same for both:
relation to the Lord not physical appetite should govern the Christian
(pp. 55f.).

For the meaning of "the body is for the Lord" see Rom. 6:12,13,19;
12:1. On "the Lord is for the body" see Hodge, p. 103; Grosheide, p. 147;
RP, p. 124; Morris, p. 100; Barrett, p. 148. Héring, p. 46, sees an
allusion to the Eucharist (as he often does!).

verse 14

ὁ δὲ θεὸς καὶ τὸν κύριον ἤγειρεν καὶ ἡμᾶς ἐξεγερεῖ διὰ τῆς δυνάμεως
αὐτοῦ—Ἤγειρεν from ἐγείρω = "wake, raise up, restore" (AG, p. 213).
Note the temporal augment ε > η, the "ε" theme vowel and the
movable "ν." Recall that in liquid verbs (HNTG, Paradigm V-4e) the
"σ" tense sign drops out. Ἐξεγερεῖ is the same verb with ἐκ-prefix. The
circumflex accent is the only signal of the future tense since the "σ"
tense sign drops out in liquid verbs. According to A. Oepke, in TDNT,
2,338, "there is no particular significance in the alteration between
the simple and compound forms [of ἐγείρω]." To whom does αὐτοῦ
refer?

Conzelmann (p. 111) notes a further distinction between stomach
and body: the one will be destroyed (vs. 13), the other raised (vs. 14).
Barrett says the reason this is so is that body means "whole person"
and thus "participates in the continuity of the resurrection life" (p.
148). Gundry (p. 54) rejects the sharp contrast between destruction
and resurrection: "The destruction of the stomach and its food need
only mean that God 'will (at the Parousia) cause such a change to take
place in the bodily constitution of man and in the world of sense
generally, that neither the organs of digestion as such, nor the meats
as such, will then be existent' (cf. 1 Cor. 15:44,51; Mk. 12:25 and
parallels). In other words, Paul simply teaches that the physical constitution of the resurrected body will be different from that of the
mortal body." His argument on p. 56 is worth pondering: namely that
in Romans 6:6 the word "abolish" (καταργέω) is used to describe what
happens to the "*body* of sin."

For the connection between Christ's resurrection and ours see
15:12–19, on which see R. J. Sider, "The Pauline Conception of the
Resurrection Body in 1 Corinthians XV.35–54," *NTS,* 21 (1974–75),
428–39.

verse 15

οὐκ οἴδατε ὅτι τὰ σώματα ὑμῶν μέλη Χριστοῦ ἐστιν;— For οἴδατε see the
notes on 5:6. Note the similar rhetorical question in 6:16,19. Μέλη,
neut. pl. nom. of μέλος = "member, part, limb" (AG, p. 502). For an

explanation of this unusual-looking ending see HNTG 21.53ff. and the paradigm on p. C–17.

"Members of Christ" anticipates the teaching of 1 Cor. 12: "The underlying thought is that of the body of Christ" (Conzelmann, p. 111). Bultmann (p. 194) argues that the parallel between 1 Cor. 6:15 ("your *bodies* are members of Christ") and 12:27 ("*you* are the body of Christ and individually members of it") shows that there is no difference in meaning between "you" and "your bodies." Gundry calls this "widely separated" parallel into question with the common sense question: "Does the general statement of Paul concerning the whole person's membership in Christ's Body [12.27] preclude his making a more specific statement elsewhere that a *part* of man's constitution belongs to Christ?" (p. 51). He continues, "In the context of an injunction against sexual immorality Paul serves his purpose better by a pointed reference to man's physique than by a general reference to the totality of man's being" (p. 61). For a bibliography of works on the church and the body of Christ see Ladd, p. 531. For Paul's use of μέλος see J. Horst, in TDNT, 4, 561ff.

ἄρας οὖν τὰ μέλη τοῦ Χριστοῦ ποιήσω πόρνης μέλη; μὴ γένοιτο.—Ἄρας is from αἴρω = "lift up, take up, pick up, take away, remove" (AG, pp. 23f.). Compare ἐκκαθάρατε, 5:7, for the loss of "ι" from the stem. Recall that in liquid verbs the "σ" tense sign drops out and in the nom. sing. participles the "ντ" infix drops ἀρ(σ)α(ντ)ς > ἄρας. Since aor. participles are often part of the action of the main verb we need not translate "having taken the members . . ." but should translate "Shall we take the members of Christ and make . . .?" Alford (p. 517), however, denies that the participle is merely pleonastic. Ποιήσω can be aor. subj. or fut. indic. Which fits the context better? Πόρνη = "prostitute, harlot" (AG, p. 700). "Perhaps we should remember that *'pornai'* were in general sacred prostitutes, slaves attached to the service of a pagan temple (notably to a temple of Venus-Aphrodite), who were supposed to put those who worshipped them in communion with the deity they served" (Héring, p. 45). See also F. Hauck-S. Schulz, in TDNT, 6,593. Γένοιτο is aor. mid. opt. 3rd sing. of γίνομαι—so common you should simply memorize this form.

Note the shift in imagery (Barrett, p. 148): in vs. 15*a* our body is a member of Christ; in v. 15*b* our members seem to be in view since we take them and make them members of a harlot. What is the basis of Paul's emphatic No to fornication? "By such a union the Christian would form one body with the person concerned, and it is impossible to belong at the same time to two bodies" (Héring, p. 46, see next verse). Héring's observation raises the question why a legitimate marriage union would not be excluded for the same reason. For Bruce's answer see p. 64 on vs. 15; for Gundry's see pp. 53f.

In the flow of Paul's argument v. 15 marks a new beginning, since in 15–20 the matter of destruction and/or resurrection of the body is left behind. Verse 15a can be seen as the fulcrum between the two arguments supporting what preceded (vs. 14—our resurrection based on Christ's) and what follows (the implications of union with Christ now).

verse 16

ὁ κολλώμενος τῇ πόρνῃ ἓν σῶμά ἐστιν;—Κολλώμενος from κολλάω = "join closely together, unite" (AG, p. 442); contract verb α + ο > ω. May be middle ("join oneself to") or passive ("is joined to"). Do not confuse ἕν with ἐν.

Ἔσονται γάρ, φησίν, οἱ δύο εἰς σάρκα μίαν.—Ἔσονται is fut. of εἰμί. Φησίν from φημί = "say, affirm" (AG, p. 864). On the μι-verbs see HNTG Paradigm V-7a. Μία is the feminine form of εἷς.

Paul quotes Gen. 2:24 from the LXX. The Hebrew reads, *wᵉhāyû lᵉbāśār 'ehād* (cf. Gen. 2:7,10). The LXX reads, καὶ ἔσονται οἱ δύο εἰς σάρκα μίαν. This is a good illustration of how Hebrew influenced Hellenistic Greek. *wᵉhāyû lᵉ* ("is unto") means "become." This construction is very literally taken over into Greek as ἔσονται εἰς ("they shall be to") = they become.

The use of body (vs. 15a) and flesh (vs. 15b) would suggest that Paul sees no distinction here, even though "flesh" is usually a negative term for him (RP, p. 127). But Barrett (p. 149) thinks that even here Paul intends "flesh" to be evil: "If one places his body at the disposal of a harlot, and so becomes one body with her, the body has taken the wrong turning, and becomes flesh." Gundry (p. 62) rejects Barrett's view and sees the parallel between flesh and body as a strong support for his thesis that "body" does not mean whole person. Conzelmann (p. 111n28) points out that the oneness of flesh spoken of in Gen. 2:24 is not true only of married partners but "simply describes sexual union in general." Precisely here lies the force of Paul's argument.

verse 17

ὁ δὲ κολλώμενος τῷ κυρίῳ ἓν πνεῦμά ἐστιν.—Κολλάω takes dat., since it means "to join *to* something."

Conzelmann (p. 112) thinks that this simply restates and explains vs. 15 that our bodies are members of Christ. Gundry cites others who hold this view (p. 65n1) but argues that Paul presents not one truth but two: "the twin truths add up to this: the whole man, body and spirit, belongs to the Lord. . . . Paul opposes the disparity between carnal union with a harlot and spiritual union with the Lord because although body and spirit differ, they belong together in the service of Christ" (p. 69). Other texts that may shed light on the spiritual union of the believer and Christ are Rom. 8:9–27; 1 Cor. 12:13; Gal. 4:6; John 15:1–7; 17:21,23. On the theology of being "in Christ" or "in the Spirit" see Ladd, pp. 479–94 (bibliography, p. 479).

verse 18

φεύγετε τὴν πορνείαν·—Φεύγω = "flee, escape, shun" (AG, p. 863). Is it present or imperative? Cf. 10:14. This is a repetition explicitly of what was demanded implicitly in vs. 15*b*. It is a specific instance of how one fulfils the command of 6:20 to glorify God in the body. Bruce (p. 65) sees an echo of Joseph's literal fleeing a temptation of this kind (Gen. 39:12).

πᾶν ἁμάρτημα ὃ ἐὰν ποιήσῃ ἄνθρωπος ἐκτὸς τοῦ σώματός ἐστιν. ὁ δὲ πορνεύων εἰς τὸ ἴδιον σῶμα ἁμαρτάνει.—Ἁμάρτημα = "sin, transgression" (AG, p. 42). Do not confuse the relative pronoun ὅ with the definite article ὁ. Ἐάν is a compound of εἰ and ἄν; its use " is all of a piece with the use of ἄν in senses corresponding with the English indefinite suffix—"*ever*" in *whoever, whenever,* etc. There is a conditional clause latent in such words" (Moule, p. 151). What mood regularly follows ἐάν? Ἐκτός = "outside" (AG, p. 245). Πορνεύω = "to prostitute, to practice sexual immorality" (AG, p. 700); do not confuse the nom. pres. participle with the gen. πορνευόντων; the genitive always has the -ντ-; the nominative never does. Εἰς in this context can mean "against" as in Luke 15:8 (AG, p. 228,4 cα), but the contrast with ἐκτός suggests that εἰς also has a spatial significance.

Verses 16 and 17 ground both 15*b* and 18*a* (which say essentially the same thing). Now in 18*b* another argument commences in support of 18*a*. How can one explain this strange argument that all sins are outside the body except fornication? After all, sins like gluttony, drunkenness, and suicide *do* strike the body (Héring, p. 46). Several suggestions have been made:

1. Paul is only speaking comparatively. Calvin (p. 131): "My explanation is that he does not completely deny that there are other sins, which also bring dishonour and disgrace upon our bodies, but that he is simply saying that those other sins do not leave *anything like the same* filthy stain on our bodies as fornication does" (ital. added). So also Barrett, p. 151.

2. Moule (pp. 196f.) thinks that vs. 18*a* is a Corinthian libertine slogan ("all sins are outside the body") and 18*b* is Paul's retort. See Barrett's (p. 150) and Gundry's (p. 73) criticisms.

3. E. Schweizer (TDNT, 7,1070) construes "body" in 18*b* as the body of Christ, the church. "In the community man is represented as united with Christ in such bodily fashion that all other sins are more readily conceivable than fornication, which accomplishes bodily union with someone else and therefore cannot take place within the body of Christ, the two being mutually exclusive." See Gundry's reply (p. 73).

4. R. Kempthorne, "Incest and the Body of Christ: A Study of

I Corinthians 6:12–20," in *NTS*, 14 (1968), 568–74, offers a combination of Moule's and Schweizer's views. Verse 18*a* harks back to the incident of incest in 5:1–5 and represents the Corinthian claim that the sin of incest lay outside the ecclesiastical body because the stepmother was not a Christian. Paul retorts that the man sins against the church because the church is *his* (the man's) body by virtue of his membership in it. See Gundry's critique (pp. 75–79).

5. Gundry (p. 72) says Alford's is the "best interpretation": "The assertion, which has surprised many of the Commentators, is nevertheless *strictly true*. Drunkenness and gluttony, e.g., are sins done *in* and *by* the body, and are sins *by abuse of* the body,—but they are still ἐκτὸς τοῦ σώματος—introduced *from without,* sinful *not* in their *act,* but in their *effect,* which effect it is each man's duty to foresee and avoid. But fornication is *alienating that body which is the Lord's, and making it a harlot's body*—it is sin *against a man's own body,* in its very nature,—against *the verity and nature* of his body; not an *effect* on the body from participation of things without, but a *contradiction of the truth* of the body, wrought *within itself*" (p. 518). See too J. Murphy-O'Connor, "Corinthian Slogans in 1 Cor. 6,12–20," *CBQ,* 40 (1978), 391–96; B. Byrne, "Sinning against One's Own Body: Paul's Understanding of the Sexual Relationship in 1 Corinthians 6:18," *CBQ,* 45 (1983), 608-16.

verse 19

τὸ σῶμα ὑμῶν ναὸς τοῦ ἐν ὑμῖν ἁγίου πνεύματός ἐστιν—Ναός = "temple" (AG, p. 535; cf. O. Michel, in TDNT, 4,880ff.). Bruce (p. 65): "Cf. 3.16, where the statement that the community is a temple of God is similarly introduced; but here the reference is to the individual believer's body as the sanctuary of the indwelling Spirit" (similarly Barrett, p. 151). Against this view Kempthorne ("Incest," pp. 572f.; see above on 6:18 #4) maintains that the singular *sōma* in vv. 19 and 20 refers to the Body of Christ. Similarly P. S. Minear, *Images of the Church in the New Testament* (1960), pp. 180–82. Gundry argues against this view on pp. 76f. and refers to 2 Cor. 4:10 and Rom. 8:23, where the singular *sōma* is used distributively.

Héring (p. 47) keenly notes the attributive position of the phrase ἐν ὑμῖν and sees it as qualifying the degree to which the Holy Spirit dwells in us: "Here it is the body of the individual which is to become the dwelling place of the Holy Spirit—not in His fullness, but in the measure in which He can reside there. (Hence wc read ναὸς τοῦ ἐν ὑμῖν ἁγίου πνεύματος and not simply ναὸς ἁγίου πνεύματος.) The ideal will only be made visibly real in the future aeon, that is, in the resurrection world."

οὗ ἔχετε ἀπὸ θεοῦ—Why is the relative pronoun οὗ in the gen. when it is functioning as the dir. obj. of ἔχετε (HNTG §35.573)? Compare 1 Thess. 4:8 on the gift of the Spirit as a motive for chastity.

verses 19b,20

καὶ οὐκ ἐστὲ ἑαυτῶν; ἠγοράσθητε γὰρ τιμῆς—Ἠγοράσθητε from ἀγοράζω = "buy, purchase" (AG, p. 12; F. Büchsel, in TDNT, 1,125). For the morphology see on ἐξουσιασθήσομαι at 6:12 above. Here there is a temporal augment and a -θη- infix. Τιμῆς is a genitive of price. Remember that punctuation is editorial not original; should the question mark (;) come after ἑαυτῶν or after the earlier θεοῦ? See the BSGNT apparatus.

A parallel is 7:23. Only in these two texts does Paul use the term ἀγοράζω in relation to Christians. "The fundamental idea of ransoming Paul derived from the Old Testament where the words are used in a wide variety of senses (e.g., Ex. 6:6; 13:13; Ruth 4:4ff.; Ps. 103:4; Is. 43:1)" (Barrett, p. 152). See the excursus in Conzelmann (p. 131) on the ransoming of slaves in that day. "In Rom. 3:24f.; Eph. 1:7 the redemption (there *apolytrōsis*) is procured through the blood of Christ (cf. Ac. 20:28; Heb. 9:12; 1 Pet. 1:18f.; Rev. 5:9), and this doubtless is the price (*timē*) here" (Bruce, p. 65).

Verses 19b and 20 seem to be a ground alongside 19a ("your body is the temple of the Holy Spirit") for 18b ("the fornicator sins against his own body") and 20b ("glorify God in your body").

δοξάσατε δὴ τὸν θεὸν ἐν τῷ σώματι ὑμῶν.—Δοξάσατε from δοξάζω = "praise, honor, magnify, glorify" (AG, p. 203; cf. G. Kittel, in TDNT, 2,253). The σα- infix without an augment means the word is what mood and tense? Δή with exhortations or commands gives them greater urgency = "now, then, therefore" (AG, p. 177).

From the context, how does one bring glory to God with the body (cf., e.g., vs. 15, also 10:31)? Note the textual variants at the end of 6:20 in the BSGNT apparatus. Metzger (p. 553) maintains that the words "and in your spirits which are God's" (in KJV) "are a gloss with no claim to be original." This is clear "(a) from the decisive testimony of the earliest and best witnesses in support of the shorter text . . . and (b) from the nature of the addition itself (it is not needed for the argument, which relates to the sanctity of the body, with no mention of the spirit [sic v. 17]). The words were inserted apparently with a desire to soften Paul's abruptness, and to extend the range of his exhortation."

THE STRUCTURE OF THE ARGUMENT

The argument in these verses is complex and does not flow neatly from premises to conclusion. In verses 15-20 there is a four-pillar foundation of the argument, each pillar of which relates to union with Christ/Spirit: vs. 15a: "your bodies are members of Christ"; vs. 17: "the one united to the Lord is one spirit with him"; vs. 19a: "your body is the temple of the

Holy Spirit"; and vv. 19*b*, 20: "you are not yours but God's since he bought you." Upon these four pillars rests the threefold hortatory conclusion in vs. 15*b*: "do not make the members of Christ the members of a prostitute!"; vs. 18*a*: "flee fornication!"; and vs. 20*b*: "glorify God in your body!"

In verses 12-14 Paul moves into the subject of fornication through the door of two Corinthian slogans (vv. 12 and 13) which attempt to justify license in one's use of the body (in eating [vs. 13*a*] and in sexuality [vs. 13*b*]). Paul's initial response is fourfold: vs. 12*a*: one should use one's freedom only to do what is beneficial (i.e., what builds up the faith and love of the church); vs. 12*b*: one should beware of falling into slavery to passions in the name of liberty; vs. 13*b*: the body does *not* exist merely to be gratified sexually, it exists for the Lord and the Lord is concerned with it (this anticipates the four pillars of vv. 15-20); vs. 14: the body is not merely transient and so ethically negligible; it is destined to be raised (and glorified, Rom. 8:21,23).

J. Héring (p. 47) makes a perceptive summarizing statement:

We are probably witnessing here [in 1 Cor. 6] the first attempt in the history of moral thought to refute libertinism in some other way than by the arguments of an ascetic, legalistic or utilitarian type which are so common in Greek philosophy.

CHAPTER THIRTY-TWO

The Hope of the Resurrection
(1 Corinthians 15:20–28)

LARGER CONTEXT

In 1 Corinthians 15 Paul treats the question of the resurrection—Christ's and the believers'. Verses 1–11 are a reminder to the church of what they had received (vs. 1) and believed (vs. 11) when Paul first preached to them the gospel, namely that Christ "was raised on the third day" (vs. 4). This original conviction Paul now attempts to reinforce by giving a list of witnesses to Christ's resurrection, "most of whom are still alive" (vs. 6). The verses thus function to establish a common ground between Paul and the Corinthians: both believe Christ was raised from the dead.

In verses 12–19 Paul begins his main argument, building on that premise. He argues that it is inconsistent to believe in the resurrection of Christ and to say "there is no resurrection of the dead" (ἀνάστασις νεκρῶν οὐκ ἔστιν; vs. 12). Not only is it inconsistent, it also implies that Paul is a "false witness" (vs. 15), faith is futile (vs. 17), the dead in Christ are done for (vs. 18), and those alive in Christ are to be pitied (vs. 19). What was the nature of the Corinthians' denial of resurrection?

1. In contemporary New Testament studies it is often argued that the gnostic leaning of the Corinthian church manifests itself in a belief that the resurrection of Christians had already occurred (spiritually, since the body was of no concern to them) and that there was no future bodily resurrection (Barrett, pp. 347f.; Lietzmann-Kümmel, *An die Korinther* [1949], pp. 192f.; J. H. Wilson, "Corinthians Who Say There is no Resurrection of the Dead," *ZNTW*, 59 [1968], 90–107). Support for this "over-realized eschatology" (Bruce, p. 144) is sought in 1 Corinthians 4:8, where Paul intimates that the Corinthians think (wrongly) that "the age to come is already consummated," they are already kings and "there is no 'not yet' to qualify the 'already' of realized eschatology" (Barrett, p. 109). Additional support is found in 2 Timothy 2:18, where Hymenaeus and Philetus are reported to claim that the resurrection of believers has already occurred (cf. Polycarp, *Phil.* 7).

2. The older view of the Corinthian error is that it was the belief that "resurrection is impossible" (RP, p. 346). As Aeschylus says through Apollo's speech, "When the earth has drunk up a man's blood, once he is dead, there is no resurrection" (*Eumenides*, 647f.). They may have thought Christ's resurrection was an isolated exception (RP, p. 346; for the Greek background to this view see A. Oepke, in TDNT, 1,396), or they may have denied Christ's resurrection also (Hodge, p. 319). The immortality of the soul after death was sufficient hope for this group. R. McL. Wilson argues that the use of 2 Timothy 2:18 in the former interpretation: "may be no more than a reading back from the Pastorals into the situation at Corinth. The most natural rendering of 1 Cor. 15:12 is not that some say there will be no resurrection (because it is already past), but that in their view there is no such thing. The verb is in the present tense, not the future. In other words, Paul's opponents would be maintaining the 'Greek' view of the immortality of the soul over against a resurrection of the body, as indeed Paul's whole argument seems to imply, with its emphasis on the fact of the resurrection of Jesus" (*Gnosis and the New Testament* [1968], p. 53).

Whichever of these views is correct (see earlier, pp. 173, 323), Paul proceeds in 15:20–28 to show that believers *will* be raised in the future and that this "not yet" event is grounded in the "already" of Christ's resurrection. For Paul's overall view of the resurrection see G. E. Ladd, *I Believe in the Resurrection of Jesus* (1975), Chapter 9 and the literature cited in his footnotes. See E. Schweizer, "1 Corinthians 15:20–28 as Evidence of Pauline Eschatology and its Relation to the Preaching of Jesus," in *Saved by Hope. Essays in Honor of Richard C. Oudersluys*, ed. J. I. Cook (1978), ch. 8 (ET from *Jesus und Paulus. Festschrift W. G. Kümmel*, edd. E. E. Ellis and E. Grässer [1975]); also R. P. Martin, *The Spirit and the Congregation* (1984), pp. 107–18 with bibliography.

NOTES

verse 20

Νυνὶ δὲ Χριστὸς ἐγήγερται ἐκ νεκρῶν, ἀπαρχὴ τῶν κεκοιμημένων—Νυνὶ δέ: "introducing the real situation after an unreal conditional clause or sentence; *but, as a matter of fact*, 1 Cor. 5:11; 12:18; 15:20; Hb. 8:6; 9:26" (AG, p. 548). Ἐγήγερται from ἐγείρω—note the unusual reduplication (HNTG §24.3148); perf. pass. does not have theme vowel. For the force of the perf. see HNTG §31.561. Ἀπαρχή = "first fruits" (AG, p. 80; G. Delling, in TDNT, 1,484ff.). Κεκοιμημένων from κοιμάομαι = "fall asleep," then figuratively "die" (AG, p. 438); note the reduplication and -μεν- participle infix.

The word ἀπαρχή is of fundamental importance here; see also its use in Rom. 8:23 (with which ἀρραβών in 2 Cor. 1:22 is synonymous). "Paul (in dependence on the Old Testament) takes the word to mean the first instalment of the crop which foreshadows and pledges the ultimate offering of the whole" (Barrett, p. 350; cf. Alford, p. 608, who sees a more precise relation to Lev. 23:10ff.). So the main point of the verse is that just as surely as the first fruits guarantee the coming harvest, so surely does Christ's resurrection guarantee the believer's future resurrection (Bruce, p. 145). Conzelmann sees another nuance: "at the same time ἀπαρχή is used to ward off fanaticism: Christ is so far the only one" (p. 268). Conzelmann assumes that the Corinthians thought the resurrection of believers had already happened (2 Tim. 2:18).

verse 21

ἐπειδὴ γὰρ δι' ἀνθρώπου θάνατος, καὶ δι' ἀνθρώπου ἀνάστασις νεκρῶν— Ἐπειδὴ γάρ = "for since" (AG, p. 284); for a similar causal use of this pair see 1 Cor. 1:21. The γάρ relates vs. 21 with vs. 20; the ἐπειδή relates the two halves of vs. 21. What verbs will you supply in these clauses? Does the γάρ supply a justification (Parry, p. 223; Hodge, p. 324) or an explanation (Alford, p. 608) of vs. 20? For further notes see on vs. 22. "The two verses may be taken together, since the latter [vs. 22] serves to make the former more precise, though the former is also important as interpreting the latter" (Barrett, p. 351).

verse 22

ὥσπερ γὰρ ἐν τῷ Ἀδαμ πάντες ἀποθνήσκουσιν, οὕτως καὶ ἐν τῷ Χριστῷ πάντες ζωοποιηθήσονται—Ὥσπερ ... οὕτως καί = "just as ... so also"; see the parallels in Rom. 5:19,21. Ἀποθνήσκω = "die" (AG, p. 90). What is the significance of the tense of this verb in this context? Ζωοποιέω = "make alive, give life to" (AG, p. 342); note the decisive -θησ- tense infix.

The effect of Adam's sin on the human race and the typology (τύπος; Rom. 5:14) between him and Christ is developed fully in Rom. 5:12–21. See also 1 Cor. 15:45–50, where Christ is pictured as the second Adam. On this motif in Paul see C. K. Barrett, *From First Adam to Last* (1962). The pertinent question is why Paul introduces the Adam-Christ contrast in this specific context. Does he see a necessary logical connection between Adam/all die and Christ/all live, so that if the Corinthians accept the one they must accept the other (in which case Paul must assume they know and agree with his view of the solidarity between Adam and humanity)? Or, apart from logical connections, is Paul simply pointing out the humanity of Christ (ἄνθρωπος; vs. 21) and a parallel between Christ's work and Adam's sin, which may help the Corinthians understand the resurrection of believers in its relation to Christ? If we omit 21a and 22a (the Adam halves), the argument of vv. 20–22 seems to be:

22b: in Christ will all be made alive;

21b: *therefore* resurrection is through a *man*;

20: *therefore* Christ is the first fruits of all (*men*) who sleep.

A tangential but important question raised by vs. 22 is whether Paul is here teaching universal salvation (cf. Rom. 5:18). Most of the commentators agree that "this can hardly be said to fit the context" (Barrett, p. 352; Conzelmann, p. 268n49), and "this interpretation utterly contradicts his eschatology" (Héring, p. 165). Two different approaches have been taken in order to harmonize this verse (vs. 22) with passages which speak of those who perish (1 Cor. 1:18; 3:17; 5:13; 6:9ff.; 9:27[?]) or of eternal destruction (2 Thess. 1:9):

1. The most common approach is to limit the πάντες in each clause of vs. 22 by ἐν τῷ Ἀδαμ and ἐν τῷ Χριστῷ respectively (Barrett, p. 352; Héring, p. 165; Parry, p. 222; Hodge, p. 325; Grosheide, p. 363). Hence we do not read simply, "All will be made alive in Christ," but rather, "All who are in Christ will be made alive." "Each of the two Adams acts as the head of a humanity—the old and the new" (Héring, p. 165). "All who are in Christ stand in solidarity with him as all men in Adam stand in solidarity with Adam. All in Adam share Adam's death, so all who are in Christ will share Christ's life" (Ladd, *Theology*, p. 326).

2. The other approach is to qualify the meaning of ζωοποιέω while letting πάντες refer to all men without qualification (RP, p. 353; Alford, p. 608). Ζωοποιέω is then taken to refer to a general resurrection of all men, which does not imply their salvation.

verse 23

ἕκαστος δὲ ἐν τῷ ἰδίῳ τάγματι—Τάγμα: of a number of persons who belong together and are therefore arranged together in a "division, group, class"; a technical military term for bodies of troops in various numbers (AG, p. 810); see G. Delling, in TDNT, 8,31f., which renders the clause "in his 'position' or 'rank'" (so also Barrett, p. 355). What verb should be supplied here? Barrett suggests "will be brought to life" from the preceding clause (p. 354). See below for further notes on the meaning of this clause.

ἀπαρχὴ Χριστός, ἔπειτα οἱ τοῦ Χριστοῦ ἐν τῇ παρουσίᾳ αὐτοῦ—Ἔπειτα = "then, thereupon" (AG, p. 284). The definite article οἱ should be translated "the ones" or "those." Ἐν has a temporal sense and should be rendered "at" (AG, p. 259, II, 2). For the religious and secular background of παρουσία see Conzelmann, p. 270n69&70 and A. Oepke, in TDNT, 5,858ff. Three types of interpretations may be considered:

1. Parry (p. 224) construes ἐν τῷ ἰδίῳ τάγματι as "in his own appointed place" (cf. 1 Clement 37:3). "As each member has now his

place and function in the Body, so, when the whole Body is quickened and raised, each will still have his place and function." Thus τάγμα = "the place in the Body, already assigned, and to be preserved in the resurrection."

2. With nuances of difference Barrett (p. 355), Héring (p. 167), Conzelmann (p. 27), and Bruce (p. 146) construe τάγμα as a reference to stages of resurrection, of which two are mentioned in this passage: Christ's and then at his *parousia* the resurrection of believers. Thus Paul stresses the reality and futurity of the believer's resurrection. Note how this guards his readers against misunderstanding teaching like Rom. 6:4 and Col. 2:12 ("you were raised with Christ") and Col. 3:3 ("your life is hid with Christ in God"). Conzelmann calls this Paul's "eschatological reservation" (p. 268n44). We have been *already* raised with Christ to "newness of life" (Rom. 6:4) but *not yet* to full resurrection life. That happens later (ἔπειτα) "at his coming."

3. The third view includes vs. 24; see on the next phrase.

verse 24

εἶτα τὸ τέλος—Εἶτα = "then, next" (AG, p. 233). Τέλος = "end, goal, rest, remainder" (AG, pp. 818f.). What verb should we supply? The third interpretation of the τάγματα (vs. 23) mentioned above views τὸ τέλος as a *third* τάγμα. For example, Alford (p. 609) sees three classes: Christ (ἀπαρχή), Christians (οἱ τοῦ Χριστοῦ); and "the rest of the dead, here veiled over by the general term τὸ τέλος." (Similarly H. Lietzmann-W. G. Kümmel, *An die Korinther,* p. 80.) See Rev. 20:5. Against this view are the criticisms of Barrett (p. 356) and Bruce (p. 147).

Some ask whether εἶτα signifies a lapse of time between the *parousia* and the end when Christ hands the kingdom over to God. Bruce (p. 147) argues that "the temporal adverb *eita* implies an interval of indeterminate duration between the parousia and the *end,* when Christ hands his dominion back to God" (similarly Ladd, p. 558). In this "final phase of Christ's kingship his people will share it with him (4.8) and judge the world (6.2)" (Bruce, *ibid.*). Alford (p. 609) locates the millennium in this period (between vs. 23 and vs. 24). Davies (pp. 293-95), however, and Barrett (p. 357) see no significant interval between the *parousia* and the end. Davies cites John 13:4f.; 19:26f.; 1 Cor. 15:5-7 to show that εἶτα need not imply an interval. On the theological significance of a millennial kingdom see Ladd, pp. 557f., 628-30; M. Rist, "Millennium," *IDB,* 3, 381f.; E. Stauffer, *New Testament Theology* (ET 1955), pp. 218f. (bibliography).

ὅταν παραδιδῷ τὴν βασιλείαν τῷ θεῷ καὶ πατρί, ὅταν καταργήσῃ πᾶσαν ἀρχὴν καὶ πᾶσαν ἐξουσίαν καὶ δύναμιν—Ὅταν is a compound of ὅτε and the indefinite particle ἄν: with the pres. subj. it means that the action of the subordinate clause is contemporaneous with the action of the main clause (AG, p. 592, 1a). Παραδίδωμι = "hand over, deliver, commit" (AG, pp. 619f.). Καταργέω = "make ineffective, wipe out, abolish" (AG, p. 418). Note the shift from pres. tense (παραδιδῷ) to aor. (καταργήσῃ). This shows that the action of the second ὅταν clause (the abolishing of the evil powers) must precede the action of the first ὅταν clause (the handing over of the kingdom to God). The trilogy of evil powers (ἀρχή, ἐξουσία, δύναμις) occurs again in Eph. 1:21; see also Rom. 8:38; Eph. 3:10; 6:12; Col. 1:16; 2:10,15. Note 1 Cor. 2:6, which speaks of earthly or spiritual ἄρχοντες being "abolished" (καταργουμένων). Barrett (p. 357) says "it is idle to attempt to distinguish between these nouns; they represent the evil powers . . . under whose control the world has come." On ἀρχή see G. Delling, in TDNT, 1,482–84; on ἐξουσία W. Foerster, in TDNT, 2,571–73; on δύναμις W. Grundmann, in TDNT, 2,295f., 307f. See, for general orientation, G. B. Caird, *Principalities and Powers* (1956); C. H. Powell, *The Biblical Concept of Power* (1963).

"In some way (never specified by Paul) authority has come into the hands of evil powers, whom God has to dispossess in order to reassert his own sovereignty. . . . Christ appears to reign during the period in which this dispossessing takes place, one enemy after another being overpowered. When the kingdom has been fully re-established, the Son hands it over to the Father, and the kingdom of Christ gives place to the kingdom of God" (Barrett, p. 357). But note well the eschatological tension: in Col. 2:15 the ἀρχαί and ἐξουσίαι have *already* been disarmed at the cross! See Heb. 2:14, according to which Jesus by his death secured the abolition (καταργήσῃ) of "the devil."

RP (p. 355) says, "What exactly is meant by παραδιδῷ τὴν βασιλείαν is beyond our comprehension." But Hodge gives four pages (pp. 330ff.) to this verse in search of its meaning. For the significance of 1 Cor. 15:23f. (with its emphasis on temporal sequence) in O. Cullmann's salvation-history scheme see *Christ and Time* (ET 1964), pp. 67, 151ff. and later discussion of this book (pp. 426f.).

verse 25

δεῖ γὰρ αὐτὸν βασιλεύειν ἄχρι οὗ θῇ πάντας τοὺς ἐχθροὺς ὑπὸ τοὺς πόδας αὐτοῦ—Δεῖ = "it is necessary," denoting compulsion of any kind (AG, p. 171); cf. W. Grundmann, in TDNT, 2, 21–25. Γάρ should alert you to think through how vs. 25 grounds vs. 24 (see Hodge, p. 331; Conzelmann, p. 272). Βασιλεύω = "be king, rule" (AG, p. 136). Note the pres. tense of the infin., whose significance Barrett (p. 358) tries to bring out with the translation "continue to reign." (When did Christ begin to reign? Ladd, p. 558; cf. Matt. 28:18; Col. 1:13, 18; 2:10.) Ἄχρι οὗ = ἄχρι χρόνου οὗ = "until the time when" (AG, p. 128,2). Θῇ, from τίθημι: the "τι" at the beginning of τίθημι is a reduplication (HNTG,

§13.24) which appears only in the pres. and imperf.; we can also rule out perf., pluperf., and fut. because there is no reduplication and no "χ" or "σ" tense sign. So θῆ is aor. The absence of an augment alerts us to the subj. mood. Thus tense and mood are the same as καταργήσῃ (vs. 24) and both have the same thrust.

Who is the subject of θῆ? In favor of Christ as the subject (Hodge, p. 331; Alford, p. 610; RP, p. 356; Parry, p. 226; Conzelmann, p. 273) it may be argued that θῆ is parallel to καταργήσῃ (vs. 24), the subject of which is Christ. In favor of God as the subject (Barrett, p. 358; Bruce, p. 147) is the loose quotation from Ps. 110:1—"The Lord said to my Lord, Sit at my right hand until I set thy enemies as the footstool of thy feet." The importance of this Psalm to the early church is seen by the number of times Christ is spoken of in terms of Ps. 110:1: Rom. 8:34; Col. 3:1; Eph. 1:20; Heb. 1:3; 8:1; 10:12; 1 Pet. 3:22; Acts 2:34; 5:31; 7:55; Rev. 3:21; Matt. 22:44; 26:64; Mark 12:36; 14:62; [16:19]; Luke 20:42; 22:69; 1 Clem. 36:5; Barn. 12:10. See D. M. Hay, *Glory at the Right Hand* (1973).

On the christological significance of the present reign of Christ see Ladd, p. 410; O. Cullmann, *The Christology of the New Testament* (1963), pp. 221ff. For those who read German an excellent article relating Christ's present rule to the Christian life is L. Goppelt, "Die Herrschaft Christi über die Welt," in *Christologie und Ethik* (1968), pp. 102–36.

verse 26

ἔσχατος ἐχθρὸς καταργεῖται ὁ θάνατος—"As the last enemy, Death is brought to nought" (RP, p. 356). Is Parry (p. 226) pressing the tense when he says, "The present tense [is used] because the destruction of death has already begun with the Lord's resurrection"? Compare Heb. 2:14; 2 Tim. 1:10 (καταργήσαντος μὲν τὸν θάνατον) and Rev. 20:14 (death and Hades thrown into the lake of fire in the last battle). Héring (p. 168) thinks this verse "precludes the possibility of something like 'everlasting torment'." Barrett (p. 358) and RP (p. 356) oppose this argument.

Paul's singling out of "death" here reminds us that his theme is resurrection. On the theological significance of death *still* being an enemy of God see especially O. Cullmann, "Immortality of the Soul or Resurrection of the Dead?" in *Immortality and Resurrection*, ed. Krister Stendahl (1965), pp. 9–53. Cullmann opposes a common sentimental view of death as a sweet doorway to heaven, insisting on its enemy-like character. For the way death has been personified in the history of religions see Conzelmann, p. 273n98; see above, pp. 46–48.

verse 27

πάντα γὰρ ὑπέταξεν ὑπὸ τοὺς πόδας αὐτοῦ—Ὑποτάσσω = "subject, subordinate" (AG, p. 855). On the morphology of "σσ" verbs see HNTG,

Paradigm V-4b and §24.252. The "σσ" is there only in the pres. and imperf. The basic stem ends in "γ" which combines with the aor. tense sign "σ" to form "ξ" here. Where is the augment? Always remember to account for the γάρ: how does vs. 27 support vs. 26? What is the subject of ὑπέταξεν? See arguments for Christ and God the Father in Conzelmann, p. 274n108.

This is a quotation from Psalm 8:6, except that Paul has changed the second person (in MT and LXX) to the third person, as he did in vs. 25 when he partially quoted Psalm 110:1. In Psalm 8 the αὐτοῦ is man, but the early church saw in it a messianic significance and applied it to *the* Son of man (Heb. 2:6–9). In Ephesians 1:20–22, Psalms 110:1 and 8:6 are again brought together, so it is possible that these two were closely connected in early Christian apologetics (Conzelmann, p. 274n103). Since the same Hebrew word lies behind θῇ (vs. 25) and ὑπέταξεν (vs. 27), Barrett (p. 358) thinks that Paul's citation of Ps. 110:1 led him to cite 8:6 as an illumination of the former. He sees rabbinic methodology at work here. For this "argument by analogy" see earlier, p. 256.

ὅταν δὲ εἴπῃ ὅτι πάντα ὑποτέτακται, δῆλον ὅτι ἐκτὸς τοῦ ὑποτάξαντος αὐτῷ τὰ πάντα—Εἴπῃ from εἶπον, "I said." The theme vowel tells us that it is subjunctive. Ὑποτέτακται is from ὑποτάσσω; note the reduplication "τε"; there is no theme vowel in perf. pass.; the voiced velar "γ" (in the stem "ταγ") assimilates to the voiceless velar "κ" before "τ." Δῆλον is from δῆλος = "clear, plain, evident" (AG, p. 177). Ἐκτός = "outside, except" (AG, p. 245). Ὑποτάξαντος: where is the "σ" tense sign for the aorist? What does the "ντ" tell us? The form is gen., after ἐκτός. Several things must be added in translation: before δῆλον we add "it is" and between ὅτι and ἐκτός we may add "they have been subjected" (Alford, p. 611).

Three differing interpretations of εἴπῃ are advocated:

1. The subject of εἴπῃ is Ps. 8:6, just cited (Barrett, p. 359). Against this is the fact that ὅταν + aor. subj. in vs. 24 and vs. 28 refers to future action. Moreover the force of the perfect ὑποτέτακται (HNTG §31.56) suggests that the subjecting is completed.

2. The subject of εἴπῃ is God (RP, p. 357; Alford, p. 611; Hodge, p. 332).

3. The subject of εἴπῃ is Christ and refers to a future declaration to the Father (Parry, p. 227).

It is so "clear" that when God subjected all things to Christ, he did not subject himself to Christ, one wonders why Paul even bothered to say this. Barrett (p. 360) proposes that it may be an attempt to counter a belief at Corinth (of which there is no other evidence, except perhaps 3:23) that at his exaltation Christ became one supreme God. Most commentators do not even raise the question. Paul's safeguard of a distinction within the Godhead may be seen in Phil. 2:11 (as noted earlier, pp. 265ff.).

verse 28

ὅταν δὲ ὑποταγῇ αὐτῷ τὰ πάντα, τότε καὶ αὐτὸς ὁ υἱὸς ὑποταγήσεται τῷ ὑποτάξαντι αὐτῷ τὰ πάντα—Ὑποταγῇ: this is a 2nd aor. pass. subj. What is the subject? Recall that neut. pl. subjects regularly have sing. verbs. This action is yet future. When αὐτός is used in the predicate position with another noun it means himself or itself (DM, p. 129). Ὑποταγήσεται: if the "θ" were present (-θησεται), the future passive would be plain.

This verse obviously supports a kind of subordination of the Son to the Father. See the helpful discussion of the christological problem in Hodge, pp. 333–36. Calvin raises the question here, which relates also to vs. 24 (Christ's handing over the kingdom to God). Do not these verses contradict the Scriptures which teach the eternity of *Christ's* kingdom (e.g. 2 Pet. 1:11)? For his answer see his commentary on 1 Corinthians, p. 327. Bruce (p. 148) also addresses the problem: "When this subjection is completed and the last enemy destroyed, Christ has fully accomplished his mediatorial ministry. He has brought the whole estranged creation back into harmony with God; now he 'delivers the kingdom to God the Father.'"

ἵνα ᾖ ὁ θεὸς [τὰ] πάντα ἐν πᾶσιν—Ἦ: pres. subj. of εἰμί. Ἵνα denotes that this is the purpose and goal of all Christ's kingly activity and his final subjection to the Father. The common translation is "that God may be all in all."

Barrett (p. 361) comments, "This is to be understood in terms of Rom. 11:36; 1 Cor. 15:54–57; 'soteriologically, not metaphysically.' . . . It is not the absorption of Christ and mankind, with consequent loss of distinct being, into God; but rather the unchallenged reign of God alone, in his pure goodness." Also compare Eph. 1:23; Phil. 2:11 (cf. R. P. Martin, *Carmen Christi* [1967, ²1983] pp. 271-83), Héring (pp. 168f.) rejects the translation, "God is all in all," because it would teach a pantheism unknown in the Bible and because ἐν πᾶσιν would then be a "stupid pleonasm." Omitting the article τά before πάντα, he construes πάντα as a single accusative used adverbially, "completely, in every respect" (as in 1 Cor. 13:7). Thus he renders the phrase, "in the whole universe and completely." RP (p. 358) suggest another slant: "The meaning seems to be that there will no longer be need of a Mediator: all relations between creator and creatures, between Father and offspring, will be direct."

THE STRUCTURE OF THE ARGUMENT

Paul wants to demonstrate in this paragraph that the past resurrection of Christ guarantees the *future* resurrection of believers at Christ's *parousia*. His argument is grounded ultimately in the revelation of God's goal in history to be all in all. We may trace the argument backwards to see how it fits together.

God is destined to be all in all. Therefore even the Son must be subject to him. But God has placed everything, including his enemies, under the jurisdiction of the Son. Therefore, before the Son is subject to the Father, the Son must bring all his enemies into subjection to himself so that when he subjects himself to the Father there will be no alien powers unsubdued. Now death is one of the enemies which must be abolished. In the context this would mean that Christ has done and will do all that is necessary to deliver his people from the shackles of death—he will raise them just as he, the first fruits, was raised. Of this the Corinthians may be sure, for God's goal is to be all in all.

Epilogue

At the conclusion of these two volumes it is well to attempt a summing-up. We have surveyed the material in the various strata of New Testament literature. The diversity of literary forms—Gospel, Acts, Epistle, Apocalypse—has become quite obvious. It is just as evident that there is diversity in the content of these books, and the presentation they give of their teaching is characterized by multiformity. Consequently, we may despair of being able to sum up under a single rubric "*the* message of the New Testament." But these various pieces of literature have been brought together into a synthetic whole, and it has been claimed that running through them we can detect the "pattern of New Testament truth."[1] Other writers are convinced that any such uniformity has to be imposed from outside, and that there is a discernible disunity within the several specimens of the New Testament "message."[2] Indeed, in the estimation of this second group, it is incorrect to speak of a single *kerygma,* and we should more accurately and honestly confess to the presence, influence, and rivalry of several competing *kerygmata.*

These matters call for extended discussion, which is not possible here. Conceding that there are differing emphases within the books of the New Testament, we may still affirm that there is an underlying and deep unity. That unity finds expression in what has come to be called the *kerygma,* the announcement of the saving events in history of God's action in his Son to reveal his character and to introduce a new age of grace and salvation. To be sure, that statement can be misinterpreted. In fact, it was misused by Paul's opponents, and we have seen that much

---

[1] See, e.g., A. M. Hunter, *The Unity of the New Testament* (U.S. title, *The Message of the New Testament,* 1944); G. E. Ladd, *The Pattern of New Testament Truth* (1968), who finds the focus of unity in "salvation history" (see below); and F. F. Bruce, *The Message of the New Testament* (1973), who writes that the New Testament authors "all bear consentient witness that Jesus Christ is Lord" (p. 12).

[2] R. H. Fuller, *The New Testament in Current Study* (1962); cf. J. D. G. Dunn, *Unity and Diversity in the New Testament* (1977). J. Charlot, *New Testament Disunity* (1970), surveys the problems from a Roman Catholic angle.

of the apostolic literature is a bid to secure the *kerygma* from misunderstanding and perversion.

When allowance has been made for differing emphases and corrective adjustment, it remains an unsettled question how best to locate and describe the center of the New Testament's deepest interest. In this epilogue we shall pass a number of current possibilities under review.

THE CENTRAL MESSAGE OF THE NEW TESTAMENT: FIVE OPTIONS

1. The traditional Lutheran position finds the heart of the New Testament in its teaching on the *justification of the ungodly*.[3] If one verse is the *locus classicus* of this message, it is Romans 4:5: the Christian is above all a believer in the God "who justifies the ungodly."

There can be little quarrel with the contention that this is a leading theme in Paul's gospel as expounded in Romans, Galatians, and Philippians. The advantages of this teaching as setting forth the New Testament message are many. It respects the Jewish background on which the teaching is set, although in direct contrast.[4] The Jewish claim that those who keep the law will be set right with God is considered by Paul a vain hope, for this class of "righteous" persons has no members (Rom. 3:9ff.), and there is no prospect of being put right with God as long as one stays with the nomistic religion of the Torah (Gal. 5:3f.). The prospect, therefore, is one of universal condemnation for the Jew as well as for the non-Jew, since all persons are sinners (Rom. 2:17–3:20) and stand under God's wrath as doomed (Rom. 1:18). Against such a tragic background of human plight and hopelessness, Paul proclaims what God has done to acquit the guilty.

The eschatological-forensic category that defines such an acquittal is equally respected. What Judaism anticipated as God's gracious intervention at the end-time, the Christian message announces as a present reality (Rom. 5:1) in the sure confidence that at the future judgment the verdict of acceptance will be confirmed (Gal. 5:5; Phil. 1:11; 3:9). Thus the tension, "already justified . . . one day to be acquitted fully," is maintained in this statement of Pauline preaching (1 Cor. 4:5).

Other aspects running deep in Paul are equally attested in this theologoumenon: the prior activity of God's grace (Rom. 3:24; 8:30, 33), the renouncing of all human merit (Rom. 3:20; 4:2; 11:6; Gal. 2:16; Phil. 3:3, 7–9), the acceptance with God built on Christ's obedience to death for us (Rom. 5:9, 18f.) and certified in his being raised to life-in-the-

---

[3] H. Conzelmann, "Current Problems in Pauline Research," *Interpretation,* 22 (1968), 178–82; J. A. Ziesler, *The Meaning of Righteousness in Paul* (1972).

[4] The lexical material is well handled by D. Hill, *Greek Words and Hebrew Meanings* (1967), pp. 82–162; K. P. Donfried, "Justification and Last Judgment in Paul," *ZNTW,* 67 (1976), 90–110. But see the objections brought by J. Reumann, *Righteousness in the New Testament* (1982), pp. 82f., and by J. A. Fitzmyer in the same volume, p. 213.

Spirit (Rom. 4:25; 8:11, 34), and the centrality of faith as the medium by which the gifts of divine grace reach the trusting person (Rom. 3:25, 28, 30; Phil. 3:9). All these emphases are picked up and extended by Paul's disciples (e.g., Eph. 2:8f.; Titus 3:5-7). They form a platform on which the Pauline believer may stand and from which he may defend the apostle's teaching against both a lapse into nomistic righteousness and irresponsible ethical indifference grounded on an enthusiastic Christianity which thinks only of present possession and forgets the future hope (Phil. 3). Judaic nomism and gnosticizing libertinism needed to be resisted in Paul's lifetime and beyond. But the limited success of Paul's gospel in the Pauline churches after his death (2 Tim. 1:15) is a reminder that his message could easily become misunderstood (2 Pet. 3:16).

The obvious deficiency in the above proposal has been addressed and remedied by recent Lutheran interpreters.[5] What is lacking in the definition that restricts justification to God's legal acquittal of individuals who are put right with him is an acknowledgment of the cosmic dimension of Paul's teaching. E. Käsemann has reformulated the nuance of divine "righteousness" in Paul to include both the stress on God's saving activity with the promise of a new creation (based on Isa. 40–55), and the idea that God has set the world right with himself in the Christ-event (2 Cor. 5:17–21). The result is that the forensic sense is diluted and the verb δικαιοῦσθαι is more widely defined as "to find acceptance" with God—a point that links Paul's message with the teaching of Luke 18:14 and brings "forgiveness" much more prominently into the orbit of justification. Points of contact with passages in the Synoptic Gospels (e.g., the controversy stories and the parables) which stress outgoing love of God in Jesus' ministry—befriending outcasts and "sinners," sharing a meal with "publicans and prostitutes," offering forgiveness as a sign of the new life in the kingdom of God here and now—help us see an underlying thread of unity connecting Jesus' ministry with the later explication of the *kerygma*.

2. Although there is much to endorse the centrality of "God's acceptance of sinners" as the ruling theme of the New Testament, W. Wrede regarded justification as a secondary polemic directed against the Jews,[6] and A. Deissmann attributed Paul's long discussions of it to the

---

[5] E. Käsemann, *New Testament Questions of Today* (ET 1969), pp. 168–82; J. Jeremias, *The Central Message of the New Testament* (ET 1965), Ch. 3; B. Reicke, "Paul's Understanding of Righteousness," in *Soli Deo Gloria:* W. C. Robinson *Festschrift*, ed. J. McDowell Richards (1968), pp. 37–49. See the comprehensive overview and discussion in M. T. Brauch, "Perspectives on God's Righteousness . . .," in E. P. Sanders, *Paul and Palestinian Judaism* (1977), pp. 523–42. Sanders's book, however, opts for eschatological participation in Christ as the central theme, particularly in Paul. See Reumann's critique, *Righteousness*, pp. 120–23 (cf. Fitzmyer, *op. cit.*, 217f., for a more positive assessment). See now for an extended critical comment R. H. Gundry, "Grace, Works, and Staying Saved in Paul," *Biblica*, 66 (1985), 1–38.

[6] W. Wrede, *Paul* (ET 1907), p. 123.

"hard fight" he had to wage against the Judaizers.[7] A. Schweitzer, in a famous phrase, referred to justification as "a subsidiary crater" within the main center of Pauline teaching which he identified as *the mystical doctrine of redemption by "being-in-Christ."*[8]

Most modern interpreters of Paul (and of the Synoptic Gospels, the Johannine literature, Acts, 1 Peter, and Hebrews) agree that the understanding of the person and place of Jesus Christ that governs these writings is the Jewish background of the two ages against which the message in all its variety is set. This is often referred to as the eschatological dimension.[9] It explains how the New Testament authors can both look back to Jewish categories of the messianic hope, the kingdom of God, and the new age of salvation, and announce that, in a new period of history which has opened up with the coming of Jesus Christ, God has inaugurated the fulfilment of the best hopes the Jewish people entertained in their long history. The fulfilment often breaks the mold and heralds some facet of God's purpose never before envisaged (e.g., a suffering Messiah, an individual Son of man, a mission to the Gentiles that makes their salvation a distinct possibility). But *Jewish* modes of thought are used, at least as the framework, however much modification is required.

Albert Schweitzer took Jewish eschatology seriously. For him Jesus could not be understood except within the format of his ancestral religion, though this posed a problem for his later interpreters, especially Paul. Paul was driven, therefore, to reinterpret Jewish eschatological hopes (which did not materialize, since the end of the world never arrived in the lifetime of Jesus) in terms of Hellenistic mysticism. And the essence of mysticism in Christian vocabulary is "being-in-Christ."

With this reinterpretation Schweitzer could account for two features in Paul's thought. One was his rationale of the time period between Christ's resurrection and his *parousia*. Clearly this interval was not envisaged in the lifetime of Jesus, who marched on Jerusalem fully expecting that the end of the age was at hand. Paul explained the post-Easter period as the time when the communion of the elect with the *Kyrios* is actual.

The second factor Schweitzer considered Paul's contribution faces the question of how the elect come to be "in-Christ." The answer is given by pointing to baptism, by which Christians come to share in a

---

[7] A. Deissmann, *The Religion of Jesus and the Faith of Paul* (ET 1923), p. 271; cf. W. D. Davies, *Paul and Rabbinic Judaism*, p. 222. J. Jeremias, *op. cit.*, pp. 58f., faults Wrede for not perceiving the ethical implications of justification, as in 1 Cor. 6:11. I may refer to *Reconciliation: A Study of Paul's Theology* (1981), ch. 3, for a further evaluation, and to some later pages in this book for a discussion of the central core of Paul's theology.

[8] A. Schweitzer, *The Mysticism of Paul the Apostle* (ET 1931), p. 225.

[9] G. E. Ladd, *Jesus and the Kingdom* (1964), pp. 110ff. (*The Presence of the Future* [1974], pp. 114ff.).

most realistic way in the life of Christ. He and his people are "physically interdependent in the same corporeity,"[10] as they enter this union by the acts of dying and rising with him in the baptismal rite (Rom. 6:4ff.).

There is a strand of apostolic teaching that strongly emphasizes the intimate union between the risen Lord and his people—a reality most clearly evidenced in 1 Corinthians 6:17: "he who is united to the Lord becomes one spirit with him." To that extent Schweitzer's stress on the believer's being-in-Christ as an essential part of Pauline teaching is a needed protest against the concept of justification by faith, which easily becomes simply a forensic formula, suggesting no more than a sterile, objective acquittal. The warmth of personal communion between Christ and the Christian (e.g., Gal. 2:20) is rightly brought to the surface in Schweitzer's exposition. Equally he has set great store by the important place of baptism as certifying initiation into Christ's body. Passages such as 1 Corinthians 12:13, Acts 2:38, and 1 Peter 3:21 have to be given their full weight when it comes to assessing the means by which the new life was communicated to men and women in the early Christian communities.

But Schweitzer has overpressed the evidence and placed a lop-sided construction on it. "Mystical union" is a questionable term to explain Paul's teaching on dying-and-rising-with-Christ. The ascription of efficacy to the sacrament of baptism, explicitly making it the indispensable and mechanical cause of the imparting of spiritual life to the convert, is hard to reconcile with the apostolic writers' teaching on faith and their safeguarding of moral requirements. Schweitzer's clear statement of what he understands baptism to effect in Paul's teaching is at odds with the same apostle's insistence on living faith as a pre-condition of salvation (Rom. 1:16; 10:17; 1 Cor. 1:21; cf. Eph. 1:13f.; Col. 2:12). Moreover, an *ex opere operato* view,[11] crudely asserting the automatic efficacy of sacramental action, is virtually denied by the repeated insistence in the Acts-*kerygma* that "faith" must accompany the rite (Acts 2:38; 8:12, 13, 35f.; 10:44; 11:14f.; 16:14f., 32f.; 18:8; 19:5); by the fact that elsewhere sacraments are said to confer no magical immunity from judgment (1 Cor. 10:1-13; 1 Pet. 4:17); by Paul's setting his baptismal practices on a lower level of importance than his proclamation of the gospel (1 Cor. 1:13-17); and by his frequent expression of the fulness of the gospel without any reference to the sacraments.[12] As a final critique,

---

[10] Schweitzer, *op. cit.*, p. 127. There is a perceptive statement and critique of Schweitzer's book in A. A. Fulton, "The Mysticism of Paul the Apostle," *EQ*, 20 (1948), 172–83. See also A. C. Thiselton, "Schweitzer's Interpretation of Paul," *ExpT*, 90 (1978–79), 132–37.

[11] Schweitzer, *op. cit.*, pp. 116f. = *Paul and his Interpreters* (ET 1956), pp. 225f. On the propriety of the term "mystical union" see E. P. Sanders, *Paul and Palestinian Judaism*, pp. 434f.

[12] A. Schlatter writes: Paul "can express the word of Jesus, not in half-measure but fully, without mentioning the sacraments at all. But if they come into view, he

we must mention that Schweitzer's intention to take the formula "in Christ" to mean a physical insertion into Christ is difficult to justify, and overlooks those instances (Gal. 1:22; 1 Cor. 1:30; 4:15; Rom. 12:5; Col. 1:2, 28) where the expression conveys an ecclesiological meaning rather than being a formula for mystical union.[13]

Nonetheless, there are at least some places where "in Christ" describes a personal union with the glorified, pneumatic Christ (2 Cor. 12:1–10), and Schweitzer's treatment rightly draws attention to this aspect of apostolic thought. Hellenistic mysticism described the quasi-physical union of the devotee with the god, yet this extension of the teaching is represented only peripherally—if at all—in the New Testament documents (cf. Acts 17:28; 2 Pet. 1:4).[13a]

3. The Graeco-Roman world into which Christianity came was peopled by men and women whose response to political upheavals, economic stresses, and intellectual ferment expressed itself in religious uncertainty. This was an age of fear and bondage to impersonal forces in the cosmos. It led to *a cry for salvation.*

An indirect witness to this ever present need is Acts 16:17. The slave girl, possessed by a python spirit, called out after Paul and Silas, "These men are servants of the Most High God, who proclaim to you a way of salvation." In the same city Paul met the heartfelt cry of the jailer, "What must I do to be saved?" with the announcement and promise, "Believe in the Lord Jesus, and you will be saved" (Acts 16:30f.). Clearly, salvation was a term readily understood in Graeco-Roman society; and it is not surprising that the earliest preachers seized on it to convey the substance, if in shorthand form, of their message. It has been appropriated, too, by some modern interpreters,[14] notably of Paul and Luke-Acts, as the key-word and epitome of their teaching. One of these scholars claims to write the whole of Paul's theology in terms of this central and inclusive concept, which "covers the initial experience, the present status and the future consummation of those who are Christians."[15]

The lexical data supporting this programmatic statement are copious. Paul can employ the aorist tense of the verb to denote what has taken place in the hour of turning to God (Rom. 8:24; the perfect tense is found only at Eph. 2:6, where the emphasis on "completed salvation" is needed to rebut the gnostic counterclaim). The present tense, "we are on

---

connects with them the entire richness of the grace of Christ because he sees in them the will of Jesus, not partially but fully expressed and effective" (*Erläuterungen,* on Titus 3, 1950, p. 262).

[13] R. Bultmann, *Theology of the New Testament.* Vol. I, p. 311.

[13a] On these two texts see W. G. Kümmel, *Man in the New Testament* (ET 1963), pp. 89–96.

[14] C. A. A. Scott, *Christianity According to St. Paul* (1927) is one of the best examples of this approach. See too A. M. Hunter's several books that pursue a similar line.

[15] Scott, *ibid.,* pp. 17f.

the road to salvation," is also found (1 Cor. 1:18; 15:2), while the future hope of eschatological deliverance at the last judgment is mentioned as well (Rom. 5:9). Romans 5:1, with its inextricable nuances, is the epitome of this apostolic kerygmatic teaching. "Let us continue at peace with God" (NEB) brings together both the present possession of the gift of salvation ("peace") and its pledge for the future.

Basic to this interpretation is the full meaning of "peace." Its Hebrew counterpart is *šālôm*, an omnibus term covering a wide range of ideas from soundness of body to the highest ideal of spiritual health and wholeness.[16] The experience of "peace" was an ever pressing need in the world of the first century, both for Jews conscious of guilt before a holy God (see Heb. 8–10) and Greek and Roman citizens crying out for deliverance from fate and the regime of the malign astral powers (see Phil. 2:6–11; Col. 1:13–20; 2:8, 15; Eph. 1:3–10; Rev. 5:1–14; Ignatius, *Eph.* 19), especially in view of the fear of death (Heb. 2:15; Rev. 1:18; cf. the synoptic stories which portray Jesus as Lord of death, e.g., Mark 5:35–43). Although the term is only marginally represented in the literature, the title "savior" (σωτήρ) spoke to a very sensitive human problem.

Salvation is depicted as a past event, and the Christian's hope of "being saved" reposes on what God has done in achieving human liberation from the thralldom of evil (Rom. 3:24; Col. 1:14). The Exodus narrative, with its Passover ritual, forms one aspect of this teaching, and Christ is widely represented as the counterpart to the Jewish paschal lamb (John 18:28; 19:14, 29, 36, etc.; 1 Pet. 1:18; Rev. 5; 7:14; 1 Cor. 5:7f.). The political dimension of this liberation is largely passed over (cf. 1 Cor. 7; Phm.; 1 Pet. 2:16); the chief concern is with freedom from the demonic powers of evil because of what Christ accomplished on the cross.

The present experience is variously described as being in a new realm (Col. 1:13) or standing on a new platform (Rom. 5:1) or enjoying a new relationship to God (Gal. 4:5–7). The effect is seen in the possession of life, which is called "eternal" (John; but the term is also in the synoptic tradition where it is an eschatological cipher for entering the kingdom, see Mark 10:17–31) and is characterized by newness (Rom. 6:4; 7:6) and the possession of the Spirit (Gal. 5:25). The chief feature of life-in-Christ, to which all the strata pay tribute, is the quality of love (1 Cor. 13) that springs from God's love in Christ for the world (1 John 4).

There are future anticipations that salvation will one day be fully realized. The new age has begun (2 Cor. 5:17), and God will bring about its completion, partly in a renewed universe (Rom. 8:18–23) and partly in a final resurrection (Phil. 3:20f.). The "hope of salvation" (1 Thess. 5:8) awaits the *parousia* of Christ from heaven—a constant theme in the literature—denied only by those who (misguidedly, accord-

16 W. Foerster, *TDNT*, 2 (ET 1964), 414f.; cf. J. Pedersen, *Israel I–II* (1926), pp. 311ff.

ing to the data that preserve their teaching) imagine that he has already come and inaugurated a heavenly existence on earth (2 Thess. 2:1f.; Mark 13:6, 21; Acts 1:11) or that he will not come (Luke 18:1–8; cf. 12:45; Heb. 9:28; 10:35–39; 2 Pet. 3:4; Acts 1:9). The exact time of his coming is unknown (in spite of those who believed otherwise; 1 Thess. 5:1f.; 2 Thess. 2:3ff.), so the insistent call is to wakefulness and constant vigilance and sobriety in personal and corporate behavior (1 Pet. 4:4, 5, 13; 5:4; James 5:7–11; and the synoptic apocalypses and the repeated appeals that punctuate the drama of the Revelation). Then "final salvation" will be attained in the resurrection of the body (1 Cor. 15), the union between Christ and believers (1 Thess. 4:17; Phil. 1:23) and the universally acknowledged lordship of Christ (Phil. 2:6–11) under God's overall monarchy (1 Cor. 15:28).

There is no doubt that "salvation" plays a significant role in the New Testament understanding of Christian existence. The outstanding objection to this type of interpretation is that it tends to be exclusively experience-oriented and narrowly individualistic. There is an undoubted personal element in the faith of the apostolic church, since the coming of Christ on the stage of human history made all the difference to the people who either came into touch with the earthly Jesus or were confronted by him as risen Lord in the proclamation of his servants (Gal. 3:1 and Eph. 2:17 refer to this "coming" of the heavenly Lord). Yet what unites the witness of the various New Testament writers is not primarily their experience but their confession that in Christ a new age has dawned and a new beginning has been made in world history. To capture this stupendous claim the proponents of salvation history have formulated a complete rationale of what the coming of Jesus Christ meant on a global scale. We turn now to consider this construction.

4. The term *Heilsgeschichte* is notoriously difficult to define satisfactorily—and thus also to translate into English—since it tends to be flexible according to the understanding of the particular interpreter.[17] "Saving history" or "history of salvation" sets the biblical drama in a framework of time. Hence O. Cullmann's title is well chosen, *Christ and Time*.[18] This book puts the emphasis on the coming of Christ as the proclamation of *a new time,* signaling the great turning-point in the history of redemption, the intrusion of a new aeon. Key verses which epitomize this model are Galatians 4:4, Romans 11:25f., and Colossians 1:26. In the Epistle to the Hebrews there is a reiterated insistence on "the last times" (1:1f.) and the "once-for-all" events (ch. 9) that mark out

---

[17] See C. K. Barrett, *From First Adam to Last* (1962), p. 4n.
[18] O. Cullmann, *Christ and Time* (ET 1951). On this book see J. Frisque, *Oscar Cullmann, Une théologie de l'historie du salut* (1960); E. C. Rust, *Salvation History* (1962); J. J. Vincent, *ExpT,* 77 (1965–66), 4–8; J. Peter, "Salvation History as a Model for Theological Thought," *SJT,* 23 (1970), 1–12; W. G. Kümmel, "Heilsgeschichte in NT" in *Neues Testament und Kirche. Festschrift R. Schnackenburg,* ed. J. Gnilka (1974), pp. 434-57.

the new order in Christ, the true and final priest. Titus 1:3 refers to "the proper time" at which God drew near to mankind in the proclamation, an event further described as Christ's coming to do away with death's power (2 Tim. 1:9f.), to usher in a new age (2 Cor. 5:17), and to inaugurate the "day of salvation" (2 Cor. 6:2) at the conclusion of which the kingdom of Christ will be openly declared (Rev. 11:15; 12:10).

It is clear even from this cursory summary that Christ in his person and work is at the midpoint of salvation history. Certain assumptions implicit in this way of putting the biblical story into a coherent pattern are listed by Cullmann:

a. Biblical understanding of time and history is progressive, mounting as on a rising line from commencement (in the creation) to conclusion, when God will consummate his purposes for the universe. On that ascending line the decisive event is Christ's victory at Easter, which has forever determined the course of future world history.

b. The whole history of God's dealings with the world may be thought of as the history of Christ, from the choice of Israel through the fate of the remnant of faithful Jews and the servant of Yahweh and Daniel's Son of man to Jesus. From that point in time, at the resurrection of Messiah, which includes his people's hope, the sweep of redemptive history moves on irresistibly to embrace the apostles, the church, and the world.

c. The centrality and cruciality of the cross are seen in that what took place on Golgotha has an ultimate significance, reaching back to explain primal history and Israel's election and stretching forward to ensure a universal redemption. Demonic forces may hinder the progress of God's plan—Cullmann later changed the metaphor of a straight, ascending line to that of a "curved" or wavy one.[19] Still the movement is rectilinear, and marks the eventual triumph of God in spite of reversal and satanic opposition.

The merits of this scheme are obvious.[20] It binds together the two Testaments in terms of promise and fulfilment; it gives a unity to the New Testament kerygma, since it offers an intelligible pattern in terms of election, substitution, and vindication of those historical events that range from Jesus' birth, baptism, and ministry to the descent of the Spirit at Pentecost and the opening of the Gentile mission. It gives a central place to the resurrection of Jesus as marking a new era in God's dealings with the world. It throws a vivid shaft of light on the place of Paul as the apostle of salvation history, both in his own self-understanding (1 Cor. 15:8–10) and in the ways he became understood (in Acts—e.g., the conversion narratives and 13:47—and in Eph. 3:1–6; even 2 Pet. 3:15).

[19] O. Cullmann, *Salvation in History* (ET 1967), p. 15. See too E. Käsemann in his *Perspectives on Paul* (ET 1971), p. 83n.
[20] The same structure is utilized in W. G. Kümmel, *Theology of the New Testament* (ET 1973), and many others.

Where this attempt to build a philosophy of (salvation) history is weak is chiefly in the area of application.[21] How can *Heilsgeschichte* so touch human lives as to make that history one of personal consequence? Cullmann's response is that "salvation history" (which tends to have a quasi-independent existence, and become an article of faith) does call us to integrate ourselves *into that history*. But exactly how we do that is not clear.

Moreover, is the Bible essentially a transcript of "events" without the interpreting commentary, the divine "word" to make their significance known to the participant and the later observer? Cullmann thinks that word and happening go hand-in-hand, and so seeks to overcome this objection. But he is still left with the surdlike problem of world history on his hands. Granted that God is the Lord of salvation-events such as the Exodus and the birth of Jesus, is he not also the God who raised up Pharaoh (Rom. 9:17) and called Nebuchadnezzar and Cyrus his servants (Jer. 25:9; Isa. 45:1) as well as the one who appointed the destinies of all men and nations (Amos 9:7; Acts 17:26)?

Finally, once we concede the importance of the narrative-events of creation, redemption, election, and atonement, we have still a sizable part of the Jewish-Christian Scriptures left unaccounted for. We need to ask about the status of those sections of the canon that do *not* reflect salvation history: the wisdom literature, the Epistle of James, or the bourgeois ethical teaching many scholars detect in the household station-codes that are akin to Stoic moral philosophy (the Pastorals, 1 Pet. 2, 3).

5. The most outspoken and trenchant critic of those who speak of "salvation history" is R. Bultmann. His review essay on "The History of Salvation and History" offers a compact statement of his objections.[22] As a counterposition Bultmann gives an interpretation of the New Testament in terms of *existentialist mythology*.

In the previous volume the place of Bultmann in the history of gospel criticism has been noted, and we have earlier (see pp. 322f.) commented on his demythologizing program. It will suffice here to mention the chief lines that inform his interpretation of the New Testament, mainly of Paul and John.[23] Both apostolic writers are believed to have their heritage in a Hellenistic-syncretistic milieu, and both employ a framework of myth into which they place the Christian message. Behind Pauline Christology in particular is the gnostic "redeemer myth," used to convey the truth of man's fear of being threatened by cosmic and alien "powers." John uses the same idea of a descending and ascending savior

[21] See Cullmann's response to criticisms, in "The Relevance of Redemptive History" in *Soli Deo Gloria,* pp. 19ff.

[22] R. Bultmann, *Existence and Faith* (ET 1960), ed. S. M. Ogden, pp. 226–40.

[23] One of the clearest expositions of Bultmann's thought is W. Schmithals, *An Introduction to the Theology of Rudolf Bultmann* (ET 1968).

figure. In both cases the point of contact is between Hellenistic man's dread of impersonal, malignant spiritual forces and modern man's existential consciousness of being imprisoned in this world of meaninglessness and despair. The Christian message comes as one of hope in both situations. Long ago the assurance was conveyed in the depiction of Christ as cosmocrator, i.e., the exalted ruler over cosmic agencies (as in the hymns of Phil. 2:6-11; Col. 1:15-20; 1 Tim. 3:16; Heb. 1:1-3; 1 Pet. 3:22; Rev. 5) and as "soul of the universe" giving coherence to all life (John 1:1-18). This mythological picture cannot be interpreted in any literal sense by us today. It requires a transposition into a modern key, where it speaks of human destiny as creatures of God under his fatherly care and control.

Bultmann's proposals to demythologize the New Testament have come under scrutiny, even when a concession is made that the parts of the New Testament that speak of pre-existence and cosmic enthronement do so in highly figurative and dramatic language. The chief accusation made against him is that he has reduced theological statements to expressions of anthropology[24] and at least given the impression that it is impossible to talk meaningfully of God except by making such statements reflexive of the human predicament and aspiration. Bultmann's preoccupation with how the New Testament is to convey its message to modern man's felt need has led him to underplay those elements in the *kerygma* that give substance to the existential call to "decision." These are divine transcendence and God's initiative in sending Jesus Christ, Christ's unique personal relationship to the Father, and the objectivity of the atonement. Without these, the summons to authentic existence and living lacks a true rationale, and represents merely an existential leap in the dark.

RECONCILIATION

Is there a more promising line of inquiry? Can we find some central idea that will do fair justice to at least three aspects of New Testament theology and religious experience? The first of these three elements is the cosmic predicament that in some mysterious way entails the disorder of nature, the opposition of demonological forces, and man's need as an alienated and disconsolate "sinner," bereft in the universe and estranged from the holy God.[25] Second is the saving action of God in Jesus

---

[24] B. Rigaux, *The Letters of St. Paul*, pp. 28, 192: "In a sense, Bultmann is not a theologian, but an anthropologist." See a clear statement in Bultmann's *Theology of the New Testament*, Vol. II, Epilogue. A better translation of Rigaux's point (from Bultmann's *Theologie des Neuen Testaments*, I [1948-53], 191) is "Paul's theology is [to be considered] at the same time anthropology," as G. F. Hasel, *New Testament Theology: Basic Issues in the Current Debate* (1978), p. 91, notes. But that Hasel's position is any more satisfactory may be questioned; see my essay "New Testament Theology: Impasse and Exit," *ExpT*, 91 (1980), 264-69. R. Morgan, *The Nature of New Testament Theology* (1973), pp. 37f., has pertinent comments on Bultmann's understanding of the kerygma's call to decision.

[25] J. Weiss, *Earliest Christianity*, Vol. 2, p. 599.

Christ, which is directed to a process of restoration that will one day lead to a reclaimed universe, at one with its creator. The effective means by which this restitution is made is spelled out in terms of redemption.[26] The mission of Jesus is uniformly described as undertaken with his passion and victory always in view. The New Testament apostles and their disciples are concerned to explicate what the cross and Easter triumph achieved; and all the documents—Gospels, Epistles, and Apocalypse—are consciously written from the vantage-point of the post-Easter experience of life in the Spirit as consisting of fellowship with the living Lord. Deliverance from demonic powers, forgiveness of sins, and the prospect of a renovated world—these are the themes that stir the apostolic authors. Barriers of separation are broken down, not only between God and a sinful race, but just as impressively between the inveterately separated groups in ancient society: Jew/Gentile; slave/free man; male/female (Eph. 2:11–22; Phm.; Gal. 3:26–29—to give only the clearest examples). Life in the society of the new creation, the church, is the sign of what God is accomplishing in the world, and a pledge of his plan to embrace the whole of humankind in his new order (Eph. 1:10).

In the third place our central idea must not overlook the ineluctably personal element in this statement. Paul remarks on this aspect in the unforgettable language of Galatians 2:20. It is a note sounded elsewhere, usually in the first personal plural, as the apostolic characters voice their convictions of what they have known at firsthand experience (Acts 2:32; 4:20; 1 John 1:1–4).

So the issue is whether we can fasten on a single term that might conceivably subsume under its rubric these manifold ideas. That term is, we believe, *reconciliation*.

Reconciliation is sufficiently broad a concept to include the pacification—or at least the neutralization—of hostile spirit powers (Col. 1:15–20; 2:14f.; Rom. 8:38f.), including both the "elemental spirits" (Gal. 4:3–9; Col. 2:20), the demonic princes of 1 Corinthians 2:8, and Satan himself (2 Cor. 2:11; 11:3, 14; Eph. 6:10–20; Rev. 12:10f.). This side of reconciliation pays tribute to the Jewish "two kingdoms" schema, which is found in the Gospels, and acknowledges the antagonistic, *Christus victor* motif that pervades the apocalyptic literature in the New Testament.[27]

Anthropological dimensions are considered in the teaching on human nature under sin in the various writers who are united in a common belief that Christ's death and victory have rescued his people from bondage to demonic evil (a theme found running from Matt. 1:21 to

----

[26] V. Taylor, *Forgiveness and Reconciliation*[2] (1946); L. Morris, *The Apostolic Preaching of the Cross* (1955), Ch. 6; H. Ridderbos, *Paul: An Outline of His Theology* (ET 1975), Ch. 5. See too the essays in *Reconciliation and Hope: Festschrift* L. Morris, ed. R. Banks (1974).

[27] See R. Leivestad, *Christ the Conqueror* (1954), and E. Stauffer, *New Testament Theology* (ET 1955).

Rev. 1:5f.), assured the church of divine pardon, and answered the elemental dread of death (Heb. 2:15; 1 John 4:13–19). Reconciliation is
closely allied to forgiveness in human experience (Col. 1:21f.; cf. Luke
15).

The locus of reconciliation is consistently traced to God's action
in Christ, even if only Paul uses the verb καταλλάσσειν—to reconcile.[28]
It is centered in the death of Christ (Rom. 5:10; 1 Pet. 1:18f.; 2:24; Heb. 9;
1 John 1:7; 2:2; Rev. 1:5f.; 5:9; Mark 10:45; and the Last Supper narratives), which is interpreted in 2 Corinthians 5:21 as an "interchange in
Christ."[28a] The ministry of the New Testament preachers is one of reconciliation (2 Cor. 5:18), with an appeal to "be reconciled to God" (2 Cor.
5:20). Completed at the cross, the reconciliation is still being fulfilled
and applied until the end-time, when the *apokatastasis* or universal
restoration will be achieved (Matt. 19:28; Acts 3:20f.).[29]

The visible paradigm of this final hope is seen in the society of
the congregations, in which "the new man" is slowly, often painfully,
taking shape (Col. 3:9–17).[30] The household rules of the later Epistles
reveal some codification of how human relationships were seen to be
understood, and—no matter what influence may be traced to pagan
sources here—there is no denying that the distinctive and controlling
motif is "in Christ" or "in the Lord." The letter to Philemon is a notable
illustration of "reconciliation" in a concrete situation.

The ultimate prospect is that of a universe brought back into
harmony with the divine intention. This is the noble vision of Ephesians
and the Apocalypse. The former document expresses in hymnlike, poetic
form the anticipation of "all things" united in Christ (1:10, 23; 4:6) when
God will be all in all and no part of the cosmos permitted to pursue a
refractory course alien to the creator's design. Whether this univer-
salism includes every person, willing or unwilling, is not specified,
though in other places in the letter (e.g., 2:3; 5:6) there is a clear
reminder of the penalty of being in an unreconciled, hostile state *vis-à-
vis* God.

The Apocalypse places the same hope of a cosmic jubilee in a
dramatic and highly pictorial setting (Rev. 20–22). There man's great
enemies are finally and forever put down (20:10–15) and life in the new
city of God repairs all the defects and liabilities of the primeval curse
(Gen. 2, 3). The assurance of "Immanuel" (21:3)—God with us—is the
token of a complete reconciliation in which no part of human society and
extra-terrestrial creation is left unaffected. The "new heaven and new
earth" (Rev. 21:1–5; cf. 2 Pet. 3:10) reverberate with a consentient Al-
leluia.

---

[28] F. Büchsel, *TDNT*, 1 (ET 1964), 255–59.
[28a] M. D. Hooker, "Interchange in Christ," *JTS*, 22 n.s. (1971), 349–61.
[29] On *apokatastasis*, see A. Oepke, *TDNT*, 1 (ET 1964), 389–93.
[30] The "new man" is a term for corporate life in the church; C. F. D. Moule,
Colossians-Philemon (1957), pp. 119f.

To summarize our survey in a sentence or two is hardly possible. But since the above suggestion that the New Testament *Hauptgedanke* or capital theme is reconciliation owes much to T. W. Manson's insights,[31] his postscript may also be taken over. The significance of Christ for the world and its history is expressible in terms of *hope;* the relationship of Christ and the church is at heart one of *love,* both uniting the Lord and his people and cementing Christians in their life together; and the bond that ties the Lord to the individual disciple is *faith,* inescapably personal yet a shared possession. "Now abide faith, hope, love; the [well-known] three" (1 Cor. 13:13*a*).

> For Paul [and the same goes for all the New Testament writers] this threefold experience means that he was a new man living in a new world as a member of a new society. It is the task of ministers of the Gospel to see to it that the Gospel we preach shall not mean less than this.[32]

As the debate to pinpoint and justify a true "center" or "heart" of Paul's gospel moves ahead — with little sign of achieving a consensus — the present writer's submission, outlined in his book *Reconciliation: A Study in Paul's Theology* (1981), may be restated in the light of some more recent studies. This is followed by a brief response to some pertinent criticisms that have been noted.

1. *Some Recent Proposals Regarding A Pauline "Core."* Recent studies have actively endeavored to ascertain whether there is a central organizing principle in Paul's theology. All students agree that Paul's thinking is not systematic but, rather, directly related to the pastoral needs of his congregations. Most interpreters believe that Paul's responses to community needs have been dictated by — and fashioned under the influence of — the adversary role he adopted in repelling what he regarded as mistaken views and in exposing deviant behavior patterns.

But there the agreement stops. When we ask about a "Pauline center" or the underlying principle of coherence in Paul's theology (to use E. P. Sanders's expression),[33] we are faced with a bewildering variety of answers. Usually the suggestions made range from being too narrow to being too wide. Proposals that say no more than that "Jesus Christ is the center of Paul's life and thought" are of course obviously true,[34] but they hardly touch on the complexity of this man's mind. Nor do they account for the flexibility of Paul's sensitive responses to situations he met, as Henry Chadwick's essay "All Things to All Men"[35] made clear.

---

[31] T. W. Manson, *On Paul and John,* ed. M. Black (1963).

[32] *Ibid.,* pp. 80f.

[33] E. P. Sanders, *Paul and Palestinian Judaism* (1977), pp. 431–42.

[34] This is virtually the conclusion J. D. G. Dunn reaches at the end of his discussion in *The Unity and Diversity in the New Testament* (1977), pp. 369f.: "The *integrating centre* [is] Jesus himself" (author's italics).

[35] *NTS,* 1 (1954–55), 261–75.

At the other extreme we encounter suggestions that have been too far-reaching. Three or four recent proposals, I submit, belong to this category.

E. P. Sanders draws attention to "two readily identifiable and primary convictions which governed Paul's life: (1) that Jesus Christ is Lord, that in him God has provided for the salvation of all who believe . . .; (2) that he, Paul, was called to be the apostle to the Gentiles."[36] Again both statements stand out as clearly demonstrable, but they do not bring us *directly* to the heart of Paul's message.

C. J. Hickling accepts the two propositions as essentially accurate but goes on to add a rider: "God has already brought about in Christ a decisive and final *transformation of time.*"[37] The basic idea is that of the "turning point of the ages" (*Aeonenwende*) — an announcement believed to be so fundamental to Paul that Hickling can write: "Here, surely, is the centre of Paul's thought, and indeed of his religion: not simply, or even principally, in the content of his assertions about God and Jesus and his own calling, but in the sense of fundamental and paradoxical contrast, as of one standing at a cosmic frontier, with which this content was perceived."[38] This slightly complex statement — if I understand it aright — brings us nearer to the Pauline center, since it recognizes the new age and the new life that came into the world through Christ; and Hickling rightly praises the novelty of divine grace.[39] Nonetheless the dualistic framework remains somewhat of an abstraction, needing to be filled with personal content and application. J. Christiaan Beker adopts a similar apocalyptic framework and regards "apocalyptic [as] the indispensable means for [Paul's] interpretation of the Christ-event."[40] He matches this schema, however, with an interface of Paul's use of "symbolic" terms in applying the conviction he had about the cosmic triumph of God to particular contingencies in the situations of his readers. Beker offers this "interaction between coherent center and contingent interpretation" as the key to Paul's hermeneutic, and indeed his theology. The outstanding question remains, however: how can a series of events on a cosmic scale be made normative to and binding on various human situations?

E. F. Osborne, on his own admission, reduces Paul's theology to one "simple theme," namely, the unity of God.[41] Such unity is expressed

---

[36] *Op. cit.*, pp. 441f.
[37] "Centre and Periphery in the Thought of Paul," *Studia Biblica 1978; III Papers on Paul and Other NT Authors. Sixth International Congress on Biblical Studies,* ed. E. A. Livingstone (1980), pp. 199–214.
[38] *Loc. cit.*, pp. 208f.
[39] *Loc. cit.*, p. 214.
[40] *Paul the Apostle: The Triumph of God in Life and Thought* (1980), pp. 15–19. In his revised edition (1984) Beker has reacted to his critics, and nuanced his position (pp. xiii–xxi). Note too his more popular *Paul's Apocalyptic Gospel* (1982).
[41] "The Unity of God in Pauline Thought," *Australian Biblical Review,* 28 (1980), 39–56.

in what God has done to reveal and convey his righteousness, which is thought of as a saving power; and it embraces the cosmos within its scope. The divine righteousness "provides a basis for ethical and political action,"[42] he rightly comments, at the close of a sustained argument based on the flow of the apostle's thought in the epistle to the Romans. But confining his attention to that one letter is a drawback and fails to gather into a synthetic statement both the pre-Pauline and post-Pauline traditions regarding that term. Moreover, even if "the righteousness of God" is seen in this dynamic way, it still remains an open question how Paul expected what God once did in saving action to provide a model for the Christian's ethical endeavor.

2. *The Need for Criteria.* Clearly before we enter the field with any further suggestions as to a *centrum Paulinum* we need to ask about the criteria by which any proposal may be justified. There is here the obvious danger of a hermeneutical circle since the criteria are drawn from the same body of data that *ex hypothesi* contains the organizing principle; and it may well be objected that we are selecting criteria that we know in advance will serve the interests of our proposed term. There seems to be no way to escape this dilemma unless we are prepared to abandon the quest and treat Paul's theology as fragmentary responses delivered *ad hoc*. Yet, provided we continue to test the criteria by the data as they are uncovered and provided we are willing to revise the initial theoretical proposal in the light of the reconstructed criteria, the enterprise is worthwhile and may be honestly and conscientiously pursued. The better way of putting the process then is to speak of a "hermeneutical spiral" by which we rise from one level to a more adequately framed hypothesis as new data are fed into the inquiry and it moves upward and forward.

The basic patterns of Paul's theological teaching, derivable from his generally undisputed letters, are as follows:

(*i*) The primacy of God's grace, which takes the initiative and promotes human recovery. (*ii*) Such an operation, while entering human history in the person of Jesus of Nazareth and at a given point in time, has repercussions that affect the cosmic scene and involve even the mysterious spiritual intelligences often referred to in Paul's worldview. (*iii*) The cross remains crucial to Paul's salvation teaching both as an event in time[43] and as related to man's need as a sinner. But with equal insistence Paul regards the cross as the instrument of self-denial by which the *sarx* is overcome and a new life, cruciform in shape and

---

[42] *Loc. cit.,* p. 54.

[43] E. Käsemann, "The Saving Significance of the Death of Jesus in Paul," *Perspectives on Paul* (ET 1971), pp. 32–59, has argued this point with great verve by showing that Paul's twin enemies were Jewish nomism and hellenistic enthusiasm. Käsemann's resistance to all kinds of *theologia gloriae,* whether triumphalistic, ecclesiastical, or evidential, raises problems for a theology of Paul that includes the term "triumph" in its subtitle (cf. Beker!).

diaconal in character, is made possible (Gal. 2:20; 6:14). (*iv*) Thus the gap between historical "is"-ness and ethical "ought"-ness must be bridged, and a rationale provided for the apostolic claim that the death and resurrection of the man Jesus impinge on human activity both as a power to break the stranglehold of evil and as an effectual summons to new life. (*v*) Finally, Paul's theology must be set in the context of his own self-description. He was both a Christian and a missionary, charged with a mandate to proclaim and live out the saving truth he claimed to have found in Jesus Christ. For Paul word and life go hand in hand; and missionary theology meant just as obviously both the kerygma and the way of life Paul exemplified and enacted in his pastoral dealings with awkward people and ugly situations.

3. *The Theme of Reconciliation.* The overall theme of reconciliation, we suggest, meets most — if not all — of these tests. This is not to say that the word-group *katallass-* is prominent in Paul's writings; manifestly it is not. Nor do we claim that "reconciliation" is used with the same nuance in those places where it does occur; obviously it does not. But our contention stands — namely, that reconciliation provides a suitable umbrella under which the main features of Paul's kerygma and its practical outworking may be set; this view also does justice to some of the main motifs in Pauline mission theology.

The term reconciliation has a pre-history in the tradition Paul gladly took over, as in 2 Corinthians 5:18–21 and Colossians 1:15–20. He was not content to leave the term open to misunderstanding, and form-critical, linguistic, and tradition-historical evidence shows how he has changed the meaning in the noun and verb by subtle editorial adaptations to the surrounding context. In particular, he has disinfected the term of its gnosticizing taint — suggested by its referring to a process of automatic fiat and physical fusion of the disparate elements in the universe — by anchoring reconciliation in the historical events of Jesus' passion and by tying in the effect of reconciliation to moral transformation in human lives.

The counterarguments in Paul are always on the level of personal relationships, of which the forgiveness of sins is the great reality shared alike by apostle and people. To that experience he appeals under a variety of images — justification, redemption, new life, sonship, the gift of the spirit, and the promise of resurrection.

Against those enthusiastic followers who believed that their baptism brought about the completion of salvation here and now, and against the intruding teachers who discounted morality as irrelevant once the spirit had been saved, Paul entered the plea of the "eschatological proviso," the "not yet" of a reconciliation that, unlike justification, is still going on and needs to be renewed continually. Hence the call to the Christians at Corinth, "Be reconciled to God" (2 Cor. 5:20), lest they receive God's grace to no purpose (2 Cor. 6:1) and fail to see his proffered forgiveness (2 Cor. 2:5–11; 6:11–13). Reconciliation is thus admirably suited to express and safeguard the existential element in Paul's moral theology. God has achieved a final reconciliation of the world, but men and women need to live with moral sensitivity and vigilance until the end comes.

The blend of God's deed and Paul's role as a reconciling agent at Corinth and in the note to Philemon illustrates how the transition from historical factuality to ethical obligation may be made. The middle term is Paul's "ministry of reconciliation" (2 Cor. 5:18) — the one clear job description Paul has left on record. What God did expressed his great love, with Christ's cross at the center (Rom. 5:1–11). Paul, as he gratefully rejoiced in that love as a fact of experience, conveyed by the spirit, saw his mission as modeling what God had done in recalling the Corinthians to their true allegiance and in urging on Philemon to consider the social implications of the new life on which he had embarked. The skeleton of an adequate ethical theory is here seen in embryo — even if it took Christians eighteen centuries to work out the force and relevance of this admonition.

Equally, the same may be said about the teaching in Ephesians 2:11–22. Here reconciliation takes on a horizontal direction. The inveterate hostility between Jew and non-Jews is overcome in the cross of Jesus who has reconciled both groups in one body. The "one new person" in place of two suggests the vision of a "third race," a new species of humankind, who in becoming part of the divine family form a microcosm of that new society which is a token in God's design to place all of conscious life under the headship of the cosmic Christ (Eph. 1:10).

4. *Conclusion.* These far-ranging and distinctive ideas, covering cosmic, personal, societal, and ethnic areas of our human story, are nevertheless part of a pattern whose picture fills the tapestry. The various strands are closely textured and intricately woven together. Yet they are not aimlessly put into a frame. There is an emerging design and a coherent picture. And the most adequate and meaningful title for the result is "reconciliation."

5. *Some Responses to Reviewers.* The elements in recent discussion, drawn from reviews, that seem to be worthy of mention are as follows.

First, several writers have queried whether it is proper to speak at all of the "center" of Paul's theology, let alone propose that it has been accurately located and identified as reconciliation. The grounds for such a denial are diverse. For some reviewers such as the Editor of the *Expository Times*,[44] Paul's thought cannot be captured in a single term. C. F. D. Moule rightly regards Paul's epistolary materials as polemically

---

[44] C. S. Rodd, *ExpT*, 94.2 (1982), 33f.

slanted with changing targets in his sights.[45] But his deduction that as "the foreground of his concern changes, [so] with it, perhaps, the centre of his picture" shifts leaves open the question how — if the center is so mobile and does not "hold" — Paul knew how to make the appropriate response in any given situation.

More reasonably Moule and others have indicted the thesis of reconciliation as the Pauline center as expressing a truism, though I should reject the inference drawn by Jeffrey W. Gillette that this exposition of Paul's gospel as intimately bound up with personal relationship is an "anthropocentric formulation."[46] Quite the opposite. The thesis repeatedly states that God's deed is the foundation, and from it Paul reasons back to human need. The cosmic setting of Paul's teaching, noted by Robin Barbour,[47] provides the backcloth; and whatever we do with the hermeneutical problem of the "principalities and powers," we must take them seriously in any understanding of the apostle's gospel.[48] But when all is said and done, the issue remains as to how Christ's death and triumph over these powers impinge on our lives today. This issue lies unresolved in J. C. Beker's work on Paul,[49] though he seeks to meet the challenge in a later, semipopular study.[50]

Second, a telling criticism by William S. Campbell asks whether the proposition that reconciliation is the *Pauli theologiae proprium,* especially in regard to the letter to the Romans, should in effect be recast. "Perhaps a modified form of [Martin's thesis] would gain wide assent, i.e., not that reconciliation *was* but that reconciliation *became* the way Paul formulated his gospel in communicating it to the Gentiles. This in turn would imply some process of development in Paul's thought so that reconciliation eventually came to stand at the apex of that development towards the end of his life."[51] This suggestion seems eminently reasonable, and I accept it.[52] Indeed, I thought I had said as much (*Reconciliation,* p. 153). But perhaps the thought needed spelling out, and Dr. Campbell has rightly done that.

Third, more than one reviewer has seen the relevance of reconciliation to both Paul's self-understanding as missionary pastor and the present-day tasks of ministry. The study leads to a "contextualizing [of] the theology of Paul"; much to be welcomed is the practical bearing of reconciliation for the ministry of the church today; one merit of this

45 *JTS,* n.s. 34.2 (1983), 599–601.
46 *Trinity Journal,* 3.1 (Spring 1982), 110f.
47 *SJT,* 37.1 (1984), 118–20.
48 See F. F. Bruce, "Paul and 'the Powers that Be,'" *BJRL,* 66 (1984), 78–96.
49 *Paul the Apostle: The Triumph of God in Life and Thought* (1980). See my review in *JBL,* 101 (1982), 463–66.
50 See his *Paul's Apocalyptic Gospel* (1982), pp. 79–121.
51 *Theology,* 86, No. 712 (1983), 300–2.
52 This position would answer D. E. H. Whiteley's question: "Is Martin right in supposing that reconciliation is central? We must ask 'central for whom?'" (*JSNT,* 20 [1984], 124).

approval to Paul's preaching is to see "how the horizontal aspect of reconciliation flows out of the vertical, the human from the divine."[53] These points of recognition and appraisal are in line with the author's intention in offering not simply a textbook for students but an exposition of Paul's teaching that at its heart has value to us because it can assist us in the ongoing tasks and opportunities of service in the church and the world. Whether the thesis stands or falls, I am content to have raised the issue and have had a hearing. If J. A. Ziesler's summary, i.e., that the author (Martin) "may well be right," speaks for several reviewers,[54] that is perhaps all I should hope for, given the jungle-like ambience of New Testament interpretations. At least one good result follows. We are faced with a continuing responsibility to make Paul's essential witness intelligible and applicable to our day. Maybe "reconciliation in Christ" will point the way.

[53] J. A. Ziesler, *The Epworth Review,* 10.3 (1983), 99f.
[54] C. H. Giblin, *CBQ,* 45 (1983), 313f. See also F. F. Bruce, *The Churchman,* 97.1 (1983), 60f.

Select Bibliography[1]

To facilitate easy reference I have placed under the heading of each chapter the titles of some significant books that are likely to be of most help to students in the early days of their studies. The number of suggested volumes has been trimmed to a minimum, so what follows should be taken as indispensable reading, at least in the present writer's judgment, in the restricted field of New Testament background and introduction.

Chapter one

Bauer, W. *Orthodoxy and Heresy in Earliest Christianity* (Philadelphia/London, ET 1971).

Longenecker, R. N. *Biblical Exegesis in the Apostolic Period* (Grand Rapids, 1975).

Marshall, I. H. (ed.). *New Testament Interpretation* (Exeter/Grand Rapids, 1977).

Chapter two

Barrett, C. K. *The New Testament Background: Selected Documents* (London, 1956).

Sherwin-White, A. N. *Roman Society and Roman Law in the New Testament* (Oxford, 1971).

Lohse, E. *The New Testament Environment* (Nashville/London, ET 1976).

Chapter three

Halliday, W. R. *The Pagan Background of Early Christianity* (Liverpool, 1925).

Grant, F. C. *Roman Hellenism and the New Testament* (Edinburgh, 1962).

Skemp, J. B. *The Greeks and the Gospel* (London, 1964).

[1] The following list of titles should be read in conjunction with the present author's expanded comments in his title *New Testament Books for Pastors and Teachers* (1984) and in the light of B. S. Childs, *The New Testament as Canon* (1984), where his chapter "Selected Commentaries for Pastor and Teacher," pp. 547–56, is apposite to the task of building a serviceable library.

Chapter four
Keck, L. E. and Martyn, J. L. (edd.). *Studies in Luke-Acts. Festschrift* for
    Paul Schubert (Nashville/London, 1968).
Gasque, W. W. and Martin, R. P. (edd.). *Apostolic History and the Gos-*
    pel. Biblical and Historical Essays Presented to F. F. Bruce
    (Grand Rapids/Exeter, 1970).
Haenchen, E. *The Acts of the Apostles* (Philadelphia/Oxford, ET 1971).

Chapter five
Johnston, G. *The Doctrine of the Church in the New Testament* (Cam-
    bridge, 1943).
Goppelt, L. *Apostolic and Post-Apostolic Times* (New York, ET 1970).
Dunn, J. D. G. *Jesus and the Spirit* (Philadelphia/London, 1975).

Chapter six
Cullmann, O. *The Early Church* (London, ET 1956).
Simon, M. *St. Stephen and the Hellenists in the Primitive Church* (Lon-
    don, ET 1958).
Green, M. *Evangelism in the Early Church* (Grand Rapids/London,
    1970).

Chapter seven
Davies, W. D. *Paul and Rabbinic Judaism*[2] (London/New York, 1955).
Wagner, G. *Pauline Baptism and the Pagan Mysteries* (Edinburgh, ET
    1967).
Rigaux, B. *The Letters of St. Paul* (Chicago, ET 1968).

Chapter eight
Munck, J. *Paul and the Salvation of Mankind* (London, ET 1959).
Ogg, G. *The Odyssey of Paul* (British title, *The Chronology of the Life of*
    Paul) (Nashville/London, 1968).
Gunther, J. J. *Paul: Messenger and Exile* (Valley Forge, 1972).

Chapter nine
Schmithals, W. *Paul and James* (London/Naperville, ET 1965).
Munck, J. *Christ and Israel* (Philadelphia, ET 1967).
Bruce, F. F. *New Testament History* (London/New York, 1969).

Chapter ten
Duncan, G. S. *St. Paul's Ephesian Ministry* (London, 1929).
Dibelius, M. *Studies in the Acts of the Apostles* (London/Naperville, ET
    1956).
Conzelmann, H. *History of Primitive Christianity* (Nashville, ET 1973).

Chapter eleven
Edmundson, G. *The Church in Rome in the First Century* (London, 1913).
O'Connor, D. W. *Peter in Rome* (New York, 1969).
Smallwood, E. M. *The Jews under Roman Rule* (Leiden, 1976).

Chapter twelve
Lightfoot, J. B. *St. Paul's Epistle to the Galatians*[4] (London/Grand Rapids, 1874).
Jewett, R. *Paul's Anthropological Terms* (Leiden, 1971).
Schmithals, W. *Paul and the Gnostics* (Nashville, ET 1972).

Chapter thirteen
Morris, L. *The Epistles to the Thessalonians* (Grand Rapids/London, 1957).
Manson, T. W. *Studies in the Gospels and Epistles,* ed. M. Black (Manchester, 1962).
Best, E. *A Commentary on the First and Second Epistles to the Thessalonians* (New York/London, 1972).

Chapter fourteen
Hurd, J. C., Jr. *The Origin of 1 Corinthians* (London, 1965).
Schmithals, W. *Gnosticism in Corinth* (Nashville, ET 1971).
Barrett, C. K. *Commentary on the Second Epistle to the Corinthians* (New York/London, 1973).

Chapter fifteen
Barrett, C. K. *A Commentary on the Epistle to the Romans* (New York/London, 1957).
Manson, T. W. *On Paul and John* (London/Naperville, 1963).
Black, M. *Romans* (London, 1973).

Chapter sixteen
Martin, R. P. *Carmen Christi: Phil. II.5–11 in Recent Interpretation* (Cambridge, 1967).
Beare, F. W. *The Epistle to the Philippians*[2] (New York/London, 1968).
Houlden, J. L. *Paul's Letters from Prison* (Harmondsworth/Baltimore, 1970).

Chapter seventeen
Lightfoot, J. B. *St. Paul's Epistles to the Colossians and Philemon* (London/Grand Rapids, 1879).
Lohse, E. *Colossians and Philemon* (Philadelphia, ET 1971).
Francis, F. O. and Meeks, W. A. *Conflict at Colossae* (Philadelphia, 1973).

Chapter eighteen
Cross, F. L. (ed.). *Studies in Ephesians* (Oxford, 1956).
Barth, M. *Ephesians* (New York, 1974).
Mitton, C. L. *Ephesians* (London, 1976).

Chapter nineteen
Deissmann, A. *Light from the Ancient East*[4] (New York/London, ET 1927).
Schubert, P. *Form and Function of the Pauline Thanksgivings* (Berlin, 1939).
Doty, W. G. *Letters in Primitive Christianity* (Philadelphia, 1973).

Chapter twenty
Cullmann, O. *The Earliest Christian Confessions* (London, ET 1949).
Hunter, A. M. *Paul and His Predecessors*[2] (London, 1961).
Hahn, F. *The Worship of the Early Church* (Philadelphia, ET 1973).

Chapter twenty-one
Mitton, C. L. *The Formation of the Pauline Corpus of Letters* (London, 1955).
Ladd, G. E. *New Testament and Criticism* (Grand Rapids/London, 1967).
von Campenhausen, H. *The Formation of the Christian Bible* (London, ET 1972).

Chapter twenty-two
Harrison, P. N. *The Problem of the Pastoral Epistles* (London, 1921).
Kelly, J. N. D. *The Pastoral Epistles* (London/New York, 1963).
De Marco, A. A. *The Tomb of St. Peter* (Leiden, 1964).

Chapter twenty-three
Cullmann, O. *The State in the New Testament* (London, ET 1957).
Moule, C. F. D. *The Birth of the New Testament* (New York/London, 1962).
Houlden, J. L. *Ethics in the New Testament* (Harmondsworth/Baltimore, 1973).

Chapter twenty-four
Bultmann, R. *Primitive Christianity in its Contemporary Setting* (London/Cleveland, ET 1956).
Wilson, R. McL. *Gnosis and the New Testament* (Oxford, 1968).
Yamauchi, E. M. *Pre-Christian Gnosticism* (London/Grand Rapids, 1973).

Chapter twenty-five
Selwyn, E. G. *The First Epistle of St. Peter* (London, 1946).

Beare, F. W. *First Peter*[3] (Oxford, 1970).
Best, E. *First Peter* (London, 1971).

Chapter twenty-six
Manson, W. *The Epistle to the Hebrews* (London, 1951).
Bruce, F. F. *Commentary on the Epistle to the Hebrews* (Grand Rapids/ London, 1964).
Buchanan, G. W. *Hebrews* (Garden City, N.Y., 1972).

Chapter twenty-seven
Tasker, R. V. G. *The General Epistle of James* (Grand Rapids/London, 1956).
Mitton, C. L. *The Epistle of James* (London/Grand Rapids, 1966).
Adamson, J. B. *The Epistle of James* (Grand Rapids/London, 1976).

Chapter twenty-eight
Caird, G. B. *A Commentary on the Revelation of St. John the Divine* (New York/London, 1966).
Bruce, F. F. *The Epistles of John* (London, 1970).
Beasley-Murray, G. R. *Revelation* (London, 1974).

Chapter twenty-nine
Cullmann, O. *Christ and Time*[2] (London/Philadelphia, ET 1962).
Käsemann, E. *New Testament Questions of Today* (London/ Philadelphia, ET 1969).
Robinson, J. A. T. *Redating the New Testament* (London/Philadelphia, 1976).

Chapters thirty to thirty-two
Barrett, C. K. *A Commentary on Paul's First Letter to the Corinthians* (New York/London, 1968).
Bruce, F. F. *1-2 Corinthians* (London, 1971).
Conzelmann, H. *First Corinthians* (Philadelphia, ET 1975).

Index of Subjects

Index of Authors

Index of References